THE ENGLISH CATHOLICS
1850-1950

A

POPE PIUS IX
Restorer of the English Hierarchy

THE
ENGLISH
CATHOLICS

1850-1950

*Essays to commemorate the centenary
of the restoration of the Hierarchy
of England and Wales*

Edited by
THE RIGHT REVEREND
GEORGE ANDREW BECK, A.A.
CO-ADJUTOR BISHOP OF BRENTWOOD

With a Foreword by
HIS EMINENCE
CARDINAL GRIFFIN
ARCHBISHOP OF WESTMINSTER

LONDON
BURNS OATES
1950

PRINTED IN GREAT BRITAIN BY HENDERSON AND SPALDING
FOR BURNS OATES AND WASHBOURNE, LTD.,
28, ASHLEY PLACE,
LONDON, S.W.I

First published 1950

FOREWORD

By His Eminence the

Cardinal Archbishop of Westminster

It was at the direct wish of the Hierarchy of England and Wales that His Lordship Bishop Beck undertook the task of preparing a volume of essays to mark the hundredth anniversary of the Apostolic Letter *Universalis Ecclesiae* by which the Hierarchy was restored.

So many-sided are the activities of the Catholic Church in this country that it was essential that each aspect should be entrusted to a Catholic writer well versed in that particular sphere. It is quite clear from this book that not merely has Bishop Beck fulfilled his editorial duties with distinction, but he has also been fortunate in having as his collaborators eminent Catholic men of letters well able to write with authority and, in many cases, from experience of their subjects.

The Catholic Church in this country is a growing community and as this process continues it will be able to play an increasing part in the life of the nation. When we consider the small numbers and meagre resources of 1850 we can but marvel at the confidence with which Cardinal Wiseman and his colleagues approached their problems. Thanks to their zeal and to the foundations laid so surely, but with such sacrifice, by the Vicars Apostolic, we have to-day arrived at a position where the Catholics of England and Wales are regarded not merely as a real force but as a body of men and women willing and able to make a valuable contribution to the life of their country.

At this time our hearts are filled with thanksgiving, first to Almighty God who has so clearly showered abundant blessings and graces upon the tender growth of a hundred years ago. We must be thankful also for those great leaders who, under God, have directed the destinies of the Church at this crucial stage. This book recalls the names of many illustrious bishops, laymen and laywomen who have won renown for the Catholic name. We must also remember with pride those lesser folk, priests and laymen, without whose labours, hidden and sometimes unappreciated, the progress from 1850 to 1950 could not have been achieved.

To-day we may face the future with confidence, that same confidence which filled the heart of Cardinal Wiseman when he first announced the glorious news to his people. But true confidence does not breed complacency, and if we are to learn from this record of a hundred years and, indeed, from the whole history of the Church since the coming of St. Augustine to this country, then we shall have before our eyes a lesson which will call forth apostolic zeal. From this book we can gain knowledge invaluable for the future. It comprises an account which can but strengthen our desire to preserve our heritage and to spread the gospel of Christ.

✠ BERNARD CARDINAL GRIFFIN,

Archbishop of Westminster

Archbishop's House,
Westminster.
July 21st, 1950.

EDITOR'S PREFACE

THE FOLLOWING pages are an attempt to show something of the growth of the Catholic Church in England and Wales during the last hundred years.

The main outlines of the story, are, of course, already known and have formed the background to the great nineteenth-century Catholic biographies—the lives of Wiseman, Newman, Ullathorne, Manning and Vaughan. While accounts of the notable personalities are not wanting, very little exact information is available concerning the details of Catholic history, diocesan and parochial, and of the growth and movement of the Catholic community. This is not entirely surprising. For at least three-quarters of the century since 1850 the bishops and the clergy found their resources and energies strained to the limit to make the most elementary provision for the maintenance of·Catholic life; and even at the present time the curial organisation in many a diocese of England and Wales is more impressive on paper than in the reality of its functioning. In such circumstances, it is not surprising that diocesan and parochial archives are scanty, incomplete and insufficiently classified or catalogued, or, for some periods of their history, practically non-existent.

Apart from the strong Catholic centres in Liverpool and Lancashire, in the North-East and in London, it may be said that the greater part of the last hundred years has been spent in bringing each diocese to maturity and that, as the centenary of the restoration of the Hierarchy is celebrated, the great majority of the dioceses of England and Wales are at least becoming what in theory they are meant to be—self-governing units of the Church, each under the jurisdiction of a bishop and each containing within itself all the elements necessary for the spiritual welfare of its members, with the Mass available to all, the regular administration of the sacraments, and the provision, from its own population, of vocations to the religious life and to the pastoral clergy.

In some senses the crowning of all this effort of a hundred years was the establishment by the Holy See in 1938 of

an Apostolic Delegation in this country. In November of that
year the Most Reverend William Godfrey, a former Rector of
the English College in Rome, was elected titular Archbishop
of Cius and was appointed first Apostolic Delegate to Great
Britain.

An Editor is only too well aware of points which are
open to criticism, and of omissions which may be noted in a
volume for which he is responsible. In a composite work of this
kind a certain amount of overlapping is inevitable. While there
may be agreement on basic facts, not all contributors draw the
same inferences or conclusions. On almost all points it has
been thought best, however, to give to each contributor the
greatest freedom in the handling of his subject, and it is hoped
that the book may have gained from the wide variety of treatment and the varied view-points of the different contributors.
Of the omissions, the most notable are concerned with
persons rather than events. All over the country the memories
of great Catholic figures, parish priests for the most part, but
layfolk as well, are remembered; the names of the clergy and
the anecdotes in connection with them are revived on those
occasions when priests meet together and have time and opportunity to speak of the past. Many of these legendary figures
are fading memories. It has not been found possible, at
short notice, to do them justice adequately or generally in these
pages, and it may justly be said that the book lacks something
of that colour and vividness which some account of these outstanding personalities, parish priests, diocesan administrators
and pioneer missionaries, might have given it. It must be left
to the piety and industry of local Catholic historians to preserve
their memory and some account of their achievements. Similarly too, this book is far from giving an adequate presentation
of the figures of prominent Catholic layfolk, particularly in
more recent years. Perhaps this deficiency will later be made
good.
Something has been said, especially in Mr. Denis
Gwynn's chapters, concerning the remarkable growth in the
number of Catholic priests in England and Wales, particularly
in the last twenty-five years. It has not been found possible,
however, to give an adequate account of the work which is

done at Ushaw, Ware, Oscott, Upholland and Wonersh, and in the other seminaries here or abroad. But nobody will doubt that upon the quality of the training which students to the priesthood receive depends, in very large measure, the future strength of the Catholic life in this country.

The editorial work entrusted to me by the Hierarchy of England and Wales has been greatly lightened by the ready help which I have received not only from the contributors to the volume but from many other sources. The secretaries of most of the Bishops have generously furnished both information and statistics concerning the history of their diocese; the Fathers of the London Oratory, the president of St. Edmund's College, Ware, Father A. Reynolds of Bishop's House, Southwark, Father J. F. Cleary of Birmingham, Father G. Collins of Northampton and Father Philip Webb of Menevia have been especially helpful in obtaining photographs and other illustrations. I am grateful to His Lordship the Bishop of Nottingham, to Father Philip Hughes and to Father Morgan Sweeney for help and advice with different parts of the book. Miss Yvonne ffrench has rendered invaluable assistance in the preparation of the illustrations which, it is hoped, may help to give the book a permanent interest and value. Though far from being complete in their scope they are representative of most aspects of English Catholic life during the last hundred years.

I must record my thanks also to Mr. J. J. Dwyer not only for his own contribution, but for pointing out a number of factual errors in the original text and also for the preparation of the Bibliography; and, not least, to the members of the staff of the publishers and printers who, by their ready co-operation, have made possible the production of so large a book in what is, comparatively, so short a time.

✠ GEORGE ANDREW BECK, A.A.,

Co-adjutor Bishop of Brentwood.

SS. Peter and Paul,
Ilford.
July 28th, 1950.

CONTENTS

LIST OF ILLUSTRATIONS

NOTE.—The illustration pages are numbered separately from the text, and are shown in square brackets.

ACKNOWLEDGEMENTS

We are indebted to the following for permission to reproduce copyright photographs in this book:

The Controller of His Majesty's Stationery Office; the Proprietors of *Punch*; Aero Pictorial, Ltd.; the National Portrait Gallery; *Picture Post* Library; the *Illustrated London News*; *The Builder*; *Country Life*; and the Topical Press Agency.

I

THE COMING CENTURY

By Philip Hughes

THE year 1850 in which Pope Pius IX restored to England its hierarchy of diocesan bishops was, by one of the accidents of history, a year which scholars were later to see as marking a great turning point in our social and economic history. This chance coincidence is a reminder, to anyone who would review the Catholic achievement of the century just closing, that although his subject is the fortunes of an entity that is supernatural he is, nevertheless, telling the story of activities that are human. The actors in that story, whether they act in harmony with the inspirations of divine grace or in opposition to them, remain natural men; they live in a natural world which not only, for its own sake, as a reality created by God, has every claim upon our attentive study, but also needs to be known well if the history of man's adventures under divine grace is really to be told at all.

We cannot safely disregard all that is implied in the principle that grace pre-supposes nature, the truth that the natural world is a fact prior to the fact of its conversion. We must not, in other words, write the history of the Catholic Church as though the Christian Life could be a matter of Faith, Hope and Charity alone; or as though the perfect Christian were pure spirit; or as though the material reality did not, in fact, ceaselessly condition man's submission to the divine ordinance that, in human life, the supernatural shall inform the natural, and, by ruling it, bring the natural creation to its own perfection.

To tell the story as though it were a matter merely of the three theological virtues, or as though the activities of popes and bishops and ecclesiastics were alone decisive, or (yet again) as though it were merely a question of the ideals and aspirations of pious souls, would be to present a fairy tale of the never-

never-land, to write history as though, in those bygone years, there had never been such a thing as that human nature which is familiar to us all; it would be not only to present a travesty of the true history but to caricature the divinely created nature of man, and the mystery of his activities under grace, so that the great drama which thereby ensues would appear as though possessed of no greater reality than that of a pageant of puppets.

So it is, then, that under pain of falsifying revealed truth itself, we need to set the events of Catholic history in the actual world where they took place—that is to say, we need to recall the natural realities which really affected those events, whatever the consciousness of particular actors at the time that these natural realities did so affect them, whatever their own awareness of this world and their understanding of it. *Ad nostram doctrinam scripta sunt.* It is axiomatic that we can never fully understand the natural without knowledge also of that other reality, the supernatural; it is no less true, and if forgotten it is no less mischievously forgotten, that we shall never understand the supernatural promises if we neglect to take into account the natural to which, and for whose saving, they were made.

We tell then the story of the restoration of the diocesan episcopate among the English people, and of what, under God's Providence, has been since attempted and achieved thereby for the extension of His reign in this land. We recall how these events took place in an age of corn laws and coal strikes, of reform bills, and political enlargement; in a time of university reform, and scientific discovery; amid an immensity of new knowledge, and of an extension of man's control over matter, and of inventions which, in fifty years, changed the order of man's life more that it had been changed in any thousand years before. It is the world of *The Origin of Species* as well as of the Oxford Movement, of the Stephensons and the Brunels, of Brassey and Bazalguette, of Kaye-Shuttleworth and Chadwick, of Lister and Simpson—to say nothing, for once, of such more familiar figures as the leaders of political life, the great writers, the artists, the scholars. It was in this world that the story which is our own particular concern all happened—in a world that men such as these were influencing, changing, improving. It was with these that the Catholic leaders had to contend, to co-operate; it was these whom they needed to understand, whom they must convince—and convert. Here is the true ruling class, already beginning to be so before 1850, and after 1850 increasingly and more really so: the national intelligence, speculative and applied.

The year 1850 that was to prove so important to the Catholics of England and Wales found the great mass of them enduring all the rigours of what has been so admirably styled " the Bleak Age "[1].

To the historian of English economic life, that year marks a turning point, as the date after which all the resources of the country are organised to assist its transformation into the classic example of the " Industry State." No less importantly, it marks another turning point also: from this time none dispute that it is the duty of all to strive to transform that " Bleak Age " into something more human. One first condition, then, of any understanding how the last hundred years have affected Catholicism in this country, must be an awareness of the forces changing English life in those years when the thirteen bishops, taking possession of the new sees, settled themselves to the task of living down the prejudice which the news of their appointment had so suddenly stirred up anew.

And first, it needs to be recalled, that it was in a generation where the reforming philanthropist, with allies now among the politicians of all parties, never ceased to be active, and when the " condition-of-England question " was accepted on all sides as a permanent concern of public policy, that the new diocesan episcopate took up its task, the work that has ever since been its ceaseless preoccupation.

The bishops, indeed, had all but everything to do, as the statistics we quote will show. They had, for example, to provide everywhere the urgently needed priests, and churches, and schools—and these schools, in that age when for poor men's children there were no schools save those which religious bodies built and maintained, were not only the security that education should be centred round the knowledge of God, but they were the sole means of instructing the working classes in the very

[1] *The Bleak Age*, by J. L. and Barbara Hammond, 1930 (Pelican Edition, 1947).

rudiments of reading and writing. They had to found orphanages and homes for the aged, refuges for the destitute and for
the morally abandoned. They had to organise the defence of
the faith against the old bitter calumnies which the educated
Englishman's ignorance and misunderstanding of the most
elementary Catholic practices and beliefs did so much to maintain in being[1a]. And they must prepare all classes of their people
against those more subtle dangers to faith which arose from
their contact with that Liberal section of the country's intelligence whence had come whatever support the Catholic claim to
a full share in the national life had ever received—liberal allies
truly, but allies whose aid was yet based on religious in-
differentism, on a conception of the state as something inevitably secular, and on the denial that religion could ever be *res
publica*. The association of O'Connell with Liberals, in the
religious sense of the word, had been a real stumbling-block to
Newman in his Tractarian days[2]; now, in the years that
followed, there was to be a wholesale reception into public life
of men, and of women too, who made no secret of their rejection
of every form of " institutional religion," who openly planned
and worked for the new non-religious century, and this in
novels and poems as well as in treatises of natural science and
social philosophy[2a].

With the appearance of this new foe to faith in the supernatural, the most characteristic spiritual offspring of the new
age, it behoved the bishops so to re-model the exposition of
Catholic belief that the faith could be seen by the outsider as a
system that did not ignore the new world which blared so
powerfully, but rather understood and took account of that
world's moral difficulties and intellectual problems, and provided adequately for both. And the chances of the bishops succeeding in their formidable task—their impossible task to the
materially minded who knew the all-but-inexistent resources,

[1a] Greville is a witness sufficiently detached to quote in illustration.
" While everything else is in a constant state of change, Protestant
bigotry and anti-Catholic rancour continue to flourish with un-
diminished intensity, and all the more from being founded on
nothing but prejudice and ignorance, without a particle of sense
and reason " (*Memoirs*, VI, 242, under date of 7th Nov., 1848).

[2] Cf. *Apologia*, 123, 125, 134, 191-2.

[2a] Cf., " the grave un-Christian philosophy of George Eliot's novels,"
Keith Feiling, *A History of England* (1950), p. 894.

in trained men, in means of training, and in money—would have seemed desperate to their very selves, had the immediate course of history been known to the bishops. For if the hundred years that followed the great event of 1850 were to be years of extraordinary growth in prosperity and in general improvement of life, years of a vast enlargement of man's control and mastery of the material creation, they were also to be years of a steady decline in purely intellectual power, in religious belief, in the domination of the material by the spiritual, and years ultimately of great moral disintegration.

It is with this terrible fact ever in mind that we recall the " watershed " events of that century, seeing them always as tending to growth or to disintegration, whether material growth and decay, or moral[3].

What will perhaps first impress whoever studies the history of the first quarter of the century that followed the great Catholic event of 1850, is that in all those years the popular agitation for social improvement and for political change did not ever really slacken. Government, for the whole of this time, was in the hands of Whig and Whig-Liberal ministries, save for the three occasions when Disraeli's successful raids put the Tories in power for a few brief months. But

[3] Newman saw, very clearly indeed, and more clearly than some contemporary Catholics liked, what the future held in store; and in a celebrated paper—*A Form of Infidelity of the Day,* written in 1854 (*Idea of a University,* 381-404)—he described the mentality of the coming generation so faithfully that, barely ten years ago, a very well-known writer, Mr. G. M. Young, could quote this passage as the exact delineation of the mind of the educated man of to-day about the unlikelihood of certitude in the matter of religion. And Newman also described the policy towards theology which the new infidelity would adopt: never to attack theology, but rather to ignore it, to " bypass " it, as we might say, and to raise up against it rival intellectual interests. What Newman did not know, in 1854, was that ten years earlier John Stuart Mill, in a letter to Comte, 3rd April, 1844, had outlined this very programme, " *Le temps n'est pas venu où, sans compromettre notre cause, nous pourrons en Angleterre diriger des attaques ouvertes contre la théologie même chrétienne. Nous pouvons seulement l'éluder, en l'éliminant tranquillement de toutes les discussions philosophiques et sociales, et en passant à l'ordre du jour sur toutes les questions qui lui sont propres.*"

the agitation for betterment and change was not a matter of party politics; change of government never greatly affected it, and the mass of new laws which it produced was in no sense the realisation of a predetermined party programme.

There were now enacted (1855-1862) a series of Limited Liability Acts to complete the work of Peel's great Bank Act of 1844 in encouraging the more rapid exploitation of new discoveries by lessening the personal risks of the investing employer. On the other hand, the friendly societies and the co-operative societies received a new legal protection, and the funds of the trades unions were made legally secure (1871). The Home Office control of conditions in the factories steadily became a greater reality, through the high personal quality of the new factory inspectorate; and the control was gradually extended beyond its first narrow field of the coal mining and cotton industries. The Ten Hours Act of 1847 really began, after its amendment in 1853, to revolutionise the working man's life[4], for it ensured in practice that no factory worked more than ten hours a day; and a supplementary Act, of 1850, secured that on Saturdays all work in factories ceased at midday. But although these principles of legal restriction of hours of work, and of a government inspectorate to enforce the law, were steadily, if slowly, extended to protect other industries (at the cost, of course, of agitation and of much parliamentary fighting) the " sweated " trades of London, and the domestic branches of the iron manufacture, remained, for yet another fifty years and more, in vivid witness to the primitive horror in which all industrial life had once been lived. Another wicked piece of human exploitation that survived until the very end of these twenty-five years was the practice of using climbing boys to sweep chimneys. Only in 1875 did an agitation that had been continuous for ninety years really begin to be successful.

It was in these twenty-five years that the new municipal corporations gradually began to make use of their powers to establish medical officers of health and a new sanitary inspectorate, to lay out public parks, to build art galleries and museums, to establish free lending-libraries and reading-

[4] For Dr. Hammond this is the Act which, above all, changes social life for the better.

rooms. And a beginning was even made of arresting the jerry-builder's long exploitation of the poor.

Also, as will be told elsewhere in some detail, it was these years that saw the gradual growth of a new political interest, a concern namely about popular education. There was no longer any need for the agitator to fight for the very principle that all should be taught to read and to write and to cipher; and, in 1870, the momentous decision was taken to establish elementary schools that should be built, equipped, and wholly maintained out of the public funds. The weaver, the coal-miner, the moulder, of 1875 was much more happily situated than his fathers had been in 1850, and his children's prospects very much less brutish than his own had been. The *polis*—society—was at last beginning to do something, as in recognition of a social duty, for the betterment of those so long condemned to mere savagery.

Finally, the urban workman was also, at last, really a citizen in 1875. The Reform Act of 1867 had given him a vote in parliamentary elections and in the elections of the municipal corporations and of the boards of Guardians of the Poor. No less importantly, the Ballot Act of 1872 had given him, with the security of secrecy, the power really to vote as his own mind decided. And all this was greatly to the good.

But, simultaneously with these happy events, another revolution was at work that was to transform the religious habits of the non-Catholic mass of the nation—or rather of that 58 per cent. of them which the census of 1851 had shown as possessed of religious habits. And the effect of this was very far from good.

In 1850 the air was still dark with the dust of a great conflict that had raged for years in the very heart of the Church of England as by law established. Nearly twenty years before this time, in what seemed the darkest hour the Church of England had known since its establishment by Queen Elizabeth, a band of young Oxford theologians had set out to renew its vitality by reviving and appropriating theories about the kind of thing the Church of Christ is, whose very existence almost all their clerical brethren had forgotten for generations. The greatest mind among these Oxford men, John Henry

Newman, taught himself, moreover, from the ancient Catholic
fathers of the fourth and fifth centuries, the whole Catholic
theory of the Church as the divinely-founded, infallible
teacher of the revelation of God to mankind; and, taking it
for granted that the Church of England as by law established
was the Church of Christ in England, he did his best to spread
these Catholic notions as being the obvious beliefs to be held
about the religion professed by the Archbishops of Canterbury
and York[5] and their flocks.

Newman lived up to his doctrines. The bishop's
" lightest word *ex cathedrâ* is heavy," he had said; for his
bishop was to him the divinely appointed successor of the
apostles. He treated the Anglican episcopate according to the
strict letter of the apostolic protocol, and in the full spirit of
what he had read about the episcopal office in the fathers.
The Church was a teacher divinely given for the very purpose
of teaching. In all questions of faith it was, then, the actual
teaching of the Church, and not the private judgment of the
believer, or the opinion of the scholar, that must decide between
right and wrong, between true and false.

These theories, that the Established Church was the
Catholic Church of Christ in the sense in which Newman had
found that Church in the ancient fathers, received, however, a
shattering blow in 1841, at a moment when Newman, at the
height of his influence, suggested that a Catholic interpretation of the Thirty-nine Articles—a " Roman Catholic " interpretation, hostile critics would call it—was what they meant
rather than that " Protestant " interpretation of them traditional since their formulation; nay, more, this Catholic
interpretation, however unusual this might seem to those now
reading the proposals of Newman's pamphlet, the famous
Tract 90, was the interpretation that all ought to put upon the
Articles; for in the Catholic Church all official statements of
doctrine must be construed in a Catholic sense, construed,
that is to say, so as to accord with the unchanging traditional

---

[5] By the Archbishops of Armagh, too, and of Dublin; for since 1801 it
was through " The United Church of Great Britain and Ireland,"
" the Protestant Episcopal Church of England and Ireland," that
the sovereign exercised his supremacy in all causes ecclesiastical.
The titles are those of the Act of Union (1800) and the Catholic
Emancipation Act of 1829.

doctrine[6]. The reaction to this, on the part of the episcopate whose chiefs were the Archbishops of Canterbury and York, was immediate, instinctive, and utterly fatal to Newman's conception of the kind of institution that body was in which, for seventeen years now, he had been ministering. It would indeed, later, be allowed that for those who held these beliefs, and practised according to them, there was lawfully a place in the Established Church, as well as for those others who, in faithful accord with the primitive reformers, with Cranmer and Jewel and Matthew Parker, looked on these things with horror as treason to Christ and an apostasy from God. What was never allowed was Newman's fundamental contention— that these " Romanising theories " were the norm of the Anglican Church's life, its official teaching, its only possible teaching, the teaching which was the sign and guarantee to its children that it was really Christ's Church[7].

How Newman, in 1845, became a Catholic, and many of his followers with him, is a story familiar to all. But it was not only Newman who was defeated in those critical years 1841-1845, and the effect of whose defeat still shook the religious world in 1850 and in the years that followed. In Newman, Catholicism yet once again went down. Once more, and most decisively, the Church of the Archbishops of Canterbury and York had rejected Catholicism, and a strong anti-Catholic reaction was inevitable; not merely a reaction against feelings of sympathy with the Church of the Popes, or against movements tending to " Romanise " the liturgical habits of the Established Church, but something much more funda-

---

[6] " . . . the doctrine of the Old Church must live and speak in Anglican formularies, in the 39 Articles. Did it? Yes, it did; that is what I maintained; . . . I believed it could be shown; . . . and therefore I set about showing it at once." *Apologia,* standard (Longman) edition, 129-30.

[7] " The only peculiarity of the view I advocate, if I must so call it, is this—that whereas it is usual at this day to make the *particular belief of their writers* their true interpretation [i.e., of the 39 Articles], I would make the *belief of the Catholic Church such.*" Newman, *Letter to Dr. Jelf* (1841), quoted *Apologia,* 131; where, also, " It is a duty . . . to take our reformed confessions in the most Catholic sense they will admit. . . ." The *Letter to Dr. Jelf* will be found, reprinted with Newman's notes (written as a Catholic in 1877 in *The Via Media,* Vol. II, 353-79; the passage quoted above is from p. 371, and the italics are Newman's.

mental than this, a reaction against the principle that the
Church is a supernatural creation, a reaction that turned
resolutely from such an idea as " mystical," and which
carried very many of the better-educated of the next generation towards that " reasonable " Christianity which had
characterised the eighteenth century. " It was the Liberals,"
Newman said, who drove him from Oxford[8]; and the result of
their victory was a generation of Liberalism triumphant. Not
the Evangelical Anglicanism of Simeon and Wilberforce and
Lord Shaftesbury was to profit from the exorcising of Tract
90, but the new Latitudinarianism of Arnold and Stanley and
Jowett, the spirit which Newman had detected, and fought in
(for example) the historical work of Milman[9]. And the victory
of the Liberals was reflected in a series of extraordinary acts
on the part of the supreme authority in the Establishment
which steadily divested it of the last trappings of its own one-
time extensive authority over the layman, forced upon it a
new conception of marriage, and tore into pieces any pretence
men might ever have made of its prelates being the authoritative
judges whether a belief was Christian orthodoxy or dangerous
heresy. That State from whose breath the Anglican Church
had received its first life, now, in a few brief years, accomplished in it some astonishing transformations—and the mass
of the nation approved them as the commonsense of the matter.

Twice, in these years, disputes between bishops and
clergy about the orthodoxy of a particular doctrine were
decided by the Supreme Governor of the nation in causes
ecclesiastical, through the court known as the Judicial Committee of the Privy Council. In each case it was the bishop's
view that was rejected and the " wider " view of the cleric he

[8] " The men who had driven me from Oxford were distinctly the
Liberals; it was they who had opened the attack upon Tract 90,
and it was they who would gain a second benefit, if I went on to
abandon the Anglican Church. . . . As I have already said, there
are but two alternatives, the way to Rome and the way to Atheism :
Anglicanism is the halfway house on the one side, and Liberalism
is the halfway house on the other." *Apologia* (standard edition),
203-4; and cf. *ibid.*, 288, " liberal in its theology, in the sense in
which the bulk of the educated classes through the country are
liberal now," i.e., in 1865.

[9] See Newman's profound analysis of Milman as a historian of
Christianity, written for the *British Critic* (Jan., 1841) and reprinted
in *Essays Critical and Historical*, Vol. II, 186-248.

opposed that was allowed: in 1850 the denial was allowed that it was the sacrament of baptism that wrought the regeneration of the soul in Christ, and in 1862 the denial that the punishment of hell is eternal. In 1857 the probate jurisdiction of the ecclesiastical courts was transferred by Act of Parliament to a new—civil—court of probate and, a much more startling change, the bishops' courts were deprived of their matrimonial jurisdiction. No prelate of the Church could, for the future, decide the question whether a marriage was valid, or a child legitimate: this, henceforth, was the business of the State alone. And the State alone would authorise married persons to separate, would declare marriages null and void, would even undo and break the bond of marriages good, valid and true, and authorise the parties to remarry whom it had thus divorced, and authorise the clergy of the Establishment to remarry them. Twelve years later, in 1869, the State made a further rearrangement, of a most serious kind, when it dissolved that entity which it had constituted sixty-nine years earlier, *The United Church of Great Britain and Ireland*, and utterly broke its own association with what, before 1800, had been the State-Established Church of Ireland, so that this henceforth was no more, in law, than a private association of individuals professing certain beliefs and owning certain properties, its constitution a private settlement guaranteed by Act of Parliament as the existing constitution of any club or friendly society or corporation is guaranteed. And, not surprisingly, in an age of such changes, there began to be talk of a disestablishment that would go further still.

These changes had found the clerical leaders of the Established Church divided. There were, of course, not wanting bishops who fought the changes resolutely until the end. They were, however, but a party. The Church as such played no part in the matter; it had no part to play, because it had no judgment to make; and, the changes legally sanctioned, it accepted the new state of things quasi-automatically. To the letter all fell out as, in Newman's vivid analysis, it is foreseen all must always fall out in the Establishment[10].

[10] The analysis is, of course, that in the first seven of the *Lectures addressed in 1850 to the Party of the Religious Movement of 1833*, reprinted in *Difficulties of Anglicans*, I, 1-227.

One last blow was struck by the State against any theory that the Church of England was held by its Supreme Governor to be the teaching voice of Christ in this island when, in 1870, it really took in hand, for the first time, the business of providing the elements of an education for the mass of the nation's children. In the course of the lengthy agitation which forced this matter upon the politicians as a really urgent necessity, it soon became apparent that there was a real antagonism between the educational enthusiasts who belonged to the Church of England and those who belonged to the various Nonconformist bodies. On what should the religious education of the children in the new schools, built with public money, be based? The solution of the educational reform league which, in politics, was akin to the Liberal government then in power, and which in its religious sympathy was Nonconformist, was that there should be no mention of religion at all in these schools: the education they gave should be wholly secular. Against this the Church of England leaders fought hard, and presently the Government found a way out, discovering a solution that has had a most curious history since, and that has fulfilled very strikingly the prophecy, made by Disraeli, greeting critically the thing's first appearance[11]. The solution of 1870[12] was that each day there should indeed be in these schools a religious hour, but that no doctrine distinctive of any religious body was then to be taught. Each child was to have his Bible, and the religious hour was to be simple Bible

[11] " You will not entrust the priest or the presbyter with the privilege of expounding the Holy Scripture to the scholars; but for that purpose you are inventing and establishing a new sacerdotal class. The schoolmaster who will exercise these functions . . . will in the future exercise an extraordinary influence upon the history of England and upon the conduct of Englishmen "; Monypenny and Buckle, *Disraeli* (1912 edition), II, 462. " [Disraeli] might have added that the clause fathered by the member for South Hants established and endowed, if it did not create, a religious sect whose standard was the English Authorised Version and whose principles of interpretation must in practice be that any explanation was valid so long as it was not contained in a creed, catechism or other institutional formulary "; J. W. Adamson, *English Education, 1789-1902* (1930), p. 359.

[12] It was a Whig, William Francis Cowper-Temple, M.P. for South Hants, who proposed the amendment that embodied this solution— whence the convenient term used to describe the new institution, " Cowper-Templeism."

teaching—a reading lesson with the schoolmaster answering what questions his scholars asked. There was not to be any guarantee given or demanded as to the schoolmaster's own religious belief—not even that he had any belief at all. And it was to this kind of religious teaching alone that the State gave the official recognition of endowment out of the public funds.

The religious history of the mass of the people after 1870, the history of the working out of the solution devised in this fundamental Act which first made education compulsory, was to be very simple. Gradually—very gradually—the new State schools would attract the mass of the non-Catholic children of the country, the number of these schools growing steadily, while the increased cost of building and upkeep brought about the surrender of thousands of Church of England and Wesleyan schools. The mass of the English people gradually ceased thereupon to have any ideas of religion that were at all definite; the mass of Englishmen gradually ceased to associate moral questions with religion, or " institutional " religion with a divine foundation and guidance. There happened what has always happened, with the vast majority of mankind: ethical teaching once divorced from revealed religion rapidly became an empty theory, more or less ideally beautiful and attractive; and then, much more rapidly, the theory began to be trimmed and altered to suit the downward pressure from the inner recesses of the human soul. It is no secret to-day that, for the great mass of Englishmen, conduct in matters of sex has long been considered lawful or otherwise according to fidelity to personal ideals, to private pacts and arrangements: it is no secret that, now, the difference between mine and thine bids fair to disappear in much the same way as the difference has disappeared between purity and impurity. These are the generalities of the hour, universally agreed, universally deplored—and they are now beginning to be all but universally associated with an acknowledged lack of religious faith, and this last with the lack of a religious teaching that is definite.

The Education Act which inaugurated the kind of religious education that is at the beginning of so much of this collapse of elementary morals, was an important part of that general mid-Victorian reaction against the idea that religion is a supernatural thing, a thing not to be arranged and docked and trimmed by man but something superior to man, something divine, according to which man should, on the contrary, arrange and dock and trim his own natural impulses and desires. A view of Christianity, of the Established Church, now began in the last quarter of the nineteenth century to dominate the educated world, in which that Church was presented as disavowing any mission to teach definitely, with authority—and with no fear that it could err when it taught—what it was that God meant when He made known the Christian mysteries; as disavowing such an office, and adopting in its place the more congenial role of reassuring the age that nothing is ultimately certain, and that religious knowledge may change just as other knowledge is rapidly changing. And it was upon a generation largely fed on such a de-supernaturalised Christianity—the better educated minority of that time at all events—nourished on this thin religious Nominalism, knowing only as Christianity this collection of habits and conventions, with nowhere an authoritative voice that even desired to say " yea " or " nay," that Darwin's *Origin of Species*, for example, which had appeared in 1859, began to work as a powerful solvent of belief. It was upon this first generation of Christians thus emancipated by religious liberalism that Huxley's militant criticism fell in the twenty years next following; and by 1890 or so the havoc wrought in the religious faith of the educated Englishman was fairly complete.

Catholics played little part in either of these two revolutions—the social or the religious—which filled the twenty-five years after 1850, save for the activities of the Poor School Committee which the bishops had set up in 1847 and which one of the most brilliant of the Oxford converts, T. W. Allies, long served as secretary. The vast majority of the Catholics were poor uneducated working people; and all too few of the better situated belonged to the class whence came the new active philanthropists, the radical utilitarians and practising Benthamites[13]. It was one of the rare converts

[13] Barely a generation away from their re-admission into the life of the community, after centuries of persecution, of political exile

from this class, Frederick Lucas—a one-time Quaker and a cousin of the Brights—who had founded *The Tablet* in 1840. His untimely death in 1855, at the height of a struggle against Archbishop Cullen's conception of himself as the chief whose political direction all Catholics in Ireland should obey, may well have been, for Lucas, the supreme relief from a situation that had long been intolerable; but it removed from the English Catholics, at the age of 43, their one publicist whose writings had showed a real and continuous understanding that the condition of the poor was a question of social justice, an able writer moreover, with the temperament of a crusader.

In the year that Lucas died the tax on newspapers was abolished, and in 1861 the duty on imported paper; whereupon all the London dailies (the only daily papers which the country yet knew) came down to a penny, except the *Morning Post* and *The Times*. And it now became possible to publish a paper which the ordinary Catholic could afford to buy. This was *The Universe*, which appeared in 1860.

But whether the Catholics read the new, cheap paper or the more expensive *Tablet* (or *The Weekly Register*) the most insistent topic, continuously, for all this quarter of a century, was the resistance of Pope Pius IX to the King of Sardinia's long assault on the Catholic Church and on the Papal State. To the English Catholic of the time this was not, and could not be, any academic problem of continental politics merely—even though, supposing the impossible, he could have prescinded from the fact that the temporal power of the popes was closely related to the independence of the Holy See in its

and of social ostracism, how could these Catholics have the habit of public action? Newman, at this very time (21st November, 1852) analysing the causes of this very weakness, and declaring that " a youth who ends his education at seventeen is no match (*cæteris paribus*) for one who ends it at twenty-two," goes on to recall how, " Robbed, oppressed, and thrust aside, Catholics in these islands have not been in a condition for centuries to attempt the sort of education which is necessary for the man of the world, the statesman, the landholder, or the opulent gentleman." The result is " a moral disability." " Their legitimate stations, duties, employments, have been taken from them, and the qualifications withal, social and intellectual, which are necessary both for reversing the forfeiture and for availing themselves of the reversal. The time is come when this moral disability must be removed " (*Idea of a University*, p. xvi).

spiritual activities. It could not be a merely academic problem
for him because England, more than any non-Italian country
in Europe, save France, was actively interested in the Italian
revolution and was interested in it in a strongly anti-papal
sense[14]. Here, in fact, was a question of domestic politics,
which filled the newspapers for years; it involved the status
of the Pope and it was a question upon which the Catholics
stood alone—so far as public speech and action went. Truly
enough, the Tory foreign policy was, since 1830, more
friendly to Austria than to France; and had the party, when
it split in 1846, not lost, with so much else, its Foreign Secretary Lord Aberdeen, the cause of the Sardinian King as the
champion of Italian unity (to which, and for whom, the rights
of every other prince in Italy must therefore be sacrificed)
would not for a generation have gone publicly unchallenged
in this country.

As it was, however, the successive Whig-Liberal
governments steadily encouraged Victor Emmanuel in his
course, through the English ambassador at the Court of
Turin[15]; and at the Congress of Paris, which closed the
Crimean War in 1856, it was the Whig Foreign Secretary,
Lord Clarendon, who made the great speech in which—as
propaganda for the Sardinian hegemony—the administration
of the Papal States was held up to reprobation as a European
scandal[16]. If France should choose to interfere in Italian
politics, and lend an army to assist the Sardinians, then,
although this meant the end of Austrian influence in Italy,
the Whig government would risk the chance that France
would dominate the country in its turn—a people would have
been liberated and, along with much else, the Papal State
would have disappeared[17].

[14] Cf. the Prime Minister (Lord Palmerston) writing, 29th June, 1856,
to the Foreign Secretary (Lord Clarendon): " I should like to see
the Pope reduced to the condition of the Greek patriarch of Constantinople, and Romagna made into a republic. . . ." Bell,
Palmerston, II, 152.

[15] The famous Sir James Hudson.

[16] " In terms as precise and energetic," said Cavour, " as the most
zealous Italian patriot could have desired." Marriott, *A History of
Europe, 1815-1923* (1931), p. 206.

[17] " I told Cavour," wrote the English Prime Minister (Lord
Palmerston) in April, 1856, " that he might say to the Emperor
(i.e., Napoleon III) that for every step he might be ready to take

And so, in 1859-60, it came to pass. Without the benevolent neutrality of the English government this revolution would never have been accomplished[18].

It is, then, hardly correct to consider the preoccupation of the leaders of the English Catholics with this question as a " distraction " from those other, domestic, matters which concerned them as Catholics no less closely. But now that the inner history of the action of the Roman authorities during the long crisis is gradually being revealed, when we learn what divided counsels tugged Pius IX now this way, now that; when we learn that, from the time of his restoration in 1850 by the armies of France, neither he himself nor his Secretary of State, Cardinal Antonelli—whom in these political matters the Pope left in supreme charge—had ever any hope but that of delaying a little further the catastrophe which they saw was inevitable, it may be permissible to regret that such a fund of energy and sincerity was devoted, in England, to the support of what, in effect, was little more than diplomatic pantomime and show—serving, very mischievously, to confirm the general Protestant prejudice that Catholics must defend the indefensible when ordered to do so, and the prejudice, also, that their religious belief was bound up with an allegiance to that whole bad order of things, social, and political, which the French Revolution had all but destroyed entirely.

in Italian affairs he would probably find us ready to take one and a half." Bell, *Palmerston*, II, 153.

[18] In the critical years 1859-60 the combination of Palmerston (as Prime Minister), Lord John Russell (as Foreign Secretary) and Gladstone (then Chancellor of the Exchequer) was especially effective. To Russell's decision to accept the Foreign Office, in the summer of 1859, " may be attributed the fact that modern Italy acknowledges that she owes more to the moral support which she received from this country than to the material support of the third Napoleon." So Russell's biographer, Spencer Walpole, *Life of Lord John Russell*, II, 309. For the history of this " moral support," i.e., a vigorous and continuous diplomatic action friendly to Sardinia and hostile to the Pope, cf. *ibid.*, 310-29. " Ever since your famous despatch to Sir James [Hudson] of the 27th [Oct., 1860] you are blessed night and morning by twenty millions of Italians . . . [who] weep over it for joy and gratitude in the bosom of their families, away from brutal mercenaries and greasy priests," Odo Russell, the Government's diplomatic agent in Rome, wrote to his uncle (Walpole, *op. cit.*, II, 328). Pius IX was surely not far wrong when he described this English Foreign Secretary, in Jan., 1860, as " our bitterest enemy " (*Ibid.*, 329).

More mischievously still, the Italian events bred new and bitter divisions among the leading Catholics in England. For there were, at the time, a minority of Catholics in England who, better informed, guessed the real nature of the crisis. Some of these were less than enthusiastic when Cardinal Wiseman and the bishops summoned the faithful to public protests against the spoliation of the Pope; and where they might make no objection to the protest against the manifest injustice, and against the no less manifest hypocrisy[19], of the Liberal sympathisers with the cause of Sardinia, and against the flood of calumny which was, as always, the staple propaganda to interest the masses and enlist their sympathy, this minority dissented nevertheless from the spirit of the official protest, and from the way in which ecclesiastical authorities, and the lay publicists most in harmony with them, tended to identify in these public pronouncements, the cause of the doomed régime in the Papal States with Catholicism itself[20].

On the other hand, this controversy which filled so much of the 1860s had the great advantage that, like the controversy over the " Papal Aggression " in 1850-51, it served to give Catholics the beginnings of an education in public action. They now first began to handle the technical business of the public meeting, with a formal resolution and set speeches in support, that was characteristic of Victorian political activity, and the most effective means of propaganda for whoever desired to influence public opinion. The layman,

[19] E.g., the suggestion, latent in the attacks on the papal administration of the States of the Church, that social conditions there were bad beyond anything known elsewhere. A contemporary, *History of Eastern England* by A. D. Baynes (Gt. Yarmouth, 1872), states that in the county of Suffolk 1 in 12 of the population were paupers and 1 in 12 of the births illegitimate. The population had increased 56 per cent. since 1801 and crime by 300 per cent.; 143 parishes were without any kind of school and the average attendance of those who attended school was two years. Of 1,219 indoor paupers only 10 could read or write well; 46 per cent. of the men and 52 per cent. of the women of this county could not sign their names at their marriage; 80 per cent. of the felons had had no education at all (*op. cit.*, p. 301).

[20] It is perhaps typical of these mischievous divisions at their worst that Newman's great sermon *The Pope and the Revolution* (*Sermons preached on Various Occasions*, pp. 281-316) could be cited as a count against him. The date of this sermon is 7th Oct., 1866.

as a force influencing Catholic policy, now first began to come into his own, the middle-class layman especially[21]; and for the first time there began to be a Catholic public action in the provincial cities and towns. The toughening effect of the bitter controversies of these years was inestimable.

For the poorer Catholics, for the great mass of the Catholic body then, the bitterness of their adversaries was a very serious reality—as Ullathorne, in 1851, reminded the Prime Minister, " The aggression is against us and our Catholic liberties. Yet, my Lord, I grieve to say it, it is not we (i.e., the new bishops) who are affected by these acts. The hand of persecution points to one class amongst us, whilst it is another that is made to suffer. The persecution falls upon the tradesmen, work people, and poor servants—upon un-offending industry and the poor seeking their bread. And see how quietly they have borne it all ''[22].

The Catholics could have pleaded other reasons, also, for being less active than their descendants might have liked them to be in the social transformation of the nation during these twenty-five years. The year 1850 had found their ex-pansion seriously threatened, after twenty years of astonish-ing success[23], by the sudden influx of the famine refugees from Ireland—thousands and tens of thousands of utterly destitute,

[21] Cf. the account in the *Tablet* for 1st March, 1851, of the great meeting at Manchester on 20th Feb., of some 10,000 " men of mature age . . . of every class " to protest against the Ecclesiastical Titles Bill. The five-column report is taken from the *Manchester and Liverpool Irish Vindicator*. The *Tablet's* own correspondent adds a description of the event which concludes (p. 132), " It is well to note, that this meeting is purely a meeting of the laity—it originated with, and was carried out by, them, and was not directed or influenced by the Clergy in any way; they attended none of the preliminary meetings, and when asked to do so said, No; they approved of the movement, but wished it to be purely laical; and some half-dozen who, out of natural curiosity, observed the pro-ceedings from a quiet corner, had carefully divested themselves of the distinctive mark—the Romish collar—for the evening."

[22] Letter in *The Times* of 11th Feb., 1851. Cf. also the *Tablet* of 17th May, p. 313, " . . . the real weight of all this agitation falls—as usual—upon the poor, and especially upon poor cookmaids, and housemaids, and maids of all work. These are Lord John Russell's victims."

[23] In 1823 there were 358 churches and chapels in England and Wales; in 1837, 433; in 1845, 509; in 1851, 586.

half-starved and fever-stricken people[24]. Here was a crisis, indeed, which they could not possibly meet as it needed, a situation that must entail heavy losses and produce, for years yet to come, a new enduring strain on the Catholics of those districts to which these poor people mostly came. Nevertheless the Catholics, in the years 1850-1874, managed to build another 439 churches, and the number of their priests rose from 826 to 1,634. Also, it was in these same years that they began to face the serious burden that they must build and maintain a whole system of elementary schools, finding the money for sites and buildings and in addition, every year, the balance between the total cost of maintenance and the meagre government grant towards it. And where in 1851 there were but 99 of these Catholic schools, with an average attendance of 7,769 pupils, by 1874 there were 1,484 schools and 100,372 pupils[25]. No section of the community made, in these years, of its own free choice, anything like so costly a sacrifice, to assist the transformation of the Bleak Age. In the debates of 1870 on the Education Bill it was the Prime Minister himself who acknowledged, in the House of Commons, that the small Catholic minority had for years made itself responsible for an amount of the nation's educational destitution out of all proportion to its own numbers[26]. For priests as for people the schools could not but be a whole

---

[24] For the conditions under which these refugees often arrived, cf. an account given to the House of Commons, in 1851, of the findings of an inquest " lately held on the child of Anne Connell, who came to England by the *Pelican* steamer from Cork. . . . it appeared that the passage money from Ireland was 2s.; that the unfortunate passengers were on deck during the whole of the journey, without covering, three days and nights; that there were 750 of these miserable creatures, in all the rain and inclement weather, mixed up with the cattle on deck; and that the unfortunate infant had died of the hardships it endured during this passage. . . . Parochial authorities in Ireland were in the habit of supplying money to pay the passage of poor creatures to get rid of them; and the summoning officer stated that he knew as many as 1,000 had been shipped from Ireland at 1s. 6d. per head."—Speech of Alexander Cochrane, M.P. for Bridport, 10th March, 1851 (Hansard, 3rd series, Vol. 114, col. 1176-7).

[25] Catholic Poor School Committee, Reports for 1851 (p. 87) and 1874 (p. 72).

[26] " Their children form probably a tenth, an eighth, or even a sixth of the educational destitution," quoted Snead-Cox, *Life of Cardinal Vaughan*, II, 89.

time anxiety that left little leisure for the study of the ultimate causes of the ills of the time, a preoccupation which badly hindered the growth of the desiderated contemplative habit, as the struggle to secure the material basis of life must always hinder it.

The general election of 1874 at which, for the first time, the electors voted by secret ballot, definitely closes the age of the uncontested political supremacy of the middle classes. Wiseman had then been dead nine years, all but three of his colleagues of 1851 had gone with him into the next world[27], and at Westminster the reign of the one-time archdeacon of Chichester was now well into its stride. The Vatican Council had been held and Manning had been one of its leading figures. In this age whose general tendency was to regard nothing as really certain but what could be tested by instruments and experiments, the council had defined that the human reason is able to arrive at a knowledge of God's existence that is sure and certain; and it had also brought to an end two famous controversies about the papacy.

The first, which went back as far as the fourteenth and fifteenth centuries, was about the relation of the Pope's primacy over the universal Church to the authority of the episcopate of the whole Church assembled in a general council; and as to this, the General Council of 1870 defined that it is indeed the Pope who is supreme as against the bishops without the Pope, and not the bishops minus the Pope as against the Pope. It defined, furthermore, that the Pope's authority is such that he is the immediate ruler of all Catholics, so that no episcopal authority can stand between his primatial act and the duty of the faithful to obey.

The second controversy which the council settled concerned the Pope's infallibility—not a controversy as to whether the Catholic Church is infallible when proclaiming a doctrine concerning faith or morals, nor as to the infallibility of the Roman Church in the literal geographico-ecclesiastical sense of that term, but as to whether this infallibility belongs to the Pope personally as he exercises his office of supreme expositor of the meaning of divine revelation.

[27] The three were Thomas Joseph Brown (of Newport and Menevia), William Bernard Ullathorne (of Birmingham), and James Brown (of Shrewsbury).

This, at the moment, was the more urgent of the
two questions, because for some years before 1870 there
had been violent controversies, in France and in Germany,
about the need to have this point settled; controversies,
whether the definition was opportune—to put the question
in terms then commonly used. In the course of these
controversies there was much wildly inaccurate statement as to
what the infallibility meant; and incredibly bitter things were
said by less than well-informed critics of the " inopportunist "
party about the orthodoxy of their opponents—by the lay-
critics especially. The small group of Catholics in England
were not spared this trial. Few indeed there were of the
publicists whose faith and knowledge were such that their
heads remained cool and their charity unbroken. And in this
very year, 1874, Newman crowned ten years of generous service of this sort to the doctrine when, answering a tremendous
attack by Gladstone on the Papacy, that sold 100,000 copies in
a matter of weeks, he explained the definition of 1870 historically, and took account of the recent controversies, in *A Letter
to the Duke of Norfolk*[28].

While the council was in session came the Franco-
Prussian War—Prussia's third, short, victorious war within
seven years; and it ended twenty years of international restlessness by finally dislodging France from the leadership of
Europe. In place of France, for the next forty years, there
dominated, naked and unashamed, the armed violence devised
and organised by Bismarck: successful, blatant, blundering,
vulgar, and by none more heartily applauded than by the
English intellectuals. And for the best part of twenty years the
new power was militantly anti-Catholic. Against this Hohen-
zollern empire of a united Germany the French set up the
republic yet once again, and this Third Republic, after some
tentative years which the Right wasted in party squabbles,
fell into the hands of the radicals and became an even more
dangerous persecutor of religion than Bismarck. These anti-
religious measures of 1874-1890—whether in France or
Germany—brought no more protests from the non-Catholic

[28] Reprinted in *Difficulties experienced by Anglicans in submitting to
the Catholic Faith,* Vol. II, pp. 171-378.

religious bodies in England than the Sardinian king's spoliation of religion in Italy had provoked in earlier years. " Rome," of course, was only reaping what she had sown, and venerable heads shook with sorrowful satisfaction at the news of her just deserts. The veteran Liberal leader, the Lord John Russell of the Ecclesiastical Titles Bill, now an old man of eighty-two, came out from his long retirement to lead an evangelical movement of thanks to Bismarck for his anti-Catholic measures; and, yet once again, the pages of *Punch* witness to the popularity of the sentiment among the middle classes[29].

Lord Russell and Gladstone, the only political leaders openly to declare themselves hostile to Catholicism, were Liberals. It was one of the ironies of political life that the first use which the new electorate made in 1874 of that secure secret vote which the Liberals had provided, was to return to Westminster a Tory majority—the first for thirty-three years. As to the Catholic electors, for a long time now resentment had been steadily driving those who were politically minded away from their traditional alliance with the Whigs and Liberals—resentment, originally, at the hypocrisy of the " Papal Aggression " campaign[30], and then at the twenty years of anti-

[29] " Friends of religious liberty, and enemies of Roman Catholicism, decided on holding a great public meeting to support the Emperor; and they persuaded Lord Russell to promise that he would preside at it " (Spencer Walpole, *Life of Lord John Russell*, II, 446). " The cause of the Emperor of Germany," Lord Russell wrote, " is the cause of liberty, and the cause of the Pope is the cause of slavery " (*Ibid.*, 448). For the letters of Wilhelm I (18th Feb. 1874) thanking Russell and " rejoicing at the proofs afforded me by your letter that the sympathies of the people of England would not fail me in this struggle," and of Bismarck (24th Feb., 1874) also, " gratified by the active interest the Nestor of European statesmen is taking in our defensive warfare against the priesthood of Rome," cf. *ibid.*, 448-9.

[30] " The whole Papist population are bursting with fury at Johnny's letter," Lord Naas wrote to Disraeli from Ireland in Nov., 1850. " If they only act up to what they say, they will never let an Irish member vote for a Whig measure." The Whig Viceroy's secretary thought Lord John's act " a stultification of the whole Whig policy towards Ireland for the last half century and more." Monypenny and Buckle, *Disraeli* (1929), I, 1084. " Can the same people," the *Tablet* wrote, 9th August, 1851 (p. 506, col. 2), " that maintain the horrors of Van Dieman's Land, and permit the scenes of an Irish famine, allow itself, without making itself ridiculous, to censure the crowded prisons of Rome? "

papal foreign policy. And it was a second irony of politics that, just at the moment when the clumsiness of these two Liberal leaders, putting the last touches to this political blundering, might be thought to alienate Catholics once and for all, there should arise a new movement in Irish politics that would, in England, rivet to the Liberal party the mass of those Catholics of the lower orders, only recently enfranchised, whom no Catholic politician had as yet thought of organising, in no matter how rudimentary a fashion. For in this parliament of 1874 a new party made its appearance—an organised, purely Irish, party—whose sole *raison d'être*, to the great merriment of the whole world of English politics, was the legislative independence of Ireland from the imperial parliament.

This new party, which was not Catholic but national, had grown out of a conference held at the Bilton Hotel, Dublin, in 1870, which conference—of men of all parties and creeds—was, to some extent, one effect of England's (as it were) jettisoning the cause of its traditional supporters by disestablishing the Church of Ireland in 1869. " The Protestants are now the sole link between the two countries," the Irish viceroy had written twenty years earlier than this, " any attempt to invade [the Established Church on the part of the government] would alienate the whole Protestant body and render them Repealers also "[31]. Gladstone's revolutionary act had not, indeed, done quite so much as that, but it had produced the Home Rule movement, the invention, in great part, of disillusioned Protestant leaders.

One effect of the appearance of this new party was a shrinkage first of all, and then the total disappearance of what, so far, had been a principal means of English Catholics being elected to parliament. In all the forty years that followed the Emancipation of 1829 very rarely indeed had any English constituency ever returned a Catholic member[32]. English Catholics who sat in the House of Commons often did so as Liberal or Tory representatives of Irish constituencies. But once the new Nationalist party was really established, the Liberals all

---

[31] The viceroy (Lord Clarendon) to Greville, in *Memoirs*, VI, 175. The date is 3rd May, 1848.

[32] The rare exceptions were constituencies where the local great landowner was a Catholic.

but ceased to win any seats in Ireland; and, outside the Dublin University and the Orange enclave in the north-eastern counties, the Tories were no luckier[33]. If Englishmen who were Catholics wished to sit in parliament they must, henceforward, persuade their parties to help them to adoption as candidates in English constituencies, and, to that end, they must make what could be made of " the Catholic vote," where this existed, or could be talked of as existing. But whatever their prospects, they were soon diminished by the hard realism of the Nationalist leaders, who grasped all the implications of the fact that the majority of the Catholics in England were Irishmen, and prepared to exploit it fully.

There were only 57 of these Home Rulers in the parliament of 1874, but the next year there joined them a young Wicklow squire, Charles Stewart Parnell. By birth he half belonged to the Ascendancy, the other half of him was a virulently anti-English American, and the whole man was a politician of genius. Four years later again, an Irishman whom the factory life of an east-Lancashire town had bred, Michael Davitt, launched in Ireland the great agrarian movement of the Land League; and a year or so later, T. P. O'Connor, with the needed modifications, introduced this political association into Great Britain as the United Irish League to be, in fact, the Irish party organisation in the cities and towns of England and Scotland[34].

From this moment, when political life generally began to be hotted up, vast numbers of the Catholics in England were at last roused by a political movement that was really their own, that offered an objective for their deepest hatreds as for their loves, and which—in the early years—thrived from the all but universal opposition of the race amid whom they dwelt. What had also arrived—though none knew this—was the hour

[33] At the general election of 1868 Ireland returned 67 Liberals and 38 Conservatives. At that of 1874, 12 Liberals and 34 Conservatives: there were also 57 Home Rulers. After the Reform Act of 1885, which gave the farm labourers the vote, the Nationalists gained still more seats.

[34] But cf. William O'Brien's *Recollections* (1905), p. 214. " It was he [i.e., Isaac Butt] who discovered the power of an organised Irish electorate in Great Britain," a reference to the Home Rule League of Great Britain which Butt had founded in the days when he was the leader of the Home Rule party in Parliament.

of Ireland's revenge on the political machine that had worked her so much ill; and before the tragedy was ended the most remarkable changes had had to be introduced into parliamentary practice, and a real alteration had been thereby effected in the balance of the constitution.

It would be altogether outside the purpose of this study even to mention the leading incidents of the great political duel that filled the fourteen years 1879-1893. But it was during these years, in which passion ran higher than in any other period of such a length in English history[35], that a bishop who proved himself a creative and unusually successful organiser, the second Bishop of Salford, Herbert Vaughan[36], founded in 1884 the Voluntary Schools Association, to enlist the interest and the political power of the ordinary Catholic in an attempt to remedy the manifestly unfair effects of the education policy of 1870 as this had been developed. And so a second political movement that concerned the ordinary Catholic mightily was launched. It was a great misfortune, in the coming years, that the bitterest opposition to the recognition of the Catholic case came from those religious bodies which were a very strong element of the party sympathetic to the national aspirations of the Irish. The other great political party, the traditional enemy of everything Catholic in Ireland, the party whose Irish wing indeed was the Orange Society, was also the defender of the schools of the Church of England, and thereby of the Catholic schools that were in the same position. That the Bishop of Salford was known to be a Conservative, and to be the proprietor of *The Tablet*, an openly Conservative weekly which, while it rallied the Catholic forces to the amendment of the Education Acts with vigour and skill, attacked the Irish nationalist movement with a zeal no mere party organ could have exceeded, even using its peculiar prestige to suggest that the movement was frowned on at Rome—all this complicated matters still further[37].

It was in these critical years, the last ten years of his

---

[35] Nowhere, perhaps, is this so well brought out as in J. L. Hammond's *Gladstone and the Irish Nation*.

[36] Who in this same year, 1884, founded the Catholic Truth Society.

[37] See *William J. Walsh, Archbishop of Dublin*, by Patrick J. Walsh (1928), for all this.

very long life, that Manning rose to the fullness of his stature
as a leader: encouraging Gladstone in his more liberal Irish
policy; advising, and indeed working with, the Irish bishops
in the critical hours when the same Gladstone was intriguing
at Rome to prevent the nomination of a Nationalist to the see
of Dublin, and Salisbury to obtain a papal condemnation of
the Nationalist movement; sympathising diplomatically with
the bishops' grievances against his brother of Salford; boldly
warning the Holy See what surrender to the intrigues of the
English government must cost. Never were Manning's gifts of
statesmanship better displayed, his understanding of the world
of men, his sense of the critical occasion, a very genius for
political action—gifts and methods that contrasted oddly with
the autocratic spirit in which he ruled his own flock[38].

And it was in these same years when, in effect, the old
cardinal enjoyed a veritable primacy of fact—to the no small
indignation of " my sister of Canterbury "—that his intervention in the great dock strike of 1889, crowning a life-time's
active interest in the condition of the poor as a matter of social
justice, lit up as with a splendid, contrasting, solitary flare the
long waste of his Catholic contemporaries' general indifference
to the question of social rights.

Manning lived just long enough to see the prospect of
better days dawning for London with the institution of the
London County Council in 1889, and to hail the *Rerum
Novarum* of Leo XIII as the most profound expression of social
justice since the words spoken in the wilderness: " I have
compassion on the multitude." For the Catholics who shuddered to see how closely he was prepared to grapple with social
evils, the old man had the same courageous scorn as Leo XIII
for the diehards of the older régime. " Do you think that
twenty legions of Pharisees would keep me from my duty?"
was one characteristic retort. Alas, the leader of genius formed
no school, left no Eliseus to catch his mantle as he sped from
earth. But the memory of his universal sympathies, of his
generous indignation, of his virile public courage remained
to animate a younger generation, to inspire through Virginia
Crawford, for example, the beginnings of the Catholic Social
Guild and to strengthen the outspoken simplicities of the great

[38] *Ibid.*, for a well documented account of all this.

cardinal of the war years, Arthur Hinsley. Nor are the echoes yet silent of Manning's mighty veracity.

The year marked by *Rerum Novarum* saw a new Education Act which, supplementing the Act of 1870, abolished all fees in the State-provided schools and in the schools founded by the various religious bodies provided for the payment out of public money of the fees of children too poor to find the few pence needed.

" We must educate our masters," the grim adversary of the extension of the franchise to the working classes had declared, as he supported the State's new interest in popular education. The system of 1870 had had barely twenty years to show what it could do to this end when a group of men, of very different type from Robert Lowe, set about the production on the grand scale of literature of such a quality that the " masters " would not need to be educated in order to be affected by it. It was in these closing years of the nineteenth century that the great move began which has effectively sabotaged the thinking power of the mass of the population. The Napoleon of the only too successful campaign was, of course, Alfred Harmsworth, Lord Northcliffe of the Isle of Thanet.

When, in the year 1855, the London daily papers came down to a penny they did not change their character. The readers they had in mind were still the middle classes, and men. The papers, therefore, remained " overwhelmingly political," and outside the leading articles they only gave the bare facts of the news; but they reported parliament at length, and the speeches of leading politicians. This was also the golden age of the new weekly and monthly reviews, where great editors like John Morley, of the *Fortnightly* (1867-1882), or R. H. Hutton, of the *Spectator* (1861-1897), exercised very real influence on English life and thought. The first sign that an age wholly different was approaching was the success of a new type of weekly, *Tit-Bits*, for example, founded by George Newnes in 1880, and *Answers*, some years later, by Alfred Harmsworth. In these new papers there was nothing to strain even the meanest intelligence. To begin with, the reader had the assurance that he would not for long have to keep his mind fixed on the matter in hand—the articles were extremely short, three or four hundred words at most; the paragraphs were short, the sentences were short, the words as close to words of one syllable as intelligibility allowed; and all was in the form of a story.

When Harmsworth took over the (London) *Evening News* in 1894 he transferred to it the technique that had made *Answers*[39] such a success that he had been able to buy the *Evening News*; and two years later he launched a new morning paper, written in the same way, to sell at the marvellous price of a halfpenny. This was the *Daily Mail*. " In a few short years "[40] the influence of this paper had all but killed the traditional journalism of the nineteenth century as a power nationally effective. The day of the " brighter " papers had now begun, in which the news is offered in pre-digested form. " The old idea [had] assumed that [the reader] was a critical person who watched events and would resent the papers missing any serious news item "[41]. But henceforward the proprietors, whose aim is merely money and yet more money, had in view a mass of readers " whose interest in politics was slight, whose memories were short, who would never know or care if half the serious news were left out, but who day by day demanded bright stories to tickle their imaginations and to talk about. To report parliament at length, or even to report it fairly at all, was to bore and to estrange them "[42]. The great objective now is to send up the circulation of the paper, and to that end " stunts " are ceaselessly devised, the best means of capturing

---

[39] And the other papers he had founded.

[40] Ensor, *England, 1870-1914,* 310.

[41] Ensor, 314.

[42] Ensor, 314. A few sentences in which Harmsworth's biographer (Hamilton Fyfe, *Northcliffe,* p. 106) describes some of his characteristics reproduce the spirit of the new press and the spirit it desiderated and encouraged in the millions who bought the papers and found in them their sole contact with things of the " mind." " Boyish in his power of concentration upon the matter of the moment, boyish in his readiness to turn swiftly to a different matter and concentrate on that. . . . Boyish the limited range of his intellect, which seldom concerned itself with anything but the immediate, the obvious, the popular. Boyish his irresponsibility, his disinclination to take himself or his publications seriously "; a man of no culture, and with no ideal except " to spawn shoals of other papers on the same mental level." Ensor, 312-3, 315.

yet more readers of the kind which the proprietors have discovered will buy these papers.

Nor must it be thought that it was merely the workman
and the kitchen-maid whom these papers attracted; that they
were, indeed, as Lord Salisbury said of the *Daily Mail* (before
his party baronetted its founder), " written for office boys by
office boys." One important part of their readers were the
businessmen, uneducated and, " outside the matters in which
they made their money, [men with] the minds of children."
This particular public the new press gathered in immediately,
for " Existing newspapers ignored their naïve tastes, while
assuming an amount of critical intelligence which they simply
did not possess."

By 1900 the *Daily Mail* was already " in such prosperity that a landslide towards [this kind of newspaper] was
bound to follow "[43]. In 1904, Arthur Pearson, for example,
bought the *Standard*—which, however, died of the change.
The London Liberal papers now all came down to a halfpenny
and were " Mailised "—which meant that in the south of
England educated Liberalism no longer had a morning paper.
And, this same year, the *Daily Mirror* began publication, as a
paper for women readers (almost failing) and then as the first
picture paper—an immediate success.

The new journalism—its daily papers, its weeklies, its
magazines for children, for women, for men, its cheap story
books, its comics, its school tales, its shockers—was already,
when the World War of 1914-1918 began, the most powerful
influence on the intelligence of the ordinary Englishman who
was under thirty. And although it had not yet proceeded to
the maximum of its possibilities in discovering what " the
public " wanted and providing this[44], it had certainly ruined
beyond recovery any chance there was—if ever there were a
chance—of realising the dreams of the social reformers of an
earlier generation, of producing, that is to say, a democracy
intelligently critical of the rulers it elected and co-operating
constructively in the restoration of a truly human life for the

[43] Ensor, 315.
[44] In 1914, Mr. Ensor notes (p. 535), the press still catered for men.
Film stars, and such, are not yet " of more consequence than
statesmen "; nor have " business and politics alike become the
merest sideshows to personal ' romance.' "

nation[45]. No system of elementary education, it may be, could
be devised that could withstand such an assault of the trivial
upon the important. Certainly the system of 1870 failed utterly
to resist it. And ability to make use of the new literature tended
to become, in unacknowledged practice, the real ultimate
objective of the only education provided for the vast mass of the
English. So was a generation bred, more and more incapable
of serious reading, of serious reflection, even of a primitive
kind. Francis Thompson, a shrewd observer of his age, noted
and shuddered at the growing popularity of the new goddess,
Gelasma.

Can this vast sabotage of the intelligence of a nation be
a matter of no concern to a religion which maintains the
primacy of the intelligence among the spiritual faculties, and
for which faith is precisely an activity of the speculative intelligence? Are not the chances of bringing " after-Christians "[46]
back to religion diminished immeasurably if their powers of
judgment are rotted with a lifetime's preoccupation with the
superficial, the ephemeral, the imaginative, the emotional?
And what has been the effect of this immense revolution upon
those popular papers which profess to give to Catholics the
news about Catholic affairs and the news of the day as it
affects Catholicism? How have these reacted? And what has
been its effect on the Catholic publicist, clerical as well as lay?

What we have been considering is, indeed, yet another
revolutionary change in the things of the spirit. What of the
religious life of England in the years when this change begins?
It was now some forty years since the *Origin of Species*
(1859) in one way, and *Essays and Reviews* (1860) in another,

---

[45] Cf. for example, Ebenezer Elliott's poem, *The Press*, quoted in
Hammond, *The Age of the Chartists* (p. 19, note 1), to illustrate
" the wild hopes about this new force that inspired democrats "
round about 1840. The last verse runs:
" ' The Press ' all lands shall sing,
The Press, the Press we bring,
All lands to bless!
O pallid want! O labour stark,
Behold we bring the second ark,
The Press, the Press, the Press."

[46] The expression of C. S. Devas, one of the rare, original and constructive intelligences among the Catholic writers of the century;
cf. his *Key to the World's Progress* (1906), pp. 42, 51-58.

first startled the religious beliefs of the educated world. Many years passed, of course, before the nature of that shock was understood and its real effects apparent—the disappearance of the educated man's certitude that " Christianity " is a reality, and the beginnings in the minds of the very clergy of an uncertainty as to how much of it is really true. In 1889 another clerical work appeared that marked a further stage along the road from Catholicism to infidelity, *Lux Mundi*. The book was read to Newman, now in the last months of his life, and remembering the school of thought that had bred its authors he said only, " This is the end of Tractarianism."

The core of English religion during all these years—of the religion of the average Englishman among those fifty-eight per cent. who, in one society or another, kept faithfully to the public worship of God—was what it has been found convenient to call Evangelicalism: those of the English who were religious were " the people of a book," the Bible; they believed that after death there is a life that is eternal—of eternal reward or of eternal punishment, according to the use made of this life on earth; and they strove to live this present life as though its sole importance lay in its being a preparation for the next. These English of this mid-Victorian period were, so the latest historian of their age considers, " one of the most religious— among highly civilised—communities the world has ever known "[47]. And it is the apparent persistence of this Evangelicalism which this author has principally in view when he describes, as all but changeless, the appearance of the mental life of the English in the forty years after 1850.

In all that time, however, it appears certain that no religious body recaptured any appreciable proportion of that half of the population which already, by 1851[48], had given up

[47] Ensor, 137, whose use and explanation of the term Evangelicalism is here adopted.

[48] That 29.4 per cent. of the total population of 1851 who, as the census of Religious Worship showed, could have attended church but preferred not to attend, i.e., 40.6 per cent. of the able-to-go-to-church population. Cf. the judgment of the census Report: " . . . it is sadly certain that this vast, intelligent, and growingly important section of our countrymen [i.e., the artisans] is thoroughly estranged from our religious institutions in their present aspect . . . [they are] as utter strangers to religious ordinances as the people of a heathen country." *Report of the Census of Religious Worship* (1853), p. clviii (for which, cf. the next section).

the practice of religion. At best, all the energies of the religious
minded had only succeeded in holding the position then
attained. But by the year 1900 the whole Victorian culture
was quite evidently falling to pieces. '' In religion, in social
relations, in politics, in business, men grown contemptuous of
the old ideals were strenuously asserting the new ones. The
former clear objectives were gone, and as yet nothing took
their place ''[49]. Most important of all was the catastrophe, now
quite evident, that had befallen the prestige of religion.

It had always been the weakness of Evangelicalism that
the basis of belief was held to be an emotional and subjective
experience—how I feel, and believe that I am led to feel, when,
in a prayerful spirit, I read the Scriptures, for example. Another weakness was the multitude of the Evangelical's social
taboos. Such a system could give no answer to the reasoned,
critical questions of the new rationalists, and so it was that it
came to lose the educated laymen who had been such a force
for good in earlier years. Evangelicalism also lost ground to
the new forces of Anglo-Catholicism—a movement which must,
however, shrink from history as its Evangelical adversary
shrank from thought; and the warfare within the Established
Church, between Evangelical and Anglo-Catholic, did much,
it has been held, to shake the ordinary man's confidence in the
clergy, the spectacle of two such very dissimilar conceptions of
the same religion.

Freethinkers had developed enormously. It was not
only a matter of the influence of Bradlaugh, a man whom
decent society refused to touch, but of the highly respectable
Huxley, and of Matthew Arnold.

New developments in social life worked in the same anti-
religious direction as the teaching of these cultured, ascetic
agnostics. For there was leisure now, as there had never been
leisure before, and recreations so varied that the leisured man
need never be bored. And there was a royal patron of the new
cult of pleasure in the person of the heir to the throne who,
for forty years, amiably led the rout, setting himself '' in minor
ways '' to wear down '' a tradition [of religious observance]
which he disliked.'' The future Edward VII is held to be one
of the chief forces that made it possible, for example, for the

[49] Ensor, 305.

gross difficulty of the Victorian Sunday to be turned, by those
of the respectable classes who preferred to observe the Sabbath
elsewhere than in church. Nor did the old habit of family
prayers survive in houses where the princely guest introduced
the new recreation of the " week-end "[50].

With the advent of this age of leisure, and with the
decline in religious belief we can link another new phenomenon
of the last twenty years of the reign of Queen Victoria: it was
now that there began that definite fall in the birthrate, which
has, since that time, sunk ever lower and lower. It seems
agreed that it was from about 1877 that this decline began,
that " by far the largest (though not the sole) cause . . . . was
that people learned to use contraceptives,"[51] and that what
" served to give methods of birth-control their first really wide
advertisement in England "[52] was the prosecution in 1877 of
Charles Bradlaugh and Mrs. Annie Besant for the obscenity of
distributing literature that described such methods. The full
tale of the decline was masked in the population statistics by
the fact that the death rate, too, continued steadily to decline[53].
This breaking up of the social and cultural unity which
we know as Victorianism, proceeded ever more rapidly as the
twenty years or so went by that lay between the death of
Manning and the first of the World Wars.

There was the last of the old imperialist wars and the last
flare up of the old vulgar, national, self-satisfaction in support
of it; the short, cheap, triumph of the flash social ideals of

---

[50] Ensor, 143.

[51] Id., 271.

[52] Id., 104.

[53] Between 1871 and 1881 the death rate was 21 per thousand; between
1886-1890, 18.9; between 1896-1900, 17.7; in 1905, 15.6; in 1912,
13.8. And the population continued to increase at rates scarcely
lower after 1877 than before: 1851-1861, 11.9 per cent.; 1861-1871,
13.21 per cent.; 1877-1881, 14.36 per cent.; 1881-1891, 11.65 per
cent.; 1891-1901, 12.17 per cent.; 1901-1911, 10.90 per cent.. But
the birth rate was dropping steadily: in 1871-1875 it was 35.5 per
thousand; 1886-1890, 31.4; 1896-1900, 29.3; in 1905, 26.9; in 1912,
24.0 A most striking illustration of what had begun to happen is
afforded by the figures of maternity benefits paid between 1866
and 1904 by the Hearts of Oak Friendly Society. In the fourteen
years 1866 to 1880 the number of payments to members for con-
finements rose by 12 per cent. (from 2,176 to 2,472); in the following 24 years the number dropped by 52 per cent. (from 2,472 to
1,165); cf. Ensor, 499.

Victoria's heir; in politics, the return of the Liberals to real power for the first time in a quarter of a century—and, as it fell out, for the last time in their history; the emergence of the parliamentary Labour party; then the last battle over religious education in the public elementary schools, the renewal of the battle over Irish legislative independence, and the new battle over the powers of the House of Lords; the Established Church in Wales suffered the fate of the Established Church in Ireland; the Home Rule Bill reached the statute book, the Orangemen prepared for armed resistance to the government, and the Nationalists reacted in like manner to this threat of civil war; there were the first big strikes and lockouts, the furies of the agitation for " Votes for Women," and then, suddenly, slicing through the welter of all these controversies, August 4, 1914, and the long-threatened European War was a fact—the date after which nothing ever would be, or could be, the same again, and the differences in kind so great, so numerous, that seemingly no one more than fifty years of age when the war broke out had any business directing policy in the critical years that followed: years when the cinema became the omnipresent institution that we know; years of the new cheap motor car, and of the motor coach, of the beginnings of the recreational use of wireless telephony, of a still more elaborate organisation of leisure and of the growth of the idea that leisure is the true purpose of life; years, also, of the new chronic unemployment, and the distressed areas of South Wales and the north-east coast, and of the so-called " dole," of the general strike and the crisis of 1931 and the means test; years, none the less, of new hopes and determination, and of an understanding—in the very worst of places—that it is indeed a new age, an age when the realisation that there are rights in social matters has established itself pretty generally, with no chance of a return to the hopelessness of the pre-war creed that status is eternally settled and a poor man's duty is to be contented with what he is; years of yet further " emancipation " in morals, with birth control at last respectable, and the wherewithal now sold openly in decent shops in the decent streets of great towns, with the number of divorces mounting at a steadily increasing rate, and extra-marital intimacy beginning to be, like birth control, something lying outside the sphere of morals; the years of the first new persecutions of Catholics, in Mexico, in Russia, in Spain, in Germany; the years of Lenin and of Stalin, of Mussolini, of Hitler—" the years between the wars."

Manning's successor at Westminster, in 1892, was his own disciple Herbert Vaughan, now 60 years of age; and within five years the new archbishop had reversed two of Manning's major policies. He had the ban removed which for a generation stood between the layman and a university education; and, closing down his own diocesan seminary, he was the main force in the creation of the Central Seminary of Oscott which was, probably, the greatest thing the Hierarchy has achieved in all these hundred years. Manning, apocalyptic and authoritarian, misled by a corrupt following of Trent and St. Charles Borromeo, had by precept and example been the means of the foundation of nine diocesan seminaries: in Westminster, Birmingham, Liverpool, Salford, Leeds, Nottingham, Northampton, Clifton, and Southwark; nine of the thirteen sees[54] each with its own college where the future priests would be trained and taught their professional sciences, philosophy and theology. With Vaughan's advent to the metropolitan see this enthusiasm ebbed as speedily as it had risen—and as expensively. At Liverpool and at Southwark alone did the new institutions flourish and survive. The Central Seminary was very speedily a remarkable success, and it gave every promise of becoming the long desiderated, national centre of Catholic thought. But Vaughan's reign was short. Within six years of the new Oscott venture he was dead; and when, in his place, the founder of the Southwark diocesan seminary was named archbishop, the older policy was restored and the Central Seminary, deprived of its main support, ceased to be: after forty years one can safely say a major tragedy.

Vaughan lived long enough to see the State acknowledge something of its obligations to those 50 per cent. of its citizens whose consciences could not accept Cowper-Templeism as religious education, when by the 1902 Education Act it undertook the maintenance of the Voluntary Schools. " Payment on

[54] By the time Manning died (1892) there were 15 sees—Beverley having been divided, in 1878, into Leeds and Middlesbrough, and Portsmouth created in 1882, out of Southwark.

account," said the veteran cardinal, to whom it never occurred to talk of the claims of minorities to special treatment.

It was upon his successor, Francis Bourne, that the responsibility fell of organising the Catholic reply to the attack on the settlement of 1902 which followed only four years later. In the Liberal government that came back to power in 1905, after a generation in the wilderness, three successive ministers of education, with three different plans, essayed the elimination of the Voluntary Schools. For the four years 1906-1909 the fight was very fierce and the anxiety grave. One happy feature of the situation was the coincidence that in the northern sees were three of the toughest men that can ever have been bishops, Thomas William Wilkinson at Hexham, William Gordon at Leeds, and Thomas Whiteside at Liverpool—the first two, octogenarian survivors of the stone age; and the third, who had the six figure Catholic population of the great seaport impatiently waiting to be unleashed, " the mildest man who ever slit a throat,"[55] whose simple reply to the threat that the day of the Catholic school was done was to say that, that being so, the Catholic children of Liverpool would soon be running about the streets until the government policy changed[56].

The Education crisis passed away, with the ordinary Catholic perhaps a little less aware than he needed to be that what had really defeated the government was the fact that its plans threatened the thousands of schools of the Established Church, in defence of which the Opposition—158 strong—rallied unanimously; that beyond this there was the all but unanimously Conservative House of Lords; and, a very real consideration, that on this question the eighty-four votes of the Irish party, normally the ally of a Liberal government, would go against it—a difference of 168 votes on a division. The day would come, a generation later, when in the Established Church the party of compromise would carry the day; when Conservatism would no longer be, as by instinct, the political arm of a Church-school party; and when there would no longer be 84

---

[55] So Augustine Birrell, the first of the Liberal education ministers whom he had to fight, after meeting Whiteside socially, many years later.

[56] And cf. Cardinal Vaughan, some years earlier, " There have got to be Catholic schools—for this reason, that Catholic children will not go to any others." Snead-Cox, *op. cit.*, II, 110.

Catholic members of the Irish party[57]. When the hour came
which simpletons had desiderated—" When there aren't any
Irish members and we will be forced to stand on our own "—
the controversy would be conducted with other weapons than
those of, say, Thomas Whiteside. And to-day we are in a worse
case than before 1902.

In the diocese of Salford the stirring events of 1906-09
had a permanent memorial in the foundation of organisations
which, had they survived, might have set England well ahead
among countries endowed with a reality of Catholic Action.
The bishop at this time, Louis Charles Casartelli, a distinguished orientalist, was a prelate singularly free from the conventional narrowness of the Victorian cleric, a man of really
cosmopolitan mind, with a breadth and variety of intellectual
sympathies that recalled Wiseman, a bishop to whom the
activities and the problems of the churches of continental
Europe were as familiar as those which faced him in his native
Lancashire. And it was with the *Volksverein* of München-
Gladbach before his mind, and the Italian *Opera dei Congressi,*
that he encouraged the movement known as the Salford Diocesan Federation; in idea (and for a few short years in reality)
the diocese in action, clergy and laity co-operating under the
leadership of the bishop. The crisis which took the reality out
of the movement was the North-West Manchester by-election
of 1908 when Mr. Winston Churchill needed to seek re-election
on his first appointment to a cabinet post. It was the moment
when two of this Liberal government's education bills had been
beaten off, and a third attack imminent—and it was a constituency where the Catholic vote was important. In the event the
new Liberal cabinet minister lost his seat; one powerful section
of the local Irish politicians blamed the Federation, rightly or
wrongly, for the defeat of their own pro-Churchill activities;
the result was much bitter feeling and a paralysis of organised
Catholic action for many years to come. The Federation, however, lingered on for the best part of another twenty years, and
the memorial of all that it had promised and of the

[57] At the requiem for John Redmond, sung in Westminster Cathedral,
Cardinal Bourne explicitly broke the rule of a lifetime to preach
a panegyric of the Nationalist leader in order, as he said, to give
public recognition to all Redmond had done in defence of the
menaced Catholic schools of England and Wales.

solution which it offered for the organisation of Catholic influence upon contemporary English life[58], will be found in the files of the monthly review, *The Catholic Federationist,* which it never failed to publish until the end, and to which the scholarly, well-informed bishop regularly contributed a signed leading article on current events.

It was from a group of Catholic trade-unionists that the initiative came which produced this remarkably well-thought-out organisation; and one of the Federation's earliest activities was an active lobbying of the Labour Party conferences to secure the deletion from the agenda of the annual resolution calling for secular education in the public elementary schools. In this the lobbyists ultimately succeeded. And there next developed, as a permanent body, the National Conference of Catholic Trade Unionists, which for years did yeoman service in the struggle to keep the parliamentary Labour Party—to which the Conference was affiliated—a non-Socialist body. The National Conference came to an abrupt end when the Labour Party " socialised " its constitution in 1918. At the meeting of the Conference held in Leeds that same year, it was resolved to ask the bishops for a practical direction, whether to continue,

[58] The Federation was organised with the parish as a unit. All Catholics over 16 were eligible, and all posts were really elective. In many respects the form of the organisation was similar to that of a Trade Union or the modern political party. Active membership would itself be an education in collective public action. Although the place of the parish priest in his own branch was safeguarded, the Federation was not clerically controlled; it was autonomous vis-à-vis the clergy, but not autonomous vis-à-vis the bishop. Within the Federation there were to be a variety of social, recreative and educational activities; rambling clubs (*lege* hiking), debating societies and a school of Social Science are some of the realised works that one recalls. It was, of course, in no sense whatever a political party, but it was definitely meant to train Catholics for active participation in whatever party their interest in public affairs prompted them to join. The plan was to inform the Catholic with Catholic social teaching, and with a judgment based on Catholic principles about all the practical questions of the day, and to send him thus informed into local public life. What such a scheme needed absolutely, if it were to surmount prejudices and suspicions too evident to need description, was the active presidency of the bishop—the bishop active in the Federation, and seen to be active by all, at every turn. In nothing could the fallacy be more fatal that, whoever is commissioned in authority's name enjoys authority's prestige, and is as effective as authority's self.

and if so how?   But to the queries put, the Conference, mysteriously enough, never received a reply, and it never met again.

The Catholic minority entered upon " the years between the wars," as little united, as evidently lacking a policy, and as badly off for constructive leadership as was the country at large. That same exhaustion of serious purpose and of appropriate initiative which afflicted the whole nation was their fate also. This state of things is all the more remarkable when it is recalled that this was the reign of the dynamic Pius XI (1922-39), from whom, year by year, there poured forth an unexampled constructive criticism of affairs, practical direction about objectives, and incitement to action more stimulating than had ever come from any Pope before.

It was the explicit instruction of those to whom this book owes its existence, that what was written should not be mere conventional panegyric, but an historical meditation upon the past such as might serve to throw light on the present and, perhaps, offer guidance for the future. History written in this spirit may contain some surprises: it will certainly offer some challenges. And to challenge a people to do better—a whole people—is the highest service that can be rendered them. The century whose many-sided Catholic achievement the pages that follow will critically record is yet that same century in which our country has slipped further and further away from belief in God. It is with the need before us to relate these two sets of facts that we ought to contemplate the achievement, and the coming years. And, since few things are more helpful than to see ourselves as we are sometimes seen, here are the recent judgments of two foreign observers, who know England well and who are neutral to all the contentions that for centuries have divided us from the mass of our fellow countrymen. The one writes of the England of to-day from his own observation of it; the other is, of all men, the one who has made the closest study of nineteenth-century England and it is of this, rather, that he writes. " Les catholiques," so M. Halévy, " étaient par naissance ou par choix, des émigrés de l'intérieur.

L'histoire du progrès du catholicisme romain en Angleterre ne peut être considérée comme faisant partie intégrante de l'histoire d'Angleterre"[59]. And M. Pierre Maillaud seems to re-echo this judgment, " The position of the Roman Catholic Church in England is not discussed here because, however powerful its influence in the past or its potential influence in the future, it does not at present penetrate the social consciousness or act upon the national way of life ''[60].

[59] *Histoire du peuple anglais au XIX siècle* (1947), IV, 357.
[60] *The English Way* (1943-4), p. 208 n.

II

THE ENGLISH CATHOLICS IN 1850

By Philip Hughes

ENGLAND, one hundred years ago, was a country whose population had just doubled itself in half a century; and this in a novel movement which, to the mingled wonder and fear of many beholders, was showing no signs of slackening. According to the census of 1851 the population then stood at 17,927,609[1], roughly two-fifths of what it is to-day.

It is of the first importance to our subject that we should form some idea how many of these were Catholics, to what sections of the community the Catholics chiefly belonged, and how they were distributed throughout the country.

The census taken in 1851 affords us a first and very valuable clue for, alone of the whole long series, it attempted to establish the numbers of the church-going population. So violent were the controversies when these figures were published[2] that the interesting experiment was never repeated. But in 1851 the buildings set apart for worship were counted, and the number of sittings each contained, and the number of those who attended the various services on a given Sunday[3]; and the totals were classified according to the various religious bodies. Now according to this census 252,783 Catholics[4] attended Mass on Sunday, March 30th, 1851; on the other hand, the same census is witness that there were at this moment living in

---

[1] Population of England and Wales.

[2] *Religious Worship in England and Wales,* London, 1853, by authority of the Registrar-General; also, by the same authority, in 1854, *Religious Worship in England and Wales, Abridged from the Official Report.*

[3] 30th March, 1851.

[4] This figure is an estimate. The actual number counted was 240,792. But of the 570 returns sent in, 27 were defective. The census officials arrived at the estimated total by assuming " that each place of worship making defective returns would have had as many attendants as the average number shown to have been present at the places of worship making complete returns." *Religious Worship in England and Wales,* p. clxxxii.

England and Wales 519,959 people who were Irish by birth. Here, in these two details, is our first clue to the actual number of Catholics.

The first disturbing fact which the figures revealed to the England of 1851 was that a huge mass of the population did not attend public worship at all—out of the total population of 18,000,000 or so, only 7,261,032 went to church on that appointed Sunday. Next it was shown that, of these seven and a quarter millions the proportion of Church of England to non-Church of England worshippers was as 52 to 48—this was the revelation around which the controversy centred; and it was also shown that while the proportion of worshippers to sittings provided—at the most numerously attended service—was, in the Church of England, no higher than 33 per cent., that proportion in the next two largest groups was much about the same: with the Independents (10.5 per cent. of the total number of worshippers) it was 38 per cent. and with the Wesleyans (14.1 per cent. of the whole) it was 35 per cent. In three-quarters of the country's places of worship, two seats out of three, then, were vacant at the best attended service of all! Such was the religious practice of the people whose indignation at the " Papal Aggression " had set the country ablaze in this very year of the census[5]. Catholics, in 1851, were in the unique condition that their attendances greatly exceeded the number of sittings—there were only 186,111 sittings for those 252,783 Catholics who went to Mass on the given Sunday. These formed 3.5 per cent., almost, of the total number of worshippers.

How shall we employ the clues which the census provides? And first, the clue of the Mass attendance figures? The officials who reported on the census allowed a margin of 30

[5] If those indifferent to " institutional " religion be set aside from the demonstrators, and the Nonconformists also, who " generally kept aloof " (so Greville, *Memoirs*, VI, 377; and cf. John Bright's testimony in the House of Commons, 7th Feb., 1851, " In the north of England the Dissenters have unanimously held aloof from the roar that has been got up in reference to this question "; Hansard, 3rd series, Vol. 114, col. 252) then these violent protestations made, in the name of the nation, by bishops, chapters and others, even had they been representative of the whole body of the practising members of the Established Church, would have been, in fact, representative of no more than 30 per cent. of the whole body of the nation.

per cent. to cover those unable to attend church—small children, the aged, the sick and so forth—and thus came to the conclusion that as well as the 7,261,032 who actually, at least once, attended church, there were another 5,288,294 who, able to attend, *neglected* to do so, i.e., the proportion of the able-to-go-to-church population who yet chose not to go was as high as 42 per cent.[6]. If we assume that the Catholics were at least as assiduous to attend Mass as were their neighbours to attend church or chapel—and if assiduousness were the only factor influencing their practice—then the number of Catholics able to go to Mass in 1851 was 435,833; and if the proportion of these to the number away from church because unable to go is, again, considered as being the same as what obtained generally, then the total number of Catholics in 1851 was 622,619, i.e., about 3.46 per cent. of the total population of England and Wales; perhaps half as many Catholics, proportionately to the total population, as there are to-day.

But I think we must consider the actual numbers of the Catholic population in 1851 as being above this figure of 622, 619, and accept it as the fact that fewer Catholics than we realise went, or were able to go, to Mass regularly in those days when churches were as few and far between as will presently be shown.

We have, in fact, other clues to the numbers of the Catholic population which must be studied, clues quite independent of that just considered. One clue is the account given to the Holy See by the bishops a few years earlier than this—and a few years earlier than what we have yet to mention, namely the huge increase in the rate of the Irish immigration into England, that followed upon the great famine of 1845-47. According to the bishops' reports there were, in 1837-40, a total of 452,000 Catholics in England and Wales. Had this increased by no more than 170,000 in the eleven years? This is, of course, a very remarkable increase, 37.6 per cent.[7]. But

---

[6] The proportion of " neglecters " to " attenders " was greatest in what is to-day the metropolitan borough of Bethnal Green, where out of a population of 90,193 only 6,024 attended church, i.e., 9.5 per cent.—a state of things approximating to the general average a hundred years later; as to morning service, out of the 90,193 only 1,796 attended.

[7] The general population increased in these years by 12.65 per cent.

—a further clue—in the ten years 1841-51 the number of Irish-born residents in England and Wales had increased by as many as 226,519 so that in 1851 the total of Irish-born residents in England and Wales stood at 519,959[8]. Now a very high proportion of these 519,959 Irish-born inhabitants of England and Wales were Catholics. It seems impossible that the total number of Catholics in England and Wales can then have been no more than 622,619, i.e., that the total of Catholics of English race and of Catholics born in England of Irish-born parents amounted to no more than the difference between 622,619 and what proportion of the 519,959 Irish born were Catholics. What was this proportion? Could it have been less than three out of four? If we reckon it at 75 per cent. then there were in England and Wales in 1851 389,970 Catholics who were born in Ireland[9]. Were there, as against these, no more than 232,619 Catholics who were born in England, whether of English or of Irish-born parents?

Again, the total number in 1851 of Irish-born immigrants who had come to England and Wales during the years 1841-51 was 226,519. The general population of England and Wales had increased during these same years by 12.65 per cent.; and at this rate the Catholic community of 452,000 described in the bishop's reports would have increased to 509,178. If to this we add the Catholic proportion (i.e., 75 per cent.) of the 226,519 Irish immigrants of these years, namely 169,889, we arrive at a total Catholic population of 679,067 in 1851[10]. Of these something like a quarter of a million possibly were of English stock[11]; seventy years earlier

[8] Of these, 386,588 were over 20 years of age.

[9] Of whom 289,941 were over 20 years of age.

[10] Very much less, indeed, than the wild estimate of a Catholic member of parliament—T. C. Anstey—on 4th Feb., 1851: that the Catholics number a million and a half; cf. Hansard, 3rd series, Vol. 114, col. 93.

[11] This is much more than such a contemporary as *The Times* would allow (10th Jan., 1854) reviewing the report of the famous census of attendance at public worship—in language which certifies how little the paper had recovered from the bigotry that inspired it, four years earlier, to exploit the legend of the " Papal Aggression." " We may very safely," said *The Times*, " put 150,000 as the sum total of the sittings required for *bona fide* English Papists; nor should we, indeed, have much hesitation in reducing even this amount by fully one-third."

Burke, following Berington, had estimated the total number of Catholics at 60,000.

But whatever their exact numbers, one important matter is certain; these Catholics were by no means evenly distributed over the face of the country; they were less evenly distributed, by far, than even their fellow countrymen were now beginning to be. For England had, in 1851, reached the central moment of her transition from rural civilisation to urban, and just one half of her people, so the census of this year demonstrates, lived in the area of 1,724,406 acres on which were built some 580 towns. The other half, dwelling in " villages and detached dwellings of the country," occupied some 35,600,000 acres. The two Englands of to-day are already remarkably distinct, in the census of 1851, and for the first time.

The London of this census has 2,362,236 people[12]— something more than one-ninth of the total population of the country[13]. But in the south and south eastern parts of the country, in England south of the line Gloucester to Grimsby, there is no other town of even 150,000[14].

The " north of England "—north that is to say of the Ribble and the Aire—touched a million and a half, a third of whom were in the industrial districts of Tyneside and Durham. Outside these districts York was the only considerable town; it had 36,000 people; Carlisle had 26,000. But Newcastle-on-Tyne had 88,000 and Sunderland 64,000; Tynemouth and South Shields had each 29,000 and Gateshead 26,000.

It was between the " north," as just described, and the line Grimsby-Gloucester that there lay the greater part of what had never been before[15] and what no other part of the world could then show, whether in pride or in sorrow, the new

---

[12] This " London " is, approximately, the area which to-day is the Administrative County of London.

[13] 17,927,609.

[14] The largest towns are Bristol with 137,000 inhabitants, Plymouth-Devonport (102,000), Brighton (70,000), Norwich (68,000), Portsmouth (62,000), Bath (54,000), Southampton (36,000), Exeter (33,000), Ipswich (just as populous) and Yarmouth (31,000), Aylesbury (28,000), the two university cities of Oxford and Cambridge (each 28,000), and Northampton (27,000).

[15] " . . . half the population urban—a situation which had probably not existed before, in a great country, at any time in the world's history." Clapham, I, 536. And in this particular area very much more than half the population was urban.

industrial districts and the new great towns. The greatest of these were in south and south-east Lancashire: Liverpool (376,000), Manchester with Salford[16] (400,000), Oldham[16a] (72,000), Preston (70,000), Bolton (61,000), Stockport (54,000), Blackburn (47,000), Macclesfield (39,000), Wigan (32,000), Bury (31,000), Rochdale (29,000). In the West Riding of Yorkshire were Leeds (172,000), Sheffield (135,000), Bradford (104,000), Halifax (32,000) and Huddersfield (31,000). The port of Hull counted 85,000 people and there were another half dozen towns of between 20,000 and 25,000. In the midlands Leicester had as many people as Bolton, and Nottingham nearly as many (57,000); Derby (41,000) and Coventry (36,000) lay on the edge of a central industrial district, where the greatest towns were Wolverhampton[16a] (120,000), Stoke[16a] (84,000) and Birmingham which, with its 233,000, was the third greatest city in England after the capital.

It is only in these industrial districts—in Lancashire especially— and in London, that the Catholics are at all numerous; here alone are they more than scattered units; it is here, too, that the Irish immigrants abound. By comparison, elsewhere and in the south especially, as the Gloucester-Grimsby line divides the country, there are—outside London—hardly any Catholics at all[17].

We may now set out in the terms of the religious census, and more prosaically than the famous first pastoral letter of the new cardinal and Archbishop of Westminster[18], what the new ecclesiastical arrangements were that he had done so much to bring about. Here, in tabular form, are the areas allotted to the thirteen sees, the number of churches and priests subject to the new ordinaries, the statistics of attendance at Mass, and of the Irish-born population, according to the census-returns.

[16] Which the census, in its general tables, combines and considers as a single unit.

[16a] The parliamentary borough.

[17] 24,521 counted at Mass in this " south " on 30th March, 1851 (as against 104,302 in Lancashire)—just under 1 per cent. of the total population, in an area that was a good half of England.

[18] For example, " until such time as the Holy See shall think fit otherwise to provide, we govern and shall continue to govern the counties of Middlesex, Hertford and Essex as ordinary thereof, and those of Surrey, Sussex, Kent, Berkshire and Hampshire with the

(Continued on page 51)

Diocese and Territory	Total Population	Churches and Chapels	Priests serving these	Catholics at Mass in these March 30th, 1851	Total Population Irish by Birth
WESTMINSTER					
Metropolitan London	1,745,601	26	72	27,494	81,453
Middlesex (*extra* Metropolitan London)	150,606	8	12	575	2,113
Hertfordshire	173,962	3	2	355	628
Essex	344,130	9	10	1,604	2,314
Total	2,414,299	46	94	30,023	86,508
SOUTHWARK					
Metropolitan London	616,635	8	19	8,500	26,095
Surrey (*extra* Metropolitan London)	202,521	9	6	1,033	2,056
Kent (*extra* Metropolitan London)	485,021	11	10	1,113	1,170
Sussex	339,604	8	8	785	2,056
Hampshire	402,016	10	12	3,082	6,701
Isle of Wight		3	3		
Berkshire	199,224	5	6	794	702
Channel Islands		3	3		
Total	2,245,021	57	67	15,307	38,394
NORTHAMPTON					
Northamptonshire	213,844	5	6	665	1,738
Buckinghamshire	143,655	3	4	322	385
Bedfordshire	129,805	1	1	50	328
Huntingdonshire	60,319	0	0	—	268
Cambridgeshire	191,894	4	2	360	989
Norfolk	433,716	7	8	1,321	1,082
Suffolk	336,136	6	6	374	704
Total	1,509,369	26	27	3,092	5,494
NOTTINGHAM					
Nottinghamshire	294,380	3	5	1,791	2,621
Derbyshire	260,693	10	9	2,499	3,979
Leicestershire	234,957	15	13	1,893	1,738
Rutland	24,272	0	0	—	82
Lincolnshire	400,236	14	12	1,596	2,344
Total	1,214,538	42	39	7,779	10,764

Diocese and Territory	Total Population	Churches and Chapels	Priests serving these	Catholics at Mass in these March 30th, 1851	Total Population Irish by Birth
BIRMINGHAM					
Warwickshire	480,120	26	34	7,889	11,894
Staffordshire	630,545	35	40	8,765	15,853
Worcestershire	258,733	12	14	3,029	2,084
Oxfordshire	170,247	8	8	928	474
Total	1,539,645	81	96	20,611	30,305
SHREWSBURY					
Shropshire	244,898	11	8	469	2,757
Cheshire	423,526	18	17	9,053	22,812
Flint		4	6	354	612
Denbigh		1	1	305	1,036
Caernarvonshire	404,328	1	1	103	583
Anglesey				—	340
Merioneth				—	77
Montgomery				—	205
Total	1,072,752	35*	33	10,284	28,422
NEWPORT AND MENEVIA					
Monmouth	177,130	8	10	2,383	5,888
Hereford	99,120	5	5	119	363
Glamorgan		3	3	2,000	9,737
Carmarthen		0	1	99	514
Pembroke	607,456	1	2	150	703
Brecon		1	1	191	674
Radnor				—	90
Cardigan				—	279
Total	883,706	18	22	4,942	18,248

* Three of these are " stations " only.

Diocese and Territory			Total Population	Chur-ches and Chapels	Priests serving these	Catholics at Mass in these March 30th, 1851	Total Population Irish by Birth
CLIFTON							
Gloucestershire	…	…	419,514	15	20	3,541	6,563
Somerset	…	…	456,259	12	12	1,321	2,222
Wiltshire	…	…	240,966	4	3	995	709
		Total	1,116,739	31	35	5,857	9,494
PLYMOUTH							
Devon	…	…	572,330	9	9	1,186	4,940
Dorset	…	…	177,095	9	9	847	916
Cornwall	…	…	356,641	11	6	459	1,541
		Total	1,106,066	29	24	2,492	7,397
LIVERPOOL							
Lancashire†	…	…	886,567	84	113	69,783	112,875
SALFORD							
Lancashire‡	…	…	1,180,834	32	37	33,029	79,635
BEVERLEY							
Yorkshire	…	…	1,789,047	61	69	20,629	43,632
HEXHAM							
Northumberland	…	…	303,568	20	23	5,564	12,666
Durham	…	…	411,679	20	20	8,346	18,501
Cumberland	…	…	195,492	9	12	2,739	9,866
Westmorland	…	…	58,397	2	2	400	607
		Total	969,126	51	57	17,049	41,640

(Footnotes on page 51)

(*Continued from page* 47)

islands annexed as administrator with ordinary powers." It hardly needs saying that such language (from the chief of the new hierarchy) was everywhere quoted as proof of " aggression," and it was made a count in the Government's case in Parliament. Greville, friendly but dispassionate, writes, " Wiseman, who ought to have known better, aggravated the case by his imprudent manifesto " (*Memoirs*, VI, 375), and when the cardinal's vicar-general, Dr. Whitty, to whom the pastoral had been sent from Rome, met Ullathorne he had a bad quarter of an hour, while the bishop lectured him for his rashness in publishing it to the world without reference to any one of the bishops, Wiseman being still abroad, no one knew exactly where.

FOOTNOTES FOR TABLE

† The hundreds of West Derby, Leyland, Amounderness, and Lonsdale; registration districts 461-7 and 481-6 in the census of 1851.

‡ The hundreds of Salford and Blackburn; registration districts 468-480 in the census of 1851. It was against the wishes of the Lancashire vicar apostolic that the county was divided into two sees. The diocese of Salford as originally cut off from the Liverpool bishop, by the bull of 29th Sept., 1850, included the hundred of Leyland. During the interval in which the new Bishop of Liverpool continued to rule Salford also (as administrator-apostolic) he procured from the Holy See a new arrangement of boundaries that restored Leyland to his jurisdiction (Litt. Apostolicæ, *Cum ecclesiasticam hierarchiam*, 27th June, 1851).

Can we draw from these figures of attendance at Mass any conclusions that are really more than guesses about the total number of Catholics in the various cities? The Report of the census, which is the source whence come these figures, gives an elaborate analysis of the returns for 61 towns of England and Wales. It will tell us, for example, that in Liverpool (a city of 376,000 inhabitants) 123,728 individuals attended church or chapel once on that Sunday, March 30th, 1851, and that 38,132 of these were Catholics present at Mass. What can we conclude from this as to the total Catholic population of Liverpool at that time? From the general, all-over, total figures of church-attenders and of people considered able to go to church, the census officials concluded that, taking England and Wales as a whole, 58 per cent. of those able to go to church actually did so; only 42 per cent. neglected to go. But in Liverpool the church going, evidently, was below this average; and study of the detail of Sunday observance in the 61 towns reveals other extraordinary differences. For example, north of that Gloucester-Grimsby line which has already been mentioned as a kind of frontier between the two Englands of 1851, out of 37 towns listed here, only six reached this " national average " of 58 church-goers to every 42 church-neglecters[19]. The great majority of the " northern " towns have less, and very much less, than the national average of church goers; while all but one of the 17 " southern " towns listed in the census have more than 50 per cent. of church goers[20], all but 11 of the 37 " northern " towns have under 50 per cent. And it is hardly possible to find a common ratio that will serve to calculate the number of Catholics in towns of such diverse habits as Liverpool, where 47 per cent. of the general population go to church, and Preston where that percentage is only 28.6. And what if we take into account the ascertained number of the Irish-born inhabitants of these towns? In Liverpool, for example, where 38,123 Catholics were counted at Mass, the Irish-born amounted to 83,813 in all; in

[19] The six were Warrington (population 23,000), where 58.7 per cent. go to church; Huddersfield (31,000), 59.0 per cent.; Leicester (61,000), 59.5 per cent.; York (36,000), 60 per cent.; Chester (28,000), 64 per cent.; and Wakefield (22,000), 73.6 per cent.

[20] The exception is Norwich (68,000 people), where the proportion of church-goers is 43.8 per cent.

Leeds, where 3,644 Catholics went to Mass there were 8,466 Irish-born; in Birmingham there were 3,383 at Mass and the Irish-born were 9,341[21].

The main resource of the new bishops as they took up the task before them was, then, the faith and goodwill of an urban population, rarely more prosperous than working class families could be prosperous in those grim times, so well called the Bleak Age[22]. And if ever our story is told it will be, inevitably, the story of the achievement of a poor, working-class population, in the main Irish by birth or by descent.

This year of 1850-51 stands out in the economic history of modern Britain as that turning point when, very definitely, and as the only alternative to national ruin, the real rulers of the country made it the goal of their activities to transform England into an " Industry-State "—into a state, that is to say, " which lives by the export of its manufactures." And this they had done because England, now, " could do no other." Proudly, ignorantly, or reluctantly, they faced the risks which this policy involved, because in this way only could the nation escape defeat in what was seen as " a question of time, a race between life and food "[23]. " Export or starve," the grim alternative was already well understood a hundred years ago.

The " Industry-State " had not indeed arrived by 1851, but by the time the young men whom these new bishops were now ordaining came to a grey-haired maturity, their country was already the classic model of all that such a state should be. And its steady development, in the forty years that followed the premiership of Peel—the man in public life who, above all others, was the very embodiment of the new Political Economy, and of the practical commercial genius of the time[24]

---

[21] A table attached to this chapter gives the population, number of church-goers, number of Catholics at Mass, and the number of Irish-born inhabitants of 50 cities and towns. As to the interpretation of these facts *unusquisque in suo sensu abundet*.

[22] Cf. the well-known work of J. L. and Barbara Hammond so entitled.

[23] Clapham, *An Economic History of Modern Britain*, II, 22-23.

[24] And heir to one of the first of the Lancashire millionaires! Peel was, no less truly, the embodiment of the new age in its serious deficiencies. " The state in his, or in other hands, lacked prescience and did not see to the end of many of its campaigns. ' Things were

—is the first natural phenomenon of the new century to arrest our reflective notice: the willed arrival of the "Industry-State," that is to say, and all that flowed from this in consequences that affected the Catholic revival, the vast mass of the Catholics in England being urban working people and casual labourers.

Meanwhile, it was " The Bleak Age."

What daily life was like for the working people of the English towns in the year 1850—and what it had been for the previous thirty years—may be read in the pages of their con- temporaries, Engels, Holyoake and Bamford, Disraeli and Mrs. Gaskell; it may be studied in Dr. Hammond's passion- ate history of the exploitation of these poor people or in the detached analyses of Sir John Clapham. But the picture varies little, whoever the painter, and it is indeed a picture of " The Bleak Age," with " the raw power of the new industrial system . . . . the arbitrary rule of capital " enjoying un- contested supremacy in all the towns it had thrown up, " the savage logic of the Industrial Revolution " working itself out unhindered by any other consideration than what would bring the maximum of profit to the fortunate owner of natural resources, of machines or of money[25].

What this spirit called into existence, in the way of towns and town life, was a horror that was not only novel, but of so recent a creation that upon these contemporaries who never had any actual contact with the industrial districts, the accounts of it would, no doubt, make no deeper impression than the story of a nightmare told at third or fourth hand. Only thirty years before our date of 1850 the typical town worker " was very far indeed from being a person who performed for a self- made employer in steaming air, with the aid of recently devised mechanism, operations which would have made his grand- father gape. . . . The representative Englishman was not yet a townsman, though soon he would be "[26]; but by 1850, if a worker, a townsman he certainly was.

And these towns, that in fifty years had sometimes quad-

in the saddle and rode mankind,' and the state let them ride . . . more often . . . because it had no clear notion of what to do for the best." Clapham, *op. cit.*, I, 378.

[25] The quotations are from *Lord Shaftesbury* (1923), by J. L. and Barbara Hammond, pp. 157, 276.

[26] Clapham, *op. cit.*, I, 74, 67.

rupled their population and multiplied it even more than
that[27], whose streets were unlit, unpaved and lacking sewerage,
whose houses lacked water supply, the streets of the working
class quarters cluttered with heaps of filth from the primitive
privies, houses black with the smoke of the manufacturies,
towns as dark by day as by night—they were indeed, " treadmill cities where the daylight never broke upon the beauty and
the wisdom of the world, raw settlements where men and women
lived as men and women live on a goldfield." This is a reflective modern historian[28]. A contemporary royal commission
said that " More filth, worse physical suffering and moral dis-
order than Howard describes [in his account of the prisons of
the 18th century] are to be found amongst the cellar population of the working people of Liverpool, Manchester or Leeds
and in large portions of the metropolis "[29]; and of such cellar
dwellers there were 20,000 in Manchester and as many in Liverpool.   These vast populations—and of necessity—lived as
filthily, said the same commission, as " an encamped horde,
or an undisciplined soldiery "[30]. And one by no means given
to sentimentalism, or to sympathy with professional reformers,
Lord Palmerston himself, when Home Secretary, declared in
1854 to the House of Commons, that the condition of Newcastle-on-Tyne " made a civilised man shudder "[31].

The Royal Commission of 1844, reporting on the state
of " Large Towns and Populous Districts," said that of 50
towns scarcely one had a good drainage system, and that in
42 of them it was decidedly bad. Six only, again, had

---

[27] Manchester-Salford from 90,000 to 400,000 (the Poor-Law district
of Chorlton from 11,549 to 123,841); Blackburn from 12,000 to
65,000; Bradford from 13,000 to 104,000.

[28] *The Age of the Chartists, 1832-1854*, by J. L. and Barbara Hammond (1930), 365; reproduced in *The Bleak Age* by the same
writers (*Penguin Edition*, p. 246).

[29] Clapham, *op. cit.*, *pp.* 537-8.

[30] Quoted *The Bleak Age*, 58.

[31] Quoted Hammond, *Shaftesbury*, 166.   Here is another, very
different, contemporary, Engels, describing the *new* parts of Manchester in 1844, " Single rows of houses or groups of streets stand
here and there, like little villages on the naked, not even grass-
grown, clay soil . . . the lanes are neither paved nor supplied with
sewers but harbour numerous colonies of swine penned in small
sties or yards, or wandering unrestrained through the neighbourhood."   Quoted, Clapham, *op. cit.*, I, 539, from the 1888 edition
of *The Condition of the Working Class in England in* 1844, p. 39.

a good system of water supply and in 31 towns this, too, was decidedly bad. " And whilst the houses, streets, courts, lanes and streams are polluted and rendered pestilential, the civic officers have generally contented themselves with the most barbarous expedients, or sit still amidst the pollution, with the resignation of Turkish fatalists, under the supposed destiny of the prevalent ignorance, sloth and filth "[32]. What wonder then that a social reformer of the day, whose personal experience of these horrors was very wide indeed, a man also who lived every moment of his life in the presence of God, the seventh Earl of Shaftesbury, confided to his diary that he held " the sanitary question, as second only to the religious, and, in some respects, inseparable from it "[33]. Such an attitude was much less common, in the ruling classes, than that expressed by another patrician, and a late Home Secretary indeed of the Enlightenment—Sir James Graham, who eighteen months earlier explained in the House of Commons that, " the lot of the labourer was eating, drinking, working and dying "[34].

" Filth and poverty were already unmanageable problems "[35] in these towns before the great disasters of the late 'forties brought to them hordes of still poorer Irish peasants, famine stricken, typhus-stricken, bred to ways of life yet more primitive and—not surprisingly—helpless before what so utterly perplexed and confounded their betters. As the cholera had swept these abominable encampments in 1832, and as it was again to sweep them in 1854, so the famine fever ranged them in the years after 1845, and a clergy who, to the general amazement, actually lived among their people, paid their toll also. In Liverpool and Leeds and Newcastle especially, they died of the terrible fever—in this last city their bishop with them. The men called to such a ministry in these great towns may be pardoned if they were less interested than the young Dr. Wiseman thought becoming, about the niceties of ecclesiastical deportment—as the bishops, largely bred of the same stock, were to be very much less than interested when the new cardinal laboured to introduce among them the fullness of

[32] So the Royal Commission of 1842 already quoted.
[33] The entry is under the date 26th Sept., 1848. Quoted in Hammond, *Shaftesbury*, 162, from Hodder's *Life of Shaftesbury*, II, 253.
[34] Hammond, *ibid.*, p. 119.
[35] *The Age of the Chartists*, p. 25; and in *The Bleak Age*, p. 38.

the protocol that governed his own appearances in public.

The critical visitor who, in 1850, complained of this hideous state of things might have been told that a new age was just about to begin; and truly enough, two years earlier, the findings of Royal Commissions had at last produced that Public Health Act which is the Magna Carta of the modern English cleanliness. For the first time, the national government made all these matters its own direct concern, setting up a centralized administration which should control the water supplies, drainage, cleaning of the streets, burial grounds, housing and offensive trades. The existing local authorities were very slow to avail themselves of their new powers, and pressure from London provoked bitter resistance. But slowly, very slowly, incredibly slowly it might seem to us, through the twenty years and more that separated that Magna Carta from the Elementary Education Act of 1870, the municipalities began to take up the new laws and put them into force. Gradually that spirit of indifference was vanquished which *The Times* had scourged when it described (November 19, 1848) how England had brought herself to the verge of bankruptcy, authorising the raising hundreds of millions of pounds to build railways and viaducts, at a time when 300 streets in a rich district of the metropolis were without a sewer[36]. It now began to be less true that " property owners still preferred dirt to expenditure "[37].

None of this reform was achieved without hard campaigning, middle-class philanthropists battling for factory legislation, and other middle-class philanthropists (who were opposed to factory legislation) battling for the abolition of food taxes; and working men, in the Chartist movement and in the new Trade Unions, battling for wages that would bring them something more than an existence that bordered on chronic starvation. In these battles all joined, historians, men of letters, novelists, and clergy; and with the rest the Prince Consort, actively interested in every practical constructive reform, and now greatly occupied with the most spectacular event of the time, the Great Exhibition of 1851. It was, then, midway through an age that was habituated to agitation on a

---

[36] Quoted in *The Age of the Chartists*, 310, and *The Bleak Age*, 223.
[37] *Ibid.*, 311 and 233.

national scale—social, economic and political agitation—and where debates no less furious had long raged about religion as this was organised in England[38], that Pope Pius IX restored the diocesan episcopate[39].

One kind of agitation, however, was as yet singularly barren; the purely working-class movement for better wages. And here we need to recall how limited, in 1851, the parliamentary suffrage remained; the constitution has still half the distance to travel that separates the Reform Acts of 1832 and 1867, and in the towns only the ratepaying occupier of premises of £10 yearly value has a vote. The whole of the working classes are thus ruled out, and so practically all of the 700,000 Catholics. Had the Catholics been then many times as numerous,

[38] Again it was the new industrial towns that were the scene of many of these quarrels. " Nobody can study the papers of this time without seeing how widespread and violent were the religious quarrels of the industrial towns. . . . Anyone who studies the newspapers and periodicals that were read by the workmen at this time must be impressed by the space and energy given to the attacks on the Church." So the authors of *The Age of the Chartists*, 26, 218 (*The Bleak Age*, 39, 116), who also note (pp. 29 and 40 of these books, respectively) that it was " into a society . . . torn by sectarian strife " that these [Irish] " immigrants from a land of poverty " poured, " bringing their own habits and religion." We may note that it was a child of the new industrial civilisation, G. J. Holyoake, who, in 1847, set the Secularist movement on its way when he founded his review, *The Reasoner*. Holyoake was none the less effective for being, like John Stuart Mill, courteous in his language. At the other pole of controversial amenity was the crude and complacent *Punch*, never so revealing of what was worst in its generation as when it mocked at the virginity of Our Lady, and at Catholic belief in the Real Presence. It is against this comic paper's general hatred of every expression of belief in the supernatural—Catholic or not—that its weekly reviling of Wiseman and Pius IX needs to be recalled. The census commissioners of 1851 spoke most gravely about the flight of the working classes from the practice of religion and about their widespread ignorance of religious truth. " The myriads of our labouring population [are] really as ignorant of Christianity as were the heathen Saxons at Augustine's landing " (*Report on Religious Worship*, 1853, p. clxii). Again " . . the masses of our working population . . . the skilled and unskilled labourers alike—minor shopkeepers and Sunday traders—miserable denizens of courts and crowded alleys . . . are *unconscious Secularists* " (*ibid.*, p. clviii, italics in original).

[39] It is little wonder that, in a matter of three months, 7,000 public meetings could be held to protest against it. For the figure, Disraeli's *Endymion*, ch. 99.

if they had been of the same social class, Catholic Emancipation (now a fact, twenty years old) must have been just as barren of effect in English public life. The Reform Act of 1867 will greatly change all that; and giving the vote to the Catholic working man, with the rest, it will also give it thereby to a multitude of the Irish, to the children, very notably, of the exiles of the Famine years; and thence, within a few years more, what strains within the Catholic body, when the hereditary Tory oppressor of Ireland is held, quasi-authoritatively, to be the only likely and to-be-trusted friend of a popular education that is religious[40]! In 1850 these are agitations beyond any man's power to foresee. Meanwhile, this voteless Catholic worker is also a man who is poor. How much is it that he is paid, and what is his day's work?

It was agriculture that was the greatest single industry in the England of 1851; and it employed about a quarter of the male population over 20 years of age. But with agricultural life and its problems the historian of English Catholicism in mid-Victorian times has all but no concern at all. After the agricultural workers the next largest class—which, however, numbers no more than a third of the agricultural workers—are the men employed in the building trades (335,663), and then the general labourers (274,079). The shoemakers and the tailors together are as many as the general labourers (173,932 and 99,633). The " new " industries account for 410,894 skilled men (cotton, 134,646; woollens, 114,350; engineering and iron, 110,055; railways, 51,843) and the coal miners number 128,086; even combined, these do not make up a very high proportion (16.6 per cent.) as yet, of the working industrial and commercial population[41], but the new industries are already important far beyond the numbers they employ by reason of their concentration in a comparatively restricted area

[40] Cf. the curious situation round about 1910, with a section of the Tory party crying " Home Rule means Rome Rule " and a section of the Liberal party protesting no less loudly against " Rome on the rates."

[41] Total number of men employed in agriculture, commerce and industry 4,323,535; total number of men employed in agriculture, 1,080,884. It is on the basis of the difference between these two figures that the percentages are reckoned.

of the country.   In the capital the percentage of men and women engaged in them was but 2.8, and in Liverpool 4.2; but in Manchester it was 30.2, in Preston 43.6, in Stockport 48.8, and in Oldham 57.3.

The most popular employment for women, one hundred years ago, was domestic service.   This absorbed one in six of all the women workers over 20[42].   Next came millinery (a term which includes dressmakers and seamstresses) and this was the occupation of a little more than one-tenth of the total of women who earned their living.[43]   " The great new raw industry of which everyone was talking "[44], cotton, employed as many as 113,775 of these women over 20; and four other textile manufactures—wool, worsted, silk and lace—accounted for a further 136,038.   Washerwomen, laundresses, and charwomen made up 177,356.   Such were the trades that occupied a good half of those two-fifths of the women over 20 who earned a wage.

These figures have for us the particular interest that they throw some light on the beginnings of a problem still with us and one which, a hundred years ago, was already a cause of anxiety to thoughtful observers, namely the effect of the factory system upon the *mores* of English women (and therefore on the future of English family life).   This problem was for no section more acute than for the small Catholic minority, composed as it was, in such great part, of the working people in the towns.   It was in the new towns, so to call them, that the majority of these urban Catholics lived; and the census of 1851 showed that in those towns where the new textile industries had established themselves, twice as many women worked for their living as in the old[45], the bulk of them, of course, in the new mills; again, many of the women over 20 who worked in these mills were married[46], and with them worked something

[42] General domestic servants numbered 339,627 in all.
[43] 226,824.
[44] Clapham, I, 72.
[45] A table is attached to show the difference, in this, between " new " towns and " old," and between those working districts where textile factories predominate and the rest.   See *infra*, p. 62.
[46] In *all* Lancs, out of women workers of the age-group 20-24 (77,344 out of a total of 111,598 women workers over 20), one in three was married; nearly one-half of this age-group worked in a textile factory.   In age-group 25-29, 29.8 per cent. of the married women

like 3 out of 4 of all the women and girls in these towns between 10 and 19 years of age.

The blackest spot of all this business was south-east Lancashire, in the main the territory which was now, in 1850, set up as the diocese of Salford. While two-thirds of the great county had remained as rural as Cornwall[47], the industrial region had, between 1801 and 1851, increased its population until it was four times as great as that of the rural part; and had increased it at nearly twice the rate at which the population of London had increased. Nowhere in the world was there then an area so large with so high an average density of population, a population, moreover, still increasing rapidly[48]. Birmingham, too, was the centre of a bad patch, but the notorious Black Country[49] was not the half in area of the cotton manufacturing district of Lancashire. And it is again a peculiarity of the cotton district that here the old traditional feminine

worked; and in the age-group 29-34, 26.3 per cent. These three age-groups (i.e., 20-34) account for three-quarters of the unmarried working women over 20, and for nearly a half of the married working women of the same age.

[47] In 1801 the population of Lancashire was 670,000, in 1851 it was more than treble this, viz., 2,067,301. The population, in 1851, of "industrial" Lancashire, 670 sq. miles, was 1,685,482; of "rural" Lancashire, 1,392 sq. miles, 381,819; of Cornwall, 1,377 sq. miles, 356,641. The exact division of Lancashire is as follows: "Industrial" Lancashire is made up of the following Poor Law unions, Liverpool, West Derby, Wigan, Bolton, Bury, Chorlton, Salford, Manchester, Ashton-under-Lyne, Oldham, Rochdale, Haslingden, Burnley, Blackburn and the borough of Preston; "Rural" Lancashire, of those of Prescot, Ormskirk, Warrington, Leigh, Barton-on-Irwell, Clitheroe, Chorley, the Fylde, Garstang, Lancaster, Ulverston, and of Preston less the borough.

[48] "A situation which had probably not existed before, in a great country, at any time in the world's history," so Clapham, op. cit., I, 536, writing, not of the particular situation in south-east Lancashire, but of the general change, brought about in only 50 years, that half the population of Great Britain was now urban. The difficulties that arose from the very novelty of the situation—whether for politicians and administrators or for Catholic bishops—must be ever before the critical student's mind.

[49] The name is used here to include the following Poor Law unions: Wolverhampton, Walsall, West Bromwich, Dudley, Stourbridge, Birmingham, and Aston; area 254.7 sq. miles. The population in this region had increased 227 per cent. in the fifty years 1801-1851. When Milner came to rule here as bishop it was 189,000; when Ullathorne came to Birmingham in 1848 it was approaching the 621,614 of the census quoted.

occupations, domestic service and millinery for example, dwindle to very nothingness[50].

How these new industrial communities were as barren of intellectual and artistic life, as they were of " amenities " for the worker, the great census is again witness. And if those

	Total of Women of 10 years and over	% of these at work	% of Women of 20 years and over at work	% of Women of 10-19 years at work	% of Inhabitants a to go to church a actuall attending
Liverpool	150,489	35.3	36.6	31.6	47.0
Plymouth—Devonport ...	37,192	38.0	37.0	38.0	53.5
Brighton	32,106	48.0	50.0	36.0	53.0
York	15,371	36.4	37.4	37.0	60.0
Sheffield	50,643	29.4	27.0	35.7	30.8
Newcastle-on-Tyne ...	34,184	32.4	32.8	33.3	40.3
Merthyr Tydfil	20,987	26.2	24.0	32.8	77.3
Wolverhampton	17,899	32.4	30.0	36.7	48.6
Dudley	13,509	32.6	30.0	32.7	51.8
Norwich	29,558	46.6	48.0	48.0	43.8
Leeds	67,909	42.6	40.0	55.6	46.6
Leicester	24,727	52.0	50.0	59.7	59.5
Preston	28,093	57.1	50.0	67.0	28.6
Oldham	27,971	55.6	50.0	71.6	26.8
Bolton	23,734	50.0	47.0	60.6	38.1
Stockport	21,971	59.0	52.5	76.3	42.1
Blackburn	17,914	61.1	57.0	70.6	48.5
Bradford	41,793	58.6	48.3	75.0	41.1
Nottingham	24,653	66.6	61.0	79.0	57.5

[50] In *Lancs as a whole*, of the age-group 20-24, 46.8 per cent. worked in textiles, and only 25 per cent. in domestic service. In *Rural Lancashire* 10,098 of the 48,877 women over 20 who worked were domestic servants; in *Industrial Lancashire*, out of 218,193 such women only 27,884. In London 70 per cent. of the women who worked were occupied with the traditional feminine crafts, domestic service, millinery, laundry, charwomen; in Liverpool, 60.8 per cent.; in Bristol, 66.6 per cent. But in Manchester-Salford only 34.1 per cent., in Leeds 32.9 per cent., in Bolton 21.2 per cent., in Preston 18.3 per cent., in Blackburn 15.4 per cent., in Bradford 15.7 per cent., and in Oldham 12.3 per cent. The table attached shows the different condition of the feminine half of the population in 19 towns of various types.

to whom it has fallen to build up the *Catholica* in these parts have enjoyed what is materially advantageous in the circumstance that their " flock " has been so singularly homogeneous, they have also suffered all the inevitable inconveniences: almost in its entirety, for the first seventy years at least, the " flock " consisted of working people whose education went no further than what the public elementary school could provide. Twenty-five years after the restoration of the diocesan episcopate the Bishop of Salford, explaining to Rome how impossible it was for Manchester-Salford to support two Catholic grammar schools, would illustrate his answer by saying that there was not a single Catholic in this vast population with means sufficient to keep a carriage. And in general resources Salford was second only to Liverpool among the new sees!

London, too, had grown hugely[51]; but London did not present a problem anything like that which vexed the Catholicism of the north-west. For London, as it extended, did not change its industrial habits. It continued to be that " home of small businesses "[52] which it had always been. There was not any invasion by the exploiters of new textile processes, nor any attempt to settle here any of the new-style engineering establishments. At such a distance from the sources of coal and iron, and with the organisation of the railways as yet so rudimentary, how could it have been otherwise? Three trades, only, stand out in the capital as forming part of organisations of any size, namely the brewers, the shipwrights and the silk weavers; and no firm engaged in these businesses is at all comparable in size to what every new town in Lancashire and Yorkshire has been familiar with for now forty and fifty years. Also, " The typical London skilled workman was neither brewery hand, shipwright, nor silk weaver, but either a member of the building trade or a shoemaker, tailor, cabinetmaker, printer, clockmaker, jeweller, baker—to mention the chief trades which had over 2,500 members in 1831 "[53]. And so it was to be for many years to come.

---

[51] In 1801, 958,863; in 1851, 2,362,236. The area—78,029 acres—is that of the districts that returned weekly *Bills of Mortality*. It is, roughly, that of the present administrative county of London.

[52] Clapham, *op. cit.*, I, 68.

[53] Clapham, *ib.*, 70.

Another striking difference between working-class life in London and in Lancashire was the extent to which children between 9 and 14 were worked. By the year 1851, thanks to the long fight for the Ten Hours Bill and to the revelations made by the Royal Commission on the Mines in 1842, the employment of children was beginning to be a burden on the national conscience. The populations of metropolitan London and of Lancashire were, in 1851, roughly equal. But while in London, out of a total of 243,648 children between 5 and 9[54] only 923 worked for a living[55], in Lancashire out of a total of 235,767 of this age there were 5,108 workers[56]. More important, numerically, is the difference between the two areas as regards the next age group, 10 to 14 inclusive. In London 38,585 of these were at work[57]; but in Lancashire, where the total number of children of this age (221,146) was approximately the same, the number at work was 85,540[58]. Of the Lancashire children between 5 and 9 who worked, 2,341 boys were engaged in the new industries—1,644 of them in cotton mills, and 293 in coal-mining; while 1,432 of the 1,842 little girls worked in textile factories, as many as 1,043 of them in cotton mills. As to the older children, nearly half of the London boys between 10 and 14 were errand boys (10,472) and about half the London girls in this group were slaveys, " general domestic servants " (6,424)[59]. Of the boys of 10 to 14 in Lancashire 29,423 were in industries[60] (21,067 of them in cotton mills, 4,190 in coal-mines); of the Lancashire girls of this age 26,019 were in textile factories, 22,350 of them in cotton mills[61].

[54] 121,254 boys, 122,394 girls.

[55] 670 boys and 253 girls.

[56] 3,266 boys out of a total of 117,774; 1,842 girls, out of 117,993.

[57] 24,625 boys out of a total of 107,231; 12,960 girls out of a total of 109,138.

[58] 48,391 boys out of 110,776; 37,146 girls out of 110,370.

[59] The total of girls of 10-14 who were " general domestic servants " in England and Wales in 1851 was 50,065.

[60] While, in London, the errand boys were 42.6 per cent. of this group of workers, in Lancashire they were but 11 per cent.

[61] Here is the number of those working in both of these age-groups, expressed as a percentage of the total number in the group, to show how London and Lancashire stand to each other, and how each

London, densely populated, manages yet once again to be *sui generis* and quite unlike the densely populated districts in the provinces. It does not yet know the new world that has grown up in the midlands and, above all, in the north; that new working class, for example, bred of factory life which, in protective reaction against the injustices of the system, is now to produce the great trade unions, the co-operative movement, and the friendly societies[62]. How important the role of these in the formation of pride of status and the preservation of self-respect, during the years when the material circumstances of life worked incessantly for the degradation of the human person to the mere individuality of the " hand," let Dr. Hammond's words tell: " Though the workmen had no votes for Town Council or Board of Guardians, there must have been great

stands to England and Wales as a whole:—

	London.	England and Wales.	Lancs.
Group 5-9			
Boys	0.56	2.0	2.78
Girls	0.21	1.44	1.56
Group 10-14			
Boys	23.36	36.6	43.24
Girls	11.93	20.0	33.3

The variation is slighter in the numbers attending school, but not in the numbers of children who are not said to be at work or attending school—the Balance, we may call them for the purpose of this table:—

	London.	England and Wales.	Lancs.
Group 10-14, at school			
Boys	46.7	39.4	38.7
Girls	44.0	41.4	36.4
Group 10-14, Balance			
Boys	30.0	23.1	17.1
Girls	42.2	37.3	29.1

Were it possible to isolate the figures for Industrial Lancashire, these contrasts would be more striking still.

[62] Halévy, *Histoire du peuple anglais au XIX siècle*, IV, 36, seems to confirm this view, when, writing of the unrest of 1842-1843 which seemed to foreshadow a social insurrection, he says " Londres qui n'assistait que de loin à la crise *dans ce qu'elle avait de plus douloureux.* . . ." The italics are mine. Any priest who came to work in London about 1931 after practical experience of working-class life in the textile towns of the north, or in the industrial parts of the north-east, would have the same impression about the relation of the London of twenty years ago to the *crise* which then gripped so high a proportion of the working-class people of the country.

numbers of working men taking part in the management of trade unions, co-operative societies, temperance societies, and friendly societies by the middle of the century. In this way scope was found for instincts and sympathies for which their occupations gave no opportunity. Men were taking decisions, assuming responsibilities, meeting and consulting . . . developing their own ideas. . . ."[63]. A French sociologist of today, Bertrand de Jouvenel, writes in a similar way of the institution in its classic Victorian days: " The distinguishing feature of trade unionism of this sort was the spiritual influence exercised on it by its membership: men who had a craft and were proud of it. They compared themselves with doctors: the craftsman has, like the doctor, had to win knowledge of his craft by study. The craftsman, like the doctor, should have his special position guaranteed him "[64].

The development of these socially educative forces—the creation of the working classes themselves—varied greatly, it is here relevant to note, from one kind of working district to another. ". . . In districts of highly diversified, and what might be called individualistic industry, as in all predominantly commercial neighbourhoods, the spread of co-operative societies had tended to be slow and patchy," in London, for example, and in Liverpool. On the other hand, " Colliers and textile workers had become good co-operators almost everywhere. . . Among the innumerable trades and manufactures of the Birmingham region, which in the pioneering days of the co-operative movement had been highly individualistic, the stores . . . had never acquired the same mastery as in places of a single industry, or of few and large-scale industries." This was true of Sheffield also, " the home of the little master." What was always required for these movements to succeed was " the group of a few earnest men." " And the evidence suggests that, however numerous and however earnest, these

[63] *Age of the Chartists*, 339.
[64] *Problems of Socialist England* (1949), p. 137, with a reference to Sidney and Beatrice Webb, *History of Trade Unionism*, p. 199. As for Catholic friendly societies at this time, cf. the account (quoted *Age of the Chartists*, 338) from the *Blackburn Standard* of 21st May, 1844, of the Whit Monday procession of 4,000 people in which, with 14 other societies, there walked " the United Catholic Brethren " and " the United Catholic Sisters."

group seeds had found the continuous uniform communal soil of coal pit or textile mill more favourable to germination and growth than the broken-up patches in little workshops and tenement factories in Sheffield, in small and varied businesses about Birmingham, or in the shifting industries of Coventry "[65].

In London the working class—and of this the Church, in London too, is mainly composed—tends to be, in the eyes of its betters, " the lower orders," rather than that community of sturdy, consciously independent spirits, whom history reveals thus socially creative, a race to whose quality conditions in the industrial areas are, in all these years, giving so notable a temper. What proportion of the Catholic people of London were able to serve the necessary apprenticeship to the skilled trades in Sir John Clapham's list, in so many of which the journeyman could, and did, become his own master? My own impression is that the great majority were never more than labourers, as were so many of the Catholics in the factories elsewhere[66]. But whatever the fact here, about one thing there is no doubt at all, namely that life for the workman in London is " different," and the London working man another type, as compared with the artisans formed by the new industries.

London, as always, is *sui generis* and so—let the question be put, it certainly never ceases to present itself to all who are not London-bred—does London as such ever understand, has it ever known, how England lives, what England thinks, and why England thinks as it does? Few questions are more important for whoever would arrive at the meaning of Catholic history in England down to the very moment the question is here posed. One problem that leaps immediately to the mind, in illustration of the need to ask the question, is the different policy and point of view that has guided the building of parish schools in, say, London and Lancashire

[65] Clapham, *op. cit.*, III, 245-6, for all the quotations in this paragraph.
[66] But not all—not even all the Irish, who, arriving (it is universally agreed) in a state of the utmost poverty and distress, sank almost inevitably to the very depths of the economic system; cf. the evidence, before a Select Committee of the House of Commons of 1825, of a Liverpool witness to the effect that the expansion of the cotton industry, in all its branches, would not have been possible without Irish workmen. Clapham, I, 61.

during the last fifty years[67]. The time lag between the publication of *Rerum Novarum* and any real official attempt to popularise its teaching is another. And if to this we add, what every national movement seems to have felt in turn, " London's compromising atmosphere!"[68]. For it is from London, since 1850, that Catholic England too is—if not governed—controlled[69].

What were the weekly wages of these Catholic artisans of the new industry, whose kind London Catholicism did—or did not—know and understand for the new force they were, a force one day to wrest a new recognition of old social truths, and to occasion the most practical of all papal returns to St. Thomas; what were the weekly wages out of which the weekly pence were so generously, so unquestioningly, given to the ceaselessly begging clergy, the steady tribute of copper and bronze from poor men's hands without which hardly anything would have been made that has been made—the outward sign of a faith which made England unique as the one country where the industrial working class was the Church's sturdiest support? Those wages were of course very scanty—at the best a mere subsistence.

In 1850 wages had been stationary for almost 20 years; but in those 20 years the cost of living had fallen, so that by 1849-50 the situation of the working classes was " relatively good "[70]. One of the best paid of all was the London bricklayer, at 5s. 3d. a day; his labourer received 3s. 6d. for the

[67] The particulars are set out in the pages of *The Catholic Directory* for whoever cares to trace this steadily widening divergence from 1902 onwards.

[68] The phrase is Dr. Hammond's, cf. *Shaftesbury*, p. 140. I do not, of course, forget for a moment the classic independence of the London working-man juries who, in 1794 and 1795, refused to find for the Crown in State Trials.

[69] In the days before the diocesan bishops were restored the London Vicar Apostolic enjoyed no precedence over his brethren. The lead fell to the senior by consecration of the four bishops—which is why Rome designed the Midland Vicar, Dr. Thomas Walsh, to be the first Archbishop of Westminster, and as a preparatory step, moved him to London in 1848. The news was public property, and the obituary notice of the old bishop (he died in March, 1849), printed in the *Catholic Directory* for 1850, styles him throughout " the Archbishop-elect."

[70] Clapham, I, 561.

same twelve hours of work—a point of interest to us, for this was the occupation of very many of the newly arrived Irish peasant immigrants. In Manchester the rates were 28s. a week for the skilled man; what the labourer was paid is not stated. The coal miner's pay varied from one locality to another. In Durham it was 3s. 9d. a day, in Northumberland and in Staffordshire it was 3s. 6d., in South Wales 3s., in Lancashire 20s. weekly.

In the new engineering trades the best paid of all were the moulders, at 34s. the week, and the turners at 30s. Neither of these touched what seems the high water mark of all wages in 1851, the 37s. that a " first class " fine spinner earned. The " third grade " spinner of coarse yarn, however, earned only 18s. a week and the woman " throstle-spinner " from 7s. 6d. to 10s.; piecers made, at the highest, 7s. 9d. The weavers seem poorly paid; a woman working two (power) looms earned weekly 10s. 2d., three looms 13s. and four looms 16s. The worst off, of all the textile workers, were the hand-loom weavers, whose craft was now in evident process of extinction. Here again was a craft in which the Irish were numerous, the setting of the workman's last, losing fight against the factory[71]. Hand-loom weaving survived longer in the woollen industry, and all through the 1850's, a man could earn 14s. and 15s. a week in Leeds. But in Blackburn, in 1841 already, the average weekly wage was only 9s. 6½d., and in Manchester, about the same time, it varied from 7s. 8¼d. to 16s. 4¾d. The silk weaver in London earned 17s. a week for work on velvets, and from 5s. 11d. to 7s. 5d. for plain silks and satins. At Coventry, the first-hand journeyman working a Jacquard loom could earn 15s. 6d.

These figures by themselves tell us little. What of the cost of living? The repeal of all the food taxes (not merely of the duty on imported cereals) between 1842 and 1846 had indeed brought down the cost of living with a rush[72]. And

[71] Clapham, I, 552, notes " the weaver's passionate clinging to his loom and his independence," and Hammond his desperate desire to save his children from the factories.
[72] The cost of living rose 23 per cent. between 1790 and 1839, but by 1848 it was perhaps even lower than in 1790. The worst, indeed, was over by 1850; but that worst had been little better

since so high a proportion of the unmarried went out to work, and of the children from the age of 10, we do no doubt need to consider the average family in the textile towns as living on " family earnings." But it is the dispassionate Professor Clapham, so fearful always that Dr. Hammond paints too black a picture, who will tell us that " relatively considerable family earnings " were exceptional in the textile towns of 1830-50. Quite a number of families, indeed, with their joint earnings were, he writes, " well above the despairing class." But of these same joint earnings he can say no more than that they were " certainly not adequate for the good life, yet not too hopelessly indequate for life "[73].

To complete the picture of the life that was the lot of the vast mass of the Catholics of 1850 we need to recall how the then new Poor Law of 1834 " did more to sour the hearts of the labouring population than did the privations consequent on all the actual poverty of the land "[74]. For it was a law that met poverty with punishment, as though it were a crime; and that treated with scorn and contumely the man, woman or child in need, and with hardship so deliberate and so systematic that it could not but seem wantonly inflicted.

Yet it was from these people, in these years, that the trade unions came, and the co-operative societies, and the friendly societies. And from those of them who were Catholics, there came a vast number of churches also[75], and of day schools, and of charitable institutions.

The senior of the eight English bishops, at the time when the diocesan episcopate was re-established, was John Briggs. He was a Lancashire man, now in his sixty-second year, and he had ruled as Vicar Apostolic since 1836, first of the old Northern District and then, for the last ten years, of the Yorkshire District constituted in 1840. Dr. Briggs had in his

than slow starvation (Clapham, I, 560). The price of the 4-lb. loaf in 1841-1849 varied from 9d. to 7d.; between 1830 and 1841 it had varied between 10½d. and 10d. (Ibid., 561).

73 Clapham, I, 566-7.
74 Alfred's History of the Factory Movement (1857), II, 76, quoted in Clapham, I, 578.
75 In 1839 there were 446 churches; in 1851, 596; in 1860, 967; in 1880, 1,134.

time served as president of the northern college of Ushaw (1833-36), after a spell of years in charge of the Catholics of Chester. He had been a consistently loyal friend to the much-abused Bishop Baines, and from the day when Lucas founded *The Tablet* was one of his warmest supporters. His views of the " forward " movement, as this was directed by Wiseman, had always been detached; and it says much for his outlook (and for his prestige) that it was Briggs whom the anti-Wiseman party hoped to see at the head of affairs once Rome was persuaded to recall the newly-appointed London Vicar Apostolic and place him, for the rest of his days, in " the golden fetters of the cardinalate "[76]. His own personal connection with Wiseman was long standing. It went back forty years nearly, to the time when this brilliant personality was a schoolboy at Ushaw and Briggs one of his masters. In 1850 the Yorkshire Vicar Apostolic became the first Bishop of Beverley, and he ruled the see until just before his death, in 1861.

Two others of these bishops had also known Wiseman since the days when, at Ushaw, they ruled him *in statu pupillari;* these were the Lancashire Vicar Apostolic, George Brown and the Northern Vicar, William Hogarth, from 1850 bishops of Liverpool and of Hexham respectively. In age the two were exactly contemporaries, and at 64 the seniors of the bench. George Brown, after he had retired from the vice-presidency of Ushaw to the charge of the mission at Lancaster, was a prominent figure in the various movements of the 1830's that worked to obtained a hierarchy of diocesan bishops conceived as a means to introduce the rule of law and to check the alleged system of rule by episcopal intuition. But once promoted to the bench, in 1840, he began to show himself something of a martinet[77], from whose decisions appeals began steadily to

---

[76] Wiseman's own interpretation of his promotion; cf. his letter to the president of Maynooth, Dr. Charles Russell, from which the phrase is quoted, Ward, *Life of Wiseman*, I, 521. See also the letter, 27th July, 1850, of Dr. Thomas Grant, rector of the English College, Rome, to Ullathorne, stating that Briggs was Rome's most likely choice as Wiseman's successor in London; Butler, *Life of Ullathorne*, I, 164.

[77] He is quoted as saying, in 1836, " If the Bishops are to be ordinaries, and the clergy remain missionaries, we shall be something like the poor frogs under the mild and paternal sway of King Stork . . . we must be parish priests with all our rights as such

flow into Rome[78]. His health had always been poor. Three years only after the great change of 1850 he had to seek a coadjutor, and was given the first of a really remarkable series of Liverpool bishops, the youthful Alexander Goss, who was to succeed to the see in 1856. George Brown's contemporary, the Bishop of Hexham, who in 1850 had been a bishop but two years, reigned longer, dying in 1866, in his 80th year, a modest, retiring, hardworking and familiar prelate, the "Bishop Billy" of Lingard's familiar correspondence, in spirit a vicar apostolic to the end.

Two of Wiseman's seven colleagues of 1850 have left all but no mark in the history of the restored hierarchy, William Wareing and William Joseph Hendren. William Wareing's promotion to the episcopate in 1840 (when he was named Vicar Apostolic of the newly-created Eastern District) was part of the clearance at Oscott necessitated by the plan to make the

guaranteed to us"; quoted in a *Proposed Address to the Rt. Rev. Dr. Briggs* . . . 1851 " from members of the Secular Clergy residing in the diocese of Beverly," printed in the *Report of the Select Committee on the Law of Mortmain* (1851), pp. 521-522. In 1847 a Preston priest writes of "the violence of the bishop, who has pronounced all rebels who petition for what he petitioned for before he was a bishop!" (*ibid.*, 458).

[78] As to appeals from clergy and laity against acts of the Vicars Apostolic in the last years before 1850 (for which see Bernard Ward, *The Sequel to Emancipation*, 1830-1850, Ch. IV and X), Gregory XVI (1831-1846) " declared that he had more trouble in the administration of church officers in his province called ' England,' than he had with the church affairs of the Universal Church "; cf. the evidence of T. C. Anstey, M.P.—a somewhat eccentric Catholic barrister, whose services this pope had rewarded with a Knighthood of St. Gregory, one of the first to be conferred— before the Select Committee on the Law of Mortmain, 3rd July, 1851 (*Report*, p. 447), reporting this as said to him in 1846 by " a gentleman connected with Propaganda " who had been sent to England to make enquiries about all these discontents, and who had " contacted " Anstey, among others. There is a vast amount of information in this Report about the internal condition of the Catholic body at this time (bishops, clergy, and the well-to-do laity) that is worth critical examination. The word " critical " might be emphasised. Wiseman himself was one of the witnesses examined, and he had to say of one accusation, brought by the Rev. Francis Sylvester Mahony, that it was " one tissue of untruths, every word of it " (*ibid.*, p. 548). The *Tablet* (27th July, 1851, p. 466, col. 4) said roundly that " the committee had become the receptacle of every possible nonsensical calumny." There is an article on Anstey in the *Dictionary of National Biography*.

newly-consecrated Wiseman president of the college[79]. Wareing was the vice-rector; and the rector, Henry Weedall, was promoted at the same time, to be Vicar Apostolic of the Northern District—an honour from which he successfully got clear by a personal, oral, appeal to the pope[80]. William Wareing became, in 1850, Bishop of Northampton, where he lasted for eight years, when he resigned. He was then 67 and thence on he lived in retirement until his death in 1865. William Joseph Hendren was a Franciscan Observant, one of the last members of the great province of the Penal Days that had given to the church the martyrs of the 17th century, and the last of the confessors[81]. In 1850 he was close on 60 and had been a bishop just two years, Vicar Apostolic of the troubled Western District and appointed thereto through Ullathorne's influence[82], whose vicar-general for that district he had previously been. He was now, naturally, named Bishop of Clifton, but within nine months he sought a refuge from the anxieties of the last two years by securing a translation to Nottingham[83]. Nottingham he endured for twenty months only, and in 1853 he retired, translated to Martyropolis, *i.p.i.* The remaining thirteen years of his life he spent as chaplain to the Franciscan nuns of Taunton, and before he died, in 1866, he was witness of the return of his order to England, and the building of the superb church at Manchester which symbolised this restoration.

The last two of the group of one-time vicars apostolic were Benedictines, both of them monks of Downside. They long outlived all their old colleagues and were both really remarkable men, Thomas Joseph Brown and William Bernard Ullathorne. They had now been in close relationship for half a lifetime, for when Ullathorne first arrived at Downside, as a lad of 17, Brown was already one of the superiors of the house and he later taught Ullathorne theology. He was a

---

[79] Ward, *Sequel, etc.*, I, 166, and II, 4, an appointment " done for the express purpose of making room for Dr. Wiseman."

[80] For these events see Husenbeth's *Life of Dr. Weedall*.

[81] Fr. Paul Atkinson, who died at Hurst Castle in the Isle of Wight in 1728, after a lifelong imprisonment, under the act of William III, for the crime of being a priest.

[82] Ward, *Sequel, etc.*, II, 216.

[83] For some account of this bishop's part in the saga of Prior Park— a history involving five episcopates in a matter of ten years—see J. S. Roche, *Prior Park* (1931).

sound and systematic student, deeply read in the Fathers, who owed his training to the last of the Benedictines of St. Maur; and he passed on the best of what he had to that pupil who was now his fellow bishop; " the only person from whose living voice I ever learnt much . . . . a teacher who spoke from the digested stores of his own mind," Ullathorne was later to write of him. Such a man, of course, was no mere pedant, and in the critical moment of Downside's fight for life with the then Vicar Apostolic of the Western District, Peter Augustine Baines, himself a Benedictine, Dom Joseph Brown rendered yeoman service to his brethren as their agent in the curia Romana. In 1850, when he was appointed to the new see of Newport and Menevia, he was a man of 52 and he had been a bishop ten years already, having been appointed Vicar Apostolic for Wales when the districts were rearranged in 1840.

Ullathorne, now 44, was the youngest of the bishops. In practical ability he stood head and shoulders above them all, one of the rare spirits with a real gift for ruling men, with ten years of pioneer life in Australia behind him and the useful experience of having figured as the unpopular centre in one of the stormiest agitations of the century, when he stood out to demand the abolition of the system of transporting convicts. He had also, since then, had four years' experience of the realities of the English mission; this was at Coventry, where he built a church and school and organised a new congregation of Dominican nuns. When, in 1850, Ullathorne was appointed to the new see of Birmingham he had already been governing this territory for two years as its vicar apostolic; and for the two years before that he had served in the same office for the Western District, in which short time he had managed to build what is still the pro-cathedral of the diocese of Clifton. It was to Ullathorne's ability as a negotiator that the restoration of the hierarchy was principally due[84], to the combination he presented of native shrewdness, great patience, a liking for hard work, a good business head, practical knowledge of the ways of the Roman officials and sound knowledge of the law. In the twenty years that followed the restoration of 1850 Ullathorne, despite his subordinate rank, was to be the real centre of English Catholic activities: the victorious

[84] So Mgr. Ward, *The Sequel to Catholic Emancipation*, II, 212.

leader of the bishops in the long drawn out contests with their metropolitan that filled so much of these years, a bishop as busy with his pen as he was fluent of speech, a real ruler, personally competent for most of the tasks he might need to delegate, a close student always and a constant reader who kept to the very best, and like his brother of Newport a model of domestic poverty and simplicity to the end of an episcopate of forty years and more[85]; all in all, surely the greatest of the ninety bishops whose lives make up the first century of the restored hierarchy[86].

To occupy the full total of the sees now created, five new bishops were needed. As late as seven months after the institution of the sees there was still no hint of any appointments and it seems to have been a kind of open secret that " authority " did not know whom to appoint. Here are two contemporary comments. The first is from a private letter by Newman, written in February 1851, " We are not ripe ourselves for a Hierarchy[87]. Now that they have one they can't fill up the Sees, positively can't. . . . We want Seminaries far more than sees. We want education, *view*, combination,

[85] It is interesting that Mgr. Bernard Ward chose as a title for the post-1850 volumes of his great work that he did not live to write *Bishop Ullathorne and His Times*: so Butler, *Ullathorne*, I, pp. v, 189.

[86] Thomas Joseph Brown died in 1880; Ullathorne in 1889, titular Archbishop of Cabasa, twelve months after resigning his see.

[87] Although Rome had consented, in 1848, to the petition of the bishops for a restoration of the diocesan episcopate, and had drawn out the full detail of the sees, it was yet quite accidental that the plan was carried out in 1850. It was not done then because the appropriate moment was now thought to have arrived. What, in fact, brought it about precisely then, was the Pope's reversing his judgment about the wisdom of allowing Wiseman to continue as bishop in London. It is Wiseman himself who is the authority for the statement that Pius IX intended him to be a cardinal in curia, and when he told Ullathorne (in a farewell conversation, July, 1850), that the pope " had stated he would provide his successor in London," he also made it clear that he hoped that successor would be Ullathorne himself. (Butler, *Ullathorne*, I, 163; quoting the bishop's *Autobiography*.) The letter of 27th July from the rector of the English College at Rome, Thomas Grant, already quoted, which speaks of Ullathorne or Briggs going to London in Wiseman's place, and more probably Briggs, gives not a hint of an idea that such a change is imminent as the restoration of the hierarchy. It was not until September that Wiseman arrived in Rome, to learn that there had been " so many and such urgent

organisation ''[88]. The second is the new cardinal, Wiseman himself, writing two months later than Newman, " As to the Hierarchy. If our body is not strengthened, and if the choice of bishops is not made with reference to this consideration as well as with regard to local wants and personal claims, not rising higher than being good and respectable, we shall never be equal to the wants of the times. If soft good persons are put in, I do not know what will become of us. I know there is little choice, but in that let us have the best ''[89].   Rumour was naturally busy. " A little while ago," *The Tablet* reported, February 1st, 1851[90], " it was supposed that all the bishop-rics were not to be filled up for a long while to come, and that several of them were to be held *in commendam*: . . . now we are told that Dr. Cox is to be the new Bishop of Southwark; Dr. Newman the new Bishop of Nottingham; Dr. Errington of Salford; and Dr. Tate and Dr. Grant of the two other vacant sees."

But to Nottingham went the new Bishop of Clifton, and in his place there was appointed Thomas Burgess, once a Benedictine and, as Dom Laurence Burgess, a highly success-ful prior of Ampleforth (1818-30) and then the principal figure among those who left Ampleforth to begin a new foundation at Prior Park under that one-time Ampleforth monk Bishop Baines. Since those far off days—twenty years ago now—he had become a secular priest, and had acted as vicar-general to the Benedictine Vicar Apostolic of Wales, serving also the mission of Monmouth. He was now a man of 60, and had only three more years of life before him. To Shrewsbury went James Brown, who was 49 and the president of the famous school at Sedgley Park which, since 1763, had been a foyer of Catholic life in the midlands[91].

remonstrances and representations against the proposal of taking him out of England '' that Pius IX had changed his plans. " This . . . precipitated the Hierarchy,'' for the new cardinal could not remain a Vicar Apostolic.   " Consequently he must return to England Archbishop of Westminster ''; cf. Butler, *op cit.*, I, 164.

[88] Newman to J. M. Capes, 18th Feb., 1851, in Ward, *Life of Newman*, I, 260.

[89] Butler, *Ullathorne*, I, 195.

[90] p. 72.

[91] The bishops of Clifton and Shrewsbury were consecrated by Wise-man in St. George's Cathedral, Southwark, 27th July, 1851. Bishop James Brown died in 1881.

The other three new bishops were all one-time scholars of the famous English College at Rome where Wiseman's happiest days had been spent as student and as rector. The senior of the three was William Turner, now 52, a classmate of Wiseman's, first at Ushaw and then as one of the little band who in 1818 had gone out to re-establish the *Venerabile* after the long twenty years in which it had ceased to function. Since his ordination, in 1825, William Turner had worked in his native Lancashire, building a church at Rochdale and serving various missions in Manchester. He had been for ten years the vicar-general for the territory he was now to rule as bishop for twenty-one years more—the most useful bishop, it may well be thought, which the see has known. Here certainly was an appointment which the event justified, and in the coming years of divisions among the bishops William Turner, by their unanimous witness, ever acted the part of peacemaker. A second Roman went to Southwark, the rector of the college, Thomas Grant, only 34 years of age, but experienced in curial ways from the years he had already spent as the Roman agent of the English bishops[92]. His services to the new hierarchy were to be invaluable in the gradual building up of a normal ecclesiastical organisation. The third Roman was, at any rate, not one of those " soft good persons " whom Wiseman dreaded might be appointed—and he was one of the cardinal's closest and oldest friends: George Errington, once Wiseman's vice-rector in Rome, and then his assistant at Oscott, now 47 years of age and serving as the head missionary at St. John's Cathedral, Salford, where he was consecrated, along with William Turner, on July 25th, 1851. Never, so far, had the combination succeeded of the unbusiness-like but large-hearted Wiseman, who found it all but impossible to say " No," and his steely, accomplished canonist friend to whom Mother Margaret Hallahan said that it was hard to believe that he had ever had a mother. Plymouth, however, was no part of West-minster, and the new bishop took to the grim poverty of his see with all his soul *naturaliter apostolica*. And then, after less than four years, Wiseman over-persuaded him, to leave Ply-

---

[92] Consecrated, at Rome, 6th July, 1851, by Cardinal Fransoni, the Prefect of Propaganda (who had been Wiseman's consecrator, too, and had ordained Newman).

mouth, to come to London, and to be once more his personal
assistant, to be coadjutor, indeed, with the right of succession
and titular Archbishop of Trebizond; and thence ensued a
tragedy that is, alas, almost all that has survived in popular
record of the cardinal's great episcopate[93].

Such were the personalities and the antecedents of the
bishops with whom the new venture began; none of them, with
the solitary exception of their chief, a great man and few to
reach more than a comfortable professional competence. And
it may be thought that as the new hierarchy began so it has
continued for the most part of the hundred years since. That
the virtues of the bishops have not been of the kind that attracts
the notice of the historian is perhaps more of a reflection on
history than on their lordships—but what of the effect of the
bishops upon their time?

" Canterbury has gone its way, and York is gone, and
Durham is gone, and Winchester is gone. It was sore to part
with them. We clung to the vision of past greatness, and would
not believe it could come to nought; but the Church in England has died, and the Church lives again. Westminster and
Nottingham, Beverley and Hexham, Northampton and
Shrewsbury, if the world lasts, shall be names as musical to
the ear, as stirring to the heart, as the glories we have lost;
and Saints shall rise out of them, if God so will, and Doctors
once again shall give the law to Israel, and Preachers call to
penance and to justice, as at the beginning "[94].

So spoke, from within, the one Doctor so far given to
the new *Anglicana;* and meanwhile a contemporary from outside its ranks drew, from the very spectacle of its poverty in all
resources, a moral that may still console the critic whose gaze

[93] The cardinals of Westminster have, all of them, had for their
biographers, distinguished laymen—and, by the fact, biographers
no one of whom was able to appreciate from the inside what they
were as churchmen, their formation as priests, their work as
bishops. Snead-Cox's life of his kinsman, Herbert Vaughan, is
the only one of the series which really makes a contact with the
heart of the matter.

[94] Newman, *The Second Spring,* a sermon preached 13th July, 1852,
in St. Mary's, Oscott, in the first Provincial Synod of Westminster:
Sermons preached on Various Occasions, 177-178.

is held—for too long, it may be—by the spectacle of impover-
ished inadequacy of means, and its inevitable fruits. By
this act of restoration, said a prominent Tory in the House of
Commons, Rome " has given the most signal, the most startling, the most transcendant homage to the voluntary principle.
For the first time in history she has connected, by the side of
an Established Church, the grandeurs of the Roman hierarchy
with the voluntary principle. . . . What makes her so powerful
nowadays—more powerful than at any time I have ever read
of in the annals of the Church? . . . One sole fact. That
day by day, and bit by bit, and degree by degree, she is withdrawing herself from State connection and Erastian domination. Thus it is that she has been enabled to present to the
world the unique spectacle of a pauper hierarchy by the side
of a largely salaried episcopate: that pauper hierarchy
recognised, and prayed for, and sympathised in by universal
Christendom; that largely salaried episcopate not recognised,
and not prayed for, and not sympathised in, out of the British
empire. At the head of that pauper hierarchy she has set a
Cardinal Prince of the Church—one, who . . . . would take
precedence even of the Prince Consort in every Court of the
Continent of Europe; but she has sent him with the wallet of
the mendicant beneath the robes of the Cardinal, dependent
upon the alms of those who choose to believe. In this, Rome
. . . . has flung far downwards the shadow of a coming truth
into a posterity which will be not ungrateful for the boon. . . .
She has read here in England the first banns of those free
nuptials between liberty and faith—between modern liberty
and ancient faith, which, in my conscience, I believe in no
remote age will yet regenerate the West "[95].

[95] The speaker was the Hon. G. A. Smythe, member for Canterbury,
the date 24th March, 1851, and the occasion the debate on the
second reading of the *Bill to prevent the Assumption of certain
Ecclesiastical Titles in respect of places in the United Kingdom;*
Hansard, 3rd series, Vol. 115, cols. 445-6. G. A. Smythe (1818-
1857), son of the sixth Viscount Strangford (whom he succeeded
in 1855), had been the leading spirit of that " Young England "
group, in the parliament of 1841, which numbered Disraeli and
Lord John Manners among its members.

APPENDIX

CHURCH ATTENDANCE IN 50 TOWNS, SUNDAY, MARCH 30TH, 1851 (see p. 53, *supra*).

Town[1]	Total[2] Population	%[3] at Church	Total Number at Church	Total Catholics at Mass	% of Mass-goers to Total Church-goers	Total Irish-born Population	Catholic Churches in the Town	Priests serving these
Bristol	137,000	55.2	52,995	2,882	5.5	4,761	4	9
Plymouth—Devonport	102,000	53.5	37,676	500	1.3	1,792	1	2
Portsmouth	72,000	50.0	24,562	931	3.8	2,729	1	1
Brighton	70,000	53.0	25,565	520	2.0	787	1	2
Norwich	68,000	43.8	21,238	250	1.2	316	2	3
Bath	54,000	79.0	29,681	645	2.2	678	2	3
Southampton	36,000	58.3	14,469	500	3.4	771	1	2
Cheltenham	35,000	62.5	15,013	325	2.2	1,134[4]	1	2
Exeter	33,000	87.0	20,005	250	1.25	309	1	1
Ipswich	33,000	69.6	15,561	200	1.3	181	1	1
Worcester	28,000	71.4	13,761	500	3.7	226	1	2
Oxford	28,000	57.0	11,463	50	0.5	154	1	1
Cambridge	28,000	63.0	12,567	260	2.1	256	1	1
Northampton	27,000	57.4	10,924	300	1.1	403	1	2
Merthyr Tydvil	63,000	77.3	34,460	600	1.7	3,051	1[5]	1
Swansea	31,000	50.0	11,020	300	2.7	1,333	1	1
Newport (Mon.)	19,323	62.2	8,400	1,300	15.5	2,069	1	3
Liverpool	376,000	47.1	123,728	38,132	30.6	83,813	11[6]	32
Manchester—Salford	400,000	37.5	79,584	19,880	25.0	52,304	7	17
Preston	70,000	28.6	14,035	5,097	30.6	5,122	4	9
Bolton	61,000	38.1	16,037	1,760	11.0	4,453	2	3
Stockport	54,000	42.1	15,995	2,000	12.5	5,701	1	2
Oldham	53,000	26.8	11,275	550	5.0	2,743[7]	1	1
Blackburn	47,000	48.5	12,529	800	6.4	2,505[7]	2	2
Macclesfield	39,000	40.7	11,454	990	8.6	2,358	1	1
Wigan	32,000	54.5	11,985	3,225	26.6	5,506[7]	2	4

CHURCH ATTENDANCE IN 50 TOWNS, SUNDAY, MARCH 30TH, 1851 (see p. 55, supra.)

Town[1]	Total[2] Population	%[3] at Church	Total Number at Church	Total Catholics at Mass	% of Mass-goers to Total Church-goers	Total Irish-born Population	Catholic Churches in the Town	Priests serving these
Bury	31,000	45.5	9,739	812	8.3	2,000[7]	1	1
Ashton-under-Lyne	31,000	42.9	9,053	500	5.5	8,090[7]	1	1
Rochdale ...	29,000	48.3	9,719	453	4.6	2,058[7]	1	1
Leeds ...	172,000	46.6	55,628	3,644	6.5	8,466	2	3
Sheffield ...	135,000	30.8	28,771	2,000	7.0	4,477	1	2
Bradford ...	104,000	41.1	29,990	3,228	10.6	9,279	1	3
Halifax ...	34,000	—	—	451	—	2,088[7]	1	1
Huddersfield ...	31,000	59.0	12,521	400	3.2	1,562	1	1
Hull ...	85,000	47.5	28,308	1,200	4.2	2,987	1	2
Leicester ...	61,000	59.5	24,747	636	2.4	877	1	2
Nottingham ...	57,000	57.5	22,528	1,420	6.2	1,577	1	3
Derby ...	41,000	55.2	15,931	1,244	7.5	1,314	1	2
Coventry ...	36,000	32.0	9,704	900	9.3	698	1	2
Stoke ...	84,000[8]	39.0	22,581	1,260	5.6	1,756[9]	1	1
Wolverhampton ...	120,000[8]	48.6	41,191	1,645	4.0	3,491	1	3
Birmingham ...	233,000	35.6	58,170	3,383	6.0	9,341	4	8
York	36,000	60.0	15,130	1,350	9.0	1,928	1	3
Carlisle ...	26,000	36.7	6,614	1,060	15.2	2,100	1	3
Newcastle-on-Tyne	88,000	40.3	24,940	3,389	13.7	7,124	2	4
Sunderland ...	64,000	44.4	20,060	950	4.8	3,601	1	2
Tynemouth ...	29,000	—	—	500	—	1,108	1[10]	2
South Shields ...	29,000	38.2	7,644	430	5.6	922	1	1
Gateshead[11] ...	26,000	30.9	5,553	500	9.0	2,195	1	
London	2,362,236	37.2	615,034	35,994	—	107,548	34	91

The London total, p. 81, is that of Division I, *Metropolitan London,* of the census reports of 1851—the census registration districts numbered 1 to 36, inclusive. It is the area of the present county of London. Since it is not possible really to treat this vast population as a unit, the details for each of the 36 districts are given in the table that follows; the present-day administrative areas to which these correspond are indicated in the second column. As to the total number of Catholics among these 2,362,236 of 1851, we have some clue in the report of the Vicar Apostolic, Dr. Griffiths, made to Rome in 1847 that the numbers of Catholics in London had increased between 1836 and 1843 from 145,000 to 195,000[96]. In a report nearly five years earlier the same bishop had explained that, " . . . of the Catholics of London three-quarters are the poorest and least religious of the Catholics of Ireland, who emigrate continually to the large towns in England "[97].

[96] Ward, *Sequel to Catholic Emancipation,* II, 177.

[97] Letter of 11th Dec., 1842, to Dr. Baggs, rector of the English College, Rome, to be communicated to Propaganda, in Ward, *op. cit.,* I, 172. This is a somewhat chill and tight-lipped summary. As a set-off to it we might quote the remarkable article *The Irish in London* in the *Rambler* for April, 1851, reviewing Mayhew's newly published *London Labour and the London Poor.* The writer of this article—critically aware of all the faults of the Irish—can say, " It is notorious that in every large town in England, and especially in the metropolis, the spiritual wants of the Irish are even less supplied than their corporal." He states that some 30,000 of the poor Catholic children in London never attend a school of any kind. " The boys and girls who *never* make their first communion must still be counted by tens of thousands. Ten times the number of clergy that we now possess, with a proportionate number of additional churches, would scarcely suffice for the ever increasing necessities of Catholic London. Then, too, see how awfully the old system of pew-renting has operated, and in many cases still operates (even when the clergy struggle with all their powers to cast it off) upon the spiritual condition of the poor. What a fearful sight it is to see a Catholic chapel, at the very time the holy sacrifice is being offered, with its largest portion, and all its best parts, half-empty, sometimes not a third or a quarter full, while below the bar where the box-keeper sits, a multitude of poor men and women are crushed together, extending not only up to the doors but through them into the street beyond. Who can wonder that the poor in England feel in many instances so little attraction for that house of God which

(*Continued on page* 85)

CHURCH ATTENDANCE, METROPOLITAN LONDON, SUNDAY, MARCH 30TH, 1851

Registration District of 1851	Modern City, Metropolitan Borough	Population of the Registration District	%[3] Attending Church	Total Attending all Churches of District	Catholics at Mass in Churches of District	Irish-born Population of District	Cath. Churches in District	Priests serving these
Kensington ...	Paddington, Kensington, Hammersmith, Fulham	120,000	32.8	27,562	1,696	4,370	3	4
Chelsea ...	Chelsea ...	56,538	40.0	15,798	770	2,450	1	3
St. George's Hanover Square	Westminster	73,230	37.0	18,855	500	2,682	1[12]	5
Westminster...		65,609	48.3	22,216		3,864	1	2
St. Martin's-in-the-Fields		24,640	50.0	8,568	800	1,250	1[13]	7
St. James		36,406	32.5	8,333	3,000	2,185	1	4
Strand		44,460	29.0	9,047	5,400	2,431	1	3
Marylebone	Marylebone	157,696	41.4	44,444		8,456	3	10
Hampstead	Hampstead	11,986	72.6	6,121	400	238	1	3
Pancras	St. Pancras	166,956	42.8	49,855	293	5,835	2[14]	5
Islington	Islington	95,329	44.5	29,697	1,545	2,420	1	2
Hackney	Hackney; Stoke Newington	58,429	58.0	23,740	300	683	1	1
St. Giles	Holborn	54,214	37.0	13,982	3,000	5,030	1	4
Holborn		46,621	33.0	10,835	400	4,224	1	2
Clerkenwell	Finsbury	64,778	27.6	12,485		1,676	1[15]	2
St. Luke's		54,055	32.0	12,066		2,192		
East London		44,406	34.0	10,604		3,626		
West London	City	28,790	30.0	6,035		1,921		
City of London		55,932	66.0	25,923	1,350	1,647	1	4

CHURCH ATTENDANCE, METROPOLITAN LONDON, SUNDAY, MARCH 30th, 1851

Registration District of 1851	Modern City, Metropolitan Borough	Population of the Registration District	%3 Attending Church	Total Attending all Churches of District	Catholics at Mass in Churches of District	Irish-born Population of District	Cath. Churches in District	Priests serving these
Shoreditch	Shoreditch	109,257	18.1	13,849		2,293		
Bethnal Green	Bethnal Green	90,193	9.5	6,024		813		
Whitechapel	Stepney	79,759	30.1	16,814	2,150	8,998	2	4
St.George in the East	Stepney	48,376	23.0	7,704	1,000	3,576	1	3
Stepney	Poplar	110,775	33.3	25,768	3,550	6,099	1	2
Poplar	Poplar	47,162	28.1	9,342	1,340	2,494	1	2
St. Saviour Southwark	Southwark	35,731	33.6	8,377	1,200	1,979	1	2
St. Olave Southwark	Southwark	19,375	51.4	6,991		2,932		
St. George Southwark	Southwark	51,824	31.4	14,991	4,000	2,467	1	4
Newington		64,816	31.7	14,432		1,336		
Bermondsey	Bermondsey	48,128	25.5	9,643	2,000	2,562	1	3
Rotherhithe		17,805	32.0	3,987		920		
Lambeth	Lambeth	139,325	32.1	31,331		4,372		
Camberwell		54,667	19.0	7,306	253	1,604		
Wandsworth	Wandsworth Battersea	50,764	66.0	23,309		848	2	7
Greenwich	Greenwich Deptford Woolwich	99,365	44.2	30,768	1,047	6,132	3	3
Lewisham	Lewisham	34,835	55.0	13,421		973		

How the bishop arrived at his figures we do not know. But eight years after the date at which he thought the total number of Catholics in London was 195,000 the census of 1851 gave the total of Irish-born as 107,548 which is considerably less than three-fourths of the bishop's figure; and it is hard not to believe that, after the years 1845-47, there were not very many more Catholics of Irish birth in London in 1851 than in 1843.

(Continued from page 82)

ought to be their own peculiar much-loved home?   Who can wonder at the eager, passionate affection which they show to those of the Catholic clergy who are enabled to escape from the thraldom of an effete and world-worshipping system, and really to become— what every Catholic priest must desire to become—the evangelists of the poor." *The Rambler,* as above, p. 292.

NOTES ON THE TABLES

1 The towns are grouped as follows: Towns south of the Gloucester-Grimsby line; new Welsh, industrial, but non-textile towns; a " new," non-textile town; the " new," textile towns of the S.E. Lancashire district; the " new," textile towns of Yorkshire and a port; the " new," industrial towns of the Midlands; two " old " towns of the North; the " new," industrial, but non-textile, towns of the North-East coast; the capital.

2 To the nearest thousand.

3 I.e., percentage not of the total population, but of the number presumed able to attend church; this number the census officials reckoned as 70 per cent. of the total population. The total number of individuals present—once at least—at religious worship, which is given in the next column, is obtained, following the method used by the census officials, by adding to the number present at the morning service, half the number present at the afternoon service and one-third the number present at the evening service.

4 Figures for the registration district of Cheltenham, not the town.

5 The church was at Dowlais.

6 This includes the church at Bootle (St. James).

7 These are the figures for the Poor Law Union and not the municipal borough.

8 These are the figures for the parliamentary borough, not the municipal borough.

9 Figures for the registration district of Stoke, not the town.

10 The mission of North Shields.

11 No church is given in the *Catholic Directory* for 1851, which says only " A new mission will shortly be commenced here. Land has been purchased for the site of a church and Presbytery."

12 This church has sittings for 500; no returns of attendance sent in.

13 This church has sittings for 550; no returns of attendance sent in.

14 No returns of attendance sent in from one of the two churches, which has sittings for 800.

15 This church has sittings for 700; no returns of attendance sent in.

III

THE RESTORATION OF THE HIERARCHY
1850

By Gordon Albion

WHEN in the Spring of 597 A.D. St. Augustine landed in Kent, he at once began the task of converting the English by setting up bishoprics at Canterbury and Rochester. In this he was carrying out instructions given him by his master, Pope Gregory the Great.

For close on a thousand years, these and other dioceses that came to be created throughout the realm of England were ruled by bishops in communion with the Vicar of Christ.

In 1559, it was precisely the refusal of the English bishops of that day to disavow this primacy of the Popes in favour of the Royal Supremacy in matters spiritual that caused Queen Elizabeth to depose and imprison the whole Hierarchy save one—Anthony Kitchen, Bishop of Llandaff, who agreed to take the Oath of Supremacy. Of the three bishops who managed to escape, Thomas Goldwell, Bishop of St. Asaph, died in Rome on April 3rd, 1585—the last survivor of the ancient Catholic Hierarchy of England.

It was two-hundred-and-sixty-five years before this country was to have another normal Catholic episcopal government and then Westminster, Southwark and the rest of the names we now know so well, were to succeed Canterbury, London, Winchester and the other age-old sees who have so unhappily lost their link with the Apostolic See of Rome.

Meanwhile the slowly dwindling number of English Catholics who stayed staunch to their ancient Faith came under a various and ill-defined leadership. In 1581, Dr. (later Cardinal) William Allen was made Prefect of the English Mission. From 1598 to 1621, three successive Archpriests were appointed leaders of the secular clergy. Then the crying need for a bishop was met by the appointment of a Vicar Apostolic, that is, a missionary, not a diocesan bishop. The experiment failed, and from 1655 to 1685 the Catholics of England had no nearer leader than their Cardinal Protector in Rome.

With the accession of the last Catholic King of England, James II, the future looked brighter and a Vicar Apostolic was again appointed. Three years later in 1688, the country was divided into four Vicariates or Districts, with a bishop over each. This arrangement had never been meant as more than an expedient until the restoration of a normal Hierarchy could be safely conceded, but it only became practicable after the grant of emancipation to English Catholics in 1829.

Nine years later, on May 19th, 1838, Cardinal Franzoni, Prefect of the Congregation of Propaganda, wrote to the English Vicars Apostolic and suggested an increase in their number as a step towards further measures. The next month, June, at their annual meeting, the four bishops, Thomas Griffiths (London District), Thomas Walsh (Midland District), John Briggs (Northern District) and Peter Baines, O.S.B. (Western District), drew up a series of propositions or *Statuta Provisoria,* which, when submitted to Rome, became known as *Statuta Proposita.*

While agreeing to the suggested increase of Vicars Apostolic and Districts, the four bishops advised delay. Then as a preliminary towards the setting up of normal episcopal government, they proposed that, whilst they retained the title of Vicars Apostolic, they should have ordinary faculties and, in addition, that they each be allowed to appoint a Vicar General, an Archdeacon, Vicars Forane and a Chapter of Canons to advise on the choice of co-adjutors, to appoint Vicars Capitular and to choose a *terna,* to be submitted to the other Vicars Apostolic, for the guidance of the Holy See in appointing successors to the Vicariates.

Although these proposals were not fully accepted, their first result was the increase of the number of Vicars Apostolic to eight. The four new districts were the Eastern, the Central, the Welsh and the Lancashire. This action of Pope Gregory XVI in 1840 was intended as a curtain-raiser to the restoration of the Hierarchy a decade later.

During these ten years, Propaganda was bombarded with memorials for the restoration sent in by various groups, lay as well as clerical, and including a Brotherhood founded for this purpose by a club of priests calling themselves the "Adelphi" and led by the learned liturgiologist, Dr. Daniel Rock.

Propaganda, in its turn, was continually asking for information on the subject from prominent English Catholics as well as from the Vicars Apostolic, especially Bishop Griffiths.

It was the latter who proposed at the annual meeting of the Vicars Apostolic in 1845 that a formal petition be sent to the Holy See for the restoration of the Hierarchy. A more urgent step was taken at their meeting in April, 1847, when Bishop Nicholas Wiseman and Bishop James Sharples were sent to Rome in the name of the Vicars Apostolic to represent to the Holy See that the restoration of the Hierarchy was the only effectual means of establishing good order and efficiency in the government of the English Catholic community.

In July, 1847, the two bishops gave an account of the English Mission to the new pope, Pius IX, and then conferred with Monsignor Palma, special under-secretary at Propaganda for English-speaking actions, and Dr. Thomas Grant, rector of the English College. The first suggestion, made by the Pope himself, was for a new Constitution and Rules for the English Mission. This was opposed by Wiseman as being only a provisional arrangement and just as difficult as the restoration of a Hierarchy for which he pressed resolutely, with the full support of the Vicars Apostolic at home and in Rome of Monsignor Barnabò, the Pro-Secretary (and later Cardinal Prefect) of Propaganda. At his suggestion, Wiseman drew up and presented a petition to Pius IX, who, after offering three Masses for guidance, expressed himself in general agreement.

But now Propaganda asked Wiseman and Sharples to reply to various objections to the granting of a Hierarchy that had been made by Charles Acton, the English Cardinal in Curia, and by Cardinal Castracane. The answer of the two bishops was made separately, for the outbreak of revolt in Italy led to Wiseman's being sent back on a political mission to the

English Government, while Sharples was soon obliged to return on account of illness.

However, in October, 1847, Propaganda ordered the English Vicars Apostolic to meet as soon as possible to draw up a scheme for the proposed Hierarchy, based on the principle of redistributing the eight vicariates into at least twelve dioceses. Thereupon the bishops met in London on November 11th, heard the report of Wiseman and Sharples and, after two days' deliberation, drew up the requested plan, adding reasons for and against a division of the London District into the dioceses of London and Southwark and of the Lancashire District into two sees. This plan appears never to have been sent to Rome, where already in October, 1847, a simpler scheme had been devised for making the eight vicariates into eight sees. At Pius IX's orders, Letters Apostolic, entitled *Universalis Ecclesiæ* and dated November 1st, 1847, were drawn up for this purpose, and briefs dated November 24th were prepared, nominating bishops to all the new sees, save Newcastle. Although these documents were never promulgated, copies were shown by the Pope to Lord Minto, then on a diplomatic mission in Rome, and were made known by him to the British Government. This fact was pointed out by Wiseman to the Prime Minister, Lord John Russell, at the time of the " Papal Aggression " outcry three years later.

The affair of the new Hierarchy took on a new turn as the result of a letter sent to the English bishops by Dr. Grant, who was their agent in Rome. He stated that he was finding it increasingly difficult to combine his office as Rector of the English College with such important negotiations pending. He, therefore, asked either to be relieved of the agency or to have a competent person from England to assist him.

At their annual meeting in May, 1848, the Vicars Apostolic discussed the matter and, after failing to persuade the historian, Dr. Frederick Husenbeth, to undertake the mission, they asked one of their own number, Dr. William Ullathorne, O.S.B., to go as their plenipotentiary to press forward the matter of the Hierarchy as an urgent remedy to the growing difficulties of the Vicars Apostolic in the control of their clergy, and to forestall misrepresentation of their own conduct to the Holy See.

Ullathorne was the ideal man for a task which he had very much at heart. He says himself that at his consecration as Vicar Apostolic of the Western District in June, 1846, he had resolved never to rest until the Hierarchy had been obtained. Later on he was to refer to the work that befell him now as " the most important and most eventful of the labours of his episcopal life."

It was the Year of Revolutions all over Europe and as he passed through Paris in the middle of May, he witnessed the abortive attempt to set up a Red Republic, watched the funeral procession of the revolutionaries killed at the Barricades and saw their leaders arrested by the army and taken to prison.

On May 26th, he arrived in Rome to stay at the English College, where he enjoyed the dual advantage of constant consultation with the Rector, Dr. Grant, and of being near Propaganda. The next day he had a long but desultory conversation with Cardinal Franzoni, to whom he had to vindicate the Vicars Apostolic whose action in various cases pending in Rome had been falsely represented. This sort of thing was in itself a strong argument for a more regular ecclesiastical administration.

But Ullathorne found his best ally not in the Cardinal Prefect, but in his energetic secretary, Mgr. Barnabò, with whom, that same day, he began a series of fruitful interviews, of which Dr. Grant or, in his absence, Ullathorne himself took copious notes.

Barnabò lost no time in plunging into the heart of the question. The chief reasons for delay in setting up the Hierarchy, he said, were first the choice of Archbishop and, secondly, the difficulty of disposing of properties held by the bishops under their present titles.

The Pope had appointed a special Congregation of seven Cardinals to cope with the question of the Hierarchy and Mgr. Barnabò promised to call them together early in June, if Ullathorne would draw up suggestions for the choice of bishops for the London, Central and Northern Districts and also see to it that the sensitiveness of the bishops would not be hurt in the event of a young man being placed over them as Archbishop. This referred to Wiseman, who was to remain in

London as Co-adjutor, even if the aged and ailing Bishop Walsh of the Central District were appointed Archbishop.

As the result of his talk with Mgr. Barnabò, Ullathorne drew up a Memorial (Document A), in which he suggested for the Northern District the then Administrator, William Hogarth. (He was actually appointed in the following July.) On the question of the new Archbishop, he pointed out that, although Bishop Walsh, as the revered senior Vicar Apostolic, would be in many ways a welcome appointment, his age and ill-health were such that he would need a co-adjutor from the start and many felt it would be better to nominate another at once to the Metropolitan See. Moreover, this nomination should take into consideration the special circumstances of London with its large Catholic population and resources and its position as the centre of the Court and Parliament. In appointing Bishop Wiseman as Pro-Vicar of the London District, the Holy See had already recognised his zeal for the Catholic poor there, as well as his outstanding literary talents and influence with distinguished converts. Therefore, even if Rome decided to make Bishop Walsh the Metropolitan, Wiseman must remain in London and this could only be as Co-adjutor with right of succession.

In a second Memorial (Document B), Ullathorne dealt with the difficulties facing Rome's proposal to increase the number of dioceses over the present figure of eight Vicariates, —in other words, the dual problem of finding suitable candidates and the wherewithal for their adequate maintenance. At present all the bishops, save two, were handicapped by poverty. Moreover, there was a great shortage of mature clergy with experience of the conditions of the English Mission. If, however, these two difficulties could be overcome, a great impulse would be given to religion, particularly in remote districts, by multiplying the centres of episcopal influence. This increase could be made at once despite the difficulties, or gradually according to plan. He himself suggested a straight change from Vicariates to Ordinary Sees, leaving the Bishops at their first Provincial Synod to subdivide according to a pre-arranged plan. Ullathorne concluded by stressing the ardent desire of bishops, clergy and laity in England to see the Church there set on the firm and solid basis of a Hierarchy as a means of ending all the present disputes and controversies, and especially the " democratic " tone creeping in, which enfeebled the spirit as well as the principle of obedience.

On June 2nd, these two Memorials were presented by Ullathorne and Dr. Grant to Mgr. Barnabò, who told them that the Pope was in favour of placing both Bishop Walsh and Bishop Wiseman in London and also of expediting the whole affair. They then urged this on Cardinal Franzoni.

The next day, Dr. Grant handed into Propaganda a third Memorial (Document G) of Ullathorne on the subject of retaining some few old titles of English Catholic sees. At their 1847 meeting, the Vicars Apostolic had been against this, so as to avoid both Protestant susceptibility and also the liabilities of the 1829 Emancipation Act, but some had since veered to the opposite opinion for weighty reasons which Ullathorne now put forward. First, to abandon the old titles altogether might be taken as a tacit admission of the validity of Anglican Orders and of continuity. It had already been argued that the Holy See had never formally condemned the Anglican position and thereby many, especially among the Puseyites, had been kept from joining the Church. If now the Holy See were to revive even one or two names of the ancient English sees in the new Hierarchy, there could be no further ground for self-deception among Anglicans.

On the second point, Ullathorne maintained that it would be difficult for the Courts to enforce a new penal law which only affected certain titles used in a certain manner, especially as English public opinion would be opposed to any act of the Government against liberty of conscience. Moreover, Catholic bishops in Ireland and the Colonies had taken titles used by Protestants without interference from the Government. For these reasons, Ullathorne suggested St. David's instead of Newport, and instead of Plymouth, Bristol. Clifton, a later suggestion he made, was the title eventually taken.

On June 5th, Ullathorne had an audience with the Pope and presented the Joint Memorial of the Bishops (Document D), drawn up by Wiseman, signed by all the Bishops and dated May 12th, 1848. It states in plain but heartfelt terms the case for the Hierarchy, which Ullathorne was commissioned as plenipotentiary to place before the Holy Father.

Ullathorne pointed out verbally to His Holiness the serious inconveniences resulting from the present state of suspense, whereupon Pope Pius expressed his esteem for the English Bishops, despite libellous misrepresentations made against them in Rome by litigious priests, and said he hoped to issue the Bull of Restoration soon.

The Special Congregation to deal with the matter consisted of Cardinal Franzoni, Prefect of Propaganda, and Cardinals Ostini, Castracane, Altieri, Vizzardelli, Orioli and Mai, with Mgr. Barnabò as Secretary. They met on June 26th and at once asked Mgr. Barnabò to tell Ullathorne of their deliberations and ask his views thereupon.

They wanted the title St. David's for Wales and thought all the Sees should be called after old ones. But was this practicable? How could the Bishops afford to pay the £100 fine?

Also they wished to divide England into twelve sees at once, so as to forestall later disputes among the Bishops. They asked Ullathorne to suggest places and boundaries. The Cardinals considered that the two objections raised, lack of money and of suitable bishops, were insufficient to delay the increase of sees, some of which could be controlled temporarily by other bishops. The Cardinals showed great interest in London. They knew that north and south of the Thames had been in different dioceses and that as far back as the time of Innocent III in 1215, the Archbishops of Canterbury, to whom the north side then belonged, had built a residence at Lambeth. The Congregation observed that to the South Thames diocese would belong important towns like Brighton, Southampton and Winchester.

While the Congregation were in session, Ullathorne sent in word that Dr. Walsh was dying, but the Cardinals' only reaction was: " Whether living or dead he shall be the first Archbishop of Westminster." They also wanted Ullathorne to transfer to the Central District, in which Oxford was situated and where they thought his influence would tell at the University. Ullathorne thought otherwise and told Barnabò plainly that he had not in reality the scholarship the Cardinals thought but recommended Dr. Grant.

On the last day of June, Ullathorne sent in to Propaganda four more Memorials (Documents I, J, K, L). The first dealt with the change-over from Vicars Apostolic to

Bishops; the second contained his suggestion of the Franciscan, Father William Hendren, as his successor in the Western District, should he (Ullathorne) be transferred.

The third Memorial (Document K) was a detailed plan for distributing the eight Vicariates into twelve Dioceses; it was accepted and incorporated into the Brief of the Hierarchy. Against his own inclination, Ullathorne attached Oxfordshire to Birmingham and not to London, kept Lancashire undivided as one see, and allowed the Thames to divide London, with Southwark as a separate see—this at the instance of Propaganda.

Some of the names Ullathorne, in consultation with Dr. Grant, suggested for the Sees were eventually changed, so his proposed London became Westminster, Bristol became Clifton, Newcastle became Hexham, though later the two names were used jointly; and lastly York was changed to Beverley. The other titles were promulgated as proposed, except that Newport was added to Menevia. Appended to this document was a map showing the eight Vicariates and the twelve Sees in different colours.

Ullathorne concluded this important Memorial with the following remarks:

" In proposing this plan of division, regulated on the principles pointed out by the Sacred Congregation, the undersigned cannot but observe that the Holy See is proposing to renew our Church as it existed in its earlier period.

" In the celebrated Synod of Arles, three British Bishops assisted, and amongst the first to sign the Acts was the Bishop of London.

" But what is more striking in the parallel is the fact that the Apostle of our Country, Pope St. Gregory the Great, in a letter to St. Augustine, contemplated erecting London into an Archiepiscopal See, contemplating the time when York might be made a second Archbishopric with its twelve suffragans.

" The Pope's words to St. Augustine are these:

' And, in regard that the new Church of the English is through the goodness of the Lord, and your labours, brought to the Grace of God, we grant you the use of the Pallium, only for use in the solemnization of the Mass;

so that you in as many places ordain twelve Bishops who shall be subject to your jurisdiction, so that the Bishop of London shall, for the future, be always consecrated by his own Synod, and that he receive the honour of the Pallium from this Holy and Apostolic See, which I, by the Grace of God, now serve.

' But we will have you send to the City of York such a Bishop as you think fit to ordain; yet so, that if that City, with the places adjoining, shall receive the Word of God, that Bishop shall also ordain twelve Bishops and enjoy the honour of a Metropolitan. For we design, if we live, by the help of God, to bestow on him also the Pallium.' ''

Ullathorne sent in with this Memorial, another (Document L) of eleven folio pages, giving a reasoned exposition upon each of the twelve titles proposed. At Mgr. Barnabò's request, copies of all these Memorials were made, one for each Cardinal of the Special Congregation.

A fortnight later, on July 17th, the Congregation was held and Ullathorne was invited to be present as the Cardinals wished to consult him on the titles of Sees, as they were particularly anxious to avoid any conflict with English Law. When, at the end of the discussions, the matter was put to the vote, the most learned canonist among the Cardinals demurred and Ullathorne was asked to withdraw.

The next day, Mgr. Barnabò told him the decisions arrived at: that Dr. Walsh, despite his dying condition, was to be transferred from the Central District to London with a view to his becoming the first Archbishop; that Ullathorne himself was to go to Birmingham, and Hendren was to succeed him in the Western District. Finally, no decision would be reached on the question of titles, as the Cardinals wished each Bishop to write to Propaganda his opinion respecting his own. This would necessarily delay the promulgation of the Hierarchy.

Thereupon Ullathorne told Barnabò, who fully agreed, that he would leave at once for England to inform the Bishops, who were about to assemble at Manchester for the opening of Salford Cathedral, of all that had happened. At Ullathorne's farewell audience with Pius IX, the Holy Father, who approved the report of the Special Congregation, asked him to tell the English Bishops of his kindly sentiments towards them and of his desire to establish them in a Hierarchy as soon as possible. He also gave Ullathorne a gold chalice to take back to the newly opened St. George's, Southwark.

Back in Manchester, Ullathorne reported to the Bishops and found dissatisfaction that Lancashire was not to be divided into two dioceses. Bishop Wiseman, after expressing his dislike of the separation of Southwark from the rest of London, spoke in warm and loyal terms of the gratitude they should all feel for what had been decided, and suggested a letter to the Holy Father gratefully accepting the arrangement, while still recommending the division of Lancashire. Ullathorne supported this in writing to Cardinal Franzoni, with the result that the twelve sees first proposed became thirteen.

All the time Ullathorne had been in Rome, the Eternal City was in a state of acute unrest, with conspiracies, plots, and assassinations an almost daily occurrence. These eventually caused Pius IX to flee to Gaeta. During the Pope's absence from Rome, November, 1848, to April, 1850, few, if any, Congregations were held, so the case of the English Hierarchy was inevitably held over until June, 1850, when, at Mgr. Barnabò's request, Dr. Grant drew up a short document making a definite request for the Hierarchy. The views of the English Bishops on their titles had been received during the summer of 1849, so the Cardinals now completed their work and the Brief was prepared. Of the final stages Dr. Grant wrote " When the Cardinals discussed the subject of our Hierarchy for the last time, late in the summer of 1850, all obstacles were removed and, after a few days' hesitation on the part of two of their number, they were unanimous in asking His Holiness to issue the Brief of September 29th, 1850."

The body of this Pontifical Decree, or Apostolical Letter[1], was drawn up by Cardinal Vizzardelli, " esteemed the first canonist in Rome," according to Ullathorne. The historical preface had been written, from material Dr. Grant provided, by Mgr. Palma, who had long acquaintance with English Catholic affairs, and had drawn up the Brief *Muneris*

---

[1] Printed *in extenso* in Appendix, p. 107.

NICHOLAS, CARDINAL WISEMAN
First Archbishop of Westminster,
1850-65

[1]

JOHN BRIGGS
First Bishop of Beverley,
1850-60

GEORGE BROWN
First Bishop of Liverpool,
1850-56

[3]

THOMAS JOSEPH BROWN, O.S.B.
First Bishop of Newport and Menevia,
1850-80

WILLIAM BERNARD ULLATHORNE, o.s.b.
First Bishop of Birmingham,
1850-88

WILLIAM HOGARTH
First Bishop of Hexham and Newcastle,
1850-66

[6]

WILLIAM JOSEPH HENDREN, o.s.f.
First Bishop of Clifton, 1850-51
First Bishop of Nottingham, 1851-53

THOMAS GRANT
First Bishop of Southwark,
1851-70

WILLIAM TURNER
First Bishop of Salford,
1851-72

GEORGE ERRINGTON
First Bishop of Plymouth,
1851-55

JAMES BROWN
First Bishop of Shrewsbury,
1851-81

Rome Sept. 30. 1850

My dear Bagshawe

I write a few hasty lines to inform you that this morning, the most memorable Consistory for England, perhaps in history, has taken place. His Holiness has proclaimed the restoration of the Hierarchy, and has conferred on one at once the twofold dignity of Cardinal & Archbishop of Westminster. In a few weeks, I shall start for London where I hope to arrive by the middle of November. I will not say a word on business. I will only say that the manner how this wonderful event has been brought about appears to every one to mark the finger of God. Till to-day all who have known what was preparing have been under strict secrecy. I send you & all your family my first archiepiscopal blessing, & am ever

Yours affect[ionate]ly +
N. Card. Wiseman

WISEMAN ANNOUNCES THE RESTORATION
in a letter to H. R. Bagshawe, September 30th, 1850

THE GUY FAWKES OF 1850

PREPARING TO BLOW UP ALL ENGLAND!

From *Punch*, 1850

THE THIN END OF THE WEDGE.

DARING ATTEMPT TO BREAK INTO A CHURCH.

From *Punch*, 1850

[14]

THIS IS THE BOY WHO CHALKED UP "NO POPERY!"—AND THEN RAN AWAY!!

From *Punch*, 1850

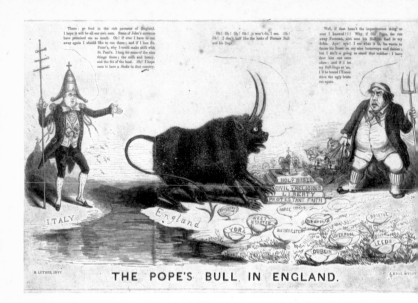

THE POPE'S BULL IN ENGLAND.

From contemporary broadsheets

JOHN BULL BETWEEN CATHOLICISM AND PROTESTANTISM.

[16]

Apostolici of 1840, increasing the Vicariates from four to eight[2].

The day after the issue of the Brief restoring the Hierarchy, the Pope held a Consistory in which Bishop Wiseman was created a Cardinal Priest[3].

On October 3rd, he received the Red Hat and, with it, the title of Santa Pudenziana. He at once requested, and received from Pius IX, the Pallium as a sign of his Metropolitan jurisdiction at Westminster.

Four days later, on October 7th, the new Cardinal Archbishop formally announced to English Catholics the restoration of the Hierarchy in his first Pastoral dated " From the Flaminian Gate of Rome," and on October 12th set out for England, fêted all the way and anticipating a triumphal welcome home.

It was on November 3rd, while driving through Vienna after dining with the Emperor, that he opened his copy of *The Times* of October 14th, to find a rude shock awaiting him. The leading article, written before the Flaminian Gate Pastoral arrived to fan and spread the flame of Protestant susceptibility, was the first indication of the hostility of English public opinion to the Pope's reaction in creating the new Hierarchy. Concentrating its attack on Wiseman, *The Times* spoke of him as " the new-fangled Archbishop of Westminster," which " signifies no more than if the Pope had been pleased to confer on the editor of *The Tablet* the rank and title of the Duke of Smithfield. But if this appointment be not intended as a

---

[2] Soon after Ullathorne left Rome at the end of July, 1848, Mgr. Palma was shot dead through a window of the Quirinal, whilst quieting the alarm of his aged mother when the Pope's palace was attacked by rebels.

[3] Since the death of Bishop Walsh in February, 1849, Wiseman had been going from strength to strength in his work in London, when suddenly in May, 1850, he had received a letter from Cardinal Antonelli, the Secretary of State, that the Pope intended to raise him to the Cardinalate. This he took as meaning that he must leave England and his work for ever, at a moment when the future held such high prospects, and would live out the rest of his life " in golden fetters," as he put it, at the Papal Court. Demur as he did, a peremptory answer came that he was wanted in Rome and that a successor would be provided for him in London. He left England on August 16th, reaching Rome on September 5th, only to find that his promotion was to be a double one and that he would after all return to lead the new Hierarchy.

clumsy joke, we confess that we can only regard it as one of the grossest acts of folly and impertinence which the Court of Rome has ventured to commit since the Crown and people of England threw off its yoke."

The Times of October 19th continued even more angrily: " Is it, then, here in Westminster, among ourselves and by the English throne, that an Italian priest is to parcel out the spiritual dominion of this country—to employ the renegades of our National Church to restore a foreign usurpation over the consciences of men and to sow divisions in our political society by an undisguised and systematic hostility to the institutions most nearly identified with our national freedom and our national faith? Such an intention must either be ludicrous or intolerable—either a delusion of some fanatical brain or treason to the constitution."

Rising to the occasion with, as Newman said later, " vigour, power, judgment and sustained energy," the Cardinal wrote that very day to the Prime Minister, Lord John Russell, deeply regretting the erroneous and distorted views printed in the papers on what the Holy See had done in regard to the spiritual government of the Catholics of England and pointing out " that the measure now promulgated was not only prepared but printed three years ago, and a copy of it was shown to Lord Minto by the Pope." Wiseman offered the Prime Minister a full explanation to remove any misconception, and went on: " I am invested with a purely ecclesiastical dignity. I have no secular or temporal delegation whatever. My duties will be what they have ever been, to promote the morality of those committed to my charge, especially among the masses of the poor; and to keep up those feelings of goodwill between Catholics and their fellow-countrymen, which I flatter myself I have been the means of somewhat improving."

Meanwhile, both the Pope's Brief and the Cardinal's Flaminian Gate Pastoral had reached Dr. Whitty, Vicar General of the London District. Whereas the Papal document gave a factual survey of the way English Catholics had been governed spiritually since the Reformation, Wiseman's Pastoral was couched in jubilant, triumphant terms, attuned to his own mood and that of the English Catholics who had waited so long for this day. But it could only serve to irritate to an extreme degree the susceptibilities of Protestants already aroused by the bare announcement of the Pope's action and by *The Times'* articles. In his natural exuberance Wiseman had forgotten that his ardent words, intended for Catholic consumption, would, on so special an occasion, receive the widest publicity.

Dr. Whitty saw this at a glance but had no means of recourse to the Cardinal, who was returning in leisurely fashion across Europe; moreover, he had no mandate either to alter the text or suppress publication. So the Pastoral was printed and read in all Catholic churches and chapels on Sunday, October 17th, and rapidly found its way into the newspapers.

The Pastoral gave a general account of the scope of the Pope's action, assuming throughout, of course, the absolute authority of the Pope over English Catholics and ignoring all spiritual authority outside the Catholic Church. Speaking of his own jurisdiction as Archbishop of Westminster and Administrator of Southwark, Wiseman wrote: " Till such time as the Holy See shall think fit otherwise to provide, we govern and shall continue to govern the counties of Middlesex, Hertford and Essex, as Ordinary thereof, and those of Surrey, Sussex, Kent, Berkshire and Hampshire, with the islands annexed, as Administrator with Ordinary jurisdiction."

Such language immediately provoked a chorus of protest, rising in a crescendo of hysterical indignation, from the Press, Anglican clergy, and leading statesmen.

" Pio Nono . . . apes the pretensions of a Hildebrand. . . . He and his clergy . . . despatch a Cardinal Archbishop to Westminster to catch fools with his title and enslave kindred bigots by his assumption of authority and state."

The Times analysed each item of the Papal Brief as if each new diocese was an added insult to the English people, utterly regardless of the fact that the Holy See had recently taken a similar step in the Colonies without any opposition from the Government.

On November 4th, while Wiseman's letter to him quoted above had just been despatched, Lord John Russell replied to the Bishop of Durham's protest at the " insolent and insidious " action of the Pope. Agreeing with the prelate's sentiments, the Prime Minister went on to say: " There is an assumption of power in all the documents which have come from Rome—a pretension to supremacy over the realm of England, and a claim to sole and undivided sway, which is inconsistent with the Queen's supremacy, with the rights of our bishops and clergy, and with the spiritual independence of the nation. . . . I confess, however, that my alarm is not equal to my indignation . . . we are strong enough to repel any outward attacks. . . . No foreign prince or potentate will be permitted to fasten his fetters upon a nation which has so long and so nobly indicated its right to freedom of opinion, civil, political and religious. . . . The present state of the law shall be carefully examined and the propriety of adopting any proceedings . . . deliberately considered."

The Prime Minister followed up this letter with a speech of the same tenour at the Guildhall, as did the Lord Chancellor at the Mansion House dinner on November 9th. Thus encouraged, the bishops of the Establishment (it is surely best to omit their names), day after day that same month, emitted phrases that rang as if resurrected from the sixteenth century or the lips of Bilious Bale. " Rome clings to her abominations . . . the slough of Romanism, the sorcerer's cup . . . crafts of Satan . . . subtle and unclean. . . . Her claims are profane, blasphemous and anti-christian. . . . England is defiled by her pollutions."

The Catholic priesthood was described as " subtle, skilful and insinuating . . . emissaries of darkness." The Pope was " a foreign prince insolent in his degradation." His action in establishing a Hierarchy, though it had passed unnoticed in the Colonies, now seemed to Protestant prelates " a revolting and frightful assumption . . . an unparalleled aggression . . . a subtle aggression . . . an indecent aggression . . . an audacious aggression." They then joined in an Address to the Queen on this " unwarrantable insult . . . this attempt to subject our people to a spiritual tyranny from which they were freed at the Reformation."

The Prime Minister's Durham Letter had appeared on November 4th—an opportune incitement to celebrate Guy Fawkes Day with special ingenuity and fervour. At Salisbury, amid a dense crowd, a torchlight procession of several hundreds, complete with brass band and carrying effigies of the Pope, Cardinal Wiseman and other bishops, marched to the Cathedral Close, where the National Anthem was played amid deafening cheers. Then the effigies were burnt over a pile of faggots and a barrel of tar, to the accompaniment of volleys of fireworks hurled at them. There followed the Morning Hymn and again the National Anthem, in which thousands joined.

The people of Ware produced a donkey to represent the Cardinal Archbishop of Westminster and, for His Holiness the Pope, had an effigy dressed in full pontificals with a triple crown, plus a large pair of ram's horns. This was first hanged from a gallows before being burned to roars of execration from the crowd.

There was a further variant at Peckham, where a van drawn by four horses stopped outside a house from which emerged a dozen men armed with various weapons, each leading a man attired in a surplice. Two others, dressed as a Cardinal and his chaplain, were led out. All were tumbled into the van. Ahead of it strode a giant of a man carrying a figure of the Pope and a document representing the Brief of the Hierarchy. The procession of at least 10,000 people marched to Peckham, where the Pope's effigy was burnt amid shouts of " No Popery! Hurrah for the Queen! No foreign priesthood!"

Unhappily such uncontrolled outbursts of bigotry were not confined to inanimate figures. At this time, the hooting and pelting of Catholic priests was not uncommon; and there were demonstrations outside Catholic churches and the smashing of their windows. Many Catholics, recalling the horrors of the Gordon Riots seventy years before, feared worse to come. Newman advised that no public action be taken till Wiseman's arrival, though a group of the Cardinal's friends were for preventing his coming at all, but Wiseman, forewarned at Bruges of what might befall him, insisted on crossing to London on November 11th, staying first at Fitzroy Square and then at St. George's, Southwark.

It was a decision of a man of great courage and simplicity. His one thought was that an enormous misunderstanding had taken place in the minds of the public, which could be put right by a frank explanation. He at once sent

Sir George Bowyer to offer this to the Government through Lord Lansdowne, Lord President of the Council, who wholly agreed and deplored the Prime Minister's Durham Letter. The Cardinal himself was the cynosure of all eyes wherever he went; at times the crowds were merely curious, but often he was hooted and his carriage stoned.

Meanwhile he, himself, pressed on with his famous *Appeal to the English People,* a pamphlet of thirty-one pages, which he wrote with great rapidity, despite the many interruptions occasioned by people coming constantly for advice as to how to cope with their particular local manifestation of anti-Catholic hostility.

The Cardinal began writing the day he arrived in London, a Monday. On the following Thursday or Friday, Dr. Whitty took the completed manuscript to the printers and, as he glanced through it in his cab, he was amazed to find not a single erasure or correction of any kind.

The *Appeal* was prefaced with a brief explanation of the true scope of the Pope's action in restoring the Hierarchy. Then came a vivid description of the agitation it had caused, particularly in the newspapers which, with a few honourable exceptions, had vied with one another in the acrimony, virulence and persistence of their attacks, refusing no anecdote however personal or distorted from the truth. Sarcasm, ridicule, satire of the broadest character—nothing had come amiss.

The Cardinal then pointed to the Prime Minister's part in sponsoring an agitation which a word from him might have allayed, as Sir Robert Peel had done some years before with the outburst over the Maynooth College grant.

In the present crisis Catholics asked no favour of the Government, but they had the right of every citizen to impartiality, so with rulers turned agitators and the Press lashing the people to further frenzy, the one hope left was to appeal to the justice and generosity of the people themselves against the misrepresentations of those in power. " To this open-fronted and warm-hearted tribunal I make my appeal and claim, on behalf of myself and my fellow-Catholics, a fair, free and impartial hearing. Fellow-subjects, Englishmen,

be you at least just and equitable. You have been deceived—
you have been misled, both as to facts and intentions."

Did the establishment of the Hierarchy deny the Royal
Supremacy? Of course it did—in things purely spiritual—as
Catholics had always done in common with the Scotch Kirk,
Baptists, Methodists, Quakers and other Dissenters. But to
identify this denial with disloyalty was to destroy all religious
liberty.

Wiseman then argued that toleration of the Catholic
religion, which was essentially episcopal, must logically include permission to establish a Catholic Hierarchy. The fallacy
that held the people in so strong a thrall was that somehow
the new bishops were claiming a new tangible possession of
the Country, something territorial, yet Wiseman showed he
had as much or as little " possession " of Westminster as he
had previously had of the London District.

As for the outcry against the Letters Apostolic, both
Prime Minister and Lord Chancellor Lyndhurst were quoted
as showing these to be inevitable to the proper appointment
of bishops and pastors for the Catholics. Hitherto such documents had been treated as non-existent in the eyes of the law.
To take cognisance of them now placed the Prime Minister
in a hopelessly illogical position.

Wiseman then quoted not only precedents for the
Colonies but the case of Anglicans doing in Jerusalem and
Malta precisely what the Pope had done in England, *viz.*,
establishing bishoprics outside the Queen's temporal domain.
How, then, was Lord John Russell justified in indicting as
" insolent and insidious " the same thing that had been
initiated and accepted by the Queen's Government?

Wiseman addressed his powerful Appeal to popular
sympathy rather than to the educated few who had deliberately
misled the people over a measure that concerned the spiritual
care of a handful of Catholics, whose main strength was the
Irish poor. Yet it had been misrepresented as an attempt to
grasp at the power and position belonging by law to the Established Church.

The circulation of the pamphlet was enormous. It
appeared in full in five London dailies on November 20th and
occupied six-and-a-half columns of small close type in *The*

Times, whose circulation was then 50,000. Yet by 4 p.m., not a copy of any of the papers printing it could be procured. In addition, 30,000 copies of the pamphlet were sold in three days.

Its effect was tremendous, commanding the silence of attention on the violent agitation that had gone on for the past few weeks. " It is so temperate and logical," wrote the *London News* of November 23rd, " as to increase public regret that it did not appear a month ago before the mischief was done, and before this angry flood of theological bitterness was let loose over the land." Other papers were equally high in its praise. " The Cardinal has astonished the natives. . . . The most astute and the most polite reasoner of his time. . . . We have seldom read an abler specimen of controversial writing."

The Times, that had led the journalistic assault, climbed down in terms that at the same time showed the limits of the general change of opinion. " If we have pronounced an opinion against the Pope and the Cardinal unheard, it has not been from any wish to deny them fair play, but because they did not condescend to give us any more tangible explanation of their acts than was to be gathered from empty gasconades and pompous manifestos . . . We congratulate Dr. Wiseman on his recovery of the use of the English language. England is suffered to remain where she is, and is no longer forced . . . to revolve round the Eternal City. . . . But let her speak what language she will, the spirit of that Church is unchanged . . . within her pale is salvation, without is heathen darkness . . . whatever is not her own she absolutely ignores . . . the existence of the Crown, of the prelates, of the mighty people of England. . . . All he (the Pope) sees is the land, a few Roman Catholics scattered up and down it, and those bishops among whom he divides it; the rest to him is nothing."

There were two other factors that aided the Cardinal's *Appeal* to soften the bitter hostility throughout the country. One was that the second half of the Prime Minister's Durham Letter was aimed at the Puseyites who found their champion in so powerful an influence as Mr. Gladstone. The other was the realization, pointed out by the well-known Catholic, Henry

Howard of Corby Castle, that Lord Russell's attack on " the mummeries of superstition " was " a deliberate insult to the faith and religious practice of at least one-third of the loyal subjects of the British realm." He meant, of course, the Catholics in Ireland and the Colonies. This gave the political opponents of the Premier, Benjamin Disraeli, and the Liberal, Mr. Roebuck, their chance to make capital of his violation of the principles of religious toleration.

As the controversy developed into a battle between High Churchmen and Liberals allied to the Catholics against ultra-Protestants and die-hards, Wiseman was anxious for Newman's influence to make itself felt and eventually prevailed upon him to deliver in the Corn Exchange at Birmingham his famous lectures on the *Present Position of Catholics*.

All along, the Cardinal had been confident that persistent presentation of the true facts of the Catholic case would prevail with popular opinion, so he himself began on December 8th, in St. George's Cathedral, Southwark, a series of lectures that were crowded to capacity by people of all shades of religious opinion. A favourite point of his was that history shows the English as capable of working themselves into a frenzy over a mere delusion. He instanced the Titus Oates Plot, the Gordon Riots, the South Sea Bubble—and now this so-called Papal Aggression. On December 22nd, in the last of his three lectures, Wiseman claimed the present persecution as fulfilling the prophecy of Christ that the world would always attack His followers.

This note was taken up by Gladstone in the House of Commons, but influential as his voice was, it could not prevent the Prime Minister, already deeply committed in this sorry affair, from introducing the Ecclesiastical Titles Bill to Parliament. This was on February 7th, 1851, and Cardinal Wiseman was present to witness a majority of 332 vote through the first reading. The second reading was passed by 433 votes against 95. The Bill received the Royal Assent on August 1st.

The Bill inflicted a penalty of £100 on persons assuming titles to pretended sees in the United Kingdom, declared all deeds and legal documents executed by such persons to be void, and all endowments of the pretended sees to be forfeit to the Crown.

Logically it applied to bishops of the Episcopal Church of Scotland, but a special clause exempted them. This was quickly pounced on by Mr. Gladstone. " If the appointment of bishops is a spiritual act," he said, " why interfere with it? If temporal, why exempt the Scottish Bishops?"

He and others maintained what most Englishmen were to admit later on, namely that the real ground of offence was the use by the Pope and Cardinal Wiseman of language that seemed boastful and so hurt the pride of the English, as the exclusive claims of Rome still do.

The Bill, therefore, meant little more than a protest placed on official record. The fine of £100 was never inflicted. The clauses invalidating deeds executed by Catholic bishops were dropped. Twenty years later, in 1871, Mr. Gladstone quietly repealed before a wholly apathetic House of Commons a Bill that had been a dead letter from the day it was passed. So poetic justice was done: an imaginary aggression had been met by an unenforced penalty in what had been from first to last almost entirely a battle of words.

The campaign was followed week by week by *Punch* in a series of cartoons with a running commentary, in both of which a deal of wit was seasoned with more than a dash of scurrility. The caricatures of *Mr. Wiseboy* and *Mr. Newboy* are excellent. When they visit Mr. Punch's office, Toby growls at Mr. Newboy who pats him, saying soothingly, " What, Toby! Don't you remember *me*, Toby?" Then when Toby makes a set at Mr. Wiseboy, Mr. Punch calls him off and lectures him: " I'll have no persecution, Toby. I say, keep your teeth out of the Cardinal's legs. . . . He has as good a right to his crimson as a Quaker has to drab and must have free leave to set up his pulpit."

When the Ecclesiastical Titles Bill is introduced, Giant Wiseman is seen being attacked by Lord Jack the Giant Killer —but his weapon is a feather. Then as the Bill runs into difficulties and Lord John prepares to modify it, *Punch* portrays him as a naughty boy who chalks up " No Popery " on Wiseman's front door and runs away.

The wishful thinking of *Punch* is expressed in a clever cartoon of a tearful Wiseman divested of mitre and crozier which are sold to a Jew. The captions " Alarming failure "

and " Must be cleared off in a few days " are placarded on
his house, while a notice informs the Puseyites (who, incidentally, are lampooned more than the Papists by *Punch*)
that " a number of Roman collars and clerical waistcoats will
be almost given away."

The best of the commentaries is *Punch's* " Decline and
Fall of the British Empire," told by an Australian historian
for the benefit of Macaulay's New Zealanders. It narrates the
persecution of St. Nicholas (Wiseman) by the tyrant Punch,
ending with the Saint's complete triumph. " St. Nicholas and
his clergy were suffered to live unmolested and continued in and
about London, making many converts. . . . " The words, in
the event, were more prophetic than their writer knew.

APPENDIX

ENGLISH TRANSLATION OF THE POPE'S LETTERS
APOSTOLIC RESTORING THE ENGLISH HIERARCHY.

THE power of governing the universal Church, confided
by our Lord Jesus Christ to the Roman Pontiff in the person
of St. Peter, Prince of the Apostles, has preserved in the
Apostolic See, during the whole course of centuries, that
admirable solicitude with which she watches over the good of
the Catholic religion in all the earth, and zealously provides
for its advancing progress. Thus is fulfilled the design of her
Divine Founder, who in establishing a Head, assured, in His
profound wisdom, the safety of the Church even to the con-
summation of the world. The effect of this Pontifical solicitude
was felt by the noble realm of England as well as by other
nations. History attests that from the first ages of the Church,
the Christian religion was introduced into Great Britain, where
it flourished until the middle of the fifth century, when not only
public affairs, but religion also, fell into the most deplorable
condition after the invasion of the Angli and the Saxons. But
our most holy predecessor, Gregory the Great, quickly sent
to that island the monk Augustine and his companions, and
after raising him and many others to the episcopal dignity, and
adding a considerable number of monks who were priests, he
converted the Anglo-Saxons to the Christian religion, and

succeeded, by their means, in re-establishing and extending the Catholic Faith in Britain, which then began to be called England. To come, however, to things more recent, nothing more evident can be found in the history of the Anglican schism, which was consummated in the sixteenth century, than the action and ever constant solicitude of the Roman Pontiffs, Our predecessors, in succouring and sustaining, by every possible means, the Catholic religion, exposed in that kingdom to the greatest perils and reduced to extremities.

It was for this purpose, not to mention other matters, that the Supreme Pontiffs, and those acting by their orders and with their approbation, exerted themselves that England should never want men dedicated to the support of Catholicism, and that Catholic youths of good dispositions should be sent to the continent, there to be carefully educated, and instructed above all in ecclesiastical sciences, in order that when they had received holy orders, they should return to their country, to sustain their compatriots with the ministry of the word and sacraments, and to defend and propagate the true faith.

But the zeal of Our predecessors will be seen more clearly in their exertions to provide the English Catholics with pastors clothed with episcopal character, after that a furious and implacable tempest had deprived them of the presence and pastoral zeal of bishops. First of all, the Letters Apostolic of Gregory XV, commencing with the words *Ecclesia Romana,* and dated March 23, 1623, prove that the Supreme Pontiff, as soon as ever it was possible, deputed to the government of English and Scotch Catholics, William Bishop, consecrated bishop of Chalcedon, with ample faculties and with the proper powers of Ordinaries. After the death of Bishop Urban VIII renewed this mission, by his Letters Apostolic of February 4th, 1625, directed to Richard Smith, on whom he conferred the bishopric of Chalcedon, and all the power accorded to Bishop. More favourable days seemed dawning for the Catholic religion at the commencement of the reign of James II. Innocent XI was quick to use the opportunity, and, in 1685, deputed John Leyburne, bishop of Adrumetum, as Vicar Apostolic over all the Kingdom of England. Afterwards, by Letters Apostolic of January 30, 1688, commencing *Super Cathedram,* he added to him three other

Vicars Apostolic, bishops *in partibus,* so that all England, by the care of the Apostolic Nuncio there resident, namely Ferdinand, archbishop of Amasia, was divided by this Pope into four districts, the London, the Western, the Central and the Northern, which then began to be governed by Vicars Apostolic, fortified with the necessary faculties and with the proper power of Ordinaries. To aid them in fulfilling the duties of so grave a charge, the Vicars received rules which were either derived from the decisions of Benedict XIV in his Constitution of May 30th, 1750, commencing with the words *Apostolicum ministerium,* or from the decisions of other Pontiffs, our Predecessors, or from those of Our Congregation for the Propagation of the Faith. This partition of all England into four Apostolic vicariates lasted until the time of Gregory XVI, who, considering the increase then obtained by the Catholic religion in that Kingdom, made a new ecclesiastical division of the country. And by his Letters Apostolic of July 3rd, 1840, commencing *Muneris Apostolici,* he doubled the number of the Vicars Apostolic, confiding the spiritual government of England to eight Vicars Apostolic of the London district, the Western and Eastern, the Central, and the districts of Wales, Lancashire, Yorkshire, and the North.

The little already said, many other matters being passed by in silence, proves clearly that Our predecessors exerted themselves strenuously to use every means which their authority offered them, to console and restore the Church in England after her immense misfortunes. Having therefore before our eyes this fair example of Our predecessors, and being desirous to imitate them and fulfil the duties of the Supreme Apostolate, and being moreover urged on by the affection of Our heart for that portion of the Lord's vineyard, We determined, from the very beginning of our Pontificate, to follow up a work so well commenced, and to apply Ourselves seriously to favour the daily development of the Church in that Kingdom. Wherefore, considering the whole actual condition of Catholicism in England, reflecting on the considerable number of the Catholics, a number every day augmenting, and remarking how from day to day the obstacles become removed which chiefly opposed the propagation of the Catholic religion, We perceived that the time had arrived for restoring in England the ordinary form of ecclesiastical government, as freely constituted in other nations, where no particular cause necessitates the ministry of Vicars Apostolic.

We thought that considering the progress of time and of events, it was no longer necessary that English Catholics should be governed by Vicars Apostolic, but that, on the contrary, the changes already produced, demanded the form of ordinary episcopal government. This opinion was strengthened by the desires which were expressed by common accord by the Vicars Apostolic of England, and by great numbers of clergy and laymen distinguished for their virtues and for their rank, as well as by an immense majority among English Catholics.

In maturing this Our design We have not omitted to implore the aid of God, who is supremely great and good, that in the deliberation of so important a matter, it might be vouchsafed to us to know and to do, that which would tend to the greater advantage of the Church. Moreover We implored the aid of the Mother of God, the most Holy Virgin Mary, and of the Saints who glorified England with their virtue, that they might obtain for Us, by intercession with God, a happy termination of this undertaking. We then confided the affair entirely to Our Venerable brothers the Cardinals of the Holy Roman Church who form our Congregation of the Propaganda. Their decision was wholly conformable to Our desire, and We resolved to approve it and put it into execution. Therefore having weighed with the most scrupulous attention everything regarding this matter, We, of our mere motion, of our certain knowledge and by the plenitude of our Apostolic authority, have decreed, and decree, the re-establishment within the kingdom of England, according to the common rules of the Church, of the Hierarchy of bishops ordinary, who shall take their names from the Sees which We by these present letters erect in the several districts of the Vicars Apostolic.

To commence with the London District, it shall form two sees, one, the see of Westminster, which We raise to the dignity of Metropolitan, or Archiepiscopal, the other, the see of Southwark, which, as also the other sees now created, We make suffragan to Westminster. The Diocese of Westminster shall comprehend that portion of the said district which extends to the banks of the Thames, and contains the counties of Middlesex, Essex and Hertford. The Diocese of Southwark will contain the portion lying to the South of the Thames, comprising the counties of Berks, Southampton, Surrey, Sussex and Kent, with the islands of Wight, Jersey, Guernsey and others adjacent. The Northern District shall be one Diocese only, taking its name from the city of Hexham, and the limits of the Diocese shall be the same as those of the District. The District of York, similarly shall form one Diocese, whose bishop shall have his see at Beverley. In the Lancashire District shall be two bishops, one of whom, the bishop of Liverpool, shall have for his Diocese, along with the Isle of Man, the hundreds of Lonsdale, Amounderness, and West Derby; and the other, who will reside at Salford, and whose see will take its name from that city, shall have for his Diocese the hundreds of Salford, Blackburn and Leyland. Cheshire, although part of Lancashire District, We adjoin to another Diocese. In the District of Wales there shall be two episcopal sees, namely Shrewsbury, and Menevia united with Newport. The Diocese of Shrewsbury will consist of the counties lying in the northern part of the Welsh District, the counties namely, of Anglesey, Caernarvon, Denbigh, Flint, Merioneth and Montgomery, to which we add Cheshire, taken from the Lancashire District, and Shropshire, taken from the Central District. To the bishop of Menevia and Newport we assign for Diocese the southern part of the District of Wales, namely Brecknockshire, Cardiganshire, Carmarthenshire, Glamorganshire, Pembrokeshire and Radnorshire, and also the English counties of Monmouth and Hereford.

In the Western District We constitute the two episcopal Sees of Clifton and Plymouth, assigning to the bishop of Clifton, for his Diocese, Gloucestershire, Somersetshire and Wiltshire. The Diocese of Plymouth shall comprise Devonshire, Dorsetshire and Cornwall. The Central District, from which We have already detached Shropshire, shall have two Episcopal sees, at Nottingham and Birmingham. To Nottingham We assign for its Diocese Nottinghamshire, Derbyshire and Leicestershire, besides the counties of Lincoln and Rutland, which we separate from the Eastern District. Birmingham Diocese shall have Staffordshire, Warwickshire, Worcestershire and Oxfordshire. In the Eastern District will be but one bishopric, taking its name from Northampton, and it will comprise for its Diocese the former Eastern District, excepting the counties of Rutland and Lincoln, which We have already assigned to Nottingham. Thus in the very flourishing kingdom of England there will be one single Ecclesiastical Province, consisting of one Archbishop or Metropolitan, with twelve suffragan Bishops, whose zeal and pastoral labours will, We hope, through the grace of God, ever produce fresh increase of Catholicism. And therefore We desire at present to reserve it to Us and Our successors to divide this province still further and to augment the number of Dioceses, as necessity may arise, and in general to establish freely new boundaries of the same, according as it may seem fitting in the Lord's sight.

We command, meanwhile, the aforesaid archbishop and bishops, to send, at the appointed times, to the Congregation of the Propaganda, reports of the state of their churches, and to be diligent in informing Propaganda of everything which they shall think profitable for the spiritual good of their flocks. We will continue, in effect, to use the ministry of this Congregation in everything which concerns the churches in England. But in the sacred government of clergy and people, and in all that regards the pastoral office, the English archbishop and bishops will from the present time enjoy the rights and faculties which are or can be used, according to the general dispositions of the sacred canons and apostolic constitutions, by the Catholic archbishops and bishops of other nations, and they will be equally bound by the obligations, by which other archbishops and bishops are bound according to the common discipline of the Church.

With regard to whatever now prevails or is in vigour, either in the ancient form of the English churches, or in the subsequent state of the missions, by virtue of special constitutions, privileges or peculiar customs, seeing that the circumstances are no longer the same, none of these things shall for the future import either right or obligation. And, that no doubt concerning this matter may remain, We, in the plenitude of Our Apostolic authority, suppress and entirely abrogate all the obligatory and juridical force of these peculiar constitutions, privileges and customs, whatever may be their antiquity. The archbishop and bishops of England shall accordingly possess the integral power of regulating all the things which pertain to the carrying out of the common law of the Church, or which are left to the authority of bishops by the general discipline of the Church. We, however, will certainly not omit to assist them with our Apostolic authority, and even with gladness will second their demands in everything which may seem to Us conducive to the greater glory of God and the salvation of souls. In decreeing, by these Our Letters, the restoration of the ordinary Hierarchy of Bishops and the resumption of the common law of the Church, We had it principally in view to provide for the prosperity and increase of the Catholic religion in the kingdom of England, but at the same time We desired to grant the prayers as well of our Venerable Brothers, who govern the church in that kingdom as Vicars Apostolic of the Holy See, as also of very many beloved children of the Catholic clergy and people, from whom We received most urgent solicitations in this behalf. Their forefathers made often times similar demands to Our predecessors, who began to send Vicars Apostolic to England, when no Catholic prelates governing their own church by ordinary jurisdiction were able to remain in that kingdom; and afterwards Our predecessors multiplied the number of Vicars and of Districts from time to time, not with the design of subjecting perpetually the Catholic Church in England to an extraordinary form of government, but rather with the intention that while they provided, according to circumstances, for its increase, they at the same time might prepare the way for the future restoration of the ordinary Hierarchy.

And therefore We, to whom the accomplishment of this great work has been vouchsafed by God's infinite goodness, do hereby expressly declare that it is far from Our mind and intention to cause the prelates of England, now invested with the name and rights of Bishops Ordinary, to be in any manner deprived of the advantages which they previously enjoyed under the title of Vicars Apostolic. For reason forbids that Our decrees, wherewith We grant the prayers of English

Catholics for the good of religion, should turn out to the detriment of the Vicars. Furthermore, We rely with firmest confidence upon the hope that Our beloved children in Christ, who during such a variety of times have never failed in sustaining by their alms and donations the Catholic church in England and the prelates who governed it as Vicars Apostolic, will display even greater liberality towards the bishops themselves, now bound by a more stable bond to the English churches, to the end that they may never want the temporal supplies needful for the adornment of churches, the splendour of Divine worship, the sustentation of the clergy, the relief of the poor, and other ecclesiastical purposes.

Finally, raising Our eyes to the hills from whence cometh Our help, We beseech God supremely good and great, with all prayer and supplication, with thanksgiving, that He, by the virtue of His Divine aid, may confirm the things by Us decreed for the welfare of the Church, and may grant the strength of His grace to those to whom appertains the execution of Our decree, to the end that they may feed the flock of God committed to their charge, and apply their zeal more and more to propagate the greater glory of His name. And, to obtain more abundant aids from heavenly grace, We lastly invoke, as intercessors with God, the most holy Mother of God, the holy apostles Peter and Paul, with the other celestial Patrons of England, and by name we invoke also Saint Gregory the Great, that, since to Us, notwithstanding the insufficiency of Our merits, was granted the renewal of episcopal Sees in England, as he in his day established them to the great advantage of the Church, so the restoration of episcopal Dioceses, effected by Us in that kingdom, may prove for the benefit of the Catholic religion.

We decree that these Our Apostolic Letters can never at any time be charged with the fault of omission or addition, or with defect of Our intention, or with any other defect, and that they can never be impugned in any way, but shall always be held valid and firm, and shall obtain effect in all things, and ought to be inviolably observed, notwithstanding general Apostolic edicts, and special sanctions of Synodal, Provincial and Universal Councils, and notwithstanding the rights and privileges of the ancient English Sees, and missions, and Apos-

tolic vicariates subsequently constituted, and of the rights of
any churches or pious institutes whatsoever, even although
ratified by oath, or by Apostolic, or any other confirmation,
and notwithstanding anything whatever to the contrary. For
We expressly abrogate all such things, as far as they contradict
this Our decree, even although special mention ought to be
made, or although some other particular formality ought to be
observed in their abrogation. We decree moreover that whatever may be done to the contrary, knowingly or ignorantly,
by any person, in the name of any authority whatsoever, shall
be null and void. We decree also that copies, even printed,
of these Our Letters, when subscribed by a Public Notary and
confirmed by the seal of an Ecclesiastical Dignitary, shall
have the same authenticity and credit, as would be given to
the expression of Our will by the exhibition of the original
Diploma itself.

Given at Rome, at St. Peter's, under the Fisherman's
ring, the 29th day of September, 1850, in the 5th year of Our
Pontificate.

(Signed) A. CARD. LAMBRUSCHINI.

IV

DIOCESAN ORGANISATION
AND ADMINISTRATION

By Morgan V. Sweeney

THE twenty-ninth of September, 1850, was a red-letter day. The reaction to it among non-Catholics, and particularly to Cardinal Wiseman's letter, with the hub-hub in Parliament, "No Popery" in the streets of London, and riots here and there in the country magnified its real effect. To Catholics who had been petitioning Rome since the end of the sixteenth century for bishops (and they meant "diocesan bishops") it seemed to be the achievement of the desired end; to the romantic-minded the link with old Catholic England was restored; to the practical-minded the anomalies of living under Vicars Apostolic were gone, and now England was under the common law of the Church[1]. None of these feelings was entirely correct. It is at least arguable, and seems to be correct, that the English hierarchy was not restored at all, but at the most refounded. The "restoration" was a polite fiction. The old hierarchy had disappeared, the outward shell with its administrative and constitutional scaffolding being taken over by the Church of England. The outlook, the customs, even the spirituality of that England had gone for ever. England had become a missionary country, and the evolution of its hierarchy had followed the usual, and to us familiar lines. In order to "hold on to the few Catholics who were left" (the words are those of Benedict XIV[2]), a Prefect of the Mission, Cardinal

[1] For many reasons much of the evidence, especially documentary evidence, on which this survey is based has come from the archives of the Diocese of Leeds. I believe, however, that the conclusions based on this have a very wide application, and that the examples of administration given can be found throughout England and Wales.

[2] *De Synodo*, lib. 9, c. 16, VIII.

Allen, had been appointed. On his death Archpriests, who were in reality Prefects Apostolic, had been in charge of the English Mission. Then came Bishops, Vicars Apostolic, and now a hierarchy was formed.

Yet the Holy See was too cautious to place England immediately under the general law of the Church. Territorial bishops were appointed, but parish priests were not; in fact parishes were only to come into being with the Code in 1918. Canons were appointed, but in a curious form, since they did not live in community nor, except on the days of Chapter meetings, recite the office in common. They were Diocesan Consultors in ermine-edged capes dignified by the title of Canon, appointed for historical and not canonical reasons. The country continued to operate under Propaganda, securing its release by " Sapienti Consilio " of Pius X in 1908. Only the progress of the Church in England, the Holy See judged, could justify the breaking of this last link with its missionary status.

With these exceptions it would be true to say that England was brought under the common law of the Church. The changeover was of some constitutional importance, though administratively is was probably unnoticed. Previously the faculties of the bishops had corresponded with those of diocesan ordinaries[3]. They appointed Grand-Vicars, though these were not strictly Vicars-General, but all their powers were delegated to them by the Bishop. Each bishop was immediately subject to the Holy See as a vicar of the Pope. It is true that the Vicars Apostolic met and consulted together, generally in London, but their common action was just that and nothing more. Each was supreme in his own sphere. This was to have effect later. The arrangements were admirable for a missionary country. The boundaries of districts and missions could be changed easily; and there was a considerable amount of freedom from established rights and vested interests that can hamper a rapidly expanding Church. The government of common law tended to be more static than the emergency government of a missionary country.

The old Vicariates were now in part broken up, but in

[3] Those of Bishop Briggs, continually renewed apparently up to his death, were in 1836 of the " second formula." Leeds Archives: Roman Documents (1819-58), no. 2.

general dioceses were not an entirely new grouping. The old London District was divided into two, Westminster taking the area north of the Thames, Southwark that south of the Thames stretching west as far as the Channel Isles. The old Northern District became the Diocese of Hexham, and the Yorkshire District that of Beverley. The Lancashire District lost Cheshire to the new diocese of Shrewsbury which took Shropshire from the Central District and North Wales from the Welsh District. What remained of the Lancashire District was divided into the dioceses of Liverpool and Salford. With the exception of Shropshire mentioned above, the old Central District was divided into the dioceses of Birmingham and Nottingham, and from the Eastern District Nottingham took Lincoln and Rutland, the remainder being erected into the diocese of Northampton. The Western District was divided between Plymouth and Clifton, and Newport took that part of Wales outside the diocese of Shrewsbury together with Hereford.

There were startling differences in the new dioceses. Outside the expanding manufacturing towns of the north, Birmingham and London, there were very few Catholics. Most of the dioceses in the south were virtually undeveloped tracts as far as the Church was concerned. The total population of the diocese of Birmingham was 1,307,198, and it was supplied by 124 priests and 86 churches and chapels, whilst Northampton with a slightly higher population had but 27 priests and 26 churches and chapels. The statistics for Plymouth are similar to those of Northampton, Shrewsbury is slightly better, and Clifton similar to Shrewsbury. Hexham had 70 priests and 51 chapels, Beverley 69 and 61 respectively, Liverpool 113 and 79, and Salford 61 and 35. Newport and Menevia had only 18 chapels with 22 priests[4]. Despairingly the *Directory* catalogues " Cardiganshire: Population 68,766. Radnorshire: Population 25,356. No Chapel! No Mission-house! No Schoolhouse! No Mission-fund! No Missioner "[5]. The new bishops appointed to the sees were faced with a truly formidable task. The population of England was beginning to increase rapidly, for the Industrial Revolution was now in its stride. With Irish immigrants to provide for, missions to found, churches to

4 For these statistics cf. *Catholic Directory* for 1851.
5 *Ibid.*, p. 66.

build, priests had to be found, and schools built and supported. It could reasonably be asked how some of the dioceses, poor in everything, could hope to survive, and from the standpoint of human prudence their foundation could be questioned. On the other hand it could well be argued that the Vicariates were too large for efficient government. Railways had not yet covered England with the network so familiar to us, and accessibility must be an important point in judging what is an efficient unit of ecclesiastical government. There was much to be said for reducing the size of units of government to make them more manageable, and the multiplication of such units by making new dioceses was obviously a step in the right direction.

So the dioceses were erected, the remaining Vicars translated to their new dioceses and left as administrators of the others until Rome could make the necessary appointments. Chapters were appointed, and it is interesting to see the Holy See suggesting that the full numbers for Plymouth should only be appointed when the diocese had enough priests[6]. Rome was prepared to wait for a while until the bishops had decided what faculties would be required[7]. It is a fitting moment to survey this new organisation.

The new territorial arrangement of dioceses has been outlined above, as has also episcopal power. The clergy had expected that the division of the dioceses into properly constituted parishes would follow as a matter of course. Before the restoration there had been inductions into missions in due canonical form[8] and the clergy might reasonably have supposed that real parishes were to be founded. The argument of the bishops was that the country was not ready for such. There were bound to be changes, the Church was bound to expand. Parishes as the clergy envisaged them were units too stable for the country in its present state. The vested rights and interests of parishes would be a bar to rapid expansion. They could well have added that it was highly doubtful whether the necessary financial stability would be forthcoming. There

---

[6] Decree of Propaganda, 21st April, 1852.
[7] Leeds Archives: Roman Documents: Rev. Thos. Grant to Bp. Briggs.
[8] Yorkshire Brethren MSS.: Hogarth, *An Account* . . . p. 411.

were endowments in some places[9], but as time went on such were to be exceptions. Bishops had tried to endow stable missions (that of Selby and Holm Beacon in Yorkshire had been so endowed at the end of the seventeenth century[10]), but the old form of endowment was not to persist. Collections, the whist drives, bazaars, dances and raffles were to be the *dos beneficii* of the future!

There seems, too, to have been behind all this a misconception about ecclesiastical government which seems to have persisted. The majority of the clergy probably held and hold to-day at least in practice that the unit of ecclesiastical government is the parish. Nothing could be further from the truth. The unit of government is the diocese. Moral theologians and canon lawyers have searched diligently for some time now to find evidence for the jurisdiction of parish priests. Their quest has rivalled the mountains in labour, and succeeded only in producing evidence of organisational rights and duties, leaving it perfectly clear that the parish priest is a coadjutor of the bishop in the government of the diocese and his real constitutional power is only delegated. The stable nature of the parish is partly due to the historical forces of feudalism and the natural anxiety of the Church that provision should be made for a secure livelihood for her priests.

The arrangements for missions under the restored hierarchy were to some extent a compromise. In order to meet the objections of the clergy certain missions in each diocese were to be given a certain stability. Their pastors were to be Missionary Rectors and could only be moved after reference to a special committee of investigation[11]. In other words certain rectors in the diocese were guaranteed a stability denied to others, a stability closely approximating to that of parish priests. In reality it was simply a form of administrative removal of parish priests. It was merely negative, and as far as the law was concerned the rector's faculties were delegated. The problem of parishes remained to be solved. In fact it was

---

[9] Cf. Y.B. MSS.: *An Account* . . . passim.

[10] *Ibid.*: Mission of Selby and Holm Beacon.

[11] *Decreta Conc. Prov. West.*, p. 61: Decree of Propaganda, Aug. 4th, 1853. The distinction is reflected in that between *amovibilis* and *inamovibilis* in the code.

not solved until the Code silently swept away this part of the legislation of the synods.

Yet the hierarchy could congratulate itself that some of its worst problems had been solved before 1850. The Old Chapter was declared to have been illegal from the beginning[12]. This is not the place to discuss its history, but its influence had gradually waned. Set up by Bishop Smith it had perpetuated itself, again quite illegally, and had a certain power of the purse. It was and it remains to this day custodian and trustee of certain funds for the Church in England. In the seventeenth century it was considered as the bulwark against the regulars, and its influence had spread throughout the country. It was a test of loyalty among the Yorkshire Brethren that its members supported the Chapter[13]. The Yorkshire Brethren Association and kindred associations had likewise privileged positions. As custodians of even episcopal funds the Yorkshire Brethren were likely to become an extra-constitutional body wielding enormous power. Archdeacon Franks in the seventeenth century frowned on their activities and ruled them with a rod of iron[14] and at the very end of the eighteenth century Bishop Gibson broke their power entirely, despite protests, by bringing their funds as far as possible under his own control[15]. His action strengthened episcopal hands but hardly improved his reputation among the clergy.

In general, too, the question of appointments to missions had been solved. As far as can be discovered there was no question of lay patronage. It is true that some lay patrons had in the course of time come to prefer regulars to seculars or vice-versa, and certain missions had come to be recognised as belonging to certain religious orders. There is a record of a personal dislike for Jesuits on the part of the Duke of Norfolk causing a change in Sheffield[16], and personal incompatibility causing one at Lulworth[17]. On the whole those lay people who supported priests were willing to accept whomsoever the Bishop sent, although there was probably some con-

[12] Ullathorne, *Autobiography*, p. 298.
[13] Y.B. MSS.: *Minute Book*, p. 107.
[14] Y.B. MSS.: *Minute Book*, p. 132.
[15] Y.B. MSS.: *Extracts* . . ., p. 74.
[16] Eyre MSS.
[17] Catholic Record Society, vol. 6, p. 366.

sultation at times between both parties. It is possible that had there been no great changes in the location of Catholics some legislation would have been required. New Missions, however, were being founded in the towns, often from the old endowed missions, and as time went on the new missions became much more important than the small country chaplaincies. The new hierarchy began free of any sort of lay presentation, and that problem was not to trouble it. The remaining difficulties were rather in the relationship between the different parties in missions supported by patrons. The Beverley Chapter noted the following in 1863: " Canon Chadwick requested Chapter to solicit the Bishop to take steps to obtain from the next Provincial Synod a definition of the duties and relations of Patrons and Chaplains, and in those Chaplaincies to which Congregations are attached, of the duties and relations of Patrons, Chaplains and Congregations. The suggestion was unanimously adopted "[18]. This request did not result in legislation. There were still, of course, houses where the chaplain was apt to be treated badly, but episcopal warnings generally wrought an improvement. On the other hand patrons were equally long-suffering, and the replacement of the chaplain has sometimes been the only solution. In short, the problems were settled by time and episcopal administrative action.

Canonically the bishops as Vicars Apostolic were independent of each other, and the problem of integrating their action would have been very difficult had not historical circumstances shown the way. Catholic Emancipation had made meetings of bishops to determine policy a practical necessity, and indeed such meetings seem to have taken place occasionally in the eighteenth century. Their yearly meetings in Golden Square were continued, generally in Low Week. Although such meetings were familiar, and although common action was the result, they did not solve the question entirely. In Canon Law eight independent bishops had met to decide common action. The personnel was almost the same, but the circumstances were different. The circumstances were to cause trouble in the future.

In their own dioceses the bishops had to solve the problem of internal organisation. Here again they had moved

[18] Leeds Archives : Canon Browne to Bp. Cornthwaite, Aug. 31st, 1863.

some distance towards a solution before the restoration. It was not a big transition from Grand Vicars to Vicars General; the institution had proved its value in the large districts, and both clergy and bishops had come to rely on them. Rural deans had been appointed. Bishop Baggs had " partitioned the Western Vicariate into four deaneries, with a view to facilitate the assembling of the clergy for the purposes of theological discussion "[19]. Bishop Briggs had a much more ambitious project, for his rural deans were armed with a formidable list of faculties including that of visitation. They were almost lesser editions of the Grand Vicars[20]. This work, even if we add to it the creation of chapters, was not enough to guarantee the easy administration of the diocese. Episcopal curias had not even begun to exist.

The other problem for solution was that of the religious orders. Their participation in missionary work in England was an historical accident. They were needed in order to guarantee an adequate number of priests in the country, and once in the country, the question of exemption was bound to arise. Benedict XIV had discussed the matter under the question as to whether regulars could hear the confession of lay persons without approbation from the Vicars Apostolic[21]. He pointed out that the matter had been raised more than once in Rome, and then noted that the answer was "no." But he did not mention the heat, the jealousy, mistrust and suspicion that had been aroused. Nor did he foresee that vested interests and established rights together with a delightful vagueness about the powers of the regulars was going to complicate the issue. The eighteenth-century peace had taken away much of the bitterness, but all the rest of the complicated issues were still there, so much gunpowder that was going to explode before the hierarchy had been restored a generation.

It was indeed in the next thirty years or so that not only the foundations, for to some extent these were laid already, but the general lines of English ecclesiastical administration were laid. It cannot be claimed that all the problems outlined above

Catholic Directory, 1851: Memoir of Bishop Baggs, p. 154.
Y.B. MSS. An Account . . . Bp. Briggs to Rev. Robert Hogarth (his Grand Vicar).
De Synodo, lib. 9, cap. 16, VIII.

were solved completely, but if they were not solved, a *modus vivendi* was established that has stood the test of time. In some ways the English hierarchy was fortunate, for the period to 1918 was one of consolidation in ecclesiastical law. The great canon lawyers had written their volumes, the problems facing the Church were more clearly understood and appreciated, especially the difficulties of dealing with a mass of law scattered in hundreds of papal and congregational decrees. Attempts were made increasingly to rationalise law and procedure, a task that had its logical termination in the codification of Canon Law, and the publication of the Code—the *Codex Juris Canonici*—in 1918[22].

The first of the problems that had to be solved satisfactorily was the relationship of the bishops among themselves. It has already been indicated that it would be strange if difficulties did not arise. The majority of the hierarchy had previously acted as independent entities, each responsible to Rome. Into this scene had been inserted a metropolitan, and the rest were suffragans under him. Now strictly this meant very little. Under the legislation in force before the Code of Canon Law the metropolitan convoked and presided at provincial councils, had to be specially vigilant on the question of the residence of his suffragans, and was a judge in appeal. These together with rights of precedence and certain other small rights were all that were left of the great powers the archbishops had claimed in the ninth century. It is true that there was the right of visitation of their suffragans, but this was so hedged round with regulations that it was virtually useless[23]. Thomassinus had shaken his head sadly over this " truly great fall in the authority of metropolitans," and found its causes obscure[24]. Phillips was similarly puzzled[25] and seems to regard metropolitans in much the same light as children look at Humpty Dumpty.

It is difficult to say whether Wiseman and Manning were ignorant of these historical facts. Sir Shane Leslie claims that Manning's championship of the metropolitan see left his

[22] It would take too long even to outline the process here. It can be studied in Van Hove: *Prolegomena* (2nd ed.), pp. 614ff.

[23] Usefully summarised in *Catholic Encyclopedia*, vol. 10, p. 244.

[24] *Vetus et Nova Ecclesiae Disciplina*, pars. i, lib. i, CXLVIII.

[25] Phillips, *Du Droit Ecclesiastique* (trans. of *Kirchenrecht*), II, p. 69

successors " so distinct a primacy to inherit "[26]. It is not surprising that he has been chided by Dom Cuthbert Butler[27]. Manning and his successors inherited no more of a primacy than Canon Law allowed, and that as has been clear was not very great. Their leadership, which is by no means the same thing, was due to their own personalities and to their position as representatives of the hierarchy and the Catholics of England in the eyes of the government. Yet neither the bishops nor the government recognised Wiseman as representative of the Church in England, but preferred to deal with Grant of Southwark[28]. The personalities of both Wiseman and Manning undoubtedly influenced the disputes, and when the accounts of these are read, one cannot but conclude that a certain ignorance of the constitutional law of the Church was present as well. It was futile to claim the mediaeval rights of Canterbury over the Church in England. It was not the first time that a romantic reading of England's Catholic past into the present had deceived English Catholics.

The cases in dispute, admirably summarised by Dom Cuthbert Butler[29], were chiefly the following: the succession of Archbishop Errington, the government of the seminaries, episcopal meetings, funds and trusts, and a dispute between the Westminster Chapter and the Archbishop. The dispute over the Westminster succession was largely a matter of personalities, and the only point that need concern us here is Rome's readiness to remove a coadjutor if his actions make the government of the diocese impossible. The dispute of the control of the seminaries was a fight by the Archbishop of Westminster for the control of Old Hall, and the Bishop of Hexham for the control of Ushaw. As far as the Bishop of Hexham was concerned, he was merely perpetuating the stand taken by Bishop Gibson, who made sure that he should control the northern half of Douay transplanted, whatever the English clergy might think about it[30]. His successor, however, had to contend with fellow bishops, not the clergy. Rome reasonably solved the question by dividing control. The same solution

---

[26] Leslie, *Henry Edward Manning*, p. 492.
[27] Butler, *Life and Times of Bishop Ullathorne*, I, p. 256.
[28] Purcell, *Life of Cardinal Manning*, II, p. 150, n. 1.
[29] *Op. cit.*, I, pp. 253 ff.
[30] Ushaw Archives: *Ushaw College History*, 6, 9, 11, 12 and 14.

was come to on the question at issue between Wiseman and
Grant about the division of the old London District funds.
One cannot help feeling sometimes that Wiseman was being
perverse, since there had been a precedent for dividing funds.
" When the Vicars Apostolic met at St. Cuthbert's College
[Ushaw], after the division of the old Northern Vicariate, it
was agreed that, in apportioning the Funds for ecclesiastical
education, the Burses should be distributed according to the
domicilium of their respective founders "[31]. It is true that
some of these were taken up as cases to Rome, but it is interesting to note that Bishop Goss of Liverpool complained that
this had been done unnecessarily[32]. Rome decided along similar
lines to this in the Westminster-Southwark dispute. The
question of trusts where the civic law was involved was left to
the individual bishops, after they had objected to being compelled to follow Wiseman's lead[33].

Although the dispute about episcopal meetings took its
rise from the charitable trusts dispute, fundamentally the
matter was of long standing. There seems no doubt that
Wiseman was unreasonably autocratic in wishing his own
opinion to prevail, and at the same time he tended to conduct
the Low Week meetings in a most unbusiness-like manner as
Ullathorne had told him as far back as 1855[34]. The conflict
came to a head over the discussions about the Charitable Trusts
Law. There was a genuine cleavage on the point as to whether
Catholic Trusts should be registered or not, which turned on
the point that the Mass was still regarded in law as a superstitious practice and any legacy liable to confiscation. The solution arrived at by Propaganda was satisfactory to both parties.
But it was Wiseman's conduct of meetings that finally irritated
the bishops so much that they appealed against him. Fundamentally and stripped of such childish objections as that
Wiseman flaunted the purple in public, the question was

[31] Leeds Archives: *Finance and Funds,* I (no date).
[32] *Ibid.*: Nos. 3, 4 and 5: Correspondence between Bishops Cornthwaite and Goss, 1862.
[33] Cf. Butler, *op. cit.,* I, pp. 220 ff. Propaganda had issued an instruction on the question on Mar. 27th, 1854, when bishops had
been told to follow the lead of Wiseman (Leeds Archives: Roman
Documents, no. 54). This is the instruction mentioned by Manning in his letter to Talbot, Purcell, *op. cit.,* II, p. 147.
[34] Butler, *Life and Times of Bishop Ullathorne,* I, p. 240.

whether the bishops met in a consultative capacity, or whether their votes had real weight. In other words, could Wiseman, as he tried to do on the question of the government of the seminaries, ignore the adverse vote as a bishop might do in certain matters with his chapter. Rome's decision that an agenda was to be circulated previous to the meeting and that the votes of the bishops were to have weight[35] was important in defining the relationship between the metropolitan and his suffragans.

The dispute between Wiseman and his chapter was likewise responsible for making clear an important legal point. In essence the dispute was part of the quarrel with Errington, and the chapter took it upon itself to criticise Wiseman's administration of the diocese. Further, on demand they refused to submit their minute-book to him. There were mediaeval precedents for such a line of action, but such were generally directed against a bishop for interfering in what was the chapter's own concern. The Westminster chapter were claiming to criticise the Archbishop as though they were Parliament and he were one of the Stuart Kings. Rome quite reasonably pointed out that, although the chapter could petition the bishop on questions of diocesan government, its discussions are limited to subjects proposed by the bishop to them and those decisions for which by law the bishop requires the advice or consent of the chapter. Other matters are outside their competence. Moreover, the whole of the chapter minutes are to be presented to him on demand, and when he is on visitation the Chapter Archives are to be thrown open to him[36].

In addition to all this the more general problems of legislation had to be faced. Canon Law in many of its aspects is broad and general and the more definite application of it is left to the province or diocese to arrange for itself. In view of the state of society in which the Church has to work, of geographical, national and historical differences, this is a wise proceeding. In the course of the previous centuries customs and practices had grown up in England which must now be checked, modified or regularised by legislation, in addition to the particular application of common law to England. This

[35] Butler, op. cit., pp. 254 ff.
[36] Purcell, Manning, II, p. 114.

legislative action was in two tiers, provincial councils and diocesan synods. Of these the provincial councils were of the greater importance, since the diocesan synods usually only reinforced the provincial legislation. There were four provincial councils, three in Wiseman's lifetime and one in Manning's. Of these the first two are important and indeed can almost be described as legislative triumphs, the third is not so satisfactory and the fourth is practically completely unsatisfactory as far as legislation is concerned.

The first two councils dealt with the important points in English Catholic life. Reasonable and necessary insistence was laid on preaching the faith and on the importance of catechetical instruction in the schools[37], on the chapters[38] and the method of the *terna*, giving three names for a vacant see, proposed by the chapter, submitted to the hierarchy and finally sent to Rome[39]. Then follow two decrees (XIII and XIV) on parochial and diocesan organisation. The next section is devoted to the sacraments, followed by a decree on the laws of the Church, on fasting and abstinence and support of pastors[40]. The twenty-fourth decree is concerned with the clergy and there are laid down the principles that have governed clerical dress and behaviour in England ever since. Then follow decrees on rectors, colleges and seminaries, regulars, nuns and bishops, with an appendix on the election and procedure of chapters. The second council tied up the loose ends with decrees on ecclesiastical goods and leave of absence for priests.

The Third Council was the scene of the dispute between Wiseman and the hierarchy on the matter of seminaries. There were grave difficulties involved. Wiseman backed by Manning wanted seminaries on the lines laid down by the Council of Trent, but English seminaries had followed the old Douay practice of educating lay and ecclesiastical students together. Manning never really understood that it supplied a need, and that it worked and had worked for a couple of centuries. In fact, close reading of Manning's correspondence seems to show that, though at times his judgment was most acute, he lacked any historical sense where English Catholicism was concerned. It was easy for him and his pitiful echo at the Vatican, Talbot,

[37] Dec. VIII.   [38] Dec. XI.   [39] Dec. XII.
[40] Dec. XXIII.

to stigmatise opposition as " Gallican," but it did not show a very high level of intelligence. In consequence of this disagreement, perhaps, decree XIII is a rather long preamble, decree XIV an interesting examination of the seminaries without the slightest attempt to evaluate what was of real importance, their spirit. It might be remarked, almost in parenthesis, that Manning never understood the unique contribution of education in freedom that Douay made to English Catholic education, which, we can believe, he would have destroyed[41]. It is not until we reach decree XV that we find any kind of legislation, and this largely on appointments and episcopal jurisdiction. Decrees XV and XVI on Mission Boundaries on the extremes of dioceses and on the payment of the *cathedraticum* reach for one brief moment the legislative heights of the first two councils.

It has been presumed that Manning must have had a hand in the work of this council on internal evidence. We know that Wiseman was responsible for the first two, and there is such a similarity between parts of the third and the fourth councils that we can conclude at least probably that Manning had a hand on the third. Certainly from the legislative point of view the fourth council is very unsatisfactory. Most of the decrees that are not hortative are copied from previous councils, and sections on clerical life read very much like advance copies of the *Eternal Priesthood*. The whole legislation reads very much like a series of preambles to Acts of Parliament with the laws left out. It is not without interest, and the ideals are excellent, but it is not legislation. Probably there was no need of further legislation. It is at least arguable that the fourth council should have sat at the end of the century to legislate in the light of the previous fifty years. In fact it was thirty years too early, and its legislative quality has suffered in consequence.

Diocesan legislation is largely disappointing in the earlier years, for it is chiefly concerned with reinforcing provincial decrees. Occasionally there are interesting particular variations, chiefly in connection with the duties of rural deans. Some dioceses (Hexham, Northampton, and Shrewsbury, for example) rule that interavailability of faculties shall cease. It seems that previously a priest coming from another district

[41] Cf. Purcell, *Manning*, II, pp. 265 ff.

could exercise faculties in the district to which he came for a month. Birmingham laid down careful notes to guide missioners in their recommendations for candidates for the priesthood. The final choice was to be made by a council of seven, three ex officio, the Vicar General and the Presidents of Oscott and Sedgley, and four appointed for three years, two by the Chapter and two by the Bishop from the clergy[42]. It is particularly after the fourth provincial council that diocesan legislation begins to be individual. Rules, sometimes originally promulgated in an *ad clerum*, have stood the test of time and are incorporated in the synod[43]. Abuses or slackness have arisen in the diocese, and Synods are used to fix the stipends of rectors and curates. On the whole the synodal legislation I have examined fulfils its duty in interpreting and applying the modifications of universal and provincial law to local conditions in each diocese. Yet there does not seem to be in England a large body of independent diocesan legislation. Perhaps the reason is that the provincial councils did settle the more outstanding problems of the hierarchy's first sixty years, and the dioceses had only to add refinements. I think, however, that this is magnifying the legislative achievement of the provincial councils. One bishop stated that "there seems to be, among some of the clergy, a want of knowledge of certain of the Diocesan Regulations,"[44] and he could have added that they knew very little about the provincial councils. What had in fact happened was that the law had become part of every-day life, was kept unquestioningly and often unknowingly, and diocesan life was governed not so much by synodal law as by administrative regulation promulgated by the various letters *ad clerum* issued from time to time.

It was this day-to-day diocesan administration that was to make or mar the Church in England. Ullathorne once said very wisely that " a long course of responsibility in ecclesiastical government cannot fail, my brethren, to give a certain facility of observation, a sort of ecclesiastical sense, I might almost say a *gratia gratis data*, an instinct acquired by contact

---

[42] Third Birmingham Synod, 1st June, 1854.

[43] Cf. First Leeds Synod, 1879, incorporating letters on Finance (1863) and on the Mutual Relations of the Missions (1866).

[44] Bp. of Leeds to the Rural Deans of the Diocese, Oct. 30th, 1906.

with the Church on many points, the result of which is like a comment on the gospel ''[45]. For some unknown reason administrative ability is often belittled, contrasted with sanctity, and dismissed as a mere nothing. There can be little doubt that we do find both together, and perhaps Thomas Grant, first Bishop of Southwark, may be taken as an example. The false separation of the two almost seems like asserting that faith will do without good works. There is not much doubt that sanctity can supply for defects in administrative ability. Sheer efficiency with all the coldness we associate with it is not going to guarantee the good health of a diocese, but in reality this coldness is a defect of administrative ability which, by being human, should be humane. If ecclesiastical administrative ability is, as Ullathorne hinted, a *gratia gratis data*, in that case a saint might reasonably expect it.

Administration never was easy, for it requires a grasp of the end to be attained, the choice of the most efficacious means, and an organising ability that prevents stultification of effort. Over and above all this, tact and diplomacy must act as a lubricant to the organisation that is set up. Bishops were compelled to deal with clergy who had inherited the spirit of independence that Douay had fostered, and in consequence the task was not easy, a judgment that is reinforced by reading episcopal correspondence. In the thirty years of the first generation a bishop could and often did act as the sole administrator. Wiseman was content to outline plans and leave the rest to subordinates to work out[46]. He was always forward-looking, more interested in far-reaching schemes than in day-to-day plodding. Manning was interested in the smaller details and, as far as he was concerned, was willing to run the diocese through secretaries[47]. He was not really worried about the composition of his chapter nor who was his Vicar General. Dr. Grant, then Rector of the English College, Rome, discussing the diocesan synod with Bishop Briggs, pointed out that the clergy were not happy about so much being reserved to the bishop, and were curious about diocesan expenditure[48]. Bishop

---

[5] Third Birmingham Synod, 1st June, 1854, Bishop's Discourse, p. 19.
[6] Ward, *Life of Wiseman*, II, p. 160.
[7] Purcell, *Manning*, II, p. 270, n. 1.
[8] Leeds Archives: Roman Documents, No. 33.

Briggs did, however, continually consult his Vicar General, and, if we are to believe his formulation of the scheme for rural deans, was prepared to delegate power and responsibility to the clergy[49]. In general it can be said that episcopal action has varied and does vary very much. A strong energetic bishop often tends to go ahead, consult his chapter or clergy when it suits him, and like Manning, once his mind is made up, shapes his course of action come what may. A weaker bishop is often run by his Vicar General or by members of his chapter. The possibilities between the two extremes are almost infinite.

The building up of a diocesan curia has varied very much from diocese to diocese. Quite early the Archdiocese of Westminster began to organise itself. In 1851 the " Weekly Board for the transaction of the ordinary diocesan business " was meeting every Thursday morning at Golden Square[50] and the Vicar General attended five mornings a week. Ten years later there were two Vicars General and by 1870 a curia had been built up consisting of the Vicar General, Oeconomus, Secretary, Private Secretary, and three other secretaries[51]. Even at this date some bishops were apparently without secretaries unless, as was probable, one of the cathedral clergy acted in that capacity. Chapters had been appointed, and the Westminster case outlined previously had determined their relationship with the bishop. Schools Committees were developed, and sometimes finance boards, but the growth o these has lain rather in the present century. The chapter, under the arrangement made by Rome, had the right to present three names for consideration when a new bishop had to be appointed. These with appropriate comments were sent by the bishops to Rome. Nevertheless considerable influence in the choice was wielded by Manning through Talbot whilst Pius IX lived[52]. It would be correct to say that all bishops appointed to English sees during this time were recommended by Manning.

Quite naturally finance was bound to be of major importance. The finances of parishes were a separate matter though the bishop generally disbursed the funds from endow

49 Y.B. MSS.: Bp. Briggs to Robert Hogarth.
50 *Catholic Directory*, 1851, p. 33.
51 *Catholic Directory*, 1870, p. 88.
52 Purcell, *Manning*, II, p. 269.

ments to the places concerned. In addition to this he was intimately concerned with the Ecclesiastical Education Fund and his own episcopal revenue. Statistics for the Ecclesiastical Education Fund are not easily obtained, and it will be sufficient to note that there was more reliance on funded monies than on collections. To-day the position is reversed. There is, however, some evidence for episcopal revenue in three documents in the Leeds Archives. Two of these are printed lists for 1862 and the third a written copy of episcopal accounts which seems to belong to a later date[53]. The sources of episcopal revenue were the Beverley share of the old Northern District funds which produced £66 16s. 6d. a year, certain miscellaneous funds producing £107 12s. 4d. a year, and the Beverley Episcopal Endowment bringing in £153 a year. The whole totalled £327 8s. 10d. The Bishop, I must add, made the total £326 3s. 6d. In 1862 the Bishop's income was £350, in 1873 it was £425. Later the bishop was requiring £500 to make ends meet. The deficit was made up by collections from the diocese. Thus the episcopal income could be in a precarious condition, and perhaps the fact that the Catholic Truth Society spent two years " dunning " Bishop Cornthwaite for £1 2s. 2d.[54] may be some indication of this. Perhaps what does emerge very clearly is that episcopal revenue tended to be insufficient and thus any hope of building up an episcopal curia was frustrated from the very beginning by shortage of money.

A brief survey of the papers of Bishop Briggs and his successor Bishop Cornthwaite will give some idea of administration during the period. As often happens we are obliged to form our judgments on what is left, for much is ephemeral, and destroyed when it no longer serves a useful purpose. Much of what survives has a connection with finance, since such papers are generally required to establish a claim or prove a payment. The nature and content of the papers do not change with the restoration of the hierarchy. There are the marriage faculties for dispensation for a number of cases, annotated by the Bishop to make sure he does not exceed the number. In the beginning notes are added to documents by Grant, who acted

[3] Leeds Archives: Finance and Funds, 8, 12, and Episcopal Acts.
[4] Leeds Archives: Various Episcopal Papers, Ia, Ic.

as Roman agent for Bishop Briggs. Sometimes it is news, sometimes as in 1850, that " Y[our] L[ordship] would please the Pope very much if you were to write to him or to the S[acred] C[ongregation] as if quite from yourself an account of your views and impressions as to the recent troubles in England and the hopes or fears Catholics have in consequence. He has not asked for such a letter, but I know it would be liked "[55]. Then Grant became Bishop of Southwark, and the Vice-rector, Dr. English, does the bishop's work[56]. A faculty to consecrate the oils with five priests for all the English bishops is a reminder that England was still short of priests[57] and a permission for three priests to wear wigs whilst saying Mass adds a very human touch to a pile of official documents[58]. The bishop objects to nuns moving out of his diocese[59], faculties are given for the appointment to vacant canonries[60], and Propaganda warns the English bishops that shortage of priests is no excuse for lowering the standard[61]. There is an interesting letter from Propaganda in answer to Bishop Briggs' *relatio* on the state of the diocese[62]. He is urged to visit his diocese, and asked why he lives in York and not in Beverley. Perhaps he did explain to Rome later that Beverley was chosen since York was a see of the Church of England, and such had been carefully avoided in choosing episcopal titles. Beverley was useless as a diocesan centre. In any case Bishop Briggs' successor must have confused Propaganda even more by going to live in Leeds! Later comes a complaint that a priest in the diocese is often drunk, and this is causing scandal[63].

After Bishop Briggs' long tenure of office, his successor, Bishop Cornthwaite, began cleaning up. There are questions as to funds[64], old quarrels are smoothed over[65]. There is an echo of the prohibition of Oxford and Cambridge to Catholics

[55] Leeds Archives: Roman Documents, No. 33.
[56] *Ibid.*, No. 39.
[57] *Ibid.*, No. 41.
[58] *Ibid.*, No. 44.
[59] *Ibid.*, Nos. 45 and 52.
[60] *Ibid.*, Nos. 47 and 48.
[61] *Ibid.*, No. 51.
[62] *Ibid.*, No. 58.
[63] *Ibid.*, No. 67.
[64] Leeds Archives: Finance and Funds, L-5, 9, etc., especially 14.
[65] Especially the Mission in Swaledale, cf. *Ibid.*, 14p.

in a letter from Charles Stourton: " I will still venture to hope that your Lordship will not consider it necessary that my son should leave before the term ending at mid-summer year "[66]. Another bishop advises him that a priest wishes to serve in the diocese, but his conduct is rumoured not to be good[67]. There are the bills for his own and Bishop O'Reilly's visit in 1874 to Rome and Lourdes. There is, too, a large collection of papers on orphanages. Bishop Cornthwaite was resolved to found one, and set about it systematically by enquiring how things were managed in the rest of the country[68]. So the day to day administration of the diocese went on, quietly, but essential to the life of the Church in England.

It should not be assumed that all the administration of the diocese was directly dependent on the Bishop. Probably, and of necessity, the bulk was done in the missions. There is little doubt that there were giants in those days among the missionary clergy. Perhaps the haze of time and distance obscures the faults of the age, but we see great administrators, bishops, and in greater abundance rectors of missions. The problems of the town mission will concern us most, since it was there that the Church's work was to assume its greatest importance. The quick growth of the towns raised among other problems a moral one, perhaps not sufficiently noticed by historians. The Catholic Church was early in the fray, and roughly and generally speaking shared the evangelisation of the towns with the Wesleyans. Later the Church of England and the Free Churches came into the towns, and the strenuous attempts at evangelisation were carried on in, needless to remark, conditions of sectarian bitterness. This was complicated by the growth of secularism smeared with " scientism " to give it an air of logical respectability. Most Catholics were very poor, the majority of them Irish immigrants whose standard of living was even lower than that of the English poor. Their houses were huddled in insanitary streets, many of which have disappeared to-day. In their midst stood the Catholic Church, presbytery and school, stone- or brick-built in the prevailing style of Victorian Gothic. The presbyteries were

[66] *Ibid.,* 14 ap.
[67] *Ibid.,* 14 ba.
[68] Leeds Archives: Various Episcopal Papers, nos. 8 a-i.

rather dark, lacking air, furnished with heavy Victorian furniture, and the rooms papered with heavily-patterned dark wallpaper.

Such is the description of the majority of our town missions. The rector was not only the spiritual father of his flock: he was their adviser, helper and leader. It was the rector who stopped the street fight when the police were afraid to intervene. He was the representative of the Catholics of the town on the School Board, where he fought for grants or for religious facilities for Catholic children[69]. He was the Catholic Church in the eyes of the town. The church and schools were built up on borrowed money, and the debt was paid by the pennies that were collected. We are struck immediately by the courage and foresight of these men. From time to time there is an agitation for a parish council to administer the temporal affairs of the Church. Such, as far as one can judge, would be very like the *consilium fabricae* in the Code[70], and the usual argument is that by means of these the parish priests would be relieved of temporal worries and would be able to devote all their attention to the spiritual needs of the parish. There is, too, the implied observation that parish priests are not good temporal managers. It is a deceptively simple argument, since it is very doubtful whether the spiritual and temporal worries of a parish can be so greatly separated. It is perhaps as well that parish councils did not exist when the missions were built up, since it is doubtful whether many of the parishes would have been founded at all. The old rectors were long-sighted in many respects. They saw the immediate need of what they were doing, and they were courageous enough to plunge into debts that would fill the ordinary man with horror, in the belief that some day by patient work the debts would be extinguished. One must wonder what the parish council would have done in the parish largely Irish where the condemnation of Fenianism caused collections to drop to almost nothing[71].

But perhaps we have moved too fast. By 1850 many

[69] Cf. Bingham, *The Sheffield School Board*, passim. The contests between Father Gos and Miss Macmillan in Bradford were almost epic.

[70] Canons 1183, § 2 and 1184.

[71] Y.B. MSS.: Rev. M. Trappes to Rev. J. Glover, 7th June, 1868.

parishes were beginning to be founded. Some of them were successors of the missions founded in the eighteenth century, others were founded from the old missions, as Hull was founded from the mission of Marston which had existed for at least a century[72]. As time went on the large missions began to split up. Mass-centres were founded, chapels-of-ease built, and at the right time the new mission was cut off from the old. We can see the process in the *Catholic Directory*. " The clergy of Brighton," we are told in 1860[73], " are most desirous to establish a mission on the West Cliff of this large and important town." That was the first step. The next we can see at Holloway[74] which, we are told, " is a station in the Rectorate of St. John's, Islington, and designed for the accommodation of residents in the outlying district of Holloway." The next stage, perhaps, is related in 1850 of Bunhill Row[75]. " There is every hope that a neat but inexpensive chapel for this crowded though poor district will be erected in the course of the year. At present the wants of the Mission are inadequately supplied by the use of the school-room for a temporary chapel." The pattern is the same all over England, except for very few cases where a mission was founded on virgin soil. A number of Catholics are on the confines of the mission. Mass is started for them, a chapel (later it was nearly always a school) is built, and then a new mission is founded. The old missions had often some endowment to depend on, and there was always the desire to give a mission stability by that means. But the Church expanded too quickly, and the congregations were too poor.

The financial problem has loomed very large in the administration of missions. It could not be otherwise. Debts were large and the ordinary running costs were a constant drain on resources. There is a letter on finance in the Leeds Synods[76] which seems to sum up the situation for the country as a whole. The principle of financial administration was that ' the definite and permanent liabilities of a Mission must be provided for before all others." The order of preference was

[2] Y.B. MSS.: *An Account* . . ., p. 195.
[3] *Catholic Directory*, 1860, p. 63.
[4] *Ibid.*, p. 48.
[5] *Catholic Directory*, 1850, p. 34.
[6] Leeds Synods: Letter on Finance, 20th Jan., 1863.

listed—debts, Mass intentions, housekeeper, insurance, maintenance, emergency fund, official expenses, salaries. Salaries
were to vary with £25 a year as a minimum rising to a possible
£50 for rectors. Administration charges were to be 4d. in the
pound, which was cheap at the price. The foundation of the
revenue was the outdoor collection, raised by the clergy themselves by house to house visits every week-end. In the diocese
of Leeds this question of collecting was the grievance that
caused the assistant priests to " strike " for a higher stipend.
They were given a rise provided the collection continued.

Yet collection of money has never been the only cause
of strong parochial life. It has been a cause, since the real
sacrifice involved undoubtedly stimulates keenness and interest. But something positive must be added, and undoubtedly
the rectors did that. Parish life was vigorous. There were
guilds and confraternities, social gatherings and, above all,
constant contact with their priests. The clergy were faced with
great difficulties. The majority of their flocks were very poor,
had little or no education, and were without leadership. Temptations to fall away from the Church were all around, slackness, possibilities of advancement, political careers, all these
things could and did make inroads. There were minor losses
such as Catholic teachers going over to Board Schools for the
sake of " greater pecuniary advantages." The hierarchy
feared they would draw the children after them, pointed out
that some of the teachers had been educated on Catholic funds
and feared in general the loss to the Catholic flock of excellent
well-trained teachers[77]. Reading of these times, one must
admire the priests who administered the missions. Their constant struggles were aimed at obtaining the very best, especially
in education, for their flocks, and it is consoling to realise how
often they obtained it.

There is another and a darker side to the excellent
development of the full parochial life. Parochialism was not
only a possibility, it was sometimes a reality. A bishop might
emphasise the constitutional position of a mission in that " all
jurisdiction in the Diocese is centred in the bishop, and by
him is delegated to you in the measure that he thinks fitting
and necessary." At the same time he must point out that " the

[77] Low Week Meeting, 1875, in *6th Leeds Synod*, p. 24.

senior priest within the limits of the mission is independent of all except the Bishop ''[78]. The rector naturally worked hard to create a real parochial spirit among his flock and, too often, found that this could be most easily created by a negative process of enmity with his neighbours. There were quarrels over boundaries, over collections, over children going to schools other than their own parochial schools. Such were commonplaces in the relationship between missions, and perhaps it is needless to remark, they were embittered if one of the missions was administered by religious. Such quarrels are apt to be exaggerated, since apparently they come under the '' man bites dog '' category. They overshadow the work described in the previous paragraph. The Church in England owes its success to a strong parochial life, not to parochialism.

Constitutionally, rural deans should form the link between the missions and the bishops. Like the deans of the Middle Ages, they should be the *oculi episcopi*, the eyes of the bishop, but like their mediaeval predecessors they often seem to have suffered from cataract. Conciliar and synodal legislation lays many duties on them, and gives them extensive delegated powers. They were expected to visit their deaneries, keep an eye on administration, spiritual and temporal, and preside over the quarterly conferences. In theory the diocese was well covered, provided the rural deans took such a high view of their office as legislators did. Perhaps legislators expected too much, or on the other hand energetic bishops found it unnecessary, and lax ones did not bother. In the course of time the rural deans gradually found a mode of action that suited them. Much of it was at an unofficial level in correcting abuses before they grew worse, and officially administering parishes in the case of illness. Much depended on the personality of the Dean for their successful accomplishment, and always will.

About the end of the period of foundation we have been considering, 1880, a survey of the constitution of the Church in this country was made as part of the case against Religious Orders which is worth noting. Bishops Vaughan and Clifford point out that there are no parishes in England, since such

[78] Diocese of Beverley: Letter on the Mutual Relations of Missions, 1st Aug., 1866.

stability would be out of place in a country where " the object is not so much the provision of the aids of religion for Catholics as to convert the heretic and so increase the number of the faithful. A parish," the argument continues, " is a territorial division of the Church founded to provide for the religious needs of a Catholic population already existing. A mission is a territorial division of the Church founded to create a Catholic population and thus prepare the way for further missions and finally for true parishes of their nature stable "[79]. This excellent summary of a situation that was to last until 1918 was a fundamental point in the episcopal case against the religious orders. I hardly think there is need to discuss the dispute so rich in personalities since good accounts are easily accessible[80]. In general the constitution *Romanos Pontifices* (May 8th, 1881) supported the bishops' contentions; whilst it safeguarded the intimate life of the religious orders, even going so far as to exempt all their houses, even the small ones; it put their missions on the same footing as the rest of the missions of the country. The elementary schools in their parishes were not exempt from episcopal visitation, though their colleges were[81]. From the administrative point of view two important questions were settled. Religious parishes could be divided and secular priests put in charge of new missions, and thus what might have been an obstacle to development was removed[82]. Secondly financial matters were put on a reasonable basis. Probably the bitterest ecclesiastical quarrels are about money or precedence, and an immediate solution is nearly always necessary for the peace and health of the Church.

The expansion of the Church continued unabated, its outward sign being the formation of new dioceses, the separation of Southwark and Portsmouth in 1882, and the division of Yorkshire, the diocese of Beverley, into Leeds (West Riding) and Middlesbrough (North and East Ridings) in 1878. Even more clearly is the expansion shown in the founding of new

[79] *Della divisone delle Missioni in Inghilterra.*
[80] Cf. Purcell, *Manning,* II, pp. 505 ff; Leslie, *Manning,* pp. 288 ff; Snead-Cox, *Vaughan,* I, chaps. 12 & 14; Butler, *Ullathorne,* II, pp. 188 ff.
[81] Summarised in the *Catholic Encyclopedia,* vol. 13, p. 154.
[82] To forestall objections, I know of at least one case where the attitude of religious did seriously delay development.

Mass centres. Figures can by no means be regarded as completely reliable, but using the dates for foundations given in the *Catholic Directory*, we can say in general that throughout the whole country there were more foundations between 1860 and 1870 than in any decade before 1900. By that date the number of churches and chapels in the country had trebled.

Organisation within the diocese did not change much. It would be true to say that until after the 1914-18 war organisation in most dioceses was rather loose despite the tight hold that strong bishops, like Whiteside of Liverpool, kept on it. Much can be said in favour of such an attitude. Expansion was the work of the missions and by the end of the century the general pattern of mission administration was settled. Things had got to the point where the bishop (knowing that the work of consolidation and expansion would go on normally) could devote his attention to slackness and irregularity. Leadership was required and given in the diocese on the Education Question, but even here the critical difficulties were to come in the next century. It is probable that in this matter mission organisation failed, not in the matter of primary education, but in that of secondary education. The normal expansion of missions was in the direction of the smaller and more manageable unit, and theory and practice had demanded that the mission unit should be entirely self-contained, church, presbytery and school. This arrangement had great advantages, for the mission's spiritual and educational requirements were at hand representing visibly the sacrifice that had gone into their erection. The Education Act of 1902 brought a new idea, for the secondary schools envisaged in the Act catered for an area larger than the mission. The problem was to become acute later, but some far-sighted rectors were already seeking ways and means to solve it.

Financial and other difficulties were still dogging the steps of central diocesan administration, and although bishops now lived apart from their cathedrals and had their own secretaries, work was becoming too much for the organisation. The story of episcopal administration is that of a large amount of work with too little staff to do it. It is true that work was delegated, but it is doubtful whether the work of the various committees was efficiently integrated unless they happened to have

the same chairman or secretary. Energy was dissipated because there was no integration, and organisation tended to be
inefficient from lack of permanent curial officials. Bishops
could find no real solution to the problem, which rapid expansion and competent rectors tended to mask, because of the
chronic shortage of priests. To a certain extent the shortage
had been relieved by a succession of priests from Ireland. This
partial solution was excellent. The majority of the people were
Irish, the outlook of the priests was right for the struggle to
maintain and extend Catholicity. They were leaders and
fighters for their flocks, and in return were obeyed and
respected. A great many of them had great powers of insight,
were towers of strength in adversity, gentle and kind to those
in trouble, strict and harsh to the wayward. They were not
popular with Catholics descended from families that had kept
the faith through penal times, but neither were the ordinary
Irish people. " All Irish, all dirty, and helpless . . . . and
unworthy objects," wrote Barbara Charlton, herself of the
Anne family and married to one of the Charltons of Hesleyside.
" I never knew," she continues, " to what degree of perfection
Irish filth could be raised until I visited the Hibernian colony
in Bristol, and duplicity went hand in hand with dirt "[83]. Of
the priest, an Irishman, she could say, " We had to suffer
from the tyranny of the priest, who never seemed to bear in
mind that but for my husband, who paid so liberally towards
the expenses of St. Oswald's Mission out of his own pocket,
he might never have been there at all "[84]. This further com-
plication time alone could cure.

So the first half-century of the restored hierarchy drew
to a close. Before twenty years of the twentieth century were
past a whole new set of conditions had arisen or were arising,
and to some extent the problems of the Church in England
changed. The time had come for thinking out new solutions.
Administratively they were never really thought out. Some
elaborate organisational schemes were drawn up in some
dioceses, for Catholic Action for instance, which never really
went any further than the paper they were written on. Parishes
tried to band together to form Catholic Action organisations.

[83] L.E.O. Charlton, ed., *Recollections of a Northumbrian Lady*, p. 228.
[84] *Ibid.*, p. 255.

By and large these did not work either, since they suffered from the double disability of being vague about the work they had to do (and not doing the co-ordinating work they could have done) and being nobody's concern. Administration and organisation began to be built up slowly with *ad hoc* committees that managed to become permanent, with experimental organisation that succeeded and was adopted in various places. In other words much of the organisation was of the " make do and mend " variety, which after trial succeeded and became permanent. To some extent diocesan and parish administration looked very like a Heath Robinson machine, but it had this virtue—it worked, and often more stream-lined paper models would not.

Any discussion in detail is useless without some understanding of the background. The whole social standing of English Catholics was changing. The generalisation that they were either of the nobility or squirearchy or else very poor had ceased to be true. There had gradually arisen a group of Catholics, small in number it must be admitted, who had obtained their wealth by the numberless avenues open to a man who was willing to combine hard work with his native intelligence. They often became important men in their civic communities and went into politics assisted by the largely Irish Catholic vote. Their names appeared on the subscription lists of Catholic charities, they helped to build churches and schools, they served on committees, gave sound unobtrusive advice and help to their rectors, and often formed the nucleus of the Society of St. Vincent de Paul. This was really only the beginning of the spread of Catholics throughout all social classes. As the twentieth century advanced the standard of living of Catholics began to improve, they began to be better educated, to take a place in society commensurate with their intelligence. The society in which they lived was in a state of flux or, according to some, in a state of moral decline. The Church in England had, then, to solve the problem of providing for Catholics gradually spreading through the social classes of this society, and to arm the faithful against the new attacks made on them.

These attacks on the Church in the twentieth century have not been so much in the nature of sectarian abuse and misrepresentation, both species of attack well-known since the Reformation, but rather the insidious infiltration of materialism, popular scientism and, much nearer our own day, Communism. Such naturally have had some considerable impact on parochial and diocesan organisation. The lectures on the faith that had been popular in the 1850's gave way to lectures on science and sociology. This is generally true despite the work of the Catholic Evidence Guild, founded to preach Catholicism in the market place. It would only be fair to comment that organised Catholic Action, despite the many associations founded to further it, has not been a success. Attempts to issue diocesan blueprints for it have only resulted in adding to the number of moribund organisations, and parochial or local organisations for rationalising or attempting to combine local societies in united action have failed. It is difficult to generalise on the causes for this failure, since many of them are local and peculiar to certain districts. Perhaps we can say that Catholics have always tended to unite on particular questions—the Schools Question leaps at once to mind—but have found other work difficult or uninteresting. Despite the good work and success of the Catholic Social Guild, the number of Catholics who are willing to train for the apostolate that undoubtedly lies about them is very small indeed. The normal parish has developed its confraternities and branches of diocesan and national organisations. There is considerable criticism of the number of such organisations, a criticism which is occasionally aired in the Catholic journals. It is not entirely true that many organisations in a parish are necessarily a sign of a healthy parochial life. They may be a sign of wasted effort. It is true that in theory each organisation is intended to cater for different classes of people, but in practice it is amazing how often the same persons appear to belong to each of the organisations. There is room for rationalisation, for combined effort at all levels, but the prospect does not seem to be too hopeful for anyone who attempts it.

The problem of catering for the spread of Catholics throughout all classes of society has not, I believe, been squarely faced. The facilities for secondary education have increased since the passing of the 1902 Act, and with this the standard of education has gone up. In many cases parishes have tended not to change their methods. It is no longer true in a great many places that the priest is the only educated man in the parish, but only too often his attitude to his parishioners is based on the misconception that he is. Gradually the Catholic graduate is finding his niche in the parish and the more general this becomes, the less likely is it that his abilities will remain unused. The problem, however, has not been attacked with any foresight, and in most cases its existence is not recognised. Yet difficulties go deeper than that. The progress of secondary school education is described elsewhere. What we are concerned with here is its impact on parochial organisation. Secondary Schools have been of necessity extra-parochial since they are compelled to take their pupils from an area covering many parishes. In consequence they have been nobody's concern. This had not been noticed since dioceses and religious orders had borne the responsibilities and financial burdens.

The suggestions of 1936 and the plans which have followed in 1944-46 Education Acts have made the problem obvious and its solution is urgent. It has been indicated that missions tended to settle into compact, self-contained units. Educational provision was parochial, and any form of it that chanced to be extra-parochial was both out of sight and out of mind. The new Act suddenly made one half of education extra-parochial, and parishes were stunned. They had developed an " elementary school mind," and now they were faced by the problem of secondary education for all. There is no doubt that the organisational problem was beyond the parishes; in fact there was a very grave danger that some larger education authorities might " pick off " parishes one by one. Moreover, the problem had to be viewed over a large area, and in order to forestall arguments, the solution had finally to be applied at a diocesan level. The advantage of a central organisation for negotiation was obvious. A Diocesan Schools Commission was not in some dioceses a new thing. The 1936 reorganisation had brought them into being, and in many cases there was a tradition of similar diocesan commissions varying from finance to fine arts. The Diocesan Schools Commissions have distinguished themselves by their energy. Generally small, staffed by experts, they have rendered excellent service in surveying the needs, planning the schools, and settling the disputes. There seems to be a future for them as a court of appeal in disputes, an advisory and negotiating body, and a stimulus to the lax.

This activity has naturally had an effect on parochial organisation. One bishop has remarked that as far as education is concerned parish boundaries must disappear. This will indeed be a revolution. Up to now the parish priest has directed the general educational policy of the parish; from now he will have to share the direction of half his children with other parish priests. This is going to raise problems of finance and of control. The financial problem is largely being solved by sharing the burden pro rata, a solution both commonsense and fair. The question of control is going to be much more difficult. It is obvious, I believe, that the solution will be made at the diocesan level and imposed from above. What the details will be cannot be predicted. There is, however, a model in the grammar school which might well be followed. The new modern schools could well be made independent of parochial direction and control. Its chapel (and it is to be hoped that the new schools will have them) could be controlled by a chaplain specially appointed by the bishop who would be in general charge of the spirituality of the school. The interested parish priests should be governors, but should not interfere with the chaplain. Such a scheme would require episcopal legislation, but that should raise no inherent difficulty.

Of the various committees that have grown up in the course of time Finance Committees are probably the oldest. Despite episcopal attempts to control finance, it is probable that only in recent times has really effective control been established. Permission to proceed with work, permission to borrow money was to be granted by these committees but, as far as can be seen, this permission was not always applied for. What is more, terms of loans were by no means uniform. Finally dioceses decided to take full advantage of the Charitable Trust Acts and secure remission of Income Tax. This involved centralisation of funds. Thus the diocese became the borrower, and in its turn lent to the parishes. The difference of the two rates of interest provided for administration, changed the need of parishes to raise money, but has put an effective break on unwise spending.

This has added a Treasurer to the list of episcopal officials. The last fifty years has seen the gradual formation of
something like an episcopal curia. Yet with the exception of
the Archdiocese of Westminster there is not much sign of its
being organised as a unit independent of parochial work in the
diocese. The difficulties of this method of organisation became
obvious when episcopal courts at the close of the war were
called upon to deal with a sudden rush of marriage cases. A
similar phenomenon was dealt with in the civil courts by
emergency measures: the canonical courts struggled through
it as best they could. Delays, perhaps dangerous delays, in
dealing with cases have not been uncommon. The obvious
solution was to have more frequent sittings of the courts, but
this solution was not easy to apply. Basically it is true that
English dioceses have not sufficient priests to meet their needs,
and the diocesan courts must be served by men who are
engaged on other duties. On the other hand the few dioceses
that have set out to form a permanent administration have not
felt the pinch as much as theorists might imagine. It is true
that episcopal incomes are often too small to pay for a curia,
yet something might be done in this direction by using convent
chaplaincies. After all the central diocesan work covering such
things as education, youth work, marriage guidance and many
other similar tasks is becoming too important and even vital to
be left to the mercies of part-time work however devoted that
might be.

The shortage of priests remarked on has been in part
caused by the increase of parishes during the last forty years.
This increase has been general and common to all dioceses, and
its main cause has been the increase in house building after the
1914-18 War, and the continuation of this consequent upon
slum clearances. The area of parishes extended, and it became
imperative to divide them. The rate of expansion has increased
steadily until the peak was reached in the decade 1930-39. The
war has put what can only be regarded as a temporary halt to
this increase, since new housing estates that are planned will
require churches. Indeed in some cases land has already been
obtained. In some dioceses the founding of schools led to this
extension; in fact one bishop would not allow churches to be
built. The whole process of expansion has generally moved

smoothly. Few parish priests have been loath to have their parishes split, in fact many have been more anxious than their bishops. It would seem that both parties have realised that the over-large parish is a definite danger to the Faith. It is easy to be complacent about the state of the parish when there are full congregations on a Sunday morning. In the large parish this may conceal an average mass-attendance of 40 per cent. or less, as against between 60 and 75 per cent., which, allowing for old people, babies and young children, and the sick, shows the parish is in a healthy state. The present generation is reluctant to walk great distances, church and schools have to be sited according to the available transport; in fact everything points to the small compact parish, easy to handle. When parish priests can no longer expect schools to hold their parishes together, a small, well-visited unit is the only guarantee of a healthy parish life.

At the higher level there has been some rearrangement of dioceses, Brentwood and Lancaster having been founded, the first out of Westminster, the second out of Liverpool and Hexham and Newcastle. The important constitutional change came in 1911 when England was divided into three provinces, Liverpool with Hexham and Newcastle, Salford, Leeds, Middlesbrough and later Lancaster as suffragans covering the North of England; Westminster with Northampton, Nottingham, Portsmouth, Southwark and in 1917 Brentwood covering the eastern side of Southern England; and Birmingham with Clifton, Plymouth and Shrewsbury covering the Western side. In 1916 the evolution of Wales was completed. In 1895 the present diocese of Menevia had been erected into a vicariate on its separation from Newport and Menevia, which latter became the diocese of Newport the following year. Two years later the Welsh vicariate became the diocese of Menevia. Both dioceses were suffragans of Westminster, and in the changes of 1911 of Birmingham. In 1916 Newport was made an Archbishopric under the title of Cardiff with Menevia as the suffragan see of this new province.

The chief constitutional changes within dioceses have passed almost unnoticed, despite their importance. All missions became parishes on the publication of the Code of Canon Law in 1918. There has been some discussion about

the matter, but the only distinction of English parishes seems
to be that there is no need to give the parish priest the greater
degree of permanence designated by *inamovibilitas*[85]. There
has, however, arisen an interesting phenomenon, the appointment of administrators to parishes who seem to be *vicarii
economi*[86]. The reason seems to have been to leave parishes
for those priests who had gone as chaplains to the forces. Yet
the practice appears to be continuing, and thus will be restored
the class of rectors removable *ad nutum episcopi* that was part
of the legislation previous to the publication of the Code of
Canon Law. That seems to be its chief use to bishops.

Diocesan administration has always to be two-tiered,
at diocesan level and at parish level. This survey of its
operation over a century shows, I believe, that there is developing a shifting of work from the parish to the diocese. Much
work cannot now be delegated with good prospect of success,
for this is the age of the expert, and the part-time authority
is not going to be a success. In the future, I believe, this
problem will have to be tackled seriously. Episcopal curias
will have to be increased, and parish priests will have to suffer
interference in spheres where they were formerly supreme.
This brings the further problem of the bishop's being screened
off from his clergy by his curia. Visitation, and the use of
quarterly deanery conferences to consult the clergy will perhaps
enable him to remain in touch. There is, too, every reason for the
chapter fulfilling its function as *senatus episcopi*. The parishes
can then be left to develop a full and close parish life. We are
in an age where the State is encroaching more and more on
individual and corporate life. The parish can give a man or
a woman a place in a family society that will stop him from
drifting into the hopeless position of a name on a card. It is
always dangerous to enter the ranks of the prophets, and
equally dangerous to offer advice, be it unpalatable or simply
superfluous. The conclusions outlined here seem to emerge
from a study of a century of administration. Administration
changes slowly, and remains almost constant under most
changes. It is, however, necessary for it to see and cater for

[85] Cf. Claeys—Bouuaert—Simenon, *Man. Iuris Canonici* (4th ed.),
I, p. 312.
[86] Cf. C. 473.

new problems that arise. The Church in England has succeeded in attaining its present position at least in part through
successful administration. For it to move forward, that administration must not become fossilised.

V

THE ARCHDIOCESE OF WESTMINSTER

By GORDON WHEELER

NICHOLAS WISEMAN, the son of Irish parents, was born in Seville in 1802. His father died in 1805 and he and his brother were sent to a boarding school at Waterford. In 1810 he went to Ushaw and eight years later to the newly-reopened English College in Rome, of which he later became Rector. He was ordained priest in 1825 and consecrated Bishop in 1840 being made Coadjutor to Dr. Walsh of the Central District and President of Oscott. Seven years later he became pro Vicar Apostolic of the London District on the death of Dr. Griffiths, and in 1850 was created Cardinal and Archbishop of Westminster.

Tall, dark, slight in his younger days and becoming corpulent in maturity, dignified, scholarly, Wiseman was a Roman of the Romans. " He had published his *Horae Syriacae* at 25; he had that devotion to Rome which had characterised the generation of de Maistre, a sympathy with the full tide of the Romantic movement, enthusiasm for Lacordaire, a fondness for happy Latin jests and a welcoming Irish impulsiveness towards each generous suggestion which might advance the Catholic Church "[1].

George Spencer, Ambrose de Lisle, Sir Charles Wolseley, Lord Shrewsbury, Kenelm Digby, the converts of the Romantic period, found a ready sympathy in him. Newman and the Oxford intellectuals who followed into the Church after 1845 found in him a scholar and a friend. Over sanguine in his expectation of England's imminent conversion, brimming over with enthusiasm for the new factors at work, he commended himself far less to the over-cautious Catholics of the old school. They distrusted the great sweep of his ideas,

[1] Mathew, *Catholicism in England*.

the new and Continental devotions which he introduced, and
his extroverted methods of approach. By the time he received
the Red Hat, he was a figure of international European distinction. He had the expansive mind of the Universal Church
and could never really understand (as he had never really
absorbed its milieu)[2], what seemed to him the narrowness of
his religious compatriots of the old school. Although they
distrusted him, they liked him. His wide and generous gestures
overcame many of their inhibitions. But his victory was not
in any sense complete until late maturity and initially he sustained a defeat which would have daunted a less magnificent
character.

On October 7, 1850, in his famous Pastoral *From Out
the Flaminian Gate* he announced the restoration of the
Hierarchy, and his own appointment as Archbishop of Westminster with all the flamboyancy of one who was quite out of
touch with the sober minds of his fellow countrymen.

The reaction of England was so violent that a repetition
of the Gordon Riots was considered likely and Wiseman's
friends did their utmost to keep him safely out of the country.
He landed unexpectedly and at once composed his *Appeal to
the English People* which, by virtue of its clarity, breadth and
apostolic charity, is one of the most remarkable documents of
the whole of the nineteenth century, and it did much to restore
the situation. It was impossible, however, to allay suspicion
entirely, and not only was the Ecclesiastical Titles Bill, against
the new Hierarchy, initiated and passed, but also an alarming
defection took place among Catholics led by the Duke of
Norfolk. Time healed the wound, and agitation against the
alleged Papal Aggression soon died. The anti-Catholic Bill was
a dead letter from the start and was quietly repealed by Gladstone some twenty years later. Newman wrote in the middle
of the agitation: " Highly as I put his (Wiseman's) gifts, I
was not prepared for such a display of vigour, power, judgment, and sustained energy as the last two months have
brought. I heard a dear friend of his say that the news of the
opposition would kill him. How he has been out! It is the

---

[2] As he wrote to Manning, October 2, 1862, " I certainly had very
few English prejudices to overcome when I reached Rome " (after
leaving Ushaw).

event of the time. In my own remembrance there has been nothing like it "[3].

When Manning preached the panegyric at Wiseman's Requiem, he took for his text: " *Let Nehemias be a long time remembered, who raised up for us our walls that were cast down, and set up the gates and the bars, who rebuilt our houses.*" It was a fitting comparison with the builder of the Second Temple; for Wiseman's constructive genius is fundamentally responsible for the renewed development of Catholic life in England as we see it to-day. In the three provincial Synods held at Oscott in 1852, 1855 and 1859 he laid the foundations of regular ecclesiastical life.

Bishop Ullathorne in his account of the restoration of the Hierarchy wrote: " For the first time since our overthrow at the Reformation were the clergy united with their Bishops in the settlement of what regarded their common interests. . . . The wisdom of retaining Cardinal Wiseman in England was never rendered more conspicuous than as exhibited in this first Provincial Council; and it may be safely said that his Presidency over the assembled Fathers, and the decrees that emanated from the Council were his masterpieces."

Wiseman's most successful rôle was in attempting to synthesise the new elements in Catholic life in England. The first of these was the increase of conversions. The second was the large-scale immigration of the Irish resulting from the potato famine. Wiseman by his capacity for administration and his breadth of vision welded these widely differing influences into something of a unity. All the time he had before his eyes the vision of an England once again Catholic. By his courses of sermons, his lectures, and other expressions of his many gifts he worked constantly towards this end, seizing all advantages and using his social gifts unsparingly to gain an entrée into all branches of society.

His first preoccupation was with the converts. He tried to persuade Newman to bring his Oratory to London and, when that was declined, welcomed Father Faber in his place. Even the flamboyant Pastoral had not stemmed the tide of conversions. " In the little dead city of Canterbury," wrote

[3] Ward, *Life of Wiseman.*

Wiseman, " under the very nose of John Bird Cantuar, twelve persons have at one time put themselves under instruction, including a niece of Sir W. Scott (Miss Peat) and Miss Stephanoff, daughter of the artist. Archdeacon Manning and Dodsworth are considered certain, and most probably Bennett and Archdeacon Wilberforce. In a few days we shall hear of Lord Dunraven and Mr. Monsell, M.P.; Lord Norreys I consider very hopeful. I saw him in Belgium and he sees Lord Arundel and Surrey almost daily; Lord Nelson likewise, and others. Mr. Rogers, Dr. Hook's curate, has been received by Oakeley." Manning was received into the Church on April 6, 1851, together with Mr. James Hope, Q.C., at Farm Street, and on the following Sunday was confirmed by Wiseman. He received the tonsure immediately and was ordained priest a few weeks later. The haste and absence of preparation were again naturally reprobated by the older Catholics. But Wiseman was quite unrepentant and the converts were grateful for one who was always anxious to smooth their paths. As Sir Shane Leslie writes in his life of Manning: " Wiseman was of the old block himself, but cosmopolitan and Roman and therefore tolerant."

After the converts, Wiseman's preoccupation was with resuscitation of religious life in England. He was convinced that communities of Religious could provide in a unique way the answer to the problems of evangelization especially among the poor. When he first came to London, apart from the Jesuits, whose splendid church at Farm Street was opened in 1849, there was not a single community of men. In a few years the Redemptorists, Passionists, Marists and Oratorians had all come and by the end of his life Wiseman had seen the establishment of fifteen communities of men and twenty-three new communities of women. In his reign as Archbishop the number of churches in the diocese was almost trebled (from 46 to 120), whilst the number of priests had all but doubled from 113 to 215[4].

In addition he decided to form a community of secular priests who should be ready to undertake any spiritual work with which they were entrusted. And so in 1857, under the

[4] *Dublin Review*, January, 1919.

leadership of Manning, he founded the Oblates of St. Charles. Two years previously he had petitioned Rome for a coadjutor, especially requesting that George Errington, Bishop of Plymouth, should be given an archiepiscopal title and sent to assist him in the administration of the diocese. "By this measure," says Dr. Mathew, "he hoped to conciliate the Bishops, the senior clergy and the laity of old-fashioned views." It turned out to be one of the few failures of Wiseman's life. Already a sick man, suffering from diabetes and frequent heart attacks, the Cardinal had more difficulty in his personal relationships than ever before. He found himself unable to delegate authority without right of appeal, and although he was rebuked by Rome the only solution was the retirement of the Coadjutor Archbishop. One can only say in passing that Errington emerged creditably from the conflict and in his retirement at Prior Park was never known to speak other than charitably of his former friend.

From 1858 until his death in 1865 Wiseman's chief and unfailing confidant was Manning. Their attitude to the Church and the world was identical and their acceptance of the extremest of views regarding the temporal power of the Papacy heralded a cleavage with Newman. This was emphasised by their united opposition to Newman's plans for an Oratory at Oxford. The hostility to the project was inspired by the recent publication of Pius IX's famous *Syllabus Errorum*.

Wiseman died on February 15th, 1865. The Requiem took place in the Pro-Cathedral at Moorfields and the panegyric was preached by Manning. The funeral procession from the church to the cemetery at Kensal Green was the most spectacular and sincere tribute to a Catholic dignitary ever seen in this country since the Reformation. He had lived down all the hatred and unpopularity of 1850 and had laid the foundations for later days. And the great-hearted man who had sobbed like a child at Newman's sermon on the "Second Spring," found his ultimate resting place in the crypt beneath the high altar of the Cathedral at Westminster for which he had prepared the way.

Wiseman, by his appointment as Archbishop of Westminster and Metropolitan of England in the Bull *Universalis*

Ecclesiae of September 29, 1850, had inherited two distinct offices of pre-Reformation times. He was the successor of the Catholic Archbishops of Canterbury, and as such held a spiritual primacy in the realm, and at the same time ruled a diocese roughly coterminous with the ancient diocese of London. With him the national and international importance of the Archdiocese of Westminster had begun. Despite the first unfavourable reactions to his appointment, intensified by the flamboyant Pastoral, he came to be accepted as an important, integral and colourful national figure. As the Victorian era swelled towards its crescendo, the stature of the Archbishop of Westminster increased in national and international, apart from merely ecclesiastical, importance. It was to attain a zenith in the rule of his successor.

II

" If Wiseman's was the pilot's venturesome arm to steer the bark of Peter through heavy seas to a safe anchorage," wrote Purcell, " it was Manning's part to make smooth the way by tact and skill and intimate knowledge of the land, for the advance of the Church into the fullness of English life."

Henry Edward Manning was born in 1808 at Totteridge. His father, William Manning, was of armigerous merchant stock and Member of Parliament for Evesham. The boy went to Harrow at the age of ten and ultimately distinguished himself by becoming Captain of Cricket. Already he had that handsome, well-mannered and agreeable air which matured into a dignified austerity. He went to Balliol in 1826 and took a First in Greats. In 1832, he became a Fellow of Merton and received Anglican orders in the same year. He married the daughter of his Rector at Lavington where he worked for seventeen years, eventually becoming Archdeacon of Chichester. " He was a Tractarian of somewhat neutral colour, an Archdeacon at thirty-two, possessed of certain Court connections, probably marked out for the episcopate "[5]. His wife died in the year that Queen Victoria came to the throne; fourteen years later, as a result of the Gorham Judgment

[5] Mathew, *Catholicism in England*.

which emphasised the erastian and latitudinarian aspects of Anglicanism, he was received into the Church. Ordained priest by Wiseman, he said his first Mass at Farm Street, and proceeded to Rome where, at the behest of the Pope, he entered the Accademia and received a Roman Doctorate. In his first year, he received seventeen converts into the Church including Henry Bowden. He had hopes that Gladstone would submit also. Wiseman found in Manning one who shared his ideas exactly and in the Errington controversy he came more and more to the fore and within a few years was Provost of the Metropolitan Chapter at Westminster. The Pope shared Wiseman's enthusiasm for the neophyte and supported him unflinchingly in his conflict with the Chapter. His appointment as successor to Wiseman, though a surprise, was unhesitatingly accepted by his former colleagues whose loyalty he completely won. He was consecrated by Bishop Ullathorne at St. Mary's, Moorfields.

" I always heard a voice saying: ' Put him there, put him him there,' " said Pius IX. The appointment was clearly providential: for despite the unfortunate and misleading verdict of Purcell's biography and the misuse of the Talbot letters (happily corrected in our own time by Sir Shane Leslie) Manning has become a legend as the great Churchman of the full tide of the Victorian age. It was not until ten years after his appointment however that he was raised to the Sacred College of Cardinals with the title of SS. Andrew and Gregory on the Coelian Hill.

Lytton Strachey, of course, followed Purcell and in his brilliant, though malicious, essay in *Eminent Victorians* based his estimate of Manning on a false premise of his subject's unbridled ambition. In this he was wrong, and the impression he gave has been corrected in our own day by Mr. Christopher Sykes in his broadcast, *A New Judgment on Cardinal Manning*[6]. " Manning indeed knew the delights of great power and of State intrigue, but for all their strength these passions were small things beside his sincere and burning faith in Christian revelation and the sanctity of the Catholic Church. For that faith Manning was prepared to throw away present

---

[6] Broadcast, November 6, 1949: I am extremely grateful to Mr. Christopher Sykes for permission to use his script.

glory, glittering prospects, the admiration of his fellow men. He did this in 1851.''

In the intrigues which preceded Manning's appointment as Archbishop, on the other hand, it is clear beyond doubt that he sought and furthered his own cause. '' People who whitewash Manning cannot explain away the very evident, the suddenly apparent presence of ambition in this phase of his life to which he partly admitted. But his detractors make an equally serious error when they see him as a mere egotist. He had a high aim. He wanted the best man to succeed, by which he meant one who could unite Catholics in England and at the same time carry out the centralising policy of Rome, a man of singular and commanding ability, and Manning sincerely and rightly believed himself to be that man.'' Strachey had no appreciation of Manning's passionate heart, of his great love for the poor. '' He hardly notices that apart from his immense public work for the alleviation of poverty, there was a daily personal drudgery from which he never spared himself, even as a very old man.''

Endowed with high talents for administration, and a great knowledge of, and access to, the rich, Manning's primary attachment was to the poor. It remained so throughout his life and his greatest work was in their regard. His first thought was for their education and in his diocese he had 20,000 for whom no provision was made. He at once founded the Westminster Diocesan Education Fund and some fourteen years later he was able with pride and thanksgiving to say: '' The work for the poor children may be said to be done. . . . There is school room for all.'' But the conflict to maintain justice for the Catholic schools was unending. Forster's Bill of 1870 introducing the School Board, after some hesitation, was accepted by Manning with the support of most of the Bishops. He was blamed for accepting secularism, but as he wrote to Ullathorne: '' My meaning is the reverse. The Boards may destroy our lesser schools at once by reporting them to be insufficient or inefficient. The effect of this in London would be to destroy one half of our schools. By opening relations with the Board, as I have with the Privy Council, I hope to save these. By standing aloof from the Boards we should be exposed to the danger of their hostility.'' The situation was met by the establishment of a crisis fund under Lord Howard of Glossop which eventually provided accommodation for 70,000 children at a cost of £350,000.

In 1885, Manning was pressing Lord Salisbury for a revision of the 1870 Act. As a result an Education Commission was appointed and Manning made one of its members. From the first he dominated its proceedings and in 1887 was able to write: " The voluntary schools were never so strong. The Board School system has not reached its strength." In the end, the former were put on the rates. He wrote to Morley in 1891: " We have at this time no system of national education, because we have two, of which neither can ever become national or universal. We need new legislation and a higher law taking up the two systems that exist. I believe that the English people ought to educate themselves with such State aid as individuals require. The State did not create our commerce nor our Empire. The intelligence and will of the people did these things." In his Lenten Pastoral of 1890, he could say that nearly 24,000 children were on the books of his parochial schools and that during the previous quarter of a century 4,542 children had been provided for in the homes of the archdiocese.

Manning was less happy in the realisation of his schemes for adult and higher education. He had convinced Wiseman and himself that Catholics could not go to Oxford or Cambridge without jeopardising their faith. The sincerity of this conviction can scarcely be doubted but at the same time one cannot help feeling that it was reinforced by his fear and distrust of Newman. It was when the latter had actually purchased land in Oxford for the founding of an Oratory there that all Manning's opposition crystallised and won the day with Wiseman and with Rome. Catholics were forbidden to send their sons to Oxford and Cambridge and Newman's project was crushed. All the same, Manning felt bound to provide an alternative Catholic University and in 1874 opened the Catholic University College in Kensington. He envisaged an organisation under the Hierarchy with examiners drawn from existing Catholic colleges with degree-conferring faculties and a senate. The idea had obvious advantages from a Catholic point of view but it was wrecked for several reasons: Newman was left out of it; the Religious Orders who wielded a paramount influence educationally were excluded from it; the old Catholics never accepted it and frequently sought and obtained from their bishops and even from the Pope dispensations to send their sons to the older universities; the Bishops themselves stood aloof and were finally, on financial grounds, hostile. And so, although a good staff was collected under the headship of Mgr. Capel, a popular preacher caricatured by Disraeli in *Lothair,* Paley, Barff, Mivart and others, the scheme was squall and squabble to the end. In 1882, it was closed down, having cost the Cardinal £10,000. He was, after all, a realist and never more splendid than in defeat. His successor, supported by the Holy See, reversed the decision to proscribe the older universities and provided safeguards against the dangers to Faith. One can only feel that this was the wisest decision and unless it had been taken Catholic influence could never have leavened the English universities in the way that it has in the twentieth century.

The education of the clergy was a subject with which he was rightly primarily concerned. He caused many heartburnings by appointing an Irish Oblate, Dr. O'Callaghan, as Rector of the English College, Rome. The Bishops complained but blamed Mgr. Talbot who certainly played a considerable part in the affair. He had said that the College attracted more Italians than converts who consequently " went sight-seeing or became Jesuits." In 1869, Manning transferred the students in Theology from St. Edmund's College, Ware, to Hammersmith, where, on the site of an old convent, he built a new and Tridentine Seminary. Ware was not sufficiently ultramontane. Something like £37,000 was spent on this project under the Rectorship of Mgr. Weathers, who remained at the helm until the closing in 1892. He was made Auxiliary to Manning in 1872 and died in 1895. Hammersmith must also be considered a failure. With the arrival of the District Railway, the country suburb was completely urbanised; and with the formation of other diocesan seminaries the numbers became insufficient to warrant the expenditure involved. Cardinal Vaughan sold the premises to the Sacred Heart Nuns in the year of his accession.

Manning's great contribution to the formation of the

highest priestly ideals is to be found in his writings and austere example rather than in his policy. *The Eternal Priesthood* and *The Pastoral Office* are his supreme legacy. He was always impatient of the idea current in some places that perfection belonged to Religious alone. He found himself in conflict with the latter over many questions of policy and jurisdiction, and was largely responsible for the issuing of the famous Constitution *Romanos Pontifices* of 1881, which settled the matter for the whole Catholic world.

The development of the diocese for which Wiseman had done so much was maintained. A number of new missions were started and ten churches built, including the pro-Cathedral of Our Lady of Victories at Kensington and the Brompton Oratory. The number of clergy increased from 215 to 358. In all the affairs of the diocese, Manning depended greatly on Mgr. Gilbert, founder of the Providence Row Night Refuge, who was his Vicar General. In 1873, the Fourth Provincial Council of Westminster was held at St. Edmund's College. All Manning's injunctions to his clergy bore the stamp of his own high asceticism. A total abstainer himself, with regard to alcohol, he recommended the same attitude to all as the surest manifestation of temperance. He allowed others to drink wine at his own table, but refused to touch it himself even *in extremis*. He constantly deplored the theatre from Grand Opera to Music Hall. He held most rigorous views about Church music and tried unsuccessfully to exclude women from choirs. In 1886, he issued a private pastoral to his clergy deploring bazaars as a means to charity. It was against his principles to dine out: but he appeared occasionally at public banquets without participating in food or drink. Archbishop's House in Carlisle Place, " which could be mistaken for a Dissenting Chapel doing duty as a railway waiting-room, was the most mournful specimen of Bleak House, with surrounding chimneys instead of trees, and for a park the open yawn in the vista of bricks, devoted to the future Cathedral, which he called his farm. He was a Londoner of Londoners, and a Cardinal to Cockneydom '"[7]. He never went on holiday and rarely left Westminster[8]. It is not surprising to find that those

[7] Leslie, *Henry Edward Manning*.
[8] It was Manning who decided to build Westminster Cathedral in

who have difficulty in distinguishing asceticism from Puritanism, regarded the Cardinal as a Manichæan. In theory, he was nothing of the kind. The rigour of his life and example certainly captured the imagination of the ordinary Englishman of his age for whom Puritanism was a religious quality. At the same time, his asceticism was a source of inspiration to his own priests and people. A steady stream of conversions continued, reaching its high water mark between 1869 and 1874. A gradual flow continued throughout the century. The converts of the Manning period came from the professions rather than the senior common rooms: Hope-Scott, Bellasis and Monsell are typical. But there were a number of figures of public distinction: Lord Ripon, who was to be Viceroy of India, Lord Albemarle, who had belonged to the Royal Household, Lord Lyons, who was Ambassador in Paris. Manning encouraged Catholics to take their full part in public life and Sir William Shee was the first Catholic to be raised to the Bench since Stuart times. He was followed later by Russell of Killowen, Mathew and others. Lord Landaff was Home Secretary in the second Salisbury Government. The Church had clearly emerged from its penal shades. In 1882, the new diocese of Portsmouth was added to the Province of Westminster, by a division of Southwark.

Manning's most important contribution to the life of the Church was the leadership that he gave in social questions. In the nineteenth century, the working class as we know it to-day emerged from the Industrial Revolution and the consequent agitations. Manning, the realist, saw the implications of justice and charity in the new situation more clearly than most of his contemporaries and realised that it was necessary for the Church to enunciate principles as well as to occupy herself with the spiritual and corporal works of mercy. We find him, therefore, in the vanguard of the working class movement, from 1872 when he supported the agricultural labourers to the great and successful climax of his life in the settlement of the London Dock Strike in 1889. In this he won, not only " the primacy of England," but the confidence of a people who have since often turned to the Church in the

memory of Wiseman. He bought the site but it was left to his successor to build.

conflict against injustice. His success in this sphere made a deep impression on Pope Leo XIII and he certainly influenced the compilation and proclamation of the great social Encyclical *Rerum Novarum*. His close relationship also with Cardinal Gibbons in these matters established a strong common link between the Catholics of England and America. By the same token of his championing the causes of the oppressed, Manning had a constant sympathy for Catholic Ireland and spared no pains to urge upon governments the necessity of a just solution to the question.

Manning was by no means merely nationalistic in his interests. In the international sphere, apart from the labour question, he emerges as the great protagonist of the declaration of Papal Infallibility at the Vatican Council of 1870. The story of his pre-eminence in those deliberations is too well-known to need expansion. On his return to England, he wrote elucidations and explanations which did much to remove misunderstandings. It is not surprising, in view of his international rôle, to find that the Conclave which elected Leo XIII in 1878 contained elements which supported the Archbishop of Westminster's own candidature.

Manning's memory is marred by one consideration: the great and perpetual rift between himself and Newman. Malice has exaggerated the fundamental incompatibility of the two great converts of the nineteenth century. On the other hand, it would be unhistorical to deny it; and if we may regret the over-sensitiveness of Newman, we must regret still more the thwarting activities of Manning in his regard. In his defence, we can say that he was convinced throughout of his own propriety and no Prince of the Church has ever paid a greater tribute to another than Manning did in his Funeral Oration for Newman.

"The impetus for the dreadful quarrel between Manning and Newman," says Christopher Sykes, "did not come, as Strachey alleges, from Manning's jealousy. It came from Ward's foolish distrust of his old friend." Manning was not a jealous person. Indeed it was his great hope to settle party differences in England altogether. But he became an extremist and the champion of the New Ultramontanes through the same influence which had begun the estrangement from Newman.

Ward is the villain of the piece.   The proceedings of the
Vatican Council in which Manning spared no pains to attain
what he considered the necessary outcome brought the conflict
to a head. And his attempt to deter Leo XIII from conferring
upon Newman the Cardinal's Hat was the unfortunate but
logical conclusion of the battle. In both cases Newman was
the victor. The wording of the definition of Papal infallibility
was extremely modest, and he was created a Cardinal. There
was never a real reconciliation between the two men. There
was room for two such dynamic influences in the Universal
Church. England was too small for them to flourish side by
side.

Cardinal Manning died on January 14th, 1892.
Herbert Vaughan was saying Mass. Dr. Johnson gave him
absolution. Dr. Gasquet closed his eyes. When Leo XIII
heard of it he said: " A great light of the Church has gone
out."

III

There seems little doubt in the mind of contemporaries
that there was only one obvious choice as successor to Cardinal
Manning. Herbert Vaughan had played his part under Wiseman and Manning in the development of the diocese of
Westminster and Catholic life in general.

Born in Gloucester in 1832, the eldest son of the
Vaughans of Courtfield, the new Archbishop sprang from an
old Catholic family of the highest integrity. His mother, a
convert, who became an ideal Catholic matriarch, had the joy
of seeing five of her seven sons become priests and all her
daughters nuns. Herbert Vaughan was at school at Stonyhurst
and went on to the Jesuit College of Brugelette in Belgium.

At the age of 19, having decided to become a priest
and to devote himself to the conversion of Wales, he began his
studies at the Accademia in Rome where he met Manning.
His health was unsatisfactory and by special dispensation he
was ordained priest at the age of 22 and at once appointed by
Wiseman as Vice-Rector of St. Edmund's College, Ware. His
magnificent presence caused him to be regarded in later years
as the handsomest man in England. " Slim of figure, his fearless blue eyes, aquiline nose, and firm set mouth, made him

in appearance an ideal Sir Galahad, setting forth in quest of the Holy Grail "[9]. Those who met him only casually considered him cold and aloof. In reality he was impetuous and warm-hearted and all his life possessed an outlook of the highest spirituality.

In 1860 he broached to Cardinal Wiseman an idea that had been developing in his mind for some time to establish in England a great Missionary College. Wiseman assented and the result was that in 1866 after a begging tour in America the College of St. Joseph at Mill Hill was opened. It was at this time that he met, through Manning, Lady Herbert of Lea who was to be the mother of his new institution and the recipient of his own deepest confidence. He had a simple devotion to the saints, especially St. Joseph and St. Peter, who seem to have aided him in all his projects in a more than ordinary manner.

His experiences in America, so magnificently unfolded in the biography by Snead-Cox, made him realise the importance of the Press and in 1868 he bought *The Tablet* which he personally edited through many stormy years. Later, too, the *Dublin Review* passed into his possession through W. G. Ward. In 1872 he was consecrated Bishop of Salford, where he brought new life to that diocese in a variety of ways and prepared himself by his experience in all sorts of projects for the wider field of Westminster. Twenty years later, and entirely against his will, he was appointed successor to Manning and was enthroned in the Pro-Cathedral at Kensington. He asked the Holy Father that the Sacred Pallium might be received in London[10] so that the ceremony should remind the English people of the apostolic source of his jurisdiction. In less than a year Leo XIII raised him to the Sacred College with the title of SS. Andrew and Gregory on the Coelian Hill.

Like his predecessor, he was at once confronted with the question of education. He saw that it was important to establish a definite policy with regard to this matter and accordingly brought into being The Voluntary Schools Association with which he had already experimented in the Diocese of Salford. This body asked for a measure of relief for all Voluntary

[9] Wilfrid Ward.
[10] At Brompton Oratory.

Schools and depended considerably on the co-operation of the interested Anglicans. Unfortunately it came at a time when the relationship was somewhat acute on account of the dispute concerning Anglican Orders. The Act which was passed in 1897 failed to admit the principle of equality, though something was gained in the way of relieving the financial burden. Cardinal Vaughan developed the just Catholic claims in the matter and was so successful in convincing public opinion thereof that the further Act of 1902 established the bedrock principle of equality.

As regards the education of the clergy, Vaughan reversed the policy of his predecessor. He did not consider the College at Hammersmith either practical or desirable. On the other hand, when it became necessary to close it, he had no intention of returning the Theological students to St. Edmund's. He thought first of sending them to Wonersh which was, however, a Tridentine Seminary in the strict sense and therefore diocesan. He turned accordingly to the idea of making Oscott a central seminary, whither all the Bishops might send their Theological students and with large numbers involved, the highest possible standard of education could be maintained. He had much difficulty in trying to convince the Bishops in this matter; but he was supported by Rome and in 1897 Oscott became *de jure* as well as *de facto* the common seminary for the dioceses of Westminster, Birmingham, Clifton, Newport, Portsmouth, Northampton, and what was then the Vicariate of Wales. Cardinal Vaughan's successor again reversed the policy and it would perhaps be true to say that the central seminary idea has never had a fair trial in this country. Its advantages are undoubtedly great. It is true that the Council of Trent required each Bishop to provide his own diocesan seminary. But it also made the proviso that poor dioceses might combine their resources. Cardinal Vaughan had long held the opinion that no diocese in England came within the rules which made it obligatory to establish a separate seminary. " Proficiency," he said, " will not come by multiplying theological seminaries, but rather by increasing the number of their students, raising the standard of their studies, and prolonging their years of culture and training." The central seminary, by pooling the resources of several dioceses, is in a position to provide the highest standard of teaching, and enables students of all parts to meet one another thus obviating a restricted outlook. At the same time, it does away with the enormous expense of maintaining separate establishments. The obvious disadvantage is multiplicity of control. All the demands of every interested diocesan cannot be met. Yet for nearly three centuries Douay was the central seminary for the whole of this country and the President, appointed by the Pope, worked harmoniously with the Vicars Apostolic. In Europe to-day the value of regional as against small diocesan seminaries is clearly realised.

In regard to the higher education of the laity, Vaughan had to face the failure of the Catholic University at Kensington and the prohibition which still applied to Oxford and Cambridge. After many consultations with the Bishops and leading laymen he came to the conclusion that the experience of thirty years had shown that Oxford and Cambridge did not present to well-trained Catholic young men the proximate occasions to the loss of faith and morals which were the grounds of objection laid down by the Holy See. Accordingly in 1895 the Bishops agreed to petition the Holy See for the withdrawal of the veto provided that there should be a resident chaplain and that instructions on Catholic philosophy and Church history should be given. Leo XIII acceded to their request. The Universities Board was established and St. Edmund's House at Cambridge was opened for ecclesiastical students.

In 1894 Cardinal Vaughan organised a Religious Census for the diocese and in 1896 appointed a board of enquiry into causes of leakage which were found to centre largely round problems of destitution. He came into conflict with Dr. Barnado when he discovered that charity was given on the one condition that the Catholic faith of the children was sacrificed. The only solution was the provision of a Home for every Catholic child who required it and accordingly he founded in 1899 the Crusade of Rescue. In 1901 this was amalgamated with an older Society and Homes were founded under the direction of Fr. Bans in which girls as well as boys could be housed. The motto of the new Society, given by the Cardinal himself, was: " No Catholic child who is really destitute, or whose faith is in danger, and who cannot be otherwise provided for, is ever refused."

Meanwhile the development of the diocese went on apace. Fourteen new churches were built in London and twenty in the Home Counties. The number of clergy increased from 358 to 448, Monsignor Michael Barry had succeeded Monsignor Gilbert as Vicar General and Provost of the Chapter in 1895. Bishop Brindle was Auxiliary to the Cardinal from 1899 until 1901 when he was made Bishop of Nottingham.

The Cardinal was dragged most unwillingly into a controversy relating to the whole position of Anglicanism *vis-à-vis* the Catholic Church. It was about this time that the late Lord Halifax, forever a protagonist of the Catholicising school in the Church of England, met the Abbé Portal and filled him with enthusiasm for the idea of corporate reunion. The Abbé visited this country but did not see the Cardinal and it soon became clear that representations to Rome were being made in the matter without the cognisance of the English Catholic Hierarchy. It is impossible for us to enter into the controversies which led up to the declaration of the invalidity of Anglican Orders in the Bull *Apostolicæ Curæ* of 1896. The Cardinal was assisted throughout these deliberations by two men of great scholarship, Abbot Gasquet and Monsignor Moyes. The part he played has been greatly misunderstood but one has only to read Snead-Cox's full account of the controversy to realise that he acted in the only way possible in a matter fraught with endless complications. As Metropolitan it was his duty to convey to Rome the feelings and judments of himself and the Bishops in a matter wherein they should have been consulted long before the affair had assumed such spectacular proportions.

The greatest event of the reign of Cardinal Vaughan was undoubtedly the erection of Westminster Cathedral whose first stone was laid in 1895. Cardinal Manning had already obtained a site and before his death managed to buy the old county prison of Tothill Fields whose position was even more suitable. Cardinal Vaughan came to Westminster and resolved to build at once. "He thought of a Cathedral primarily, perhaps, as a House of Prayer, but also in a very real sense as a living organism from which should radiate all sorts of spiritual influence. To use a phrase which was often on his lips during the last years of his life, he wanted ' a live Cathedral.' He wanted a Cathedral which should be the head and heart of the life of the Church in England, and the vivifying centre of its spirit and worship '"[11]. But he had other ideas as well. He wanted it to be a place in which the full Liturgy of the Church should be celebrated and the Divine Office publicly recited or sung. He wanted it to be above all a centre of worship and suitable for congregational use. As to its architecture, he would avoid the Gothic and the Classical, in view of the proximity of the Abbey and St. Paul's; and so Joseph Bentley was commissioned to design a Byzantine edifice. From the point of view of funds the whole matter was put into the hands of St. Joseph.

Money began to pour in and the Cardinal himself was tireless in asking for donations for this great purpose. Monsignor Fenton, now Auxiliary Bishop, was sent to Italy and brought back a gift of £1,000 from Leo XIII. Father Kenelm Vaughan was sent to beg in Spain and then in Spanish America. He was able to bring back more than £18,000 for the Blessed Sacrament Chapel. Different individuals were invited to be responsible for the building of various parts, and although the work was delayed from time to time, it was never for want of money. At the beginning of 1898 the foundations had been laid and the walls had risen to a height of nearly 30 feet. A year later, these stood at 85 feet and after ten million bricks had been laid the walls waited only for their crown of domes. In 1902 before the Cathedral was completed Bentley died and the Cardinal wrote of him as follows: " The Cathedral will be his monument. For myself, I have a gratification in the thought that I gave him a free hand. Having laid down certain conditions as to size, space, chapels, and style, I left the rest to him. He offered me the choice between a vaulted roof and one with saucer domes; I chose the latter. He wished to build two campaniles; I said one would be enough for me. For the rest, he had a free hand '"[12]. The Cathedral was opened for the first time for public service in June, 1903, in the presence of the dead body of its founder.

[1] Snead-Cox, *Life of Cardinal Vaughan*, Vol. 2.
[2] *Ibid.*

It had been the Cardinal's idea to entrust the singing of the Divine Office to Benedictine Monks and negotiations with the English Benedictines had been initiated. For various reasons they did not fructify. For this the blame has frequently been laid at the door of the English Benedictines. In justice to them, we cannot do better than quote the account of the negotiations given by Abbot Hicks in his *Life of Abbot Ford*[13]: " Prior Ford (of Downside) signified his readiness to fall in with the Cardinal's proposal, but he explained that if several monks were to live in a monastery attached to the Cathedral it would be vitally necessary for them to have some active work to do in the parish." " Only a small percentage," he said, " of the young and robust men competent to carry out efficiently the choral duties of the Cathedral would be able to spend the rest of the day in quiet study in their cells." Unfortunately the Cardinal was unwilling to hand over the parish to the Benedictines, but he did not at once make his views clear to Prior Ford. Instead of replying to the Prior in this sense, he wrote to the Abbot of Solesmes enquiring as to the possibilities of his taking over the Cathedral duties. The Abbot of Solesmes answered that he would be ready to take responsibility, but only on the understanding that several monks of the English Congregation were lent to him to do at least half the work, and that they should be his subjects while at Westminster. The Cardinal now felt that he had found a solution, and he was both surprised and grieved when Prior Ford pointed out to him the many objections, theoretical and practical, to such a proposal. In consequence of all this, the original scheme came to nought, and the present arrangement of a choir of the secular clergy took its place. For this purpose, he obtained permission from Rome to increase the number of Canons of the Metropolitan Chapter from twelve to eighteen, and make provision for a body of eighteen Cathedral Chaplains. A choir school was also founded and on May 7th, the even of the Ascension, 1902, the Divine Office was sung for the first time in the Cathedral Hall. " Whatever sentimental regrets may be felt," writes Abbot Hicks, " on historical grounds, that the Benedictine monks are not again at Westminster, no one can deny that the Divine Office and

[13] Published by Sands and Co.

the Liturgical services are carried out in the Cathedral to-day in a manner comparable to that which obtained in the great abbeys of England before the Reformation.''

Cardinal Vaughan's high conception of Liturgical worship has been made a lasting influence through the adhesion in the main to his plans for the Cathedral. He was a man of deep traditional spirituality and it was his custom to spend an hour every night in prayer before the Blessed Sacrament. His book *The Young Priest* was his legacy to his clergy and his outlook had less rigour than that of his predecessor. Many works of spiritual and material importance in the life of the Church began in his time: The Catholic Truth Society, The Converts' Aid Society, The Catholic Social Union, and others. He died on the Feast of the Sacred Heart, 1903, and after the stately Requiem at Westminster was buried in the garden of his beloved Missionary College at St. Joseph's, Mill Hill. His memorial in the Cathedral is the Vaughan Chantry where the Cardinal's Hat hangs over a recumbent statue. The whole building is his epitaph. His death marks the end of an epoch of gigantic personalities and already the " lines of connection of the See of Westminster with the general English life were becoming primarily administrative and philanthropic, concerned with war and peace, the relations between England and the Vatican and national questions ''[14].

IV

Leo XIII died a month after Cardinal Vaughan, and one of the first acts of his successor, the saintly Pius X, was the translation of Bishop Bourne, then in his forty-third year and Bishop of Southwark, to the See of Westminster.

Francis Bourne was born at Clapham in 1861 of an English father who was a Civil Servant and an Irish mother. From birth he was attached to the capital and profoundly English in his sympathies. At the age of eight he was sent to Ushaw, which in those days was a hard school for young boys. Eight years later he went to St. Edmund's College, and at the end of his philosophical studies, for a short interlude, tried his vocation with the Dominicans at Woodchester. In 1880 he

[14] Mathew, *Catholicism in England.*

proceeded to the college at Hammersmith and in the following year went to St. Sulpice in Paris. He ever afterwards regarded his two years there as one of the greatest graces of his life. " The Sulpician recollection and devotion remained with him always and a sympathetic understanding of French Catholicism "[15]. He completed his studies at Louvain and in June 1884 was ordained priest at Clapham. After gaining parochial experience at Blackheath, Sheerness and Mortlake, he was sent in 1889 to Henfield and West Grinstead, where he began the foundation of the Southwark Diocesan Seminary which in the following year was moved to Wonersh[16]. In 1896 he was consecrated Bishop of Epiphania and Coadjutor to Dr. Butt, Bishop of Southwark. Although he was a young man when he was translated to Westminster, Bishop Bourne had already gained great experience in all spheres of priestly work.

Of middle height and with hair becoming white " above a pleasant, frank and rather heavy countenance, he had a dignity of bearing which never left him and he was perhaps seen at his best in some of those great ceremonies in the magnificent setting of Westminster Cathedral[17] which he carried through so perfectly "[18].

He was at once confronted, as his predecessors had been, with the question of education and his consistent policy over a long period established a Catholic attitude to the question which, general speaking, encountered success. There had been much dissatisfaction on the part of anti-Catholics with the Act of 1902, and with the catchphrase " Rome on the Rates " Birrell, Runciman and McKenna had attempted to change its provisions. A great demonstration in the Albert Hall called by the Archbishop and supported by the Duke of Norfolk and other leading laymen rallied Catholics of every political creed to the defence of the schools. Archbishop Bourne's tenacity resulted in the rout of his opponents in 1908.

---

[15] Mathew, *Catholicism in England*.

[16] Throughout his life he was to be noted for his devotion to the Salesian ideals. At Blackheath and West Grinstead, he had had to do with orphanages and had learnt much from Don Bosco with whom he had stayed at Turin.

[17] It was he who appointed Mgr. Canon Martin Howlett Administrator of the Cathedral, a post which he filled with distinction for over forty years. He died in 1949.

[18] Mathew, *Catholicism in England*.

During the rest of his reign this conflict over the schools was to be maintained in a greater or lesser degree. In 1929, the Hierarchy had again to reiterate Catholic principles. Standing firmly on the principles of parental rights he maintained a strong and united position and whilst welcoming educational reform in its best sense he was constantly opposed to anything which would deprive parents of their rights or the Church of her responsibility.

Archbishop Bourne was primarily concerned with the education of his future priests. Almost immediately he had decided that all the diocesan students should receive their full course at St. Edmund's College, Ware. Since the closing of Hammersmith they had been sent for their theological studies chiefly to Oscott or Valladolid. The Archbishop set to work at once on the enlarging of St. Edmund's and in 1904 the new Divines wing of the College, eventually called Allen Hall after the Founder of Douai, was opened. A shrine chapel was also built to house the relic of St. Edmund of Canterbury. There were now 25 Divines and nearly 200 lay boys at the College. Ten years later Allen Hall was burnt down but it was soon rebuilt on a grander scale by the ever patient Cardinal. The gradual improvement of St. Edmund's was his life-long pre-occupation. Just before the First Great War " he built new dormitories and classrooms for the lay boys, as well as an airy and handsome refectory for the philosophers and theologians of the Divines side "[19]. Ultimately as an offering of thanksgiving for the protection of his diocese during the war, he built the Galilee Chapel in which he is buried.[20] He also made what he called a return to old English ideals by recreating the school department of the college on the House system, reserving the old central college building for the residence of the Church boys, and setting up Houses for the lay boys under House Masters. He did not favour the idea of sending boys to the English College, Rome, but preferred that they should go to the Eternal City after ordination for higher studies.

Cardinal Bourne has been criticised for his concentra-

[19] Oldmeadow, *Francis Cardinal Bourne*.
[20] At the time of the Golden Jubilee of his Priesthood in 1934, he panelled the walls of the Sanctuary in the College Chapel, laid a parquet floor and marbled the steps.

tion on St. Edmund's to the detriment of provision for primary education in the new suburbs. There seems to be some justification for this. Before Cardinal Hinsley's time, there was no Diocesan Schools Commission and educational enterprise was left entirely to parish priests who received little or no direction in the matter, though when they initiated schemes they received encouragement and sometimes financial support. It is quite clear now that in Cardinal Bourne's time schools should have been built at Camden Town, Copenhagen Street, Hammersmith (St. Augustine's), Hampstead (Kilburn), Harrow Road, Kentish Town, Stoke Newington, Stroud Green, and Tollington Park. The deficiencies in Middlesex and the Hertfordshire towns cannot be laid so clearly at his door since their development took place largely in the 'thirties and his active life ended in 1932, although he lived on for another two years. But between 1930 and 1940 there should also have been schools at Dollis Hill, Ealing, Golders Green, Kenton, Kingsbury Green, Palmers Green, and New Southgate.

There is some criticism also of his concentration on the " St. Edmund's ideal " and questions are asked as to its realisation and value. It is thought by many to-day that he made a great mistake in departing from Cardinal Vaughan's idea of a central seminary, and that by pouring all his resources into St. Edmund's, he narrowed the outlook and potentialities of many students who might otherwise have been sent to Oscott or Rome. The School at St. Edmund's has scarcely become " The Catholic Winchester " that the Cardinal so earnestly desired. On the other hand, there is much to be said for the study, piety and learning of the Edmundian training.

Anti-Catholic feeling had to be encountered in spheres other than education. Great resentment was aroused over the marriage of the Princess Victoria Eugenie (Ena) to Alfonso XIII and her reception into the Church. But greater still was the feeling over the Eucharistic Congress of 1908. Cardinal Vannutelli was the Papal Legate for the series of splendid functions which surpassed in solemnity and devotion anything that had happened in England since the Reformation. By the intervention of the Prime Minister, Asquith, the Procession of the Blessed Sacrament through the streets had to be abandoned, and Archbishop Bourne in deference to authority gave orders for its cancellation. The nation-wide Press was on the side of the Church and *The Spectator* wrote: " The honours of the controversy rest with the Archbishop of West-minster, while the Home Secretary's (Herbert Gladstone's) letter is a lamentable exhibition of the abnegation of responsi-bility." Throughout his life Archbishop Bourne developed a singularly harmonious relationship with the Government. The " silent Cardinal " was always dignified, never irresponsible. He could speak when need be: never without necessity, and this was increasingly appreciated and stood the Catholic Church in this country in the greatest good stead. His happy relations with the first Lord Baden-Powell and his encourage-ment of scouting for Catholics reflect his realisation of civic values and ideals of service in the Commonwealth of nations. With regard to Anglicanism, his attitude was much the same as that of his predecessors, and later on, in the " Malines Conver-sations," he found himself in almost the identical position of Cardinal Vaughan at the time of *Apostolicæ Curæ*.

On October 28th, 1911, the Apostolic Constitution *Si Qua Est,* rearranged England ecclesiastically into three Provinces, making Liverpool and Birmingham metropolitan in addition to Westminster. The last-named retained North-ampton, Nottingham, Portsmouth and Southwark as suffragan sees. (Brentwood was added in 1917 on its creation with Mgr. Ward of St. Edmund's as its first Bishop.) At the same time, certain new distinctions of pre-eminence were granted to the Archbishop of Westminster so that unity in government and policy might be preserved. It was decreed that he was to be permanent Chairman at the meeting of the Bishops of England and Wales; that he should take rank above the other two Archbishops; that he should enjoy the privilege of wearing the pallium, of occupying the throne and of having his cross carried before him throughout the two countries; and that in all dealings with the supreme civil authority, he should in person represent the entire episcopate of England and Wales. Great progress had been made since 1850. As Archbishop Bourne himself pointed out: " The two new provinces each possess more churches and larger bodies of clergy than were contained in the whole country in 1850: while the third and smallest province falls but very little short of the same degree of expansion." In Westminster alone the number of priests had been multiplied by five, the number of churches by four, and the Catholic population had been increased by one hundred and fifty thousand.

In November of the same year, 1911, the Archbishop of Westminster was raised to the Sacred College with the title of St. Pudenziana which had been Wiseman's. He was to take his place in two Conclaves: that which elected Benedict XV in the year of the outbreak of War and that which chose Pius XI in 1922. The Cardinalate gave him a new and recognised ascendancy in his own country and enabled him to emerge as a great spiritual leader during the War. His love for France stood him in good stead also. The establishment of the Legation to the Vatican in 1915 and the whole course of the relations between England and Rome was partly his work. " He laboured without stint for the bodily as well as the spiritual welfare of the soldiers and sailors and their dependants "[21]. A round of visits began not only to camps in the homeland but across the Channel to the fighting front. After Jutland, he was for some days the guest of Admiral Jellicoe. In 1918, before the end of the War, he wrote his Pastoral on the New Order inculcating the principles of the Encyclicals and the conditions for a just and lasting peace. " Peace without justice," he said, " is not worth having. . . . Human nature is still the same, the old passions and sins may easily revive and may work among conquerors and conquered the old prolific evils which ultimately give rise to civil contest and war of nations. The world is not at rest. Even within our own borders, there are portents of danger." Indeed they were many: the unsolved Irish Question, Zionism, unemployment and moral issues.

Cardinal Bourne has sometimes been regarded as unsympathetic in relation to Ireland. This is based on three main charges: that he did not share the enthusiasm of the Bishop of Southwark for the cause of Terence MacSwiney; that he remained aloof in the affair of Archbishop Mannix; and that he allowed and participated in the Requiem at Westminster Cathedral for the English Catholic victims of " the Dublin murders."

[21] Oldmeadow, *Francis Cardinal Bourne.*

The hunger-strike of the Lord Mayor of Cork, imprisoned on a political charge at Brixton, raised a doubtful moral point. Was he committing suicide or sacrificing his life for a glorious ideal? The Cardinal did not see the answer as clearly as Dr. Amigo; but anyhow, it had not happened in his diocese. Archbishop Mannix was prevented by the English Government from visiting Ireland after journeying all the way from Australia. The Cardinal stood aloof in this matter also and avoided a meeting which would have been perhaps embarrassing to both parties. When he was accused of conspiring with the Government against the Archbishop, he issued a statement in which he said: " I desire it to be known that neither directly nor indirectly was I consulted in any way on this matter." With regard to the Requiem, as Mr. Oldmeadow says: " To have allowed the Catholic Three to be trundled off to suburban cemeteries, unwept, unhonoured and unsung . . . while their comrades-in-arms, the Protestant Nine, were being wept honoured and sung in the Abbey would have been ' taking a side ' indeed."

The Cardinal was a Home Ruler in the modified sense. He always wanted the widest possible self-government for Ireland compatible with the maintenance of the link with the Crown and the safeguarding of the essential defences of the Empire. How far these provisos were justified is another question and beyond our scope. But he certainly had all the moral teaching of the Church behind him in the condemnation of secret organisations and the excesses on both sides. And he spared no pains in doing all he could to obtain a just and peaceful settlement of the question. There is no doubt, however, that his attitude was always coloured by his belief in the Empire: " The protection of the Empire," he said, " is as important for Ireland as for us: and it is as important for civilisation, I think, as for us both. Given *that*, I am for Irish self-government as far as the Irish people themselves desire it. I want England to trust Ireland and Ireland to trust England, for I love them both as I love justice and peace." He was present at the Eucharistic Congress in Dublin in 1932. He received a great reception: for after all he was a Prince of the Church and the son of an Irish mother.

In the wider field there was much for which to be

thankful.   Apart from its obvious defects which a man of Cardinal Bourne's perspicacity could not fail to recognise, the League of Nations was at work. The number of conversions to Catholicism had greatly increased in the war period and in 1922 G. K. Chesterton was received into the Church. The Cardinal himself gave thanks for the Silver Jubilee of his episcopal consecration in 1921, and the Society of St. Augustine was founded to assist with the maintenance of Archbishop's House. The building of churches and some schools went on apace throughout his reign. The Cardinal Vaughan School had been started. The number of clergy had increased also. In his book, *Ecclesiastical Training,* Cardinal Bourne left them a legacy, as his predecessors had done, on his own ideals of the priesthood. Apart from *Occasional Sermons,* it was his only publication. Sulpician in its inspiration, it reflected the mature conclusions of a spacious mind which had rated priestly formation before any other episcopal work.

In 1926, from the pulpit of Westminster Cathedral, he condemned in no uncertain terms the General Strike for which, he contended, there was no moral justification. Speaking on May 9th at High Mass he said: " The time through which we are passing is of exceptional character, and the present strike is of a nature quite unlike the many others which have preceded it. It is necessary that Catholics should have clearly before their minds the moral principles which are involved: —

" 1.   There is no moral justification for a general strike of this character. It is a direct challenge to a lawfully constituted authority and inflicts, without adequate reason, immense discomfort and injury on millions of our fellow-countrymen. It is therefore a sin against the obedience which we owe to God, who is the source of that authority; and against the charity and brotherly love which are due to our brethren.

" 2.   All are bound to uphold and assist the Government, which is the lawfully constituted authority of the country, and represents, therefore, in its own appointed sphere, the authority of God Himself.

" 3.   As God alone can guide both rulers and ruled to a wise and successful understanding, it is the duty of all to pray earnestly and constantly for His guidance, that the day may be hastened when these unhappy conflicts shall terminate in a just and lasting peace." He was an authoritarian in the right sense, and his action won admiration from many quarters, though " it also caused a lessening of his popularity among those big Catholic town populations which were attached to the Labour interest "[22].

The Cardinal's journeys were always undertaken with a high sense of responsibility, and it would be impossible to over emphasise the salutary effects of his visit to Canada in 1910. In 1918-19, he had made a tour of the Near East. In his own words: " The purpose of the journey was two-fold—official so far as the visit to the Catholics in the Navy were concerned; quite unofficial, but perhaps no less useful on that account, to Church and State in all its other aspects. . . . It was felt by the competent authorities, at home and abroad, that the presence and passage of a British Subject holding high ecclesiastical rank through countries in which the problems of the future were likely to be specially acute would make clear the relations between the British Government and the Catholic Church at the present day; would allay groundless fears; and might gather at first hand information more readily given, perhaps to one coming in this two-fold character . . . for both Church and State "[23]. The national and international importance of the Archbishop of Westminster was never more fully recognised by a British Government than on this occasion. Doubtless the recognition was opportunist. There was great fear on the French side that British post-war policy in the Near East would seek to bolster up the advance of Protestantism at the expense of Catholicism and Orthodoxy. The Cardinal's official tour, accompanied with full honours, was meant to allay this fear. Perhaps he allowed himself to be too closely associated with the mind of the Government in all this. There is no doubt however that he was absolutely convinced of the Government's complete integrity. Speaking in French at Cairo, he said: " There is one word in your address of welcome which is not acceptable. You have spoken of my country as a Protestant State. . . . I would rather say that our Government is a Christian Government. . . . From my own ex-

[22] Mathew, *Catholicism in England.*
[23] Oldmeadow, *Francis Cardinal Bourne.*

perience I can declare that there is nothing to fear. One may openly be a Catholic, a practising and even a militant Catholic."

In 1927, he visited Poland; in 1931 he was Papal Legate at the St. Joan celebrations in France[23a]; in 1932 he attended the Eucharistic Congress in Dublin. He was to be Papal Legate for the second time at Buckfast. Perhaps the apogee of his career was reached at the magnificent celebrations held to commemorate the centenary of Catholic Emancipation in 1929.

In 1933, ill-health made itself apparent and the Cardinal had to curtail his engagements. In 1934, however, he was able to celebrate the Golden Jubilee of his priesthood and opened the New Chapter House at Westminster. The new pulpit in the Cathedral also commemorates this occasion. His last great act as spiritual leader of his country was to be present at Walsingham on August 19th, 1934, when the Shrine of Our Lady was set up once more in the Slipper Chapel. It was an occasion which rejoiced his heart and a fitting conclusion to a great episcopal reign. His love for Our Lady of Walsingham and the English Martyrs is indicative of his essential patriotism. He died peacefully in the early hours of new year's day, 1935. The memorable Requiem was held in the Cathedral and burial took place in the Galilee Chapel at St. Edmund's College, where the Hat now hangs.

The late Viscount Fitzalan of Derwent spoke of him: "To understand the Cardinal, one had to be on intimate terms with him. He had a reserve which sometimes gave an impression almost of coldness, but to an individual in a time of trial or sorrow he would unbend with an overwhelming rush of sympathy. . . . His rather cold and calm reserve concealed a profound spirituality which was known to very few and meant that this close communion with his God was the chief feature of his life." In official circles he was appreciated for his frank sincerity. "You always know where you are with Bourne" was an expression often to be heard. The very sad lack of a comprehensive and understanding biography of this great priest is an indication, not that the subject is deficient, but

[23a] He had been present at the Orleans celebrations two years before (1929).

that biographical capability in the world of letters has sadly deteriorated. His greatest tribute comes from the hearts of the many priests of his diocese who loved and trusted him as a great father in God.

V

On March 25th, 1935, Pius XI translated Archbishop Hinsley to Westminster. The appointment caused no little surprise as the new Metropolitan was in his seventieth year and relatively unknown in his own country. Yet the events of the next few years were to show that no more distinctively English a character could have been chosen.

Arthur Hinsley was born in Yorkshire in 1865. Educated at Ushaw and the English College, Rome, he returned later to the former as a Professor and to the latter as Rector from 1917-1930. He was also a curate for a time in the West Riding and headmaster of St. Bede's School at Bradford. After a quarrel with Bishop Gordon of Leeds, he spent twelve years in the Southwark diocese at Amberley, Sutton Place and Sydenham, until 1917. As Rector of the Venerabile, he was made first Visitor and then Apostolic Delegate in Africa, and consecrated Bishop in 1926 (being raised to the rank of a titular Archbishop in 1930). On his return from Africa, he was made a Canon of St. Peter's and everyone thought that his career had terminated. It had yet to reach its zenith. In December 1937, when he had been Archbishop of Westminster for just over two years, he was raised to the Sacred College with the title of St. Susanna.

" It should not be invidious to say that no English Cardinal since Cardinal Manning has made a deeper impression on his own community and on the national life "[24]. If this judgment is not certainly true of the former, it is undoubtedly so of the latter. What was the secret of Cardinal Hinsley's emergence as the greatest of all religious leaders in Britain in so short a span? It must be put down first and foremost to his distinctively English character. He had all the warmth of northern origins, the downrightness and brogue of a Yorkshire-

[24] *Daily Telegraph,* March 18, 1943.

man, a native simplicity and straightforwardness, a deep Faith, an overwhelming humility coupled with a mastering sense of duty. He was the blunt Englishman possessed of a great innate dignity divorced from all attachment to pomp or ceremony. His sincerity was unquestionable. He believed in the justice of all British administration. He was the perfect Christian patriot. He had in addition absorbed a wealth of experience of all kinds, in the purely pastoral sphere of parochial administration, in secular and ecclesiastical education, above all, perhaps, in Africa. He loved companionship and especially that of the young. He was impulsive and sometimes unguarded in his pronouncements[25]. Even these frailties served to endear him still more to his fellow countrymen; for he was a real person. But above all, he had a deep-rooted devotion to the Person of Christ and the English Martyrs who inspired his shield.

Secondly, the circumstances of his reign as Archbishop afforded full scope to the play of his qualities. War intensified and clarified all his predilections and called him out of a circumscribed field to be a great spiritual leader for the whole land, and " probably the best loved Cardinal England has ever had "[26]. He cared nothing for all this except in so far as it might mean a new advance for Christian and Catholic principles.

For the first four years at Westminster, Archbishop Hinsley concentrated on the administration of his diocese. He had come at a disadvantage compared with all his predecessors. He knew little of ecclesiastical affairs in England, apart from his contacts with the English Hierarchy at the Venerabile. He knew none of his clergy. To remedy this, he at once set out to visit them in their own homes and to establish personal contacts. It was not easy for a man of his age and his memory for faces was not all that it had once been. They liked his informality and approachability but they could never feel that he had his finger on the pulse of their activities. The long and fatherly reign of Cardinal Bourne had made it difficult for anyone to take his place in their particular sphere. Arch-

---

[25] The reference to the Holy Father in his sermon at Golders Green on October 13, 1935, during the Abyssinian War is an example.
[26] *Daily Mail*, March 18, 1943.

bishop Hinsley ordered a General Mission throughout the diocese in which he participated to the full. He sought advice in everything and from many quarters. There was no autocracy. Perhaps he did not always sufficiently realise that bureaucracy has its dangers too. " In addition to the Diocesan Council, which advises on clerical appointments and general affairs, he inaugurated a Schools Commission and a Finance Board. There was set up, also, a considerable number of minor Boards to advise and guide the Archbishop. Moral Welfare, youth, Catholic Action, art, music—every aspect of diocesan activity, in fact, provided a sufficient reason for forming a committee usually composed both of priests and laymen "[27]. From the Autumn of 1939, when the Cardinal became more and more occupied with national and international affairs, the routine work of the diocese was increasingly delegated to the Auxiliary Bishops and the Vicars General.

The question of education was to the fore again. " The fate of Catholic schools remained the Cardinal's chief preoccupation to the end of his days. It is permissible to suspect that his fear of impending injustice may have hastened his end "[28]. And this despite his conviction that Catholics would receive justice if only Englishmen could be made to understand the true issues. He seized upon every opportunity in letters to *The Times* and pronouncements on other occasions to state in reasonable terms the Catholic claims. He fought for the most part a lonely battle. The Anglicans were giving up more and more of their own denominational schools. The Nonconformists had few strong feelings in the matter. Rising costs after the First World War had made it increasingly difficult for Catholics to build new schools or improve existing ones. The school-leaving age was being raised and standards of building were becoming increasingly exacting. The Act of 1936 met these difficulties to some extent by giving power to local authorities to pay up to 75 per cent. of the cost of new schools and improvements to existing ones. Many Catholics felt that even this should be opposed as an inadequate half measure. But three-fourths of a loaf is better

[27] Heenan, *Cardinal Hinsley.*
[28] Heenan, *Cardinal Hinsley.*

than no bread and the act was welcomed as a precedent in the right direction. Unfortunately its effects were nullified by the Second World War and in 1944 the whole educational system in this country was to be revolutionised by an Act which repealed that of 1936. Cardinal Hinsley saw this coming and was horrified by the vision of a completely State-controlled system which seemed in so many ways to embrace the very principles which we were fighting in the war with Nazi Germany. He was afraid that " the craze for monotype education, made popular by the misleading slogan ' equality of opportunity,' would produce an unspiritual and highly un-desirable youth of State pattern. For this reason he viewed the sudden interest shown by the Board of Education in youth organisation with qualified enthusiasm "[29]. In the event, his fears were to be more than justified.

If the British public showed little understanding of the education question, they were on the other hand deeply in-terested in Cardinal Hinsley's exposition of Christian Social doctrine. For them, he appeared in the rôle of another Manning. That he was a friend of the people was manifested by his pronouncements at the time of the Golden Jubilee cele-brations of *Rerum Novarum* and by his ardour for the lay apostolate expressed in the Joint Pastoral of the Hierarchy in 1936. His elucidation of conceptions of Christian justice in-creased in crescendo with their revocation in totalitarian countries, and his vigorous broadcasts were regarded as great patriotic contributions to a conflict with evil concerning the righteousness of which he had no doubts. It was this above all which won him " the primacy of England." It was the Manning touch completed by an endearing capacity rarely surpassed. His love for Poland and all victim nations, his impatience with Pacificism, his approval of the United Nations, his hatred of tyranny, his admiration for Malta, his pride in the heroism of his people, made him one with them in the widest of all fields. Like his predecessor, he personally visited Army camps, R.A.F. stations and Naval units.

Perhaps his greatest achievement in the eyes of his non-Catholic contemporaries was the inauguration of the

[29] Heenan, *Cardinal Hinsley*.

Sword of the Spirit, on August 1st, 1940. One of its first-fruits was the initial proclamation signed by the Archbishop of Canterbury (Dr. Lang), the Cardinal, the Moderator of the Free Churches (Dr. Armstrong) and the Archbishop of York (Dr. Temple), and published in *The Times* on December 21st. It was the explicit acceptance of the Five Peace Points of Pope Pius XII. The original idea of the *Sword* was the unification on an international scale of all Catholic social effort. With her many exiles and refugees, London had become more international and Catholic than ever before. The Cardinal wanted to unite these elements with his fellow countrymen in an organisation which would aim at the restoration in Europe of a Christian basis for both public and private life, by a return to the principles of international order and Christian freedom. Christopher Dawson was appointed as Lay Leader. The campaign of the *Sword* swept the country in an extraordinary manner and gained support on all sides. It caused disappointments and misunderstandings as well. The Cardinal had to make it clear that co-operation with members of various religious bodies did not involve any revision or compromise of Catholic doctrine. Full membership was for Catholics only. The *Church Times* and other publications expressed disappointment, but through the good offices and understanding of people like Dr. G. K. Bell, the Anglican Bishop of Chichester, charity was maintained and the good work continued. It is only right to record that it was distrusted by many Catholics, especially in the North, from the start. In historical retrospect it will surely be regarded as at any rate indicative of the great power of Catholicism in the land.

Cardinal Hinsley's reign also saw the establishment in 1938 of an Apostolic Delegation in London for Great Britain. This at first caused some alarm and questions were asked in the House. It was welcomed by Cardinal Hinsley, and the Apostolic Delegate, Archbishop Godfrey, formerly Rector of the English College Rome, has been an entirely reassuring influence and achieved during the War great alleviation of suffering through diplomatic channels which otherwise would have been impossible. The Delegation is an established factor in the Catholic life of England and marks an important advance—perhaps the most important since the restoration of the Hierarchy—in ecclesiastical organisation.

Cardinal Hinsley died on March 17th, 1943, at Hare Street, the country house bequeathed by Mgr. R. H. Benson to the Archbishops of Westminster. The Requiem in Westminster Cathedral was a spontaneous reflection of a nation's grief. Here there was no question of mere official representation. The Government was present almost *en masse* to pay tribute to a great Father of the People. The body was interred in the Cathedral in the Chapel of St. Joseph and the Scarlet Hat, like a gigantic pendulum whose motion has ceased, hangs over a simple marble slab.

In conclusion, we may soliloquise that God has bestowed singular graces upon our Church and country in the men He has raised up to be our pastors in the last hundred years. Each Cardinal Archbishop of Westminster has been in his own time the providential leader of his people. The very variety of their characters and gifts has borne witness to the unity of their principles. They have spoken " with authority "—an authority symbolised by the Sacred Pallium imparted by the Apostolic See—and they have left no one in doubt or uncertainty with regard to their Christian responsibilities. They have shown themselves one with Augustine and Theodore, Thomas of Canterbury and the English Martyrs: and for this we render thanks.

VI

THE BISHOPS OF THE CENTURY

By Philip Hughes

NINETY-ONE bishops, since the Restoration of September 29th, 1850, have ruled " by the grace of God and favour of the Apostolic See " the dioceses then created, and those subsequently formed from them[1].

These ninety-one diocesan bishops have, all but seven of them, been taken from the secular clergy—an astonishingly high proportion, it might seem, in a country where for most of the century a good third of the parish clergy have been regulars. Of the seven regulars, five were Benedictines[2], one a Friar Minor[3], and one a Redemptorist[4]. Four of the secular clergy bishops have been members of a congregation of secular priests, Manning, Herbert Vaughan and O'Callaghan[5] being Oblates of St. Charles, and Bagshawe[6] an Oratorian. Ten of the bishops were Irish by birth[7].

The great majority of these bishops[8] came to their charge after a life spent wholly in parish work—as missionary priests, in the terminology still in use for many years after the restoration of 1850. Some 18 had served as rectors[9] of seminaries; two had been priors of monasteries[10]; three were headmasters of schools[11] at the time of their appointment. No fewer than six were rectors of the English College, Rome, called the *Venerabile*[12], from which in all 21 bishops of the 91 have come. Seven of the bishops were converts, four of

---

[1] By sees the 91 bishops are thus divided:—Westminster 6, Birmingham 5, Cardiff (the one-time Newport and Menevia, then, after 1895, Newport) 5, Liverpool 6, Beverley (and then, after 1878, Leeds) 5, Clifton 7, Hexham (since 1861 Hexham and Newcastle) 8, Northampton 7, Nottingham 7, Plymouth 6, Salford 6, Shrewsbury 7, Southwark 7. In the sees founded since 1850 there have been: Middlesbrough (1878) 2, Portsmouth (1882) 4, Menevia (1897) 5, Brentwood (1920) 2, Lancaster (1924) 2. There have been no more than 6 translations of bishops from one English see to another in all these 100 years: Hendren (Clifton to Nottingham)

them convert clergymen[13]; nine only of the 91 have come
from the nobility and landed gentry[14].

This chapter, for all that the *debitum pietatis* is very
evident and must somehow be met, can, however, hardly fail
to be the least satisfactory in the book. Four alone of all
these prelates[15] have found a biographer; and, whatever the

in 1851, Vaughan (Salford to Westminster) in 1892, Bourne
(Southwark to Westminster) in 1903, Keating (Northampton to
Liverpool, as archbishop) in 1921, Mostyn (Menevia to Cardiff, as
archbishop) in 1921, McGrath (Menevia to Cardiff) in 1940.

2 In Newport and Menevia (later (1895) Newport, and then (1916)
Cardiff) a see confided in 1854 by Rome to the monks of the English
Benedictine Congregation, Thomas Joseph Brown, 1850-80; John
Cuthbert Hedley, 1881-1915; James Romanus Bilsborrow, 1916-20.
In Birmingham, William Bernard Ullathorne, 1850-88. In Lan-
caster, Thomas Wulstan Pearson, 1925-38.

3 William Joseph Hendren, Bishop of Clifton 1850-51, of Nottingham
1851-53.

4 Robert Coffin, Bishop of Southwark, 1882-85.

5 Bishop of Hexham and Newcastle, 1888-90.

6 Bishop of Nottingham, 1874-1901.

7 James Chadwick, Bishop of Hexham and Newcastle, 1866-82;
Bernard O'Reilly, Bishop of Liverpool, 1873-94; Richard Lacy,
Bishop of Middlesbrough, 1879-1929; William Cotter, Bishop of
Portsmouth, 1910-40; John Kiely, Bishop of Plymouth, 1911-28;
Richard Downey, Archbishop of Liverpool, 1928; Thomas Shine,
Bishop of Middlesbrough, 1929; William Lee, Bishop of Clifton,
1930-48; Michael McGrath, Bishop of Menevia, 1932-40, Archbishop
of Cardiff, 1940; Henry Vincent Marshall, Bishop of Salford, 1939.

8 60 out of the total 91.

9 Cambridge, St. Edmund's House: Williams, McNulty, Petit. Leeds
Seminary: Gordon, Poskitt. Mill Hill, St. Joseph's: Vaughan.
Old Hall Green, St. Edmund's College: Ward. Upholland, St.
Joseph's: Bilsborrow, J., Whiteside. Ushaw: Briggs. Wonersh:
Bourne, Doubleday.

10 Brown, T. J., of Downside; Burgess, of Ampleforth.

11 Brown, J., of Sedgley Park; Casartelli, of St. Bede's, Manchester;
Williams, of Cotton, St. Wilfrid's.

12 Wiseman, Grant, Cornthwaite, O'Callaghan, McIntyre, Hinsley.

13 *Manning* (Westminster, 1865-92), *Coffin,* C.SS.R. (Southwark,
1882-85), Wilkinson (Hexham and Newcastle, 1890-1909), *Brownlow*
(Clifton, 1894-1901), Thorman (Hexham and Newcastle, 1925-38),
Youens (Northampton, 1932-40), *Poskitt* (Leeds, 1936-50); italics
mark those once clergymen of the Church of England.

14 Clifford is the solitary son of a noble. The other eight are: Cary-
Elwes, Errington, Mostyn, Riddell, Wilkinson, and the three
Vaughans (William, Herbert, Francis).

15 Grant of Southwark, Amherst of Northampton, Ullathorne of
Birmingham and Hedley of Newport. The only other bishops who
have tempted biographers are the first five archbishops of Westminster, Wiseman, Manning, Vaughan, Bourne and Hinsley.

worth of their work to their own time and to us, the great
majority of the bishops have left little behind in the tradition
of the sees they ruled but memories which, as is inevitable,
grow ever fainter year by year. Few things so bring home to
a priest how the years are passing more swiftly than he has
realised, as to see the good story about His Lordship, that
once shook the table, met with a polite, non-comprehending
smile, and "Would that be the last bishop, Father?" The
thought of the oblivion that comes even upon the mitred dead
caught the magnificent imagination of Villon five hundred
years ago:

> Mais où sont ly sainctz Apostoles,
> D'aulbes vestuz, d'amicts coeffez,
> Qui sont ceincts de sainctes estoles,
> Dont par le col prent ly mauffez,
> De maltalent tout eschauffez?
> Aussi bien meurt filz que servans,
> De ceste vie sont bouffez.
> Autant en emporte ly vens.

> Prince à mort sont destinez,
> Comme les plus povres vivans:
> S'ils en sont courcez ou tennez,
> Autant en emporte ly vens.

"Pontifical death," indeed! And here, with *Alibi aliorum
sanctorum, martyrum, confessorum atque sanctarum virginum,*
the chronicler free to choose his subject and concerned, like
any other artist, to choose what can at least be successfully
attempted, would, if he were wise, leave their lordships. *Fecit
ordinationes decem,* and so forth, and almost no more, says
the Breviary record, of a whole string of the martyr popes
of the primitive Church. The real work for which the Providence of God has instituted the episcopate must ever escape
the scrutiny of man; and although it is far from being "interred with their bones," it does not so live after the prelates,
in the sight of man, as do their more ephemeral effects, good
or bad. "The duties of a bishop," says the Consecrator, to the
priest upon whom he is about to lay the *onus episcopale,*

" are to rule, to teach, to consecrate, to ordain, to offer [sacrifice], to baptise and to confirm."

The task set by the office is one impossible, of course, to nature alone—calling more and more (if the natural alone be regarded) for such an assembly of the talents as is rarely found among the children of men. The Church usefully reminds the biographer (to say nothing of the critic) that the function is primarily sacramental, that the office has regard to the " Fides Christi et sacramenta fidei " which is the very being of the Catholic religion, and that it is a man whom the powers conferred through sacramental rites presuppose as their subject. Why then, despite the misleading (and increasingly mischievous) incitement of popular press headlines and adjectives, seek there, and demand as the primal necessity, universal genius? the scholar, the man of affairs, the speaker, the preacher, the authority omniscient if not infallible on politics domestic and foreign, the diplomat—in fact, all and everything, the arbiter of the elegancies barely excepted? The Church herself is simpler. She asks no more than the saint.

" The new bishop," Pennyalinus once wrote in a Catholic newspaper, " is one of the greatest theologians in the diocese of X "—the said diocese numbering barely sixty priests, theologians and all. We can all smile easily at the folly; and in the midst of our superiority the bitter reminder will stab us that, like the rest, we too love a hero, must have one of our own and, if one is not provided by grace or by nature, will speedily provide one from our own imagination. It remains true, however, here as everywhere else in matters Catholic, that to desert the ideas which are the Church's own (even for the ideas of those of her children who are courtiers by profession, by necessity—or by instinct) is to risk considerable trouble. The sacraments are not magical; genius is everywhere rare; sanctity is the one *carriera* open to all. And if bishops are to be assessed, judged, " placed," it is only according to the standard which God Himself has fixed; and to apply that standard is His sole right. As bishops alone can speak with knowledge of " those cares and that grief, which in varying but sure measure fall to the lot of every bishop,"[16]

---

[16] Bishop Burton, preaching at the funeral of Bishop Hedley, November, 1915.

so it may be left to them, as they ask for prayers over the remains of bishops lately dead, to utter the saving bluntness about " the last farthing of a bishop's heavy debt ''[17]. Who that was there will ever forget the lesson of Cardinal Bourne's funeral, when, at the dead bishop's express command, not a single word of panegyric disturbed the Requiem?

> I will not perturbate
> Thy paradisal state
> With praise
> Of thy dead days.
>
> To the new heavened say,
> Spirit, thou wert fine clay[17a]

Among our 74 bishops deceased there were all types, of course; and whatever the goodness of the best, none of them so far evident as subjects occupying the time of the Congregation of Rites. Here and there is the prelate of whom his friends would mournfully say *capax nisi imperasset*, brilliant promise, until the test came of that unique unknown for which no conscious training can prepare. Here and there is the elderly eccentric, in his time the delight and the dismay, turn by turn, of his clergy and his brethren (and even of " the faithful of the said diocese "). There is a small handful of really outstanding personalities, and a few who survive as traditionally the " great " bishop of the see they once occupied. But the average bishop is very like the average man; finding " the daily round, the common task "—the correspondence, the interviews, the committees, the visitations of parishes, convents and schools, the conferences about money (the necessary, and where to get it), the social events, the annual meetings, the endless speeches *de omnibus rebus et de quibuscumque aliis*—finding all this sufficiently occupying; and as for being a master in Israel and a herald to his time,

[17] Bishop Hedley, preaching at the funeral of Bishop Thomas Joseph Brown, 1880.

[17a] This, of course, is Francis Thompson on Manning, *Lines to the dead Cardinal of Westminster*.

lucky if, amid the press of affairs, he can keep abreast of what
ever lore was his in days less filled with inescapable engage
ments.

It is perhaps not surprising that writers have been rar
among the bishops, although those who wrote before findin
themselves *in altissimis* seem to have found a means to con
tinue this apostolate—Wiseman, for example, contrived t
supply one article at least to almost every number of th
Dublin Review that appeared in the 1850's, years when he wa
ceaselessly in demand, in every part of England, as th
universal champion of the Church in the pulpit and on th
platform. And these review articles covered every topic of th
day, sociology, literature, the arts. From Manning, too, ther
came a succession of books, doctrinal and controversial, com
posed, once again, by a man whose written correspondence o
public engagements would crush the moderns. The two Bene
dictines, Ullathorne and Hedley, are also exceptions to th
common run of non-writing bishops for whom the Church c
their day was assuredly deeply grateful. But the tradition o
Challoner and Hornyold, and Walmesley and Milner has hardl
been maintained. If to the bishops just named we add th
mid-Victorian convert Brownlow, of Clifton, we have told th
tale of writing bishops.

It is more surprising, perhaps, that not many of th
bishops could be counted as of the company of the grea
preachers—even in the late nineteenth century marked by goo
preaching in every denomination. Wiseman there was, of cours
and perhaps *facile princeps* from the point of suitability t
his own particular time; possessed of a rich, warm, imaginativ
eloquence; able to present, in the simplest way, a vast learnin
that seemingly covered the whole range of knowledge and a
its latest developments. Manning, too, is among them, mor
formal, drier, less pleasing to the hearer, but dominating, eve
apocalyptic at times. Roskell knew great fame in his day, bu
no tradition of him has survived; and Clifford also, of thes
early bishops, had a scholarly eloquence. Ullathorne preache
well, as he did all else well—the unusual personality (a
always) never failing to hold his hearers, by the hour ordi
arily and on occasion for much longer. The greatest of all—
and yet in no way a speaker—was Hedley, the only bisho

HENRY EDWARD, CARDINAL MANNING
Second Archbishop of Westminster,
1865-92

HERBERT, CARDINAL VAUGHAN

Third Archbishop of Westminster,
1892-1903

[18]

(Picture

FRANCIS, CARDINAL BOURNE
Fourth Archbishop of Westminster
1903-35

ARTHUR, CARDINAL HINSLEY
Fifth Archbishop of Westminster,
1935-43

RICHARD ROSKELL
Second Bishop of Nottingham,
1853-74

ALEXANDER GOSS
Second Bishop of Liverpool,
1856-72

WILLIAM JOSEPH CLIFFORD
Third Bishop of Clifton,
1857-93

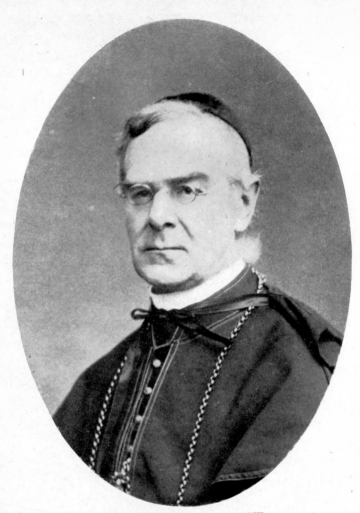

ROBERT CORNTHWAITE
Second Bishop of Beverley, 1861-78
First Bishop of Leeds, 1878-90

JOHN CUTHBERT HEDLEY, o.s.b.
Second Bishop of Newport, 1881-1915

[25]

ROBERT BRINDLE ^(Picture Post)
Fourth Bishop of Nottingham,
1901-15

[26]

LOUIS CHARLES CASARTELLI
Fourth Bishop of Salford,
1903-25

THOMAS WHITESIDE
Fourth Bishop and first Archbishop of Liverpool,
1894-1921

RICHARD LACY
First Bishop of Middlesbrough,
1879-1929

JOHN VERTUE
First Bishop of Portsmouth,
1882-1900

[30]

FRANCIS MOSTYN
First Bishop of Menevia, 1898-1921
Second Archbishop of Cardiff, 1921-39

BERNARD NICHOLAS WARD
First Bishop of Brentwood, 1917-20

whose sermons have survived publication for more than his own time, to be republished continuously for their unique achievement that they convey the very substance of doctrine, set out in a highly finished style whose one aim is clearness, and in a well-planned order, designed to make certain beyond a peradventure that every point reaches its mark and there abides. In later years, there were, in the first quarter of the present century, a trio of really eloquent bishops, variously gifted but all preachers well beyond the average of good preaching—Keating of Northampton was one (a product of Northcote's Oscott) and McIntyre, first auxiliary and then Archbishop of Birmingham, from that same first Alma Mater, was another. The third was the prelate who, in all the century, stands in a class apart for the distinction which marked his whole episcopal action, George Ambrose Burton, Bishop of Clifton 1902-30, a spirit touched with genius, who never realised all his quality promised, so exacting was his taste; a rarely cultivated mind; theologian, scholar, and artist breathed into a sturdy north-country character as forthcoming and blunt as Ullathorne or Hedley.

From this attempt to portray the Hierarchy of the century, the present-day episcopate is naturally ruled out— —which brings the formidable total of 91 down by 17; and, since it is not possible to say anything but the conventional commonplaces about them, those bishops also are passed over who have died so recently as the last 20 years, which lowers the task of the chronicler by another 22. Of the remaining 52 bishops, two are separately treated in a paper on the cardinals, and something has already been said about the personalities of the bishops who first filled the original 13 sees. The total number of prelates about whom something remains to be said is, then, 37. And since it is just not possible to deal intelligently even with this reduced number, save in a meaningless kind of miniature biographical dictionary, I propose to make a selection; its principle, in many cases, must be little more than personal recollection of things heard about bygone personalities. And for confirmation of such recollections, beyond what is to be found incidentally in the lives of contemporaries, I have gone no further than the accounts of the bishops published in the Catholic press when they passed from the scene[18].

II

Wiseman himself was afraid that Rome, yielding to the pressure of local feeling that X or Y should not be passed over, would appoint to the sees priests admirable in all respects save their lack of gifts appropriate to leaders of the " flock." How far he had any influence in the appointments beyond what his rank as metropolitan allowed, discussing with the other bishops the *terna* presented by the chapter of the vacant see, is not known. But all six of the appointments made between the final establishment of the Hierarchy and his own death, 14 years later, were admirable.

Richard Roskell's appointment to Nottingham, in 1853, was the first of these. He was born at Gateacre, near Liverpool, in 1817—young to be made a bishop by 1853, and (a novel experience, surely!) he found himself on taking over his diocese, younger than the youngest priest in it. His early education he had from the old school founded by Challoner at Sedgley Park, near Wolverhampton, and thence he went, by way of Ushaw, to the English College, Rome, where Wiseman was now in the last stages of his rectorship and Roskell one of the last of the many friends the college had brought him. It was in the chapel of the college that Wiseman was consecrated bishop, and there the following day he held his first ordination, to confer the priesthood on Roskell.

Wiseman came back to work as a bishop in the English midlands, and Roskell to his native county, very young and

---

[18] How far this must be from anything like an adequate account of the matter may be gathered from some of the omissions, e.g., Richard Lacy, the first Bishop of Middlesbrough 1879-1929; Edmund Bagshawe, Bishop of Nottingham 1874-1901; Edward Ilsley, Bishop and Archbishop of Birmingham 1888-1921. If local patriotism in the various sees has not been sufficiently interested, if the successors of these prelates upon whom the burden fell of laying foundations have not been interested, who shall be expected to preserve their memory?

gay and as lighthearted as his Irish mother; and also, that somewhat rare spectacle, a fully-fledged doctor of divinity. For seven years he served as curate to the vicar general, William Turner, at St. Augustine's, Granby Row, then " the leading mission of Manchester and of the entire district of East Lancashire," until, in 1847, there occurred at St. Patrick's the famous first-class " stirr " between head-priest and assistant about which the old people still talked 60 years later. The head-priest was one of those figures of heroic stature, then to be seen in every part of England laying foundations that still endure, men like Thomas Doyle in London and Thomas McDonnell in Birmingham. The Manchester pioneer, Daniel Hearne, was the founder of the mission, the parishioners took sides, and the bishop began his solution by moving both the priests, and putting Dr. Roskell, not yet 30, in charge. The story long survived of the new rector's hostile reception, of how he called in the supernatural in the person of Dr. Gentili, and of the marvellous six weeks' mission that followed and the quasi-transformation of the parish into a kind of religious community that the great Rosminian effected. Three years later came the erection of the see of Salford, William Turner became the bishop and Richard Roskell was named first Provost of the Cathedral Chapter, the head of the diocesan clergy. This was in 1852, and barely twelve months later the Provost was Bishop of Nottingham.

" As a bishop Dr. Roskell was of too retiring a disposition," said the writer of his obituary; and so the chronicler may think also, as he becomes aware that to all intents and purposes Dr. Roskell was the first bishop and that he ruled the see for 21 years. In all the disputes between Wiseman and his suffragans, that began about this time, disputes about policy in the matter of the registration of Catholic trusts, about the control of the various colleges and about the relation of archbishop to suffragans, Roskell stood consistently by the cardinal —often the only bishop to do so. He was a singularly fluent Italian speaker and writer, reputed a good canonist, a most generous-hearted man, and " as exact as one of his own dear father's chronometers." He was only 57 when his sight began to fail—cataract threatened him with complete blindness—and he resigned his see. Six years later a stroke paralysed him badly and in 1883 he died, at Whitewell in Yorkshire at the opening of the Trough of Bolland[19].

Diffidence, luckily for Liverpool Catholics, was not a characteristic of Alexander Goss whom the ageing first bishop of the see secured as his coadjutor with the right of succession in 1853. The new bishop was then 39; and he was the real ruler of the diocese from the day of his consecration until his death, brought on by 20 years' continuous overwork, in 1872. The great Lancashire city was already a good quarter Catholic when the see was founded, and it enjoyed the somewhat unusual distinction of being the seat of a bitterly hostile and militantly anti-Catholic opposition. Dr. Goss's episcopate was stormy, and he never ceased to fight. " Goss with his usual rough violence—the crozier hook and point," said Manning, as yet no more than a priest, of an occasion when the bishop held his own against the protonotary's conception of what that " own " should be. " Strong and resolute almost to vehemence " was the more politic phrase he used preaching, as Metropolitan, at the bishop's funeral, and acknowledging that it was to his energy and administrative talent that " Liverpool owes its formation as a diocese "—acknowledging also that it was only in the last two years of his life he had really come to know the bishop. The best testimony to the great service his life had been were the words of the (Liverpool) *Daily Post*, remarking of his funeral that " such a demonstration of respect was never witnessed in Liverpool before," and attributing the influence " in a Protestant community " of this " untitled bishop of an unestablished church," not to his social rank, or genius, to " any obsequiousness or mastery of the ingratiating arts," but to his " hearty and manly devotion to the duties of the Christian episcopate."

" When we speak of the pastor who folded one flock in one place, of a tiller of the earth who ploughed and sowed and reaped in one field, and that a field calm and practical under the light of this western sun, theirs is no long history to tell."

[19] Dr. Roskell makes an effective appearance in the life of Cornelia Connelly, foundress of the Society of the Holy Child Jesus, advising this much-tried and saintly woman in the troubles that the vanity and incompetence of the local ordinary had brought upon her institute.

So said Manning at Goss's funeral. And the same words describe well the 30-years episcopate of another Lancashire man, his contemporary Robert Cornthwaite, who came to be Bishop of Beverley at 43 years of age, five years after Goss had succeeded to Liverpool. Like Goss and Roskell, this bishop, too, had gone, first to Ushaw and then to the *Venerabile*. Seven years he spent as Rector of the college, then ill-health forced him home, to the charge of the mission at Darlington and the post of vicar-general to William Hogarth. As Bishop of Beverley Robert Cornthwaite established a diocesan seminary at Leeds (1876) and by preaching charity sermons all over his diocese, he collected personally the greater amount of what it cost. His predecessor had lived at York, but Cornthwaite made Leeds his residence; and when, in 1878, he secured from Rome the separation of the East Riding from his jurisdiction he broke with the archaeology that had fixed Beverley on him for a title, and the new sees were placed at Middlesbrough and Leeds. As the first Bishop of Leeds he reigned another twelve years. When he died the *Leeds Mercury's* chief impression was the " gentle, unassuming nature of the deceased prelate," and though it was one of the great preachers of the day who spoke at his funeral, Wiseman's one-time secretary John Morris, now a Jesuit these many years, the sermon had nothing to add, the preacher nothing to report, beyond a life of industrious devotion to the never-ending small tasks, and of fidelity to God.

Episcopal life in Yorkshire and Lancashire, whatever its anxieties, was lotus eating by comparison with what, in the mid-nineteenth century, awaited bishops in the west of England and in Wales—the Western District of the days of the Vicars Apostolic.

At Plymouth, Errington, the first bishop, had barely time to survey his diocese when he was translated to archiepiscopal Trebizond, *in partibus,* and promoted as coadjutor to Westminster with the right of succession, a dizzy eminence in which he has had no successor. This was in March, 1855; but so soon did the new archbishop and his principal come to realise that, in official relationship, their ancient incompatibility still continued, that before a successor was given to Errington at Plymouth, he was already back in the west of England, ruling the neighbouring see of Clifton as Administrator Apostolic. And it was one of the canons of Clifton, William Vaughan, whom in October, 1855, Rome chose to be the second bishop of Plymouth. He was to rule the see for 47 years, and to be, by hard personal effort and resolute patience, the very real founder of its Catholic life.

When William Vaughan was consecrated on November 16th, 1855, he found the clergy of the three counties in his charge, Devon, Cornwall and Dorset, to consist of the eight canons of his Chapter, 15 other secular priests, and a few unattached regulars. Within three years, said the bishop who preached at his funeral[20], six of the canons and five of the priests " dropped away one by one, and left him almost alone." The bishop held on, and " somehow or other, by the grace and favour of God, priests began to come to him, and after many dreary years the day came " when there could really be said to exist the beginnings of a diocese of Plymouth. When, after 36 years of single-handed effort, he obtained from Rome an assistant bishop, he had added 40 new missions, each equipped with a church, there were eight convents and sixteen parish schools " and not a mission with a debt "—an immense work evidently, and, said the *Western Morning News,* all done " without any parade or ostentatious display." William Vaughan, who is surely one of the heroic figures, was in his 42nd year when he succeeded to the see, one of the Courtfield family of this name and a younger brother of the Vaughan who was the cardinal's father. William Vaughan was born February 14th, 1814, and educated at Stonyhurst and at Oscott, at that time a school for boys as well as a seminary. His first choice of a career was the army, and it was when, somewhat abashed, he was considering the defects in his character which a military friend warned him must be remedied if he were to succeed as a soldier, that the thought came to him of another life that better deserved the toil of such a *conversio morum.* So Vaughan returned to Oscott, to study for the priesthood. It was Bishop Baines who ordained him, in March, 1838, and for the next 17 years he worked continuously on the mission: at

[20] Robert Brindle, Bishop of Nottingham, 1901-15, who had lived with Vaughan as one of the Cathedral clergy and then its administrator, from 1862 to 1874.

Lyme Regis, until 1847; at St. Mary's, Bristol, for a year; and then, from 1848 to 1855, at the pro-cathedral Clifton. When the chapter of the new diocese was set up, in 1852, he was named Canon Penitentiary. Bishop William Vaughan died on October 25th, 1902, towards the close of his 89th year.

When William Vaughan went down to Plymouth to take possession of his see, he found there, administering the diocese as Vicar-Capitular, a young priest of 31 who, four years earlier, had been his own curate at Clifton; this was Dr. William Clifford, Canon Theologian of the cathedral chapter these two years, and already very much a *personaggio*; for the brilliant and scholarly priest was also the son of Lord Clifford of Chudleigh, and Lord Clifford, a Devon magnate, was indeed a power in that age when peers really led the social and political life of the communities where their properties lay.

William Clifford's education, too, had begun with the Jesuits, at Hodder, the preparatory school for Stonyhurst; and then he had passed to the school at Prior Park lately opened, with a great flourish, by his own bishop, Dr. Baines. And when he finally settled to study for the priesthood he went to Rome, to the famous *Accademia* for Noble Ecclesiastics. This was in 1840—the year Wiseman left Rome to begin his life as a bishop in England. In the next ten years, spent continuously at Rome, Clifford, to whom all houses were open, for Cardinal Weld had been his uncle and he had relatives by marriage among the Papal aristocracy, made good use of his time in every respect. He laid the foundations of a really good formation, both in theology and in canon law; he became an accomplished Italian speaker; and he learned the business of finding his way about in that world of the Curia Romana where to live is itself a great art. It was indeed a young man of promise whom Bishop Hendren ordained priest on August 25th, 1850, and who took his doctorate in theology just a year later, September 16th, 1851.

The see of Plymouth was erected in the interval between these two events, and it was to the joint office of secretary to the new bishop, George Errington, and priest of the mission of Stonehouse, that William Clifford was appointed in April, 1852. The three years he now spent with Errington—who worked the mission as its rector—living in the same house and sharing the bishop's anxieties and the daily life, knit Clifford very close to the man who was his senior by a good 20 years; their kindred tastes, as students of theology and of law, no doubt accounted in part for their friendship, and the fact also that they came from the same social world. Clifford remained ever afterwards Errington's loyal friend. Without any clamour he stood consistently by the Archbishop of Trebizond in the bitter tragedy that ended his association with the English Hierarchy. He supported, in the most striking way open to him, the vote of the Westminster chapter in 1865 that Errington should be Wiseman's successor. He gave him a home at Prior Park, in the archbishop's last years, and there in the cloister the two prelates lie buried, side by side.

Errington's successor at Plymouth did not long enjoy the advantage of an assistant of William Clifford's quality. He had scarcely made him his vicar-general when, during a visit to Rome, Pius IX appointed Clifford to the vacant see of Clifton —the youngest priest ever put in charge of a diocese in this country[21]—and the pope emphasised the personal nature of the choice by himself consecrating the new bishop, February 15th, 1857.

William Clifford's appointment to Clifton was the fourth change of ruler the see had known since its constitution, six and a half years before. He was indeed its third bishop, and during a large part of the two years since the death of the second bishop it had been ruled by Errington as Administrator-Apostolic. The trouble was simple enough—the see was all but bankrupt, seemingly vowed to bankruptcy in perpetuity, as a result not merely of the financial methods by which Bishop Baines, 25 years before this, had raised the immense sum needed to buy Prior Park, but of the crushing disaster of the great fire which had burned down so much of the property before the college was really under way. From 1836 onwards, calamity had never ceased to dog the steps of the successive bishops, five of whom were popularly thought to have succumbed[22], in one way or another, to the invincible anxieties of

[21]   He had just passed his 33rd birthday.
[22]   Baines, who died in 1843; Baggs, died in 1845; Ullathorne, translated in 1848; Hendren, translated in 1851; Burgess, died in 1854.

this situation. The iron-minded Errington had lately some-what simplified the situation, selling up the college and its contents by public auction.

As with William Vaughan at Plymouth, it was Clifford's first great merit that he lasted—conferring on the Catholics of this much afflicted see the benefit of 36 years of a continuous, stable administration; an administration, moreover, that was extremely competent. No doubt the most striking evidence to his people of the new bishop's ability was that he bought back Prior Park, re-opened it, and made it for all his own time a real success. They had also the satisfaction that their bishop was one who " mattered " in local affairs, and this on his own merits. While, as a theologian and a man of scholarly interests, he intervened with some credit in the burning question of the day, the reconciliation of the biblical account of the creation of the world with the discoveries of the new geological science, he was also, for many years, an active member of the Somerset-shire and Gloucestershire Archaeological Association, and many of his papers survive in its proceedings.

Of the prominent part which Clifford played in the Vatican Council something will be said presently. It may be noted meanwhile that, as he stood by Errington so he was always Newman's staunch friend and champion against the malice of the Catholic underworld and its never-ceasing " whispering " campaign of misrepresentation. Fittingly, it was the Bishop of Clifton whom the Oratorians asked to preach at the Cardinal's funeral.

At one moment in his life the votes of his episcopal brethren seemed to foreshadow for him a higher destiny than the small see of Clifton. This was in 1865 when, on Wiseman's death, the Westminster chapter proposed to the Holy See, as the *terna* for the succession, the names of Errington, Clifford and Grant; and the bishops (with whom it lay to modify, or to quash, this vote) sent on the *terna* to Propaganda approving it. It is one of the familiar incidents of this famous story that both Clifford and Grant then wrote to Rome withdrawing their names, so that Errington alone stood presented to the Holy See as the English choice and preference. "Clifford is the very soul of chivalry—no braver bishop in Rome," the Bishop of

Kerry wrote to Newman during the Vatican Council[23]. His action in 1865 was typical, and in character; and in a generation where differences over policy degenerated only too easily into bitter personal squabbles, Clifford managed easily to observe the mean and to avoid anything like " party " action. His last appearance in the affairs of English Catholicism as a whole was his collaboration (at the request of the Hierarchy) with Manning and Herbert Vaughan in the Roman litigation that preceded the Bull *Romanos Pontifices* (1881), which clarified and remodelled the relations of bishops and regular orders in what regards the rights of regulars who are parish priests or administrators of parishes[24].

William Clifford, who was almost the last survivor of the bench over which Wiseman had presided, and who outlived Manning too, and Ullathorne, died on August 14th, 1893, in some sense unexpectedly, and still in full episcopal activity, not quite 70 years of age.

With the names of Clifford and of William Vaughan there needs to be associated, whenever the marvellous work accomplished in the west is recalled, that of the one time Prior of Downside, Thomas Joseph Brown, who, first as Vicar Apostolic of Wales and then as Bishop of Newport and Menevia was responsible for South Wales, Monmouth and Hereford during 40 years (1840-80). Here, again, a fine character and gifts that would have brought distinguished recognition from a wider world were generously given to create a diocese where the monk-bishop found a desert[25]. The friendly association, through the best part of a long lifetime, of these three selfless and competent administrators, by which Catholicism was at last re-established in the west of England, must be considered one

23 Butler, *History of the Vatican Council*, II, 30; letter of February 20, 1870.
24 The history of this will be found in Snead-Cox, *Life of Cardinal Vaughan*, Vol. I.
25 In 1840 there were in all Wales together with Monmouth and Hereford only 17 missions, and a total of 5,000 Catholics; 2,000 of these were in Monmouthshire, 550 in Herefordshire, and 12 of the 17 missions were in these two counties. In Glamorgan there was not one church. Most of the " churches " were garrets or lofts. The annual collection for the bishop's maintenance brought in £10. The *évêché* was a tiny cottage at Bullingham. Wilson, *Life of Bishop Hedley*, 99, 135.

of the most singular accomplishments of the restored Hierarchy.

III

The new Hierarchy's most spectacular hour was its participation in the Vatican Council—the first General Council to be held for three hundred years, and known to all as the Council which defined the infallibility of the Pope. To the place of this Council in what may be called the general history of the English Catholics, some reference has already been made. No more will be said about this here; but, however briefly, some record should be made of the part taken in the Council by the English bishops.

The Council, summoned by the Bull *Aeterni Patris* of June 29th, 1868, held its first public session on December 8th, 1869. Its first dogmatic " constitution," *On the Catholic Faith*, was voted in the third public session, April 24th, 1870; the second dogmatic " constitution," *On the Church of Christ*, which contains the definition about the infallibility of the Pope, in the fourth public session on July 18th. Just a day later the long Franco-Prussian crisis came to a head with Napoleon III's declaration of war. Two months later, on September 20th, the armies of the King of Italy captured Rome. On October 20th Pius IX suspended the Council indefinitely.

Manning, as is well known, was one of the central figures of the Council, as he had been a central figure in the general international controversies which preceded it. But the metropolitan did not, by any means, act his suffragans off the stage once the Council had assembled. There were no sees vacant in 1869, and all the bishops appeared in the Council but two: the senior bishop, Brown of Newport and Menevia, who stayed in England, " in charge," and Goss of Liverpool, laid low by illness en route. Neither of these was of Manning's mind. Goss, says the most recent historian of the Council, was " a Gallican "[26]; and the untheological extravagance of Manning's personal views was little in keeping with the sober, trained judgment of the Benedictine bishop. In fact

[26] Whatever this may mean! Butler's authority (*History of the Vatican Council*, I, 206) is a letter from Goss to Newman, which, however, he does not quote.

the only one of the bishops revealed as really in sympathy with Manning was Cornthwaite, of Beverley[27].

Ullathorne, and Grant also (whom Ullathorne considered " our best theologian "[28]) were from the beginning supporters of the policy for the definition of the infallibility, but in no sense associated with Manning whose peculiar point of view they by no means shared. Neither Roskell, of Nottingham, nor James Brown, of Shrewsbury, are mentioned at all by Abbot Butler. Turner of Salford, Amherst of Northampton, and William Vaughan, he sets down as disposed to think the time had not come for the infallibility to be defined[29]. Clifford was as outstanding a figure, among the bishops of the minority, as was Manning among the majority bishops; he was " the only member of the English Hierarchy to take a strong inopportunist line " and " to throw in his lot heartily with the Minority "[30]. Errington, restored to episcopal activity by the Pope's decision to accord titular bishops a vote in the Council[31], shared Clifford's views, and usually acted with him. All we are told of Chadwick, of Hexham and Newcastle, is his vote in the last session.

Once the 800 bishops had arrived in Rome and the Council got under way, their life was very gruelling—endless meetings of committees, long hours of debates, with only the occasional holiday of a major feast, and after Easter the weather hotting up furiously to the greater discomfort of many of these elderly and very elderly men. Presently petitions began to descend on the pope for " sick leave." The Englishmen seem to have stood it well, down to the last few weeks; but Grant, who fell ill early in March, died in Rome on June 1st. And when the day came to vote on the infallibility question, Turner, Brown (of Shrewsbury), Roskell and Amherst had gone home.

The procedure adopted for transacting the Council's business was that the bishops should, in a body, debate the drafts of definitions or regulations put forward by the Holy

27 Butler, I, 206, says " an extremist of the Manning type."
28 Butler, I, 181; for Butler's opinion of Grant, *ibid.*, 175, 206.
29 Butler, I, 206.
30 So Butler, I, 137, 206.
31 Butler, I, 92; no date given.

See. When a question had been fairly thrashed out, this General Congregation of the Council would vote on the draft as a whole and, if the vote was favourable, it would then be promulgated in a Public Session. To consider the new points that must arise during these debates, committees of bishops (24 members to each) were elected by the whole body—the so-called *Deputations,* of which there were four, one for questions concerning Faith, one for questions about religious orders, a third for Eastern Rites and the Missions, the fourth for questions of ecclesiastical discipline and diplomatic procedure. The bishops of the various countries met to nominate candidates for these and, to Manning's surprise, the English bishops proposed Grant as their candidate for the all-important deputation *De Fide.* It was, however, Manning who was elected—Grant being chosen for the committee on Eastern rites and the missions. Two others also of the ten English bishops were chosen to serve, Clifford on the deputation for the regular orders, and Ullathorne for that on ecclesiastical discipline.

As might be expected, there was as much episcopal activity outside the council chamber as within, an endless activity of groups with ideas about improving the procedure, groups anxious to see their own pet schemes given priority, groups suspicious of " less intelligent " groups, and the less intelligent suspicious of the activities of the others. Whence petitions, and demands for audiences, and counter-petitions and counter-demands. It is one of Ullathorne's distinctions that, active-minded as he was, understanding to the full all the issues, and familiar with the leading personalities, by no means unconscious of his own diplomatic abilities and of the prestige that accrues from 25 years of an unusually successful episcopate, he resolutely kept himself clear of what may be called these parliamentary activities. In a sense, it is true, he could well afford to do so: he was of the majority—but he was fair-minded enough to have no desire to hinder the other side from the fullness of its lawful freedom. And like all the truly fair-minded of his race he had no fear of other good men's freedom—and took it that his fellows were as good and well-intentioned as himself. Clifford was not so happily placed. He was among those bishops openly spoken of, by the clique whom Ullathorne styled the *zelanti,* as the enemy: bishops very varied indeed in character, and varied in the reasons that made them reluctant to see the infallibility defined here and now, but put on the defensive from the moment the Council met by the challenging acts of the *zelanti*.

One of the first of these acts was the " monster petition "[32] to the Pope issued for signature on December 30th, 1869, urging that the question of the Pope's infallibility be brought before the Council (as yet it had not even been mentioned). The organisers of this petition ultimately secured 380 signatures to it, but, besides Manning, only two of the Englishmen signed, Grant and Cornthwaite[33]. Six months later, on June 13th, 1870, there appeared another petition from bishops of the majority party (to the cardinals presiding over the debates) asking that the closure be now applied to the discussion on the infallibility. As it bore only nine signatures (when ten was the minimum required) the legates ignored it. Cornthwaite and Manning were two of the nine signatories[34].

Clifford's name—Errington's also—appears on a memorial of 44 bishops sent to the presiding cardinals (April 18th, 1870) in strong support of an important amendment proposed by Ullathorne[35]. Ten days later he is spoken of as one of a deputation about to propose to the Pope that the infallibility question be postponed for a year, acting in this with Kettler of Mainz, Kenrick of St. Louis, and Moriarty of Kerry, among others[36]. As the end of the infallibility debate draws near, Clifford once again joins with those who think like him to protest, on July 9th, about a matter of procedure[37]; and his signature is among those of the 55 bishops who, after voting against the definition on July 13th, write to the Pope that they propose to absent themselves from the Public Session on July 18th, since " filial piety and reverence . . . do not allow us in a cause so closely concerning Your Holiness to say ' non-placet ' openly and in the face of the Father "[38].

Four of the English bishops spoke in the Council:

[32] Butler's phrase, I, 203.
[33] *Ibid.*, 206.
[34] *Ibid.*, II, 81.
[35] *Ibid.*, I, 281.
[36] *Ibid.*, II, 40.
[37] *Ibid.*, II, 88.
[38] *Ibid.*, II, 160; text of the letter, 158-9.

Vaughan, Errington, Clifford and Ullathorne. Vaughan intervened, on April 30th, in the discussion whether there should be one uniform elementary catechism for the whole Church, in order to protest that Bellarmine's catechism, proposed as its basis, was " as an elementary catechism for children, of all known to him, the least adapted to the needs of our time." The Bishop of Plymouth was nervous but, reported Ullathorne, " he got through very well "[39]. Clifford's first speech, on January 25th, was also on a practical question. He protested that some of the proposed regulations for clerical life were impracticable, and he asked for a reform of the rubrics of the breviary, to secure that the whole psalter was read weekly[40]. On April 30th he again spoke, following Vaughan "with a conciliatory speech "[41].

Ullathorne spoke, on March 24th, to propose an amendment in the very opening words of the first dogmatic constitution. The text proposed read: *Sancta Romana Catholica Ecclesia credit et confitetur* (the Holy Roman Catholic Church believes and confesses). To prevent any possibility of future controversialists misrepresenting this as evidence in support of the theory that the one Church of Christ is actually divided into Roman Catholic, Greek Catholic and Anglo-Catholic branches, Ullathorne proposed that the text should read " the Holy Catholic and Roman Church," or that, at any rate, a comma be placed between " Roman " and " Catholic." Clifford spoke in support and finally, on April 19th, it was decided to amend the text to *Sancta Catholica Apostolica Romana Ecclesia credit et confitetur* (The Holy Catholic Apostolic Roman Church believes and confesses[42]).

Ullathorne also intended to speak in the debates about the definition of infallibility, but a sudden illness struck him on the very day appointed him (June 25th) and so, losing his turn, he could do no more than send in his matter for the consideration of the deputation *De Fide*. He had already, in March, when the drafts of the proposed decree were first circulated, written in to propose the use of the familiar term *ex*

[39] *Ibid.*, I, 230.
[40] *Ibid.*, I, 227.
[41] So Butler, I, 231.
[42] Butler, I, 278-80.

cathedra, and so many other bishops supported the suggestion that, although the deputation did not favour it, the Council adopted it [43]. Now, in June, Ullathorne wanted to see the phrase *ex ecclesiae magisterio* inserted into the very heart of the definition[44].

Clifford's speech on the policy of now defining the doctrine had been made a month earlier, on May 25th[45]. It was made under the disadvantage that he had to follow Manning who, " obviously anticipating Clifford "—so Ullathorne[46]—had spoken for an hour and three quarters[47]. Clifford made the point that the authority and infallibility of the Pope should not be treated apart from the authority and infallibility of the Church. Amid some interruption he said that the definition would be used by English Protestants to justify the existing prejudice that the Pope is a despot and a tyrant in the Church. In July Clifford proposed to speak a second time, in the debate on the actual text of the definition. But when, after eleven days (June 15th to July 4th), 57 bishops had spoken, and the leaders of both sides agreed to propose that the others who wished to speak should resign their right, all sixty of the intending speakers did so, Clifford with the rest[48]. Errington, meanwhile, had spoken on June 20th: a brief, businesslike recommendation to speed up the procedure, and a proposal to use the word " magisterium " and not " infallibility "[49].

In what Butler calls " the trial vote "—the final vote of the bishops in a General Congregation on the constitution *Pastor Aeternus,* as a whole (July 13th, 1870)—the total votes were: *Placet* (Ayes) 451, *Non Placet* (Noes) 88, *Placet iuxta modum* (Ayes, but conditionally) 62[50]. Six of the English

---

[43] Butler, II, 92.

[44] Butler, II, 111-12.

[45] Butler, II, 52.

[46] Butler, II, 68.

[47] " The speech was one of the triumphs of Manning's life," Butler, II, 50. " I saw dear old Cardinal de Angelis look in despair at the cardinals next to him," wrote Manning, " as if he thought I should never end. But the bishops never moved till I had done "; quoted, *Ibid.,* 50-1.

[48] Butler, II, 106.

[49] Butler, II, 100.

[50] *Ibid.,* II, 49.

bishops were among these 601—Cornthwaite and Chadwick voted *placet;* Ullathorne *placet iuxta modum*[51]; Vaughan, Clifford and Errington *non placet*[52]. Those who voted with a condition, now set out in writing what it was that kept them from a simple assent. Ullathorne's point was that " the introduction of the anathema [which closed the canons attached to the constitution] had been made by the deputation at a time when there was no longer any opportunity of discussion "[53].

The doctrine, then, it was now certain, would be defined in the Public Session announced for July 18th. At the solemn definitive voting on that day, only two bishops voted *Non Placet*[54]. Among the 533 who voted *Placet* were Ullathorne, Vaughan, Cornthwaite and Chadwick[55]. Neither Clifford nor Errington was present.

IV

James Chadwick, the bishop who with Cornthwaite voted *placet* through all the debates on the *Pastor Aeternus,* was the first of the " post-Wiseman ". bishops, consecrated to Hexham and Newcastle on October 28, 1866. He was also the first of the bishops Irish by birth. On his father's side he came of a Lancashire family. But the father had migrated to Drogheda in the early years of the century, and the bishop's mother was an Irishwoman. It was at Drogheda that the bishop was born, April 24, 1813. He was sent to Ushaw as a boy of twelve, and here he was to remain for thirty out of the forty years before his consecration. After his ordination, in 1833, he taught philosophy and then theology until, in 1850, he joined a group of diocesan missioners who worked from a centre at Wooler in Northumberland. In 1856 he returned to Ushaw for three years; and he returned to the college a second time in 1863, after a spell as chaplain to Lord Stourton at Allerton Mauleverer. His career as bishop, said Provost Consitt, preaching at the funeral, " was not a very eventful one "

---

[51] *Ibid.,* II, 154, 165.
[52] *Ibid.,* II, 151.
[53] *Ibid.,* II, 154.
[54] *Ibid,* II, 163; Fitzgerald of Little Rock (Ark.), U.S.A.; and Ricci of Cajazzo.
[55] *Ibid.,* II, 165.

—by which was meant, no doubt, that all the bishop did in sixteen years was steadily to increase the number of churches and schools and priests. But in 1877, at a crisis of Ushaw history, Bishop Chadwick, at the request of the northern bishops, returned to the college yet a third time, to rule it as president for a year, still, of course, retaining his see[56]. The bishop died May 14th, 1882.

Of Thomas Grant, the first Bishop of Southwark, an Irishman who, by the chance of war, was born in France[57], this at least should be said, that all his contemporaries held him to be a saint. As a little boy of ten he attracted the notice of John Briggs, then in charge of the mission of Chester, where the boy's father's regiment was quartered, and it was the future Bishop of Beverley who sent him to Ushaw in 1829. In the next seven years he showed himself a consistently brilliant student, and his later career at Rome, 1836-41, fulfilled all his early promise. For the first two years after his ordination, in 1841, he served Cardinal Acton as his private secretary, and so obtained a most valuable initiation into the practice of the canon law and the business methods of the Roman Curia. In 1844, still two years short of thirty, he was named rector of the English College and Roman agent for the English bishops; and in this post he rendered the most vital services of all once the discussions began about the restoration of the Hierarchy. Ullathorne, in his *Autobiography*, gives Grant the highest praise, " His readiness of resource, his practical knowledge of Roman business, his acquaintance with the Cardinals, his intimacy with Monsignor Palma, whose long and intimate experience in English ecclesiastical affairs gave him great weight in Propaganda, and his promptitude in making himself useful on every occasion . . ."[58].

When Thomas Grant died, prematurely worn out by

[56] As Bishop John Briggs had ruled the college from 1833 to 1836 and as Bishop Thomas William Wilkinson was to rule it from 1890 to 1909.

[57] Where his father, a sergeant in the 71st Foot, was serving in the army of occupation after Waterloo.

[58] Quoted from the second edition of the *Autobiography*, edited by Shane Leslie (1941) under the title *From Cabin Boy to Archbishop*, p. 285. This is the only complete publication of Ullathorne's text.

overwork and the racking complaint of a cancer, it was
Ullathorne again who commemorated him—a man so able, so
loveable, so saintly that it is hard to understand how his
memory has ever been obscured, and his remarkable life given
not a beginning even of the cultus that might have seemed its
due.   Something of what Ullathorne then wrote ought to find
a place in this centenary commemoration of bygone bishops.
" A saint has departed from this world," he wrote, in a letter
of June 1st, 1870.   " The singleness of his heart and purpose
was the same from his innocent childhood to his innocent departure.   His conscience was tremulously delicate.   He was a
child of prayer, and a slave of duty and of charity.   A great
sufferer, physically and spiritually, and that for many years,
he never relaxed, even to the last moments of his life, from
incessant work.   He was always praying, reading, writing;
thinking of everybody but himself.   So many consulted him
on all kinds of subjects, from theology and canon law and
civil law, from cases of conscience and the business and trials
of life, down to the records of past events, points of literature.
. . .   His memory was prodigious, almost miraculous in
its capacity . . .   and accuracy.   His correspondence
was more extensive than that of all the other English bishops
put together. . . .   He moved incessantly through his
diocese, did everything himself, and yet he took care that his
clergy should know where each day the post would find him.
. . .   He has been dying for the last two years . . .   yet
death, repeatedly close to him, neither changed the tone of his
mind nor the unwavering good humour of his character.   He
made no scenes, he took no attitudes, he drew no attention to
himself, his conversation went on in the same agreeable flow
. . .   writing his letters just as usual. . . .   Look at
the diocese of Southwark as it was when he took it, and as it
is now. . . .   All our really successful negotiations with
Government for military chaplains, for mitigation of aggressive laws, for the navy, for workhouses, etc., etc., have been,
directly or indirectly, accomplished through him.
        " He was not only the light of our episcopal meetings,
but the laborious drudge . . .   [work] often done in a
state of great and distressed suffering. . . .   It will never
be known in this world to how many persons of all ranks and

of many countries, he has been a light in darkness, a friend
in need.   In the General Council   .   .   .   perhaps there was
no other single bishop who was so widely and generally known
by bishops of all nations, or of whom, as to sanctity, learning,
and excellent practical sense, there was a higher opinion ''[59].

Thomas Grant's second successor, Robert Aston Coffin,
should also find some place in this scanty chronicle, and that
not merely for his personal merits, but also because he is the
solitary diocesan bishop in all these hundred years chosen from
the regular clergy[60].   At the time of his appointment Robert
Coffin, now a man 63 years of age, was Provincial of the Redemptorists in England, an office he had held for many years.
He was born at Brighton in 1819, educated at Harrow (1834-
36), and at Oxford (Christ Church, 1836).   Charles Bagot, the
Bishop of Oxford so sympathetic to the good intentions of
Newman and his party, ordained Coffin, now an ardent Trac-
tarian, and in 1843 he became vicar of St. Mary Magdalen,
Oxford. He became a Catholic some eight weeks after
Newman, who assisted at his reception into the Church at
Prior Park, December 3rd, 1845.   Fourteen months later he
joined Newman, St. John and others in Rome and with them
made his novitiate as an Oratorian. He was ordained on All
Hallows eve, 1847, and when the property that is now Cotton
College was made over to the Oratorians he was appointed
superior of the small community.   In 1850 he left the Oratory
to become a Redemptorist.   From 1855 to 1865 he was rector
of the house of his order at Clapham, and from 1865 to his
consecration he served as Provincial. The business of a general
chapter brought him to Rome while the see of Westminster

---

[59] *Letters of Archbishop Ullathorne*, 243-9, for the full text of this
touching remembrance.

[60] Of the five Benedictine bishops, Ullathorne and Brown were already
bishops when the Hierarchy was restored; Hedley and James
Romanus Bilsborrow were bishops of the see which, in 1854, the
Holy See " made over " to the English Benedictine Congregation;
Thomas Wulstan Pearson, first bishop of Lancaster, was the first
fulfilment of the quasi-pledge of Rome, after the surrender of the
diocese accepted in 1854, that one of the bishops would always be
an English Benedictine.   Outside the special case of these monk-
bishops, Coffin is the only regular, so far, to rule a diocese as its
ordinary.

was vacant, and Manning's nomination hung in the balance. Some words of Coffin to the influential Cardinal Reisach are thought to have played a part in strengthening the decision of Pius IX to pass over Propaganda's choice (Ullathorne) and appoint Manning. In these long years of Redemptorist life Robert Coffin translated many of the works of St. Alphonsus and he won a great name as a preacher, especially of retreats to the clergy. But he reigned too short a time to leave any mark as Bishop of Southwark[61].

As the Downside Benedictine, Ullathorne, dominates the twenty-five years that immediately followed the restoration of the Hierarchy, so it is the Ampleforth monk, Dom Cuthbert Hedley, who is the outstanding bishop in the generation that follows. But before treating of this truly great figure, whose episcopal life covered the long period of forty-two years, we may first consider a group of five bishops, none of them ordinary men, who were roughly his contemporaries.

The first of these is the third bishop of Northampton, Arthur Riddell, one of the few bishops of the last hundred years who have come from those old Catholic families that were in earlier times the sole support of the Church[62]. That he was such and that, at his death, he was last survivor of his own family, are, however, facts probably less interesting than that the Curé of Ars foretold to his mother that her two-year-old baby would one day be a bishop. And it was seemingly at Riddell's suggestion, presiding (as senior bishop of the province) at the bishops' meeting to consider a successor to Cardinal Vaughan, that the name of the junior bishop, Francis Bourne, was added to the terna[63]. Bishop Riddell, a kinsman

---

[61] March 1882 to April 6, 1885; from July 1884 he was seriously ill and slowly dying, at the house of his order Teignmouth, Devon. He is said to have received into the Church " upwards of 90 Protestant clergymen "; *Tablet*, April 18, 1885, p. 623.

[62] A striking reversal of the older order, for the Vicars-Apostolic from 1688 to 1790 were almost all of gentle birth.

[63] So the late Mgr. Canon Ross to the writer. According to this account the bishops " dropped " from the terna the name of Mgr. Merry del Val on the ground that he was not an English subject, and substituted Bourne's name. The other two names were the Benedictines, Hedley and Gasquet, and the chance intervention at Propaganda of the Cardinal Archbishop of Sydney, Patrick Moran, who had spent a lifetime rooting out all trace of the English Bene-

of the Vicar Apostolic of that name who died of the typhus ministering to the poor of Newcastle in 1847, was born in York in 1836, and he came to the episcopate after twenty-one years of parochial work (1859-80), first at Hull, where he built a church and schools, and then at Scarborough. The *Tablet*, which records " his loveable nature, quiet but unceasing work, tact and affability," notes how, in the vast area of the seven counties confided to him, the number of the Catholics rose in the thirty-seven years he was bishop[64] from 6,000 to 13,000, the churches from 47 to 65 and the priests from 34 to 78.

In the neighbouring see of Nottingham, considered sixty years ago almost as testing as Northampton to the virtues of patience and endurance, this Yorkshire bishop had for a colleague, in the last years of his life, the Lancashireman Robert Brindle—a singular and striking figure of whose record all Catholics of those days were very proud, for twenty-five years of his life had been spent as an army chaplain, and in that time he had managed to see active service in every campaign the army fought. And when he died, an old man of 78, there were still alive witnesses who came forward, with an abundance of stories, about all that his endurance had done to hearten the troops, and about a priestly spirit that frequently touched the heroic—men who had seen him toiling at the oars as Wolseley's army made its way up the Nile in the vain endeavour to rescue Gordon, and who knew of ten-mile tramps across the desert by night to give the last sacraments to fever-stricken soldiers. It was the Khartoum expedition that won him the D.S.O. The bishop was born at Liverpool in 1837, and through a relative, that Dr. Brindle who was the right-hand man of Bishop Baines (another Liverpool worthy), he came to be associated with the west of England. He was a pupil of the English College at Lisbon (later legend said he ran away to fight in the Crimean War) and for the first twelve years after his ordination (1862-74) he was attached to the cathedral at Plymouth. He came out of the army in 1899 to be appointed auxiliary bishop to Cardinal Vaughan, and in 1901 became the fourth Bishop of Nottingham, which see he ruled

dictine work in Australia, was a turning point in the history of Catholicism in this country.

[64] Consecrated June 9, 1880; died September 15, 1907.

for fourteen years until his resignation, at the age of 77, in 1915. He died June 27th, 1916.

John Bilsborrow, the third bishop of Salford, has a claim to remembrance as a principal leader in the most successful of the educational fights to establish the rights of Englishmen not " Cowper-Templeist " in religion to an equal share of public monies with those who are. " There is little doubt," said the *Manchester Guardian,* recording his death in March, 1903, " that his influence in moulding the educational policy of the Catholic hierarchy during his episcopate has been very considerable, perhaps only second to that of Cardinal Vaughan himself." The Education Question, as it was in those days, he knew in all its detail; he saw it as the simple matter of principle it has always been, and he was able to demonstrate his case with lucidity and force and a simple Lancastrian indignation that never failed to be effective. And yet he was a bishop of whom the same paper could truly say, " He never took the prominent position in the public eye which his distinguished predecessor, Dr. Vaughan, occupied for twenty years. He was rarely seen on public platforms or at social gatherings. He was most at home in the pulpit, where he was forcible and impressive, and spoke with an earnestness of conviction that was decidedly striking."

John Bilsborrow came of farming stock and, like a good score of the bishops of the penal days and sub-penal days, he came from the Fylde of Lancashire, where he was born, at Singleton Lodge, March 30th, 1836. His studies were made at Ushaw, in the heyday of Mgr. Newsham's presidency (1851-65) and after his ordination he served for seven years at Barrow-in-Furness, where he built a church and schools. Then, to recover from a severe illness brought on by years of hard work, he was sent in 1872 to his own home countryside, as priest in charge at Newsham (1872-9). It was about this time that the Bishop of Liverpool[65] was planning the new seminary of Upholland. John Bilsborrow, intended for one of the chairs, gave up his parish and resumed his studies at the Gregorian University. It was not, however, until 1885

[65] The third bishop, Bernard O'Reilly, a first-cousin of Bishop James Chadwick, born at Drogheda 1824, educated at Ushaw, ordained before his time to replace priests who died of the famine fever, in 1847; Bishop of Liverpool 1873-1894.

that he received his appointment as Rector of the new seminary and in the meantime he served the missions of Ainsdale and Grange-over-Sands, where also he built a church. It was, then, a native of the county and a man of wide practical experience that Salford received as its bishop in August, 1892, upon the translation of Herbert Vaughan to Westminster; and the ten years of his effective, but in no way spectacular rule, saw great advances, due entirely to the initiative of this far-seeing and kindly old man, *tam pater nemo*, whose episcopal device might well have been set by way of epitaph over his grave in the grim cemetery where he lies, *I have compassion on the multitude*.

John Bilsborrow, a solidly read man, would have distrusted instinctively anyone who spoke of him as a scholar. But the last two of this particular group of bishops, William Robert Brownlow and Samuel Webster Allen, were scholars essentially, and to the end, despite a lifetime given entirely to parochial work.

William Robert Brownlow, Bishop of Clifton, 1894-1901, was born on July 4th, 1830, the son of the rector of Wilmslow, Cheshire. He was educated at Rugby (where he missed Arnold's care by a matter of months only) and Trinity College, Cambridge, where he graduated ninth senior optime in 1852. He took orders in the Church of England and after serving various cures for ten years he became a Catholic in 1863. " It was history more than anything else," he was to write later, " that brought me into the Church," words which re-echo those of the priest who received him, Newman, " To be deep in history is to cease to be a Protestant." After three years in Rome, at the Collegio Pio, Brownlow was ordained priest, for the diocese of Plymouth, on December 22nd, 1866. His first appointment was to Torquay, where he had held his last Anglican curacy. For the next twenty-eight years he filled a variety of diocesan posts—inspector of schools, canon of the cathedral chapter (1878), vicar-general (1888), provost of the chapter (1893)—while serving various missions. And during these years he never ceased to study and to write. With Dr. Northcote he published a classic work on the catacombs, *Roma Sottereana*, and two historical books, *The Early History of the Church of God* and *Slavery and Serfdom in Europe*.

Brownlow was almost 64 when he was consecrated fourth Bishop of Clifton on May 1st, 1894, and he ruled the diocese for barely seven years. But in those seven years he won a place in the public life of the great city of Bristol that makes him unique among the bishops of this see. In all its social activities he was a much welcomed leader, and especially in the work of the Royal Society for the Prevention of Cruelty to Children. He died on November 9th, 1901.

Samuel Webster Allen, the fourth Bishop of Shrewsbury, was also a short-lived prelate. He was born at Stockport in 1844, and after studies at Oscott and the English College, Rome, he was ordained on December 4th, 1870. During the Vatican Council he had the interesting experience of serving as one of the official shorthand writers who recorded the debates. After his ordination he served as secretary to the first Bishop of Shrewsbury, James Brown, until his death (1871-80), and at the same time as curate and then administrator of the cathedral—which last appointment he held until his own nomination to the see in 1897[66]. Meanwhile Allen played his part in public life with general credit, as vice-chairman of the Poor Law Guardians and vice-chairman also of the local School Board. The bishop was an accomplished Italian scholar, but his lifelong predilection was the new field of oriental studies— Syriac and, more especially, Egyptology; and he built up a remarkable Egyptological library. He was barely 53 when appointed Bishop of Shrewsbury, but his time was to be short, for he died on May 13th, 1908.

" This day a Prince has fallen in Israel," said the *Tablet*, announcing in November, 1915, the death of Bishop Hedley and appropriately putting the page into mourning. He was, indeed, and he had been for years, as Cardinal Bourne declared, " the leader of the bench of bishops "; and this position he owed, in the first place, to the possession of a fine mind, cultivated and developed through a lifetime's study of the best, and ceaselessly exercised upon all the thought of the

[66] This unusual circumstance, of the whole of his priestly life spent in the same cure, was to be repeated in the career of this bishop's nephew, Ambrose James Moriarty, who served this same cathedral church from his ordination to his own appointment as Bishop-coadjutor of the see (1895-1932).

day, secular and religious, the theology, the philosophy, the
history, the natural sciences. " He could give an appreciation
of Professor Zahm," his biographer wrote, " he could advise
Baron von Hügel or correct Professor Mivart; he could offer
a criticism of Herbert Spencer; he could appraise the work of
Darwin and Huxley and adjudge its influence on current
thought"[67]. And the scholar so gifted was at heart an artist.
Here, indeed, to speak of natural endowments, lay the secret of
his power over two generations of English Catholic life.   In
many respects one is tempted to compare him with that other
scholar among the bishops who was a writer and a preacher,
Wiseman—but while Wiseman was interested in all the arts
to the point of fascination, it was rather as a learned connoisseur.   Hedley was a practitioner; and—unlike Wiseman—
one whose instructed senses were grimly intolerant of all but
the perfect.   The art to which he gave himself was the use of
his own native tongue, and in his mastery of this most difficult
business the musician is apparent, as he is apparent in the
faultless rhythms of Newman, Hedley's master and acknowledged such.   Of this discipleship and its effect it was right
that the prelate who preached at the funeral should speak,
" Among our modern Catholic writers he is inferior to one only,
and yet with that one he might have said: ' I think I never
have written for writing's sake: but to express clearly and
exactly my meaning ' "[68].

The artist's characteristic weakness, to make his art an
end in itself and the main end of his life, has no place here.
What is operative is the commonsense of Aristotle, informed
by the supernatural and subdued ultimately to ends that are
divine, art being a right way—and, precisely, the right way of
making.   Hedley, austere of aspect, sturdy, Northumbrian in
every feature and in every fibre of his natural being, his will
disciplined to devotedness by the firm grasp of his intelligence
on all the essentials, with " short shrift for sheer silliness,"
and " an excellent sense of humour which officialism did not
dull," in an episcopal life of forty-two years—surely the Eng-

[67] Wilson, *Life of Bishop of Hedley,* 56.
[68] The preacher was George Ambrose Burton, Bishop of Clifton, from
whose sermon come all the quotations that follow, except they are
otherwise noted.

lish monk to perfection—once unwittingly, in a score of words, described his own lifetime's aim (and his great achievement), as he explained to beginners what it is that is found " virtually nowhere except in the Fathers of the Church." In the Fathers, he thought, we have " the inestimable advantage of hearing our religion put into words by a man with a personality, a style and a distinction of his own . . ."[69]. In seven books[70] published during his time as a bishop, in scores of pastoral letters and in numberless sermons and addresses, Dom Cuthbert Hedley was all this for a good forty years to the Catholics of this country, a candle set, indeed, " upon a candlestick, that it may shine to all that are in the house."

In his writing the bishop " is always straight to the point, the foe of nebulosity and muddle, in diction copious, often majestic, always abounding in apt imagery "; and so it fell out that, " the Bishops of England possessed in him not only one who could aid them with his ripe experience, but upon whom they could count, whensoever the need arose, to give fitting and noble expression to their united deliberations and feelings."

How all this was achieved the simple record of the bishop's early life soon reveals, and a moment's consideration of the ideal to whose formative influence he had surrendered himself, once for all, in early boyhood. Achievement, of course, it was; something done, whatever the aids, *per proprias operationes*. Personages whose gifts are infinitely below those which glorify the great writers can still stare as they hear the Bossuets complaining how they need to chain themselves to their desks. And if this monk, who " made leisure, by the wise disposal of his time, to write and publish for the edification of all," was the bishop of a diocese that ranked among the smallest, there came upon him, by reason of its very exiguity, what comes to every priest single-handed in a small parish, the daily need to turn his hand to every variety of

[69] *Lex Levitarum,* 73-4.
[70] Three collections of sermons, *Our Divine Saviour, The Light of Life, The Christian Inheritance*; a collection of pastoral letters, *The Bishop and his Flock; Lex Levitarum, or Preparation for the Cure of Souls; The Holy Eucharist; A Retreat.* Two other books—*A Retreat for Priests, A Retreat for Religious*—were published posthumously.

tasks: the diocese of Newport and Menevia had no staff of canonists and financiers and secretaries to take the hack work of administration from a gifted bishop's shoulders—had he desired such relief. When Hedley, in 1881, entered on his life as its hard-working bishop, there were only 13 secular priests at work in the diocese—eight of them lent by other bishops—and 47 churches and chapels. When he died there were 54 secular clergy belonging to the diocese, and the churches and chapels had risen to 80[71]. He had 40,000 Catholics to care for when he succeeded to the see, and these had doubled by the time he died[72]. It is little wonder that, " In the early days his appointment as bishop came as a disappointment to many, who regretted a genuine literary vocation should be spoilt"[73].

John Hedley (he was Cuthbert by religious profession) was born at Morpeth in 1837, and in 1848 he was sent to the Benedictine school at Ampleforth, then in its heroic age, slowly recovering from the assault which had left it for dead by the road. At the end of his studies he offered himself as a postulant and he was professed a monk in 1855. Seven years later he was ordained priest, and then, just as the priory might hope to see its school profit from the most brilliant recruit thirty years had brought to it, he was appointed to teach in the newly established general house of studies at Belmont Priory near Hereford. The church of this priory was the pro-cathedral of the diocese of Newport and Menevia, and from its monks the cathedral chapter of the see was formed. Though Dom Cuthbert could not have guessed it, he had reached the land where he was to live and work for the rest of his long life, fifty-three years.

At Belmont he was set to teach the young monks the theory and the art of preaching, and then philosophy and then theology; and for eleven years he worked himself—and them —very hard. This was long before the days of Leo XIII's fruitful imposition of St. Thomas Aquinas as *doctor communis,* but at Belmont, under the strong influence of this very young

[71] And this in a diocese diminished, since 1881, by the loss of the south Welsh counties.
[72] For the figures, Wilson, *Life of Bishop Hedley,* pp. 127-8 (1930).
[73] *The Tablet,* November, 1915, in a leading article.

monk, no time was wasted on the superficialities of the rhetorical apologists of the early nineteenth century. Standards were high, as the work was hard. And like Ullathorne, and his own Benedictine ordinary, Thomas Joseph Brown, once Ullathorne's master, Hedley became a great reader of the Fathers. And it was now that he began to write, and to be published.

Dom Cuthbert Hedley was just under 36, and Canon Theologian of the chapter when, in 1873, at the petition of Bishop Brown now in his 75th year, he was named auxiliary bishop. Some years later the old bishop died, and after an interval of nearly a year the bishop-auxiliary was appointed in his place (1881). Three years before this, in 1878, he had accepted the editorship of the *Dublin Review*, in succession to W. G. Ward and he retained it for three years more. And it was about this same time (1884) that Hedley made his first declarations (if that be the right word) in favour of the ban being lifted that kept Catholics from the universities of Oxford and Cambridge, about which most important activity of the bishop's life something is said elsewhere in this volume. Like all the strict ecclesiastics whose strictness is rooted in theological principles really and fully understood, and not in a personal attachment to the appearances of things, Hedley had not a touch of fanaticism in his character; and as he knew no fear, save that of offending God, so was he wholly inaccessible to panic, and ready to direct others—and save them from their own weaker selves—on broad, simple lines. Here again, what is active is the monastic tradition; and in the bishop's attitude in the controversy whether Catholics should be allowed to go to Oxford and Cambridge he is, it seems, the heir and disciple to that still stiffer character his predecessor in the see. The same unhurried, instructed judgment, and the calm, courageous confidence it produces, are again to be seen in Hedley's action during the crises that followed Pius X's exposure of the miserable superficialities of the movement called Modernism. Here he kept his head, as Ullathorne kept his head in the Second Spring; and, like Ullathorne, he was no doubt the cause of others keeping their heads too[74].

St. Gregory the Great, dedicated to an apostolate of

---

[74] For this, cf. *Insurrection versus Resurrection*, by Maisie Ward, 1937, Chapters XI-XV.

active charity, is the pattern of all true monks no less surely
than St. Benedict himself, their patriarch. And it is with some
of Hedley's own words about St. Gregory, spoken in Westminster Cathedral, that we may leave the memory of this great
English monk who so glorified the Hierarchy of this country,
words which, once again, reveal the real heart of all his own
life. " The soul is ' enlarged,' says the saint, by the sight of
God. *Videnti Creatorem angusta est creatura;* to him who
looks on the Creator, narrow, narrow is all that is created.
Narrow indeed! What was the Roman emperor, what was the
fierce Lombard, what was the ocean, what were earth and
space, to the man who sat near the tomb of St. Peter and had
his spirit and heart filled with the communication of the mighty
spirit of the Lord of heaven and earth? . . . That terrible time
when St. Gregory thought the last days were near—it seems,
in his writings, to have been almost a time of peace. He lives
and acts as if there was nothing to disturb him. . . . He shows
that he is solidly at peace . . . his heart is steady, his vision
clear, his will is with his God "[75].

[75] *St. Gregory the Great*, a sermon preached . . . at the centenary
celebration, March 12, 1904; printed in *Lex Levitarum;* the quotation is from page iv.

VII

OLD CATHOLICS AND CONVERTS

By David Mathew

THE actual restoration of the Hierarchy does not appear
to have been of deep concern to the old English Catholic
body. Their principal representatives had been much
more disturbed by the incursion of clergymen which had followed upon Dr. Newman's submission. They were affected
by the impact of Father Faber and his Wilfridians on their
old-fashioned ways. Profoundly conservative in their outlook
the rich Catholic landowners were only now accustoming themselves to their political freedom. The Queen had been on the
Throne for thirteen years and had endeared herself to her
Catholic subjects; her sharp comments on their Faith were
very seldom known to them.

The core of the hereditary Catholic position was the
network of estates in Northumberland and Durham and the
farming stocks in Lancashire and especially in the Fylde. In
Yorkshire there were certain pockets, particularly in the North
Riding, and throughout the North and Midlands a proportion
of Catholic labourers and farmers could still be found among
the tenants of an estate whose owners had remained faithful to
the Old Religion. In East Anglia and in the southern and
western counties the Catholic village unit was normally of
minor consequence. At Oxburgh, Costessey, Thorndon,
Mapledurham, Buckland, Tichborne, Chideock and Ugbrooke
the Catholic population was not considerable. It was rather
more impressive at East Hendred and Lulworth and at
Wardour and in the town of Tisbury. In spite of patronage
from the great house the tendency in such parishes was for the
congregation to diminish. The chapels were in some cases
maintained to a large extent by the indoor staff, who now for
half a century had tended to belong to that phalanx of English
Catholics in domestic service whose numbers filled every post

of trust in the fine mansions. There appears to have been no general effort to attract Catholic tenants when the farms fell vacant. It may be that the atmosphere of genial tolerance tended to militate against this practice. The old English Catholic stocks were absorbed in the routine of rural life. It was not as yet the custom for the eldest sons of squires to purchase a military commission. The universities were still closed to them and there was as yet no widespread desire on the part of Catholics to attend them. A certain amount of travel was customary but does not seem to have made a great appeal. There was a good deal of contact with Paris and a number of Catholic girls were brought up in French convents and were associated with an Anglo-French Catholic group in Paris. The parents of Roger Tichborne belonged to this circle, which was without any definite French political affiliation. In general the eldest sons of squires would settle down in early manhood on their fathers' acres. The eighteenth-century practice of many younger sons living at home was still continued. The estate agents on the larger properties were, too, often members of a wide cousinage. Three generations of Mostyns acted in this capacity for the Dukes of Norfolk. Neighbourly ties united Catholic and Protestant landowners. Attachment to their own countryside and a certain absence of outside interests tended to increase the local influence of the Catholic squires.

If the squires seldom moved, the first stirrings of industrialism had an effect upon their tenants. The history of Catholicism in the Army has not as yet been studied, but it would not appear that that life attracted the agricultural labourer. These were lured by the prospects of the growing towns. It is interesting to speculate to what extent the young men coming from these Catholic " islands " strengthened the town parishes of the Industrial Age. In Preston, St. Walburge's was founded in 1850 and St. Augustine's and St. Gregory's had been established in the fifteen years preceding the restoration of the Hierarchy. These developments were the immediate results of the movement of the population from the hereditary Catholic farm lands of the Fylde. In this connection it would be of interest to study the two streams of Catholic labour, that coming into Preston from the Fylde and converging upon

Liverpool and Chorley from their rural hinterland, and the Irish immigration pressing to the Mersey ports and Manchester and spreading fanwise from Wigan to St. Helens.

The development of Middlesbrough belongs to a later period than that which we are now considering and the early Irish immigration in the North-East would seem to have been concentrated on Tyneside. In both Northumberland and Durham there was a long-established Catholic rural population which would be drawn upon by each successive opening of industrial plant. In the North of England there would appear to have been a definite proportion of Catholics working upon the construction of the railway system which marked these years. Catholics in independent business gained reinforcement from the country parishes. In Northumberland and Durham many families in business in the growing towns traced back their roots to the villages dependent upon Croxdale and Felton, Swinburne, Stella, Minsteracres and Hesleyside. It would be valuable to investigate to what extent the young men coming from the Catholic " islands " strengthened the town parishes of the Industrial Age. At a later date some of the leading Cardiff families sprang from the tenant farmers at Courtfield and Llanarth.

It is probable that the old Catholics benefited less than any other section of the community from the new industrial prosperity. They had always had their substantial merchants of whom Bishop Challoner's friend Brian Barret of Milton may be cited as an example. They had their conveyancers and physicians, their wine merchants and printer-booksellers. These, however, were the old professions and respected trades. There were Catholics among the men and women who laboured at the new machines but very few among those who drew their profit from them, a few families in the wool trade and some mill owners whose children's names are in the old registers of Ampleforth and Stonyhurst.

Similarly there were few Catholics among the class of new investors, for the squires were as a rule conservative in this matter, preferring to put their money into house property or land. There were whole sections of English life which the Catholic community did not penetrate, the clerical and academic worlds, the new industrialism, the groups from which the Civil Service was then recruited. The great mercantile grouping of the City of London was alien soil to them. Yet these were the quarters from which so many of the men would come who joined the Church through the Oxford Movement. At the moment it was the landed interest and that alone which was predominant in the Catholic body.

Returning to a consideration of the landowners, it may be said that it was the squirearchy rather than the peers which gave the tone to the climate of opinion. The leading Catholic in the Upper House was the sixteenth Earl of Shrewsbury, an elderly man, serious and splendidly generous but in character in no sense typical. He lacked the mark of an essential insularity. His tastes were cosmopolitan and he was much at ease in the Rome of Gregory XVI; his two daughters were married to Roman princes. Lord Clifford was of the same way of thinking without Lord Shrewsbury's patronage of Pugin or his ascetic and Gothic sides. He was a son-in-law of Cardinal Weld and had a villa at Tivoli: his son William, later Bishop of Clifton, was a student at the *Accademia degli Ecclesiastici Nobili*. Much more in keeping with the general traditions of their grouping were the four sons of the seventeenth Lord Stourton whose names and properties, all situated in Yorkshire, illustrate the system of accretion and re-dispersal that was going on continuously among that enclosed cousinage; Lord Stourton of Allerton, Sir Edward Vavasour of Haslewood, Charles Langdale of Houghton and Philip Stourton of Holme-on-Spalding-Moor. Among these figures Charles Langdale is the name to note.

In any case the Catholic peers were as a factor inconsiderable. Out of a total of some twenty or so, including the holders of Scottish and Irish titles, they could muster only twelve votes in the House of Lords. These were further reduced by the fact that two votes were pledged to the Whig Government on every issue, while Lord Howden, the only convert, was *en poste* at Rio de Janeiro.

Some points may be made in regard to the old landed stocks. In 1850 they still sent a proportion of their sons into the Religious Orders and many daughters into convents of every kind. Jean-Nicholas Grou, the author of the *Maximes spirituelles*, had been chaplain at Lulworth Castle and had died there; he had had a certain direct influence on this grouping. Their piety had a light-hearted note: in a sense the shadow of the Georgian world lay on them, the moral, domesticated, yet outspoken world of King George III and Queen Charlotte. They were one of the few religious groups in England which were not subjected to the influence of the Evangelicals. In this connection it is worth considering the case of the Vaughan family. Old Bishop William Vaughan of Plymouth was a nephew of Cardinal Weld and had all the familiar old Catholic characteristics, but Herbert Vaughan and his brothers and sisters and nephews were a very different proposition. Here it was the influence of the mother that was decisive. Mrs. John Vaughan had been brought up a Welsh Anglican of Evangelical principles. This is surely reflected in the nature of her children's piety, which was so self-confident and warm and uninhibited. Their deep sense of " separateness " suggests an Evangelical family background rather than the rollicking schoolrooms of the Catholic squirearchy. In later life Herbert Vaughan would find his affinity among converts of a certain school. Few others approached the influence which Manning and Lady Herbert of Lea exercised on him. From a different angle it may be noted that Herbert Vaughan and his brethren and Manning and Lady Herbert all took ecclesiastical rank with an almost painful seriousness. It was a matter to which they gave much thought; such was not the practice of the Old Catholics. At the same time these points are just suggested and not pressed. In other respects, such as their deeply conservative approach and their unbreakable fidelity, the Vaughans conformed to the old Recusant pattern.

As a general rule the wealthier members of the Catholic community travelled less than their fathers had done; they settled down easily to what was now becoming the organised life of the hunting counties. Their property was for the most part in agricultural land and they were in consequence little touched by the new developments. In this regard the position of the Towneleys at Burnley was exceptional. Some families had fairly extensive holdings in London ground-rents. The Tichbornes owned Doughty Street until the houses were sold one by one to meet the costs of the Tichborne Trial. The great families usually recognised their obligation to provide churches

where they held much property, as the Dukes of Norfolk built
St. Marie's, Sheffield. Landowners of position often acknowledged their duty to construct or to join with other gentlemen
to construct a Catholic church in the county town. A private
chapel was invariably attached to each Catholic mansion;
Wardour Chapel is perhaps the finest example in England.
Such chaplaincies were usually but not invariably served by
the regular clergy.

In their approach to the new century the old Catholics
were in general not reactionary, but they were markedly
detached from current political problems. A vehement dislike
of railways was mainly found among the fine old Tory Protestants. On the other hand Mr. Charlton of Hesleyside was an
active promoter of the new lines. Usually the men who
opposed the railways opposed Tract XC.

It must not be thought that there was among the
Catholic squirearchy any ill will towards converts. They were
however, expected to accept the general way of life of those
who had maintained the ancient Faith through the hard centuries. Bishop James Yorke Bramston after going down from
Trinity College, Cambridge, had been a pupil of Charles Butler
and it was the latter's personality which had led him first to
enquire about and then to join the Catholic Church. He was
Vicar Apostolic of the London District from 1827 until 1836
and was a good example of a man who had accepted the outlook and the values of the old stocks. Sir Charles Wolseley
and Ambrose de Lisle may be mentioned as young squires of
large fortune who proved acceptable. It was a question of those
who were prepared to enter within the citadel. After these
preliminary comments the other groups and their interactions
can be examined.

The work of the prominent members of the laity has
been affected in a greater or a less degree by the climate of
ecclesiastical opinion and it is of interest to examine the different situations which arose in the second half of the nineteenth
century. There were three groups varying very greatly in
numbers and opportunity within which leadership might be
discovered, the old Catholics and their tenants and satellites,
the compact although cleavage-ridden body of the converts
and the large masses of the Irish immigration. This third

group was extremely numerous and after the extension of the franchise politically significant; from its midst there came those leaders who swung the Irish vote in the years when Home Rule became an issue. For the rest it was the old Catholics and the converts who alone possessed the advantages which would enable a man to attain to prominence in the middle period of Victorian England.

The life of Charles Waterton is characteristic of the vitality and originality of the old landed stocks whose members would sometimes amass expert knowledge provided that this was kept free from mere book learning. Waterton was sixty-eight years of age at the restoration of the Hierarchy and survived until 1865. He was a naturalist of distinction and was praised for his attractive style by Sydney Smith. In the museum at Stonyhurst there is a delightful picture in which he is shown riding on an alligator, a cayman, on the banks of the Essequibo river. He had the independence of mind of an earlier time and a ready acceptance of each adventure. He was a man of simplicity and found all ways made smooth for him. In his early life his uncle had introduced him to Sir Joseph Banks, who will always be remembered for his consignment of bread fruit trees in that voyage of the *Bounty* which ended in mutiny. Like all those squires of his generation, to whom political life made no appeal, he had never suffered from persecution. His contacts with his neighbours were easy and they were proud of him. Waterton's sympathies were not confined to those of his own tradition; his favourite author was Laurence Sterne.

In spite of his unique charm and what may be held to be his eccentricities, he was yet in some ways not untypical. He belonged to that generation in which Catholics of position, and especially those few with scientific tastes, were regarded with a tolerant generosity by the powerful interests which had desired or had consented to Emancipation. In that old world it was, perhaps, not hard for Catholics to win recognition. In the period before the Oxford Movement it was a satisfaction to men of Liberal sentiments to note that members of the Church of Rome were not denied an allotted place. This can be seen in many different fields. Thus in regard to historical study it may be held that Lingard's later influence was curtailed unduly, but the actual reception of his *History of Eng-land* was at the time of writing on the whole friendly. Sir Arnold Knight was welcomed as a physician and in the civic life of his own town. It was during these years that Mr. Stonor sat as a member of Parliament for Oxford City. With the exception of Mr. Stonor, afterwards Lord Camoys, the men mentioned here did not belong to the squirearchy, but they were to some extent established in their positions as a result of the prestige, arising from social consequence and landed wealth, which attached to that body.

It may be suggested that the Whig, although not the Tory, political grouping was conscience-stricken in their regard. There was a certain unexpressed desire to make amends Catholics in the services and the professions therefore gained as a result of the general sense in influential circles that the Penal Laws had been both unjust and anachronistic. It is probable that the Catholics who first entered into these fields the Howards and Jerninghams in diplomacy and the Cliffords and Dormers in the army, made at least as much progress in these careers as might have been expected from their abilities and influence. The last word is crucial for in the period of nominations to the foreign service and the purchase of commissions the notion of influence was inseparable from the development of any career other than the commercial. Cardinal Wiseman came to Westminster in the heyday of family influence and during the last years of sinecure. It is worth noting that Anthony Trollope's novel *Phineas Finn* was not published until 1869; that work is a contemporary study of political manipulation by a patron or patroness. The hero is one of Trollope's few Catholic characters. Throughout the years of Wiseman the life of the Catholic laity was conditioned by the climate of mid-Victorian patronage.

At this period, and for motives different from those which have just been considered, Irish Catholics who had been educated in England and had entered Government service were received with a certain degree of favour. In 1850 the brothers Sir Justin and Richard Lalor Shiel held the posts of British Minister to the Shah of Persia and the Grand Duke of Tuscany. The veteran Sir Martin Archer Shee was in his last year as President of the Royal Academy. Linked with this grouping but not related to them was Serjeant Shee who was to be the first Catholic to become a justice of the Court of Queen's Bench since Emancipation. He was the son of an Irish merchant settled in Finchley, who had married into the old Recusant family of Darell of Scotney. Except for the forensic power of Richard Lalor Shiel, no especial abilities need be attributed to these four men. They had come to their successes easily and the tide was with them.

It was in accordance with the tradition of the times that a considerable public prestige was accorded to the lay spokesmen for the Catholic body. These included at that date the Hon. Charles Langdale and Lord Howard of Glossop, who were in succession chairmen of the Catholic Poor School Committee from the beginning of this period until 1877. The men who now came to prominence were nearly always either wealthy or at least possessed of adequate resources. Dickie Doyle, the illustrator who resigned from *Punch* on account of that paper's attitude towards " Papal Aggression," was one of the few exceptions to this rule. Many prominent Catholics in these years of Cardinal Wiseman were closely attached to the Society of Jesus; they were the penitents of those old fathers who had taught at Stonyhurst before any one had thought about the Oxford Movement. Politically the Catholic landed grouping had still certain ties with the Whigs, but it was a type of affiliation which it is difficult to define. They viewed the Radicals with sharp distaste and the Tories had opposed Emancipation. It was left for the next generation to move over to support Disraeli and Lord Salisbury. Sir John Pope-Hennessy, who entered Parliament in 1859, was the first Catholic member to sit as a Conservative.

In considering the old Catholic grouping and their supporters and the men who came forward to some extent beneath their influence it is interesting to observe an almost complete absence of prominent lay women. In the generation which was between fifty and thirty in 1850 there is an effect of dullness. Emancipation had been won, and men were inclined to rest on what O'Connell had achieved for them. They gave expression to their loyalty to the House of Brunswick. A certain freedom of manners had survived from the eighteenth century, but with some exceptions they conformed to a rather rigid social and political orthodoxy. In general they may be looked upon as the men whom the Oxford Movement put upon their guard.

In their minds conversion was linked up with the notion of enthusiasm, which in turn suggested Methodism. They had been brought up to a strict reticence in everything that related to religious practice. The only type of convert they accepted was the layman who adopted their own code. The Evangelical note, which was a constituent element in the Tractarian outlook, was profoundly uncongenial. The parsons to whom they were accustomed were well-mannered and convivial and with sporting proclivities. They disliked a clergyman who might show himself excitable or emotional; not such were their own priests. As a group they were united in their reactions to Father Faber's words and writings. The sons of these men were sometimes the devoted followers of John Henry Newman. Among other qualities it was, perhaps, his reticence that appealed to them. This, however, belongs to a later period when the *Apologia pro Vita Sua,* which was printed in the year before Wiseman died, had brought Dr. Newman to his great fame. The old Catholics and their followers were certainly a stalwart generation. Did Manning gain the confidence of any one of them?

The converts present a very different picture but one which lacks the unity that springs from several generations of proscription. There were for the most part directly or indirectly Newman's disciples and none of the laymen were over forty in 1850. Even Ambrose de Lisle, who had been converted at Cambridge a quarter of a century previously, was only born in 1809. The greater number came from the universities, and many of the more vital from clerical-landed or mercantile-landed stocks. None of the peers who came with this first wave were men of any considerable attainments.

It was characteristic of the Oxford Movement converts that so many of them should have retained through life the contacts, if not the unimpaired friendships,. which they had first formed when undergraduates. So many of them moved within a closed academic circle which was small, secluded and intimate but ultimately influential. No clearer impression of the atmosphere of the old common rooms can be obtained than that provided in the Memoirs which Mark Pattison, who once was Newman's disciple, wrote when Rector of Lincoln. The picture is almost photographic with Pattison's sharp, arid comment in the settled calm of the eighteen-eighties. Newman kept his private world and communicated in what was almost a private language. At the same time the circumference of his discipleship was central to the mid-Victorian scene in thought and letters. Thus Tennyson and Ruskin had close contacts with its members. Many of the converts had self-confidence and an adventurous spirit. These qualities are apparent in William George Ward's friendship with John Stuart Mill.

An interesting feature in the lives of the laymen from the Oxford Movement was their relation with the clergy. It was singularly independent whether in criticism, friendship or dislike. In the case of Richard Simpson, the editor of the *Rambler* and biographer of Campion, his attitude was marked by an irreverent independence which had no counterpart among the standpoint of his new English co-religionists. On the other hand there was maintained between Ward and Manning a curiously equal friendship which on both sides had something of the proprietary. The converts were often without that sense of distance which marked the approach of the old Catholics to all priests except those who were members of their own family. They had, too, an approach to the Roman Curia which was wholly novel. In regard to the Court of Rome the men of the old tradition were accustomed to assume one of two attitudes, either what could be termed a mild Cisalpine outlook which bore some resemblance to a loyal and detached Gallicanism or else that filial and respectful distance which the Jesuits of the older school would inculcate. Ward, of course, was an exception, but his efforts to influence Pio Nono in the matter of the nomination of Manning to Westminster was something that had not been seen before. Equally unmeasured was Coventry Patmore's expression of intense dislike for the same prelate.

It seems exact to suggest that the majority of the converts were conscious of the ecclesiastical world. They included those who listened to and read Fr. Faber, those who were in at least a remote fashion Newman's disciples and that small but significant grouping who were Manning's friends and admirers. As a body they had an attitude or rather a series of attitudes

towards church music and church architecture and also broadly
speaking to spiritual writings and methods of devotion. A
considerable proportion were sons of the clergy and nearly all
had been brought up in that strict circle where the day began
and ended with the reading of the Bible and family prayers.
In certain convert households whose records have come down
to us there was a Sabbatarian strictness and almost a sense of
Election: the mid-Victorian converts owed more to the
Evangelical tradition than they ever admitted.

They may be said to have offered a corporate immola-
tion of the chances of worldly success. It is difficult to recall
the name of any convert of that first generation who made a
really great worldly career. James Hope-Scott for all his
wide practice at the parliamentary Bar yet never made that
progress through forensic triumphs to judicial honours that
had been predicted for him. It would be a mistake to over-
emphasize this point; it is, however, clear that among the
early waves of converts the lives of many were both canalized
and deflected. This was perhaps the case with Robert Ornsby
and Thomas William Allies and John Hungerford Pollen; all
three were drawn into Newman's university venture in Dublin
The career of the biologist St. George Mivart was clearly deflected by his acceptance of a " chair " in Manning's late
experiment in South Kensington.

There was often an element of difficulty in the life of the
Anglican clergyman who remained a layman after his conversion, like Richard Simpson and Allies. Such men were in
general cut off from the university circle in which they had
sometimes been for long established. In the case of Allies
it may be suggested that it was neither academic opinion in
England nor his co-religionists in his own country but rather
Catholic opinion on the Continent which valued his eight
volumes on *The Formation of Christendom*. In a wholly new
way the converts looked to Pius IX and later to Leo XIII as
their fatherly and immediate protector. To those of an older
tradition they appeared to be preoccupied with the personal
aspects of the Papacy. This was reinforced by the fact that
the bulk of the converts either came of Tory stock or adopted
Conservative principles before conversion. They abhorred
those who attacked their legitimate rulers. The sufferings of

the Sovereign Pontiff at the hands of the Piedmontese were an outrage to their convictions and called forth a filial and chivalrous devotion for the venerable person of Pius IX.

This matter, however, belongs rather to the consideration of the second wave of conversions; but there are one or two points that might be made in regard to the position of the predominantly clerical body of converts who were received into the Church between 1845 and 1850. A high proportion of these men were young unmarried clergy who entered the Religious Orders or helped to form the Oratories or joined the ranks of the secular priests. As such they are outside the scope of the present essay, although it would be interesting to note the factors that separated them from or linked them to the priests of the old tradition. It is probably accurate to suggest that their acceptance was a very gradual affair; it was perhaps most rapid in the case of those who, like Frederick Oakeley, placed themselves under the direction of the Society of Jesus which had always had a strong following among the Recusants.

In general it may be said that it was suffering which commended individual convert leaders to the laymen and clergy of the ancient stocks. In that sense it was the Achilli trial which did so much to establish Newman. In this instance Newman was sentenced by an English court and browbeaten by an English judge for the crime of telling the truth about an arrant scoundrel. Such circumstances would appeal to the most philistine. This was in 1853. Following out the argument it may be hazarded that there were few English Catholic gentlemen who would not feel more warmly towards the Oratorian once they knew that Dr. MacHale of Tuam was opposed to him. His English co-religionists were riveted to Newman by the attack made by Kingsley in 1864. Suffering, and especially public suffering, formed a link between Newman and the men who did not forget the proscribed centuries. This was a bond that Manning always lacked.

Once the stream of conversions had begun it was to prove continuous, although there were certain peak periods like the year immediately following on Newman's reception into the Church, the months that followed the publication of the Gorham Judgment in 1850 and the eighteen months in 1868-69 when Lord Bute's conversion occasioned the writing of

Disraeli's *Lothair*. Once Dr. Newman had set the example there was always a certain number of young men who joined the Catholic Church during the undergraduate stage or at the beginning of their professional life. Thus Francis Burnand, afterwards the editor of *Punch*, John Francis Bentley the architect of Westminster Cathedral, Edmund Bishop the liturgiologist and historian, and Gerard Manley Hopkins were all received into the Church in the ten years following 1857. These later converts were for the most part not associated with that particular clerical-academic group which had been so strongly represented among Newman's immediate followers.

One aspect is worth remarking. The effects of foreign travel coupled with the fact of Newman's action began to tell. It is noticeable that prior to 1845 conversions to Catholicism among the English people who visited or even lived in Italy or France were very rare. After that date there was a change. Thus the years spent on the Ligurian coast seems to have played some part in the conversion of Mrs. Thompson, the mother of Alice Meynell and Lady Butler. There is reason to suppose that Mrs. Gaskell's constant travel and perhaps especially the visit made to Rome in 1857 induced the sympathetic approach towards Catholicism which marks her later work. She was retentive of impressions and had moved out from the prejudices of her Unitarian family circle. Gradually, too, conversions were made among those who had little or no explicit experience of the Church of England. Coventry Patmore had no Anglican links either in his upbringing or in his first wife's family. It is also true that the converts scattered far and wide. Mr. Gurdon on resigning his family living settled in Biarritz and his son Dom Edmund Gurdon was for many years prior of the Carthusian monastery of Miraflores. By 1865 the convert element had lost the relatively homogeneous character which at first marked it. At the same time converts began to penetrate the new bureaucracy a full generation before the hereditary Catholics of any grouping had found their way there. As early as 1866 Sir Peter Renouf and Scott Nasmyth Stokes both held the appointment of chief inspector of schools.

In contrast with the situation in the old Catholic grouping women played a prominent part among the converts. In this connection it is difficult to exaggerate the significance of

Lady Georgiana Fullerton. Respect was paid by politicians and men of letters to her novels and for the last twenty years of her life she was the very pattern of the great lady wholly given over to works of charity. In so brief a survey we cannot assess but only note the influence of those convert peeresses who were so often linked with Fr. Faber's Oratory. The more remarkable members of this group with which the Vaughan and Howard daughters can be held to be associated were characterised by a dominating and self-sacrificing energy. A whole development of Religious Orders and organised good works came from this impetus; the Poor Servants of the Mother of God founded by Lady Georgiana Fullerton's friend Mother Magdalen Taylor, a convert who had worked as a nurse with Florence Nightingale; the Sisters of Charity of St. Vincent de Paul, the Good Shepherd nuns and the Poor Clares; the Carmelites from the Rue d'Enfer. The preoccupation with active works of charity and a readiness to move forward and to adventure in this field was in some ways a special contribution of the convert grouping, although all shared in it. The same preoccupation is seen reflected in the time given by Lord Ripon to the work of the Society of St. Vincent de Paul. On this name we may pause. The third Marquess of Bute gave the work of his mature years to Scotland and his labours as a munificent ecclesiastical antiquary really belong to the history of Catholicism in that country. The only political figure of real significance who joined the Catholic Church in the second half of the nineteenth century was George Frederick Samuel Robinson, Marquess of Ripon.

There were many circumstances in his position that were unusual. He had been born in Downing Street, while his father was Prime Minister. The heir to great wealth he belonged to a family with a political tradition dating back to the reign of George II, but without any permanent link with either party. His background was deeply Evangelical and in his youth he was a disciple of Tom Hughes and F. D. Maurice. His ideas never lost some traces of the Christian Socialist movement which had dominated his thought when he first entered Parliament as the Liberal member for Huddersfield. These early enthusiasms gave way to an instinctive sympathy for such radical solutions as commended themselves to what was now emerging as the Liberal Party. It was this Liberalism, which was separate in its inspiration from any Whig policy or sentiment, that later commended Lord Ripon to Mr. Gladstone. He entered the cabinet in Palmerston's last administration at the age of thirty-six. When he became a Catholic eleven years later, in 1874, he had served as Lord President of the Council in Gladstone's first administration and had presided at the War Office and the Colonial Office. He had received the Garter and was grand master of the English Freemasons.

Lord Ripon was one of the half-dozen leading political figures in the second half of the Queen's reign who owed their influence to hereditary landed wealth backed up by a tradition of public service and a manifest integrity. Gladstone early noted in him the mark of persistency. At the time of his conversion his political position was long assured and he held office in every Liberal administration from 1886 until his death in 1909. He was the only Catholic ever to hold the great post of Viceroy of India. The letters exchanged with his cousin Lady Amabel Cowper, who became a Catholic at about the same time but from the more explicitly Whig circle of the Cowper family, throw an interesting light on the approach to the Church of those who were politically Liberal and had never had Tractarian sympathies.

In close association with Lord Ripon was the fifteenth Duke of Norfolk who, from the time when he attained his majority in 1868 until his death in 1917, was the lay spokesman of the Catholic body. Politically the two men were far apart and this became still more evident in later life when Lord Ripon was Liberal leader in the Upper House. There was even in old age a secular optimism and a Liberal hope in Ripon's approach to general questions which was very far removed from the Duke's unimpassioned Conservative principles. There were, however, clear resemblances. As leaders of the English Catholics they had a definite idea of what was practicable in the existing political situation. They were both mastered by a sense of duty. Neither of them had great originality of thought and their very strong political position was based on a combination of inheritance and character. They were both drawn to those works of charity which Frédéric Ozanam had founded and developed.

In addition the Duke of Norfolk had a deep interest in all church matters. He and his brother, afterwards Lord FitzAlan, were pupils and disciples of Cardinal Newman and educated in the Oratory School which he founded at Edgbaston. They belong, like Wilfrid Ward, who came to the same standpoint in early manhood, to the first generation of Newman's Catholic discipleship. They were the men who from boyhood had known him as the author of the *Apologia*. All those who came in these later years to this intimate relation retained throughout life the note of reverence in their approach to the Oratorian Cardinal.

In many ways the 'eighties were a hopeful decade for English Catholics and landmarks were by then established: the Brompton Oratory and St. Philip's Church at Arundel, which indicate the taste of the Duke's early manhood. This was the last church built by Joseph Hansom as architect and was by far his most successful work. In these years the Duke carried out great building schemes at Arundel Castle, but as he grew older his mind was increasingly concentrated on church architecture and principally on the completion of St. John's, Norwich.

The political outlook of the Duke of Norfolk was congenial to Lord Salisbury, but apart from holding the postmaster-generalship in that premier's third administration he did not take office. The political contribution of the Norfolk Howards was made by his brother Lord FitzAlan and his nephew James Hope. The period when the Duke's influence in Catholic affairs was most in evidence was during the eleven years in which Cardinal Vaughan occupied the see of Westminster. The two men shared the same political approach and there was an easy intimacy between the Vaughan and Howard families. The Duke of Norfolk had a unique effect upon the Catholic body. He spent himself in the service of the co-religionists with an ungrudging and patriarchal charity.

It was in this period that the amalgamation of the old Catholic and convert groupings may be held to have approached completion. It is always difficult to generalise on such points, but it would seem that henceforward the explicit convert groupings faded away. The men who had been Tractarians were dying. An easing of the Catholic position was at this time discernible in many fields. In 1877 Dr. Newman was elected to an honorary fellowship at Trinity. This was the gesture by which the University made peace with her great son.

The progress of Catholics in public life was now apparent. In 1886 Henry Matthews became Home Secretary, the first Catholic to join the cabinet since Emancipation, while in the same year but in another administration Sir Charles Russell was appointed Attorney General. In the time of Lord Ripon's viceroyalty Sir Frederick Weld was Governor of the Straits Settlements and Sir John Pope-Hennessy Governor of Hong Kong and Mauritius. These were the early years of the two Catholics who were to leave the deepest mark on colonial administration, Sir Hugh Clifford and Sir Herbert Murray. When Ripon sailed from Bombay Sir Antony Macdonell was in the middle and Sir Michael O'Dwyer at the beginning of his service in India. Sir Nicholas O'Conor was gathering that unique influence at the Foreign Office which was to lead to his thirteen years tenure of the St. Petersburg and Constantinople embassies. It was, indeed, a situation which was still unclouded by the educational struggles of later years and by the division of opinion within the Catholic community in England which the introduction of the Home Rule Bills would bring about. This calm, this atmosphere of benevolence owed something to the last sunset period of Cardinal Manning's life, to his wise preoccupation with social questions and to the great prestige which he enjoyed throughout the country.

A few references can help to measure the spread and diversity of the Catholic life in these years of the late 'seventies and the 'eighties; Arthur Conan Doyle left Stonyhurst; Francis Thompson left Ushaw; Edgar Wallace was christened in the Catholic church at Greenwich. Among the young married couples living in London were the Wilfrid Meynells in Inkerman Terrace and the Ernest Cassels in Orme Square. Thomas Garner, who was to build the choir at Downside Abbey, was in the later stages of his partnership with G. F. Bodley; Edward Elgar was organist at St. George's, Worcester; Richard Terry was organist in the Anglican Cathedral at

Antigua. To speak of those now dead who were then children, John Wheatley, later the first Catholic member of a Labour Government, had left the parish school at Baillieston to go down the coal mine where his father was working. Maurice Baring was at Eton; Gilbert Chesterton entered St. Paul's in the year of the Queen's first Jubilee; Eric Gill was the small son of the minister of the Brighton chapel of the Countess of Huntingdon's connection. The Catholic Church went forward receiving its new recruits from many quarters.

In some respects it was a peaceful scene containing many unstable features. The Catholic landowners were now aligned with the general body of Conservative opinion. In that period of moderate publicity they received a deep respect. Financially their situation was very satisfactory. A proportion of the landowners, possessing house-property, had benefited by the spread of the industrial townships which still grew continually. Sir William Harcourt's Death Duties were ten years ahead. This was probably the moment when the incomes of the landed class had reached their maximum. The surviving strength of their political influence is reflected in the novels of Mrs. Humphry Ward. The number of Catholic undergraduates at Oxford was very limited and at Cambridge smaller still. On the other hand the number entering Sandhurst was by this time relatively considerable, although a good many only served in the Army for a few years.

A marked weakness in the general Catholic position was the absence of secondary day schools for boys. There was as yet nothing on the Catholic side to correspond to the many grammar schools which served the rest of the population. And this more than any other single factor accounts for the trivial impact made by the Catholic body on the commercial life of the Queen's reign and on industrial management. Provision was being made, especially in the cities and industrial towns, for Catholic schooling, but it was for that elementary schooling of which Cardinal Manning saw the sharp necessity. The term the Catholic Poor School Committee is sufficiently indicative of the approach.

The movement of population was slowing and the principal recent developments were the influx to the steel works at Ebbw Vale and the building up of the industrial life of

Cleveland which had necessitated the creation of the diocese of Middlesbrough. The scattered country parishes remained fairly steady during this period for the big house still gave employment, there was a distaste for any form of emigration and, except in certain areas, there was no startling growth of industry. These were the years before the coming of the motor car. After the tireless energy of Manning there came the decade of Vaughan's consolidation. Looking back on them the changes in English Catholic life, apart from the great church building in the towns, do not seem very striking in the first fifty years of the restored Hierarchy. The old Queen died and then Lord Salisbury, and early in 1903 Cardinal Vaughan retired to St. Joseph's, Mill Hill, to pass the last months of his life in the house which he had founded. The Catholic life in England opened on to the new century.

VIII

CARDINAL NEWMAN

By Humphrey J. T. Johnson

IT is idle to ask the question what would have been New-man's future had he remained an Anglican. We can picture Manning as an Anglican bishop, possibly even as an arch-bishop, but we may demur to the suggestion that without R. H. Froude, Newman might have been a leader of liberal thought or an Evangelical divine. So acute a mind could never have rested content in Anglicanism, the intellectual paradise of men who hold that religion loses its beauty and its freshness if we seek to be too logical about it. The bent of Newman's mind would have driven him towards Rome and, had he rejected grace, he would have been most likely, not a Low churchman or a Broad churchman, not even a typically liberal agnostic, but a Voltairean of aristocratic sympathies who, though the most subtle anti-Christian writer of his day, would have stressed the social utility of Christianity.

More discerning treatment by the bishops might have kept Wesley within the Anglican fold but no amount of sym-pathy or encouragement could have done so with Newman. If this be grasped the judgments pronounced on his conversion by two great political leaders a generation after it took place lose much of their force. Disraeli said that by leaving the Church of England Newman had dealt it a blow under which it still reeled, his opponent that the effects of Newman's secession were so great as to be still unmeasurable. The fact is that Newman, being what he was, could not have remained in the Church of England, though his temporary sojourn in it had the effect of strengthening rather than of weakening that body.

Newman's life as a Catholic was to last forty-five years all but two months. During this period he devoted his atten-tion to a surprising number of problems though on many of them he left nothing published. The way in which his mind travels from subject to subject, from the development of doctrine to the theory of education, the relations of religion and science, the inspiration of scripture, the intellectual basis of belief, the position of the Church on modern society and the respective limits of civil and ecclesiastical power might convey to some the impression of a restlessness which was scarcely wholesome. But external circumstances more than once were the cause of diverting Newman's attention from one question to another. Sometimes he seemed forced to leave one because in the existing temper of public feeling he judged that it was impossible to say anything useful on it. At others he felt compelled to take up a subject because there seemed no one else capable of handling it. Such was the case when he answered Gladstone's strictures on the Vatican Decrees. He did this, not because he had made a life-long study of the relations between Christianity and the civil power, but because he was convinced that the task of dealing with Gladstone could not be safely left to Manning. But a unity lies behind all Newman's work as a Catholic. All was written, either directly or indirectly, in defence of the claims of revealed religion as embodied in the Catholic Church, though sometimes he was thereby led into controversy with opponents of dogma and at others with believing Christians of another denomination. During his first years as a Catholic he was fighting on a single front, engaged in warfare against liberalism in religion. From 1860 onwards we find him engaged on a second one, against those elements in the Church which he believed to be needlessly exacerbating her relations with the modern world. Many learned men can study a subject for years, master the great majority of its details, and yet say nothing which really illuminates it. Newman's genius lies in this that he touched upon nothing without saying one thing at least which threw some light upon it.

It is never a good thing for a convert to hear it being asked what the authorities of the Church mean to do with him. In Newman's case it was inevitable, since both in Rome and in England was spread the facile delusion that our country was on the brink of conversion. That Newman would be ordained was a matter about which there seems to have been no doubt, but whether he would join the ranks of the regular or the secular clergy was for a moment uncertain. We cannot imagine him in a religious order or congregation in any other capacity than that of Superior for life, and we may be tempted to believe that he joined the Oratory of St. Philip Neri because of the facilities which it provided for such a solution. This was not because Newman wished to domineer over others. He was indeed always most respectful in his attitude to the personality of other people. It is because he could not work easily in the capacity of a subordinate. No doubt the Oratory appealed to him because it was the nearest approach to be met with in the Catholic Church to the life to which he had been accustomed —that of an Oxford College, with its celibate fellows, in the days before the Royal Commissions. But Newman's devotion to St. Philip was genuine, and resemblances between the two, though sometimes doubted, are visible. Both men drew their inspiration from the early centuries of Christianity rather than from the Middle Ages or the Counter-Reformation. Both felt a call to the spiritual succour of those who were passing from boyhood to manhood. When the present writer mentioned these likenesses to one who had known Newman, his attention was directed to a third resemblance lying in the fact that St. Philip and Newman were alike in aiming at being ordinary men in whom their contemporaries would see nothing artificial or theatrical. In this Newman differed from Faber who, despite his genuine devotion to the saint, was given to mimicking St. Philip, a thing Newman never did. The problem of how the ecclesiastical authorities were to make use of Newman while the conversion of England was taking place did not arise since that conversion never came about.

Unlike the great majority of his fellow Catholics, Newman did not anticipate it. Yet he knew that those who had initiated or followed the movement of 1833 had an attitude towards the Church different from the rest of the nation, and to them he addressed a special appeal. This took the form of a course of lectures on " Difficulties felt by Anglicans "[1], given in London during the first half of 1850 at a time when the Bishop of Exeter was making one unsuccessful move after

---

[1] Later editions of this work include Newman's replies to Pusey's *Eirenicon* and Gladstone's *Vatican Decrees*.

another to prevent the institution of Mr. Gorham to the living of Brampford Speke on account of his disbelief in Baptismal Regeneration. Though the present-day reader may find these lectures at times rather long-winded and feel that the argument would have been better stated if set forth more briefly, they contain a profound analysis of the spirit of Anglicanism. The Church of England, the lecturer told his former associates, was no body politic but a department of the State, a collection of officials depending on the Civil Power. Elizabeth boasted that she had " tuned her pulpits "; Charles forbade discussion on Predestination; George on the Holy Trinity; Victoria allowed differences on Holy Baptism. The Movement of 1833 was something alien to the National Church. Though neither Lutheranism nor Calvinism was the exact doctrine of the Church of England either heresy easily coalesced with it. With Catholicism it was otherwise. A riot caused by the refusal of an incumbent to recite the Athanasian Creed, as many did so refuse, was unthinkable. The Established Church could not therefore be used to combat the spirit of the age except as a drag on a wheel. It had changed and was changing with the nation. To seek to make England Catholic by means of the Church of England was like trying to evangelize Turkey by means of Mohammedanism. Not even the Non-jurors, in whom the early Tractarians felt so much interest, had a coherent body of doctrine.

In his judgment of individual Anglicans Newman gives the impression of being more severe than was Manning in his old age. Twelve months later he delivered in Birmingham his lectures on the " Present Position of Catholics in England," which may be read in conjunction with the former. They were given in a different atmosphere; for the " No Popery " agitation and the " Ecclesiastical Titles Bill " had intervened. The gist of the contention embodied in these lectures is that the main opposition to the advance of Catholicism in England was to be found, not in Protestant argument, but in the Protestant tradition, which dominated all except the Tractarian and Rationalist minorities. Under its influence Englishmen had come to identify Protestantism with good sense. Protestantism had become " the intellectual and moral language of the body politic."

The reader of these lectures can have but little doubt
left as to why Newman did not share the current expectation
of the conversion of England. His position at the time was
somewhat tragic. No Catholic seemed more fitted than he to
make the Catholic religion comprehensible to the English
people, yet no means by which he could do this lay at hand.
Suddenly and unexpectedly there opened before him a prospect of advancing the Catholic cause, if not in England, at
least in the British Isles. No opportunity for a University
education existed for Irish Catholics. In 1850 the Synod of
Thurles, though only by a narrow majority, it is true, condemned the Queen's Colleges instituted by Sir Robert Peel
with a view to remedying this defect. The ground of the condemnation was the danger to Faith involved in " mixed "
education. A solution of the problem thus created seemed to
be suggested by the recent revival in Belgium on Catholic
lines of the ancient University of Louvain. There was
obviously no one in the three kingdoms so fitted as Newman
to become Rector of a like institution in these islands and the
Irish bishops invited him to occupy this post. The offer was
accepted, and its acceptance added a classic to English literature, though it did not fulfil its primary purpose.

Before taking up his new task Newman wrote his discourses on the " Scope and Nature of University Education "
delivered in 1852[2]. The author defines a University as a place
where universal knowledge is taught. Its object is intellectual
not moral, and it aims at the diffusion of knowledge rather
than its advancement. If the object of a University were
discovery, it need not have students; if it were a place of
religious training, it could not be the seat of science and
literature. Its object is to initiate the student into " the largest
and truest philosophical views," so that he will feel nothing
but impatience and disgust with " random theories and imposing sophistries." The lecturer passes on to themes suggested by the foundation twenty-four years earlier of the un-
sectarian University College in London, in the establishment
of which Liberals, Jews and Socinians had taken part. If the

---

[2] These lectures have been incorporated in a larger work, *The Idea
of a University*. They have been republished by themselves in
Everyman's Library.

pursuit of universal knowledge was the object of a University such an aim must include what was known to us by revelation, as for instance that Antichrist was to come. We could not believe the Christian religion to be true and thrust aside what it taught us. This would have been admitted by the early Protestants, but modern Liberals and Latitudinarians asserted that it was " as unreasonable to demand for Religion a chair in a University, as to demand one . . . for fine feeling, sense of honour or patriotism." Theology had at least as good a right to claim a place in a University as Astronomy. If any science drops out of the circle of knowledge its place cannot be kept vacant. It is forgotten and the other sciences intrude where they have no right. If Theology were put out of possession it would be the prey of a dozen other various sciences.

As an example of the neglect of the claims of Theology Newman cited Dean Milman's *History of the Jews*, a subject which the author had sought to assimilate as closely as possible to secular history by omitting the Providential element from the narrative. From this error, by which he had been guilty of at least bad judgment, he would have been preserved had he been a Catholic. Another science the teaching of which led to ill results, if divorced from Theology, was Political Economy. For in such circumstances it engendered cupidity.

The range of studies pursued in a University should be as wide as possible; though no individual student could pursue each one, all would indirectly benefit by this width. For in an assemblage of learned men, each zealous for his own science, everyone learns to respect, consult and aid the others. Thus is created " a pure and clear atmosphere of thought." The student who breathes it comes to profit by an intellectual tradition and his education can be called " Liberal." The effect of such an education is " to open the mind, to correct it, to refine it . . . to give it power over its own faculties, application, flexibility, method, critical exactness, sagacity, resource, address and eloquent expression." Not many, it is to be feared, of those who pass through a University come near to this ideal, and probably we should rest satisfied if we could feel sure that each student who did so was able to gain possession of one of the qualities here enumerated. The ideal of a Liberal Education was not, so Newman considered, fulfilled in men who were merely well-read or well-informed. It was not realised in those who are only " possessed by their knowledge and not possessed of it." " The memory can tyrannize as well as the imagination." The practical error committed by educationalists in the preceding twenty years had lain in trying to teach so much that nothing was properly learned at all. Liberal knowledge must be distinguished from intellectual recreations and from what are called accomplishments. " Do not say, the people must be educated, when after all you only mean amused, refreshed, soothed, put into good spirits and good humour, or kept from vicious excesses." " Education is a high word; it is the preparation for knowledge and it is the imparting of knowledge in proportion to that preparation. . . . A University is . . . an Alma Mater, knowing her children one by one, not a foundry, or a mint or a treadmill."

Mere enforced residence together of a number of young men, as was the case at Oxford at the end of the eighteenth century, was a training moulding and enlarging the mind which fitted them for secular duties and produced better public men than would a University which dispensed with residence and tutorial superintendence. As health ought to precede labour of body so general culture of mind is the best aid to professional and scientific study. The man who has learned to think and to reason and to compare and to discriminate and to analyse, who has refined his taste, and formed his judgment, and sharpened his mental vision, will not indeed at once be a lawyer, or a pleader, or an orator, or a statesman, or a physician . . . but he will be placed " in that state of intellect " in which he can take up any one of these sciences or callings. In this sense mental culture is emphatically *useful*.

A University is not the birthplace of poets or of authors of immortal works, of founders of schools, leaders of colonies, or conquerors of nations. It is a great ordinary means to an ordinary end; it aims at raising the intellectual tone of society, at cultivating the public mind, at purifying the national taste, at supplying true principles to popular enthusiasm and fixed aims to popular aspiration, at giving enlargement and sobriety to the ideas of the age, at facilitating the exercise of political power, and refining the intercourse of private life.

In his last lecture, which deals with the duties of the

Church towards Liberal knowledge, there is to be found Newman's eloquent plea for the study of secular Literature in a Catholic University; if Literature, he argues, " is to be made a study of human nature, you cannot have a Christian Literature. It is a contradiction in terms to attempt a sinless Literature of sinful man."

No University has ever attained to Newman's ideal, which proved unrealisable in his own hands. He expected too much of human nature. But the failure of the Dublin University scheme was due to a combination of several causes. Whether with truth or not, it has been said that Newman lacked organising ability. Absence of governmental recognition was certainly a drawback. Perhaps he himself was too easily discouraged. He did not work readily with the Irish bishops. He seems to have thought them anxious to keep too much in their own hands. This might have affected him less had the See of Dublin itself had an occupant in sympathy with Newman. But Dr. Cullen had been translated to it from Armagh soon after Newman had accepted the University Rectorship. A potent factor adverse to him was that although he was a warm friend of Ireland his University, had it succeeded, would have inevitably been a means of increasing English influence in that country to the detriment, as some thought, of an Irish national culture. Newman, moreover, so long as Pius IX lived would have been unable to count on very much sympathy in Rome. For the Papal Brief setting up the University envisaged an institution not altogether like that which he had planned. This document, drafted it is thought by Dr. Cullen himself, presupposed something more nearly approaching a sort of lay seminary.

Newman was never again to be occupied in a practical way with University teaching, or administration, and it was ironical that members of his own religious community had to qualify themselves for teaching posts by means of degrees obtained at the undenominational University of London, of whose foundation he had himself so strongly disapproved. Yet the problem of how to provide a University education for such young Catholic Englishmen as were fit to receive it could not escape his attention. The solution that he would have liked best, an English Louvain, was obviously out of the question, at least, at that time. In default of this the best thing to do seemed to be to send Catholic young men to Oxford and Cambridge after taking adequate precautions for the protection of their faith, and indeed a few of them were already beginning to go there. Could the problem be solved by establishing a Catholic College at Oxford, to be followed by one at Cambridge, which had for its tutors men trained at such places as Stonyhurst and Ushaw? There had been no precedent in either University for any institution of this nature at the time when Newman began to turn over this question in his mind. But the idea may have been suggested to him by the fact that as far back as 1845 the Tractarians had been mooting the possibility of a new College at Oxford for the purpose of perpetuating their principles, a possibility eventually realised in Keble College.

Newman never thought of going to Oxford with an aggressive purpose, though undoubtedly he would have liked to defend the Catholic position there and explain it to the University. In 1860 he wrote to Canon Estcourt, " While I do not see my way to take steps to weaken the Church of England, being what it is, least of all should I be disposed to do so in Oxford, which has hitherto been the seat of those traditions which constitute whatever there is of Catholic doctrine and principles in the Anglican Church "[3]. He looked back affectionately to his old University. " Catholics did not make us Catholics," he said, " Oxford made us Catholics. At present Oxford surely does more good than harm." The moral dangers of Catholics going to Oxford were less than those to be encountered elsewhere[4]. " A boy of 19 goes into a London office with no restraints. At Oxford and Cambridge he has at least *some* restraints."

It was at the time when he was encouraged by the reception given to the *Apologia* that the idea of returning to Oxford took possession of Newman, at first in the shape of a Catholic College, and when this was dropped in that of a Catholic Oratory. In 1864, without any concrete plan as to how they were to be used, he bought for £8,400 five acres in Oxford, fronting on Walton Street, and the knowledge that he

[3] *Life,* by Wilfrid Ward, II, p. 57.
[4] *Ibid.*

had done this spread alarm in those Catholic circles where Newman was distrusted.

The attitude both of the English Hierarchy and of Propaganda to Newman's Oxford plans is described by Mr. H. O. Evennett. Here it will be sufficient to mention the psychological factors which influenced his English opponents. Manning, the chief of these, though opposed to the idea of a Catholic College and to that of Catholics going to other Colleges, was seemingly still more opposed to the possibility of Newman himself going there in any capacity. Both he and Wiseman were obsessed by dread of Catholics whom they considered unsound on the question of the Pope's Temporal Power, and Manning, shortly to become Archbishop, was filled with apprehension lest the atmosphere of Oxford should turn into miniature Actons the more intellectual of the Catholic youths who went there. Ullathorne, after momentarily favouring the idea of a Catholic College at Oxford, altered his mind but was ready to give the mission there to the Oratorians. There can be no doubt however that in whatever capacity Newman had gone to Oxford his residence there would have had the effect of encouraging more Catholics to attend the University, and his projected migration thither was discountenanced by Propaganda in 1867.

Among converts to the Catholic Church there are to be found those whose main anxiety is to discover how little it is possible to believe, while yet remaining orthodox, and those who think that there is some peculiar merit in believing as much as possible. The former class is as a rule the more intelligent since it consists for the most part of those who are aware that difficulties exist. But among the latter will be found cultivated persons, yet timid and scrupulous, who deceive themselves into thinking that the spirit of intellectual inquiry is the fruit of pride and confound credulity with humility.

Newman, unlike Faber, never entertained any special predilection for a theological proposition merely because it was shocking to Protestants, but he felt at first that it was pious to believe more than he was obliged to. In his early years as a Catholic he held that the Pope received a much larger measure of divine guidance than he afterwards thought to be the case. Whether or no Newman was actually superstitious during his first years as a Catholic, he was uncritical. He accepted the story of the translation of the Holy House of Loreto because he found that everyone in Rome believed in it and so it appeared to him unfilial not to do so. If God, so he reasoned, could have floated the Ark of Noah on the billows of the world-wide sea why should we hesitate to give credence to the belief that angels had borne the Holy House from Nazareth to Italy? Had Newman remained in this state of mind, though he would have had a large circle of pious readers, he would be less sought after by intellectual inquirers. But the world was changing and Newman changed with it. By 1850 the intellectual revolution was well under way and it was as though there had been a sudden drop in the temperature. " If an Oxford man," says Mark Pattison in his *Memories,* " had gone to sleep in 1846 and had woke up again in 1850, he would have found himself in a totally new world. . . Theology was totally banished from the Common Room, and even from private conversation." There is perhaps some exaggeration in these words but they show the direction in which the wind was blowing. The decade following 1850 saw the revolution advance by giant strides. First came the *Politique Positive* and then *The Origin of Species.* By 1860 a new phase in the intellectual history of Europe had opened.

The Catholic religion was beginning to find its most formidable antagonist not so much in the liberalism which Newman had known at Oxford as in a materialism which claimed to base itself on the findings of natural science. Allied to this was a destructive criticism of the Old and New Testaments bolder and more confident than it had been thirty years before. The echoes of the storms raging on the other side of the Channel and the North Sea reached the narrow cultured fringe of the English Catholic body. But Newman quickly grasped that a new apologetic was needed if highly educated men were not to be further alienated from the Church, and intelligent Catholics then growing up to manhood were not to be left without help and guidance. Could he himself do something to meet these needs? When Newman and his associates had sought to combat the drift towards liberalism in theology at Oxford they had relied mainly at least on a reassertion of traditional principles. This was possible because the liberalism of that epoch was based more on sentiment than on a case built up out of new facts. But a method of apologetic which could pass muster in 1845 was largely outmoded by 1860. Opponents of dogma claimed support from branches of knowledge out of reach of the Fathers of the Church, the Reformers and the theologians of the Counter-Reformation. They could not be effectively refuted by a mere appeal to general principles. Specific answers which took cognizance of new knowledge were demanded. What were these answers to be?

At the age of sixty Newman began to address himself to these problems. He had had no special training to qualify him to face them in their details, but he was gifted with an intellect quick enough and penetrating enough to see in most cases where the real difficulties lay. But quickness of intellect in such matters was a two-edged sword. On the one hand it enabled its possessor to say things which would be helpful to the ablest young Catholic students, whether clerical or lay, but on the other hand it made him able to see much further than the great majority of contemporary bishops and theologians imbued with a marked distrust of " novelty." Such men, far from cognisant of the issues under consideration, would naturally scent heresy in solutions which seemed contrary to their notions of orthodoxy, and so it would turn out that what was helpful to the minority would appear scandalous to the majority.

In the relations between faith and science Newman saw far. That the world as we know it had been created in six days of twenty-four hours each had of course been abandoned by the most enlightened theologians in 1860, but the separate creation of species was held to be indisputably taught in God's Word. Newman on the other hand found a want of simplicity in the idea of " the creation of trees in full growth or of rocks with fossils in them."

Such a speculation would have come quite naturally to the author of the *Essay on Development*. From it he passed on to a yet more daring and in the eyes of his contemporaries impious one. It was, he thought, as strange that monkeys should be so like men if there were no *historical* connection between them as to suppose that there was no course of history by which fossils got into rocks. " I will either go the whole hog with Darwin, or, dispensing with time and history altogether, hold not only the theory of distinct species but also of the creation of fossil-bearing rocks."

Such sentiments are not of course to be found in Newman's published writings. Obviously they could not have been. They are found in a note written in 1863[5] which shows us how his mind was affected by the burning controversy of the day, and how far he was ahead of his time, something which is also brought home to us by perusal of the ill-informed letters on the subject of evolution which still appear in the Catholic press. Had Newman been able to reconcile the theologians of his time to a spiritual conception of evolution an unhappy chapter would not have had to be written. But such a thing could not have been[5a].

If in the field of the relations between religion and science Newman left no published contribution at his death, to that of biblical exegesis he made one which has been considered by many as of dubious orthodoxy. If neither Germany nor France produced a Darwin, England had neither a Strauss nor a Renan. The Higher Criticism of the Bible came later and its most gifted exponents were conservative and reverent. Yet Biblical criticism raised issues which affected all countries and English Christians could not adopt ostrich-like tactics and assert that for them these controversies were devoid of meaning. Newman saw that the Higher Criticism must be faced and set himself to study, though only in broad outline, the problems which it raised. Unlike Pusey he had never acquired any first-hand knowledge of German speculations in this field. Nor does it seem that he seriously attempted to do so. The translation of Ewald's *History of Israel* lies with its pages still uncut on the shelves of his room. But though he gained

[5] This note was published by the present writer in the *Dublin Review*, July, 1934.

[5a] In 1875 the Catholic biologist and evolutionist, St. George Mivart, asked Newman to accept the dedication of his *Lessons from Nature*. Newman's reply has not been published, but Fogazzaro says that it showed clearly the identity of the views of the ecclesiastic with those of the layman (*Ascensioni Umane*, 1918, p. 25). In the dedication Mivart speaks of Newman's ability to unite the theistic and naturalistic conceptions of the world.

no mastery over the intricacies of Pentateuchal criticism he knew that difficult problems were demanding a solution along Catholic lines.

It is uncertain whether Newman was at any time troubled by the moral difficulties raised by the Old Testament. He evidently knew little or nothing of the light which could be thrown on them by the study of Comparative Religion. He reconciled himself to the slaughter of the Canaanite children by reflecting on the holy thoughts with which he supposed the minds of the slayers to have been filled. He did not seek an explanation by setting the story against the background of contemporary life. The difficulties which Newman felt touched rather on the accuracy of the Bible in minor matters of fact, and were occasionally concerned with literary problems such as questions of authorship and plurality of sources.

At the end of October, 1864, Arthur Stanley, who had been made Dean of Westminster a year earlier, after preaching in Birmingham, called at the Oratory. The leader, so far as it had one, of the Broad Church party he questioned Newman on his views about the Higher Criticism[6]. Did not he recognise a difference between the shadowy character of the history in Genesis and the clear outlines of the biography of David? Newman playfully assumed the rôle of *advocatus diaboli* and said that the story of Saul's fall seemed to him as much like a poem as anything in the Bible. The Dean passed on to the delicate question as to whether a composite character could be recognised in Genesis. It was one calculated to throw many men into a state of mental anguish as they had to make up their minds whether the idea must be rejected as a temptation against faith or whether it was a speculation in which it was lawful to indulge. Newman adhered to the second alternative at least as regards the early chapters[6a]. " It struck me," he said, " the first moment I read these chapters in Hebrew. There must be two documents. And I mentioned it to Pusey who seemed to acknowledge it. Would he acknowledge it now?" Stanley thought that he would not. Yet Newman's admission was made, not without a sense of fear. For having

---

[6] We have, of course, only Stanley's account of the conversation.
[6a] On this point see also Tract LXXXV reprinted as Part III of *Discussions and Arguments*.

allowed himself to recognise a compilatory character in Genesis he confessed to seeing the same thing in the Gospels which seemed " not a regular history but biographical anecdotes strung together." The Dean asked whether such speculations on the character of the sacred books were not barred by the Council of Trent. Here Newman seemed sure of his ground. " Not in the least," he replied firmly. Stanley then asked him a question which has no doubt many a time been put by a Protestant to a Catholic. Why were Catholics so unwilling to face the problems raised by the Higher Criticism, when one would have supposed that it would have been much easier for them than for Protestants to do this, since Catholics had the Church to lean on as well as the Bible? " You, if any, are called to the task and you do not help us." Newman's answer was interesting. " I grant it. We can do nothing. Our ' School ' is scattered. We have no theologians left; the French Revolution has spoiled us of our revenues. We are powerless "[7]. The two men then rejoined Tom Arnold in the School Library.

Stanley's recollections shed a partial light on Newman's thoughts touching these matters. Unpublished notes written during the early 'sixties show that he twice contemplated a treatise on the Inspiration of Scripture and twice gave up the task. In certain problems of literary criticism he was ahead of his time. He admitted the pseudepigraphical character of Ecclesiastes. But the notes make clear also that he felt that the question must be faced whether it was any longer possible to reject the view that the sacred books contained erroneous statements. He instanced the census said to have taken place during the governorship of Quirinius, a difficulty not yet fully resolved. In the second of these abortive treatises Newman adumbrated a theory designed to harmonise Inspiration with modern difficulties. It was that in each book of the Bible inspiration was accorded to the writer in the way demanded by the character of the writing, whether it were history, prophecy or doctrinal or moral exposition.

Twenty years later, when he had passed the age of eighty, Newman returned to the subject of Inspiration, urged

[7] Prothero & Bradley. *Life and Letters of Dean Stanley*, II, 340-342.

thereto it seems by Renan's taunt that the biblical scholar would find the little finger of the Catholic Church thicker than the loins of Protestantism[8]. Was error compatible with Inspiration? Newman appears to have considered that it was, provided that the error was confined to the *obiter dicta* of Scripture. Dr. Healy of Maynooth replied that error could no more co-exist with inspiration than could grace with sin. To which Newman rejoined that sin and grace could be found side by side in the same person. Did the Christian religion stand or fall by the truth of every factual statement in Scripture? Newman could not bring himself to believe that its fundamental verities would be undermined if, for instance, St. Paul, through a slight failure of memory, had stated that he had left with Carpus at Troas the cloak which he had in fact left elsewhere. After his death, his successor as Superior of the Birmingham Oratory, Father Ignatius Ryder, in the American *Catholic World* explained Newman's concept of *obiter dicta* in Scripture as something which embraced the choice of the literary vehicle made use of by the author whether it be prose or poetry, a treatise or a letter.

Of Newman's views on Evolution we may say that they are now becoming increasingly acceptable to Catholics and of his views on the bearing of the Higher Criticism on the doctrine of Inspiration that they are likely to receive more attention in the future than they have done in the past. The like must be said of the two most important of Newman's writings, the *Essay on Development* and the *Grammar of Assent,* neither of which exercised a marked influence on his contemporaries though both, profiting by a certain weariness with scholasticism, are to-day receiving greater attention[9].

There were those among Newman's Catholic contemporaries who hoped that he would have produced a new *Summa* to meet the needs of the nineteenth century. Such could not have been. Not only would the minds of his contemporaries have been quite unripe for his conclusions but the subject-

---

[8] *Stray Essays on Controversial Points* (privately printed 1890). The first essay dealing with Inspiration appeared in the *Nineteenth Century* for February, 1884.

[9] The latter was, however, brought to the notice of the public through Sir William Harcourt's reading of a long extract from it to the House of Commons.

1atter itself would have been in many instances in a state of
uidity. Yet a careful student could construct a posthumous
umma from Newman's works.

It is not to Philosophy or Theology or speculations on
1e relations of faith and science that we must look if we are
) measure Newman's influence on the England of his day.
3ut for two men, Charles Kingsley and William Ewart Glad-
tone[10], Newman's life after his conversion might have been
1at of a figure almost forgotten by the public. These two
ntagonists gave him an opportunity, not merely of revealing
eep trains of thought, but of displaying literary and dialec-
cal skill in a way which delighted readers. The *Apologia* was
niversally applauded, though some of the applause may
ave come from those who regarded Newman as a stick with
7hich to beat the Pope. Few non-Catholic readers could, of
ourse, follow its arguments but many could appreciate and
/ere delighted with the author's love of truth and his
1oroughly English outlook. Englishmen knew that Catholic
eers and country gentlemen (at least those who were not con-
erts) on all except strictly religious questions thought and
elt very much as their non-Catholic neighbours thought and
elt. Converts they distrusted, mainly of course owing to their
islike of the religious doctrines they had embraced but also
ecause, rightly or wrongly, they associated with them a lack
f frankness. An individual priest might be well liked by the
'rotestants of his own town or village but to the average
on-Catholic reader of the *Apologia* the Catholic priesthood
7as a body actuated by standards of truth and honour which
iffered from his own. It was obviously far beyond the power
f any single man however gifted he might be to allay the
uspicion of the Church of Rome which was to be met with in
ll classes of Englishmen and Newman himself could obviously
1ake no appeal to the masses; but so far as any one man could
o he lessened this suspicion among educated persons, though
'anny Kingsley derived some comfort from letters she received

[10] It is gratifying to recall that these controversies left no legacy of
personal bitterness. Newman said a Mass for Kingsley when he
died, feeling confidence in his salvation on account of his defence
of the Athanasian creed against Archbishop Tait. One of the last
presents which Newman must have received was a reading-lamp
given him by Gladstone.

from working men telling her that they knew from persona
experience that her husband was right in his view on the
Roman clergy after all. Doubtless there were not a few who
reflected with pleasure that there was room in the Roman
Catholic Church for a Newman as well as for an Antonelli, a
Manning or a Cullen.

Yet simultaneously with the benevolent regards of his
non-Catholic fellow-countrymen Newman had to endure the
suspicious looks of many of his fellow Catholics. There was
widespread among them a temper of mind which he found un
congenial, both in speculative and in practical matters. When
Faber's book, the *Blessed Sacrament*, appeared, though
graciously dedicated by the author to himself, Newman said
that he knew of no book which would so readily turn him into
an infidel. With Manning's views on the Temporal Power of
the Pope, Newman was also out of harmony. To be accused
of being " unsound " on this question was the most deadly
charge which could at the time be levelled against a Catholic
Newman rejected the extreme clerical or, as it was then called
ultramontane standpoint. He denied that the Papal Govern
ment was a theocracy and that its overthrow could be equated
with Israel's rejection of that form of polity. It seems clear
also that he would have approved of some sort of agreemen
between the Pope and the Italian Government and he took a
more favourable view of Napoleon III than was generally
taken by Catholic opinion. But in the ten years following the
appearance of the *Apologia*, if he was frequently in the
thoughts of the ecclesiastically-minded, he was little in the
public eye. The occasion of his return to the limelight was not
a direct attack upon him, but a controversy as to the import
of the Syllabus of Errors and the Vatican Decrees.

In 1866 W. E. Gladstone had been in Rome listening
to voluble friars who compared Protestants with toads and
reptiles. Little did its authors know what a hornet's nest
their oratory was stirring up. What would become of the
liberties of non-Catholics if the Roman Catholic Church gained
the upper hand was a question on which the English statesman
began to brood. At length on his retirement from the premier
ship in 1874 he put pen to paper and in what Newman described
as a " powerful pamphlet " attacked the Syllabus and the

Vatican Decrees. Behind Gladstone stood Acton, and at Acton's side was Döllinger. Newman was under no illusion with regard to the formidable nature of the onslaught, rendered more and not less formidable by the fact that it came from a deeply religious man. Yet to Newman personally it gave an opportunity which was not unwelcome. For it enabled him, under cover of replying to Gladstone, to utter some severe words against what he regarded as the almost criminal irresponsibility of Manning and W. G. Ward[11]. Newman's pamphlet took the form of an open letter to the young Duke of Norfolk and its main contention was that none but the *Schola Theologorum* was competent to determine the force of papal and synodal decrees. Manning himself had also replied to Gladstone and had written as though the *Schola Theologorum* did not exist. Newman's words about it must have seemed to some like an attempt to reduce the Papacy to a constitutional monarchy. But Pius IX himself, while remarking that there were expressions in Newman's letter which were not free from objection, said that he had been told that it had done good. What many, perhaps most, Catholic theologians of the day might have found disquieting in the open letter was the author's readiness to uphold in certain cases the rights of the individual conscience against ecclesiastical authority, not excepting that of the Pope. To them it may well have furnished evidence that Newman had never been completely converted from Protestantism. But he appealed to the authority of St. Francis de Sales who, in a letter to the Présidente Brulart, when she questioned him about the authority of the Pope over princes, deprecated extreme opinions put forward by hotheads who make themselves " *les bons valets, soit du Pape, soit des Princes.*"

In England the open letter created some impression. It made Newman again a centre of public attention, interest in it being aroused as soon as it was known that the writer was at work. It was conceded by some that if the author were Pope the Syllabus and the Vatican Decrees might be so mildly and so liberally interpreted that the Roman Catholic Church might be shown to be after all something different from what

---

[1] The later Manning, fierce critic of a papal policy of the *Non Expedit* and friend of liberal causes, had not yet developed.

she was feared to be. *The Times,* however, in a five-column review of the " open letter " doubted whether Newman's persuasiveness could allay suspicion since he took it for granted that all the world was a theologian.   Anti-clericals seem to have feared that Newman would take the wind out of their sails. For the belief that Rome at heart repudiated him stood them in good stead. Arnim, the German ambassador in Rome, prematurely announced that Newman's manipulations were not accepted at the Vatican, a judgment with which Acton, much as he disliked Newman, was forced to disagree on the ground that they received an indirect sanction when Leo XIII raised him to the purple. At the reception given at Norfolk House on this occasion, as the representatives of the old Catholic families and the converts knelt to kiss his ring, Matthew Arnold shook hands with the new Cardinal and made a deferential bow. The act was symbolic. The literary world of the great Victorian Age had come to regard the Roman Catholic Church as an institution with which relations of civility might be maintained and the largest share in bringing this about belonged to Newman.

Eleven years later he died and *The Times* said " whether Rome canonizes him or not he will be canonized in the thoughts of pious people of many creeds in England "[12] Not less moving is the judgment pronounced on the Cardinal by an eminent Anglican divine who was far from being a High Churchman, Professor W. Sanday.   " No man," he wrote " living or dead, ever did so much to give English people a *chastened* religion."[13]

If we seek to judge his influence by asking ourselves what the world would be like if Newman had not lived, at what conclusion shall we arrive? He failed to arrest the progress of liberalism in the Church of England but this was a task in which no man could have succeeded. More than any other man could have done he strengthened the hands of those in that body who were fighting on behalf of dogma. A High Church revival there would have been had there been no Newman, but it would have gone less far and it would have drawn fewer within its influence. If Newman could not have stemmed the advancing tide of liberalism in the Established

[12] August 12, 1890.
[13] *England's debt to Newman,* p. 13.

Church still less could he have called a halt to the slow but progressive dechristianization of England. But those who were working for that end would have readily admitted that his was the most outstanding personality on the other side and have reckoned him as the supreme example of the subtle influence wielded by superstition over a highly-gifted intellect. Certainly the English Catholic community gained something in popular estimation from the fact that the greatest religious personality of the century belonged to it. English Catholics were proud of Newman though few would have understood the deeper trains of his thought. Many of those who became Catholics under his influence would doubtless have done so, treading other paths, had he never lived. But others would have remained in the Church of England and others again most likely have drifted into unbelief.

Newman's influence on the Catholic Church in England is not, however, to be measured solely by the number of converts directly or indirectly brought into the Church; it must be measured also by the way in which the respect that he was held in by the non-Catholic world broke down its isolation and did a little at least to mitigate the contempt with which it was regarded. Yet to English Catholics of the present day Newman seems to mean less than he did to those of half a century ago[14]. This is not merely because the lapse of time has dimmed his memory but because a generation of Catholics has grown up dominated by interests which were not his. Newman was not interested in social reform. He owned that he had never asked himself the question whether the number of public-houses in England was excessive. Men to whose minds the thought of the Last Judgment is ever present as a stupendous reality tend to have their enthusiasm less easily aroused by schemes of social betterment than those to whose minds the thought of it but rarely occurs. The philosophy called Chestertonianism would have been distasteful to Newman. He would have distrusted tabloid apologetics. The interest aroused in Catholics by the Newman centenary in 1945 was mainly emotional and, except in the case of a small

[14] An Australian student of Newman recently told the present writer that he believed that there was no country where Newman was at present less appreciated than England.

minority, divorced from any serious attempt to study his thought. The young Catholic of the present day has a belief in the perfectibility of this world quite alien to Newman's more sombre outlook.

Out of England it is otherwise. After the First World War a serious interest in Newman's writings showed itself in France and Germany alongside of a more popular Newman movement in America. The latter has no doubt been stimulated by the paucity of native Catholic authors of repute. The mainspring of the former is provided by a certain impatience with the categories of scholastic thought. How far such a trend is likely to go it is not as yet possible to predict, but some of those who do not make their judgments lightly assert that the former Tractarian leader will one day hold a place in the history of Christian thought comparable to those of St. Augustine and St. Thomas.

IX

THE IRISH IMMIGRATION

By Denis Gwynn

FOR more than a century Irish immigration into Great Britain has been one of the most important factors in the Catholic revival. At the period during and after the disastrous potato famine of 1845-47, the influx of poor Irish labourers, who came in search of food and employment on any terms, was so overwhelming that the Church in England and Wales soon consisted chiefly of Irish Catholic immigrants. Cardinal Manning's experience was mainly confined to London and to the great industrial cities which he visited from time to time; but he was a shrewd and vigilant observer of every aspect of Catholic life. The reminiscences which he set down in the closing years of his long life show repeatedly how conscious he was of the preponderance of Irish Catholics. Thus, at the close of 1882, he wrote[1]: " I remember saying that I had ' given up working for the people of England to work for the Irish occupation in England.' But that occupation is a part of the Church throughout the world, of an empire greater than the British." Nearly five years later, in February, 1887, he reflects, when reading the life of Lord Shaftesbury, that " I have spent my life in working for the Irish occupation of England." And again in the summer of 1890, when he wrote his last memorandum on the " Hindrances to the spread of the Catholic Church in England," he observes[2]: " We have a million of people, priests, or faithful of Irish blood, faith and civilisation in England." That estimate of their number was impressive; but the proportion to the total was still more remarkable. In a letter to his successor Cardinal Vaughan, who at that time controlled the *Tablet*, Manning wrote in the

[1] Purcell's *Manning*, II, pp. 677-8.
[2] *Ibid.*, p. 775.

same period a warning that he should bear in mind that
" eight-tenths of the Catholics in England are Irish. Two-
tenths, say two hundred thousand, are English, but a large
number are in sympathy with Ireland."

The proportion of Irish Catholics had been important
since long before the great exodus from Ireland which followed
the famine. It had grown steadily in the seaports and the new
industrial areas which formed during the early years of the
century. There was a constantly expanding flow of young
Irish labourers who found work in the docks and in the mines
and the new factories of the north and the midlands. There
was a large seasonal immigration also at harvest time, which
spread much farther afield and established connections which
developed and attracted much larger numbers in the years that
followed. They came only for a few months and went home
again with the earnings which helped to pay the rent and tithes
at home. While they were in England or Scotland they were
away from contact with the Church, and they did not remain
long enough to form even the nucleus of congregations. At
a later period, when they became much more numerous, their
need of religious assistance provoked the pity of some of the
richer Catholics, and especially of pious converts, who felt it
their duty to provide chapels for them. A tradition of estrangement and even of hostility persisted, however, for several
generations. Writing in 1890, Cardinal Manning recalled[3] how
" once it was my fate to ask the people at St. Mary's to sign
a petition to Parliament. The Petition lay for signature in the
school next to my house. I found that a young Irishman had
emptied the ink-bottle over it as a protest against Parliament."

The million of Irish Catholics in England [he went
on] are not only alienated from our laws and legislature, but
would upset the ink-bottle over the Statute Book. So long
as this habit of mind lasts we shall never have a Civil[4]
priesthood; and so long as our priesthood is not Civil it will
be confined to the sacristy, as in France, not by a hostile
public opinion, but by our own incapacity to mix in the

[3] Purcell's *Manning*, II, p. 775.
[4] Manning is here referring to a statement by Gioberti that the
Anglican clergy were *Un clero colto e civile*.

Civil life of the country; and this incapacity hitherto has sprung from hostility, suspicion and fear. A capacity for Civil and public action needs, of course, a training and education, but it springs from a love of our country. The Irish have this intensely for Ireland, but can hardly have it as yet for England.

Manning wrote those reflections so late as 1890. But even he was scarcely acquainted with the conditions which had arisen soon after the famine, when Wiseman had recently become the first Archbishop of Westminster. The searing memories of hunger and helpless destitution in those early years were shared by few of the Irish Catholics whom Manning knew afterwards in London. There were districts even in the 'fifties where the Irish immigrants still spoke Irish habitually. A. M. Sullivan, who afterwards became one of Parnell's party in the House of Commons, and was father-in-law to Mr. T. M. Healy, visited the Irish colonies in the Midlands in 1856 as a special correspondent for the Irish *Nation*. " It is lives that are bought and sold in the furnaces and forges of South Staffordshire," he wrote[5] after visiting Darlaston and Oldbury and Wednesbury. Thousands of famine refugees had found employment in these towns, in the most laborious and exacting work among " mounds of fire and sheets of flame, with a forest of stacks belching out smoke." In these appalling conditions, where safety precautions were still almost unknown, the Irish labourers soon died of overwork and exhaustion, and only the powerfully-built country-bred men could even attempt it.

Most of them, he found, still talked Irish constantly: and of Wednesbury he wrote that " in very many of the houses not one of the women could speak English, and I doubt that in a single house Irish was not the prevalent language." It was to this Black Country district Father Sherlock was sent, to Bilston, because he could hear the confessions of the Irish labourers and their families in Irish. In the shipping centres, such as Liverpool especially, and Cardiff and Hull and New-castle, there were still more who could scarcely understand English when they arrived on the immigrant ships, or as stowaways. In South Wales about the same time the Italian

[5] *The Irish in Britain*, p. 418.

Father Signini had found it necessary to compile for his own use a small conversation book in Irish, so that he could hear confessions.

Many Irish priests had been coming to minister in England for years before the Hierarchy was restored, and their number increased rapidly when the bishops with regular sees were able to arrange for new parishes and appoint the clergy to the places where they were most needed. The English priests often found great difficulty in getting on terms with their immigrant congregations, but many of them showed a noble gift of sympathy. At Wednesbury A. M. Sullivan was deeply impressed by the generous attitude of Father Revell, and he reported gratefully that " it is not always that the claims of a common faith ensure for our people from an English-born clergyman that forbearance for their peculiarities, that merging of the national antipathy in the religious accord which alone can reconcile him to a congregation of Celts."

Even the Irish priests who came to work in the new parishes, where the refugees were crying out for spiritual assistance, were often appalled by the conditions that had arisen after years of sweated labour since the escape from famine at home. The industrial cities were expanding with phenomenal rapidity, and they had become centres of great prosperity and wealth, which made the misery of the un-organised manual labourers all the more galling. An Irish Vincentian priest, Father Murphy, has left a poignant record of his first impressions on going to open a new Mass centre in a house at Sheffield in the 'sixties:

The morning was cold, the room was scarcely half-filled by a badly dressed, poor, perished-looking congregation. This beginning was not very encouraging. At that time the trade of Sheffield was most prosperous and the abundance of all material things, money included, was literally teeming and flowing over. Yet our poor people, through neglect, disorderly habits, and most of all through drink, were in a state of the deepest poverty and degradation. However, the gathering at the eleven o'clock Mass was better, and in the evening was even larger, and the mission had " got a good start." I shall never forget the opening of the Sunday school, or catechism, in the afternoon of that day. The few children who assembled in the lower school room were like wild Indians; they seemed never to have seen a priest before; and their wild disregard of order or of authority almost disheartened me.

Similar testimony from many places could be multiplied almost indefinitely. The picture lightens as the years pass, and the next generation consisted either of children who had grown up in the Irish settlements which had formed after the first flood of immigration slackened, or of immigrants who at least were not fleeing from actual famine and destitution. Yet their general poverty was still appalling; and it was congregations of this kind who first produced the humble Mass houses and halls and schools, or even churches of some sort, which brought so many parishes into life. Their achievements in this respect were remarkably recognised, forty years ago, by Bishop Bernard Ward, who had no recollection of the earlier phase and whose instinctive sympathies were naturally repugnant to the Irish Catholics in England. Bishop Ward's father had been one of the foremost figures in the Oxford Movement, and his family tradition was that of the landowning gentry. As a convert, W. G. Ward had found little difficulty in associating with the old Catholic families who were also land-owners. He and they had nothing but the Catholic faith in common with the mainly Irish congregations who formed so large a proportion of the Church in England.

They would have found nothing to offend them, for instance, in the attitude of that typical grand lady from Northumberland, Mrs. Charlton, whose lively reminiscences[6] have recently been published. She describes, for instance, how in 1847 two members of her family had arranged to " share the expense of setting up a school for Catholic children just behind St. Oswald's Church, whose priest should give religious instruction to the scholars. At that time there had been a small discovery of iron ore at Bellingham, and the place was full of dirty ill-conditioned Irish labourers whose children sadly needed education, and to be taught better ways than their

[6] *Recollections of a Northumbrian Lady* (Jonathan Cape).

parents." Many schools and Mass-houses in those earlier years were provided in this spirit by wealthy Catholics, who combined their traditional piety with a social life of balls and shooting parties and foreign travel, and were horrified to find these swarms of uncouth and hungry labourers arriving in their neighbourhood, demanding religious as well as material assistance. In 1860 Mrs. Charlton describes a typical house party at the Marquis of Westminster's, where some embarrassment was caused at dinner by disparaging references to Roman Catholics. When the Marquis attempted to spare her feelings by mentioning that she was a " Roman Catholic lady," she retorted at once, " Yes, but an English Catholic, not an Irish one, which is all the difference in the world. English Catholics are responsible beings who are taught right from wrong, whereas Irish Catholics, belonging to a yet savage nation, know no better and are perhaps excusable on that account."

Bishop Ward, in writing his monumental volumes on the history of the Catholic revival, was fully aware of how much these English aristocratic families had done during the earlier years, in lending the services of their chaplains, and in providing temporary buildings where the Irish poor could attend Mass and be taught their religion. But with that full knowledge, and as the son of one of the most prominent and zealous of the Oxford converts, he wrote in 1909 that the Irish immigration after the great famine " affected the future of Catholicism in this country more even than the Oxford Movement, for it was the influx of Irish in 1846 and the following years which made our congregations what they are and led to the multiplications of missions." He continued:

> Up to that time the English Catholics relied for the building of their churches almost solely on the donations of the few hereditary Catholics and others of the upper classes; after the great Irish immigration it became possible to build from the pennies of the poor. Many missions owe their very existence, including serviceable churches and schools, to the large Irish congregations. If proof be wanted of the importance of the immigration, it is only necessary to cast our eyes on those parts of England, as, for example, East Anglia, whither the Irish hardly penetrated, and to see the

desolate state of those counties so far as the Catholic religion is concerned. Even in Lancashire and the northern counties generally, where the number of English Catholics was far greater than in other parts of the country, the congregations were largely increased and many missions established due in great measure to the influx of Irish immigrants.

That story can be traced in the annual volumes of the *Catholic Directory*, which show the dates of the foundation of missions, and their gradual expansion as the Irish colonies became established and grew in numbers. It was many years before the first colonies of starving refugees had found even a sense of security and hope, in the new industrial areas to which their labour had contributed so largely under the ruthless exploitation of mid-Victorian days. There were enterprising and hard-working men and women among them, who made fortunes by industry and trade, even before the famine years. In time the new class of successful merchants and large employers in great provincial cities like Manchester and Liverpool and Birmingham and Newcastle and Bristol included a considerable number of Irish Catholics. In the professional classes also they gradually gained prominent positions, in spite of their handicap in being unable to obtain even secondary education.

But in general the Irish Catholics remained congregated in the congested areas, which had been built without any plan and without any regard to the requirements of decent housing while the industrial expansion was in full tide. If trade declined, the Irish labourers were the first to suffer unemployment, and the insecurity of their position made them the more anxious to remain together for mutual help in bad times. Whole areas of slum property became their recognised quarters; and their sense of isolation in a strange and often unfriendly country kept them together, prepared to accept a lower standard of life than other people. But their Catholic faith united them even more than their sentimental attachment to Irish ways. The churches and schools became the chief centre of their life, with Irish priests who had volunteered for service in England and dedicated themselves to their protection.

Only a few typical instances can be quoted here, of the process by which parishes were gradually formed from the humblest beginnings in various parts of the country. Every biography of the Catholic pioneers during the century contains similar illustrations. Few records of any sort remain concerning the parochial priests who laboured in poor parishes and whose names are not now remembered. But in the memoirs of converts who entered the Catholic priesthood there are many glimpses of what was happening all over England. Newman's former disciple at Littlemore, for instance, Father William Lockhart, was first deputed by Cardinal Wiseman to open the new Mass centre at Kingsland, in north London in 1854. A record by one of Father Lockhart's colleagues of its opening explains how Mr. Thomas Kelly, " a zealous Irishman who had risen in the world by his talent and industry to become a master builder and contractor " offered the use of part of his own house for the mission and to provide board and lodging for one priest.

To carry this out, Mr. Thomas Kelly gave up the whole of the principal floor in his house. The drawing-room and back parlour communicated by folding doors, and this served for chapel and sanctuary, whilst the two rooms on the other side of the entry served for Father Lockhart's study and bedroom. The first Mass was said with a congregation of some twelve or fourteen persons; but as the news of the opening of a new mission spread, other Catholic families residing in this neighbourhood made themselves known, so that before the end of the year, the parlour and entry were unable to contain the worshippers.

A timber yard with carpenters' shops lay behind the house: these Mr. Kelly rearranged, and the additional bench room thus afforded enabled him to give up the space under one of his shops as a chapel. This chapel was supposed to seat about 75 persons. Two bays were next added to the chapel, which, being curtained off, served for a school during the week. Towards autumn, 1855, Father Lockhart thought we were sufficiently established to do something for ourselves, and on October 16th we slept for the first time in our own hired home. In October, 1855, a paper-staining manufactory in Tottenham Road, adjoining Mr. Kelly's yard, with the corner house in Culford Road, was purchased by our Fathers.

The factory was opened immediately as a temporary church, whilst the second floor was being removed to make a more permanent church, with a western gallery on the first floor.

Mass was said here, on the site of the church of Our Lady and St. Joseph, on June 29th, 1856.

Father Lockhart, as a convert with private resources, was able to contribute personally towards church building; and at a later period he was even able to buy at auction the beautiful old pre-Reformation church in Ely Place, off Holborn, which Manning then entrusted to the Fathers of Charity. Another of the early converts who entered the priesthood with personal resources of his own was Earl Spencer's son, Father George Spencer, who subsequently became a Passionist. His first appointment for missionary work in England was at Walsall, to assist Mr. Martyn, who had been saying Mass on Sundays in a temporary chapel at West Bromwich. At that time it was not even marked on the maps, though its new industries were attracting large numbers of Irish labourers. Father Spencer was able to contribute £2,000 towards the building of its first church, and he soon had started three schools and begun preparations for building a church at Dudley. But even those few priests who could contribute money themselves for building had to rely chiefly upon collections from their poor parishioners. It was the poor who, literally with their penny contributions, provided whatever personal income the priests could count upon. Mr. John Denvir, in writing[7] of the Irish colony in the London docks, recalls how in 1856 Cardinal Wiseman opened a new church in east London and '' described how it had been erected by the penny contributions of Irish labourers, bargemen, bricklayers, hodmen and other toilers. So could Cardinal Manning tell of similar work done all over London, in connection with well nigh a hundred Catholic churches, and with numerous schools and religious houses.''

[7] *The Irish in Britain.*

But it was in the crowded northern cities chiefly that the hundreds of thousands of poor Irish Catholics contributed most decisively to Catholic progress. Mr. Thomas Burke's invaluable *Catholic History of Liverpool,* published in 1910, abounds in information concerning the growth of churches and schools and the means by which funds were raised through the whole century to provide for the Irish immigrants. Even in the 'thirties, when larger churches had become an urgent necessity, and committees were formed to undertake the collection of funds, the " humble Catholics living in the neighbourhood " had become a chief source of support. The first attempt to build a permanent church at Liscard, for instance, originated among them. Previously there had only been Mass on Sundays in the upper room of a small hotel. In the 'forties, when St. Anthony's Chapel was being built in northern Liverpool, a committee was formed[8] among the small number of influential Catholics, who did not then include even one Irish name. In a report issued after some years, during which litigation over the site had caused much delay, it was explained that " the only funds for carrying the vast enterprise into effect were the voluntary donations of a few wealthier Catholics, and the weekly penny subscriptions of the labouring class." But " the population in the district, chiefly by the continued influx of fresh comers, had increased to many thousands. For this multitude, the erections essential for the preservation and practice of religion, as well as for the education of crowds of destitute children, had to be provided."

By the early 'fifties, when the Irish famine had overwhelmed Liverpool with immigrants, the provision of schools had become the most urgent need. Father O'Carroll, who died soon afterwards from his exertions and anxieties, was able to enrol 300 girls and 100 infants in his new school on the first day, but had to turn away hundreds more for lack of room. Father Noble, of the Oblates of Mary Immaculate, found that in his own parish he had some 2,500 children between the ages of four and fourteen in need of school accommodation; and the Oblates decided to take no steps towards building a permanent church before schools had been provided. A priest of great energy and apostolic zeal, Father James Nugent, soon

[8] Burke, p. 56.

became the chief organiser of Catholic education for the poor, and his influence extended far beyond Liverpool.

Churches had to be built as well as schools, and the building of St. Vincent de Paul's church in St. James' Street was an instance[9] of what faith and courage were needed. The new church was to replace the wooden shed hitherto in use, and Bishop Goss had no funds at first even to pay the £6,000 needed for the site. But the foundation stone was laid by the bishop in April, 1856, and after his sermon " the Irish ship carpenters of the parish passed in single file, each laying one day's wages on the newly blessed stone. Then followed the dock labourers with their offerings, the total offering amounting to £101 9s." Within a year the site had been paid for; and while the weekly collectors continued to bring in their collections of pennies to Father O'Reilly, the church was built. When it was opened in August, 1857, this poor Irish congregation had by that time contributed £6,500.

It was inevitable that, with such inadequate buildings for worship, a proportion of the Catholic population gradually fell away and ceased to come to church. By 1861 Father Nugent was asserting boldly that there were 150,000 Catholics, or one-third of the entire city population, in Liverpool. But the attendance at Catholic schools, in spite of all efforts to build and support them, was far below the known total of Catholic children. Father Nugent declared openly that there were already some 23,000 children " roaming about the streets and docks "; but persistent pressure by the clergy could not compel them to attend school until compulsory education was enforced by law in 1870. To demand compulsory school attendance meant adding enormously to the provision of Catholic schools, and Father Nugent's fearless campaign for compulsory education encountered much opposition among Catholics who believed that their resources could not rise to its needs. But he persevered valiantly; and even in 1870, when the poverty of the Catholic population was less intense than in the earlier years, he showed that the Catholic school attendance ought to be 11,000 instead of the 6,000 on the rolls. One reason was that the poor families needed the earnings of their children; and so long as young children could

[9] Burke, p. 126.

legally be employed, the temptation to allow them to earn wages was overwhelming. The poor themselves had to provide most of the cost of the school buildings, besides contributing to the churches and to the salaries of the teachers. Some relief came with the generous donations of the Duke of Norfolk, Lord Bute and other wealthy Catholics to the general fund which was raised for the Catholic schools when the Education Act of 1870 became operative. A new middle class was also gradually arising, and it subscribed handsomely in every district. Even so, Father Seed could announce that in his own parish, St. Alban's, some £5,700 had been given in pennies alone, for the new parish schools.

South Wales was the most destitute of the chief centres in which congregations formed rapidly through Irish immigration. Almost all the Catholics there were Irish immigrants. They had been arriving since before the Hierarchy was restored, and the first colonies attracted others. During the famine, Irish refugees came to South Wales in great numbers, many of them landing as stowaways on potato boats, or by any means of escape. The conditions which they found on their arrival became much worse when they increased the overcrowding and the unemployment in what are now prosperous industrial cities. A vivid description of conditions in 1841, the year after a separate Vicariate of Wales was established, is contained in a letter[10] from its first bishop, Dr. Thomas Brown, O.S.B. Bishop Brown there explains that the missions at Bangor, Merthyr Tydfil, Cardiff, Newport and Wrexham were all quite recently founded, and that the actual buildings in use could only be justified by " absolute necessity such as that which drove the primitive Christians into catacombs and caves." As an instance he describes the mission " chapel " at Merthyr Tydfil, with an entirely poor Catholic population which fluctuated from 500 to 1,000.

The very best place that can be obtained for Catholic worship is a loft reached by a ladder, ill-ventilated, low, narrow, dark, without ceiling, not secure against wet and wind, and running over the public slaughter-house of the

[10] The letter was published from the diocesan archives by Father J. M. Cronin in *St. Peter's Magazine* some twenty years ago.

town, whence issues the confused bellowing, bleating and screaming of pent-up and butchered oxen, sheep and swine, and whence oftentimes ascend through the floor, odours exceedingly offensive. At Cardiff we are now, principally through the charity of a deceased Catholic lady, Mrs. Eyre, of Bath, erecting a capacious church. But meanwhile, as long since, the divine mysteries are offered, from want of means to procure a more becoming house of worship, on the ground floor of a small cottage crowded almost to suffocation up to the very altar, mostly with very poor Irish, behind whom are hundreds of others extending down an open back yard, and exposed to all the inclemency of weather; from which those in front and the priest at the altar are not secure, owing to the removal of the window at his back, in order that he may be heard by those who are in the yard.

At Abersychan, the only place which can be procured for the congregation (fluctuating according to the varying demand for labour in the iron works from 300 to nearly 1,000) is a club room in a public house. At Swansea, a large town and a noted watering place, the chapel is a miserable building scarcely sufficient to accommodate half the ordinary congregation. Its floor is giving way in all parts, and its roof is so rotten that there is reason to apprehend its falling in upon the priest and congregation. At Bangor, the chapel, besides being too small for those who frequent it, is in a very unfinished state—the inside walls being not yet plastered.

Only a few years after that letter was written, the flood of refugees from the Irish famine poured into all these centres, and the labour of the priests became more overwhelming. Bishop Brown's letter explained how, even in 1841, the clergy depended for their support almost entirely upon the contributions of poor labourers, many of whom were frequently unemployed. Their numbers increased greatly in the following year, but they were so destitute that their need for assistance far exceeded what they could contribute. At Cardiff at this time Father Millea's income during most of the spring " did not exceed eight, sometimes not five, shillings per week." At

Merthyr Tydfil the bishop had given permission to its laborious missioner, Father Carroll, to earn a little money, both for his own maintenance and to provide alms for the destitute, " by carrying on (under the name and by the agency of one of his congregation) a merchandise of salt provisions which he obtains at a low price from a charitable friend in Ireland, himself being exculpated in so doing, by absolute necessity." At Abersychan the missioner's poverty was even worse, and his weekly income during part of the summer had been less than half-a-crown. " I am almost certain," the bishop added sadly, " that the great reduction of the number of workmen in the iron trade at Abersychan during the present winter and of the price of labour, must cause a suspension of this mission until the return of better times." But the need for that mission, and of many others in South Wales, became vastly more urgent, whether the prospects of trade were better or worse, when the famine refugees arrived in tens of thousands soon afterwards.

In such surroundings, and with no recollection of any decent standard of life and no hope of better prospects intemperance was a constant temptation among the multitudes of poor Irish Catholics. Drunkenness became widely prevalent among them, and continued so for many years. The same problem had arisen in Ireland before the great famine, when millions of smallholders and labourers had lived entirely on potatoes as the Indians lived on rice. Even milk had been a rare luxury for their large families of children as well as their parents. Strong drink had been their greatest temptation in those days. Father Mathew's temperance campaign had produced a revolutionary change until the three consecutive years of famine broke down all restraints, and demoralisation set in again. As refugees in the new industrial areas of England without access to Mass and the sacraments, and with no priests to minister among them, they had recourse to drink again as the only alleviation of their miserable lives. Father Mathew died a few years after the famine abated, but other pioneers of temperance arose in England, of whom Cardinal Manning became the most powerful. When he was appointed as Wiseman's successor in 1866 he had recognised that the multitude of poor Irish Catholics were now incomparably the most important factor in the Church in England. He saw, too, that intemperance was their chief failing; that it arose from the misery in which they lived, and that improvement could come only by a campaign to prevent drunkenness and by large measures of social reform, which would ensure fair wages and shorter hours of work and so restore the possibility of a decent Christian family life. In that conviction Manning launched his League of the Cross, for temperance, which acquired the character of a religious crusade, combined with real effort for social reform.

In his invaluable study of *The Irish in Britain,* which Mr. John Denvir published in 1892, full tribute is paid to the value of Manning's efforts in this direction. Mr. Denvir was an Irish Catholic journalist from Liverpool who became the first editor of the *Catholic Times* when Father Nugent bought it as an organ for the northern Catholics. He had acquired an unrivalled knowledge by his close study of the Irish electorate, as the chief organiser of the United Irish League of Great Britain. Most of Mr. Denvir's work is concerned chiefly with Irish politics, but there are nearly a hundred pages which give detailed accounts of Irish Catholic settlements in all parts of Great Britain. His analysis of the Census returns is only partially illuminating, because the statistics available could only show the number of Catholics in each county or borough who were actually of Irish birth. Even in the 'sixties and 'seventies, there was already a large proportion of Irish Catholics who had been born in England or Wales but who still retained their strongly Irish tradition. The proportion who had come direct from Ireland decreased rapidly; because the influx of immigrants declined when the main stream was directed to America and Australia, and because the proportion who had been born of Irish parents in England was increasing steadily.

An estimated total of Irish-born persons in England and Wales is given in each of the decennial Census reports; but the figures cannot be reliable, especially for the earlier periods when so many of the Irish immigrants had no settled residence. Such as they are, the figures must be considered in relation to the total population at each period. In 1841 the recorded total was 420,000 out of 16 millions. By 1851 it had increased to 520,000 out of 18 millions, and by 1861 to 600,000 out of

20 millions. It had fallen to 570,000 in 23 millions by 1871, and it was again 570,000 in 26 millions in 1881. By 1891 it had declined to 460,000 in 29 millions; and by 1901 to 420,000 in 32 millions. In 1911 there were some 360,000 Irish-born in 36 millions; and in 1921 some 370,000 in 38 millions. In 1931 there were some 380,000 in a total of 40 millions.

The figures of Irish-born population are therefore misleading as totals; but their distribution reflects closely the general outline of the Irish settlements. The immigrants, once they had found employment, tended generally to remain in the same districts. Their families and descendants multiplied there without spreading further afield. So the general Census report for 1881 notes that " the distribution of the Irish was most unequal. In the purely agricultural counties their numbers were insignificant, while in the great manufacturing and mining counties they formed a not inconsiderable fraction of the population. Thus in Lancashire they formed 6.1 per cent.; in Cumberland 5.6 per cent.; in Durham 4.2 per cent.; and in Cheshire 3.7 per cent. of the population." These figures, it should be noted, include only the Irish born. Even they, in 1881, were also over 2 per cent. in Middlesex, Monmouth, Northumberland and Glamorgan. They were least numerous in Cardigan, Merioneth, Carmarthen and Radnor, Norfolk, Suffolk, Cambridge and Huntingdon, Wiltshire and Buckinghamshire.

But their chief concentration was in the new cities, especially in Lancashire and Cheshire. In Liverpool the Irish-born alone in 1881 were nearly 13 per cent.; in Birkenhead and St. Helens nearly 9 per cent., and 7.5 in Manchester and Salford. The other cities in which they were most numerous were Middlesbrough, Stockport, Cardiff, Gateshead, Preston, Bolton, Bradford and Oldham. A broader calculation shows that among the inhabitants of London and all the other towns which then included over 50,000 people, the general average was 3.3 per cent. of Irish-born persons, while the average for the rest of the country was only 1.5. Roughly speaking, therefore, by 1881 four-fifths of the Irish-born people in England were living in big cities. Another calculation, based on the same figures, reveals how clearly defined was their general distribution. Roughly one-sixth of the whole Irish total was resident in London, and almost an equal proportion in Liverpool and Birkenhead; and about half as many more in Manchester and Salford. The three next centres in importance were Leeds, Bradford and Birmingham. Apart from these principal cities, the Irish born were similarly concentrated in a small number of counties. Lancashire—which at that time included many towns which are now treated as county boroughs—contained nearly two-fifths of all the Irish born who were not in the cities, while London with its closely-adjacent counties had nearly one-fifth more. Yorkshire had about one-tenth, while Durham and Cheshire had another tenth; and the only other counties with any considerable number were Cumberland, Staffordshire and Northumberland, Glamorgan and Hampshire. All these counties were the chief centres of industry or mining or shipping, with the exception of Hampshire, where the Irish contingent always consisted largely of soldiers quartered around Aldershot or sailors around Portsmouth.

This analysis for 1881 shows the broad pattern which had emerged when the main influx of Irish immigrants had almost ceased. This pattern persisted until the first considerable upheaval came after the First World War in 1914. A much greater dispersion began in 1939; but the general outline of Irish distribution prior to 1939 can be simply stated. Until then, the Irish Catholic population had continued to live and to multiply in the cities where the Irish immigrants first found employment and made their homes. Direct immigration had become a relatively small factor before the end of the century. But the Irish Catholics continued to increase steadily, as their families grew, most of them marrying people of their own race and faith. In consequence the Catholic population of England and Wales became increasingly localised, so that the northern ecclesiastical province of Liverpool contained three-fifths of all the Catholics in England. The provinces of Westminster and Birmingham had similar local concentrations in the areas where the Irish colonies had produced the chief centres of organised Catholic life. These conditions changed relatively little, except for a gradual expansion outwards from the cities into the suburban areas, until the outbreak of war in 1939 produced a wholesale evacuation from the cities where the Catholics were most numerous.

Any statistical study of the Catholic Church in England and Wales during the past century is therefore largely a study of the Irish immigrants and their descendants. It was they, as Bishop Ward has pointed out, who first formed the principal congregations, about the time that the Hierarchy was restored, and whose religious needs produced the churches and schools that they required. Some reservation must be made in regard to certain areas of Lancashire and Yorkshire particularly, where the old Catholic element in northern England was still relatively numerous, and where churches and schools had existed for years. But it is broadly true that the churches and schools came into being mainly to provide for the Irish Catholics. The large increase in the number of priests was likewise due chiefly to the Irish immigration. A great proportion of the priests came direct from Ireland, and in increasing numbers, to minister to their own people in England.

The general picture lightened, with the growth of a new generation who found more skilled employment at better wages, while the Catholics in the professional classes, as civil servants of all sorts, or doctors or lawyers, began to establish their positions, and many others achieved some degree of prosperity in trade or as employers of labour. But the mass of poor Irish Catholics were still chiefly engaged in casual labour, which the trade union movement had not yet been able to organise—as dockers or building workers or in the heaviest forms of work, or as agricultural labourers who had to subsist on seasonal earnings. In the cities, the degrading conditions which prevailed everywhere affected them most of all. Drunkenness was the most demoralising and debasing feature in the whole social life of the poor of all sorts during the later years of the century. Among the Nonconformist social reformers total abstinence has become almost an article of faith; and even among the Catholic reformers Manning's League of the Cross represented the most powerful influence for counteracting the tendencies which kept the poor in their abject condition. Education and total abstinence became linked as two chief factors in every effort for social advancement.

In the north, Father Nugent had found it impossible to

make headway without preaching strict temperance, just as
Manning had done in London. Their denunciations of drunkenness and its social consequences are scarcely intelligible to a
later generation.   Even in their own day they were often
regarded as a calumny on the poor Catholics. Father Nugent
certainly did not lack sympathy with them. He had made himself their foremost spokesman in Liverpool, where he established the weekly *Catholic Times* as their outspoken organ.
Yet even he in 1870, after a tour of Canada and the United
States, incurred many reproaches for his exposure of conditions
in Liverpool when he appealed[12] for help to keep the Catholic
children off the streets.

> Let any man walk our streets, let him go along
> Marylebone, Vauxhall Road or Scotland Road, and his heart
> will sink as he sees not only poverty, but naked, disgusting
> pauperism. When I see so many poor girls crowding the
> workhouses and prisons: when I see the noblest race God
> has ever created degraded and demoralised in our large
> towns, is it not the duty of every man who has a spark of
> humanity in his veins, to stretch out his hands, and give the
> warm feelings of his heart, to put them in a position where
> they can be self-reliant, where they can gain their bread
> without becoming a race of paupers?

In London, as in Liverpool or Manchester or Newcastle
or Cardiff or so many other congested cities, the conditions
were similar. The Catholic populations which had formed in
them were still largely working in the casual trades, most exposed to unemployment and least capable of asserting the right
to fair wages and working hours. They provided a constant
surplus of cheap labour, which kept down wages in the largely
" unskilled " occupations which they followed.   The rise
of the " New Unionism," with John Burns and Ben Tillett as
its principal agitators and organisers, gave them their first
chance to join trade unions, which had to fight hard for recognition. Cardinal Manning in London had already become
recognised as a vigorous social reformer with radical views,
and his close relations with the Irish labourers encouraged
even the most fiery of the young trade union leaders to seek

[12] Burke, p. 195.

his advice and help. The climax of his efforts for social reform came in the great London dock strike of 1889, when the whole trade of London was held up by a dispute in which the dockers asked for an extra sixpence, " the dockers' tanner," a day. It seemed impossible that, with so large a pool of unemployed labour, the new trade union could hold out indefinitely against the employers' refusal. After all other attempts to reach a settlement had failed, Manning, in his venerable old age, was implored to take a hand in bringing both sides together. By using his personal prestige and influence, he obtained concessions which he could bring to the dockers, at their headquarters; and when his proposed terms met with opposition he played his last card successfully by threatening to appeal to the Irish dockers in the parishes which he knew well.

Manning's triumph in settling the London dock strike of 1889 marks the end of the earlier phase. In forty years since the Hierarchy was restored, the Irish Catholics had become thoroughly established in England, and no longer regarded themselves as aliens. Immigration still continued steadily, but on a greatly reduced scale, and the later immigrants were no longer destitute or homeless. On the contrary, many of them were young people who came fully trained for commercial or professional life. In England new generations had arisen among the children of the earlier immigrants, and they obtained employment easily in the general expansion of English life. They had been finding their place increasingly in the better paid occupations, and many were now engaged in trade, in teaching, or in the civil service, journalism and the other professions. Anglo-Irish trade has always been one of the very largest markets for both exports and imports; and the commerce between the two countries, besides the shipping and transport which it involved, was largely conducted by Irish settlers in England.

As the years passed, many Irish Catholics in England grew prosperous through such commerce, especially in the provision trade in the big cities and in the cattle and coal trades. Many more became prominent as professional men, or in local affairs. In law, for instance, Lord Russell of Killowen had become one of the most eminent barristers and judges of his time, and there were many other distinguished Catholic bar-

risters and solicitors and judges. Still more numerous were
the Irish Catholics who achieved eminence in the medical profession; particularly in the Army Medical Service, of which
General Sir Alfred Keogh became the first head, and the
precursor of other famous Irish Catholics in the service. In
journalism Irishmen have always been conspicuous, especially
among political and parliamentary correspondents where
names such as Sherlock, Macdonagh and Herlihy have
abounded. T. P. O'Connor, as founder and first editor of the
Star newspaper and of other successful periodicals, was one
of the most typical figures of his generation. Another famous
Catholic of Irish origin was his contemporary in Galway,
Sir Anthony MacDonnell, who, after great distinction in the
Indian Civil Service, held high positions in Whitehall and in the
city.

In the mid-Victorian period the mass of Irish Catholics
in England still retained a tradition of active hostility towards
the British Government. The Fenian movement had wide
support in England, in spite of the constant denunciations of
secret societies by Manning and the bishops. But a new phase
opened when Parnell organised a vigorous Irish National Party
at Westminster, with the double programme of achieving the
reform of land tenure in Ireland and the establishment of Home
Rule. His incursion into British politics was so dynamic, and
his personal leadership so dramatic, that he soon galvanised
support among all the Irish settlements in England. In the
great cities he could count upon rallying immense audiences;
and the organisation which arose in those years became extremely powerful in the places where Irish Catholics were
numerous, as the United Irish League of Great Britain under
the presidency of T. P. O'Connor. Even in the early 'eighties
it became possible to secure the election of T. P. O'Connor as
an Irish Nationalist member for the Scotland division of Liverpool, and he retained that seat until 1929, becoming eventually
Father of the House of Commons and a Privy Councillor. No
other English constituency would actually return an Irish
Nationalist member; but there were scores of constituencies
in such cities as Manchester, Newcastle, Hull, Leeds, Sheffield,
Bristol or Cardiff, or even in parts of London, where the Irish
Catholic voters could decide the result of an election.

The Catholic masses had become enfranchised, and they found leaders, especially in local government, among the younger generation or among the older immigrants who had acquired important influence in trade or the professions. There had been so much " leakage " among the Irish Catholics during the earlier years that some typically Irish leaders like J. R. Clynes, who were Irish in origin, had ceased to be Catholics. But their following was chiefly among the Irish Catholics; and the Church could always count on the Irish vote whenever its religious needs were involved. In the long conflict over the religious schools, both in Parliament and with the local authorities, the Irish vote was an extremely important asset. It was all the more important when the Liberals were in office, because the Liberals were generally hostile to religious education, but had to avoid estranging their Irish supporters in many constituencies. On the schools question, the Irish Nationalists in the House of Commons, who numbered some eighty members, could also be counted upon to support the Catholic claims. Before the Irish Nationalist Party had disappeared from Westminster, one of its Whips, Mr. John Boland, was awarded a papal knighthood by the Holy See in recognition of his services to Catholic education in England. Mr. Boland remained on in London, and for some thirty years gave devoted and invaluable service to the Catholic Truth Society as its general secretary.

Parnell's Home Rule agitation in the 'eighties had brought the Irish Catholics in England into closer relations with English political life. Manning, also, by his open support of the Irish national demands, had won their confidence and sympathy, besides the respect and gratitude which he had earned by his years of work for the Catholic schools and church building and by his temperance crusade. He utilised their support fully for the protection of religious rights in Parliament. There had been a gradual but always increasing assimilation to English life and ways; and the continual intermarriage between English and Irish men and women was breaking down the old sense of separation. One of the most conspicuous examples of such parentage was Cardinal Bourne, whose mother was an Irish Catholic, while his father was an English convert. Cardinal Hinsley likewise had an Irish mother, while his father was of old Yorkshire Catholic stock. In time the strongly Irish tradition, which had still been intensely active in Manning's days, lost most of its force. The Irish enthusiasm which had been kindled by Parnell's agitation subsided for years after his death, and only came to life, in a much less intense form, when Redmond's agitation for the Home Rule Bill revived the former organisation of Irish voters, during the years before 1914. But by that time support for Home Rule was general among all members of the Liberal and Labour parties, and the old sense of racial antagonism in England had largely disappeared.

When war came in 1914, the Irish Catholics in England gave it their unqualified support. Among the first military formations to be raised for the new armies were such groups as the Tyneside Irish Brigade and the many battalions of the London Irish and Liverpool Irish. Priests of Irish origin volunteered in large numbers as chaplains to the fighting forces; and in the whole war record of those years Irish Catholics in England played their full part. At the conclusion of the First World War there was an active, but transient, revival of anti-English feeling, during the final campaign for national independence in Ireland by the young Sinn Féin movement. The employment of military coercion in Ireland, the wholesale arrest of Irish elected representatives, and the disgraceful atrocities carried out by the Black and Tans around 1920, stirred up bitter feelings for a time. But peace came quickly when Lord FitzAlan had been sent to Dublin as the first, and the last, Catholic Viceroy, to replace Lord French. Since the establishment of the Irish Free State in 1921 there has been no serious interruption in the general process of fusion in England.

Two personal instances may be mentioned specially as typifying that process. The High Commissioner for Ireland in London, Mr. John Dulanty, C.B., whose services have contributed immeasurably to the improvement of Anglo-Irish relations during the past thirty years, was born in Manchester of Irish Catholic parents. At an extremely early age he became a member of the executive of the United Irish League of Great Britain, representing the Manchester district. During the First World War he was on active service in France before rising to the highest levels in the Civil Service, first as Deputy Director of the Ministry of Munitions and later as Establishment Officer in the Treasury. He gave up a career of extraordinary promise to accept the invitation of the new Irish Government to assist them in their London office. Among Mr. Dulanty's contemporaries, as another young organiser of the United Irish League, was the late John Scurr, who became one of the most prominent young members of the Labour Party during Ramsay MacDonald's first period of office. When the Labour Government in 1926 adopted a policy which threatened disaster for the hard-pressed Catholic schools, Mr. Scurr led a revolt in Parliament against his own party, which successfully protected the Catholic interests. In so doing, he sacrificed his political future, after years of work in East London.

It was significant that, with the rise of the Labour Party after 1918, the Irish popular vote in England was transferred almost solidly from the Liberals to the Labour side. When T. P. O'Connor retired in 1929, the Liverpool constituency which he had represented for nearly fifty years as an Irish Nationalist, went to Alderman Logan, the leader of the Labour Party in Liverpool and a prominent representative of the Irish Catholics. The Catholic voters in England and Wales are still chiefly concentrated in the industrial areas, and their direct representatives in Parliament have been almost all members of the Labour Party. Mr. Jack Jones, for many years the dockers' member for Silvertown in East London, was a very typical representative of the older generation of immigrant labourers from Ireland. In the present House of Commons, another much more recent immigrant from Ireland, Mr. Delargy, M.P., typifies a very different generation. But the Irish Catholics in Parliament have by no means all been members of the Labour Party. Sir Patrick Hannon, who is also of Irish birth and education, was for years a most popular representative of the big industrial interests in Birmingham of which he was a prominent director. Among other Irish Catholics in the Midlands who are associated with large business interests is Sir Martin Melvin, G.C.S.G., whose enterprise has made the *Universe* the most widely read Catholic newspaper in England. Another outstanding Irish Catholic, born and educated in Ireland, was the late Edward Eyre, a director of finance banking who commanded great influence in London and in both North and South America. He was one of the most devotedly generous benefactors of the Church in the previous generation.

A final note must be added concerning the Irish clergy in England. In the earlier phase, when parishes were still taking shape, the priests who arrived in scores from Ireland literally laid the foundations of the subsequent progress. As pioneers, unknown and unremembered to-day, they established a connection which developed and broadened, with a regular supply of young Irish priests for missionary work in England. Some of them came at first only to gain experience; but the majority remained in Great Britain until their death, labouring under enormous difficulties. They faced, one after another, the formidable tasks of providing new churches and schools, even when a beginning had already been made. Their days were spent in ceaseless ministrations to congregations of poor and defenceless people, who were often in dire distress and who frequently had been demoralised and degraded by the conditions in which they lived. All through the chief centres of Irish population these Irish priests continued to develop what they found already available, and to meet the constantly changing needs of the time. Even where dignified churches had been built, to replace barns or sheds, they were usually too small after a short time, and other and larger churches had to be built to supplement them. The schools' problem was still more pressing and most onerous; because the Catholic schools had to compete with those provided by the superior resources of other denominations, or with the bottomless purse of State education. Through it all, the problem of " leakage " persisted always, and the energies of the priests were constantly taxed to bring back lapsed Catholics. At the same time they had to provide for those who remained faithful, but could scarcely contribute anything themselves.

One question must occur to every student of the problems who is aware of the vast efforts and the spiritual zeal of the Irish clergy through all these years. Why did so few of them—though they were so large a proportion of the whole

clergy in Great Britain—become outstanding national figures.
The fewness of bishops of Irish origin did indeed become a
matter of comment and even of resentment, among the Irish
Catholic community generally, from time to time.

The Irish clergy, however, fully understood the
problems that were involved. Many of them had political
sympathies which were scarcely compatible with promotion
to episcopacy in England. Many more had brought with
them that old tradition of intimate relationship between the
Irish priest and his parish which they valued far more than
any advancement elsewhere. Moreover, in many dioceses
the resources available for a bishop's maintenance were so
small that it was almost indispensable to choose some priest of
social status who could provide from his private resources for
the decent upkeep of his position. It was scarcely less necessary that he should be a priest who had no political affiliations
or ties, which might cause embarrassment in dealing with
unfriendly local authorities and with the Government of the
day.

But the chief reason why the Irish clergy figured so
little in the ranks of the Hierarchy lay in their previous training in Ireland, and in their own dedicated services as parish
priests. Maynooth, in its long tradition, had aimed always at
producing zealous missioners, rather than men of spectacular
gifts and individual distinction like Wiseman, with his vastly
different Roman training. They were not trained to be either
diplomats or administrators, or scholars intended for the
Catholic universities. Their whole training and their subsequent experience on the English mission, whether in the congested cities or as pioneer missionaries in remote places, had
been for directly personal work among their growing and
precarious congregations. As such, they lived and laboured
until death took them. Their monuments are to be seen in the
flourishing churches and schools and institutions which have
arisen from their personal labours, each man performing all
that lay within his power while he lived, and relying upon his
successor to continue and to develop further what he had
begun.

X

CATHOLICS AND THE UNIVERSITIES, 1850-1950

By H. O. EVENNETT[1]

WHEN, in surveying the educational policy and achievements of the English Catholics since 1850, we pass from school to university level, we are at once struck by one very important difference. England to-day is covered with a network of Catholic elementary schools and a sprinkling of secondary schools, but there is no Catholic University. We have no Louvain, no Fribourg; there is no English counterpart to the Catholic University of America, the Sacred Heart University at Milan or the many other Catholic universities produced by the intellectual revival of the 19th century. The Church, indeed, claims equal authority in the higher and the lower spheres of education alike, but in England it has come about that Catholics go for their university education to Oxford or Cambridge, to London or Durham, or to the newer universities and university colleges in the provinces. That we have no Catholic University is due partly to the comparative poverty of Catholic intellectual resources and the lack of co-ordination among them, partly to the mishandling of the attempts to found a Catholic University College in the later decades of the 19th century, and partly also to lack of incentive, seeing that during the last fifty years the ecclesiastical toleration of Catholics going to Oxford and Cambridge—granted originally in 1895—has developed *de facto* into definite approval and positive encouragement. This last factor, together with the rise of the provincial universities—and all that

I am grateful to His Eminence Cardinal Griffin, Archbishop of Westminster, to His Lordship the Bishop of Northampton, to the Abbot of Downside and to the Master of St. Benet's Hall, Oxford, who have kindly allowed me to see and use material in their custody. Also to Monsignor Kerr McClement, Father Sebastian Redmond, A.A., and Father Philip Hughes for the help they have so willingly given me.

this implies—has entirely transformed the whole nature of th
problem of a Catholic University in England.

The present situation, then, has existed only since th
turn of the century. For some forty years previously, a grea
educational issue of extreme importance for English Catholic
was fought out against the complicated and changing in
tellectual background of mid and later Victorian England—
indeed, against the even wider background of the political an
intellectual vicissitudes of 19th-century Catholicism as a whole
The issue was this. Should the English Catholics—takin
advantage of the gradual abolition of religious tests at Oxfor
and Cambridge—throw in their lot with the national univer
sities and face all the rocks and shoals of English universit
life as it then was, or should they attempt to create a universit
of their own in which a specifically Catholic learning an
culture might arise as a rock of salvation amid the all-engulfin
tide of liberalism and scepticism? To many minds—and no
only those of Manning's cast—so noble and ambitious a proje
as an English Catholic University, seen as an intellectua
coping-stone to the achievements of the second spring, mac
a powerful appeal. This was the bright vision, which in th
'sixties sprang before the minds of Ward and Manning an
Acton, even, indeed, of Newman himself, and which was th
necessary accompaniment to the strong ecclesiastical admon
tions which, in the interests of their faith, officially kep
Catholics from Oxford and Cambridge between 1865 and 189!
But the vision faded, languished, and eventually expired i
the suburban air of Kensington. Manning proved himse
unable either to conceive or to organise an Institute of Highe
Studies capable of providing an intellectual training of equa
breadth and quality with that of Oxford and Cambridge or c
making a successful appeal to the Catholic laity, who wer
acutely conscious of the social, political and cultural advan
tages of which their sons were deprived by exclusion from
Oxford and Cambridge. For there was an important socia
(using the word in its broadest sense) as well as a purely in
tellectual side to the whole matter.

The Church in England in 1850 was not without me
of real distinction in scholarship—Wiseman himself, Lingard
Rock, Waterworth, Acton, not to mention the Oxford conver

nd others such as Renouf and Mivart and Paley. But their
xistence in no way compensated for the lack of an institution
t which Catholics could obtain a university education. They
ight, indeed, go to Cambridge as undergraduates—Cardinal
cton had been among the few who had done so—for no
eligious test was exacted there at matriculation. But a
ambridge degree was impossible and at Oxford even matricu-
tion was barred by religious tests. The disadvantages of this
tuation had not been lost upon the leaders of the Church.
Viseman is said at one time to have favoured the notion of a
atholic college or hall at Oxford, as part of his vision of the
turn of Catholics into every branch of English life. But
ere can be little doubt that the Vicars Apostolic as a whole
ould have been more favourable to a Catholic University
ollege under direct clerical control, such as Bishop Baines—
ith Wiseman's support—had abortively planned at Prior
ark in the middle 'thirties.

The recent conversions, however, had served to set
xford more prominently before the Catholic consciousness,
d to bring into the Church men of high intellectual standing
ho knew Oxford from the inside. But it was a changing
xford and, moreover, an Oxford about the future of which
ese men were uneasy. The Oxford Movement was a protest
ainst the spirit which was threatening to transform the
niversities from orthodox and exclusive Anglican strongholds
to centres of mid-Victorian liberalism and scepticism. The
ry movements of university reform which in the 'fifties
moved the religious tests at matriculation and graduation
d so opened up Oxford and Cambridge degrees to Catholics,
ere part and parcel of a broader intellectual movement of
iticism which was making the atmosphere of the universities
ore dangerous to religion and adding scepticism and rational-
m to Protestantism among the dangers which Catholics would
ve to encounter there. No one knew this better than the
xford converts themselves—Newman, Ward, Manning,
akeley and the rest, among whom there was at this time com-
ete agreement over the acute dangers to faith which a
atholic would meet with at an Oxford college. Moreover, it
as precisely at this period, in the middle 'fifties, that Newman
Dublin was working out the theory and vainly endeavour-

ing to give flesh and blood to the reality of a Catholic Unive
sity, not only in order to provide an alternative to Protesta
Trinity and the secular Queen's Colleges at Cork, Galway an
Belfast, but also with the ambition of creating a university
high standing which would be capable of serving English an
Irish Catholics alike.

Liberalism, however, was more than a merely Englis
phenomenon. The conflict between the Oxford Movement an
the new trends of thought was reproduced on a wider Cathol
stage and with greater variety of manifestation by an intens
intellectual and ecclesiastical struggle within Europea
Catholicism as a whole. The most far-reaching issues we:
involved: the extent of the Church's " magisterium "; h
attitude towards independent learning and science and to tl
new principles of criticism; the position of the lay schola
problems concerning the spiritual as well as the temporal pow
of the Pope. Many decades were to pass before these problem
were to find some solution, and meanwhile there was muc
conflict and passion and tragedy. The English " Liber
Catholicism " of the *Rambler* and of the *Home and Forei*
Review was the counterpart of more intensive movements
Germany, France and Italy, but " Liberal Catholicism
represented an attitude which the Papacy and at length tl
whole machine of ecclesiastical government rallied to denoun
and suppress. It is impossible to appreciate the atmosphere
which the question of Catholics going to Oxford or Cambrid
was debated in the 'fifties and 'sixties without understandi
both the contemporary developments within the universiti
themselves and the wider European background formed by tl
tremendous issue of Liberalism versus Ultramontanism.
must be remembered too, that the restoration of the Hierarcl
had not removed England from the control of the Congreg
tion of Propaganda, and thus the bishops were under t
necessity of frequently consulting this body which had
fingers on the pulse of Catholicism all over the world.[2]

The intellectual controversies of the hour, howeve
only helped to make the lack of proper university opportunit

[2] Most of the letters of Propaganda to the English bishops si
about 1865 are preserved in the Westminster Archives. For 1
other side of the correspondence access would presumably be
quired to Propaganda's own papers.

or Catholics more acutely felt. Newman failed in Ireland, and
t had been in any case somewhat unreal to conceive of Dublin
is an intellectual magnet for Englishmen. The new London
University, to which many Catholic colleges were now
' affiliated," might be degree-giving but except for students
t University or King's College was hardly educational. It
vas perhaps no wonder, despite the storm centres in the intel-
ectual sky, that many of the English laity should feel, after
he first removal of the religious tests, that if Catholics were to
olay their legitimate part in English public life, and if Catholic
Emancipation were to be fully exploited, it was vital for
Catholic young men to be able to open the many doors to
vhich Oxford and Cambridge held the key. It was not, as
Manning somewhat unjustly remarked later, the latchkeys to
Berkeley Square that they coveted, but access to the full cul-
ural and political opportunity that the universities, and the
iniversities alone, afforded. A self-denial that had been the
eroic virtue of necessity in Penal Times might well be foolish-
iess after Emancipation. The larger social aspect of the ques-
ion might be ignored by Rome and minimised by rigorist
heological opinion in England, but it necessarily bulked large
n the eyes of the laity.

Schemes—perhaps not always very carefully thought
ut—began to be mooted for enabling Catholics to go to
Oxford without becoming members of a college as a certain
umber now began to do. Proposals for a Catholic hall
vith Catholic Tutors, and even—should it be constitutionally
ecessary—with a non-Catholic as nominal head, gained the
upport of eminent converts such as Oakeley and Renouf, and
n 1864 a hundred laymen presented a supporting petition in
Rome. But they were strongly opposed by others, of whom
Manning (not yet a bishop) and W. G. Ward were the leaders.
'his party pointed out that such a hall could not be hermetic-
lly sealed off from dangerous contacts with the rest of the
University of a kind calculated to de-Catholicise the minds and
norals of its members. And, furthermore, they asked, with
ome reason, why, if isolation were indeed regarded as possible,
. would be desirable to have the hall at Oxford at all? But
iey also held that even if Oxford did not actually destroy
aith, it would certainly serve to " liberalise " it and to

produce " minimising " Catholics of the " liberal " type
They believed, moreover, in the intellectual mission of
Catholicism to save England from what was killing Oxford—
the new liberal and rationalising influences. Thus for them the
university question concerned not merely a few individuals but
the whole future prospects of religion in England. In his well
known article in the *Dublin Review* of July 1863 entitled
" The Work and Wants of the Catholic Church in England "
Manning set out with great lucidity and fairness the pros and
cons of Oxford and Cambridge. He reckoned the foundation
of a Catholic University as well within the powers of " a body
which has in one day founded thirteen dioceses."   All the
elements, he maintained, existed in the " four greater colleges
of Stonyhurst, Oscott, Old Hall and Ushaw " together with the
" eight lesser colleges of Sedgeley Park, Mount St. Mary's,
St. Edward's, Downside, Ratcliffe, St. Beuno's, Beaumont
Lodge and Ampleforth." It became current doctrine, in Rome
and England alike, for the next thirty years, that in the
aggregation of English seminaries and secondary schools under
both secular and regular clergy (collectively but in this context
perhaps misleadingly known as " The Catholic Colleges "
there somehow existed the makings of a university. But in
what exact sense, save perhaps that of forming an examining
body, was never completely clear.   With a revealing lack
of historical sense Manning in this article wrote of Ushaw
and Oscott as " living witnesses of what mediæval
Oxford and Cambridge were." If further resources were
needed, he went on, foreigners could be enlisted. The Church
was universal. " The Society of Jesus alone contains in itself
men capable of holding professors' chairs in all the chief faculties of arts, literature and science."

Less surprising, perhaps, than this willingness of
Manning to rely on the Society of Jesus is his ignoring of the
Oxford converts as a special class in the intellectual resources of
English Catholicism and the omission from the list of Catholic
" colleges " of Newman's four-year-old Oratory School
though the yearling Jesuit Beaumont was included. But the
force of Newman's name could not be ignored, and though
Cardinal Barnabò, Prefect of Propaganda, had his attention
first seriously drawn to the Oxford problem by Manning in

connection with the schemes for a Catholic hall in the University, it was in fact Ullathorne's two invitations to Newman to make an Oratorian foundation in Oxford which brought the matter to a head. Although Ullathorne had principally in mind the better efficiency of the Oxford mission, which the Jesuits had given up in 1860, Newman himself, not regarding purely parish work as proper to the Oratorians, saw an opportunity of being helpful to such Catholics as might be found—converts or otherwise—in the University. He was willing to agree " not to take part in University education " and indeed held strongly that Catholics who went to the Oxford colleges ran serious risks. But he assumed that somehow or other some Catholics would be found in the University (converts, for example) and he welcomed the chance of assisting them spiritually. But to Manning and Barnabò it seemed—and perhaps not unreasonably so—that Newman's mere presence in Oxford would suggest an encouragement to Catholics to go there, and they believed that at the Oratory School Newman was systematically preparing boys to do so[3]. The two unsuccessful projects for an Oxford Oratory put forward successively in 1864-65 and 1866-67 form the immediate background to the Roman and episcopal decisions of those years against Catholics going to Oxford or Cambridge. In the larger background loomed the Munich Congress of 1863, Pius IX's Munich Brief, which was so bitter a disappointment to the Liberal Catholics, and finally the Syllabus Errorum of 1864.

Propaganda, at the instigation of Manning and Ward, exhorted the bishops to discuss the whole university question. At their Low Week meeting in 1864 the bishops condemned the project of a Catholic hall at Oxford and decided that parents were to be dissuaded from sending their sons to the universities. But no public pronouncement was made. To Manning's disappointment they also decided that a Catholic University was not practicable, for which reason Ullathorne and some of the other bishops were said to be opposed to a formal public prohibition of Oxford and Cambridge. Wiseman's health, however, was now breaking up, and from outside the episcopal body Manning continued, through Talbot and

---

[3] In fact only one boy was being so prepared at the time, at his parents' request.

Barnabò, to force the pace. The bishops were instructed by
Rome to meet again on the same matter, which they did on
December 13th. Nine days previously a series of leading
questions on the probable effects of Oxford on Catholic young
men had been circulated over Wiseman's name to a large
number of Oxford converts. Newman, however, did not receive a copy; instead, though himself the greatest intellectual
force in the Church in England, engaged at that very moment in
writing his famous *Apologia,* he was receiving sharp reprimands
for his alleged preparation of boys for Oxford at the Oratory
School. Although Clifford of Clifton and Vaughan of Plymouth
were said to have spoken in favour of a Catholic hall, the
bishops at their December meeting drew up and unanimously
signed a letter to the Holy See giving their reasons for holding
that the establishment of Catholic colleges at Oxford and Cambridge could not be approved and that parents must be dissuaded from sending their sons to the Universities. In a reply
dated February 5th, 1865, a copy of which was sent to each
bishop, Propaganda confirmed these decisions as consonant
with its own principles of opposition to "mixed education" and
exhorted the bishops to take steps to perfect the education
already given in the Catholic schools[4]. In a circular letter o
March 24th, five weeks after Wiseman's death, the bishop
informed their clergy of these decisions and the Roman con
firmation, but there was still no public pronouncement
Thus things remained until Ullathorne's revival of the
Oxford Oratory project in 1866 which drew from Propaganda
on March 12th, 1867, a letter to Manning, who now sa
in Wiseman's archiepiscopal seat at Westminster, saying
that the bishops were again to consider the university
question and to communicate with Propaganda upon
the measures to be taken for preventing Catholics from
studying at Oxford. When they met on April 30th the bishop
decided that it was inexpedient to publish to the faithfu
Propaganda's letter of February 5th, 1865, but that all priest
should be told that the Holy See enjoined them to carry out it
provisions. They were also conscious of the difficulties in re

[4] This letter, frequently cited in later documents, but never printe
or published, is in the Archives at Archbishop's House, Westminster
Roman Letters, I, fol. 3. Another copy, fol. 49.

gard to converts at the University[5]. A letter was sent to Propaganda embodying these and other points and stating the episcopal wish to make known by Pastoral Letters and through the clergy the grave dangers to be incurred by those who might enter the universities in spite of the admonition of their pastors. The result was the well-known rescript of Propaganda of August 6th, 1867[6], which together with its predecessor of February 5th, 1865, remained the operative document until 1895. In obedience to its injunctions, all the bishops at Advent addressed Pastoral Letters explaining its contents to their clergy and laity. So far as the laity were concerned, these Pastorals were the first official utterance of the Bishops on the University question.

The rescript of Propaganda was not couched in terms of formal legal prohibition. But it declared, in effect, that any Catholic going to Oxford or Cambridge would commit the grievous sin of knowingly exposing himself to a proximate occasion of mortal sin. "You will clearly explain in your Pastoral Letter the doctrine of the Church on avoiding the proximate occasions of mortal sin; to which occasions no one without grievous sin can expose himself, unless under the pressure of grave and adequate necessity, and unless such precautions be taken as shall remove all proximate danger. And in the present case, where, as His Holiness has declared, there is an intrinsic and very serious danger to purity of morals, as well as to faith (which is altogether necessary for salvation), it is next to impossible to discover circumstances in which Catholics could without sin attend non-Catholic universities." To all intents and purposes, therefore, the prohibition under grave sin was absolute and the matter presumably one for the confessional. It became the accepted doctrine that only a bishop was competent to detect the "next to impossible circumstances" and to declare that one of his subjects might attend Oxford or Cambridge without incurring grievous sin. Later on, when such special episcopal permissions increased, it was feared that measures would be taken to stop up even this loophole. But, in the next thirty years, some Catholics there must have been

[5] Minutes of the Episcopal Meeting.
[6] Published both in Latin and English, in Guy, *Synods of Westminster*, I, 254-5; II, 330-2.

who went to Oxford or Cambridge, or remained there after conversion, without episcopal licence, and so far as is known without outward sanctions being imposed.

Propaganda followed up the decisions of 1867 by pressing for the foundation of a Catholic University, which project the bishops discussed in some fulness at their Low Week meeting of 1868, and again in 1869. It was vital to do something to offset the virtual prohibition of Oxford and Cambridge. The Jesuit Provincial, Father Weld, had a scheme for an Institute of Higher Studies centred round the studies of the Jesuit scholastics; Manning spoke of the creation, as a first step, of a Board of Examiners, perhaps with the example of London University in his mind. But there was considerable misgiving over the prohibition in some responsible ecclesiastical quarters, and this was seen in 1871-2 when on their return from the Vatican Council the bishops again broached the vexed question of Higher Education. In 1871 a meeting of bishops, heads of Catholic colleges, and superiors of Orders was convened to discuss the betterment of Catholic secondary education, and to consider the possibilities of providing some higher education at university level. A sub-commission of five was appointed to gather information and opinions. It circularised a number of clergy and laymen. Though the question of Oxford and Cambridge was of set purpose not raised in the questionnaire sent out, a number of those who replied expressed the opinion that only by the foundation of a Catholic college or hall at Oxford or Cambridge could adequate facilities for higher education at a university level be provided for the Catholic laity. To Manning's dismay this opinion was warmly supported on the sub-commission itself by persons no less important than the President of Oscott, Canon J. Spencer Northcote, and the Rector of Stonyhurst, Father Purbrick. In separate personal reports both these able men argued cogently in favour of a Catholic college at Oxford or Cambridge and analysed very clearly the weaknesses and impracticabilities involved in any possible form of independent Catholic institution of a university type. Father Purbrick said that he assumed that the Rescript of 1867 referred only to Catholics going to the existing Oxford and Cambridge colleges, and not to the foundation of a Catholic college. Both he and Canon

Northcote quoted Newman for the view—which indeed needed expressing and was too often lost sight of—that any university experience worthy of the name must involve to some extent a risk of unsettlement. The case against Oxford and Cambridge was voiced on the sub-commission by the Rev. F. Wilkinson of Ushaw. His report was a shrewd, matter-of-fact document which made some telling points, but which did not attain the breadth of view of those of his opponents. The other two members, Dom Norbert Sweeney, O.S.B., one of the outstanding members of the Downside Community and an M.A. of London, and Father Hutton, President of Ratcliffe College, wrote much more shortly in their separate reports. Both disclaimed all personal knowledge of Oxford and Cambridge but both were impressed by the points made by those who had written in favour of them, and both thought that the question of founding a Catholic college at one or even both the universities should be given serious consideration[7].

These reports came before the bishops at their Low Week meeting in 1872. They seemed to their Lordships merely to show that the decisions of 1865 and 1867 were still not sufficiently well known and ought therefore to be printed. The Benedictine Bishop Brown of Newport, according to his own account, was the only bishop who did not, at the morning meeting, assume that the whole matter was irrevocably decided[8]. But in the afternoon, his fellow-Benedictine Ullathorne of Birmingham again raised, in addition to plans for a Catholic University, the question of a Catholic college or hall at Oxford or Cambridge. Clifford of Clifton, probably having in mind the final removal of religious tests in the previous year (1871) whereby Catholics might not only graduate but also become members of governing bodies in Oxford and Cambridge, proposed that before any decision was come to, Rome should be informed as to certain altered circumstances.

---

[7] These five reports were privately printed. They may be found in the library of the London Oratory—Pamphlets. David Lewis Collection, 101. I am grateful to the Fathers of the Oratory for permission to use their library. MS. copies of the reports of Canon Northcote and Father Purbrick are among the Hartwell de la Garde Grissell papers at St. Benet's Hall, Oxford: also the printed questionnaire received by Grissell on which is scribbled the draft of his answer.

[8] Wilson, *Life of Bishop Hedley*, p. 230.

Northampton, Plymouth, Shrewsbury and Newport (but not Birmingham) voted with him. All the rest (except Liverpool, who was absent) were against. Next day Shrewsbury proposed that enquiries should be made as to the practicability, from the Universities' point of view, of a Catholic college or hall and how far episcopal control of it could be permitted. Manning at first consented to make such enquiries, but on an amendment to the motion secured unanimous agreement that Propaganda should first be informed as to what was actually being done about higher education and should be asked for " rules to guide them in deciding on the course to be pursued." He himself was requested to draft the Report, together with Ullathorne and Clifford[9]. But Propaganda did not change its views. Reiterating its frequently stated case against " mixed education," it continued to press for the establishment of a Catholic University. The documents condemning attendance at Oxford and Cambridge were incorporated into the decrees of the 4th Synod of Westminster in 1873, and in a Synodal Letter of August 12th of that year the bishops announced that the earlier decisions still stood, despite the complete removal of the religious tests in 1871—which to Cardinal Barnabò, indeed, seemed to increase rather than to diminish the dangers. In 1874, somewhat hastily, and after renewed promptings from Rome, the Catholic University College at Kensington was opened.

Despite the eminence of many members of its staff—Mivart, Barff, Seager, Paley, Devas—and despite the high tributes to its teaching paid by able men who passed through it, such as Abbot Cuthbert Butler of Downside and Wilfrid Ward, there was a world of difference between the reality of Manning's Kensington and the ideal of Newman's Dublin—and one difference was, of course, the absence of Newman himself. In addition, the virtual exclusion of the Orders, the close clerical control exercised by the Archbishop, the impossible constitution, the lack of academic autonomy, and finally the disastrous and inexplicable appointment of Mgr. Capel as Rector, all revealed the narrowness and limitations of the

---

[9] Minutes of the Bishops' Meeting. The Report to Propaganda was printed and may be read in the British Museum. Ullathorne afterwards complained of its unfairness, see Butler, *Life of Ullathorne*, II, 35.

academic ideas of the former Fellow of Merton who now wore the mitre at Westminster. Might a more generously conceived plan, giving freedom of action to an inspiring Rector, and involving a wider pooling of intellectual resources, have succeeded in laying the foundations of an effective Catholic University? Who can say? What is undeniable is that the unhappy experiment at Kensington, for better or worse, gravely prejudiced a second attempt ever being made. The laity would not send their sons to Kensington. The Rector mismanaged its affairs. And Manning, stoically and uncomplainingly, bore the whole brunt. In 1878, in circumstances amounting almost to financial scandal, the college beat a retreat from Wright's Lane to the Cromwell Road. In 1882 what remained was incorporated into St. Charles' College in Bayswater.

The failure of Kensington strengthened the case for a reconsideration of the prohibition of Oxford and Cambridge. Gradually the climate of opinion underwent modification and new actors began to appear on the stage. This was increasingly apparent in the 'eighties. After the climax of the Vatican Council, Catholicism felt itself on surer ground. A less astringent intellectual atmosphere characterised Leo XIII's Pontificate. The revival of Thomism and the pronouncements of the new Pope on the study of History induced greater self-confidence and a less timid attitude towards contact with non-Catholic scholarship. W. G. Ward died in 1882 and his son Wilfrid, who had been denied Oxford, became a champion of the forbidden fruit. In 1871 the Jesuits had resumed the Oxford Mission and many of their priests were supporters of the University. There seems no evidence for Wilfrid Ward's opinion that the Jesuits were opposed to Catholics going to Oxford out of jealousy for Stonyhurst where the advanced Philosophers' course was open to boys after leaving school[10]. It may be noted that Francis Urquhart did this course before passing on to Oxford in 1890 with an open Exhibition at Balliol—and a London degree behind him. The Benedictines, too, now began to figure more prominently.

[10] Yet as late as 1895 there was apparently much difference of opinion within the Society. See Maisie Ward, *The Wilfrid Wards and the Transition*, pp. 271-2.

Hedley, the enlightened and influential Ampleforth monk who succeeded Brown at Newport in 1881, was, like his predecessor, favourably inclined towards Oxford and Cambridge. At Downside, in the 'eighties, the great convert scholar Edmund Bishop, though not himself a monk, was inspiring the movement of monastic scholarship which produced Dom Aidan Gasquet, Dom Cuthbert Butler, and others, and which would ultimately turn towards the universities.   Most important of all, at Oxford and Cambridge themselves the intellectual air was calmer.   There was less open hostility to Christianity, and liberal criticism was less aggressive.   New Schools and Triposes were coming into existence and speculative philosophy was less prominent.   In 1883 Baron Anatole von Hügel became Curator of the Museum of Archæology and Ethnology at Cambridge and with the encouragement of his brother Friedrich began to work for the removal of the prohibition.   At Oxford the protagonists were more numerous—including B. F. C. Costelloe, Hartwell de la Garde Grissell and others.   By the early 'eighties an Oxford University Catholic Club had been founded to induce Catholics who had been through the University to replace their names on college boards and to exert Catholic influence in Convocation. Lists exist, compiled by Grissell[11], which give the names of 47 Catholics who matriculated as such between 1867 and 1887, and over 100 between 1887 and 1894.   When account is taken also of converts—Grissell made a list of about 130 received either as undergraduates or in later life between 1871 and 1897—the number of Catholics at Oxford between 1880 and 1895 cannot have been inconsiderable. As early as 1888 the Newman Society for Catholic undergraduates was founded.   How many of these undergraduates had episcopal permission?   Foreigners, Irish, and Scots—it must be remembered—would not need it. While accounts continued to be heard of apostasies, they were countered by an increasing number of favourable reports on the behaviour of the majority.   Catholics prominent in public life began to urge a reconsideration of the official position. Chief among these were the Duke of Norfolk, Lord Braye, the Etonian convert, and T. W. Allies.

The 'eighties saw a series of attempts to bring about a

11 Grissell papers at St. Benet's Hall, Oxford.

change. In 1882 indeed, at the Low Week meeting, the bishops resolved once more to call the attention of the faithful to the ban on non-Catholic universities and schools—but at the same meeting Mgr. Lord Petre, a supporter of the universities, had an interview with the bishops on the subject[12], and a few days earlier Bishop Hedley, Lord Braye and Grissell, with Newman's blessing, had raised the matter at an audience with Leo XIII, and had presented a memorandum. Rome now asked all the bishops to give their views separately and independently. Hedley's, in favour of a tacit permission provided there were also a strengthening of the Oxford and Cambridge missions, is published by his biographer from his draft. Ullathorne seems to have held and communicated substantially the same views, though, as in 1872, he was opposed to the bishops' themselves asking for the question to be re-opened. In 1885, however, Cardinal Simeoni wrote officially that the rescript of 1867 still had full force. Other moves in 1889 and 1890 were equally unsuccessful, in spite of the subject having been aired in a number of pamphlets. Among the authors were the Rev. R. Belaney, a Cambridge graduate, and Alexander Wood. One pamphlet, written by a Roman canonist, Carlo Menghini, in the form of a letter to Grissell, suggested that the rescript of 1867 was defective both in form and in mode of promulgation and maintained that each individual might decide whether the university would be an occasion of sin for himself or not. It was very severely handled in the *Tablet*[13]. While Manning lived, in effect, nothing could be done, for he had the ear of Rome, and held that Oxford and Cambridge were as dangerous as ever and fundamentally hostile to Christian faith and morality. Grimly determined against all concession, he expressed his views with all the old vigour. His Easter Pastoral of 1885 on this subject is a magnificent piece of powerful and moving writing, appealing from " worldly motives " to the highest principles of spirituality.

Manning died in January, 1892, having survived Newman by seventeen months. As an old Oxford man—who

[12] Minutes of the Bishops' meeting.
[13] Grissell papers. Grissell's correspondence reveals widespread lay and clerical support for Catholics being allowed to go to Oxford.

still in a sense loved and valued his Alma Mater—he had spoken with authority on the universities, even though his views in his latest years might perhaps have been regarded as out of touch with the realities. Vaughan had no personal knowledge of Oxford or Cambridge. He saw them entirely through Manning's spectacles and had been a faithful follower of his policy. He was said to entertain a highly unreal view of the average undergraduate's preoccupation with and capacity for speculative philosophy. Yet he was capable, as Manning was not, of yielding to the pressure of opinion and of resetting his course; and it was under him, and in a certain sense because of him, that the change of policy came about in 1895.

There is, however, every evidence that right up to the very eve of the change, Vaughan's determination not to abandon Manning's principles remained firm and unaltered[14]. The universities—he believed—were centres of infidelity and worldliness. No social or worldly advantages could offset this. The increasing number of permissions given by bishops to individuals, especially the permission given to the Duke of Norfolk's nephew, James Hope (afterwards Lord Rankeillour), by the Bishop of Southwark, outraged him as it had outraged Manning. With such an example, what might not follow! In February, 1893, he was angered by the action of Anatole von Hügel who, attired in Cambridge M.A. gown and hood, had presented to Leo XIII an address and a gift from the Catholics of Cambridge University at the Audience given to the English pilgrims on the occasion of the Pope's episcopal jubilee[15]. But Vaughan was driven to realise that the existing position was rapidly becoming untenable. He sounded the laity but was firmly told that no support would be forthcoming for a new attempt at a Catholic University College. Only two courses were open; either to restate the prohibition so as to exclude the possibility of individual permissions, or to extend a general toleration with such safeguards to faith and morals as might appropriately be devised. Many influential men among the laity—Norfolk, Wilfrid Ward, Anatole von Hügel—feared, and not it would seem without reason, that Vaughan at one time contemplated the former course. At the end of May, 1894,

[14] But compare below, p. 308—Bishop Casartelli's opinion.
[15] See *Dublin Review*, April, 1946.

he virtually forbade a summer school for Catholic Elementary Teachers to be held at Oxford. This had been suggested by a Miss Donelan at the instigation of Father Nugent, who had brought back the idea from America. It had been organised by a group of Catholic social workers (including a number of Oxford men) who had founded Newman House in Kennington, and it enjoyed the full support of the Bishop of Birmingham. Vaughan's grounds for his action were that the school, having been arranged to take place at Oxford and in an Oxford College (albeit in vacation!), would indirectly encourage " mixed education and the frequentation of non-Catholic universities by Catholic youth." The annoyance aroused by this high-handed intervention over Bishop Ilsley's head led to a step being taken which seems to have been in contemplation ever since the return of the pilgrims from Rome in the previous year. In June the Duke of Norfolk called a meeting of interested laity at which it was decided to draw up a petition to the bishops in favour of the opening of the universities to Catholics under adequate safeguards. The secretaries of Newman House, the Hon. Everard Feilding and Sidney Parry, were deputed to make a draft, together with Wilfrid Ward, and the first rough sketch of points in Parry's hand still survives in the pages of a notebook containing—in the same hand—his minutes of the meetings at which the arrangements for the abortive Oxford Summer School were recorded[16].

The Petition was ably and tactfully drawn up. No attempt was made to argue that the original prohibition had been a mistake, but it was pointed out that the Church had always been ready to moderate her objection to " mixed " university education when her own ideals were unattainable and it was represented that changed circumstances now made this desirable in England. The hostile infidelity that had earlier characterised the universities had died down. Catholic works were used in the Oxford History School and no one was

[16] This note-book is preserved in the archives at Westminster. The Summer School incident was described by Sidney Parry himself in *The Month*, March, 1933, in an article on Newman House in which Vaughan's letter of prohibition is published. See also the *Tablet* for 26th May and 9th June, 1894. The whole affair should be read in conjunction with my account of the origin of the Petition in the *Dublin Review*, April, 1946.

obliged to study philosophy. Experience had shown that the dangers to faith and morals at Oxford and Cambridge were now less than those encountered in the Army, the professions or student life in London. Clerical witnesses from Oxford and Cambridge—including some Oxford Jesuits—testified to the excellent record and behaviour of Catholic undergraduates. It was impossible for Catholics to play their full part in the life of the country without the advantages of an Oxford or Cambridge education. A London degree was not enough, and it was pointed out how great a work had been done for Catholicism by the Oxford converts. The desirability of taking special measures to safeguard the spiritual interests of Catholics at the universities was alluded to and references made to Pusey House and Mansfield College as possible examples of what was required. The whole affair was treated as one of urgency. It may be added that although the Petition was originally intended to be exclusively lay, in fact about 80 of the 436 signatories were priests—practically all of them graduates of Oxford, Cambridge or London. It is important to realise that the movement had widespread clerical support, and from secular priests as well as regulars.

During July Vaughan was told of the Petition and its main points by the Duke of Norfolk, with whom he was always in close and friendly relations. He then expressed his opinion that " the present state of affairs was unsatisfactory . . . . and that if the Holy See thought well to change its policy he would be quite willing to concur "[17]. During the summer he made up his mind. Perhaps he had already been subconsciously moving towards this. Bishop Casartelli, who knew Vaughan well at Salford, believed that the process of his conversion had been going on even before he had left Salford. He ascribed it largely to the influence of Canon Moyes, whom Vaughan took with him from Salford to Westminster; no doubt Casartelli himself may also have played some part.[18] At any rate, on September 26th Vaughan wrote to Hedley

[17] Maisie Ward, *The Wilfrid Wards and the Transition,* p. 268.
[18] See the report of an address delivered by him at St. Bede's to Catholic Teachers (no date) in the St. Bede's Magazine—*Baeda,* New Form No. 3, June, 1941, pp. 8-9. Casartelli favoured Catholic secondary school-boys going to their local universities and condemned the London External Degree examinations as a " tyrannous fetish " destructive of true culture by the kind of preparation they entailed.

saying that he was now prepared to advocate a solution of the university problem " in the only way it will work " and enclosed a memorandum, summarised in Snead-Cox's biography, in which some of the main points to be made in the Petition were repeated[19].   He then seems to have consulted some of the other bishops, after which he summoned a special meeting of the Hierarchy for January 4th, 1895.   At this meeting, which presumably had the Petition before it, though additional signatures were still being collected, the Hierarchy decided by " a good majority " that they would themselves petition the Holy See to remove the prohibition of Oxford and Cambridge, and that they would place themselves at the head of the movement and take steps for providing spiritual safeguards for Catholic undergraduates[20].   Minutes of this meeting (from which Hedley was absent) do not seem to be extant but it is clear from later correspondence that about four or five bishops were in opposition (certainly Riddell of Northampton, Gordon of Leeds, Lacy of Middlesbrough and Bilsborrow of Salford) and did not believe in the " altered circumstances." They were shocked and amazed at Vaughan's change of attitude, which they attributed to the pressure of the laity; and later, when the Joint Episcopal Instruction to parents and superiors was in preparation they questioned the accuracy of the statement that the Petition had been drawn up " on hearing that the question had been re-opened by the Hierarchy." And indeed Vaughan's later contention that the whole initiative had originally come from the bishops themselves is hardly borne out by the existing evidence.   The Petition was decided on in June and revealed to Vaughan in July.   In September we have Vaughan's own word that he had made known his change of attitude to none of the bishops save Hedley.   It is true that the opening words of the Petition appear on the face of things to give support to Vaughan's contention, but the final text was not fixed until quite late in the year, after it was known that Vaughan had in fact decided to ask the bishops to reconsider the matter.   Yet it is interesting to note that the first draft of proposed points for the Petition in the

[19] Snead-Cox, II, 81.
[20] Snead-Cox, II, 83-4.   It may be noted that only one of the English diocesan bishops was a university man—Brownlow of Clifton, who was a member of Trinity College, Cambridge.

Newman House note-book begins: " (1) Bishop of Birmingham's letter implies that whole question of Univ. Education is likely to come before Hierarchy." In the letter referred to, however (the text of which may be seen in the *Tablet* of June 9th, 1894), the Bishop of Birmingham, in conveying to Parry Vaughan's virtual ban on the proposed Oxford Summer School, had merely written that the Cardinal considered the matter of the School so important that it ought to come before the Hierarchy as a whole and, if necessary, be put before Rome. The larger implication suggested by Parry's note would hardly seem warranted.

In spite of earlier history and of Propaganda's strong words in the past about mixed education, no objection seems to have been voiced in Rome to the new proposal even though it was now not a question of a Catholic college, but of Catholics going to the existing colleges. What would have happened if a similar proposal had been put forward by Manning at any time between 1864 and 1892? Would Propaganda have deferred to any proposal coming from the whole English Hierarchy—or a large majority—and had it in fact all along done no more than act as Manning's and Ward's mouthpiece? It is not easy to say. But now in fact the proposal to tolerate Catholics going to Oxford and Cambridge under certain conditions (seeing that there was still no Catholic University) was immediately accepted by Propaganda on March 26th, approved by Leo XIII on April 2nd and communicated to Vaughan by Cardinal Ledochowski in a letter of April 17th, 1895. The conditions were, first, that no young man should be allowed to benefit from the toleration unless he had previously had a sound Catholic upbringing and was personally suited for the university, and secondly, that regular courses of lectures, attendance at which was to be compulsory, should be given on Philosophy, History and Religion by Catholic " professors " in order to fortify the minds of the Catholic undergraduates against error. The bishops and a mixed committee of clergy and laymen were to make these and any other necessary arrangements. The idea of the lecture courses almost certainly reflects Vaughan's personal ideas as to what was necessary, and shows his preoccupation with the alleged philosophic problems of undergraduates. The Universities Catholic

Education Board[21], when it came into existence and could call on the advice of experienced university men such as Urquhart and Hope and others, saw that the proposal of compulsory lecture courses was impracticable. Instead, weekly conferences were instituted. In addition, special Chaplains were appointed for the undergraduates, a proposal not directly envisaged by Propaganda, but subsequently sanctioned by it in a letter of June 10th, 1896, which laid down that should the bishops think that priests other than those on the local mission were required specially for the undergraduates, the Ordinary should give faculties to any priest or priests appointed for this purpose by the whole body of bishops[22]. Out of these beginnings have developed—with the help of local university Catholic associations—the flourishing Oxford and Cambridge chaplaincies housed to-day in the Old Palace and Fisher House respectively, centres of active Catholic life and influence. It will be seen that no attempt was made in 1895 to found a Catholic college or hall for laymen at either university, which up to the early 'eighties had been the sole proposal.

The toleration was warmly welcomed by the laity and the Catholic schools. At the first meeting of the Catholic Headmasters' Conference in 1896 Father Norris of the Oratory School spoke enthusiastically of the benefits to be expected from Catholics going to Oxford and Cambridge, and the controversies of the 'sixties can hardly fail to have been recalled when two Oratory boys won at Oxford the first open scholarship awards to be gained by Catholics after Urquhart. As time went on Vaughan became increasingly happy and even enthusiastic about university developments, and showed his real greatness thereby. Bourne set the seal on the episcopal encouragement of Catholics going to Oxford and Cambridge by his patronage of the Newman and Fisher Societies and by the ideas which he at one time entertained for a Catholic " faculty " or " institute " at Cambridge. The Modernist crisis occasioned, it would seem, no qualms.

But, at the outset, the bishops were at pains to stress that it was toleration merely, and not encouragement, that was given in 1895. This was apparent even in Hedley's ex-

---

[21] Now the Oxford and Cambridge Catholic Education Board.
[22] Westminster Archives, Bishops' Printed Circulars, etc., II, 201.

cellent and judicious article in the *Ampleforth Journal* of July, 1896. It appeared more uncompromisingly in the *Instruction to the Parents, Superiors and Directors of Catholic Laymen who desire to study in the Universities of Oxford and Cambridge* issued over the names of all the bishops in August, 1896, the tone of which seemed calculated almost to encourage the faithful to look the gift-horse in the mouth. Even this, however, was not sufficient for Riddell of Northampton, in whose diocese Cambridge lay. For in sending the *Instruction* to his clergy he drove home all its points in a special covering letter in which he compared the toleration of Oxford and Cambridge to the toleration of mixed marriages and '' hoped against hope '' that such Catholics as ventured to attend the University of Cambridge might '' pass through the ordeal unscathed.''

This official caution on the part of the Hierarchy, however, was already to some extent being contradicted in practice not only by Vaughan's personal attitude but also by developments which were a further reminder that the movement in favour of Oxford and Cambridge was not exclusively lay. Soon after Propaganda's pronouncement of April, 1895, the Jesuits established a house of study for their own subjects at Oxford and were soon followed by the Benedictines of Ampleforth, whom they encouraged and aided. These two foundations are now Campion Hall and St. Benet's Hall, which enjoy the status of Permanent Private Halls in the University. At Cambridge, the Downside foundation of Benet House was soon being arranged, while the initiative of Mgr. Ward, President of St. Edmund's College, Ware, and later Bishop of Brentwood, together with the generosity of the Duke of Norfolk, enabled the latter's long-cherished hopes of seeing secular priests and students for the priesthood enjoy the benefits of a university education, to be fulfilled in the establishment of St. Edmund's House. In this venture Cardinal Vaughan himself took an enthusiastic part. All this, however, did not go unchallenged. The minority among the bishops—especially Leeds, Middlesbrough and Northampton—were dismayed at the idea of clerical students going to Oxford and Cambridge. They pointed out that such an idea had not even been mooted, let alone discussed or approved, at the bishops' meeting, and

that clerical students were not referred to in Propaganda's pronouncements. The matter was submitted to Rome early in
1896. But the hopes of the minority were disappointed, for
Rome gave consent, on condition that the clerical students
should live under strict ecclesiastical discipline[23]. But the
minority had perhaps some justification for their resentment
that a decision of which they very strongly disapproved should
have been taken without discussion by the whole episcopal
body, and they were not mollified by Vaughan's pointing out
that toleration was not encouragement. It was owing to differences of opinion on this matter and the refusal of the minority
to sign any joint statement appearing to give approval to the
idea of clerical students going to Oxford or Cambridge that the
issue of the Joint Episcopal Instruction referred to above was
delayed for over six months.

At Oxford the Capuchins and the Salesians, and at
Cambridge the Friars Minor, the Christian Brothers de la Salle,
the Irish Christian Brothers and the Rosminian Fathers have
since added to the clerical houses established for university
study. Other Orders and congregations, too, have taken advantage of the facilities offered by Campion Hall and St.
Benet's Hall at Oxford and by St. Edmund's House at Cambridge, while the return to Oxford of the Dominican house of
provincial studies has exercised a powerful influence on
Catholicism in the University[24]. In addition to those, therefore, who have been at the University as laymen, the number
of clergy, secular and regular, who have been through an
Oxford or Cambridge course as clerics, is growing. The motive
of bishops and superiors, however, would seem to be mainly
that of providing a supply of graduates for school teaching,
and it may be permissible to regret that less stress seems to be
laid nowadays on what in the beginning was at least an equal
motive—the educational interests of the clergy themselves and
the development for its own sake of Catholic learning and
scholarship. The original purpose—to take one example—of
the Downside foundation at Cambridge was to further, in the

[23] Letter of Cardinal Ledochowski of 5th June, 1896. Westminster
Archives, Bishops' Printed Circulars, etc., II, 201.
[24] The Dominican foundation at Cambridge is not specifically a house
of studies, though Dominicans have taken degrees from it and one
of the community is now a University Lecturer.

work of Dom Cuthbert Butler and Dom Benedict Kuypers and their hoped-for successors, the movement of monastic studies which Edmund Bishop had inspired at Downside and of which Dom Aidan Gasquet had hitherto been the main product[25]. Pressure of other work and the inexorable increase of new commitments inevitably make it difficult for individual clergy, either secular and regular, to become scholars. But scholarship, if it is to be fully effective and fruitful, demands the whole of a man's working time. Until we have become accustomed to the notion of scholarship as a priestly work and are prepared to recognise that gifted amateurs with insecurity of tenure in their facilities for regular study cannot build up a first-class tradition or make an adequate mark in the world of learning, we shall never reproduce in England the professional " learned abbé " of the continent or lay the foundations of a Catholic University.

Strongly as the episcopal minority in 1895 disliked the toleration given to laymen to attend Oxford and Cambridge, their dislike of clerics going to them had been even stronger. Fearful of unhappy repercussions on traditional seminary training, they did not perhaps reflect upon the unfortunate results which might have followed from the laity receiving a type of higher education from which the clergy were excluded. In the event, the educational and cultural outlook of the clergy has been widened without detriment to the normal ecclesiastical training or studies, which in fact are often completed—at least in major part—before the priest or religious goes to the university. In a sense the clergy were quicker off the mark than the laity to take advantage of the changes of 1895 for the numbers of laymen at Oxford and Cambridge did not rise very substantially until after 1918, when the habit of university-going began at last to be formed. There are to-day about 500 lay Catholics at Oxford and about 300 at Cambridge[26], together with a sprinkling of dons—considerably larger at Oxford than

[25] At the same time, far-sighted men such as Dom Edmund Ford, Dom Cuthbert Butler and Dom Henry New at Downside, Dom Anselm Burge at Ampleforth and Father Norris at the Oratory, realised that contact with Oxford and Cambridge could not fail in time to have a transforming effect on the Catholic schools.
[26] Both figures include women, for whose attendance special permission was sought for and obtained at Rome in 1907.

at Cambridge. In all walks of life where an Oxford or Cambridge education makes a difference, Catholics in increasing numbers have felt more on a level with others. And, indeed, in addition to the cultural benefits which they have reaped, the stimulus to understand and explain their faith has also been positively valuable. Much of the older fear of Oxford and Cambridge proceeded from a concealed uneasiness in regard to the level of religious instruction in Catholic secondary schools and its power to deal with new intellectual or social experiences. There can be no doubt but that the challenge of university experience has contributed greatly to the raised efficiency of the teaching of religion and its application to modern social and intellectual problems in the Catholic schools.

By the beginning of the twentieth century, then, the period of self-imposed isolation was at an end and English Catholics were free to go up to the Oxford and Cambridge colleges. But Oxford and Cambridge, while still in a category apart, no longer stood alone in the English university world. Though never at any period the exclusive preserve of the rich or aristocratic, the two ancient Universities were now unable to meet the increased volume of demand for university education that was brought about by the spread of secondary education into whole new ranges of English society and by the stimulus of the 1902 Education Act. The last fifty years have seen not only great developments in the early nineteenth-century university foundations of London and Durham, but also the rise of the newer universities and university colleges in the provinces to a place of high significance and import in English education. English Catholics contributed to all this in a double way; first because their own provision of secondary education for the middle classes on more modern lines had even before 1900 made considerable strides, thanks largely to the work of the orders of Teaching Brothers, and secondly because by the turn of the century the Catholic faith was in the process of making those great advances among the middle classes which have transformed the social structure of English Catholicism during the last fifty years. The university question for Catholics in the twentieth century has been no longer a matter affecting merely the 200 or so scions of leisured or wealthy families in terms of whom Bishop Hedley and the Duke of Norfolk thought in the 'eighties[27]. A body not only much larger but socially much more highly diversified has had to be considered.

The pronouncements of Propaganda against the dangers to Faith and Morals of " mixed education " had sometimes referred to Oxford and Cambridge specifically and had sometimes employed such expressions as "Protestant universities" or " non-Catholic universities," all no doubt intended as synonymous. Though at the outset Newman had understandably supposed that the document of 1867, in which the operative phrase was " non-Catholic universities," would apply to London as well as to Oxford and Cambridge, it became clear in time that it was not to be taken as so doing. London and the newer provincial universities, notwithstanding that all were frankly secular, were not, it would seem, ever regarded as " dangerous occasions of sin." No doubt this was because of their largely non-residential character and because of the absence of corporate college life and the personal tutorial system. At Oxford and Cambridge these could bring dangerous influences to bear in powerful and subtle manners. Also, no doubt, because speculative philosophy—that great bugbear—featured less prominently in the studies and traditions of the newer institutions. The early history of Catholics at the provincial universities might make an interesting story if fully worked out. The friendly relations between Ushaw and Durham (to which the College was at one time actually affiliated) are well known. Many Catholic schools and colleges were at one time similarly affiliated to London, on whose degrees Catholics, both clerical and lay, relied almost entirely for their teaching qualifications during most of the nineteenth century[28].

In 1898, however, the University of London, hitherto exclusively an examining body, became a normal university providing teaching for its examinations and embracing a number of different institutions of a collegiate kind,

27 Wilson, *Life of Bishop Hedley*, p. 232. In a letter written in 1867 Bishop Brown, O.S.B., of Newport, said that only one family in his diocese could possibly be affected by the rescript of that year.
28 This chapter was already in proof when I came across Father Henry Tristram's interesting study, " London University and Catholic Education," in the *Dublin Review* for October, 1936.

the number and variety of which have greatly increased during the past fifty years. In size, quality and prestige, London University has grown very rapidly. To-day it numbers over twenty-six thousand internal students, not to mention an almost equal number of external ones, and it is hardly surprising, therefore, that there are considerably more Catholics among them—2,000 is a very conservative estimate—than at Oxford and Cambridge put together. A very high proportion, however, come from overseas, especially from the colonies, and the bias of their studies leans more heavily towards medicine, economics and law than towards either the humanities or pure science. A large number of clerics and religious of both sexes still take London degrees or teaching diplomas—often by dint of hard work in their exiguous spare time. Since 1910 the Catholic students at London have had their own chaplain. But only since 1934 has he been full-time and unencumbered in his university work by other commitments, and only very recently has he acquired a suitable chaplaincy around which to co-ordinate the necessarily peripatetic and far-flung activities of his work. In recent months a second chaplain has been appointed.

It is impossible to arrive at anything like an accurate estimate of the number of Catholics—even perhaps of regularly practising Catholics—in the English and Welsh provincial universities. The figure 3,000 has recently been suggested as a possible total for the Catholic " student population " of Great Britain[29]. But if we deduct from this a suitable figure for the Scottish universities, and if we accept 2,000 as the figure for London, and 800 for Oxford and Cambridge combined, it is clear that the grand total must be placed much higher. In 1947 there were 61,000 full-time university students in England and Wales[30] out of a total population estimated at about 43,500,000. Assuming a Catholic population of 3,000,000 (a moderate estimate) the same proportion would give about 4,200 as the Catholic student population of England and Wales. Allowing the figures given above for London, Oxford

[29] *Unitas* (the Bulletin of the Newman Association) for Dec., 1949-Jan., 1950 (Vol. III, No. 83), p. 180.
[30] Report of the University Grants Committee on University Development, 1935-1947.

and Cambridge this would leave 1,400 for the 18 provincial universities or university colleges. There is no reason, however, to suppose that the proportion of university students in the Catholic body is the same as for the country in general.

A perhaps somewhat tardy recognition of the growing importance of the newer universities has led to the recent movement for the appointment of provincial university Catholic chaplains. The appointments are made not, as in the case of the national universities of Oxford and Cambridge, by the Hierarchy as a whole with the advice of the Oxford and Cambridge Catholic Education Board, but as at London, by the local Ordinary. This is surely suitable since, despite the special circumstances which in the post-war years have drawn men and women from all parts of the country into the provincial universities and thus somewhat modified their local character, the provincial universities are probably destined in the long run to remain strongly and permanently associated with their own regions. There are now 18 Catholic university chaplains in the provinces. Of these, however, only two (Liverpool and Manchester) have an established chaplaincy centre and are full time. At Cardiff there is a chaplaincy centre but the chaplain is not full time. Elsewhere there are as yet neither special centres nor full-time chaplains.

The work of the chaplains at London and in the provinces necessarily differs in some important respects from that of their longer established colleagues in Oxford and Cambridge. London, of course, is *sui generis,* and both because of its intrinsic importance and its location in the heart of Empire, cannot properly be regarded as provincial. Yet the life and spirit of London University have much in common with the provincial universities which differentiates them all from Oxford and Cambridge. For all the recent multiplication of halls and hostels, the modern universities are essentially non-residential, and whereas at Oxford or Cambridge the chaplain's work revolves primarily around the Sunday Mass in his special chapel, in London and elsewhere his task is wholly a week-day one, the students, even those whose homes may be elsewhere, going to their parish churches on Sundays. Thus the provincial chaplain tends to meet his flock very much in their special capacity as students and as members of their University Catholic Student Society. The provincial Chaplains, are, in fact, much more nearly Chaplains to Societies as such than are their Oxford and Cambridge colleagues. Students' Unions are of great importance in London and the provinces, and the strength of the Catholic Societies and the activity of their members are far more important to the Chaplain and his work than are the activities of the Newman and Fisher Societies at Oxford and Cambridge. Another distinguishing feature in London and the provinces is the absolute equality of the sexes. The nature of the Catholic societies, their activities and their relations to the Chaplain must necessarily be influenced by this circumstance. In many places, indeed, women may be in a numerical majority. In Oxford and Cambridge not only do the women have their own colleges, but their proportion within the university as a whole is strictly limited. Thus at Oxford, where the Chaplaincy is mixed, the Catholic women form a substantial though permanent minority. At Cambridge the Catholic women have the benefit of a Chaplain and Chaplaincy of their own.

It is from London and the provinces that the main support and drive have come for the promotion of larger unions and federations of Catholic students. This is understandable, since it is these modern universities which have done so much to promote a conception of an estate of studenthood till lately foreign to English undergraduates. In 1922 the University Catholic Federation of Great Britain was established in order to link together the Catholic societies in the British Universities. It was federated to Pax Romana, the international federation of Catholic University Societies founded at Fribourg the previous year, and undoubtedly owed much to this organisation. In 1942 the undergraduate and graduate elements within the Federation re-organised themselves into two bodies called the Union of Catholic Students and the Newman Association respectively, retaining, however, strong mutually co-operative links as sister members of Pax Romana. Since 1947 Pax Romana has transferred its headquarters to Rome where it enjoys the privilege of having a Cardinal-Protector.

The Union of Catholic Students bears witness to the religious zeal and high sense of social responsibility which animate Catholics studying at the universities and which are to be found in Oxford and Cambridge, in London, and in the provincial universities alike. The Union runs a Journal of its own and its yearly Directory gives details of the various ways in which it aims at bringing Catholic influence to bear in problems connected with university work and life. It sends delegates to conferences at home and abroad—such, for example, as those of the National Union of Students—and its Catholic Action service is active and zealous in a number of different ways. The Newman Association from an initial membership of 70 in 1942 now numbers more than 1,500 Catholic graduates drawn from various professions and walks of life. It has a flourishing permanent centre in London and a number of active local branches. It publishes a monthly bulletin—*Unitas*—and engages in a number of valuable and enterprising activities. Its Summer Schools, lecture courses, University Extension work (some of it recognised by the University of London Extension Board) and kindred activities are already doing much to suggest the useful work that might accomplished by a Catholic Higher Institute, while renewed interest has been aroused in discussions on the conception of a Catholic University. Fifty years ago both the Newman Association and the Union of Catholic Students would have been inconceivable.

In scholarship and culture, then, Catholics in England are now far less isolated than they were a hundred years ago. Their own tradition of scholarship has greatly benefited in quality and morale from contact with the high standards of the English universities, and their presence in these has contributed to a valuable process of intellectual cross-fertilisation. It has been estimated that there are at least 150 practising Catholics who are professors or lecturers at the British universities, and the intellectual claims and standing of Catholicism are far more generally appreciated than was once the case. But English universities are not intellectual centres only; they are also (especially Oxford and Cambridge) social organisms, membership of which imparts, in the widest sense, a social education which contributes to the integration of national life. It is surely in accordance with the English genius that, in answering the nice question whether the Church should con-

ract out of the organs of secular and national society or
whether she should work in and through them, the ecclesiasti-
al authorities in England should so largely have chosen,
wherever possible, the second way.   It is, no doubt, very
esirable that Catholic scholarship in England should even-
ually find some adequate and appropriate institutional ex-
ression of its own, in the form perhaps of a Higher Institute
t which subjects of the greatest moment for religion—
Theology, Philosophy, History, Sociology—should be taught
nd studied at the highest level.   Such an Institute, command-
ig intellectual respect, might find itself endowed with the
ower of growth.   But it is difficult to imagine a general retreat
rom the existing universities on the part of Catholics in
eneral; and the idea of a full Catholic University to which
ll English Catholics desirous or deserving of a university
ducation would normally go, would seem, in any foreseeable
uture for England, to belong to the realm of the Platonic.

M

XI

SECONDARY EDUCATION FOR BOYS

By W. J. BATTERSBY

IN the middle of the last century, Catholic Higher Education
was confined to a small group of Colleges which catered for
the sons of the upper classes. These schools, apart from
a few recent foundations, were of long standing, and had all
grown up on the Continent during the Penal Times, except for
two established on English soil itself by Bishop Challoner.
They represented the old Catholic tradition in education, and
they were closely connected with that body of staunch
Catholics who had weathered the bitter years of persecution.

The development which has taken place during the
hundred years from then till now was initiated by those forces
which brought the Catholic Church as a whole in this country
out of the Doldrums of the 'forties into the spring breezes of
the 'fifties. The Industrial Revolution, which changed the
face of Britain, created a new and powerful middle-class among
the people, and led to an insistent demand for secondary education of a utilitarian type, midway between the primary grade
of the elementary schools and the classical education of the
Colleges. The Oxford Movement, on the other hand, which
brought into the Church numbers of converts whose background and mentality differed radically from those of the old
Catholics, necessitated a certain adaptation of the education
provided for the upper classes, and a closer orientation of the
Colleges towards the older universities. As a result of these
two forces, therefore, we find the emergence of a type of higher
school for boys of middle-class families, which had hitherto
been a feature lacking in the Catholic system of Education,
and we find a new impetus being given to the existing Colleges.

The Colleges were of two kinds: those conducted by
Religious, and the Seminary-Colleges run by the secular clergy.
The Jesuits, formerly of St. Omers and Liège, were at Stony

hurst since 1794; the Benedictines of St. Lawrence's, Dieule-ward, were at Ampleforth since 1802, and those of St. Gregory's, Douai, at Downside since 1814. The Dominicans, after the failure of Carshalton, which was the continuation of Bornhem, in 1810, had made a fresh start at Hinckley in 1823. The secular clergy of Douai had migrated some to Old Hall Green, whither Challoner's school of Standon Lordship had been transferred, and others to Durham, settling finally at Ushaw in 1808. Challoner's second school, that of Sedgley Park, had evolved into the seminary-college of Oscott.

By 1850, a small number of new foundations had been added to this group of old schools. Bishop Baines had opened Prior Park as a seminary-college for the West in 1830, and five years later he had confided it to the Rosminians. The Rosminians themselves had established Ratcliffe College in 1847. The Jesuits founded Mount St. Mary's in 1842, and the same year the fifth seminary-college, St. Edward's, Liverpool, was begun.

Finally, there were some seventeen establishments of less ambitious proportions; preparatory schools and private boarding schools, run by Catholic laymen, but catering for the same clientèle. Of these, typical specimens were Mr. Dunn's " Prospect House," at Bristol, and the " Priory," Edmonton, where Mr. Murphy conducted a school of twenty pupils at 25 guineas a year. In a somewhat different class was St. Mary's, Woolhampton, which had been opened by the secular clergy in the same year as Prior Park.

Such was the equipment of Catholics in the sphere of Higher Education in 1850. At St. Edmund's, Old Hall, the ecclesiastical students and lay pupils followed a syllabus of studies which comprised English, French, Latin and Greek; Italian and German; Reading, Elocution, Writing, Arithmetic, Mathematics, History, Geography and Natural Philosophy. At St. Mary's, Oscott, where Nicholas Wiseman had been President 1840-41, and where the fees were 50 guineas for boys under fifteen and 55 for boys over that age, the subjects taught were the same, with the addition of " other branches of learning." Sedgley Park, which had been founded by Challoner for the mercantile class, still retained some of its original characteristics. The fees were comparatively low, £23 a year, and the Prospectus stated that " the object of this establishment is to give a useful English education to those who are intended for mercantile pursuits, and also an elementary knowledge of the classical languages." Prior Park, on the contrary, was very expensive. It was divided into two colleges: St. Paul's for students of advanced age, and St. Peter's, where the course of studies was " directed towards the ecclesiastical state, the learned professions or commercial pursuits." The original Prospectus stated that " the education is conducted by a competent number of Catholic clergymen, under the immediate direction of the resident Bishop," and that " the object of the institution, its course of studies and general system of discipline are similar to those of the other English Episcopal Colleges."

With regard to the Colleges conducted by Religious, Stonyhurst and Mount St. Mary's represented the long-standing and well-tried Jesuit tradition in education. In the earliest Prospectus of Stonyhurst in the *Catholic Directory* for 1797, the fees were given as 40 guineas, and the syllabus of studies included Latin and Greek; all the branches of classical education; sacred and profane History; Geography, Arithmetic, and, for more advanced pupils, Algebra, Geometry and all the other parts of Mathematics. The school year began with a three-day retreat for the older boys, and religious training was thoroughly attended to. At the head of the school was " The Philosophers " section, which included those boys who had finished the ordinary school course, and which supplied something in the nature of a university course at a time when Catholics were still barred from Oxford and Cambridge.

The Benedictine Colleges formed a type apart. They represented in modern times what the monastic schools of the Middle Ages had been. Their ideal was to make the " school " as much like the " family " as was consistent with sound discipline, and their chief and peculiar power as educational centres lay in the unseen influence of the cloistral exercises upon the students. Unfortunately, in the 1850's, Ampleforth and Downside were only just emerging from a very critical period occasioned by the action of Bishop Baines, but they were soon to enter a period of prosperity under the leadership of remarkable men: Dom Aidan Gasquet, Dom Edmund Ford,

Dom Cuthbert Butler and Dom Leander Ramsay of Downside, and Dom Oswald Smith of Ampleforth.

The first result of the new spirit introduced into Catholic Education by the converts was the foundation of the Oratory School in May 1859. The conditions prevailing in the existing Colleges were not altogether acceptable to those who had been educated in the great Protestant Public Schools and the older universities. They desired for their sons a school run on lines which would be less ecclesiastical and monastic, and where feminine influence would be real and constant. Newman took the idea up, and planned an establishment where the fees would be £80 a year, " the school hours, order, discipline and books those of an English Public School, so far as they are consistent with Catholic habits and requirements," and where there would be " houses " " superintended as at Eton by Tutors and Dames."

After a somewhat difficult beginning, the school prospered, and it gained an added significance from its close connection with Newman over a period of thirty years, and from the fact that it was his sole permanent contribution to English Catholic Education. To-day it continues at Woodcote, near Reading, whither it was removed from Caversham in 1942. It passed out of the control of the Oratorian Fathers in 1930, and is now under a Governing Body, with a secular priest as Headmaster and a lay teaching staff.

The only other school of similar standing founded before the 1870's was Beaumont. This College on the banks of the Thames, begun in 1861, completes the trio of Jesuit Public Schools covering the North, Middle and South of England respectively, and to-day, with its Prep. School of St. John's and a total of 276 boys, it ranks in size practically equal to St. Mary's with its Prep. School, Barlborough Hall.

It was to be expected that, in the 1870's, when secularism was the fashion and when not only the Church but the very basis of Christian belief was being attacked on all sides by the advocates of science and progress, the Catholic Colleges and their system of education should have been very closely scrutinised. The evidence supplied to the Sub-Committee on Higher Catholic Education, which had been appointed in November 1871, was to the effect that, " in morality, our

Colleges are infinitely superior to non-Catholic schools; they conscientiously train all comers, the dull as well as the clever, and secure a higher average standard of knowledge in a wider range of subjects. Still, if a comparison be made between the highest and cleverest boys at each respectively, I think we do not come near Eton, Rugby, Cheltenham, Wellington, and some other non-Catholic schools in three particulars, viz., first in scholarship; secondly, and much more, in composition, some varieties of which, for instance, Greek verse, are utterly unknown amongst us; thirdly, in expansion of mind, earnestness of purpose, definiteness of aim.'' The writer attributed this to '' our small numbers . . . . to the advanced age and backwardness of many when they come to us; to the stimulus which the prospect of a University career, of University distinctions, of University emoluments, gives to one and all of the great Public and even private non-Catholic schools; to the strange absence of foundations for great prizes, such as abound even in recently established non-Catholic colleges . . . . and lastly, to the terrible *vis inertiae* of comfortable, self-satisfied, mediocre, unambitious traditions.''

In the *Tablet* of January 19th, 1878, one reason for the deficiencies of Catholic Colleges was pointed out. '' For those who are laymen, a Professorship in a Catholic establishment offers such a poor opening that almost any other pursuit is more lucrative and attractive. . . . Our old Catholic Colleges too constantly hesitate to devote the necessary funds towards the payment at the market rate of Professors and tutors of first-rate ability.'' It was thought also that there was room for at least one more Catholic College; a school of the expensive type like Harrow or Rugby, for Catholics of the highest social rank. These opinions were concurred in by the Hon. Rev. William Petre, an Old Boy of Downside, who had himself recently founded a school at Weybridge. He added that, whereas reasons diocesan, local and economical were such as to guarantee the continued prosperity of existing Catholic institutions, there still remained a certain number of Catholics who were warranted in looking for a school conceived on more comprehensive ideals.

It was recognised, however, that the Catholic Colleges were not without some scholarly success. In the Schools Inquiry Commission, Lord Lyttelton had been struck by the evidence given by some Examiners of the University of London to the effect that Stonyhurst boys went up " better prepared than perhaps any school in England with regard to Classes." The proportion of Catholic candidates who obtained high classical honours, moreover, was so great as to show that, had a proportionate number gone up to the examinations, the palm would have been carried over Protestant rivals. It was admitted, nevertheless, that among the Catholic aristocracy, " there is a pretty universal sense of intellectual inferiority, by some acquiesced in, by some resented, by all deplored."

But if the question of Catholic Colleges for the well-to-do was important, the need for meeting the growing demand for middle-class secondary education was even more pressing. In spite of their shortcomings, the Colleges were, in the main, fulfilling their function, whereas in the sphere of Catholic middle-class education, everything had to be created. In fact, the rise and growth of Catholic secondary schools is one of the striking developments of the last century.

In 1850, there existed only two small beginnings, both of which were in Liverpool. The Jesuits had opened St. Francis Xavier's Day School in Soho Street in 1840, and a Catholic Middle School had been begun in Rodney Street at the instigation of Fr. Nugent and under the patronage of Bishop Brown, in 1850. The former had little success at first owing to the fact that it kept too close to the " classical " tradition, but when the syllabus was adapted to meet the needs of sons of Liverpool merchants, the situation improved. Only after 1866, however, did the numbers swell above the 80's. The Catholic Middle School, on the other hand, gave from the beginning a commercial education combined with religious instruction at a low fee of 4 or 5 guineas a year. There was a library and a reading room, and evening classes were held.

The need for secondary schools was not confined to the Catholic body alone, but was the great want of English Education generally at this time. Even eighteen years later, the Schools Inquiry Commission reported that, " of public boarding schools there is a large supply for those boys who are intended to stay until 18 years of age. There is a smaller supply for the second grade (i.e., for boys up to 16). . . . For the third grade (i.e., for boys up to 14) the Shoreham school, established by Mr. Woodard, is an almost solitary example." Matthew Arnold's opinion, after visiting the schools abroad, was that " our middle classes are nearly the worst educated in the world."

The demand was for cheap schools with a curriculum of " modern " studies, as opposed to the costly Public Schools with their " classical " education. The problem for Catholics and non-Catholics alike was to supply these requirements at a time when no help of any kind could be expected from the State. For Catholics there was only one possibility. Since the efforts of the clergy and the laity were wholly directed towards maintaining the elementary schools, the provision of secondary education had perforce to come from the Religious Orders. These alone, thanks to the vow of Poverty of their members and the pooling of resources by a centralised administration, were in a position to shoulder the serious financial burden of setting up schools where the low fees would yield little or no profit to cover initial outlay.

It was an event of some significance, therefore, when the Brothers of the Christian Schools (De La Salle Brothers) opened a boarding and day school at Clapham in 1855. It was the first step towards providing the required type of school on an adequate scale, and marked the beginning of that extensive work in Catholic secondary education which has been undertaken by the various Orders of Brothers during the past century. In their Prospectus, the Brothers at Clapham adapted themselves immediately to the situation. " The course of studies embraces Religion, Sacred History, Reading, Writing, English Grammar, Composition, Geography, the Elements of Physics, Chemistry, and Natural History, Drawing, Vocal Music, the French and German languages, and, if required, Italian and Spanish." The type of education was, therefore, non-classical, and the scale of fees was suited to the pocket of middle-class parents: £21 per annum for boarders, and £9 for day boys.

Schools now multiplied rapidly. The De La Salle Brothers opened a second at Southwark in 1860, and the same year the Jesuits began a Catholic College at Preston. Two years later, the Xaverians opened a College in Manchester, and in 1868, their school at Mayfield. The Augustinian Fathers began St. Monica's Priory, Hoxton Square, in 1864, and the Josephites came to Croydon in 1869. Meanwhile, Manning, two years before his nomination to the See of Westminster, had started St. Charles's College, Kensington, with his Oblates of St. Charles, and thus showed his marked interest in middle-class education.

By 1870, there was the nucleus of a system of Catholic secondary schools. With regard to the success of these schools from the outset, we have the testimony of Mr. Fitch in the Report of the Schools Inquiry Commission. " The only proprietary schools which have succeeded," he wrote, " are those founded by religious bodies for the education of their own children, and managed on more or less exclusive principles." After illustrating this, and giving an account of several boarding schools belonging to Religious Orders, he continues: " The curriculum of instruction in all these schools differs in one important respect from that of the ordinary grammar school. English grammar and composition, geography, history and physical science, receive much attention; ' fancy classics,' as they are sometimes called, are discarded." The general opinion of the Commissioners, in fact, was that " the educational character of proprietary schools stands very high."

An important factor meanwhile in the development of middle-class education was the institution of public examinations. These supplied a recognised test, and consequently a guarantee to the general public of the proficiency of private schools. The College of Preceptors, which represented the private school masters as a body, began to examine pupils and to award certificates in 1850. Seven years later, the Oxford and Cambridge Locals were instituted, and in 1858 the London University emerged as an examining body for external students. The consciousness of responsibility for national education thus shown by the universities was immediately appreciated, and the " Middle Class Examinations " gained wide repute. These examinations, in fact, soon became more than a mere incentive to study and a standard of school work. From 1854 they were required for admission to the Indian Civil Service, and from 1855 for entrance to the Royal Military College, Woolwich, and to certain positions in the Home Civil Service.

In due course, even the pupils of the Colleges and Public Schools entered for these examinations, which thus became a unifying influence on the syllabus of studies of all schools whether middle or higher class. For Catholic schools they had the additional advantage of creating a uniform standard between them and the other secondary schools of the country, and of thereby lessening the sense of isolation. The general effect of these examinations on Catholic schools may, in fact, be judged from what was said in the Special Report of the Sub-Committee on Higher Catholic Education in 1871 concerning London University. " Our connection with London has had, as far as it goes, an undoubtedly beneficial influence on the state of the studies in some Colleges. The hope of obtaining a degree has attracted a certain number of young men. . . . A still greater benefit has been felt both at Ushaw and at Stonyhurst, from the stimulus given to boys in their earlier studies, from the partial removal of the sense of isolation, and from the effect of the application of an external test to the proficiency of our boys."

Before the 1880's were reached, the whole course of studies throughout the entire system of Catholic higher education was directed towards the attainment of examination results. The situation was summarised in 1884 by Dom Cuthbert Butler, then Prefect of Downside: "The present age is emphatically an age of examinations; competitive examinations have been carried to the most extravagant pitch; hardly any career in life is open without one or more of these ordeals at the outset; it is impossible to stand aloof; the most independent schools have been obliged to yield more or less to the current of public opinion."

The examination system which thus dominated secondary education till the Butler Act of 1944, however, was not without its serious disadvantages. The Spens Report pointed out that: " The principal weakness of the secondary curriculum, taken as a whole, is that too often it is not centred around any core, or related to any one main stem of learning, or way of looking at life." It was, in fact, merely a curriculum of examination subjects with no unifying educational aim, and the danger from the Catholic point of view was that

Religion, which ought to permeate the whole school course and create its atmosphere, tended to become just one of the subjects taught.

Meanwhile there had been additions to the number of Catholic schools of both types. Cotton College was inaugurated by Bishop Ullathorne in 1873, and two years later, at the instigation of Bishop Vaughan, St. Bede's, Manchester, was founded. St. Cuthbert's, Newcastle, followed in 1884. The Franciscans began St. Bonaventure's in 1877 at Stratford, but moved it to Forest Gate in 1884. The Oratorians founded St. Philip's, Birmingham, in 1887, and, following the death of Manning, the Jesuits opened schools in the London area at Wimbledon (1893) and Stamford Hill (1894). The Xaverians added Clapham College to their list of secondary schools in 1897, and four more Congregations entered the field of Catholic Higher Education: the Brothers of Mercy with St. Aloysius' College, Highgate, in 1879; the Marist Brothers with St. Bede's, Jarrow, in 1876; St. John's, Islington, in 1881; and Notre Dame des Victoires in 1892; the Salesians with Battersea College in 1887 and Burwash in 1897, and finally the Irish Christian Brothers who took over Prior Park in 1895, and the following year began St. Brendan's College, Bristol.

An important step in co-ordinating the work of the boy's schools and in providing a channel for the interchange of ideas, was taken in 1896 when the Conference of Catholic Colleges was founded. With one exception, in 1915, the Conference has met yearly since its inception.

But now State interest, which had hitherto been confined to the sphere of elementary education, began to extend to the secondary. The first signs were the appointment of a series of Commissions of Inquiry: the Clarendon in 1861, the Taunton in 1864 and the Bryce in 1894, leading eventually to the legislation of 1902-3 which became the starting point of our modern system of education. The Act of 1902 laid upon County Councils and Boroughs the office of Local Education Authorities with responsibility, as far as higher education was concerned, " to consider the educational needs of its area . . . . to supply or aid the supply of education other than elementary, and to promote the general co-ordination of all forms of education." Thus the State was henceforth committed to supplying higher education, and also to co-ordinating elementary and secondary by assuring a normal progression from one to the other. By the Free Place System, begun in 1907, it sought to implement this.

Catholic schools were now in the position of " non-provided " schools as against " provided " schools built and fully maintained by public money. In the period 1902-8, therefore, the denominational issue, which had waged so long over the elementary schools, was broadened to include secondary schools, and three Government Bills were introduced to effect a just settlement, but without success. It was possible for Catholic schools under certain conditions to claim aid from the authorities, but, in fact, discretion to refuse aid on denominational grounds was exercised against them in some areas.

The early years of the present century, however, were particularly fruitful in Catholic foundations. This development was occasioned not only by the Balfour Act and the stimulus it gave to secondary education as a whole, but by the fact that the anti-clerical legislation in France, beginning with Jules Ferry's Education Laws of 1881-6 and followed by the Loi d'Association of the Waldeck-Rousseau régime in 1901, led to an increasing influx of French teaching Religious into this country. In 1900, Fr. Hinsley (later Cardinal) began St. Bede's, Bradford, and the same year the Irish Christian Brothers opened St. Edward's, Liverpool. The Benedictines of Downside founded a Priory at Ealing in 1902, and Douai took possession of Woolhampton the following year. The Salesians established schools at Farnborough (1901) and Chertsey (1902); the Marist Brothers their College at Grove Ferry (1903) and St. Mary's, Middlesbrough (1904), and the Jesuits St. Michael's, Leeds (1905).

During the years preceding the Great War, with the State assuming wider responsibility and administrative machinery becoming increasingly elaborate, this activity in Catholic education continued. The year 1908 saw three foundations: St. Boniface's College, Plymouth, and St. John's College, Southsea, by De La Salle Brothers exiled from France, and the Xaverian College, Brighton. In 1911, the Marist Priests entered upon the scene with St. Mary's, Sidcup, the same year as the De La Salle Brothers added St. Helens Grammar School to their list. And just before the war broke out, the Vaughan School was founded as a Memorial to the Cardinal who had done so much for Catholic education.

The war itself brought a clear realisation of the importance of education in moulding the temper of a nation, its ideals and its standard of values, as well as in the advancement of science and learning. It came to be recognised that the development of education would have to form a primary object of post-war reconstruction and, for this reason, important legislation was passed even before the cessation of hostilities. The Act of 1918 was " prompted by deficiencies which had been revealed by the war," and was directed " to repair the intellectual and physical wastage." The co-ordination of all forms of education was carried a great step forward, and it became ever more imperative for Catholics to direct every effort to prevent their children from drifting into non-Catholic schools. As a result, existing establishments were enlarged; further foundations were made; still more Orders were roped in to undertake educational work, and the number of lay members on the staff of schools was greatly increased.

The new foundations between the two wars included five by the De La Salle Brothers, four by the secular clergy, including the John Fisher School, Purley, four by the Irish Christian Brothers, three by the Salesians, two by the Jesuits, the Marist Priests, the Marist Brothers and the Xaverians respectively, and one by the Brothers of Mercy. The Benedictines of Belmont Abbey, Hereford, opened a boarding school in 1926; the Dominicans Laxton Hall in 1924, and many Colleges began Prep. Schools; Downside at Worth, Stonyhurst at Hodder, and so forth.

The new Orders which entered the field of secondary education were the Lamennais Brothers with St. Mary's, Bitterne, in 1922, and Market Drayton in 1928; the Assumptionists with St. Michael's College, Hitchin, taken over from the Fathers of St. Edmund in 1925 and the Becket School, Nottingham, in 1931; the Salvatorians in 1926 with a college at Harrow Weald; the Presentation Brothers in 1931 with a college at Reading, and the Carmelites the same year with a school at Aberystwyth.

The increasing participation of the laity of recent years in Catholic secondary education has been a highly significant development. Some schools, while remaining under the authority of the clergy or a religious body, have come to be wholly staffed by lay-masters, as for instance, St. Philip's Grammar School, Birmingham. Many others have a proportion of half or more. On the whole, schools run by teaching Orders have fewest lay-masters, but even in these the number is on the increase. In one sphere closely connected with Catholic secondary education, laymen have been independently active and particularly successful, namely, in Preparatory Schools. At the present time there are at least seventeen such schools of deservedly high repute. Ladycross has over 100 boys, as also has St. Bede's, Stafford; Wellbury has 90; Penryn School, Worcester, 75, as also St. Philip's, Kensington, and Avisford.

The co-operation of the laity is now recognised as being not only highly beneficial but absolutely necessary. Despite every effort, the supply of Catholic Colleges and secondary schools remains wholly inadequate, and the demands made upon the clergy and the Religious Orders, in respect both of personnel and finance, have become increasingly impossible to meet. Hence the Hierarchy in 1947 " approved the suggestion that the Catholic laity should be invited to undertake the work of opening some of the new boarding schools required." A possible future development lies, therefore, in this direction.

The 1944 Act, by raising the school leaving age to fifteen, and by offering free secondary education of one kind or another in State schools to all, has had far-reaching consequences. The onus has been thrown on Catholics of supplying their own secondary schools and of bringing them up to the high standard now required, in order to be able to come to an arrangement with the Ministry or the Local Authority whereby their children will have the same facilities as are offered to non-Catholics in State schools built and maintained wholly at the public expense. Existing Catholic secondary schools have for the most part assumed the status of Grammar Schools, and have struggled valiantly to obtain recognition as efficient either as Direct Grant Schools, Voluntary Aided or Independent, according to the particular circumstances of each. Catholic secondary schools of the " modern " or " technical " type, however, are very few, and the provision of such schools on the scale required is among the many serious problems awaiting solution.

Since the 1944 Act and the end of the war, a few more schools have been founded, notably, St. Bernardine's Franciscan College, Buckingham, St. Peter's, Guildford, and the Dominican school at Llanarth Court, Monmouthshire. If the educational needs of the Catholics of this country are to be satisfied, however, the speed with which new foundations are made will have to be greatly accelerated.

The general situation of Catholic secondary schools to-day is one which causes grave concern. The efforts made during the last hundred years have been tremendous, yet the results fall far short of the requirements. They are even inferior to what they could be. The system of Catholic secondary schools suffers from two main defects: inadequacy and lack of diversity. The overwhelming proportion of schools is of the grammar type, catering for one particular class of boy. And even in this restricted sphere the provision is insufficient. The Report of the Special Committee set up by the Hierarchy showed that the number of boys in the boarding and grammar schools in 1948 was 19,000, leaving some 5,000 unaccounted for. In these same schools, however, a large number of places were occupied by non-Catholics (240 in the boarding schools and 12 per cent of the total in the day schools), which means that the residue of 5,000 Catholic boys unprovided for is much larger than it need be. The cause is to be found in the haphazard development of the system whereby the initiative has been left to the clergy and the Religious Orders without guidance from a central authority. While many large towns are unprovided for and whole industrial areas under-served, localities of comparatively small importance possess large schools too big for the number of Catholics and are compelled to accept non-Catholics to fill their places. It seems imperative, therefore, to prevent the continuance of this unguided development in the future.

No less important is the question of co-ordinating the system. Modern administrative policy since the Balfour Act, and more especially since the Hadow Report, the Spens Report and the Butler Act, has been towards integration, and if the Catholic system is to keep pace with the national system, it will have to equip itself with the parts required and co-ordinate them. Pupils leaving the primary schools must have not only grammar schools to go to, but all the other types of secondary school into which they may be graded. The financial burden weighing on the Catholic body for rebuilding and adapting the schools is so enormous, however, despite government aid, that it would seem that the task of providing the new schools required (for which no financial aid is available) will have to fall to the Religious Orders as in the past.

The principle of integration applies also to the details of the curriculum. Developments following the Butler Act, whereby external examinations have been reduced to a school-leaving certificate to be taken at the age of sixteen or later, clear the way for reorganisation. A splendid opportunity is offered Catholic schools for co-ordinating the course of studies in closer accordance with the aims and ideals in view. Proposals to this effect have already been put forward at the Conference of Catholic Colleges, notably in 1942, and with a view to arranging studies on a frankly Christian basis. It is now time to elaborate these proposals and to devise some plan in which Religion will take its correct place in Catholic education as the core and centre of the course of studies, and permeate the whole as its living soul.

XII

EDUCATIONAL WORK OF THE
RELIGIOUS ORDERS OF WOMEN:
1850 - 1950

By W. J. Battersby

THE SITUATION IN 1850

I F we are to appreciate at its true value the work of nuns during this period, not merely in the sphere of Catholic education but of English education as a whole, we must bear clearly in mind the conditions which prevailed a century ago. The evolution of our present-day system of education for girls and women is one of the striking developments of the past hundred years, a change so complete as to require an effort of the imagination to visualise the state of affairs in the eighteen-fifties. It is no exaggeration to say that the Religious Orders have contributed enormously towards the progress realised, and in some respects have led the way.

The situation in the middle of the last century was chaotic. Girls had the same advantages in the sphere of elementary education as boys, but they had little else. There were no Public Schools for girls and few endowed schools, while the Universities were closed to them. There were private governesses, usually foreign ladies, for those who could afford them, but they taught nothing more than superficial accomplishments. As late as 1868, the Schools Inquiry Commission emphasised the poor quality of female education, and commented on " a want of thoroughness and foundation; a want of system; slovenliness and showy superficiality; inattention to rudiments, undue time given to accomplishments, and want of organisation." Contemporary evidence is abundant to prove this, from Frances Power Cobbe, who, in her autobiography, speaks of the fashionable boarding school to which she was sent in 1836 as teaching everything in inverse ratio to its importance, to Charlotte Brontë, who ridiculed the one school which did attempt to provide a good education at small expense, the Clergy Daughters' School at Cowan Bridge, of which she had been a pupil.

The reason for all this is not hard to find. With the suppression of the convents at the time of the Reformation, many of the ideals of Christian womanhood had disappeared. Hence respect for the feminine intellect, after two centuries of decline, had now reached its lowest ebb. Girls were no longer offered any serious instruction, for they were deemed incapable of assimilating it. A learned lady was regarded as a monstrosity; the Blue-Stocking became the target of universal satire. Teaching was considered no profession for a woman; it was the acknowledged resource of middle-aged spinsters, and the one thing that anybody could do, since it required neither knowledge nor experience. Marriage alone filled the horizon of mothers and daughters, and the one aim of feminine education was to enable a girl to shine in a frivolous and unintellectual society, and thus secure for herself a husband. Even when Bedford College was founded, in 1849 (the second attempt to provide something for women after F. D. Maurice's venture the previous year), it was not intended as a place of learning, but as a school where girls of professional and middle class could be given some culture that would help them to be better wives and mothers. Mrs. Reid's project was regarded as so daring, in fact, that it was described as " The Voyage of Adventure," and popular prejudice was so strong that it required forty " Lady Visitors," whose function it was to chaperone pupils at lectures, to allay suspicion.

It comes as a complete surprise, therefore, to people who read all this in text-books, to find that Catholics in the eighteen-fifties, who formed only a tiny minority of the total population, could point to an imposing selection of convent schools, and to a number of private " Academies " which provided a good education for Catholic girls.

In the first place there were the historic schools of long standing. The Bar Convent, York, run by the daughters of Mary Ward (The Institute of the Blessed Virgin Mary), had continued on English soil unperturbed for a hundred and seventy-five years. For over fifty years, ever since their return from the Continent after their exile during the Penal Times, Canonesses, Dominicanesses, Benedictines, Franciscans, and even Poor Clares had boarding schools in various parts of the country. The Canonesses of St. Augustine, founded at Louvain in 1609, were at Spetisbury, Dorset; those of the Holy Sepulchre, founded at Liège in 1642, were at New Hall, Essex. The Dominicanesses, established at Brussels by Philip Howard (afterwards Cardinal) in 1660, were at Atherstone; the Franciscans from Bruges (originally Brussels, 1619) at Taunton, and the Poor Clares from Dunkirk (a filiation of Mary Ward's convent at Gravelines founded in 1608) were at Scorton, Yorkshire. The Benedictines of the first English house at Brussels (1597), were at Winchester; those of its Ghent filiation (1624) at Caverswall Castle, Staffordshire, and those of the Dunkirk filiation (1662) at Hammersmith. The Benedictines of the distinct Cambrai foundation, dating back to 1623, were also engaged in teaching at Stanbrook. Added to all these English convents were two French Congregations: the Benedictines of Montargis who were at Princethorpe, and the Visitation nuns at Westbury-on-Trym.

These historic schools had behind them a long tradition and experience in education. Their record was a proud one, for their influence had been powerful in maintaining the Catholic faith in England. But the fact that these Orders, except for Mary Ward's Institute, were contemplative and cloistered, made them conservative and retired, a thing by no means wholly bad in education, but tended also to keep them somewhat out of touch with a rapidly changing world. The old Orders, in fact, were not primarily intended for teaching, but represented the tradition which for so long had been maintained in the Church, and against which Mary Ward had struggled so desperately. New Congregations had now arisen, however, embodying a different concept of the Religious Life, and better adapted to the work of education. These now began to arrive in England, and by 1850 a number of them had already established themselves.

Viscountess Bonnault d'Houet, foundress of the Faithful Companions, had come to this country in 1839 and had taken over Abbé Carron's schools at Somers Town. Since then her nuns had spread to Hampstead, Tottenham and Birkenhead. Another foundress, Catherine McAuley, came over from Ireland in November 1839 with her Sisters of Mercy, and took over schools at Bermondsey. Within a week there were six English postulants, including Lady Barbara Eyre. Thereafter her foundations multiplied with amazing rapidity. In less than ten years there were schools in London at Chelsea, Blandford Square and Moorfields; and in Birmingham, Nottingham, Derby, Leamington, Sunderland and Cheadle. Other nuns from Ireland, the Sisters of the Presentation, had already established themselves in Manchester in 1836.

Several other Congregations, with whose names we have since become familiar, had also started work. The Sacred Heart nuns were at Berrymead Priory, Acton, since 1842; the nuns of the Institute of Charity (Sisters of Providence) at Loughborough, since 1843, and the Notre Dame nuns had followed the Redemptorists to Penryn in 1845, and to Clapham two years later. The Sisters of Charity of St. Paul had arrived at Banbury in 1847, and the Sisters of the Christian Retreat had come to Peckham the same year, and were now at Plymouth. The Daughters of the Faithful Virgin were established at West Norwood since 1848; the Sisters of the Immaculate Conception at Penzance, and finally, in 1850, the first English house of the Sisters of the Assumption was opened by the saintly Mother Thérèse Emmanuel at Richmond, Yorkshire.

Besides these Congregations of French or Belgian origin, there had also been a small crop yielded by English soil itself. The Sisters of the Infant Jesus had been established at Northampton; the Dominicans of St. Catherine of Siena had been founded by Mary Hallahan and Bishop Ullathorne at Coventry in 1844, and the Sisters of the Holy Child at Derby two years later. Mother Connelly, the foundress, had since moved her headquarters from the Midlands, however, and was now installed at St. Leonards.

Thus, in 1850, there were over twenty different Orders of nuns engaged in the work of education at every social level. The historic schools corresponded to the Public Schools and offered a select education to the upper classes. Some of these convents eventually gave up teaching; the Benedictines of Stanbrook and the Poor Clares after a short time; the Dominicanesses after their transfer to the Isle of Wight in 1866, and the Benedictines of Winchester (later at East Bergholt) in 1877. The others, however, continued with acknowledged success to the present day, though some have changed their original locality. Thus, the Benedictines of Caverswall went to Oulton in 1854, and now have some thirty pupils in their Abbey School. The Canonesses of Spetisbury are now at Newton Abbot, where they conduct a large establishment with 240 pupils; and their Bruges filiation, which returned to the Continent in 1802 after eight years at Hengrave Hall, Essex, is back again with a High School at Haywards Heath of 175 girls. The Franciscans continue at Taunton with some forty pupils, and since 1860 have a filiation at Woodchester.

The new teaching Orders differed from these foundations in three respects. They dropped the idea of strict enclosure; they were organised on a central basis and multiplied communities all over the country; and, from the beginning, they undertook a double mission, that of parochial schools and of secondary schools for the middle classes. Thus, the Faithful Companions, who were the first in the field of elementary education, taught the poor in schools in London and conducted a convent school at Oxton, Birkenhead, for children in more favourable circumstances; while the Holy Child nuns at St. Leonards taught in the poor school, and at the same time had a school for the upper classes at their convent. Some Orders catered specially for the poor and orphans. Sisters of Mercy had charge of the Liverpool Catholic Female Orphanage and similar institutions in other towns, while the Daughters of the Faithful Virgin looked after orphans at Norwood. But other Congregations also shared in this charitable work. The Sisters of the Assumption began with an orphanage at Richmond, and the Dominicanesses had a female charity school at Hinckley.

To complete the picture we might add that besides this large number of schools run by Religious Orders old and new, there were some fourteen private " Ladies Schools " in 1850, conducted by Catholic lay-women. The majority were in the

London area, but there were some at famous Catholic centres such as Ladyewell, Fernyhalgh.

Such was the promising position in the sphere of Catholic education for girls at the beginning of our period; a position in sharp contrast with the deplorable conditions prevailing in the country as a whole. But not only were the schools surprisingly numerous; they were taught by capable women who looked upon their work as a sacred calling and performed it with wholehearted devotion and great conscientiousness. In the convent schools, girls were instructed in a wide range of subjects. Besides a sound course in Religion, they were taught History, Geography, the use of the Globes, Botany, Writing, Arithmetic and all kinds of needlework, useful and ornamental. The Congregations of Continental origin brought with them new ideas, which, with the increase in the number of English members in their communities, were gradually adapted to the conditions prevailing on this side of the Channel. They were able to offer the pupils in their schools excellent facilities for the study of foreign languages, as well as finishing courses in branch convents abroad. The English Congregations were obviously fitted from the outset to supply the special needs of Catholics in the social life of the country, and they evolved a very advanced system of education.

An outstanding example of this is to be found in the *Book of Studies* (1863), which embodied the educational ideas of Mother Connelly and formed the basis of the method followed by the Sisters of the Holy Child. Mother Connelly had herself been educated in America and on the Continent, and she brought to her task a mind fresh and unfettered by the bonds of established attitudes and customs. As a convert, moreover, she was in a position to understand the requirements of the time, when the Oxford Movement was sweeping large numbers into the Catholic fold, and she imposed upon her nuns the duty of " meeting the needs of the age." To the teaching of Religion she attached the greatest importance. This lesson was placed at seven in the evening, when the work of the day was over, and the children were made to feel that it was quite different from all the others. The younger children were taught about God as a loving Father, with no mention of the punishment of sin until they had learnt to love Him for His goodness. The list of other subjects taught reminds us of the syllabus of Miss Beale at Casterton and Cheltenham. It included English, French, Writing, Arithmetic, Geography, History, Singing, the principles of Church Music, Drawing, Plain Needlework, every kind of embroidery, together with the cutting out and making up of vestments. After a few years, Philosophy, Logic and Astronomy; Geology, Architecture, and Heraldry were added as well as Latin and Greek, and there were readings and recitations in German and Italian.

In view of this amazing range of subjects, it is surprising to find that very much more than a mere superficial knowledge was nevertheless acquired, and that the girls, on leaving school, were in a position to reach real proficiency in, and to attain a life-long enjoyment of things of high cultural value. The thoroughness of Mother Connelly's methods, in fact, is beyond question, and may be judged from such experiments as bringing specialists from London for gold work, lace-making and fine embroidery; paying professional workers in plaster to give the nuns lessons in modelling, and asking Pugin to design church carpets. She aimed at the very highest standard and would tolerate nothing less than the best. The church singing was magnificent, and it was taught in such a way that the children enjoyed it. She did not indulge in theories and topical discussions as to whether girls should learn the same things as boys and compete in the same examinations, but she aimed at providing a type of education which would produce truly cultured women. She carried out her ideas with complete fearlessness as may be judged from the fact that, at a time when play-acting was considered the acme of worldliness, she prepared and executed some first-rate pieces on the convent stage, and set up a high standard of performance because she considered this to be part of the pupils' training in good taste and ability.

With regard to the success of Mother Connelly's system, we have the testimony of a Government Inspector. " It is impossible to witness without admiration the results obtained in this very interesting school," wrote Mr. T. W. M. Marshall in his Report in 1853. " Consummate skill in the art of teaching, unwearied patience, and the most persuasive personal influence have combined to accomplish all the rarest fruits of Christian instruction. The school is now one of the most perfect institutions of its class in Europe.''

Equally good work was being done by some of the other Orders as is evident from further Reports by the same Inspector. Concerning the schools of the Sisters of Mercy in Birmingham, Mr. Marshall wrote: '' All the results which flow from solid and judicious instruction, diligent and affectionate supervision, and the most unstinted liberality, continue to be realised in these admirable schools in which it would not now be easy to detect any defect.'' After giving a detailed account of his investigation he added: '' I have only to report my unqualified admiration of all which is done in these schools, and of the spirit which animates both the managers and the teachers.''

The significance of all this becomes apparent when we consider that, even twenty years later, it was admitted that '' the importance of attending more systematically to the education of girls . . . . is still most completely ignored in practice. . . . Girls are sent to school merely to keep them out of the way for a while, until they are old enough to be of use; to be taught to read and write, without which acquirements they would of course be uncivilised; and, if they belong to the middle and upper classes, to become acquainted with a few accomplishments intended to help their appearance in society, and to assist them in arriving at the great end of getting married ''[1].

At the opening of our period, therefore, in the middle of the last century, Catholics could claim to have a system of education for girls, whereas the country at large could not. This system was to extend its scope gradually to all parts of the country as the Religious Orders spread, but the important thing was that a system existed, complete in all its parts, with primary and preparatory schools; boarding and day schools; orphanages and charitable institutions of various kinds. In all, the basis was Religion, and a thoroughly Christian and Catholic education was given by dedicated teachers.

It is significant that when an effort was made by Nathaniel Woodard in 1855 to provide Church of England girls' schools, he declared that '' religious homes and convents

[1] *The Education of Girls,* F. J. Faraday, 1872, p. 1.

are more in harmony with my ideas," and when he established St. Michael's School, Bognor, as the first of a series, his plan was that it should be governed by a body of teaching " Canonesses." Thus esteem for the Catholic system of education was made evident by imitation.

UNDER CARDINAL WISEMAN, 1850-65

It was Wiseman who, as Coadjutor Bishop for the Midland District and later for the London District, had encouraged Cornelia Connelly to found her new Congregation, and who by his personal influence had helped to bring about the influx of teaching nuns from abroad. After his elevation to the See of Westminster, he invited still more Congregations to this country, for he esteemed that there could be no more powerful instrument for the conversion of England, which he so ardently desired, than Catholic schools. During the fifteen years of his episcopate, thanks to his encouragement, ten Orders of Sisters added their efforts to what was already being done for the education of girls, and he himself created the Poor Sisters of Nazareth.

The care of the poor was, in fact, his first concern. At the very beginning of his reign the Cardinal declared that the portion of Westminster which most interested him was that wherein lay concealed " labyrinths of lanes and courts, and alleys and slums, nests of ignorance, vice, depravity and crime, as well as of squalor, wretchedness and disease; whose atmosphere is typhus, whose ventilation is cholera; in which swarms a huge and almost countless population, in great measure, nominally at least, Catholic; haunts of filth, which no sewage committee can reach, dark corners, which no lighting board can brighten." It was owing to his endeavours to find a home for a greatly afflicted child that the Sisters of Nazareth came into being. They formed themselves into an independent branch of the Little Sisters of the Poor, and established themselves at Hammersmith in 1851. The educational work for the poor and orphans which they have since accomplished is beyond all praise. To-day, after one century of existence, they are to be found in practically every diocese, and twenty-seven towns in England now have their Nazareth House.

Another teaching Order of English origin which appeared upon the scene at this time was that of the Daughters of the Holy Cross and Passion. This Congregation, founded in Manchester for the purpose of providing homes and educational facilities for factory girls, and schools for the poor and middle classes, had within a few years establishments at Bolton, Salford, Sutton, Dewsbury and Huddersfield. At the present time, there are communities in a dozen other towns of Lancashire and Yorkshire, and one at Islington.

The Ursulines, who arrived in London in 1851, represented an Order famous in the history of Education, with a tradition of three hundred years behind them. It was fitting that at this moment they should have added their influence to the general effort in the great surge forward which characterised the Catholic Church in England. They began work in elementary schools in London, at Broad Street and Moorfields. Five years later they moved to Oxford, but eventually were obliged to return to Belgium. Soon they were back again, however, and opened a boarding school at Upton in 1863. To-day, the Ursulines have eight High Schools, all of which, with the exception of Brentwood with 740 pupils and Kettering with 250, belong to the Roman Union.

An important acquisition was made when the Congregation of the Holy Union of the Sacred Hearts came to this country. The three pioneer Sisters, two of whom were English, arrived on the last day of the year 1859, and under the auspices of the Benedictine Fathers who were friendly with their Founder, Abbé Jean-Baptiste Debrabant, took over the elementary school at Bath, hitherto taught by the Sisters of St. Paul. They began in much poverty, but their work was so far successful that, within three years, they were able to begin a boarding school. With a far-sightedness somewhat rare in Continental Orders, they immediately opened a novitiate in England, and thereby ensured their rapid and prosperous development. To-day, with nine schools and a Training College, they rank among the most important Congregations engaged in educational work.

It was doubtless a great event when the Sisters of Charity of St. Vincent de Paul first came to this country in 1857. At the present time they are the most numerous of all the Congregations in England, but education is only one of the many forms of charitable enterprise which they undertake. They have a secondary school for girls at Darlington, but, for the most part, they specialise in institutions. They have the only Catholic asylum for the blind in this country, at Liverpool; the only Catholic school for deaf and dumb children, at Boston Spa, Yorkshire; an orthopaedic hospital and school for crippled children at Northwood Hills, Middlesex, and a home for mentally deficient at Sheffield. They run Homes for Rescue Work, as at Gravesend; Poor-Law Schools, as at Hereford; Probationary and Approved Schools, as at Newcastle and Liverpool; orphanages, as at Newcastle and Hull, and an Open Air School at St. Leonards. Both in scope and in character, their work is absolutely admirable.

Of the other Congregations which came to England at this time, that of Jesus and Mary, deserves special mention. These Sisters opened the first Catholic school in Ipswich since the Reformation, in 1860, in the parish organised by the French émigré priest, Abbé Simon. To the day school with which they started, they soon added a boarding school and a night school, and by courageous work amidst much hardship resulting from poverty and anti-Catholic prejudice, they greatly assisted in rekindling the faith in this part of the country. In 1886 they undertook more pioneer work by opening an elementary school at Willesden. To-day, the convent school there numbers some 500 girls, and a Preparatory School flourishes in the next parish. Their establishment at Ipswich continues as a High School with 260 pupils, and there are other schools at Felixstowe and Bletchley with 170 and 120 girls respectively.

It was under the encouraging patronage of Cardinal Wiseman and the Hierarchy of the restoration that the first Catholic Training Colleges were opened. The pupil-teacher system, whereby would-be teachers were given a four years' course of practical training before entering a College, had been in operation since 1846. By 1854 there were 137 pupil teachers in Catholic boys' schools and 243 in the girls' schools. " What now remained above all things needful," wrote the Secretary of the Poor School Committee, " was that these apprentices should be turned into accomplished teachers." The main difficulty was to find the money. In 1850 a Training College for men had been established at Hammersmith at a building cost of £8,000, and although £2,500 had been contributed by the Privy Council, the strain on the slender resources of the Committee had been very heavy. It was a great relief, therefore, to those responsible for Catholic elementary schools when Religious Orders of nuns came forward and supplied the desired Colleges at their own expense.

Mother Connelly accepted the offer of a Government Training School in 1855, and took upon herself the responsibility of supplying the necessary building and equipment. With the adaptability which enabled the Sisters of Charity to apply themselves to every good work, and which led the Sisters of Mercy and the Daughters of the Faithful Virgin to set out for the Crimea as voluntary nurses with Miss Nightingale, the Holy Child nuns forthwith prepared and entered for public examinations, an unprecedented venture, and obtained the Teachers' Certificate. By the following February a qualified staff was ready, and the Training School was opened with nine Queen's Scholars. The work was well planned, the students responded enthusiastically and the numbers rapidly increased. Unfortunately, owing to administrative difficulties, this School had soon to be abandoned. A similar Training College begun about the same time in Liverpool had also to be given up.

The Training College established by the Notre Dame nuns was destined to be more durable. It was the outcome of a request made in March 1855 by Mr. T. W. Allies, Secretary of the Poor School Committee, to the Mother General of the Order. Notre Dame Sisters were already teaching in Liverpool, having taken over St. Nicholas' poor school on the invitation of Fr. Nugent four years previously, and since then they had accepted the Female Orphanage from the Sisters of Mercy, and established a boarding and middle school at Mount Pleasant. In October, Sister Mary of St. Philip, with three companions, was sent to obtain the necessary qualifications for the new mission, and on the Feast of the Purification the next year, the Training College was opened at Mount Pleasant with twenty-one students. It was an important event, for Our Lady's Training College now stands as the oldest and the largest of the imposing group which the nuns of various Orders have established in this country.

It was fortunate that the provision of Colleges for Catholic women teachers was no longer delayed, for serious difficulties lay immediately ahead in the path of Catholic elementary education. The first of these, arising from the application of Lowe's " Revised Code," which instituted the system of payment by results, had a serious effect on the Training Colleges themselves. Up to this time, 1863, full grants for tuition and maintenance had been paid in respect of all students in residence, with an additional allowance for books in the case of First Class Queen's Scholars. With the introduction of the new principle, however, grants for students were deferred until after they had left College and had secured two favourable reports, with an interval of twelve months between them, in their schools. At the same time personal allowances were discontinued, so that the College authorities were obliged to provide from fees and private subscriptions one fourth of the cost of maintenance and tuition of the students. The financial strain thus became unbearable. It was at this time that St. Leonards' Training School collapsed, and Mount Pleasant might well have shared the same fate had it not been for the generous benefactions of the wife of the Hon. Edward Petre, who, after the death of her husband (1848), had entered the Congregation of Notre Dame as Sister Mary of St. Francis.

Further difficulties arose later as a result of the Education Act of 1870, but these are bound up with the developments during Cardinal Manning's reign. Meanwhile, it is clear from this brief survey of Wiseman's episcopate that great strides were made towards providing Catholic education for girls on an extensive scale during these first fifteen years of our period. Elementary schools were multiplied, and a provision of trained teachers was assured. The number of convent secondary schools likewise increased. The initiation of charitable enterprise in favour of the destitute and orphans, however, was perhaps the most significant feature of this development. The condition of the poor, so graphically described by the Cardinal in his *Appeal to the English People,* presented a problem of the utmost urgency. The work begun by Wiseman was continued by his successor, and became, in fact, Manning's primary preoccupation.

UNDER CARDINAL MANNING, 1865-92

In the Pastoral Letter issued only fourteen days after his consecration, Manning pointed to " the tens of thousands of poor Catholic children who are without instruction or training. . . . The lowest estimate reaches 16,000, a more probable estimate raises it to 20,000." He enumerated the institutions already in existence: the two orphanages of North Hyde and Norwood; the Boys' Reformatory School at Blyth House, Hammersmith; St. Nicholas' Industrial School, Walthamstow; St. Margaret's Industrial School for girls at Queen's Square; the Refuge at Finchley and the Orphanage for boys at Hendon, and he emphasised the insufficiency of this effort. In the next Pastoral he enlarged on the subject, and drew attention to the number of children who fell under the operation of Law for offences, or were committed as friendless and abandoned. " The late Acts of Reformatory and Industrial Schools enable us to provide for them with greater facility," he said, " but so great is our poverty that we are not able to keep pace with the need, and many of them have been sent to Protestant institutions." Others were in workhouses where " the education is exclusively Protestant—books, catechisms, prayers, teachers, worship." Manning placed the number of these children at " more than a thousand," but he soon found that the figure was twice as great. With characteristic energy, therefore, he organised public meetings and opened a Diocesan Fund to cope with the situation. The direction which his educational policy would take was thus clearly indicated.

Inevitably, the nuns were appealed to and forthwith they set about the work to the full extent of their resources. The Sisters of Charity built a school for 200 boys at Mill Hill at their own expense, and took over another started by a secular lady at Leytonstone. The Sisters of Mercy opened an Industrial School for girls at Eltham at their own expense, and similar schools were established by other nuns at Finchley and Isleworth.

It was providential that an English Congregation which was founded at this time should have been devoted to work of mercy. The Poor Servants of the Mother of God owed their origin to the conversion of Fanny Taylor, a nurse in the Crimea, and developed under the encouraging patronage of another convert, Lady Georgiana Fullerton. Typically enough, the Foundress began her career by looking after a girls' Industrial School under the Oblates of Mary Immaculate at Tower Hill, and the work of her first nuns was in poor schools at Roehampton and Beaumont (1871-72). In 1880, when a convent school was opened at Brentford, the Sisters also took charge of the poor school there. Even when the great Providence Hospital was begun at St. Helens, four years later, a night school for miners was appended to it. Thus, the education of the poor became one of the aims of the new Order and remains so to this day. The Poor Servants of the Mother of God are now widespread in England, and although they have convent schools at Beccles, Chippenham, Amersham and Portslade, they are mainly concerned with primary schools, as at Gloucester and Clifton; Children's Homes, as at Brighton, Freshfield and Liverpool; Homes for feeble-minded girls as at Brentford, Weston-super-Mare and Roehampton; and Preservation Homes, as at Streatham and Liverpool.

But Manning was not permitted to give his undivided attention to the working of the Poor Law and the Reformatory and Industrial School Acts. In 1870 came the re-organisation of elementary education on national secularist lines, and the great effort on the part of the Catholic body, as described earlier, to prevent the children from drifting into the Board Schools. Upon the Training College at Mount Pleasant fell the task of supplying qualified teachers for the new schools and classes, and buildings were planned to double its capacity. In 1870, the Sacred Heart nuns established the Wandsworth Training College to share in the work, and five years later the Holy Child nuns opened a Pupil Teachers' centre at Preston, where young girls of twelve and thirteen who taught all day in the schools, came for lessons from 6 to 8 p.m. during the week, and on Saturday mornings.

To meet the need of the time, Religious Congregations already engaged in elementary school work did all in their power to extend their efforts. This was all the easier as three Orders which had arrived in the last year of Cardinal Wiseman's reign were just settling down. The Poor School Sisters of Notre Dame established themselves at Birmingham, Southend and Woolwich; the Servite nuns took over poor schools at Arundel and Stamford Hill, and the Sisters of St. Joseph of Annecy did the same thing in the West of England; at Devizes (1864), Newport (1873) and Malmesbury (1883).

Other Congregations now appeared on the scene. The year previous to the passing of the 1870 Act, the Daughters of the Cross of Liège, came to England and established themselves at Cheltenham, from whence they moved to Chelsea and spread to Bury and Manchester. By 1893 they had added Carshalton to their list. The Sisters of the Sacred Heart of Mary came to England in 1873, and began work in the North at Bootle and Liverpool. Eleven years later, Bishop Bagshawe founded the Sisters of St. Joseph of Peace at Nottingham, whence they have spread to Leicester and Grimsby. Finally, the Kulturkampf was responsible for the arrival of the Sisters of the Poor Child Jesus from Germany in 1873, who took up in this country the work they were not permitted to do in their own.

In this way, at a critical period, the teaching Orders of nuns rendered invaluable assistance in the sphere of elementary education. It is significant that the Cross Commission, in their final Report (1888) on the working of the Elementary Education Act, after mentioning the vast increase in the number of Voluntary Schools since 1870 " in most of which the whole basis is religious," and which were " erected and maintained at great pecuniary sacrifice on the part of their supporters and held in much favour by large masses of the population," made special mention of the work of the nuns. " It is admitted and proved very conclusively," said the Commissioners, " by the remarkable results of the labours of members of religious communities in Roman Catholic schools, that the employment as teachers of women of superior social position and general culture has a refining and excellent effect upon the schools in which they teach." (Report, p. 80.)

But, while these efforts were being made to cope with the needs of Catholics in the sphere of elementary education, secondary schools were not neglected. This was all the more important as everything pointed to a development of State enterprise in this direction also. Although Manning did not live to see this take effect at the turn of the century, he must have felt it coming. Considerable significance, therefore,

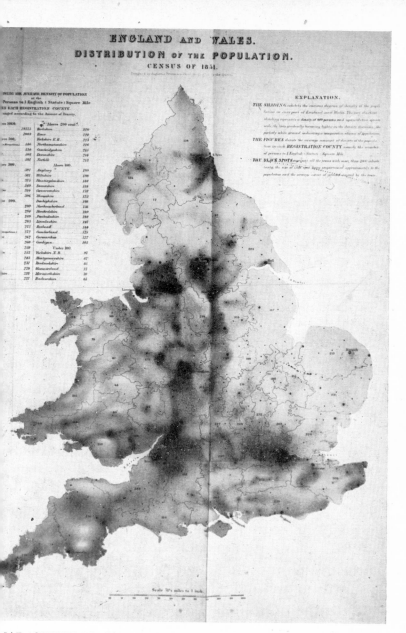

MAP SHOWING THE DISTRIBUTION OF POPULATION
IN ENGLAND AND WALES, 1851
From the Census return of the Registrar-General

[33]

USHAW in 1850 and at the present day

[34]

(Aero Pi

St. EDMUND'S COLLEGE in about 1865 and at the present day

UPHOLLAND

(Aero Pictorial)

STONYHURST the West Front

AMPLEFORTH in 1840, and at the present day

(Aero

COTTON COLLEGE

ST. ANGELA'S, FOREST GATE in 1862, and at the present day.

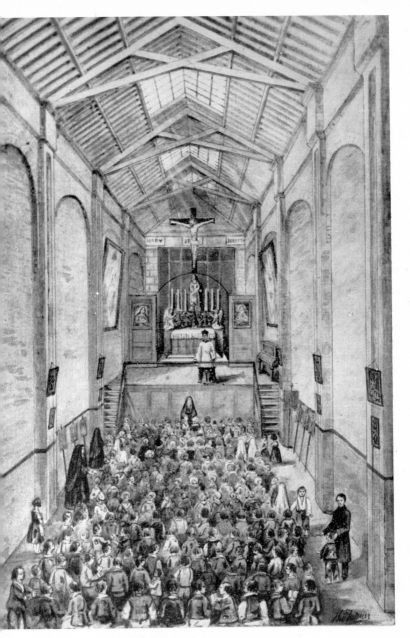

THE LONDON ORATORY
The Ragged School, Dunne's Passage, in 1852

[45]

CHURCH OF THE IMMACULATE CONCEPTION,
FARM STREET, in 1850

ches to the foundations made by the daughters of Mary
rd at this time, at Gloucester in 1862 (which moved to
land's Lane ten years later and subsequently to Hamp-
d), at Ascot in 1885, and at Cambridge in 1897, and also
he arrival of four Congregations which have been particu-
y successful in the higher education of girls: the Religious
ie Cross; La Retraite; the Dames of Christian Instruction;
the Ladies of Mary.

The Ladies of Mary followed the Josephites to Croydon
869, and opened the Sacred Heart Convent, " Coloma,"
ch to-day has grown to a school of 530 pupils. A dozen
rs later they began at Scarborough where they now have
girls at Notre Dame du Sacré Coeur and a parish school.
nore recent years they have established other schools: St.
ie's, Sanderstead (1909), with 500 pupils; St. Winifrede's,
st Hill (1915), with 200, and St. Clare's, Coalville (1930),
l 120 girls.

The Religious of the Cross began at Bournemouth, in
1, the work they now continue in High Schools for girls at
combe, Waterlooville and in the Isle of Wight. La Retraite
ted their first school at " The Willows " in Clapham High
et in 1880. At present their day school at Clapham Park
450 pupils, while their boarding school at Burnham, which
opened at Sevenoaks in 1883, has some 120 girls. In
tion they now have large day schools at Clifton and
ton-super-Mare, and a Preparatory School at Tooting with
pupils. Finally, the Dames of Christian Instruction, a
gian branch of St. Sophie Barat's Congregation, began their
l-class school for girls at Sherborne in 1891, and now have
cond similar school at Effingham, Surrey.

In addition to these Congregations we might mention
Dames of Nazareth who settled at South Ealing in 1880
evote themselves to the higher education of young ladies,
the nuns of the Most Holy Sacrament who began a board-
ind day school in Golden Square in October 1874. Blessed
ament Convents have since grown up at Brighton (1888),
ling (1903) and Tunbridge Wells, while two schools in
don were destroyed during the war.

The twenty-six years of Manning's episcopate, which
e to prove crucial in the history of Catholic Education, were

N

thus rich with educational developments initiated by the Religi
Orders of women. While legislation seriously threatening
very existence of Catholic elementary schools proved a stim
to action, and the sight of swarms of neglected children in
great cities excited the flame of charity, the anti-religious l
of France and Germany drove to our shores at an opport
time large numbers of exiled nuns to reinforce the Congre
tions already established and enable their work to spread.
provision of Catholic schools for girls was in this way grea
increased, and offered a promising beginning for the twent
century.

THE DAWN OF A NEW ERA

As the nineteenth century drew to a close, serious p
blems affecting the education of girls loomed on the horiz
These problems arose from the wider issues of " The Right
Women " and the changing position of the female sex
modern society. The influences which were to lead ultima
to the present day situation wherein women stand on an ec
footing with men, were already at work, and were reflected
far-reaching changes in the educational sphere. Efforts v
being directed towards obtaining for girls the same advanta
as were enjoyed by boys, and towards securing for women
possibility of a university education on a par with men. Th
movements achieved a measure of success in a comparati
short space of time, and it became necessary for those resp
sible for the education of girls to prepare their pupils for a
of vastly greater opportunities than had existed before.

In a single generation the whole aspect of female edu
tion had altered. Cheltenham Ladies' College, founded in 1
as a counterpart to the Boys' College, had, under the heads
of Miss Beale (1858-1906), achieved a resounding success
set the fashion for Public Schools for girls. The Endo
Schools Act (1869) had encouraged the erection of girls' sch
by the application of surplus funds from old trusts, while
newly formed Girls' Public Day School Trust had founded
first schools at Chelsea and Croydon in 1873 and 1874. I
Davies, the foundress of Girton College, and Miss Clou
foundress of Newnham, had begun the assault on Cambri
University, while at Oxford the " Association for the Edu

tion of Women " resulted in the foundation of Somerville College and Lady Margaret Hall in 1879, of St. Hugh's in 1886, and St. Hilda's in 1893. In 1878 London University had thrown open its degrees to women students; the newly formed Victoria University had done the same shortly after, and in 1892-93 the Scottish Universities and the University of Wales followed suit.

This tremendous advance was made amidst a welter of new ideas which required the most careful sifting, and was accompanied by much experimenting in pedagogical methods, as for instance co-education at Lady Barn and elsewhere. The pursuit of higher studies became a craze, when the modern Blue-Stocking appeared in the attractive gown of a University graduate.

In the face of all this " progress " and the strong tide of public opinion, the Religious Orders relied on the anchor of established traditions. They stood sufficiently aloof from the current of worldly affairs to be able to form balanced judgments, and they professed definite principles regarding the education of girls, from which they were not prepared to depart. Thus, while the future appeared to them full of hope, they were not blind to the dangers of following a course of events which, at accelerated motion, was outstripping the thought which should guide it.

" Our girls are in danger of drifting and floating along the current of the hour," wrote a brilliant and saintly representative of one of the great teaching Congregations[2]. " In the work of educating girls, every generation has to face the same problem and deals with it in a characteristic way. For us it presents particular features of interest, of hope and likewise of anxious concern. . . . We have our splendid opportunity and are greatly responsible for its use."

Could it be taken for granted, as it seemed to be, that what was suitable for boys and men was necessarily good for girls and women? " If we want a girl to grow to the best that woman ought to be," continued Mother Stuart, " it is in two things that we must establish her fundamentally—quiet of mind and firmness of will. . . . Catholics have been spurred into the movement (towards higher studies) by those who are keenly

[2] Janet Erskine Stuart, *The Education of Catholic Girls*, 1911.

N 2

anxious that we should not be left behind. . . . But, may it be suggested, in their own education, a degree for a man and a degree for a girl mean very different things even if the degree is the same. For a girl it is the certificate of a course of studies. For a man an Oxford or Cambridge degree means an atmosphere unique in character, immemorial tradition, association, all kinds of interests and subtle influences out of the past, the impressiveness of numbers. The difference is that of two worlds. . . . Atmosphere is a most important element at all periods of education, and in the education of girls all-important, and an atmosphere for the higher education of girls has not yet been created in the universities. The girl students are few, their position is not unassailable, their aims not very well defined, and the thing which is above all required for the intellectual development of girls—quiet of mind—is not assured.''

Thus, the attitude towards the new opportunities was at first one of caution. That this was not due to excessive conservatism is obvious from the subsequent record of nuns themselves and of their pupils at the universities, but it was typical of the seriousness with which the mission of Catholic education was envisaged.

Meanwhile, every boat from the Continent brought its contingent of nuns. The folly of French politicians which deprived their country of the services of thousands of experienced teachers because they belonged to Religious Congregations, enriched England to a corresponding degree by strengthening the ranks of those Orders which were already established, and by bringing still more Congregations to share in the work. Thus, in 1894, the Sisters of the Christian Schools of Mercy arrived at Bracknell (Berks), and subsequently established themselves at Reading, Birmingham and Worcester, where they now have secondary schools with 420, 120 and 330 pupils respectively. In 1897, the Bernardines re-appeared on the scene. They traced their origin to a pre-Revolutionary community of French nuns which, in 1792, had come to England and set up a school at Islington, but which had returned to France some years later. Political events once more drove them to these shores, and they opened a boarding school at Slough which is now a Recognised High School with some 570 pupils. In 1910 they took over an elementary and secondary school at High Wycombe from the Daughters of the Holy Ghost, and two years later began teaching at Westcliff-on-Sea where they now have over 700 pupils in two schools. In 1902, Mother Cabrini, the saintly foundress of the Missionary Sisters of the Sacred Heart, established her first convent in this country, and two years later, the Sisters of St. Martin of Tours began their convent at Muswell Hill. In 1911, a community of English Canonesses of St. Augustine which had been founded at Paris in 1633 and which, with the Benedictines of Ypres, had been the only community to survive the Revolution without leaving the Continent, came to England and established themselves at Ealing. To-day, their High School there counts some 250 pupils.

At the beginning of the century (1901) there originated also the Congregation of the Sisters of the Sacred Hearts of Jesus and Mary as an independent English branch of the parent Order, who took up a specialised branch of educational work, namely, schools for delicate and mentally deficient children. To-day they are widely scattered with establishments at Chigwell, Liverpool, Hayling Island, Herne Bay, Farnham, Godalming, and several houses in the London area.

Other developments of considerable significance began during this period, namely, the foundation of more Training Colleges. In 1896, the Holy Child nuns, at the desire of Cardinal Vaughan, opened a College for Catholic secondary school teachers. Students reading for London degrees also attended the College, and among them a number of members of other Religious Congregations. To-day, Cavendish Square Training College offers a one-year course for post-graduate students, and, since the Curtis Report, a course in " Child Care " for workers in Catholic Homes. The nuns of the Holy Union opened a Training College at Southampton in 1904, and to-day it has 137 students following the two-year course.

The progress of this important work of teacher-training by nuns has been one of the noteworthy features of recent years. There are now eleven Training Colleges, nine of which are recognised by the Ministry. The Faithful Companions have 168 students at Sedgley Park College, Manchester; the Assumption nuns have 140 at Kensington Square; the Sisters of Mercy train 168 at Endsleigh Training College, Hull; the Sacred Heart nuns have 140 at Digby Stuart College, Roehampton, and 180 at St. Mary's College, Newcastle, and the Sisters of Charity of St. Paul have some 80 students at Newbold Revel, Rugby. Mount Pleasant now has 220 students and is thus the largest of the group. Besides these Colleges offering the ordinary two-year course, there are two Froebel Training Colleges, one at Croydon with 40 students, conducted by the Ladies of Mary, and one at Wandsworth under the Sacred Heart nuns. Between them, the various Orders train some 1,300 women teachers for Catholic schools. This number would be considerably greater were there more accommodation. For the 1946-47 session, for instance, Mount Pleasant was obliged to refuse 62 students, Roehampton 60, St. Mary's, Newcastle, 55, and Croydon 20.

The period between the two wars was one of consolidation and expansion. Many convents sought to profit by the advantages offered by the Balfour Act of 1902 and the Fisher Act of 1918 to obtain official testimony of their educational standing or to alleviate their financial difficulties. They invited inspection, and the outcome was that, even before the Butler Act, the Board of Education's Efficiency Recognition was held by some 100 schools, over sixty of which received aid from public funds. Hitherto, Catholic secondary schools had been built and maintained entirely at the expense of the Religious Orders responsible for them, even the salaries of lay-teachers being paid out of the resources of the school. The great financial strain was met in each case by pooling the funds of the Order, by school fees, by salaries earned by nuns teaching or holding headships in elementary schools, and by contracting debts. Now it became possible to apply for " Direct Grant," whereby a capitation allowance was given for each pupil over ten and under nineteen years of age, or to obtain a " deficiency grant," a sum equal in amount to the deficit between fee income and expenditure. The stipulation was that the school should reach the level of efficiency required by the Ministry, in buildings, staff and equipment, and that it be open to inspection.

Meanwhile, the number of schools increased enormously. This was due not only to the spread of Congregations already at work, but to the arrival of still more to augment the variety. This multiplication of distinct Orders, a phenomenon of modern times, has been such as to defy even enumeration. To the lay-man, in fact, the position is confusing in the extreme. Not only are there as many as 84 different Congregations of nuns, each with its distinctive name and habit, in a single diocese, but several Congregations with the same name and apparently of similar type all engaged in educational work. Thus, there are no fewer than eight Orders of Sisters of Charity, four Congregations of Sisters of St. Joseph, besides a number of different Congregations of Dominicans and Franciscans of the Third Order.

This has not passed without comment. Some maintain that religious life would gain in strength, dignity and influence were its forces, instead of being dispersed, gathered into a few great Orders. Women, however, more than men, cling to individuality. This diversity, moreover, results from a variety of aims pursued by the different Congregations with the encouragement of the Church; for, as the Secretary of the Poor School Committee pointed out a century ago with regard to Religious Orders of women: " Good work thrives under them; and, it would seem, under them alone." (Report, 1850.) If new Congregations arise it is in answer to imperative calls for help in the varied spheres of Catholic activity. Education greatly benefits from new foundations for very often teaching is taken up as a supplementary work even when the primary aim is quite different, and thus the list of Orders engaged in Education reflects the same diversity. It is remarkable, for instance, that the 336 schools grouped in the Association of Convent Schools in 1948, belong to practically 100 distinct Congregations[3].

The contribution of individual Congregations to Catholic education, however, is widely different. The great teaching Orders, founded specifically for educational work, have a larger number of schools and may be expected to achieve greater efficiency than Congregations which pursue a multiplicity of aims of which Education is only one. Thus, we find that the Sisters of Mercy have 28 schools which are

[3] The Association of Convent Schools was founded in 1928, the object being to maintain the Catholic tradition and character of the schools; to facilitate the exchange of ideas and information, and to work in conjunction with the Conference of Catholic Colleges. Membership qualification is a minimum of fifty pupils and a course of general education reaching a satisfactory academic standard.

members of the Association of Convent Schools, Notre Dame 20, and the Faithful Companions 17, whereas there are some 30 Congregations which are represented by only one school each. But, in the arduous struggle to provide Catholic schools, every little counts, and small Congregations which gallantly attempt with limited resources to maintain schools in remote districts for the sake of a small number of Catholic children, perform an invaluable service even though such schools stand little chance of reaching a high degree of efficiency. The existence of many schools of this type helps to explain the preponderance of Catholic girls' schools over boys' schools; a preponderance of more than five to one.

The extent of the educational work accomplished by the united efforts of the Religious Orders of women in recent times is very considerable, and covers all branches at every level. The large majority of Catholic Institutions are run by nuns. They have seven '' Approved '' schools; four for girls and three for junior boys. For blind, deaf and other handicapped children they have a dozen establishments. For orphans and abandoned children they have some thirty residential homes and schools for girls, and seventeen for boys. In the sphere of primary education their contribution is very great, while the entire system of Catholic secondary schools, with the insignificant exception of a couple of establishments such as Rye St. Anthony, Oxford, is in their hands. In these boarding and grammar schools they educate a total of 27,000 Catholic girls, besides several thousand small boys in the preparatory departments. Moreover, in these same schools they have over 20,000 non-Catholic children[4].

The fact that so many non-Catholic parents send their daughters to convent schools even in preference to schools academically superior, is no doubt a testimony to the esteem in which these schools are held even outside the Catholic body, and denotes a certain appreciation on the part of these parents that nuns have something valuable to impart in the preparation of children for life besides mere instruction. To Catholics, however, who are aware that some 146,250 Catholic girls between the ages of 11 and 16 need education, the fact that non-

[4] Report of the Special Commission appointed by the Hierarchy, 1948.

Catholics occupy 43 per cent of the places in Convent schools appears altogether incongruous. To remedy such a misplacement of effort must be one of the tasks of the future; a difficult one, no doubt, for the situation as it exists is the result of compelling forces, chiefly financial. Convent schools, for their very existence, have had to depend on school fees, and have had to limit their clientèle to pupils who could afford them. Thus the number of free places which could be given was strictly limited, and in the case of boarding schools, a serious liability. Hence non-Catholics who were able to pay the fees were taken in, while Catholic girls were left out, owing to their inability to do so.

The abolition by the Butler Act of all fees in State secondary schools brought matters to a head. Catholic schools found themselves in the position of either having to come to some arrangement with the Ministry or the Local Authority whereby the school fees would be paid out of public money, or of continuing to impose an unfair burden on Catholic parents. As a result, most schools, except those which catered specially for the upper classes, applied for recognition in one form or another, so that by 1948 the number of " recognised " schools had risen to 109, and the number in receipt of public money to 73. To achieve this, the Religious Orders concerned shouldered heavy building programmes and made tremendous efforts to attain the high degree of efficiency required by the Inspectors.

The period following the Butler Act, in fact, has been one of re-adjustment to the new conditions created by that Act. Not only did individual schools have to reconsider their position with regard to State-built establishments staffed and equipped with an unstinted supply of public money, but the schools of each administrative area had to be considered together as forming one educational whole. Considerable adaptation was necessary, with the co-operation of the Educational authorities, and in the sphere of secondary education the burden of this re-adjustment fell largely on the Religious Orders. Nor was it a light one. Provision was made in the Act for financial assistance being given to secondary schools for modernising, rebuilding and enlarging (up to half of the cost in the case of " aided " schools), but this still left the balance to be supplied by those responsible for the school, and the sum was frequently very large. In the County Boroughs of East and West Ham, for instance, where the secondary education is being undertaken by two multi-lateral schools, the Ursuline Convent of St. Angela and the Franciscan school of St. Bonaventure, these two schools between them have shouldered a financial responsibility amounting to £200,000.

The desperate struggle which all this has entailed was accepted willingly as the final result will yield, it is hoped, precious advantages. Catholic children will be able to enjoy a secondary education in Catholic schools irrespective of their ability to pay fees; and convents will no longer be obliged to close their doors to Catholic girls in favour of non-Catholics. If the schools are brought up to the standard of modern requirements, the ever-present danger of Catholic children drifting into the better equipped schools of the State will be averted.

CONCLUSION: THE FUTURE

The history of the educational work of Religious Orders of women during the last hundred years presents the picture of an apparent relative decadence. Whereas in the eighteen fifties and for many years after, Catholic schools were far in advance of those of the rest of the country, the situation to-day shows Catholic schools to be in a position of inferiority as compared with the schools of the State. This has come about owing to discrimination in favour of undenominational schools in the course of the development of our national system of Education, and Catholics have had to pay a heavy price for their faith.

The present inferiority, however, is more apparent than real, for to a large extent it is a question merely of bricks and mortar. A system of education, in the last analysis, must be judged not by buildings and equipment, but by the teachers and what they teach, for the results will depend far more on these factors than on anything else. If Catholics have all along maintained their schools despite the heaviest handicaps, it is in the belief that their system, based on sound religious principles and administered by dedicated teachers, is, judged by moral standards, immeasurably the best. For this reason the fight for the schools will continue whatever the sacrifices imposed by unfair discriminating legislation.

But the support of the Religious Orders is now more than ever necessary. There are no organisations better able to face a financial crisis than those whose members are vowed to poverty, and precisely because the provision of Catholic schools has always been, and still is, fraught with well nigh insuperable financial difficulties, the Religious Orders have had, and still have, an essential part to play. Without them a large percentage of the Catholic schools which cover the country to-day would never have come into existence. Now, the financial burden weighing on the Catholic body is immeasurably greater than it has ever been, and clouds the future. Not only are there tremendous liabilities involved in re-organising and rebuilding the schools which already exist, in order to meet the requirements of the 1944 Act, but many new ones have still to be supplied. In the sphere of secondary education particularly, the Catholic system needs completion, and as under the new dispensation no financial assistance is obtainable for this purpose, it must fall to the Religious Orders to cope with the problem.

To accomplish the task which awaits them and on which the future of Catholic Education so largely depends, the Religious Orders need one thing: vocations. In the past the Continent supplied vast numbers of members, and Ireland has been a fruitful source of postulants. It is now time that English Catholics provided the quota required, especially as the teaching Orders, generally speaking, are now equipped with novitiates in this country for the training of their recruits. No doubt, the re-organisation of schools has resulted in the increase of the number of qualified lay-mistresses on the staffs of convent schools, and it seems likely that in the future, with salaries paid by the State, the lay element will increase still further. Yet while this will ease the situation and offer more encouraging prospects to Catholic women teachers, it cannot do away with the need for vocations, for on these the Religious Orders absolutely depend, and without them the whole fabric must eventually collapse.

The primary source of vocations is the schools themselves. If Religion forms the basis of all instruction, and a religious atmosphere permeates the whole, vocations should develop as surely as seed in good soil, despite all the adverse conditions of modern life. One precious advantage of the recent re-organisation, in fact, has been the liberation of secondary schools from the constraint of an externally controlled syllabus. This offers a unique opportunity for reconstituting the course of studies in Catholic schools in accordance with the Catholic philosophy of Education, and of placing Religion in its right place as the focus of all. Significantly enough, this all-important question formed the main theme of discussion at the annual meeting of the Association of Convent Schools in 1948, and it is to be hoped that practical results will not be long delayed.

XIII

THE STRUGGLE FOR THE SCHOOLS

By A. C. F. BEALES

I. INTRODUCTION: TO 1850

T is quite certain that, from the Elizabethan Religious Settlement of 1558-63 down to the first Relief Act of 1778, the policy of the Government had been to make a Catholic education in England impossible. It is no less certain that the attempt had failed. For while it cannot be claimed that the exiled colleges and schools in the Low Countries and in Spain were linked with and served by a system of preparatory schools at home, it is known that at least 120 Catholic schoolmasters were teaching clandestinely in England in the 17th century and at least 135 in the 18th; and that during those two centuries over 220 Catholic schools, of intermittent and hunted existence, were functioning at one time and another, at least three of them with unbroken continuity from about 1650. By the time the exiles returned, under cover of the wave of British sympathy for those persecuted by the French Revolutionary leaders of 1789, a movement of popular Catholic education was already under way in this country; and its consolidation between then and 1850 makes the Restoration of the Hierarchy the beginning of the second chapter in modern Catholic education rather than the first.

The difference in the picture as it stood in 1829 (Emancipation year) and in 1850 is immense. In 1829 the Catholics were educationally isolated; they knew nothing of the Public Schools and Universities. The aloofness of the Catholic aristocracy, natural in a body trained for so long to unobtrusiveness during Penal Times, was equally naturally misunderstood by the new tolerant, English " liberal " society. Politically also they stood alone; there was no hope of a joint civic campaign

for educational rights on the part of the various minoriti
above all with the Nonconformists and the Jews, for suspici
of the Pope as a " foreign sovereign " lived on. The report
a Select Committee in 1835 gave the total of Catholic scho
in England as 86 day, 62 Sunday and one infants' scho
The total for Scotland was 20.

The change in the general Catholic position in the ne
20 years can be sensed from background influences. T
Dublin Review was begun in May, 1836, to supply the ne
for a Catholic periodical of high literary merit that would co
mand the attention of non-Catholics. *The Tablet* followed
1840, at the instigation of a stormy and implacable controve
sialist, Frederick Lucas. The same year also brought fr
abroad three orders of Religious, on the invitation of I
Wiseman, to widen the field of Retreats and spiritual dedic
tion among all classes. The revival of the school at Fern
halgh, Lancashire, in 1842 (one of the few with an unbrok
career going back to the 17th century), was felt to be
omen.

By 1840, in short, the Catholic body had taken t
field with an educational campaign. The main spearhead
this campaign was lay in character: the Catholic Institute, s
up in 1838 as successor to a long series of similar bodi
stretching back to the Cisalpine Club of 1792. But the Institu
like its predecessors, ultimately failed.

At the instigation of Charles Langdale there arose—
take over its educational work and its funds—the Catho
Poor School Committee of 1847 (September 27th), establish
under the patronage of Our Lady and St. Joseph, and acti
as the accredited instrument of the eight Vicars Apostolic
their educational relations with the Government. This Co
mittee was a lineal successor, in fact, of both the Catho
Institute and the threefold Associated Catholic Charities
1815. In turn it was to give place to the present Catho
Education Council in 1905. Charles Langdale was its fi
president. It was expressly an official body established
receive grants from the 1839 Committee of the Privy Coun
on Education, side by side with the (Anglican) Nation
Society and the (Nonconformist) British and Foreign Scho
Society, which had been receiving such grants ever since 183

The work was to concentrate immediately on the two key-problems: primary schools and the training of teachers.

Self-help on a gigantic scale is the main explanation of the multiplication of Catholic elementary schools by 1850. In 1843, when the ill-fated Catholic Institute canvassed every parish in the country for statistics, the Catholic population (under a million as yet) possessed 236 day and 60 Sunday schools (33 of them in London), catering for altogether 38,207 children. But the number of children *without* schooling was estimated at 101,930.

The teaching in the schools was on the Monitorial lines of Lancaster and Bell as modified by the Christian Brothers of France and Ireland.

The first Catholic Training College for men (the only one till 1947) was founded at Hammersmith in 1850, as an instrument of the Poor School Committee's policy, and at first on the lines of the Lamennais Brothers of France. The first Catholic school inspector, the Rev. T. W. Marshall, was deploring at the time the lack of anything for women teachers comparable to Hammersmith, or to the work of the De La Salle Brothers. A beginning had been made, none the less, among the teaching Orders of women; for training was going on sporadically inside the Communities at Birmingham, Derby and Northampton. And the first Catholic Orphanage had been founded by Dr. Manning at North Hyde in 1847.

If the restored Hierarchy inherited an Irish and an industrial and (through the hordes of unschooled) a " leakage " problem, they nevertheless inherited, then, the firm foundations of a " second spring " in popular education. During the century now being celebrated, their Lordships concentrated with singleminded devotion on the " schools' question "; so much so, that whereas the story of Catholic secondary education is the story of the Religious Orders, that of the primary schools for the masses is the story of the Bishops, to an extent which makes the two parts of the picture delineable separately without doing violence to the whole.

II. FROM 1850 TO 1870

Until 1850, the keynote of Catholic policy had been to secure an equitable share of the central Exchequer grants available for school-building. From then till 1902, punctuated by the crisis of the Education Act of 1870, the keynote was to secure an equitable share of the local rates. Although the problem on the surface is financial, the underlying principles of political and religious freedom are marked from time to time; especially as the Government had not itself a coherent educational policy till after 1870. By that date at all events the basic claims of the Catholic minority had become clear, namely that the parent has a natural right to have his child educated according to his conscience, and a civic right that this shall not cost him relatively more than his neighbour. The key to the schools' campaign since 1850 lies in that twin assertion. Gladstone's policy, of " completing " and filling the gaps in that denominational " voluntary system " which, despite its Anglican and Nonconformist and Catholic pioneers, had been unable to provide school places for all the nation's children, was thoroughly in tune with the age: an age which, long after the rise of a " secularist " outlook after 1836, was still " religious " in its view of education. The long line of abortive Bills from 1830 to 1870 shows this " climate " only too clearly. The shoal on which they all foundered was not whether there is an inviolable unity in religious and secular education, but how this unity could best be preserved, by legislation, amid a variety of denominations each at war with the others, and all at war against the entrenched position of the Anglican Establishment. This was a situation which, if it defeated the Catholics in 1870, defeated Forster and Gladstone too.

The Establishment was indeed entrenched. Not only can it claim the lion's share of the work in the days prior to the 1870 State system, but right down to 1902 fully half the country's elementary schools were Anglican foundations. It was a divided Church, as the meeting of the National Society in 1851 showed, with its cleavage between the traditionalists and those who would make concessions in return for Government grants. But its strength appeared triumphant in such reminders as that of Mr. Henley in the Commons in 1858, that " God has pointed out to us in the clearest manner, from Genesis to Revelation, that life is not to be gained through the tree of *knowledge*," and that of Mr. Borthwick in 1846, that

ducation wrongly imparted only has the tendency of
ing a criminal a more clever criminal." Here was the
wer to a rising secularism.

The Nonconformist view crystallised during the period
an "undenominationalism" of which the British and
ign School Society's Memorandum of 1855 is a classic
sition:—

> We have often expressed our opinion, and now
> peat it, that the B. and F. School Society was founded on
> e principle of religious equality as regarding all profess-
> g the Christian faith; that in order to carry out this
> inciple the Scriptures were to be read in all schools, care-
> lly excluding all Catechisms and all Formularies of Faith;
> d that this principle was to be applied in all oral teaching,
> well as to the books read.

the Nonconformist ranks were likewise divided. The
Methodist leader, Jabez Bunting, roundly condemned
education which looks only at the secular interests of an
idual, which looks only at his condition as a member of
society, and does not look at him as a man having an
rtal soul." J. E. Rigg, similarly, who knew Manning
devoted his *Essays for the Times* (1866) to urging a
ninational system of rate-aided schools.

For the politicians, Lord John Russell had given it as
r Majesty's wish " in 1839 that " the youth of the
lom shall be religiously brought up, and that the right
science should be respected." Inside the Education
tment, Sir James Kay-Shuttleworth's *Memorandum on
ar Education* in 1868 proposed the extension of the
ninational system by means of rates; and moderate
n in both Parties supported him. On the eve of the crisis
70 *The Times* declared that " we must in some way
t a really national character to the Denominational
n."

The Catholics alone presented throughout a completely
front. Divided they might be on the liturgy, on church
d as between the newer, " Oratory Catholics," and the
" Garden of the Soul Catholics "; but on the schools'
n they spoke as one.

In 1851, Milner Gibson raised the rates-issue squarely

in the Commons. His own solution was that the school
rate-supported, must be neither secular nor denominationa
neat forecast of what 1870 in fact tried to do). Within
years of this, the heat engendered was such that Lord Sha
bury felt " it had better be called a water-rate, to exting
religious fire in young people."

The great irony is that the principle of *no* denom
tional teaching in schools provided out of public money
shrined in the Act of 1870, and Government policy ever si
had already been negated by law, and was to be again.
there are four statutes relating to publicly-provided schoo
which the State is even charged with the duty of ascertai
the religion of the child, so that he can be sent to a scho
that denomination (These are: the Reformatory and Indus
Schools Acts of 1866, the Act of 1893 for Deaf and D
Schools, and that of 1899 for Defective and Epileptic Child
All this, moreover, to say nothing of State-salaried denom
tional chaplains in the Navy and Army and the prisons.
is denominational teaching clearly " on the rates "[1].

By the time the storm broke, however, much had
pened to consolidate the Catholic position.

The most far-reaching work of " salvaging "
children was that done among the destitute and criminal cl
by Wiseman (till his death in 1865) and Manning.
" leakage " of Catholics into infidelity was seen to be d
two main causes: insufficient places in the Catholic school
reasons of general poverty in this age of voluntary effort
the non-Catholic atmosphere of the Reformatory and I
trial and other schools run by the Home Office and Poor
Guardians for the poor and delinquent. Wiseman and Ma
made this problem of the " underdog " their main educa
concern.

The first Catholic Orphanage was opened in 18
North Hyde, in Middlesex; the first Reformatory in 18
Blyth House, Hammersmith; and the first Industrial S
also in 1855, at Walthamstow. Within two years there
six Catholic Orphanages and 18 Reformatory and Ind

[1] These institutions were the domain of the Home Office, th
Office and (later) the Ministry of Health, and not the Minis
Education—whose " tradition " since 1870 is, therefore, tech
consistent.

Schools, all maintained by voluntary effort. For ten years thereafter the problem was to identify Catholic children in need of these institutions (who were sent automatically to Poor Law schools). It says much for the persistence of the two prelates that, in 1862, Parliament was prevailed upon to vote £500 for R.C. chaplains in seven prisons, and that the Reformatory and Industrial Schools Acts of 1866 laid it down that Catholic delinquents and destitute should be housed in the denominational Catholic institutions, henceforth rate-aided. From then onwards the task—at times a most bitter struggle— was to persuade anti-Catholic Boards of Guardians to transfer Catholic children. Manning was still engaged in this remedial work when he died in 1892. It served to mitigate one aspect of the leakage question; the lack of school places. Voluntary efforts meanwhile secured that, where in 1850 there had been 41,382 Catholic elementary school-places, by 1870 there were 101,556—more than double.

The other cause of leakage was the acute shortage of trained teachers. In 1860 the average salary for Catholic men teachers was £50, and for women £26, figures that were depressed still further by the grant conditions of the Revised Code after 1861. This inevitably deterred the higher pupils from enrolling as pupil-teachers. Moreover, as late as 1867, there was still a prohibition (dating from the 1829 Emancipation Act) against Religious Orders. The men's College at Hammersmith established a lay department as early as 1854; and the prevailing discouragement of women pupil-teachers who found no College available on completion of their apprenticeship was met a year later by the foundation of the Liverpool (Notre Dame de Namur) and the St. Leonards (Holy Child) Colleges. By 1860 there were eight teaching Orders of nuns at work in the country, instructing over 12,000 girls. The Wandsworth Training College (Sacred Heart) followed in 1870.

But in so far as education is, to the Catholic, a unity of the religious and the secular formation in a theological atmosphere, religious instruction was vital. And, by the concordat with the Privy Council in 1847, religious instruction was outside the Inspectors' purview. There was, therefore, no organised means of assessing and improving it; and the *unaided* Catholic schools were, of course, not inspected at all. As early as 1852 the Hierarchy decided to set up their own inspectors of religious instruction, on a diocesan basis, with a system of prizes and rewards, and the Catholic Poor School Committee offered to finance such a scheme. Four years later the plan came into operation, with a Syllabus of Religious Instruction for the pupil teachers, a rota of diocesan specialists, and two Ecclesiastical Inspectors appointed by the Bishops and financed by the Committee. This is the germ of the system of diocesan inspection existing to-day.

All these problems loomed large in Manning's famous Education Pastoral of 1866, on the first anniversary of his consecration as second Archbishop of Westminster: an utterance which *The Times* commended for its freedom from exaggeration. But what loomed largest was the question of cost. Manning, therefore, followed up the pastoral letter at once by establishing the Westminster Diocesan Education Fund—the first of a series of " Crisis Funds " that is not yet ended. It was to cater for those without schooling; those who had broken the law and were in schools for delinquents; the 1,000 Westminster children in Workhouses; and Catholic elementary education in general. Within a year £7,855 had been raised, and 20 new day schools started.

Such was the *tempo* during the first half of Thomas William Allies' secretaryship of the Poor School Committee (1853-90). Allies, an Oxford Movement convert, and the right-arm of the Hierarchy, is undoubtedly the greatest of the Catholic lay leaders in the entire century. He ran the policy of the Poor School Committee on three maxims: " There can be no sound education without religion; As is the teacher so is the child; As is the trainer so is the teacher."

This was said at a time when only one Catholic child in three was in a Catholic school, when most of those attending were under 8, and when only a third even of these attended for more than a year. Its long-term importance becomes apparent against the secularist background of the discussions on the Butler Bill in 1943-44. Meanwhile the Revised Code of 1861, in relating curriculum-grants to the Three R's only, put a premium on " no straining after higher classes, as the grant will not depend on them "; and, by discouraging entry into the teaching profession, it threatened to sap the whole of the laborious Catholic consolidation.

All the more need, then, for Government action to create a national system. And, given the known desire of Gladstone to supplement rather than supplant the historic Voluntary System, the dominant question was bound to be the kind of religious teaching to be given in any publicly financed schools.

Public opinion in 1870 fell broadly into four camps. The National Education League was openly secularist, and the enemy of the Voluntary Schools; the National Education Union, as an Anglican organ, wanted the Voluntary System retained, supplemented and rate-aided; the moderate Nonconformists (led by Dr. Henry Allen) inclined to the same view, but they were a minority; the Catholics insisted unequivocally on a Voluntary System fully rate-aided.

The Government's own view was by now clear. W. E. Forster (the Vice-President of the Council and, till 1849, himself a secularist) was determined " not to destroy anything in the existing system which is good." His initial Memorandum (October, 1869) accordingly rejected the secularist solution. But he also rejected the completely denominational solution of the Anglicans and Catholics on the ground that, even with rate-aid, they lacked the administrative and other resources to compel a really national system. He was fully alive to the ethical implication of rates: " It would not be fair to tax a Roman Catholic to teach Methodism . . . (but) it would not be unfair to levy a rate on a Roman Catholic for the *secular* education of a Methodist." Gladstone's view, as Prime Minister, is best seen in his comment on this Forster Memorandum:

> Why not adopt frankly the principle that the State or the local community should provide the secular teaching, and either leave the option to the ratepayers to go beyond this *sine qua non*, if they think fit, within the limits of the Conscience Clause, or else simply leave the parties themselves to find Bible and other religious education from voluntary sources?

When the Bill was introduced (February 17th) it did not rule out rate-aid by local authorities to the denominational schools. There was to be a period of grace, moreover, for the Voluntary bodies to provide schoolplaces for everybody, and thereafter new schools publicly provided by local School Boards would fill the gaps.

This meant that, out of 178,000 Catholic children needing schools, and with only 100,000 already being schooled, some 78,000 (44 per cent.) might now be lost, by being compelled to attend Board Schools, unless schools could be created for them within the period of grace, after which building-grants would cease. Manning issued a memorandum, which took " Christian education as the *genus* and denominational as the *species*," in the hope of making possible a joint denominational stand. Allies added that, if compulsory schooling were necessary (and he insisted that it was), that only made a denominational system an " absolute right," any alternative being an affront to parental conscience.

> The moment this truth is made clear, the question of primary education is settled for Catholics. " Catholic schools for Catholic children " must be their motto.

There is the origin of a famous formula. Catholic activity in terms of it was strenuous from the moment the Bill was introduced. The Catholic Poor School Committee met nine times, petitioned the Commons, and interviewed the Catholic M.P.s and the Government four times.

But the Catholic case was heavily handicapped. All the Bishops were abroad, attending the Vatican Council in Rome. Nor was any plea advanced for Catholic schools to " contract-out " of the general terms of the Bill, as Forster expected them to do (and as the Jews in fact did). More lamentable still, the first personal contact between the Bishops and the Poor School Committee occurred on the day the Bill received the Royal Assent (August 9th).

Manning had in the meantime kept up a spirited correspondence with Gladstone from Rome, trying to head him off from a solution of " common (undenominational) schools," lest the English Catholics, like the Americans already, be forced to eschew a national system of which, in their hearts, they longed to become part. " I do not see," he wrote,

> why the school-rate should not be granted in proportion to private efforts by enactment of Parliament. In the last three years we have opened in London 30 new schools, and have

gathered out of the streets 3,000 children. Give me time, and just proportionate help, and there will not be one of our children without a school . . . . (March 20th).

By March 19th the Catholic claim had crystallised out under five heads: public support, where the parents asked and the number of children warranted a school; increased building-grants; power to lease and hire and mortgage; a longer period of grace; and care in the definition of " parent " so as to protect the child to the utmost. The famous " Crisis Fund " of June 13th (which raised ultimately £390,000 and created 71,518 school-places) was launched on that basis. But the opposition of secularists, who could not suffer the Established Church to reap so much rate-aid, and those who feared that a precedent of rate-aid for denominational teaching in England must be extended also to Ireland, proved too strong. On June 16th the Prime Minister told the Commons that the new School Boards should give no aid to the Voluntary Schools, but that the Government would itself proffer them increased Privy Council grants.

Then came the " Crisis Day " (June 30th), when the Cowper-Temple clause was adopted. This was the clause which forbade in Board Schools the teaching of " religious catechism or religious formulary distinctive of any particular denomination," thereby declaring for " undenominational " religious instruction. Disraeli, echoing words of Lord Brougham as long ago as 1820, had already said of this clause (June 20th) that the teacher nevertheless

cannot teach, explain and enforce the Holy Scriptures when he reads . . . . without drawing some inferences and conclusions, and what will these inferences and conclusions be but dogmas? . . . You are inventing and establishing a new sacerdotal class.

Cowper-Temple himself said that: —

the exclusion of catechisms and formularies left the opinions and faith of the teacher untouched, and dealt only with lesson-books which bore upon the title-page indications of their origin.

But subsequent wistful opinions that the clause, therefore, did allow denominational teaching have been answered by eighty years of practice, reinforced by the high improbability that those who " excluded documents intended to admit doctrine.' The undenominationalism of the Cowper-Temple clause is accordingly still to-day the kernel of Government policy, and a major reason for the enactments of 1944 on the same subject. What the clause did was to render impossible any relations between the Voluntary Schools and the Board Schools—thereby wrecking Gladstone's original plan.   His last word (on the Third Reading, July 22nd) is worth recording:—

> It was impossible for us to join in the language, or to adopt the tone, which was conscientiously and consistently taken by some members of the House, who look upon these Voluntary Schools, having generally a denominational character, as admirable passing expedients, fit to be tolerated for a time . . . . but wholly unsatisfactory as to their main purpose, and therefore to be supplanted by something they think better.   That . . . . has never been the theory of the Government.

" Our best course," wrote Manning to Ullathorne in September, when the Bill had become law, " is to co-operate to the utmost of our power," though " the Boards may destroy our lesser schools by reporting them to be insufficient or inefficient."   But he held the Act to be a breach with long centuries of Christian education, a divider of the nation in that one-third of the children would be educated as Christians and two-thirds " indefinitely," and a blow at the very root of England's Christian inspiration.   Nor was he alone: Gladstone himself spoke tartly of " the popular imposture of undenominational instruction."   Allies, looking to the future, impressed on the Hierarchy the now urgent need for trained teachers, the short-sightedness of using any untrained teachers because they were cheaper, the obligation to keep the schools efficient, and the need for a *national* Catholic policy.

> As the State deals in its unity with the whole mass of the population, the Church must do the like—consider the needs of the whole body, and call upon the whole body to supply them. . . .   But it is not in human nature, not even in regenerate human nature, to lend such co-operation without being proportionally trusted in the distribution of these funds. . . .   It is the more easy for this trust to be

given to the Catholic laity because, by the very principles of their Faith, there can be no interference on their part with the teaching which concerns faith and morals (November).

The Education Act, as finally passed, bore on the Denominational Schools, then, as follows: The Timetable Conscience Clause provided for the withdrawal of children from religious instruction at the request of parents; the Cowper-Temple Clause meant that denominational children in the Board Schools would find no unity of secular and doctrinal instruction; the year of grace was reduced to six months; building grants were to cease at the end of the year; and rate-aid was withheld altogether. Hence the unequal Dual System of the newer (undenominational) schools, entirely provided and maintained out of public funds, and the older (denominational) schools, provided by voluntary subscription and helped only by Privy Council grants.

III. FROM 1870 TO 1902

Except on one occasion, immediately after 1870, when there was Catholic criticism of Manning for " co-operating " with the new Act, and because he restricted the crisis-money, raised in 1871, to " those schools which have accepted the Government's terms," the Catholic education front was solid. The Cardinal's own views soon stiffened, indeed, when T. B. Huxley and the secularists came fully into the open. His Pastoral of 1872, on *National Education and Parental Rights,* is the most forthright of the long series he was to issue before his death. Education, he said, " is the field on which I should most wish to fight a general action. A large part of the English would be with us, or would not fight against us."

The most enduring of the portents that appeared during these final years before the victory over rate-aid, could be seen quite early on from the relations between local School Boards and the denominations. Manchester is a not untypical example. Its School Board comprised representatives of three parties. But, within five years of the Act, a compromise had been arrived at between the Unsectarians and the Anglicans, whereby a modicum of Natural Religion should be taught in the

Board Schools. In so far as this " broke down the barrier of principle between them," it had two consequences; that there were now virtually only two parties on the Board (the four Catholics, the 11 others), and that the Protestant denominations began to surrender their schools to the Board on the strength of the compromise. Generalised over many parts of the country, this meant that by 1883 no fewer than 478 Voluntary Schools had been so transferred, and over 1,200 by 1895 (though, of course, none of them Catholic). Here is the beginning of what has now become, since 1924, the " Agreed Syllabus " policy of the non-Catholics at large. The other direct result was that, shorn of support by their Protestant colleagues, the Catholics were sometimes at the mercy of unfriendly School Boards, and found their proposed schools vetoed as " unsuitable " or " unnecessary."

More immediate and universal was the incidence of inequitable financial help: the rates. " An educational rate raised from the whole people," said Manning, " ought to be returned to the whole people in a form or forms of education of which all may partake "; whereas the 1870 rate was " sectarian," given to only one class of schools, representing only one form of opinion, pressing unequally on rich and poor, and carried with the help of Nonconformists who had only recently denounced Church Rates as persecution. His own solution was that of financing education entirely out of taxes; and if this were resisted as using public money for religious teaching, why had the critics tolerated that very thing ever since 1833? The prevailing system, declared the Hierarchy in 1885, was " using *two* measures in appraising the value of the work done " (grants; grants plus rates). With education compulsory, this penalised poor parents; and it " threatened the extinction " of the Voluntary Schools. Allies' replies to the Cross Commission in 1886 made it clear, moreover, that the Catholics were adhering to Manning's policy of defending *all* the Voluntary Schools. Would he allow Protestant children to have a school at the public expense? Certainly—" I only claim what all may claim; I stand upon a common ground."

In this unequal setting, the Voluntary School population nevertheless increased to over two millions in 14 years while that of the Board Schools reached less than a million. Academically the products were best, moreover, in the Catholic schools, whose record of " complete passes " each year, till 1875, was the highest of all (72.14 per cent.). But the Board Schools drew 17s. per child from the rates, to the Voluntary Schools' 6s. 10d. from charity. Hence a marked poverty in buildings, equipment, teachers' salaries and size of classes. Hence, too, a disparity in the children schooled " free " because penniless (in 1884: Anglicans 2.6 per cent., School Boards 4.2, Catholics 13.1). And all the time, a Voluntary School, when built at private expense, was at once rated for the upkeep of the Board School. The phrase " voluntary subscription " becomes a mockery.

What irked most in all this was that, despite the struggle and the examination results, the Catholic Managers, in having to watch the pennies, and the Saturday night street collections, were reaping a public reputation (which they have hardly lost yet) for being against *material* advances in education. But this was bound to continue as long as the four main impositions endured. These were: the rating of Voluntary Schools (above); the fact that the State grant (maximum 17s. 6d.) was related to the total of voluntary subscriptions (and thereby made these, is effect, compulsory); the impossibility of securing a grant where the local School Board said *it* could accommodate the denominational children; and the loss of time and wages involved by indigent parents having to apply to the Boards of Guardians personally, in the daytime, for remission of fees.

It was because these burdens were common to all denominations that Herbert Vaughan, both as Bishop of Salford, and as Manning's successor at Westminster after 1892, tried intermittently to mobilise a united Christian front. When he founded the Voluntary Schools' Association in February, 1884, he made it expressly interdenominational. " The Catholic schools may be the iron head to the spear, but the iron head will make but a poor weapon unless it have the weight of the wooden shaft behind it." He summoned as recruits all who believed in " definite and dogmatic religious instruction in schools " and were ready to demand a 25 per cent. rise in grants and the removal of the four evils just dis-

cussed. Consistently with this he resolutely resisted attempts
to buy off the Catholics by separate treatment—as in the
Minority Report of the Cross Commission in 1888. And in his
third year at Westminster (1895), he upheld the Nonconformists in their protests at having—in hundreds of localities—to
send their children to an Anglican school, because the ratepayers were forbidden by law to provide one that suited the
Nonconformist conscience. Full public support, incidentally,
he had not, as yet, asked for his own Catholic schools. But
the Nonconformist acceptance of undenominationalism, and
the divisions among the Anglicans, made a united Christian
front impossible; while the Agreed Syllabus policy, since
developed, has now removed all hope of one.

All these issues came to a head together in the Cross
Commission Report (on the working of the Act of 1870) in
1888: albeit the Government was to do nothing in the way of
essential remedies till 1902. Cardinal Manning was a member
of the Commission, and T. W. Allies and five other Catholics
gave evidence before it.

In the previous fifty years, the Catholic body had
created 680 elementary schools and three training colleges.
The grant-aided schools had risen from 28, in 1850, to 328
(1,862 departments); their population from 38,000 to 173,000;
and the annual Privy Council grant to £194,000. But though
the maximum building-grant had been raised in 1870 from
one-third to a half (as a consolation for loss of rate-aid), rising
costs had offset this to the extent that the cost per child in
Voluntary Schools could amount to only £1 14s. 7d. per year,
as against the Board Schools' £2 1s. 6½d. There had to be 20
per cent. remission of fees in the Catholic schools through
poverty; for the Board Schools were now admitting the middle-
class, and leaving the " arabs " to the denominations. And,
as a consequence of Payment by Results, the Catholic recruit-
ment of pupil-teachers in the last five years had fallen from
1,632 to 1,125. So precious were teachers now, that the Principal of Hammersmith Training College explained that he
kept in touch with students when they left him, and knew
exactly where every past student now was. Even so, there was
only one male teacher to every four women—an explanation of
why the " lay " girls' schools were, in fact, the better.

It is true that these disabilities could be removed over-
t, as Anglican and Nonconformists were finding, by hand-
the schools to the School Boards. But this could be done
' at a price which the Catholics could not even contem-
e—the abandonment of that organic Catholic school
mosphere '' which could not be guaranteed except by the
y contact of believing teacher with believing child.

The evidence, and the manifest devotion of the Volun-
Schools, impressed the Cross Commission to the extent
they recommended, as follows:—

183. That there is no reason why the principle of
oluntary Schools receiving annual aid from the rates should
t be extended, and rate aid, in respect of their secular
iciency, should not be given to Voluntary Schools (as it
now given to Industrial and Reformatory Schools), with-
t the imposition of the Cowper-Temple clause, which,
der the Act of 1870, affects those Schools only which are
ovided and supported entirely by the rates. . . .
We should regard any separation of the teacher from
igion as injurious to the morals and secular training of
scholars.

But the only immediate implementation was to make
entary education free, by the Act of 1891. This the
olics had hitherto feared, believing that an abolition of
would apply only to the Board Schools, and, therefore,
ps kill their own.

In so far, though, as there are two sides to every pic-
it has to be recognised that more could have been spent
atholic schools by temporarily spending less on churches.
policy that had made the first foundations possible, after
had been to build the school first, and use the school-
l as a church *ad interim*. Further, less dispersal of funds
duplication of building-costs might have been secured by
ater centralisation. This also would have conserved teach-
ower.

While the Cross Commission is thus a landmark in the
y of Catholic education for a variety of reasons, the chief
n is that from then on the Catholic educational claim
to grow towards the cry for full and equal *maintenance*,
ually achieved in 1902. When the *Westminster Gazette*

pointed out, in 1895, that by now only 30 per cent. of the c
came from subscriptions, *The Tablet* retorted that the soo
the term " Voluntary " could be forfeited altogether,
better: —

> The single thing we want is equality of educatio
> opportunity for all parents, whether they value defi
> religious instruction or not.

An intensive series of pronouncements by the Hierar
had by now been in full swing since 1892. The Bishops ca
specifically for a fair share of the rates; they appealed to
Natural Law as demanding that schools should be managed
persons who had the confidence of the parents; and they s
Cardinal Vaughan and the Duke of Norfolk to ask Lord Sa
bury, as Prime Minister, whether the day of discrimina
and palliatives should not now give place to the day of just
It was at this point (1895) that the internal divisions am
the Anglicans slowed down the pace, and, while the Natio
Society itself adopted a resolution claiming rate-aid, the A
bishop of Canterbury deplored the policy as " dangerous
and an Anglican deputation to the Prime Minister deprived
Catholic spearhead of its shaft.

This is mainly why the last two Government meas
before the close of the century were still only palliatives.
John Gorst's Bill of 1896, which would have gone so fa
to allow " reasonable arrangements " to be made for
aided religious instruction in Board Schools at the par
request (thereby torpedoing the Cowper-Temple cla
failed. The Education Act of 1897, which did pass, aboli
the 17s. 6d. grant-limit and the rating of Voluntary Sc
(as well as Payment by Results), but introduced no new
ciple; and Cardinal Vaughan took it " on account."

Of immense importance for the future was the elec
in the same year, of Fr. William F. Brown, of Southwar
the School Board for London. This brought into publi
as great a figure among the clergy as Allies was among
laity. For Fr. Brown (subsequently Bishop of Pella) wa
many years to personify the " Catholic Schools' questi
in the eyes of the whole kingdom.

Cardinal Vaughan's last word on the old system

one of disgust. In 1899 an Education Department circular threatened that, where a school's voluntary contributions were " less than might be reasonably expected," the grant would be reduced. It added that the contributions could be kept up by greater attention to " collections, bazaars, entertainments and the like." A system, commented the Cardinal, in which schools could only survive " on a basis of bazaars " was a *reductio ad absurdum*; and its days were already numbered.

The Hierarchy canvassed successively two positive propositions to replace it. The first, in 1891, was the one actually adopted ten years later. It involved the abolition of the School Boards, and the transfer of school-control to the new County, etc., Councils. This was elaborated in the *School Guardian* in January, 1895, and is claimed to have influenced Balfour in drafting his Bill. The other plan, in 1901, was to introduce into England the 72nd section of the Scottish Education Act of 1872, which had left it to the Scottish School Boards to give different kinds of religious instruction according to the wishes of parents (usually, by having denominational teachers in proportion to the children on the roll). The suggestion marks the first step towards a belated striving by English Catholics after educational solutions which, despite risks, their Scots brethren had accepted while still open.

Mr. A. J. Balfour's mind was already made up by 1896, as a result of the abortive Gorst Bill. In general, the prevailing educational chaos, as between " elementary " and " secondary," must be reduced to order. In particular, the denominational schools must be saved from ruin. " The Board School . . . . is, and ought to be, merely the supplement to Voluntary Schools when Voluntary Schools fail to do their duty." Since, however, the Cabinet's first draft Bill (in December, 1901) confused the issues of aid and control, the real architect of the Bill was the Permanent Secretary of the 1899 Board of Education, Robert Morant, who realised, from the Anglican and Nonconformist opposition to the Gorst Bill, that no Government could repeal the Cowper-Temple Clause and live. The Balfour Bill eventually took nine months to pass through Parliament. The Prime Minister undertook, as our duty, as far as we can, to see that every parent gets the kind of denominational teaching that he desires—

a principle that he quoted to great effect in countering the
objections of the Nonconformists led by Dr. John Clifford.
The Bishop of Pella afterwards said that, given the heat of
the 1902 debates, only a vast Bill dedicated (as this one was)
to a complete reform of the entire educational system could
at the same time contrive to help the Voluntary Schools.

The Act, as finally passed, put the Voluntary Schools
" on the rates." Provided by the denominations as to sites
and buildings and structural repairs, they were thenceforth to
be maintained financially by the new Local Education Authorities. Their teachers were to be appointed by the School
Managers, subject to a veto on educational grounds by the
L.E.A.; the secular education was to be controlled by the
L.E.A., the religious by the Managers (who were to comprise
four denominational and two L.E.A. representatives).

In securing this signal result, the Hierarchy had the
support of John Redmond's Irish Party in the Commons,
despite Allies' taunt that the English Catholics did not want
help from " traitors to their Queen." J. H. Haldane and Lord
Hugh Cecil were also towers of strength, the former wanting
the Voluntary Schools mended, since they could not be ended,
the latter abhorring any solution that would give the child " a
clear field to the negative movement which we say is the real
peril of the future." The Nonconformists protested bitterly at
" Rome on the rates." Cardinal Vaughan replied that the
schools and the teachers " are ours—we paid for them "; that
Catholic teachers would have to teach somewhere, and so why
not where wanted? and that too much ought not to be read
into the word " Managers," since those functionaries would
have nothing to do but appoint teachers. *The Tablet* declared
that " the assertion of this great principle of the fundamental
equality of *all* the public elementary schools in the country is
a matter of such far-reaching consequences that it dwarfs all
the details of the Bill." The Cardinal agreed that " we are
not likely ever to get a more satisfactory settlement." Twenty-
five years later, Cardinal Bourne qualified this:—

> There was *no bargain*. We had to accept what we
> could get. We were told that it was quite impossible to give
> us any further assistance from the taxes, and that we must

come under the control of the L.E.A.s to get help from the rates.

Hence, in 1902, the claim to rate-aid was met, though the claim to full equality was not. The record of those fifty-two years is explicable only in terms of the tolerant bearing of English public opinion, then not yet " post-Christian," when really informed on an issue it believes to be fundamental; and of that unanimity on such an issue which only the Catholics, united by their transcendental allegiance, could show. The record explains, in its turn, one curious historical fact. It has been said that the Catholic authorities always preferred not to make themselves responsible for any detailed scheme, but to make their net demands and leave the Government of the day to meet them. Subject to the exceptions we have noted, this is true. But, with the English Catholics by 1902 still a small minority, and with no real educational system in exist-ence till after that date, no more comprehensive policy was possible.

IV. FROM 1902 TO 1939

The Dual System had been " ratified," and accord-ingly the Catholic claim outstanding was now for full equality within the new national system of education—a claim that would now include the secondary school field, with which this chapter is not concerned. But, until the War of 1914, every-thing hinged on attempts to reverse the clock by eliminating the Dual System altogether.

The spearhead of these was the Cliffordite Noncon-formist passive-resistance after 1902, which took the form of refusing to pay rates towards Anglican or Catholic religious teaching—to the extent of over 20,000 summonses and dis-traints by the end of two years. Though this campaign never enjoyed widespread popular support—since most ordinary people failed to appreciate the grounds of a resistance limited to rates and not including taxes—it profoundly influenced the Catholic prospects in two ways.

There was, first, a policy of killing the Denominational Schools by " administering " them out of existence, in defiance of the Act of 1902. In 1905-06, the Merionethshire County

Council, for example, refused statutory grants to the Voluntary Schools until penalised by the Board of Education to the same amount; the Catholic school at Keynham Barton was told (illegally) to provide its own furniture; the West Riding County Council truncated teachers' salaries for the time spent in religious instruction—till it was called to order on appeal to the High Court; and attempts were made to oblige Denominational Training Colleges to admit applicants of any creed or none.

The other Free Church threat was openly legislative—the four Education Bills of the Liberal Government of Campbell-Bannerman in 1906-08. The Prime Minister himself had declared for " perfect freedom of conscience, and equal treatment." The President of the Board of Education, Augustine Birrell, was likewise personally friendly to the Anglicans and Catholics. But Nonconformist pressure made the Birrell Bill of April 1906 a death-knell to the non-provided schools. Only Council Schools were to be recognised by the State; the L.E.A.s were to appoint all teachers; rate-aided religious teaching was to be undenominational; and the Voluntary Schools should be transferred to the local authorities—even perhaps by compulsion. Certain provisions, which seemed to offer the Catholics a less speedy death, prevented any united Christian front (even had Cardinal Bourne wished for one). It was left to the Lords to amend the Bill so drastically as to kill it, thus saving an estimated Catholic loss of over one half the schools.

The attempt of Birrell's successor, Reginald McKenna (a Cliffordite), was to secure the same end in 1907, under cover of a Money Bill (which the Lords had no power to amend). When this failed, he put up in 1908 a national, undenominational system from which the Catholics and Anglicans could contract-out by forfeiting their share of the rates—unless their school was the only one in the neighbourhood—in which case it would be expropriated. The Catholics estimated that this would involve their having to keep their schools up to minimum legal efficiency on one-third the income of the Council Schools. The final attempt reverted to the line of treating the Anglicans and Nonconformists together, and the Catholics separately. When its financial provisions were published, they provoked an outcry, led separately by Cardinal Bourne and the Archbishop of Canterbury, and the Bill was dropped.

These were the highlights of the pre-war years. Altogether some twenty proposals were made before 1914 for ending the Dual System. One local attempt, at Bradford, where certain Catholics in 1905 went so far as to agree to the appointment of their teachers by a joint committee of the City Council and the school's trustees, dumbfounded the Catholic Education Council. The most far-reaching of the paper schemes, sponsored by Catholics, was the " Manchester Concordat " of 1910 (the work of Mgr. Joseph Tynan), based on the following spirited principles: —

> If liberty, economy and efficiency have to ride the same educational horse, two must necessarily sit behind— Liberty has first place in this scheme.

The whole output together serves to concentrate attention on the three crucial questions involved in any ultimate solution of England's Dual System. One is curricular—Is religion the core of education, or only a subject? One is administrative— Shall there be national control or local autonomy? The third is political and theological—Is the obligation to educate the parents' or the State's?

Though the English Catholics have been behindhand in policy and promptitude since 1902, their answer on these three questions was never in doubt. It can be gleaned from Cardinal Bourne's annual addresses to the National Catholic Congress after 1903, and from his Pastorals, until formulated in the Declaration of the whole Hierarchy in 1929.

The foreground is seen in the multiplication of Catholic Action organs: Catholic Education Council in 1905, incorporation of the Crusade of Rescue in the same year, Catholic Social Guild in 1909, Catholic Workers' College at Oxford in 1921, University Catholic Federation in the same year (on a national, not a diocesan basis), and many others. The background is the episcopal pronouncements. Cardinal Bourne repeated in 1903 that " those who regard a sound dogmatic teaching as the foundation of all true education " should not have " less favourable treatment " than their fellow-citizens; in 1905, that the Anglicans might, in time, make their own honourable

peace with the State, and leave the Catholics to stand alone;
in 1906, that the teacher represents the parent and not the
State, and that the State " is only the representative and embodiment of the parental mandate "; in 1911, that while " no
claim has been made, or ever will be made, for the public
remuneration of definite religious teaching," it was iniquitous
to make Catholics (and others) provide their own sites and
school buildings; in 1912, that the teacher is the key to education—" and the long chain of organisation which separates
the teacher very far from the parent does not weaken the
fact." The more he clarified the position, the more he felt that
the Catholics would stand henceforth alone. So much so, that
when Anglicans and Nonconformists together sought his
collaboration in a joint *demarche* during the First World War
he declined—for between the Catholic and the non-Catholic
connotation of " definite " religious teaching there is a gulf.
The days of united Christian fronts on education had, unhappily, gone; they had never indeed arrived.

The Hierarchy's Declaration of 1929, which marks an
epoch, has not since been surpassed : —

1. It is no part of the *normal* function of the State to *teach*.
2. The State is entitled to see that citizens receive due
   education sufficient to enable them to discharge the
   duties of citizenship in its various degrees.
3. The State ought, therefore, to encourage every form of
   sound educational endeavour, and may take means to
   safeguard the efficiency of education.
4. To parents whose economic means are insufficient . . . .
   it is the duty of the State to furnish the necessary means
   . . . . from the common funds arising out of the taxation
   of the whole country. But in so doing the State must not
   interfere with parental responsibility, nor hamper the
   reasonable liberty of parents in their choice of a school
   for their children. Above all, where the people are not
   all of one creed, there must be no differentiation on the
   ground of religion.
5. Where there is need of greater school accommodation,
   the State may, in default of other agencies, intervene to
   supply it; but it may do so only " in default of, or in
   substitution for, and to the extent of, the responsibility
   of the parents." . . .

6. The teacher is always acting *in loco parentis,* never *in loco civitatis,* though the State, to safeguard its citizenship, may take reasonable care to see that teachers are efficient.

7. Thus a teacher never is and never can be a civil servant . . . . Whatever authority he may possess to teach and control children, and to claim their respect and obedience, comes to him from God, through the parents, and not through the State, except in so far as the State is acting on behalf of the parents.

Meanwhile, post-war educational reconstruction had begun in terms of the Fisher Act of 1918. This left the Dual System untouched (though an abortive Bill in 1920 would have had the L.E.A.s appoint all teachers). And if the Fisher Act's great innovation of Day Continuation Schools failed in the country at large, the Catholic Day Continuation School set up under the London County Council (St. Vincent's) managed to prosper. The year 1918 is much more significant for its Scottish precedent.

The Scottish " Concordat " (section 18 of the Education [Scotland] Act of 1918) was in large part the work of the Bishop of Pella, whom the Pope had appointed Apostolic Visitor to Scotland in the previous year. Building on the natural religiosity of the Scottish nation, his negotiations with Sir Robert Munro and Sir John Struthers brought off a definite solution of the Scottish Catholic Schools' question, and completed a development begun in 1872. The fundamental issue was precisely the same as in England. On the one hand, the local authorities wanted " administrative dualism " of control to go; on the other hand, the Bishops, in order to preserve the Catholic character of their schools, wanted " religious dualism " to stay—of which the only acceptable guarantee would be that of " Catholic teachers for Catholic schools." The Concordat satisfied both parties, by provisions for appointing the teachers whereby the religious authority was first to be satisfied on religious grounds before the local authority appointed; and, in return, the Catholic schools were transferred to the L.E.A.s, and the Catholic unequal financial burden of the past disappeared. This administrative framework has since been extended to each new development in educational progress.

At the time, the Scots Catholics were dubious: as also were their Bishops. In the end the Holy See, by its only intervention in the entire century, instructed them to accept. The settlement is now regarded as the best in the world. But the question as to whether the *English* Catholics could also have secured this " Concordat," in 1918, is largely idle. Apart from the difference of scale—not 500 but over 1,000 English Catholic schools, and with their distribution far less homogeneous than in the Catholic " belts " in Scotland—the English Catholics had no positive policy. They declined to consider any change in the 1902 system of appointing teachers; but, for the rest, the Bishops were known to be divided and, in point of fact, the issue was not raised in England. Despite a successful motion in the Commons on it in 1923, by T. P. O'Connor and Sidney Webb, it was not till 1931 that the Catholic Education Council declared in favour of a " Scottish Concordat " for England, and that Cardinal Bourne expressed a willingness to consider a change in the method of appointing teachers. The only alternative afterwards put up—the Cardinal's interesting project for " Universal Scholarships " in 1926—came to nothing.

The other significant trend apparent all this time was the steady disappearance of the non-Catholic Denominational Schools, as a result of the device of " Agreed Syllabuses of Religious Instruction " begun in Cambridgeshire in 1924. Here was a bargain which, on Anglican and Free Church and local authority premises, was scrupulous and satisfactory. The local authority negotiated a syllabus with these bodies, and agreed to teach it in all Council Schools; whereupon the denominational Schools were handed over, and the Protestant financial burden disappeared. Hence it is that, whereas in 1870 every elementary school prior to the Gladstone Act was a Denominational School, and the Anglican and Free Church Schools stood in 1902 at 12,202, they subsequently fell to 11,703 in 1926, 9,319 in 1935, and 9,098 on the outbreak of war in 1939. In 1948 the total school-*departments* were; Anglican 9,098, Free Church 117. This explains the inevitable loss of support for the Catholic case among other Christians.

It also points the contrast with the Catholic curve itself; for, unable to accept the principle that there can be an " agreed minimum " body of doctrine (which is heresy), the Catholics have gone on building. The figures over the same period are: 1,066 (1902), 1,230(1935), 1,266 (1939) and 1,828 *departments* in 1948. But to-day, while Denominational Schools are still half the total schools of the land, they house less than a third of the children—a fact which influenced the National Government in 1944. Moreover, unless the trends alter, the Protestant Schools will now virtually die out, leaving in the country two mutually-exclusive systems, one Catholic, one secular: as Lord Hugh Cecil had prophesied in 1902, Allies in 1883, Manning in 1870 and W. G. Ward a century ago.

The 'twenties, however, were preoccupied with *immediate* costs. By 1926 the cost of a Catholic school-place, which in 1870 had been £1 5s. 5d., and in 1918 £10, was £23 10s. Rising post-war prices, and the need for larger, as well as more schools, especially secondary, and above all in new suburbs, were harrowing the clergy universally. Then came the 1926 Hadow Report on *The Education of the Adolescent*.

The Hierarchy acclaimed its bold proposal that the old era of separate, parallel, elementary and secondary systems should be superseded by a new age of unified, end-on, schools, with a diversified education after the age of eleven, according to criteria which Mr. R. A. Butler was later to call " the Three A's—age, ability, aptitude." But the cost of reorganising all schools on these lines would clearly cripple the Denominations. Between 1914 and 1930 the Catholic body had built 96 schools, with 60,000 places, at a capital expenditure of £1,700,000. Half that number, built and enlarged five years later, were to cost £4½ million.

The Labour Government of 1930 appreciated the impossible position, and endeavoured to mitigate it. Sir Charles Trevelyan offered grants to all grades of Denominational Schools for the reorganisation of buildings under the Hadow Scheme. But, in return, the teachers were to be appointed by the local authority, subject to certain teachers being " reserved " to the Denominations. This the Catholics rejected; an amendment by a Catholic M.P. (John Scurr) was carried against the Government, and the Bill was thrown out by the Lords.

There is a colossal irony in this. For it was soon *afterwards* that Cardinal Bourne declared himself ready to consider modifications in the method of appointing teachers (Lent, 1931), and the relief ultimately given (by the 1936 Act) was on worse terms than those of the Trevelyan Bill, since it was confined to senior schools. Once again the Catholics had been too timid and too late.

The 1936 Act empowered the local authorities to make grants of up to three-quarters of the cost of reorganising Denominational Schools. In return, the L.E.A. was to appoint all except the " reserved " teachers, and there was to be Agreed Syllabus religion for those non-Catholics desiring it. But the grant was permissive only, not mandatory; it was for senior schools only, whereas the greatest need was for junior school reorganisation; and only proposals agreed and sent to the Board of Education within three years would be considered. The alternative, of course, would be *un*reorganised Catholic senior schools, and the consequent loss of their children, who would gravitate to the better-equipped Council Schools. Archbishop Hinsley, who had succeeded Cardinal Bourne a year earlier, decided to accept the offer gratefully, and work to it without stint, to preserve Catholic primary schools, which now held not 1 in 17 of the country's children, as in 1902, but 1 in 14, with 532 secondary schools, the whole staffed from the output of nine training colleges.

Within the next two years, five Catholic proposals had gone through (to 11 Anglican), and the only English borough without a Catholic school was Morley (near Leeds). On the other hand, nearly one-fifth of the Catholic children in the country were not in Catholic schools at all. Reorganisation in rural areas, involving the creation of Central Schools, was retarded by distance, and transport complications, and threatened to disrupt parish life. In the towns the pace was faster. Many authorities (including London) were willing to give the full 75 per cent. grant; some others, 50 per cent.; Lancashire gave a lead in its assurance that head teachers would be " reserved " and the rest be proportionate to the roll; and Surrey a lead by drawing up short-lists of applicants, and leaving the final choice to the Managers. The first Agreement arrived at was that with Southport in January, 1936.

Some authorities offered grants, but no transport (e.g. Warwick), others refused any grant at all (e.g. Llanelly, Swansea, Caernarvonshire). The one notorious case was Liverpool, where the City Council refused grants, and the excitement was intensified when Archbishop Downey, with the fate of 42,402 Catholic Liverpool children at stake, called on his flock to make it an issue at the forthcoming local elections. The result was a resounding defeat for the Catholics, but the Board of Education stepped in (July, 1938)—as it had done in 1908 in Merionethshire—and withheld £180,000 of its grant to the Liverpool authority. Eventually, by means of a private Act, a solution was reached whereby the Archbishop *rented* Schools from the L.E.A.

By the time the war broke out in September 1939, Catholic school-department reorganisation had reached 44.8 per cent., to Anglican 45.7 per cent. This compared unfavourably with the Council Schools (71.7 per cent.). And no fewer than 399 Catholic school buildings, which had been pioneers in their day but were now decrepit, were still on the Board of Education's " Black List " as late as 1942. The war, however, curtailed more reorganisation than this; for only the nine Catholic schemes approved (out of 289 submitted under the 1936 Act) went ahead, as the guillotine date had been reached.

The end of an age had already been reached. During this period, from 1902 to 1939, too, one Catholic leader passed and another arrived. Sir John Gilbert, the successor of T. W. Allies as Secretary of the Poor School Committee and Education Council, and at the same time Chairman of the London County Council, died in 1934; while in Cardinal Arthur Hinsley the Church, and indeed the whole country, was to find a champion as spiritually young as he was physically venerable.

V. FROM 1939 TO 1944

The aim of the Education Bill of 1944 was to complete, at last, a coherent national system of primary, secondary and further education, as sketched in the Hadow and Spens

Reports. This inevitably meant that the denominational question would henceforth exist in secondary, as well as primary
schools; for the line between these was henceforth to be one
merely of age, through the transfer of *all* children at eleven
to varying kinds of secondary education (grammar, modern,
technical) all equal in status and amenities. The Dual System,
therefore, *must* be settled.

In settling it, the National Government's attitude was
determined by several definite convictions. From none of these
did it depart in the end. The denominations were to be treated
together—no separate settlement for the Anglicans and
Catholics (though the Nuffield Report suggested that Catholics
and Jews might be so accommodated). There was to be no
abolition, nor modifying, of the Cowper-Temple clause—
religious instruction in all L.E.A. schools must be by Agreed
Syllabus. The Dual System was not to be extended; there
would be no grants for the building of *new* Voluntary Schools;
and there was not to be a " Scottish " solution (for reasons
considered **earlier).**

The opponents of the Dual System, on the other hand,
were most formidable. They comprised the National Union
of Teachers (which objected to 10,000 denominational
" closed " headships, to " tests for teachers," and to the
clerical " right of entry " into secondary schools); many of
the local authorities (eager to secure equalised building standards); all the Free Churches (in the light of their policy since
1870, and of the fact that over 400 schools were the Anglican
schools of " single-school areas," and—frequently—from
declared anti-Catholicism); and many of the Anglicans (satisfied with Agreed Syllabus religious teaching). To these were
added the Trades Union Congress, the Workers' Educational
Association and the Co-operative Union.

The Catholic attitude was that, on grounds of equity
and history, there should now be 100 per cent. grants for
Catholic schools; that " tests for teachers," the hallmark of
that " pluralism " which alone could withstand the totalitarian
mind, were vital; but that the 13 Catholic " single-schools "
could be ceded, and also the appointment of teachers, if there
were satisfactory guarantees.

Mr. R. A. Butler, who succeeded to the Board of Edu-

cation in July 1941, had to frame a Bill that would accommodate as much of these conflicting and fiercely held views as
humanly possible. By dint of consummate Parliamentary
skill, he was to do so.

The Government produced several plans in turn,
maturing in detail but essentially the same. The *Green Book*,
early in 1941, conceived its Voluntary School provisions in
terms of the time-honoured principle that the grant of public
money involved a degree of public control. For primary
schools the local authority was to pay all costs and appoint
the teachers (except " reserved " teachers). For secondary
schools there was to be the same future, unless they could find
half the costs of their own reorganisation. To this the Catholic
Hierarchy countered in June with a plea for either the Scottish
solution, or an extension, to the whole country, of the Liverpool Act of 1939. This was followed up in October by a letter
from Cardinal Hinsley, and in November with a deputation
to Mr. Butler, led by the Bishop of Pella and Canon Vance.

The second Government plan (March, 1942), while
never wavering in aim or basis, repeated the " options ";
there could be complete transfer of a Voluntary School to the
Local Authority, or the school could find half the costs of
reorganisation and retain its independence. How far these
were really " options " is a question. In terms of financial
resources, the first alternative smacks of compulsory transfer.
The other alternative, the Bishop of Salford described in his
1943 Lenten Pastoral, as follows: " We have made you pay
for a dinner, but if you wish we will . . . . allow you not to eat
it." It emerged afterwards that the first alternative was intended for acceptance by the Anglicans, the second by the
Catholics.

The Catholic Bishops, standing firm, now made public
their willingness to concede the appointment of teachers in
return for guarantees (Bishop of Salford, May 9th; Catholic
Education Council, April; Bishop of Northampton, Novem-
ber). But there was clearly some confusion on this, since
Mr. Chuter Ede (the Under-Secretary) told the Commons on
January 21, 1944, that the Hierarchy had not offered the
Government the Scottish solution, but only enquired the
Government's own views on it. On June 21st appeared the

Joint Pastoral on the Social Question, point ten of which laid it down that

> religious education, to meet the wishes of the parents, should be available to all school children, and on such conditions that the general education of the child should not suffer in any way from its parents' insistence on religious education.

The second Catholic proposals to the Government were tendered on the same day. The Bishops again offered either the transfer of all Catholic schools to the local authorities, with prior approval of a teacher on religious grounds before the local authority should appoint, or else the *renting* of new school-buildings from the local authority, as in the Liverpool Act. These proposals without details were made known at the Catholic Teachers' Federation meeting on June 24th by the Bishop of Leeds.

The third Butler plan, in September, appeared on the surface to be identical with Plan Two. But, in detail, its provisions as to " reserved " teachers were tighter, while, on the other hand, the " contracting-out " was extended beyond Modern Schools to cover all schools. In a letter on September 16th to Archbishop Amigo of Southwark, following a visit from the Bishop of Pella, Mr. Butler widened State help for " alterations " to include " replacement " of a school, but he stood firm against grants for new schools. The Advent Pastorals of the Bishops reiterated that there would be no surrender of schools. The year closed with a letter from the Cardinal to all parents asking the prayers of their children for the safety of the schools.

In the New Year, 1943, the Catholic negotiating body was enlarged to take in representatives of parents, teachers and the secondary schools. After the shock of the Cardinal's death in March, the leadership of this body passed to Archbishop Downey of Liverpool, and, at this point, a full-scale Catholic agitation began.

The Catholic rank-and-file had been irked at the " secrecy " surrounding the Government's early proposals, and at a lack of factual information to reinforce their own efforts. They had been enraged at a Trades Union Congress decision in the previous September in favour of abolishing the denominational schools—a decision which the late Cardinal had deplored because it " sounds the tocsin of domestic strife in the midst of the country's peril." Catholic Parents' and Electors' Associations had begun to arise (on the model of Bradford in November, 1942) and had been approved by the Cardinal in February; and the plan of campaign of his own Sword of the Spirit movement for 1943 was to concentrate entirely on the Schools' Crisis. In a few places there was even joint Christian action on this ticklish question of education—on a basis of parental and civic rights. The Catholic agitation of 1943 was such that by November there were 60 Parents' Associations in Westminster alone. An energetic band of lay leaders, from all the wings of the Catholic Action lay apostolate, marshalled a nation-wide campaign of public meetings, the like of which had not been seen even in 1870.

The White Paper, *Educational Reconstruction,* marks the point at which Mr. Butler, having achieved the " balanced settlement " he was contriving, finally deprecated joltings from any quarter whatsoever. The unknown quantity had been the Anglicans, for the other " vested interests " were solid in their several views. The Archbishop of Canterbury, Dr. William Temple, had told the Church Assembly in 1942 that " if we wish to avoid totalitarianism, there is merit in the very duality of the Dual System." But he was subsequently to call the *White Paper* a " glorious opportunity " for the Church of England. It can be seen today that, by November, 1942, when the Archbishop of Canterbury was able to win over the Assembly to endorse the Government's Plan Three, the Board of Education had only the Catholics to deal with on any crucial point. The Council for Education Advance (comprising the T.U.C., N.U.T., W.E.A., etc.) deeply disliked the Dual System but was not prepared to press to extremes and wreck a Bill. It is not too much to say, then, that by the beginning of 1943 the future Bill was safe, but for two dangers. One of these was that Catholic intransigence might provoke the anti-denominationalists into canvassing a secular system altogether, and carrying it in Parliament; the other was that any Government yielding to the denominationalists by increased grant offers, or on new schools, might have the same result.

This explains to some extent the vitriolic attack on the Catholics in the Free Church Press in 1943—when the *Baptist Times* went to the extreme of charging them with teaching children " dogmas which are subversive of the State—as we see from Italy and Spain." On the other hand, Mr. Butler's " balance " was not appreciated in the hurly-burly of the various public campaigns, and intense negotiations accordingly continued with all parties as to details within his framework—they to contrive modification, he to avert it.

Early in 1943 Cardinal Hinsley had drafted a Memorandum epitomising the Catholic case. It is a statesmanlike document. The existing defects in Catholic schools, he said, were due to rising costs, war damage, the movement of population, and (behind this) the long penalisation of the Catholic ratepayers. The maximum Catholic claim now was 100 per cent. public financial support. The minimum claim should include debts from the past and the needs of new centres of population. This the 50 per cent. offer would not meet. The Catholics would, however, try to make do on an all-round grant of 75 per cent., supplemented by Treasury loans. In return, the appointment of teachers could be ceded (with guarantees) and also the single-schools.

On January 15th the Cardinal saw Mr. Butler and asked for 75 per cent. grants, but to no purpose. After his death, the Hierarchy's Low Week Statement applauded the educational provisions foreshadowed, and restated the fundamental moral issue:

> The State should provide schools to which Anglicans and Free Churchmen, Catholics and Jews may send their children, with a good conscience, always supposing that there are a sufficient number of such children in a given area to warrant the establishment of a school. The present educational system of England and Wales is unjust because it discriminates unfairly . . . . Scotland has a fairer system. We trust that the Government will give England and Wales a settlement at least as equitable as that. . . .

The *White Paper* (July 16th) reflects the skill with which Mr. Butler had navigated. In so far as the Voluntary System was to be retained and blessed, its enemies had failed and were chagrined. In so far as the Voluntary Schools could preserve full freedom only by financing half their reorganisation (and in the case of new schools all of it), they themselves had failed and were chagrined. The daily act of worship and the Agreed Syllabus enjoined on all council schools were certainly a refutation of those who feared a paganising Government—albeit the Anglican *Church Times* was to dub all this " Mr. Butler's National Christianity," and the Catholic *Universe* to liken it to the " Birreligion " of 1906. But the options open to denominational schools had now hardened out. They could have " aided " status if they could find the 50 per cent., " controlled " status if not, or " special agreement " status if they had a 1936 Act proposal that could be revived.

The Catholic reaction was one of dismay; and, to increase the force of the agitation, the Catholic Parents' and Electors' Associations in August hurriedly organised themselves on a national basis, jumping diocesan frontiers. It says much for the balance of Catholic perspective that the Hierarchy, in the midst of a life-and-death struggle, felt able to declare that they " do not approve the formation of the National Federation." But, with it or without, the popular campaign went ahead at every level of public life.

In September Mr. Butler went to see Archbishop Williams of Birmingham, then to Ushaw to meet all the Northern Bishops, and then (October 19th) he met the entire Hierarchy in London. A Joint Pastoral at the beginning of Advent explained to the public how and why the *White Paper* was unacceptable as it stood, and declared the Board of Education to be the " odd man out " in refusing public money for denominational teaching, since the Home Office and War Office and Colonial Office had long allowed it. A Sword of the Spirit letter in *The Times* (November 11th) recalled the scrupulous justice of the Scottish and Irish and Dutch solutions—to which Lord Eustace Percy (ex-President of the Board of Education) replied, begging the denominationalists not to widen the area of discussion at this late stage.

On November 24th the Board gave the Bishops a departmental estimate of the Catholic costs, on the basis of a 35 per cent. addition to 1939 costs for school-places. It put the total liabilities at just under ten million pounds. Then, just before Christmas, the Bill was introduced into Parliament and seen to be in all essentials unchanged.

The debates throughout the 1944 Session were remarkably placid. It was, indeed, but for the Catholics, an agreed Bill. It took 19 Parliamentary days to pass the Commons, as against 59 in 1902. The Hierarchy said categorically, on January 5th, that they would " never accept the Bill as it now stands." The Bishop of Lancaster described its financial provisions as " lunacy." Lord Perth and Lord Tyrrell asked, in *The Times*, why the principles of the Minority Treaties imposed on the Poles and Czechs, by the victorious Allies, in 1919, could not apply at home.

The fateful interregnum at Westminster finally ended two days before the second reading, with the enthronement of Dr. Bernard Griffin as successor to Cardinal Hinsley on January 18th.

The unopposed second reading produced support for the Catholics from outside their ranks: for the abolition of the Cowper-Temple clause (by Mr. Henry Brooke) and for interest-free loans (by Mr. Liddell). Five Catholic members spoke. Mr. Butler saw the new Archbishop on the following day, and was asked, yet again, for a 75 per cent. grant and interest-free loans. *The Tablet*, looking ahead, reflected gravely that Parliament was accepting

> the idea of a non-institutional Christianity . . . . in some sense Christian without being either Church or Chapel. Few men appreciate the immensity and the revolutionary character of what is being attempted.

It was no accident, added Mr. Woodruff, that the Board of Education was having to attract by increased salaries, and the teaching Orders were not.

During the Committee stage, in February, the Catholic members sought to pare what could be pared from the inevitable bill of cost. They tabled amendments asking for a clause to be inserted safeguarding the rights of parents, and secured it; for an increase of grant, unsuccessfully. A concession on Treasury loans was ultimately won, not interest-free but at 4½ per cent. interest-and-redemption-charges, amounting on a Government calculation to £430,000 a year. No " ceiling " was attached to this clause, despite repeated warnings in both Houses that, within a very few years, the Treasury calculation would have become hopelessly out of date and the liability correspondingly vaster. After some fifty amendments, the Bill passed the Commons on May 12th. Lord Rankeillour made one more unavailing attempt in the Lords to have the " 35 per cent. over 1939 costs " basis revised. The Royal Assent to the Bill was given on August 3rd.

The settlement thus offered the Voluntary Schools three " optional " futures. They could become " aided " by paying half costs; " controlled " by failing to—thereby losing their denominational character, except for two periods a week; or " special agreement " schools under the 1936 Act. It was only too obvious that the Dual System was not going to be extended.

Within this setting, certain hardships were foreseen by the Catholics all along. The denominations could hardly provide secondary schools of all three kinds for themselves (grammar, modern and technical), and could not know in advance the proportions of their children to earmark for each in planning buildings. They feared too a serious loss of senior children to the better-equipped Council schools. As for costs, it would mean finding a half for modernisation, rebuilding on new sites, substitute schools, and the accommodating of displaced pupils; from a quarter to a half for special agreement schools; and for new schools the whole cost of sites and buildings. This was to be tempered by the two Amending Acts of 1946 and 1948, but it was still subject to vagaries of the price-level.

During the first few years, down to the end of our century, the Act of 1944 was administered on the whole as favourably to the Catholics as its limits allowed. Where Local Authorities tended to interpret their duties narrowly, the disputes usually had to do with freedom of parental choice of school at the age of eleven, or on transfer to a new home, and with the payment for playgrounds, medical services and religious books and equipment. The most serious of the open conflicts involved a parents' strike for six months at Barking in 1947.

The prospects were least good in Wales, which had

been the storm-centre of Nonconformist resistance in 1902. As late as 1949 the North Wales Council of Evangelical Churches sought a concerted policy with the Local Authorities against Catholic Schools. This foreground, and the background of a sparsely-populated land in which, even to-day, there are only 41 Catholic schools in the Archdiocese of Cardiff and 16 in Menevia, was certain to make the task for long years to come as pioneering as it had been when the modern Missions were started (in Swansea before 1800, Newport 1808, Cardiff 1828).

When Miss Ellen Wilkinson succeeded Mr. Butler at the General Election of 1945, she took in hand the question of Catholic " Direct Grant " secondary schools, so that, by May, 1946, fifty-one were on the Ministry of Education list, and only eleven had been refused. Her successor, Mr. George Tomlinson, showed a marked sympathy towards the struggling Catholic Schools. He decided in their favour many of the appeals against L.E.A. decisions. On his opening a Catholic school at York on October 2nd, 1948, he said:

> Catholics can rest assured that the Government will respect their rights. Schools like this are the only antidote to the many problems facing us in the world to-day.

All the same, he warned the Bishop of Hexham and Newcastle a year later that

> I am sure that no new settlement which could be negotiated would be as favourable to denominational interests as that of 1944.

The great nightmare was soaring costs. School-places had stood at roughly £60 in 1939. By 1949, when the Hierarchy issued up-to-date estimates in the light of post-war experience, the cost of a school-place varied, according to diocesan returns, from £191 to £400. The Treasury calculation of 1943 was seen to have been as fleeting as the Catholic M.P.s had prophesied at the time. The total Bill had risen from ten millions to over sixty millions.

Hence the campaign with which the century closed: the " School Crisis " of early 1950. The Bishops had issued a statement in the previous June, calling attention to the astronomical rise in costs, and insisting that there must be a " ceiling " to the cost per school-place, together with interim help, pending an Amending Act in the next Parliament. Then,

n October, the Hierarchy decided to broach a permanent settlement of the whole school question, based on two principles.
The Catholic schools should be *leased* to the L.E.A.s at nominal
rentals, save where local Catholic managers had an outstanding
liability themselves—in which case the annual rent payment
made by the L.E.A. should balance the managers' outgoings in
interest and redemption charges on their own loans. And the
local authority would henceforth appoint the teachers in the
Catholic schools, subject to a guarantee (as in Scotland) that
the teacher be satisfactory to the religious authority on religious
grounds.

These proposals, even when it was made clear that
neither the Ministry of Education nor the political Parties
would countenance any interference with the balance and
framework of the 1944 Act, were made the basis of a nation-
wide Catholic campaign during the General Election of 1950,
under the guidance of the special " Action Committee " set up
by the Hierarchy, but with the initiative coming from the
parishes and the lay organisations. The scale of this campaign
dwarfed even that of 1870 and 1885; and certainly that of
1943-44. Practically every Parliamentary candidate in the
625 constituencies was interviewed by a local Catholic deputation, in order to make sure that all candidates were at least
informed on the matter, and in order to make known to Catholic
voters up and down the country the general tenor of the
replies.

There was small likelihood that the Bishops' proposals
would be considered in their entirety by the new Parliament.
But there was every likelihood—attested by questions on the
impossible burden saddled on the Voluntary Schools, tabled by
Catholic and other members immediately the new House of
Commons met, and by the fact that the Minister of Education
was himself obliged to ordain a " ceiling " for school building
costs—that amelioration short of upsetting the Act of 1944 was
at last being definitely investigated by the Government. It
is on that note, of suspense and anxiety, that the century ended.

VI. CENTENARY CONCLUSION

Our survey has shown that Governments were increasingly favourable to the Denominational Schools down to 1902,

but thereafter less so. Mr. Gladstone was determined that the Voluntary System should be completed; Mr. Butler that it should not be extended. What was in 1870 a factional opposition to denominationalism by Nonconformists and convinced secularists alone, is now the opposition of the professional bodies and leaders of all the learned societies. The country has steadily lost its religiosity and become " post-Christian." Where that has not happened, on the other hand, in Scotland and Eire and Holland, solutions to the denominational question have been found that satisfy all the parties to the historic disputes. In those lands the case to be met has been rightly appraised as one of parental and minority rights in conscience. But in England and Wales in 1943-44 there was no longer an effective public opinion persuaded that religion is indeed the core of education.

Till then, the century under review had shown that at each turning-point the Catholic demand increased. From 1847 till 1870 it was for State grants. From 1870 till 1902 it was for rate-aid and full maintenance. After 1902 it gradually became the claim for complete equality. The root principles were asserted each time (long before their ultimate codification in the Encyclical *Divini Illius Magistri of* 1929), the fact that the English Catholics were living in a land of mixed religion was acknowledged as inevitably limiting their full recognition, and the detailed demands were always determined by the historical and local context. That is the perspective from the Catholic side. The explanation of why the campaign succeeded till 1902 and thereafter failed lies in the wider, national perspective of religious drift.

Moreover, the success was always greatest when the Catholics had a clear objective in view, and planned for it in advance; notably in 1847, and in Cardinal Vaughan's remarkable campaign from 1884 to 1902. At the other key-dates there was either no unified leadership on the spot, as in 1870 when the Hierarchy were in Rome, and in 1943 during the Westminster *interregnum,* or else there was no unanimity, as in 1918 and 1930.

To say that there is no longer a real public opinion in England on religious education—that the " God dimension " is lost; that the Scottish solution was not considered seriously by the country at large; that what prevailed in 1944 was the "sectional" interests of the Free Churches and the professional organisations—is only half the matter. The other half is the presentation of the Catholic case, and the effort to recreate a public opinion and instruct and mould it.

On this, it has to be said that, throughout the hundred years, the fundamental point was always, and consistently, "equality of opportunity." This was a claim resting, throughout the period, on the right of the parent to have his child schooled in his own faith and at no more cost than his neighbour's. And it was a claim all the more arresting in view of the Government's own inconsistency over the principle of "no public money for denominational teaching." In adopting that principle, Gladstone, having failed to satisfy everybody, satisfied nobody. But the Agreed Syllabus policy has now made Cowper-Temple more permanent than ever, because it has at last satisfied almost everybody, except the Catholics. Here is a reason why by 1950 the Catholics had to break with tradition and strive for separate treatment.

Where the ethical claim for equality of opportunity became in detail a matter of hard cash lies in that, whereas the total Catholic costs were always a generalised sum, they were also always an individualised burden. The total affected the national Budget; the burden affected the lives of individual children from day to day. It was not, for all that, properly a financial issue at all: especially as, come what might, Catholics would not consent to go to any but Catholic schools.

To the extent that all this had been made clear, from 1847 on, to the nation's leaders, the Catholic defence was sound and effective. But that defence also had its shortcomings. There was throughout too little done to prevent the easy assumption, by outsiders, that it *was* "out-of-date bricks and mortar" the Church was defending. There was insufficient stress—or alacrity—in welcoming the *material* side of educational advance on which the country outside the Church set such increasing store. There was too little recognition that the statesmen were indeed doing (according to their lights) the best they knew. There was a too great afterglow of that introverted demeanour of Penal Days—which others came to mistake for an imperious aloofness. There was all the time a vicious circle in which the penurious Catholic laity lacked a full formation in theology and philosophy, and the Hierarchy, therefore, distrusted lay initiative. All these things were symptomatic. And the temptation to assume that the country was still actively anti-Catholic persisted long after the nation had become (in fair weather) religiously indifferent. Nor was this lack of contact mitigated by a Catholic Press whose columns on education caught the imagination least when there was no crisis.

The insulation here revealed explains also why the Catholics have so often misread the signs of the times, for all that Belloc wrote *The Servile State*. The Education Act of 1944, Archbishop Downey has said, was less favourable than that of 1936; the Act of 1936 less favourable, said the Bishop of Pella, than the Trevelyan Bill of 1930 (which the Catholics had rejected); and the Bill of 1930 less favourable than the Scottish Concordat of 1918 (which they had allowed to pass them by). Here are thirty years of lost leeway: and the tide was ebbing, as it still is.

Only twice, too, was a resolute attempt made to recruit allies from outside—by Manning in 1870 and by Vaughan in 1884. Before that it had been unnecessary, for all the denominations were urging the same case (though separately). Later on it was not the policy of Cardinal Bourne, and in any case it was impossible; for even Cardinal Hinsley's daring effort at joint, civic, Christian co-operation in 1940 brought him only individual outside support in the hour of the Schools' crisis. The revulsion caused among Protestants by Cardinal Bourne's aloof attitude, and among Catholics by the lack of effective response to Cardinal Hinsley's, served to demobilise the Christian forces, though the country's religious " climate " was still deteriorating. An attempt " next time " at separate treatment, on its merits, as a minority, became, for this reason also, the most practicable course for the Catholic body.

The century thus leaves three long-distance tasks for the English and Welsh Catholics in the field of popular education. One is to recreate a public opinion alive to the fundamental religious issue. This can hardly be done till past mistakes of psychological approach are taken in hand. A second task is, thereby, to change the *nature* of the demand made by the Government next time—to secure, after all, an equitable treatment as a citizen-minority. This can hardly be done without a sustained campaign of public instruction, such as the Hierarchy called for in the summer of 1949. The third task is to keep the Catholic schools in existence meanwhile, despite the rise of their bill to £60 million for the next twenty years. And this last can hardly be done short of a national Catholic trust fund, as T. W. Allies urged in his own day, available from a central pool, for help locally where the shoe pinches hardest, diocesan frontiers notwithstanding.

Such an equitable settlement, operative today in two parts of the British Isles, is impossible in England and Wales today for historical reasons, which a survey of the last hundred years makes only too incontrovertible. Whether the prospects in 1950 are better than they were in 1850 is an open question. Then, it was a matter of winning recognition from a public that did believe in the unity of religious and secular education. Now, it is a matter of maintaining that recognition amid a public opinion which believes so no longer. Mr. Gladstone, by supplementing the Dual System, advanced it. Mr. Butler has halted it, and outflanked it. Over half the Anglican schools were expected to opt for " control." Few except the Catholics have now any over-mastering, transcendental drive to prevent the changed trend from running its logical course. Few, except the Catholics, see any longer anything vital to salvation that an Agreed Syllabus cannot give; for few, except the Catholics, subscribe any longer to the bedrock educational truth, that the Christian formation of the child can be secured only by a dedicated partnership of the home, the church and the school, through the trinity of parent-priest-teacher.

In England and Wales today the Catholic Schools are more than ever, then, missionary schools. In measurable time they may be the only ones left. Were they to be lost to the country, as God's Church sees it *all* would be lost. Wherefore, by that dispensation with which Providence chastens its children, it was the task of the Bishops in the last century to create these schools, but, in the next century, to preserve them from extinction.

NOTES TO MAP ON PAGE FACING

The purpose of the map is to indicate the burdens and problems special to the various dioceses, which can be arranged in groups, i.e.:

Group A—(dioceses all but wholly rural) the dioceses of Menevia, Nottingham, Northampton, Portsmouth, Clifton and Plymouth.

Group B—(dioceses all but wholly industrial) the dioceses of Liverpool, Salford, Leeds, and Hexham and Newcastle.

Group C—(dioceses mainly rural, but responsible for " urban concentrations," shown specially shaded) the dioceses of Lancaster, Middlesbrough, Shrewsbury, Cardiff and Birmingham.

Group D—(the special case of the dioceses responsible for Greater London) the dioceses of Westminster, Brentwood and Southwark.

The 1949 figures are given because these are the latest complete statistics published. They are taken from the table in the *Catholic Directory for 1950*.

				Schools	Children in these
Group A	...	...	...	207	26,510
Group B	...	...	...	522	195,112
Group C	...	...	...	372	89,377
Group D	...	...	...	281	52,202

Liverpool diocese (77,972 children) has almost three times the number of children in Group A.

Salford diocese (48,286 children) has almost twice that number.

Hexham and Newcastle diocese (39,517 children) has almost one and a half times the number.

The total (1949) population of the area in Group A is estimated by the Registrar-General as 10,731,563, i.e., almost a quarter of the estimated total population of England and Wales, and perhaps a million more than that of Greater London.

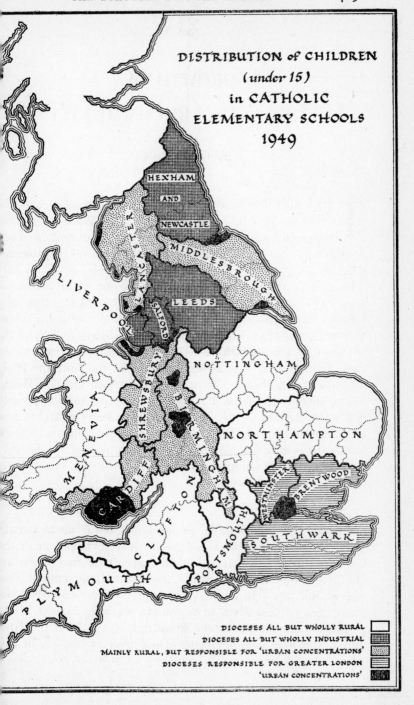

DISTRIBUTION of CHILDREN
(under 15)
in CATHOLIC
ELEMENTARY SCHOOLS
1949

HEXHAM AND NEWCASTLE
MIDDLESBROUGH
LANCASTER
LIVERPOOL
SALFORD
LEEDS
NOTTINGHAM
SHREWSBURY
MENEVIA
BIRMINGHAM
NORTHAMPTON
CARDIFF
CLIFTON
WESTMINSTER
BRENTWOOD
SOUTHWARK
PLYMOUTH
PORTSMOUTH

DIOCESES ALL BUT WHOLLY RURAL
DIOCESES ALL BUT WHOLLY INDUSTRIAL
MAINLY RURAL, BUT RESPONSIBLE FOR 'URBAN CONCENTRATIONS'
DIOCESES RESPONSIBLE FOR GREATER LONDON
'URBAN CONCENTRATIONS'

XIV

GROWTH OF
THE CATHOLIC COMMUNITY

By Denis Gwynn

THE crude figures which record a continual increase of the
Catholic population in England and Wales since the
restoration of the Hierarchy need a great deal of inter
pretation, although they obviously reflect unbroken progress
The broad totals are familiar to most people; with roughly
2,650,000 Catholics in England to-day out of an estimated
population of 40 millions; and 110,000 in Wales out of a
total of three millions. But their distribution during the whole
century since 1850 has been strongly localised; and until the
outbreak of war in 1939 it followed generally the remarkably
clear pattern that was already defined at the time the Hier
archy was established. In the years between the two World
Wars there was some modification of the former closely
restricted pattern, with a persistent increase of churches and
of priests in the districts which had been previously most
backward. But the Catholic population was still relatively
very small in the counties which were gradually being developed by new missions.

I

In general, Catholic progress had been, up to twenty
years ago, a consolidated and methodical development of the
Catholic missions which had taken shape at the time when the
Hierarchy was restored, while the great Irish immigration
was in full tide. In a previous chapter I have described the
main lines of that Irish immigration, showing how it led to
permanent settlements in the industrial areas where the Irish
immigrants found employment. These were principally in and
around the seaports and in the new industrial areas which

ere then expanding rapidly. The pattern of Catholic dis-
ibution in England up to 1930 was still virtually the same,
nd there had risen a thoroughly organised Catholic life, which
as beginning to expand deliberately into wider areas. A
loser analysis of progress at different stages during those
ighty years could only indicate the process of growth, without
evealing any vital change in distribution.

It is moreover necessary to emphasise the vagueness of
uch statistics as are available for comparison. The *Catholic
Directory* published no statistics of Catholic population from
ear to year until 1900. Since that time the figures have been
nore or less regularly supplied. But even in the years prior to
939 (when accurate returns became impossible under the
hifting conditions of the war years) they could never pretend
o be accurate. In compiling the annual *Catholic Directory*,
he regular method was to obtain official information direct
rom each parish priest or head of a religious house, and then
ubmit the proofs for verification to the bishop's secretary.
Delays, and discrepancies in detail, were only to be expected.
But it was found impossible to establish any uniform system
or recording even the most important totals. Some dioceses,
or instance, would send an approximate total, in round num-
ers, for the Catholic population, while others would be
recise. Some would make no alteration whatever for a
number of years, and then substitute another round figure
vhich was obviously guesswork. Others would give precise
otals; but it was always impossible for parish priests in
rowded districts to know just how many Catholics were living
n the parish at any time. There was no conceivable method
f discriminating between lapsed and practising Catholics
mong those who were known to be there.

Even in the statistics for baptisms and for conversions
here was chaos. Some dioceses would deduct the number of
onverts from the total of baptisms, while some would count
hem twice, both as converts and as newly baptised. Persistent
equests for the adoption of some uniform method only pro-
luced explanations which showed how many difficulties existed
vhich made accurate returns impossible. Of the various returns
—which were all carefully sifted before publication—those of
Catholic marriages and of Catholic school attendance were

the most reliable. But even they were obviously incomplete
as a picture of actual conditions: because Catholics might
marry outside the Church and then have their marriage
regularised, or the school attendance figures might be either
above or below the total of Catholic children in any parish.
These difficulties were still apparently incapable of solution
in 1939. The difficulties at an earlier stage were so much
greater that it would be foolish to take the earlier statistics too
literally. Nevertheless they provide a rough index to Catholic
progress; and the totals of priests and churches and religious
houses are particularly revealing.

The clearly defined concentration of Catholics in the
industrial areas, from the 'forties onwards, contrasts curiously
with the earlier pattern of Catholic survival.   Lancashire,
and to a lesser extent Yorkshire, had remained the principal
strongholds of Catholic life in the eighteenth century.   But
these surviving Catholic centres were quite incapable of providing for the multitudes of poor Irish immigrants who flocked
into the new industrial districts.   They were by no means even
in the same places where the industries and mines developed
so rapidly.   And as many of the clergy, before the Hierarchy
was restored, were still directly attached to the old landowning
families who had their own private chapels in their homes,
the priests whom they maintained were unable to devote themselves to the areas where they were most urgently needed.   The
old families had a strong tradition of generosity towards the
Church which they had kept alive, and in many instances
they did provide buildings, or contribute towards the funds
needed, for places of worship and for schools which were required for the Irish immigrants.   But their private chapels
were too remote, and much too small even if they were not
too remote, to make any serious contribution towards providing for the multitudes of Catholic immigrants.

It is important to stress this point, because there was
for years a clear distinction, even in Lancashire, between the
English Catholic communities and the far more numerous Irish
Catholics who crowded together in the new urban areas.   The
priests who ministered to them were not the same; for the
English clergy were still largely tied to the scattered Catholic
settlements.   The Irish immigrants attracted priests of their

wn race from Ireland, or became the concern of the religious
rders who began to work among them. The Vicars Apostolic
ad not the necessary authority to appoint or transfer priests
ɔ the places where they were most needed; while they were
aturally obliged to provide chaplains for the old families
ho had kept the local missions in existence for centuries.
t was the influx of new Catholic settlers, chiefly from Ireland,
nat made it necessary to double the number of Vicariates in
840, ten years before the Hierarchy was restored. The great
nvasion of refugees from the Irish famine had not then begun,
ut the number of immigrants was rising steadily, and especi-
lly in the north. In London the immigration was more mixed
han in the northern and midland cities. It included many
'rench Catholics who had remained on, since their escape
rom the revolution. There were large numbers of Italian
Catholics as well. Wiseman's famous series of lectures in
London in 1835, which attracted such remarkable audiences
n his first public appearance, arose from his having under-
aken to deputise for a friend at the Sardinian chapel in Lin-
oln's Inn Fields. Some twenty years later, when he had
ɔecome Cardinal Archbishop of Westminster, he was to leave
vivid picture of another crowded part of London, where he
vent to attend an evening mission in the open air near
)xford Street. In a letter to Mgr. Talbot in Rome he describes
ow he

found the place crammed from end to end, all round and
behind the platform. Every window was filled with tiers of
faces, the whole line of roofs covered with legs dangling
over the parapets—most with candles in their hands and
every window illuminated, while against the walls were
illuminations with lamps; so that altogether, on coming to
the entrance and looking down, it had the appearance of a
street Madonna festival in Rome. On alighting I went into
the crowd, which made way and our procession formed. I
was in my usual black dress, black cassock and red fariazolo,
with biretta, cross, etc. After a hymn, I addressed the
people who listened intently. I preached on perseverance,
especially in sobriety, going to their duties, peaceableness
and not sending their children to Protestant schools. They
all with one voice promised fidelity.

There was not even a temporary chapel in this crowded part of London; though St. Patrick's, Soho Square, had been built in its first form, St. James's, Spanish Place, existed, and the Jesuit church at Farm Street was established. Wiseman told his poor congregation that he had found a room where Mass would be said for them in future and he promised to provide a priest. They had cheered wildly, he told Mgr. Talbot; and as he went off, " the cheering as we went along to the carriage must have been heard for miles. I never heard anything like it." Many similar glimpses of such open-air missions and processions could be quoted, for the various districts in which these Catholic congregations were rapidly forming, and waited anxiously for priests or churches to be provided. The difficulties were enormous; and even the introduction of religious orders was often disappointing.

The old conflict of authority between the Vicars Apostolic and the heads of religious communities had been largely overcome since the Hierarchy gave to the bishops the general administration of their dioceses. But in practice it was found that religious communities became anchored in one place, and groups of priests would live and work together in one house instead of spreading their activities further afield. An account of these difficulties, which had their counterpart in all the crowded industrial districts, is given in a letter[1] which Wiseman wrote to the convert Father Faber in October, 1852, when Faber was preparing to establish the Oratorians in London.

When I first came to London I saw that the neglected part was the poor, and to that I resolved to give immediate attention. After having consulted some zealous priests, I concluded on the plan of local missions in the midst of them. At the very same time the Rev. Mr. Hodgson proposed a similar plan, and I embraced it. He gave up the best mission in the district, and gave himself up to the work. God blessed it, and three permanent missions arose from it; two most flourishing on this side of the water (the Thames) one on the other. But these permanent results could not be

<hr>

[1] Purcell's *Life of Manning*, II, pp.2-9.

verywhere secured for obvious reasons, as proximity to the
hurch, want of a place for a chapel, poverty, etc. I there-
ore felt more and more the conviction strengthened that I
1ad from the beginning entertained, that steady, continual
1nd persevering work among the dense, sinful masses could
only be carried on by religious communities. . . .

When I came to London, there was not a single
community of men. There were two Jesuits *en garçon* in a
1ouse, that was all. Now it is different.

(1) The Jesuits have a splendid church, a large
1ouse, several priests, besides Westminster. Scarcely was
I settled in London than I applied to their superior to estab-
ish here a *community* in due form of some ten or twelve
Fathers. I also asked for missionaries to give retreats to
congregations, etc. I was answered on both heads that
dearth of subjects made it impossible. Hence we have
under them only a church, which by its splendour attracts
and absorbs the wealth of two parishes but maintains no
schools, and contributes nothing to the education of the
poor at its very door.

(2) The Redemptorists came to London as a missionary order, and I cheerfully approved of and authorised
their coming. When they were settled down I spoke to
them of my cherished plan of missions to and among the
poor. I was told that this was not the purpose of their
institute *in towns*, " and that another Order would be required for what I wanted." . . . They have become,
as far as London is concerned, a parochial body, taking
excellent care of Clapham (having five or six priests and
abundant means for it), and they have given two or three
missions with varied success in chapels; but no more than
they have done in Birmingham and Manchester. . . .

(3) The Passionists I brought first to England, in
consequence of having read what their founder felt for it,
and of a promise I made to Father Dominic years before.
I got them placed at Aston Hall, and consequently they
have spread. I gave them a house; after a time they emi-
grated to the Hyde, thence into the fields, and now they
have come to St. John's Wood. They have never done me
a stroke of work among the poor, and if I want a mission

from them, the local house is of no use, and I must g
person from the provincial as if it did not exist.

(4) The Marists I brought over for a local purp
and that they are answering well. I hope for much g
from them in Spital Fields; but, at least at present I d
not ask them about general work.

(5) And now last, I come to the institute of whic
almost considered myself a member, San Filipp
Oratory. . . .

His letter was an urgent appeal to Father Faber to
whether the restrictions upon the activities prescribed by
Oratorian rules could somehow be overcome. He knew v
the zeal and the wholehearted earnestness of the religio
orders, but he found in every case that his own hopes of act
assistance were frustrated by the rules which bound each Or
to its special purpose. He concluded with a lament wh
illustrates one of the most difficult problems of the wh
period:

> Having believed, having preached, having assu
> bishops and clergy, that in no great city could the salvat
> of multitudes be carried out by the limited parochial cler
> but that religious communities alone *can* and *will* underta
> the huge work of converting and preserving the corrup
> masses, I have acted on this conviction. I have introdu
> or greatly encouraged establishment of five religious cong
> gations in my diocese; and I am just (for the great wo
> where I first began! Not one of them *can* (for it cannot
> want of will) undertake it. It comes within the purpose
> none of them to try.

These criticisms were to some extent an exaggeratio
but it is easy to understand Wiseman's passionate desire
the help of some body of " diocesan missioners " who wo
devote themselves entirely to missionary work. He esta
lished such a society himself before long, in the Oblates
St. Charles, with Manning at their head, in the rapidly e
tending district of Bayswater. In other districts, especia
in Leicestershire and in South Wales, the Rosminian Fath
of Charity undertook similar work; but even they found

JOHN HENRY NEWMAN

a group taken in Rome on the occasion of his visit to be made a Cardinal, 1879

THE FIRST PROVINCIAL SYNOD OF WESTMINSTER, 1852

From the unfinished painting by James Doyle at Oscott.

Sir George Bowyer

Mgr. Searle Rev. J. Wheble

?   Provost Whitty   ?   Thomas Grant (Southwark)   ?

Dr. Crookall   Nicholas Wiseman (Westminster)   William Wareing (Northampton)   Rev. R. Bagnall

Canon Cookson   John Briggs (Beverley)   William Ullathorne (Birmingham)   Provost Roskell

?   Thomas Joseph Brown (Cardiff)   George Errington (Plymouth)   J. H. Newman

Canon McGuire   William Hogarth (Hexham & Newcastle)   James Brown (Shrewsbury)   H. E. Manning

Provost Weedall   William Turner (Salford)   ?

Canon Hunt   Thomas Burgess (Clifton)   Provost Husenbeth

Very Rev. D. Aylward, O.P.

Very Rev. Etheridge, S.J.

Very Rev. J. Molyneux, O.S.B.

Provost Crook

Very Rev. Fr. Eugene, C.P.

Very Rev. J. B. Pagani, Inst. Ch.

THE FOURTH PROVINCIAL SYNOD OF WESTMINSTER, OLD HALL, WARE, 1873

Not all those present can now be identified. But the Bishops are grouped in the centre as follows :

JAMES BROWN
(Shrewsbury)

WILLIAM VAUGHAN
(Plymouth)

RICHARD ROSKELL
(Nottingham)

HENRY EDWARD MANNING
(Westminster)

WILLIAM ULLATHORNE
(Birmingham)

FRANCIS KERRIL AMHERST
(Northampton)

HERBERT VAUGHAN
(Salford)

THOMAS BROWN
(Newport & Menevia)

JAMES DANELL
(Southwark)

BERNARD O'REILLY
(Liverpool)

JAMES CHADWICK
(Hexham & Newcastle)

WILLIAM CLIFFORD
(Clifton)

ROBERT CORNTHWAITE
(Leeds)

THE CARDINAL-ARCHBISHOP OF WESTMINSTER AND THE BISHOPS OF ENGLAND AND WALES,

1897

Back row, from left to right:

WILLIAM GORDON (Leeds); THOMAS WHITESIDE (Liverpool); WILLIAM BROWNLOW (Clifton); FRANCIS MOSTYN (Vic. Ap. of Wales); RICHARD LACY (Middlesboro'); THOMAS WILKINSON (Hexham and Newcastle); ARTHUR RIDDELL (Northampton); FRANCIS BOURNE (Southwark); SAMUEL WEBSTER ALLEN (Shrewsbury).

Front row, from left to right:

JOHN CUTHBERT HEDLEY (Newport and Menevia); EDWARD BAGSHAWE (Nottingham); WILLIAM VAUGHAN (Plymouth); HERBERT VAUGHAN (Westminster); EDWARD ILSLEY (Birmingham); JOHN VERTUE (Portsmouth); JOHN BILSBORROW (Salford).

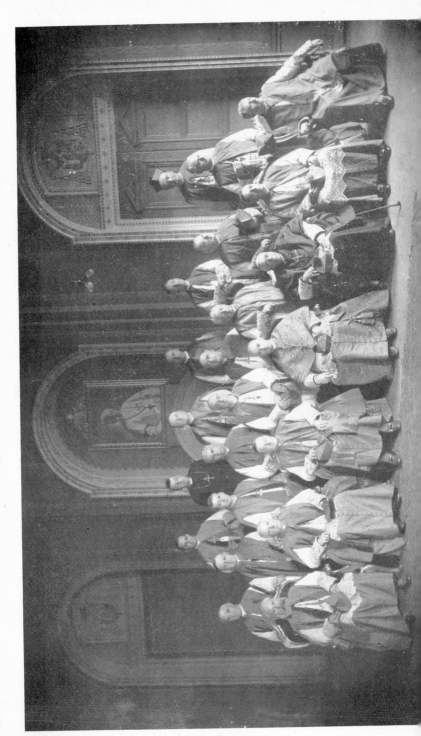

THE ARCHBISHOPS AND BISHOPS OF ENGLAND AND WALES,
1912

Back row, from left to right :

?; GREGORY THOMPSON (Gibraltar); RICHARD COLLINS (Hexham and Newcastle); JOSEPH BUTT (Aux. Westminster); JOHN McINTYRE (Aux. Birmingham); ?.

Middle row, from left to right :

HUGH SINGLETON (Shrewsbury); JOSEPH COWGILL (Leeds); FREDERICK KEATING (Northampton); PETER AMIGO (Southwark); LOUIS CASARTELLI (Salford); WILLIAM COTTER (Portsmouth); PATRICK FENTON (Aux. Westminster); JOHN VAUGHAN (Aux. Salford); JOHN KIELY (Plymouth).

Front row, from left to right :

HENRY HANLON (Vic. Ap. of Uganda); RICHARD LACY (Middlesboro'); THOMAS WHITESIDE (Liverpool); FRANCIS BOURNE (Westminster); JOHN CUTHBERT HEDLEY (Newport); FRANCIS MOSTYN (Menevia); GEORGE BURTON (Clifton).

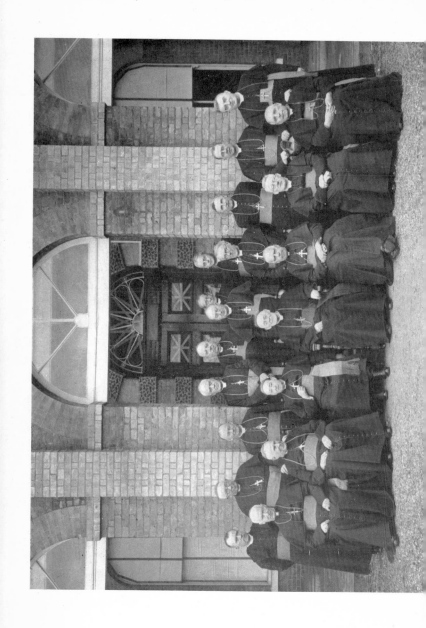

THE ARCHBISHOPS AND BISHOPS OF ENGLAND AND WALES,

Low Week, 1941

Back row, from left to right:

DANIEL HANNON (Mcnevia); THOMAS FLYNN (Lancaster); JOHN FRANCIS MCNULTY (Nottingham); AMBROSE MORIARTY (Shrewsbury); WILLIAM LEE (Clifton); JOHN BARRETT (Plymouth); JAMES DEY (Army Bishop); JOHN HENRY POSKITT (Leeds); JOHN HENRY KING (Portsmouth); LEO PARKER (Northampton); JOSEPH MCCORMICK (Hexham and Newcastle); HENRY MARSHALL (Salford).

Front row, from left to right:

THOMAS SHINE (Middlesboro'); PETER AMIGO (Southwark); RICHARD DOWNEY (Liverpool); ARTHUR HINSLEY (Westminster); THOMAS WILLIAMS (Birmingham); MICHAEL MCGRATH (Cardiff); ARTHUR DOUBLEDAY (Brentwood).

THE HIERARCHY IN 1950

Back row, from left to right:

GEORGE BRUNNER (Aux. Middlesboro'); JOSEPH RUDDERHAM (Clifton); FRANCIS GRIMSHAW (Plymouth); EDWARD ELLIS (Nottingham); JOHN PETIT (Menevia); JOHN MURPHY (Shrewsbury); CYRIL COWDEROY (Southwark); GEORGE ANDREW BECK (Aux. Brentwood).

Front row, from left to right:

HENRY MARSHALL (Salford); JOHN HENRY KING (Portsmouth); JOSEPH MASTERSON (Birmingham); RICHARD DOWNEY (Liverpool); BERNARD GRIFFIN (Westminster); MICHAEL McGRATH (Cardiff); JOSEPH McCORMICK (Hexham and Newcastle); THOMAS FLYNN (Lancaster); LEO PARKER (Northampton).

CARDINAL MANNING'S LAST RECEPTION, 1891

From the painting in Archbishop's House, Westminster.

H. E. CARDINAL MANNING *sits talking to* THE DUKE OF NORFOLK.

Behind the table stands THE MARQUESS OF RIPON.

Standing at the back, from right *to left, may be seen the following:*

The Bishop of Salford (HERBERT VAUGHAN); RT. HON. W. MATTHEWS, Q.C., M.P.; COL. PRENDERGAST; MR. JUSTICE DAY; SIR CHARLES RUSSELL, Q.C., M.P.; CANON JOHNSON; ALDERMAN STUART KNILL; FR. HAYES; BERNARD WHELAN, ESQ.; J. F. BENTLEY, ESQ.; F. C. BURNAND, ESQ.; W. S. LILLEY, ESQ.; CHARLES KENT, ESQ.; the Bishop of Emmaus (JAMES LAIRD PATTERSON); WILFRID MEYNELL, ESQ.; J. G. COX, ESQ.; FR. GRAHAM; the Bishop of Amycla (WILLIAM WEATHERS); HERMAN LESCHER, ESQ.; SIR CHARLES CLIFFORD, BT.

"RAISING THE (TRADE) WIND."

Cardinal Manning. "There, that's right! Both be Reasonable, and work together.
Bless you, my Children!"

THE DOCKER'S CARDINAL
From *Punch*, 1889

necessary to appoint certain priests specially as Itinerant Missionaries, just as the Passionists did. Every religious order inevitably followed the same course, establishing local houses where their priests could live in community. But these houses in time became the centres of intense Catholic activity. The very houses of which Wiseman complained in 1852, that they tied up numerous priests who might otherwise have separately worked far afield, were to become before long main sources of Catholic progress. The work of the Jesuits in Farm Street, or of the Passionists at Highgate, of the Redemptorists in Clapham, of the Oratorians in Kensington, or the Franciscans at Stratford, was to extend far and wide, though it was focused in one place. And in every one of the great centres of Catholic population the religious orders made an immense contribution by solid and constructive concentration over a period of years.

While the poor Catholic populations clamoured for priests or local churches and schools, " leakage " became an extremely serious problem in the places where priests and schools were lacking. But it was less devastating than might have been expected, because the poor Catholics, being mainly Irish, continued to live in colonies, and so kept their religious tradition, even though many of them became negligent in going to church. In time the work of the itinerant missionaries, the constant expansion of the religious orders, and the creation of new temporary Mass centres while churches and schools were being built, provided widely for the needs of the Catholic population. It was an immense and providential advantage that they were inclined to settle and multiply in the same restricted areas where they first arrived. Mixed marriages, between Catholics and Protestants, resulted often in increasing the Catholic members of the next generation, though they frequently resulted in estrangement from the Church. And so long as the Irish Catholics, who formed so large a proportion of the whole body, continued to live in the same districts, there was always a probability that those who had lapsed would come back again.

What Wiseman had not foreseen was the great influence that was exercised by these growing Catholic centres, at a later period, among the Nonconformist sects, who gradually declined in numbers. His attention, in regard to the prospects of England's conversion, had naturally been focussed upon the Tractarian movement. He was almost alone in showing active sympathy towards Newman and his Anglican friends. Newman's conversion, which was followed by so many gifted and influential members of the High Church party, had vindicated his generous encouragement of their desire to revive Catholic practices and traditions in the Church of England. And the problem of finding scope and employment for the Tractarian converts was one of the most pressing calls upon Wiseman's energies and resources. But as the years passed, the main stream of converts was less from the Church of England than from the Nonconformist churches. The possibilities of making converts in great numbers among them had been discovered even before Newman's conversion, when Father Gentili had preached with such surprising success, and laboured almost without assistance, in the remote Leicestershire villages while he was acting as chaplain to Ambrose Phillipps at Grace Dieu. Gentili and his friends had been obliged, by the sudden immigration after the Irish famine, to abandon those efforts and minister among the hundreds of thousands of destitute Irish Catholics who needed religious assistance. But his brief experience in Leicestershire had shown, just as Father Dominic Barberi had found in Staffordshire, that there were masses of earnest people who had joined various sects in despair of finding spiritual comfort in the Church of England at that time. They had responded eagerly to the Catholic missionaries, even when they spoke English with difficulty.

Until Wiseman had died in 1865, all hopes of extending the Church in England by making converts had been based principally upon the Oxford Movement and its consequences. Some of the most outstanding priests in England, besides Newman and Manning, were themselves convert clergymen who had been closely connected with the Tractarian movement. And besides the convert priests, there were many pious laymen and women of important social position, and sometimes of considerable private means, who helped immensely by their generosity in building churches and in subscribing to Catholic funds for extensions of all sorts. The work of consolidation and expansion continued with ceaseless activity and perseverance through Manning's long rule at Westminster. But the

Oxford Movement had become a spent force by the end of the century, and new opportunities had arisen with the decline of the Nonconformist churches.

II

Conditions in London were fairly typical; and the Catholic position at the opening of the new century can be traced clearly in a remarkable survey which was undertaken by the *Daily News* in 1903 and edited in book form by Mr. Richard Mudie Smith[2]. In a large volume containing many detailed maps and statistical tables for each district, it provided a complete analysis of religious life in London, based upon months of carefully conducted observation by a team of trained enumerators. They recognised, for instance, that in reckoning the attendance at Catholic churches it was necessary to " include the attendance at every Mass from 6 a.m. to 12 a.m. inclusive," because Mass attendance was compulsory, whereas other denominations sometimes attached more importance to evening services[3]. They made careful observation

[2] *The Religious Life of London,* Hodder & Stoughton, 1904.

[3] This is one of the reasons why the survey undertaken in 1886 by the *British Weekly* is so inadequate. No account was taken of attendances at any service held prior to 11 a.m.

Other references to Mass attendance in the *Daily News* survey are worth noting. Thus, with regard to North London, Mr. W. R. Warren notes: " In the case of Roman Catholic places, the overwhelmingly large gatherings in a few centres are entirely due to the celebration of Mass. Everything begins and ends with that " (p. 155).

With regard to South London, Mr. Masterman notes: " Space forbids the discussion of many other points of interest in these figures. There is the smallness of number and magnitude of congregation of the Roman Catholic churches, revealing both the poverty of this body in South London and the readiness of its members to travel considerable distances to fulfil their obligations of attendance at Mass " (pp. 205-6). And he adds a comment as apt to-day as it was almost 50 years ago: " The reformers of the sixteenth century endeavoured to restore the worship to the people in the vulgar tongue. Unfortunately, the Reformation was in essence aristocratic, never, as the Reformation abroad, awakening response from the masses of the population. The churches passed from the hands of the people, who ceased to take a pride in them; the Church services became more and more an inheritance of a limited aristocracy; the search for something more warm, human, and inspiring contributed largely to create the great independent bodies which in all the subsequent centuries have formed minor

everywhere of the members who attended more than one service on Sundays, and they even allowed for wet or fine weather during the observation. The net result for all London was to show a total of 1,250,000 worshippers; of whom 538,000 were of the Church of England, 545,000 were at the Nonconformist churches, 96,000 were Catholics and 72,000 others. The survey revealed particularly how large was the Nonconformist proportion in certain parts of London.

In East London it had been generally believed that the Church of England was strongest, because of its many active and philanthropic clergymen there. But even in East London the Church of England had only 60,000 worshippers on the Sunday when the census was taken compared with a total of 82,000 Nonconformists, of whom the Congregationalists were 24,000, the Baptists 19,000 and the Wesleyans 13,000. In the more prosperous West London districts the Church of England was greatly preponderant, with some 25,000, against 8,500 Catholics, and some 7,000 Nonconformists. But the position in South London was specially revealing. Mr. C. F. G. Masterman, who contributed this chapter, gave as his general conclusion that

In South London the poor (except the Roman Catholic poor) do not attend service on Sunday, though there are a few churches and missions which gather some, and forlorn groups can be collected by a liberal granting of relief.

The working man does not come to church. A few small communities of Primitive Methodists, Baptists, Salvationists, and similar bodies, as a general rule represent his contribution to the religious life of the nation.

The tradesmen and middle class of the poorer boroughs exhibit an active religious life, mainly gathered in the larger Nonconformist bodies, especially the Baptists.

The residents in the suburbs crowd their churches and chapels, and support with impartiality and liberality all forms of organised religion.

centres of worship. I have no hesitation in saying that, for the majority of the poor, our services are as incomprehensible as if still performed in the Latin tongue. The central service of the Roman Church, indeed, with its dramatic and appealing character, is far more intelligible even to the humblest worshipper."

These revelations of a general decline of religious worship were discouraging enough, even at the opening of the new century. Conditions in London were generally similar to those in all the industrial cities. The Church of England had already lost its hold upon the people, except in the more prosperous districts. But the Nonconformist churches still drew crowded congregations, especially in the suburban areas. In Wandsworth and Lambeth the Church of England still accounted for half the small total of church attendance, and the combined Nonconformist churches accounted for most of the remainder. In Woolwich, out of 31,000 in all, roughly 12,000 were Church of England, and some 11,000 were Nonconformists, half of them being Baptists. In Southwark the Church of England had 12,000; the Wesleyans and Methodists 5,500; the Baptists over 9,000 and the Congregationalists 4,000; while the Catholics were 4,500. For " Greater London " outside the inner districts, the Nonconformist totals were also very considerable. While the Church of England had a church attendance of 235,000, the Baptists had 54,000, the Congregationalists 53,000, the various Wesleyans and Methodists 66,000, the Presbyterians 13,000, the Plymouth Brethren 14,000, the Salvation Army 16,000 and the Catholics 31,000.

These figures suggest the background to the fifty years of Catholic expansion that followed, while they show how relatively small was the proportion of Catholics, even among the dwindling numbers of those who attended any church at all. The decline of the Church of England continued steadily, but the decline of the Nonconformist churches was far more rapid. It was among these hundreds of thousands of Nonconformists, whose organised religious life was already falling to pieces, that converts to the Catholic Church were largely gathered in the subsequent years.

Mr. Percy Alden, commenting on " the problem of East London," indicated that so far as the Catholic body is concerned the question was one of maintaining standards of practice rather than of making new converts. The churches were not big enough to meet existing needs and the natural increase of the Catholic body, and the main concern of the clergy, was to exhort and encourage—and sometimes to bully—slack members of the congregation to more frequent and regular attendance at Mass and the Sacraments together with facing the constant preoccupation of raising sufficient funds to keep the Catholic schools going. He wrote as follows:

The Roman Catholics occupy a somewhat unique position in East London, a position analogous to that of the Jews: it is not for them to convert or proselytise—they could fill all their churches to overflowing if professing Catholics alone attended. Their priests experience in very poor districts the same difficulty in getting a regular attendance that other denominations find; a further proof, if proof were required, that poverty is a bar to attendance at church. They are least successful in the Isle of Dogs, where the conditions are all against them, and where other denominations suffer in equal measure. Men like Father Gordon Thompson, who works in the Devons Road area, are able, however, to influence the poor Irish labourers who have grown careless about their religious life, and it must be admitted that both he and the Catholic priests generally seem to succeed in making the poor pay much of the cost both of the church and of the school. At the Limehouse Mission there is an organised school collection from house to house every Sunday afternoon; no doubt this will be dropped as a result of the London Education Act, but the people will still be expected to give the same amount of money in other ways.

III

By the end of the nineteenth century, the general framework of the Catholic community was already formed. Within its last twenty-five years the number of churches and chapels in England and Wales had grown steadily from 1,000 to 1,500, and the priests from 2,000 to 3,000. In the main Catholic centres the ground was already organised, and it had become necessary to build and to plan ahead on a much larger scale than formerly. The years of persistent planning and industrious perseverance had produced great results; and the fact that the Catholics had tended to remain together in the same districts had made it possible to concentrate the Church's resources where the large communities lived.   Cardinal

Vaughan's decision to build a vast Catholic cathedral in Westminster as a memorial to Manning was one indication of the larger scale on which plans were being made. It was so ambitious that Vaughan was accused of megalomania; but within a few years after the great cathedral had been opened, it was found to be too small for the needs of the Eucharistic Congress of 1908. In our own time it has been filled to overflowing again and again, even on diocesan or local occasions.

The new churches and schools and religious houses were being planned everywhere with a sure confidence of future expansion; and the growing resources of the new Catholic middle class made it possible to work on larger lines. At the same time the era of urban expansion was beginning, with large suburbs spreading out around all the cities where Catholic life was now sufficiently organised and prosperous to assist in wider developments. In the first years of the new century, up to the outbreak of war in 1914, there was a continual extension of churches and religious houses in the new suburban areas all over England. The war gave a sudden impetus to Catholic life, partly because war always stimulates a religious revival while it lasts, and partly because war in Europe established much closer connections between England and Catholic countries. Army and naval chaplains became a regular and permanent institution; Catholic churches, especially in London, became a recognised focus of public functions in relation to the war. Cardinal Bourne particularly acquired the status of a national figure, by virtue of his office. The increased diplomatic activity in London, and nationally important functions such as the public requiems for Allied military leaders or statesmen, compelled the Government to apply frequently for his advice or his collaboration. By the end of the First World War the total of priests, secular and religious, had risen to some 4,000, compared with 3,000 at the beginning of the century. Churches and chapels had increased from about 1,500 to 1,900: the total Catholic population from about 1,300,000 to 1,900,000.

Moreover, the general fusion of the diverse elements in the Catholic community was now largely complete. Cardinal Bourne himself, as the son of a convert English father and an Irish Catholic mother, was typical of the general assimilation of converts and Irish immigrants with the definitely English tradition, which had been so much modified since the first years of the revival. The gradual expansion of the main Catholic districts into a wider circumference around the earlier centres had helped to reduce the sense of restriction and of isolation which had kept the Catholic population closely united, and largely class-conscious. And as the new suburban areas extended, and more and more churches and schools were built to provide for their Catholic residents, the continual increase of converts became more widely representative.

The most outstanding sign of consolidation and continual growth was the decision by the Holy See to create three metropolitan provinces in 1911, with Archbishops for Birmingham and Liverpool as well as Westminster. Wales also was created a separate province in 1916, with an Archbishop in Cardiff, and Menevia as a suffragan see. A further division was made in 1917, when the county of Essex was separated from Westminster as the new diocese of Brentwood. Seven years later there was a similar rearrangement in the north, when the diocese of Lancaster was formed, to include the thinly-populated counties of Cumberland and Westmorland (which were formerly in the diocese of Hexham and Newcastle), and the northern part of Lancashire which was formerly part of Liverpool archdiocese.

These developments in ecclesiastical organisation reflected the expansion and increase of Catholic population which had continued ever since the restoration of the Hierarchy. It is impossible here to examine that process in detail. The development of Southwark under Archbishop Amigo's rule was broadly typical, though few of the other dioceses could show such striking results. Similar conditions can be seen in the much more recently established diocese of Lancaster. In each there was in one part a main industrial concentration, well provided with churches and schools and a large Catholic population. So, from South London in Southwark, and from the industrial centres around Lancaster, there has been a steady outward expansion into the modern suburban areas. Along the coastline in both dioceses, there are large and growing holiday resorts such as Brighton or Blackpool, and important shipping centres such as Dover or Barrow-in-Furness. Converging, both from the coast inwards and from the cities out-wards, there has been a systematic development of the smaller centres of population in between. At the same time there has been a vigorous organisation of new missions in the less populous counties where Catholics were previously few and scattered. The result in Southwark was astonishing after some forty years of Archbishop Amigo's rule. There were only 150 churches and chapels in Southwark when he became bishop in 1904. By 1914 there were 222, by 1939 there were 274; and at his death in 1949 there had been a further increase to 280, in spite of all restrictions on building and though many of his churches, including St. George's Cathedral, had been wholly or partly destroyed during the war.

As the new suburban communities developed, new Mass centres and churches became necessary. The new parishes were no longer similar to those which had been typical Catholic urban development in the Victorian era. The days of stone facings and pseudo-Gothic architecture, with tiled or stone flooring, pitch pine benches, ornate sanctuary rails, and the massed stone or marble reredos of wedding-cake construction, were now giving place to a less pretentious and possibly more func-tional building, often in yellow or red brick of simple line and austere decoration with neo-liturgical ornamentation begin-ning to be evident particularly by the flat altar table, the domed and completely veiled tabernacle and the generous use of Gothic vestments. Some of the new churches, particularly the more recent ones, were of the bungalow type. It is interesting to notice in the diocese of Southwark for example the districts in which this expansion took place. The following is a list of places in Southwark where, since 1925, new churches have been opened, the dates of opening being given in brackets:

Addiscombe (1925), Ash, Aldershot (1934), Ashtead (1944), Aylesham (1930), Bagshot (1927), Banstead (1931), Beckenham (1938), Bellingham (1928), Bexley Heath (1936), Biggin Hill (1931), Billingshurst (1925), Blackfen, Sidcup (1937), Bostall Park (1936), Carshalton Beeches (1934), Cheam (1937), Cranleigh (1929), Downham (1928), Eden-bridge (1931), Horley (1929), Lancing (1935), Lingfield (1940), Mongeham, Deal (1933), Morden (1930), Mottingham (1927), Petts Wood (1937), Purley (1931), Selsdon (1927),

Send, Woking (1939), Stoneleigh (1937), Wadhurst (1929), West Wickham (1936)[4].

IV

Even twenty years ago, when the rapid expansion of modern suburbs was beginning, it was apparent from the figures in the *Catholic Directory* that, in roughly half the counties of England and in four-fifths of Wales, the Catholics

[4] Similar developments north of the Thames are as follows:—Abbots Langley (1928), Barkingside (1928), Boreham Wood (1925), Burnt Oak (1928), Chadwell Heath (1935), Cockfosters (1936), Dagenham (1926 and 1930), Eastcote (1935), East Ham (1926), Elm Park (1939), Epping (1932), Greenford (1928), Gunnersbury (1931), Hampton-on-Thames (1927), North Harrow (1939), South Harrow (1933), Hatfield (1930), Heston (1928), Hillingdon (1937), Hornchurch (1931), Kenton (1932), Kingsbury (1930), Kingsbury Green (1926), Knebworth (1929), Loughton (1927), New Barking (1935), Northfields (1926), Osterley (1934), Perivale (1936), Puckeridge (1926), Rainham (1938), Redbourn (1936), St. Margaret's-on-Thames (1930), St. Quintin Park (1937), Tollington Park (1925), Walthamstow, Chingford Road (1932), Watford North (1925), Welwyn Garden City (1925), Wembley Park (1932), West Green, Tottenham (1927), Wheathampstead (1936), Whetstone, N.20 (1926), Whitton (1934).

The pattern for Liverpool is as follows:—Wavertree (1925), Fazakerley (1929), Garston (1926), Gateacre (1947), Mossley Hill (1926), Allerton (1936), Speke (1940), Stanley (1927), Knotty Ash (1931), East Lancashire Road (1937), Norris Green (1928), Peel Road, Bootle (1926), Orrell Road, Bootle (1932), Hillside Avenue, Huyton, Liverpool (1938), Baker's Green, Huyton (1948), South Dean Road, Huyton (1934), Roby (1934).

In the diocese of Middlesbrough the following new churches or Mass centres have been opened since 1925:—Cottingham Road, Hull (1925), Grove Hill, Middlesbrough (1926), Southcotes Lane, Hull (1926), Guisborough (1927), Cottingham (1928), Swanland Road, Hessle (1928), Hornsea (1928), Saltburn (1928), Newport, Howden (1929), Hipswell Road, Catterick Camp (1930), Boothferry Road, Hull (1930), Linthorpe Road, Middlesbrough (1931), Spring Bank West, Hull (1932), Lealholm, Yorks (1932), York (1932), Hall Road, Hull (1933), Ulshaw Bridge, Middleham (1933), Northallerton (1934), Acklam, Middlesbrough (1934), Whitby (1935), Marske-by-the-Sea (1936), Redcar (1937), Linthorpe, Middlesbrough (1938), Dormanstown (1939), Redcar (1939), Burdyke Avenue, York (1942), Huntington Road Soc. Hall, York (1942), Ampleforth (1942), Brompton-on-Swale (1943), Hopewell Road, Hull (1944), Goatland (1946), Lea Smith Street, Hull (1946), Redcar Road, Ormesby Village (1946), Danby (1947), Lealholm (1947), Keld, Richmond (1947), Gunnerside Lodge, Richmond (1947), Low Row, Richmond (1947), Scorton (1949), Thorntree, Middlesbrough (1949), Green Lane, Scarborough (1949), Sleights (1950).

were still an extremely small and scattered minority. In wide districts there was not even a Catholic church or priest to be found. That was still the general position in all Wales, except for the two southern counties of Monmouth and Glamorgan, which contained very large Catholic populations in the industrial and shipping centres. It was the same in the whole diocese of Plymouth, including Cornwall, Devon and Dorset: in the diocese of Clifton, including Gloucestershire, Somerset and Wiltshire: in the immense diocese of Northampton, including the seven counties of Bedford, Buckingham, Cambridge, Huntingdon, Norfolk, Northampton and Suffolk. In the three dioceses of Menevia, Clifton and Plymouth there was not one county which contained 10,000 Catholics; and many counties had not even a few thousands. Similar conditions prevailed also in most of the diocese of Nottingham, where Lincolnshire, Rutland, and even Nottinghamshire each had less than 10,000 Catholics. Even the new see of Lancaster had extremely few Catholics in Westmorland and Cumberland though they were very numerous in the northern end of Lancashire, which it included. And there was another large area in the southern midlands where Catholic churches were still extremely few—in the three adjacent counties of Oxford and Buckingham and Berkshire.

A map indicating the distribution of Catholics by counties even twenty years ago thus showed that, if England and Wales were taken together, more than half of the country was still deplorably backward in Catholic population. Apart from the large local concentration in two counties of South Wales, the whole western side from Anglesey down to Portsmouth was still undeveloped. Across the centre, only Staffordshire and Warwickshire made a break in the similar emptiness, which stretched from the west coast of Wales to the coastline of Lincolnshire, Norfolk and Suffolk. There were four special areas alone in which the Catholic population was really large and important. The area of London, north and south of the Thames, included fully 300,000. The industrial area around Cardiff had some 80,000. The Tyneside area round Newcastle had about 150,000. The other main concentration was much larger in extent. The diocese of Leeds, as the western half of Yorkshire, had about 150,000. The small diocese of Salford had nearly 300,000, and the archdiocese of Liverpool had nearly 400,000, in addition to the adjacent concentrations of some 80,000 in north Lancashire and some 50,000 or more in Cheshire.

Hence, in 1930, in more than half England and Wales the Catholic population was still extremely small; while it was really numerous and strongly organised in Lancashire and western Yorkshire, on the Tyneside, in London, and in the cities of South Wales. But there were a number of counties, adjacent to these larger Catholic centres of population, in which twenty years ago progress was already evident. Birmingham itself had for years had a considerable Catholic population, and there were flourishing Catholic centres in various parts of Staffordshire and Warwickshire; but they were still few and widely scattered in Oxford and in Worcestershire. There were important centres also in Derbyshire, and they were numerous also in the East Riding of Yorkshire. Around London also there were clear signs of real progress. Hampshire had always contained a good many Catholics, in the military area round Aldershot and in the seaports of Portsmouth and Southampton; and they were steadily spreading out. In Essex there were already nearly 50,000. Middlesex likewise was being rapidly developed, and also Hertfordshire. And in the three counties south of the Thames (Kent, Surrey and Sussex), there had been a continual expansion. About half of the 180,000 Catholics in Southwark diocese were in London; but there was a steady and continual increase in the suburbs which were expanding southwards, besides large Catholic parishes in the seaside resorts along the southern coast.

I have taken the picture as it stood twenty years ago, because the dispersal into the suburban areas of the great cities was then beginning. But it had not yet assumed the dimensions of the much wider extensions into the suburbs which followed, between the two World Wars. Still less could it be compared with the sudden and far-reaching dispersal which came with the outbreak of war in 1939, and was intensified by the destruction by bombing in so many cities and the growth of new centres which arose during the war. But by 1930 the Catholic population was already beginning to spread outwards from the few main centres in which it had been concentrated for the previous eighty years. On the other hand, the chief concentrations were still strongly apparent.

The broad totals for twenty years ago could be further simplified. The northern province accounted for about three-fifths of all the Catholics in England. Their distribution was clearly defined. There were two main concentrations in the industrial areas. The main concentration was based upon Liverpool and Manchester. The dioceses of Liverpool and Salford together counted some 670,000 Catholics; to which must be added roughly 80,000 from Lancaster diocese and perhaps 70,000 more from the diocese of Shrewsbury (which counts as part of the Birmingham province). This whole area may be described as the Industrial North-west, with a total Catholic population of 820,000.

If we count the diocese of Leeds together with Hexham and Newcastle and Middlesbrough, as the Industrial North-east, there was here another concentration of some 440,000 Catholics. The only substantial concentration in the whole Midland province, apart from Cheshire (which, in fact, was a direct overflow from the Liverpool area into Birkenhead and its surroundings) was in Birmingham itself and a few other cities of the northern midlands. The Catholic population in the Industrial Midlands was not more than roughly 100,000. Another main concentration of Catholics was gathered in the Greater London region—comprising the areas where Brentwood, and the northern part of Southwark and the southern part of the archdiocese of Westminster converged. A total of about 400,000 could be attributed to this London area. Thus the general picture for the whole country would show, for twenty years ago, some two million Catholics in all; of whom roughly 800,000 were in the Industrial North-west and 450,000 in the Industrial North-east; 100,000 in the Industrial Midlands and 400,000 in Greater London.

That left very roughly 250,000 Catholics in all the other counties of England, but even in them the distribution was similarly localised in clearly defined districts. In the diocese of Northampton there were just over 20,000 Catholics and only 59 churches registered for marriages in the whole seven counties. In the diocese of Plymouth, with only 21,000

for the three counties of Devon, Dorset and Cornwall, they
were even more sparsely scattered; because it included the
city of Plymouth and several other large towns which had
substantial parishes. In the diocese of Clifton, with 28,000
Catholics, the position was much the same, because the congregations and priests were chiefly in a few cities like Bristol,
or around important Catholic centres like Downside. In the
Portsmouth diocese, with 53,000 Catholics between the two
counties of Hampshire and Berkshire, it was the same story;
with scarcely any churches or congregations in either county,
apart from the crowded cities of Portsmouth and Southampton
and a few special centres in Winchester and Aldershot and
Reading. Even in the archdiocese of Birmingham, with
130,000 Catholics altogether, Worcestershire was as backward
as almost any part of Wales or of East Anglia, and in Oxfordshire there were fewer than twenty Mass centres. The industrial
areas, however, were vigorously developed and Birmingham
itself had the first Catholic cathedral to be built since the
Reformation.

V

Comparative figures for churches at the present time
have been largely invalidated during the past ten years. So
many churches in all parts of the country (and often they were
the largest and most important) were destroyed and cannot
yet be rebuilt. On the other hand many temporary churches
and chapels and Mass centres were established during the war,
to provide for Catholic residents in the new industrial or
military centres which formed in those years. Some of these
centres have since been almost abandoned, while others have
become permanent and have attracted large populations.
Statistics of local Catholic populations have been similarly
affected by the years of upheaval. For a general comparison
it is more reliable to contrast the figures of 1939 with those of
1914, which show the position on the eve of the two wars.
Thus, Westminster in 1914 had some 256,000 Catholics,
whereas in 1939 the same area (now divided into the two sees
of Westminster and Brentwood) had 370,000. Liverpool in
1914 had less than 400,000 Catholics but there were roughly
500,000 in the same area (including part of what is now

Lancaster) in 1939. The total Catholic population of England and Wales, which was 1,870,000 in 1914, had grown to 2,360,000 in 1939.

This increase of some 500,000 Catholics still indicated the old concentration in clearly defined areas. Industrial Lancashire alone had contributed some 200,000 to the increase; while Greater London had contributed 150,000, though this area was largely changed in character, because of the vast expansion of the London suburbs during that period. Of the remaining increase of 150,000, by far the largest part had been contributed by the other three principal industrial areas of South Wales, Birmingham and Tyneside. That general distribution has not even been modified since, as a result of dispersal during the recent war; and the old pattern still persists.

While the increase of Catholic population was thus encouraging, the increase of churches was most remarkable, and the increase of priests has been still more promising for the future. The total of churches in each province shows the following comparison between 1939 and 1914. The southern province of Westminster had 882 churches instead of 705. The Midland province of Birmingham had 510 instead of 380. The northern province of Liverpool had 921 instead of 679, Wales had 174 instead of 127. The total of churches and chapels had thus risen, within twenty-five years, from 1,891 to 2,475. In Northampton, where Catholics were so scattered over seven counties, the 25 new churches was an increase of nearly 30 per cent. In Clifton the increase was nearly half the previous total; and the archdiocese of Birmingham had gained nearly 50 more, principally in the outlying districts. In the north the diocese of Leeds had increased its churches from 111 to 188, again in the more remote parts of western Yorkshire.

While this extension into formerly backward districts was so apparent in the years between the two World Wars, the statistics did not reveal the many cases in which existing churches had been enlarged or otherwise improved. The scale of church building had become more ambitious everywhere, and it was always necessary to plan for larger congregations in the future. The most outstanding instance of this new spirit of confidence was Archbishop Downey's decision to build a new cathedral in Liverpool which was to be the cathedral for the whole northern province for great occasions. It was to be far larger in size than Westminster Cathedral, which had seemed fantastically large when Cardinal Vaughan had undertaken to build it, but had already been found too small, again and again, for special religious celebrations.

Coinciding with this rapid increase of church building between the two wars, was a similar rise in the number of priests in every diocese. The seculars and the religious congregations must here be considered together, for lack of space; though the progressive increase of religious orders and of nuns was of special interest. The combined total of priests rose from some 3,800 in 1914 to over 5,600 in 1939. Here, even more than for the churches, the statistics revealed a deliberate expansion into new areas. For Northampton the total had doubled, rising from 90 to 180. In Nottingham it had risen from 120 to over 200; in Clifton from 120 to nearly 200; in Plymouth from about 100 to 170; in Shrewsbury from 80 to 150. In Menevia, the most thinly populated of the dioceses, comprising nearly all Wales, there were nearly 160 priests instead of 90. Even in the more crowded dioceses with small territories the increase was most impressive. Salford had over 500 priests instead of 350; Westminster had over 860 instead of 650; Birmingham 460 against 300; and Liverpool over 600 against 460.

When war came again in 1939, the picture had therefore been full of promise on all sides. The old pattern of localised Catholic distribution still persisted in its general outlines, but the areas of concentration were more numerous. They were all expanding steadily, pushing out new missions from the various centres, and building new churches from year to year, while each new parish became a focus for wider expansion. No other religious denomination in England could even contemplate such steady expansion anywhere in England and Wales. Most of them were facing a continuous and demoralising decline in their numbers. The Nonconformists especially were being obliged to relinquish churches whose congregations had melted away, and the buildings were soon sold and converted to other uses.

Yet the growth of the Catholic population by natural increase ought to have been very much larger than it actually was, even without the continual accession of converts, who brought in new blood and a constant renewal of religious energy and fervour. But the Catholics still benefited from the tradition which had kept them for generations living in close proximity within clearly defined areas, where Catholic social and religious life had become so well organised that Catholics had little difficulty in finding wives or husbands of their own faith. Year after year, Catholic numbers were steadily increasing; and, as new parishes were constantly being formed in the previously backward counties, there was always less risk of losing contact with Catholic worship when Catholics moved from their former homes to other districts.

Nevertheless, the impact of war in 1939 upon the Catholics of England and Wales brought a far more drastic upheaval to their religious life and their social traditions than to any other denomination. The first shock came in September, 1939, with the sudden evacuation of children from all the principal industrial cities, which were expected to become the targets of attack from the air. The cities and industrial areas from which evacuation was at first almost compulsory were precisely those in which the Catholic population was chiefly centred—Liverpool, Manchester, Leeds, Sheffield, Newcastle, Birmingham, Cardiff, Portsmouth and Southampton and London. Almost without preparation hundreds of thousands of Catholic children and their mothers were uprooted from their previous surroundings in the cities, and sent to remote places in the countryside. The cities from which they were evacuated had been for generations the chief strongholds of organised Catholic life. The country places to which they were sent were the remote counties in which Catholic expansion had scarcely yet made any effective penetration. In those first anxious months of the " phoney " war it became apparent how little real progress had even yet been made in extending the Catholic Church all over England; and how enormously important had been the more recent formation of parishes in remote places.

In hundreds of distant and lonely missions, where some modest church had been recently built as an act of faith in the future, the local priest would find during that time that he was overwhelmed by a temporary incursion of Catholics. Military and Air Force centres brought their quota of Catholic men and women in the fighting services. Evacuation of banks and commercial houses, of universities and civil service departments and of many diverse groups of people, resulted in large congregations where there had been only a handful before. It was a chaotic situation all through the war, because the evacuation was often only temporary. It might recede and then be resumed again, either through fear of air raids or because of devastation in the cities when the air attacks actually began. New war industries arose, some of which were closed when the war ended; or great camps and air bases were formed, which were usually demobilised after the return of peace. But in many places the war buildings have since been put to some other use; and everywhere there has been an upheaval of population. Great numbers have moved from one place to another, in search of a new permanent home. Many more who would have wished to go back have found it impossible to obtain houses in the devastated cities. It is too early yet even to guess what form the new pattern of distribution for the whole people will ultimately take.

After ten years since 1939, the statistics in the annual *Catholic Directory* can only reveal a shifting situation. So many of the large churches in the cities have been wrecked or utterly destroyed. So many temporary Mass centres have become redundant since the brief local increase of population during the war: while others have already formed the nucleus of future parishes. Rebuilding has in many cases been impossible in the blitzed cities, partly because of Government restrictions on building licences, and still more because of the overwhelming cost of replacement. Building of new churches has been almost impossible, while the acute shortage of houses persists. Even in regard to payments in compensation for destroyed property, the Catholic community has suffered more severely than the other denominations. Almost every other religious community had been faced with declining church attendance, so that the existing churches were larger than was really needed. But the Catholic churches everywhere were experiencing the need for enlargement. Compensation for churches of all sorts has been fixed on the basis of actual replacement in the simplest form, with a strong tendency to reduce the claims for replacement, on the plea that the previous churches were larger than was really necessary. In a great number of cases, with other denominations, the congregations had fallen far below what the destroyed churches could accommodate. The Catholic churches, on the contrary, were usually too small for their regular congregations, or had been built recently with ample reason to expect a future increase.

Notwithstanding all these difficulties, it is most remarkable that the *Catholic Directory* should show a quite substantial increase in the number of churches and chapels between 1939 and 1949. Most of the increase is probably due to the acquisition by religious congregations of houses in which they have established a public church or chapel of some kind. But since 1939 the total of churches and Mass centres in England and Wales has actually risen from 2,475 to 2,821; and this increase of nearly 350 is made up by small additions in almost every diocese. The most notable increases, however, are in the formerly neglected areas which came to active life for a period during the war. Thus, Northampton now has 151 churches against 105 ten years ago, and Nottingham 175 against 129. Birmingham has risen from 214 to 270 and Clifton from 111 to 139. Menevia shows an astonishing rise from 58 churches to 102[5].

The estimates of Catholic population for each diocese must be more than ever uncertain while economic and social conditions are so unsettled, and there is still so much movement

[5] This dispersal into new areas is emphasised by the figures for Easter duties. A few examples from parishes in the Northampton diocese will make this clear.

Parish.	*Easter duties.* 1931	*Easter duties.* 1949
Aylesbury... ...	131	782
Bedford	640	1,660
Cambridge ...	752	2,134
Dunstable... ...	40	440
Luton	440	2,243
Peterborough ...	468	872
Slough	689	2,407
Sudbury	97	439
Wellingborough ...	252	469

from place to place. But the gross total of Catholic population, which is unaffected by movements from place to place, rose within ten years from 2,375,000 to 2,650,000. That increase of 275,000 Catholics is remarkably high in comparison with a total estimated increase of less than 550,000 for the whole population of England and Wales. A broad comparison by provinces is still fairly reliable, even though so much disturbance continues; and the general totals are revealing. Each province showed a substantial increase, but the northern preponderance is greater even than before. Out of 2,650,000 Catholics, 1,465,000 are in the northern province, showing an increase of 215,000 in ten years. The southern province had increased by 75,000, from 705,000 to 784,000; and the midland province still more in proportion, from 313,000 to 400,000. In Wales, where population had declined severely during the pre-war economic depression, the increase was least rapid, from 100,000 to 111,000.

The most striking feature of the returns during the past ten years is the large increase in the number of priests. Upon the clergy chiefly must depend all future expansion and consolidation. Space does not allow of any analysis of how far their numbers are derived from English seminaries or from the assistance of Irish or foreign priests, or how far the religious congregations are contributing to the tasks of future development, in a situation which has altered greatly since before the recent war. But within ten years the total of priests in England and Wales has risen from 5,642 to 6,643. In Wales alone it has risen from 329 to 385. In the northern province of Liverpool it has risen from some 2,200 to nearly 2,500; in the province of Birmingham from under 1,000 to over 1,200; in the province of Westminster from 2,130 to over 2,500. An examination of the figures by dioceses shows some remarkable local results. Thus Westminster and Cardiff show only a slight increase, while Liverpool has a rise from 613 to 720. Lancaster similarly has increased from 190 to 227. Hexham and Newcastle, with 412 priests, has over 60 more than ten years ago. But the most striking proportional increases are in some of the dioceses which were most backward for years. Northampton's clergy have increased from 177 to 213; Nottingham's from 202 to 255; Portsmouth from 272 to 383 (which is presumably due in part to military and naval bases); Southwark from 687 to 772; Birmingham from 465 to 557; Clifton from 195 to 252 and Menevia from 156 to 202[6].

These figures obviously cannot be taken as any indication of relative activity in each diocese. The clergy who were trained in the archdiocese of Westminster, for instance, or Liverpool or Birmingham, may be found working in other dioceses. But the total increase of 1,000 priests within ten years would have seemed scarcely conceivable in the days when the Hierarchy was restored, a hundred years ago. There were not 800 priests in all England and Wales in those days, and many had died during the recently preceding years from sheer overwork, or from the " famine fever " which the Irish immigrants brought with them. " The labourers are so few " was the burden of countless letters which survive from those days: and it was recognised on all sides that if there were more labourers in the untilled fields, the prospects of England's return to the Catholic faith would be immeasurably improved[7]. The recent war, by its upheaval of the whole population and the vast social changes which it has wrought, has created conditions of transition which may also be compared to those which resulted from the great Irish immigration of a century ago. The Catholic Church in England and Wales now at least possesses a large body of highly-trained and experienced priests, who are devoting themselves to consolidating and expanding the work of the earlier pioneers. They have moreover at their disposal a wide and flourishing organisation of churches and schools and religious institutions already in existence, no matter how heavy may be the burden of continuing and developing them.

[6] The total number of priests in England and Wales at 10-year intervals is as follows:—1910, 3,835; 1920, 4,528; 1930, 4,484; 1940, 5,642; 1950, 6,643.

[7] The annual number of ordinations to the priesthood among the secular clergy and the religious orders almost doubled between the two wars. In 1913 the number was 119 and in 1939 it was 215. In the five years prior to 1939 the totals were 228, 227, 260, 238 and 219.

1850

MAP SHOWING THE NUMBER OF PRI

IN THE ORIGINAL DIOCESES

DIOCESES WITH LESS THAN 100 PRIESTS

~ ~ FROM 100-200 ~ ~

1900

MAP SHOWING THE NUMBER OF PRIESTS

IN THE ORIGINAL DIOCESES

HEXHAM

LIVERPOOL

BEVERLEY

SALFORD

NEWPORT AND MENEVIA

SHREWSBURY

NOTTINGHAM

BIRMINGHAM

NORTHAMPTON

WESTMINSTER

CLIFTON

SOUTHWARK

PLYMOUTH

DIOCESES WITH LESS THAN 100 PRIESTS

FROM 100~200

200~300

300~500

1950

MAP SHOWING THE NUMBER OF PRIES[T]

IN THE ORIGINAL DIOCESES

HEXHAM

LIVERPOOL

BEVERLEY

SALFORD

SHREWSBURY

NOTTINGHAM

NEWPORT AND MENEVIA

BIRMINGHAM

NORTHAMPTON

WESTMINSTER

CLIFTON

SOUTHWARK

PLYMOUTH

DIOCESES WITH FROM 200 ~ 300 PRIESTS

300 ~ 500

OVER 500

L.P.

MAP SHOWING BY COUNTIES THE DISTRIBUTION
OF CATHOLICS IN ENGLAND AND WALES
IN 1950
BASED ON THE ESTIMATES GIVEN
IN THE CATHOLIC DIRECTORY

AREAS * CONTAINING LESS THAN 15,000 CATHOLICS

FROM 15~30,000

30~50,000

50~80,000

OVER 80,000

'' areas '' is meant counties or parts of counties where differently shaded.

XV

DEVELOPMENT OF
THE RELIGIOUS ORDERS

By Edward Cruise

THE memorials in stone left to us in the ancient abbeys even when ruined or dismantled, indicate something o the past glories of the religious life in England. These buildings remind us of the profound loss to England that wa: effected by Henry VIII's suppression of the religious houses It was not only that centres of charity, of study and of fine workmanship disappeared. These could be replaced in othe: ways. It was centres of prayer also which were destroyed places where men and women devoted themselves primarily to the worship of God, to prayer and to their personal sanctifica tion, and secondarily to pastoral work, to works of charity and to study. Religious, by so maintaining the practice and ideal of prayer, perform a vital function in society; their houses should be centres of spiritual energy, and by their very exist ence a reminder to others of the primacy of the spiritual and of the Christian's obligation to pray. But Henry VIII and his successors had done their work well, and by 1850, although there were some who were maintaining the ideal of the religious life, they were sadly few in number. We are still far to-day from having undone Henry's work, but the last century has been one of remarkable growth and development.

The contrast between the numerical strengths of the religious orders in England in 1850 and in 1950 is most marked At the beginning of our period there appear to have been 10 orders or congregations of men with perhaps 275 priests (although this number is hard to check accurately) as against over 70 orders at the present day with some 2,360 priests In 1850 there were 14 orders of women in 53 convents as against over 140 orders of women in 1,075 convents in

England at the present time. The bare figures, however, indicate inadequately the weakness of religious life in England in 1850.

Only the Jesuits could be described as being in a strong and flourishing state. The English Province had been started in 1621, and was divided into 12 colleges or districts with their own Rectors and officials but with no buildings of any sort. For more than 200 years they had maintained an average of 20 novices a year. Even during the period of their suppression the Fathers in England, largely through the influence of Bishop Challoner, continued their work and remained in their districts, living of course as secular priests, and with their vows no longer recognised.

After the restoration of the Society in 1814, the quarrel between the Jesuits and the Vicars Apostolic, which had its roots in the earliest days of the Province, continued, unfortunately, unabated. There was, for instance, the occasion in 1830 when the Vicar Apostolic in London tried to persuade the British Government to express its distaste of Jesuits to the Pope. But the Jesuits appeared to thrive on this opposition, for in the period up to 1850 and beyond they expanded rapidly in numbers and converted into fact parishes and colleges which had existed only on paper since the earliest penal days. By 1850 Stonyhurst had already been established for half a century at the house presented by the Welds of Lulworth. It had over 200 pupils and a heterogeneous but fine group of buildings, in which was given the full traditional Jesuit education, but in an atmosphere that was inescapably and almost aggressively English. Mount St. Mary's College had been founded more recently. The church in Farm Street, which was to play a central part in the Catholic life of the next century, was, with Cardinal Wiseman's support, opened in 1849.

Of the other orders of men in England in 1850, the Benedictines grouped together in the English Congregation were the most numerous, and had behind them a great tradition of work for the Faith in England. They were, however, going through a difficult period. Till the French Revolution the monks were trained in monasteries abroad, and then in the great majority of cases went to work on the mission in England, nine of them being martyred in penal times. At the Revolution their monastic properties were confiscated, and there was at one time a fear that it would not be possible to maintain the separate corporate existence of the communities. In the event Downside, Ampleforth and Douai survived. The communities had, however, hardly become firmly re-established before the existence of the two first named was seriously threatened by the work of Bishop Baines, an Ampleforth monk who became Vicar Apostolic of the Western District. He drew away some of the leading Ampleforth monks to work with him while he tried to turn Downside into a seminary for his Vicariate. Possessed of a powerful personality and grim determination, he weakened and nearly destroyed the English Congregation[1].

A more glorious cause of the temporary weakening of the Congregation was the number of the outstanding monks who had the honour of playing such a large part in the foundation of the Australian Hierarchy. For instance, it was the labours of Dom Bernard Ullathorne that led in 1840 to the establishment of the Australian Hierarchy, and the first Bishop of Maitland and the first two Archbishops of Sydney were Downside monks.

As a result of all this it can hardly be said that the Benedictines were at first in a position to react vigorously to the stimulus offered by the Oxford Movement and the re-establishment of the Hierarchy. It is not without significance that in contrast to many of the other orders none of the distinguished converts found his vocation with the Benedictines.

The Dominicans, the other order of men which had been long established in England, were in a much worse plight. They had never been as vigorous in post-Reformation England as the Jesuits or the Benedictines and in the period before 1850

---

[1] It is often told at Downside how Fr. Brown (later to become Vicar Apostolic of the Welsh District), a Downside monk who was the principal proponent at Rome of the case against Bishop Baines owed his ultimate success over Baines in Rome partly to his prowess in skipping. He arrived in Rome in mid-winter and used to skip at night to warm himself. The noise at first caused much mystification, but this turned to astonishment and delight when Fr. Brown was later persuaded to give public performances. It is said that when Cardinal Cappellari, who as Prefect of Propaganda was judge of the case, saw the performance he clapped his hands and fairly shouted with delight and was from that time most friendly towards Fr. Brown!

heir continued existence hung for a long time in the balance.
They had been re-organised into a Congregation and later into
a Province (operating from Flanders since 1622), and they con-
inued their work in this way till the French Revolution. In
810 the Province had reached its lowest ebb and during the
ext generation only just managed to carry on. Although it was
ittle affected by the Oxford Converts or the Irish Immigration,
turning-point came with the acquisition from the Passionists
n about 1850 of Woodchester Priory. This became the centre
f a revived attachment to an austere standard of observance,
nd the order gradually began its return to a more important
osition in English Catholic life.

The Franciscans were even less fortunate. All three
ranches of the First Order had died out in England before
850. The Friars Minor Conventual, historically the main
runk from which the other branches sprang, were suppressed
y Henry VIII and did not return to England till 1906. The
Second Province of the Friars Minor had been established in
629, but by the beginning of the 19th century the vigorous life
t had once shown had ebbed from it and the last Chapter was
eld in 1838. A new start was made from Belgium in 1858,
argely owing to the persistence of the Abbess of the Franciscan
ouse at Taunton, a start that was in time to lead to the Third
Province set up in 1891, and which has to-day some 200 friars
n 18 Friaries and is responsible for missions in South India
nd the Transvaal. The Anglo-Irish Province of the Capuchins
ied out in 1802, but there was a return of these friars to
England in 1850, followed by wonderful pioneering work,
specially in South Wales. Altogether they founded some 35
arishes, which they nursed and, when strong, handed over
o the bishops to be taken on by the secular clergy. In 1873
n English Province was set up.

Already by 1850 these orders of men which had main-
ained or nearly maintained a continuity in England had been
oined by others. In 1837 the Cistercians returned to England
o give expression once again by their lives to the importance
ttached by the Church to the contemplative life. It was
hrough the aid of Ambrose de Lisle Phillipps and the Earl of
Shrewsbury that a group of monks went from Mount Melleray
n Ireland to Mount St. Bernard's, Coalville, Leicester, where

the monks immediately set themselves to putting up building
partly designed by Pugin. In 1850 Mount St. Bernard's wa
raised to the dignity of an Abbey, and England had her firs
mitred Abbot since the Reformation.

A more controversial note was struck by the newe
orders, the Rosminians, Redemptorists, Passionists and
Oratorians, when they first came to England. Some of th
members of these orders were Italians, and most of them en
couraged Italian forms of piety and practices which shocked
many of the old-fashioned English Catholics brought up on th
solid austere piety of Challoner. Thus Dr. Lingard wrote to
fellow priest in February, 1850, suggesting as a subject fo
discussion at one of Dr. Wiseman's *soirées*, " How to send
away those swarms of Italian congregationalists who introduc
their own customs and by making religion ridiculous in th
eyes of Protestants prevent it spreading here?"

The new religious on their part thought the English
Catholics backward, stagnating, lacking in zeal and infected
by the Protestants among whom they lived. By their ow
methods they hoped to convert England quickly. A greater
knowledge and the obvious sanctity of many of the new religi
ous soon softened hard feelings. And there can be no doub
that a new rich element was added by these orders to English
Catholicism.

The Rosminians had the saintly Fr. Aloysius Gentili in
their ranks. Archbishop Ullathorne bears witness to the extra
ordinary effect that missions given by him had in Coventry
and Bristol. In the latter town he says, " It began a new orde
of things." Ratcliffe College, which they founded, had as its
President from 1851 to 1880 a great classical teacher in Fr
Hutton. The school has continued to prosper and develop
especially under its late President, Fr. J. C. Emery, the presen
Provincial.

When Fr. Dominic Barberi, the first Passionist to come
to England, arrived in 1842, he entered upon the work fo
which he had for many years been longing. His zeal wa
rewarded in his reception of Newman into the Church. A
convert parson, Fr. Ignatius Spencer, the son of Earl Spencer
was one of the first Englishmen to join the Passionists. With
an evangelical fervour that shocked some Catholics almost a

uch as it shocked Fr. Ignatius's relations, he preached
roughout the country the power of the crucifix and a Crusade
Prayer for the conversion of England. To-day there is an
nglish Province of the Passionists with about 100 priests in
ine houses.

Another modern order, that of the Redemptorists, which
ad come to England in 1843 with the similar object of preach-
g, giving missions and Retreats, especially to the most
eglected, was soon greatly strengthened by the reception of a
ries of distinguished convert novices. Perhaps the name of
r. Bridgett, the biographer of St. John Fisher and St. Thomas
lore, is the best known. A man of great integrity of character,
e brought many to the Faith by his writings and preaching,
hich continued incessantly from his ordination in 1856 till
is death in 1899.

The Oratorians were introduced to England in 1847 by
ewman. They settled in Birmingham two years later, where
ie work of the distinguished group, whose names are enshrined
1 the concluding words of the *Apologia,* was somewhat over-
nadowed by the great Newman, whose spirit to this day seems
） pervade the Birmingham Oratory. Newman's work and in-
uence were so great that he seems hardly to belong to one
rder or indeed to England only but to the life of the whole
hurch in the second half of the nineteenth century.

Cardinal Wiseman persuaded Newman to send a group
nder Faber to found an Oratory in London. There, under
aber's influence, the characteristic approach of the newer
eligious orders could be seen in its full glory. The traditional
straint or timidity of the English Catholics was replaced by
amboyant and self-confident display. The decoration of the
hurch (which was at first just off the Strand) was as bright
nd Italian as were the devotions, the hymns and the manner
f preaching of Faber. Many of the hereditary Catholics were
ismayed (almost as dismayed as was the Gothic-loving Pugin
t the post-Tridentine architectural tastes of the Fathers), while
rotestant bigotry had plenty to feed on. But there can be no
oubt about the wonderful work they did. The small com-
iunity, with the help of some Sisters of Compassion, were
aching perhaps 1,000 children in several schools, they were
ringing Catholic life to the faithful who continually crowded

their church and they gave missions and lectures which won
stream of converts. In 1853 they were so cramped for spac
that they moved out to Brompton, where gradually there aros
the present Oratory and church, the product of the devotion c
a series of benefactors[2].

The way in which the Brompton Oratory has come t
be looked upon as a natural and essential element in Englis
Catholic life is symbolic of the way in which the newer orders
coming to England in a steady stream throughout the century
strengthened and embellished the older Catholic tradition i
England.

If we turn to examine the position of the religious order
of women in and after 1850, we find that the large number c
convents, with a wonderful continuity of tradition alread
dating back two hundred years and more, creates the greates
impression. For instance, among the Benedictine nuns ther
were at least six houses in England that were founded betwee
1598 and 1662. They had all suffered greatly at the Frencl
Revolution. The Stanbrook community, for example, wa
imprisoned at Compiègne for 18 months, daily expecting th
sentence of execution that came to the Carmelites, their com
panions in prison. The communities had found the re
establishment in England, whither they all returned from th
continent, very difficult; but by 1850 those houses that sui
vived had entered upon a great period of development
Churches were built and consecrated; and suitable conventua
buildings encouraged regular observance and the fitting an
dignified carrying out of the Divine Office. The most ancien
house (now at Haslemere) was that founded at Brussels i
1598 by Lady Mary Percy, youngest daughter of Blessee
Thomas Percy. But possibly the most distinguished of th
houses has been that founded at Cambrai in 1625 and now a
Stanbrook. Partly through the influence of Dom Laurenc
Shepherd, who became their chaplain in 1863, and partl

[2] The Oratorians tell of the following incident when Anne, Duches
of Argyll, who was to be one of their greatest supporters, firs
called at the Oratory and, wishing to be received into the Church
asked for Father Faber. " The church verger, by name Munster
looking critically at the very plainly dressed woman, said: ' Fathe
Faber is engaged: go off to Dr. Manning, he is good enough fo
the likes of you!' " She obeyed, but later returned to the Oratory

through the inspiration given by two distinguished Abbesses, Dame Scholastica Gregson and Dame Gertrude d'Aurillac Dubois, they played a leading part in the restoration of plain-chant. This work has received special recognition from Popes Pius X and Pius XI. A parallel revival of the chant can be seen in the other five Benedictine houses and in those that came to be founded during the course of the century. St. Mary's Abbey, Colwich, was the first House of Perpetual Adoration in England. The devotion has been established since 1829. To-day there are 16 Benedictine houses of women in England.

The Carmelites had in England in 1850 two venerable foundations at Lanherne and Darlington. Their traditions flowed direct from St. Teresa's reform. The first English nuns were trained in the Carmels in the Low Countries by such immediate disciples of St. Teresa as the Venerable Anne of Jesus and Blessed Anne of St. Bartholomew, in whose arms St. Teresa had died in 1582. The Carmel now at Wells was founded from Lanherne in 1864; the Carmel now at Chichester (a foundation dating from 1678) came to England in 1892.

In the penal times probably no English convents on the continent maintained such a reputation among the English Catholics as those of the Canonesses Regular. Their schools were famous, and they educated the daughters of most of the Catholic nobility. Of these the house now at Newton Abbot (at Spettisbury in 1850) can claim not only to carry on the great mystical tradition of Windesheim but to have direct continuity with pre-Reformation Catholicism in England. The Canonesses of the Holy Sepulchre at New Hall have an almost equally venerable tradition.

The Poor Clares of the First Rule had one convent in England in 1850. It is the present Abbey at Darlington, which can trace its traditions to the first English post-Reformation Poor Clare community established in 1607. The first of a series of foundations of the Strict Observation of the Poor Clare Colettines was made at Baddesley Clinton in 1850. The Cistercian Abbey at Stapehill deserves to be grouped with these ancient English foundations. Its connection with England dates from 1801 when the community sought protection here from the Revolution. In their austerity of life these nuns have

remained true to the spirit of Val-Sainte, a reform more rigorous
than that of de Rancé, which influenced them in the period
immediately prior to their coming to England.

Nearly all the ancient English foundations are of a more
or less strictly contemplative nature, but there was one, the
famous Bar Convent at York, which belonged to an Institute
founded expressly by Mary Ward (1585-1645) to carry out
an active apostolate similar to that of the Jesuits. As Peter
Anson says, " it required great courage for a woman to convince the Holy See that the legislation of the Council of Trent
needed modification; and that unenclosed nuns were essential
for the welfare of souls and the preservation of the Faith "[3]
And indeed at one moment Urban VIII suppressed her first
community and imprisoned Mary Ward. But eventually Mary
Ward's sanctity triumphed over all obstacles and an Institute
of the Blessed Virgin arose which has to-day in its two branches
some 5,400 sisters. The Bar Convent is descended from a
convent founded in England in 1669. They moved to York
in 1686 where they started what is the oldest existing convent
in England. Gradually other houses of the Institute, all of
them with schools, have grown up, Ascot, the Provincial and
Novitiate House, with its well-known boarding school, being
pre-eminent.

The common law of the Church of enclosure for nuns
was modified early in the nineteenth century, and the result has
been the extremely rapid growth of many active orders of women.
With the number of women religious increasing twice as rapidly
as that of men during the century, the multifarious activities
of these orders has been one of the most striking features of the
modern Church. England has taken her full part in this
development and an ever increasing number of orders and
congregations came to work beside the older ones[4]. It is impossible here to do more than mention a few of the outstand-

[3] *The Religious Orders and Congregations of Great Britain and Ireland*, p. 318.
[4] It is interesting to note that English opinion was already in 1851
becoming conscious of the growing number of convents. Dislike
of them was expressed by some members of the House of Commons
who introduced in that year a Bill for the half-yearly inspection of
convents " to make provision for preventing the forcible retention
of females in houses wherein are resident persons bound by monastic
vows."

ing personalities who have played a leading part in this development.

One of the most remarkable was Cornelia Connelly, who founded in England a new congregation, the Society of the Holy Child. An American, she married an Episcopalian clergyman, Pierce Connelly. Shortly afterwards they both became Catholics and with the permission of Pope Gregory XVI he was ordained a priest and she, after living for some time in a convent with her two children, felt called to found a Congregation in England for the education of Catholic girls. Supported by Cardinal Wiseman, she opened a convent in Derby but soon moved to St. Leonards-on-Sea, which became the first Mother House. The Society, which was to show forth the simplicity, obedience and love of the Holy Child, prospered despite the great trials of Mother Connelly (her husband, for instance, gave up his priesthood, lapsed into Protestantism and gained control of their two children). The Congregation was finally approved by the Holy See in 1893 (14 years after Mother Connelly's death) and now has many convents, including five in Southern Nigeria, where the Sisters do missionary work.

Another English Congregation was founded by a woman perhaps even more remarkable, Mother Margaret Hallahan. When Dom Bernard Ullathorne was at Coventry she became his housekeeper and sacristan and the teacher in the primary school. But that does not begin to suggest the work she did, for she proved to have a remarkable influence on the young factory women whom she gathered together in the evening to teach their religion and she appears to have taken care of many of the destitute of the parish. It is hardly surprising that Ullathorne, with such an assistant, made a hundred converts a year or that he encouraged her not only to become a nun but to found a new congregation of Dominican Conventual Tertiaries. It was in June, 1844, that she and three other postulants were clothed. Soon afterwards the new convent followed Ullathorne to Bristol and then finally settled at Stone when he became Bishop of Birmingham. Ullathorne, who was, by agreement with the General of the Dominicans, superior for life of the Congregation she had founded, described her as " the most remarkable religious woman of our age and

country," and he summarizes her work by saying she wa
" foundress of a Congregation of the great Dominican Order
she trained a hundred religious women, founded five convents
built three churches, established a hospital for incurables, three
orphanages, five schools for all classes, including a number fo
the poor." And reading her life one gets a wonderful sense o
the degree to which the supernatural had become natural t
her. To-day the Congregation has many convents and some
400 religious.

The Sisters of Notre Dame first came to England in
1845, but the extremely rapid development of the Institute in
England dates from the reception of the habit in 1850 by Laura
Jerningham, daughter of the Earl of Stafford and widow of the
Hon. Edward Petre, who had died in 1849. It has been said
that " to her zeal and breadth of vision and to the scope permitted to her by her superiors was largely due the rapid
expansion of that province, chiefly in the industrial towns o:
Lancashire between 1850 and 1870." In 1854 Frances Lescher
joined them and in the following year was sent to undertake
what was to be her life work, the founding and building up o:
the great Catholic Training College in Liverpool for teachers
which has been one of the principal pillars in the whole of this
period of our educational effort in this country. The part played
by Laura Jerningham in the first generation of the Institute in
England was continued by Mary Elizabeth Towneley, another
descendant of a staunch English Catholic family, who became
a novice in 1872 and through her great gifts of personality and
intellect came more and more to control and inspire the English
Province till her death in 1922. To-day the Institute does work
in every branch of the educational field in England, having
the care of over 50,000 pupils.

The Nazareth Houses, which are to-day so much prized
for their devoted work for the aged and for children, originated in 1851. The Poor Sisters of Nazareth were founded by
Victoire Larménier with the support and guidance of Cardinal
Wiseman. Their first house in Hammersmith is to-day the
headquarters of a Congregation which has houses in North
America, Australia and New Zealand.

In turning to consider the developments in the religious orders of men in the central section of our period, we can have little doubt that the most important single event was the return of the Carthusians to England. As Pius XI has said, ' It is highly important for the Church . . . that there should never be lacking men of prayer, who, unimpeded by any other care, would be perpetually beseeching the Divine Mercy and would thus draw down from heaven benefits of every sort upon men, too neglectful of their salvation '' [5].

The last English Carthusian had died in 1825, thus ending that line of Carthusians which stretched back 650 years into the Catholic past of England and, with John Houghton and his companions, had given the first English Martyrs to the Church under Henry VIII. The question of a new foundation was first raised by Mgr. Clifford when he visited the Grand Chartreuse in 1863. He suggested a site in Somerset, near Witham, which had been, in the twelfth century, the first English foundation. But difficulties arose which made it impractical, and although the Bishop of Southwark then attempted to gain them for his diocese, saying, '' I have no greater desire than to have contemplatives in my diocese,'' the Franco-Prussian War intervened and the matter was dropped. In 1873 the question of a foundation in Southwark was again considered and this time effected. A property in the parish of Cowfold, near West Grinstead, was purchased. The monk who came to sign the agreement was dressed as a Russian nobleman (he was a former Governor of the Caucasus) for fear of exciting the anti-Catholic prejudices of the owner, a Mr. Boxall. On February 6th, 1873, the first Carthusians took possession of Parkminster. There was a scare when the Bishop of Cork nearly persuaded the Grand Chartreuse to make the foundation in his diocese instead. By 1875 normal monastic observance was established and plans were drawn up for building a large monastery on traditional Carthusian lines. It was to be one of the largest Charterhouses in the world, as it was to be used as a house of refuge if religious persecution broke out on the Continent. In 1883 Dom Victor Doreau was appointed first Prior of Parkminster, and on May 10th of the same year the new church was consecrated.

[5] From the Bull *Umbratilem,* 8th August, 1924.

Visitors found, as Cardinal Manning said, that " the Carthusians have built, not a convent, but a city." And, indeed, it was at that time easily the largest monastic building in England. At the end of the day of consecration Bishop Coffin proclaimed the perpetual enclosure and the 12 Fathers and 10 Brothers were left to lead in silence and solitude that life, hidden with Christ in God, which is the Carthusian vocation. The monastery has prospered and to-day there are about 30 choir monks and 18 laybrothers.

At the same time that the Carthusians were settling again in England there was a dispute going on between the Bishops and some of the Regulars which had the fire and the fierce cut and thrust that you only find in a fight between powerful contestants convinced of their principles and their integrity. It was the climax to a struggle that had gone on for 300 years. The immediate *casus belli* was the opening of a school in Manchester at the order of Fr. Gallwey, the Provincial of the Jesuits, without the permission of Bishop Vaughan. When the matter was discussed at the Low Week meeting of the bishops in 1877, it was decided by Manning to challenge the Regulars (the Jesuits and, to a lesser extent, the Benedictines were chiefly concerned) over the whole field of the privileges and exemptions from the Canon Law of the Church which they claimed had come down to them from penal days. Ullathorne and Clifford were deputed to draw up the bishops' case, which asked in particular for decisions on twelve specific points all concerned in one way or another with exemptions on the part of the Regulars from the authority of the bishops. Clifford and Herbert Vaughan then took the case to Rome where it was contested for four years. It is pleasant to note that during the struggle Bishop Vaughan, an old Stonyhurst boy, chose an English Jesuit House in which to make a Retreat.

The decision finally came with the publication in 1881 of the Bull *Romanos Pontifices,* which was favourable to the bishops. Eleven of the twelve points which they raised were decided as they desired. That the Bull has been productive of immense good there can be no doubt. As Ullathorne, a Benedictine, said, " there is nothing more injurious to any religious body than a false tradition fostering the corporate pride of men who are individually humble "; while the Jesuit General told Vaughan nine years after the condemnatory Bull that " he would not have *Romanos Pontifices* changed in anything." It gave the bishops that power in their dioceses which the proper exercise of their office requires, while taking from them the fear that the English Church might be controlled by the religious orders, a fear which had so dominated Manning that although he realised the need for secondary schools he would never allow the Jesuits to open one in his life-time in Westminster.

The dispute did not affect the work of the Jesuits, which was of a quite outstanding character during this period. Their school at Stonyhurst continued to develop rapidly, and a series of buildings and reconstructions, culminating in the complete rebuilding of the playground front from 1876, produced by 1889 what is still essentially the present college of Stonyhurst. It makes with its frontage of 830 ft. as imposing a group of buildings as that of any school in the country. And, although the great days of Oscott under Dr. Northcote should not be forgotten, there can be no doubt that through the second half of the nineteenth century and beyond there was no Catholic school that could pretend to rival Stonyhurst. A series of Rectors and Fathers, among whom Fr. John Gerard must be ranked high, influenced generations of boys for good. Beaumont was founded in 1861. Similar in many ways to Stonyhurst, it has, however, been more affected in its organisation of work and discipline by the customs of the non-Catholic Public Schools. For instance, Fr. Joseph Bampton, who became Rector in 1901, introduced the prefect system, as it is understood in those schools.

At the same time Farm Street was exercising a remarkable influence. Throughout its hundred years of existence it has averaged 73 converts a year, but there was a period at the turn of the century when half the Catholic books being produced were being written by the Fathers there, and when attendance at some of the sermons was a social necessity. In the field of literature, the names of Fr. Gallwey, Fr. Rickaby, Fr. Coleridge, Fr. Gerard, Fr. Pollen and Fr. Thurston come to mind, while it was Fr. Bernard Vaughan who exercised as a preacher such a compelling attraction. Fr. Vaughan was a brother of the

Cardinal. It was while he was at Manchester, whither he went in 1883, that he first became noted as a preacher. Fr. Martindale in his biography of him tells how he soon came to be looked upon by the city as a civic asset. " Very hand-some in a large and massive manner; having a voice still flexible and ' golden ' when he willed; and with that quality about the whole of him which his fellow-citizens were the very men to observe and appreciate—of being certain to ' get there ' whatever walk in life he chose." He had a genius for publicity. The bazaars, for instance, which he ran were fan-tastic. One was on such a scale that the Lancashire and York-shire Railway had to run special trains for it. His public and social works were such that no civic occasion was complete without him. He became more than a local figure by his sermon on gambling, which he had the good fortune to have taken up first by a Nonconformist minister and then by the very anti-Catholic Anglican Bishop of Manchester. From then onwards he was almost a national figure, and his sermons, lectures and articles were in demand in all parts of England. In 1901 he was moved to Mayfair and his series of sermons on the Sins of Society were the talk of the season. But Fr. Vaughan was very much more than a successful publicist. He dealt in the sensational, but his life showed that this was only a means. In his years in London he was as well known in Commercial Road, where he taught Catechism to a 1,000 children, as he was in Mayfair. " A noble-hearted man, simple as a child, very wearied of the world and yet on fire to help it, in such ways as he knew, for the love of God and of Our Lord."

It is perhaps more surprising to find among the Jesuits in the same period a poet of outstanding quality, and yet such Gerard Manley Hopkins certainly was. Born in 1844, he went up to Balliol in 1863, was received into the Church in 1866 and the following year took a first in Greats. He entered the Jesuit Novitiate in 1868 and died in 1889. He had written some poetry before becoming a Jesuit but it was some years before he returned to what he felt at first was perhaps something of a luxury. The bulk of his poetry remained to the end small, and even the greater part of that was not published by Robert Bridges, to whom he entrusted it, till 1918. But his influence since then on English poetry has probably been greater than that of anyone except Mr. T. S. Eliot. Few have written better of the wonderful " freshness deep down things " than he; and his sonnets on the miseries of the human soul being purified by God's love are unique in our literature. His influence on modern poetry has been exercised principally through his experiments in new rhythmic forms. But this holy Jesuit is truly great because he managed to create a Catholic poetry within the framework of the non-Catholic English literary tradition.

In this same period there were most important developments among the Benedictines in this country. These developments were the outcome of a battle of ideas which raged within the English Congregation for the last twenty years of the nineteenth century. " On one side," Abbot Hicks has written, " in this ' battle of ideas ' were ranged all the higher Superiors, the General Chapter, and the bulk of the rank and file of the various communities; while on the other side was a small but faithful band of young men at Downside, guided, inspired and led by one man—Hugh Edmund Ford "[6].

By the Constitutions of the Congregation power was vested not in the Superiors of the various houses, Ampleforth, Downside and so on, but in the General Chapter which met every four years. For instance, at it the Superiors of the various houses were elected. During the interval between the chapters all power was vested in the President and three Councillors elected by the Chapter. They even had the right to move a monk from one monastery to another or to a parish or mission and so on. The monk took his vow of obedience not to the Superior of his house but to the President. In the parishes the monks were governed by Provincials, who were again elected by the Chapter. The monasteries were looked upon as little more than Seminaries in which the monks spent a few years of their life preparing themselves for their *real* work, the Apostolic Mission. Such Constitutions had been framed to allow the English Benedictines to concentrate all their energies upon missionary work at a time when the number of secular priests were woefully inadequate.

No one thought that such a state of affairs was in harmony

---

[6] *Hugh Edmund Ford, First Abbot of Downside,* by Dom Bruno Hicks, p. 100.

with the Rule of St. Benedict or with Benedictine tradition. In these all the emphasis is placed upon the individual monasteries which are practically autonomous and upon a life led in the monastery in which the Work of God, the Office said in choir, is the centre. Dom Edmund Ford and a group at Downside claimed that, with the growth in the number of the secular clergy, the assistance of the monks on the parishes was not of such paramount importance and that the monastic life should again become the predominant factor in English Benedictine polity. This view was resisted, as we have said, by the majority of the Congregation, but in 1880 Mgr. Weld, an old friend of Downside's, asked at Rome that an Apostolic Visitor be sent to examine the organisation and constitution of the Congregation. The following year Dom Boniface Krug, the Prior of Monte Cassino, was appointed, and his advent opened a period of vigorous controversy on the subject within the Congregation, which was to continue unabated till Pope Leo XIII's personal intervention in the Bulls *Religiosus Ordo* and *Diu Quidem* nearly twenty years later. By them the more strictly monastic character of the English Congregation was re-established. The missions or Benedictine parishes were recognised as part of the work of the Congregation, but the emphasis was placed on the individual monastic houses. These were raised to the rank of abbeys and it was to his Abbot that the monk made his vows; and it was the Abbot and not an outside Superior who controlled the appointment to the missions attached to the abbey.

It was natural the Downside monks should have chosen Dom Edmund Ford as their first Abbot. He was of slight build and delicate health but possessed of wonderful moral courage. He was a great leader of men, affectionate, cheerful, persistent in pursuing his purpose, with a clear intellect and a grasp of principles. He had an interior religious spirit that made him completely unselfish and able to work against the ideas of his superiors in the Congregation while submitting to authority and not offending against charity or obedience.

This controversy is central to the history of the Benedictines in this period because it is largely as a result of its outcome that the number of monks and of monastic buildings with their great Abbey Churches has grown so rapidly in the

resent century, making a greatly strengthened monastic observance possible. But it must not be allowed to obscure other
developments. In 1859 Belmont was opened as a common
novitiate for the Congregation and was made a Cathedral
Priory by Pope Pius IX on the pattern of those existing in
England before the Reformation. In 1876 a foundation was
made in Scotland at Fort Augustus, largely owing to the
generosity of Lord Lovat and the zeal of Dom Jerome Vaughan,
brother of the Jesuit and the Cardinal. In 1903 Douai Abbey,
an old community of the English Congregation, was forced
by persecution to leave France and to settle at Woolhampton, near Reading, where the monastic buildings
and the school have been growing steadily ever since. As soon
as the ban on Catholics going to the Universities was lifted,
both Ampleforth and Downside opened Houses of Study, one
at Oxford and the other at Cambridge, the effects of which
both on scholarship within the monasteries and on the development of the monastic schools have been most marked.

Of the distinguished Benedictines of the period there is
no doubt that Bishop Hedley and Cardinal Gasquet are pre-
minent. The first, a monk of Ampleforth, became auxiliary to
Bishop Brown of Newport, a monk of Downside, in 1873 and
succeeded him in 1881. During his long life as bishop (he died in
1915), he showed himself to be in the best tradition of the
mediæval monastic bishops. He combined learning with wisdom
and holiness. He possessed a Northerner's independence of mind
and bluntness of expression and came to hold a unique place
in the English Hierarchy, of which he was, apart from
successive Archbishops of Westminster, the most distinguished
member. His *Retreat* has become almost a classic in its own
field and his other works show him a good theologian.   He
never allowed himself to become cut off in spirit or affection
from his much-beloved Ampleforth. Dom Aidan Gasquet became Prior of Downside in 1878 at the age of 32 and held the
office for seven years. By his energy and force of character
he made it a period of great development in the school, in
monastic building and above all in the field of scholarship.
He himself wrote a series of historical studies which have had a
permanent influence on English opinion about mediaeval
religious and monastic life. In 1900 he became President of

the Congregation and in 1907 was called to Rome to become President of the newly-formed Vulgate Commission, being made a Cardinal in 1914. From then till his death in 1929 he played his full part at Rome, holding a series of important offices and during the First World War being the most forceful spokesman at the Vatican of the Allied cause. His *Religio Religiosi,* a small work written after he became a Cardinal, is a fine expression of his monastic ideals.

Among the modern orders who came to England during this period, the Salesians are the most important. The order was founded at Turin in 1868 by St. John Bosco. Its extremely rapid development throughout the world is paralleled only by that of the Cistercians in the twelfth and the Jesuits in the sixteenth centuries. There were over 1,000 members of the Congregation at St. John Bosco's death in 1888, and over 10,000 at the time of his canonisation in 1934; there are over 16,000 to-day. That wonderful growth has been reflected in the English Province which has now over 400 members. The first house was founded at Battersea in 1887 at the direct instance of St. John Bosco, whose thoughts had been directed to England some years previously when the boy Dominic Savio, who is being beatified this year, had a vision of the English people groping in a fog which was eventually dispelled by the Pope bearing a torch representing the light of Faith. This remains the principal house of the English Province, but there are now nineteen houses (with a twentieth being planned) which undertake all the traditional Salesian works. There are agricultural colleges, colleges for arts and trades, a number of secondary schools or colleges, a house of studies just outside Oxford, a missionary college, and even then the list is not complete. Great as St. John Bosco was in his life-time as a miracle worker, nothing he did is more marvellous than the development of his Congregation since his death.

Another order of recent foundation which is bringing new spiritual vigour to England is that of the Augustinians of the Assumption. Founded by Father Emmanuel d'Alzon in 1845, they first came to England in 1901. They have so far developed in this country that an English Province was set up in 1946. There are eight houses and over 70 religious.

The expulsion of many of the religious orders from

France was indirectly advantageous to England. Many of the orders opened houses here for their religious, and most of them stayed here even when the period of persecution was over. The figures for the number of religious priests in England tell their own tale. In 1901 there were 990; in 1902, 1,107; in 1905, 1,280; in 1910, 1,514. There was a similar increase in the number of nuns working in England, the Sacred Heart order, for instance, giving refuge to about 300 of their religious from France.

The chief characteristic of the period among the religious orders of women is the immense growth in the number of nuns fulfilling the active works of mercy in England. The Sisters of Charity of St. Vincent de Paul and the Irish Sisters of Mercy multiply their convents till they become a familiar sight in our cities. The Little Sisters of the Poor have opened from 1861 onwards a number of houses to take care of the aged poor of either sex. The Good Shepherd nuns develop their special work of looking after unmarried mothers and their babies; the Little Sisters of the Assumption come to England to fulfil their vocation of ministering to the sick poor in their houses. Many fresh orders come to join those of the Faithful Companions, the Ursulines and others which are already doing teaching work in England.

There were at least two more English Congregations founded, one, that of the Poor Servants of the Mother of God, by a remarkable woman, Fanny Margaret Taylor. She had the odd distinction of having founded *The Month* (in 1864) and of keeping it going for a year before handing it over to the Jesuits. And it was to her that Cardinal Newman gave the *Dream of Gerontius* to publish, taking it from his wastepaper basket to do so.

A religious girl, she joined an Anglican Sisterhood and then when the Crimean War broke out went out to help Florence Nightingale nurse the wounded. It was while nursing under appalling conditions in the Crimea that she received the gift of Faith. This she attributed under God to the example of the Irish soldiers she nursed. But there were also some English nuns working with her, and writing to her mother some time before her conversion, she said, " I do love them so, they are so gentle, loving and courteous, such a contrast to some people!''

Slowly, with the help of such priests as Dr. Manning and the Jesuit Fr. Gallwey (it is pleasant to see the two sharing in the good work!), it became clear to her that she was called to found a congregation that would be dedicated to the service of God in His poor. It was in 1870 that Fanny Taylor and three companions began their novitiate. Under the leadership of Mother Magdalen Taylor (as the foundress came to be called) the Congregation prospered, and the new Constitutions (based on those of the Society of Jesus) were approved by Leo XIII in 1885. To-day there are convents in England, Ireland, Italy, France and the United States, where thousands of the poor, especially orphans and the sick, are looked after.

A similar Congregation, that of the now famous Blue Nuns, The Little Company of Mary, was founded by Mary Potter and approved by Leo XIII in 1893. There are now some 700 nuns whose principal work it is to assist the sick and dying in hospitals and private houses. Their Mother House, the convent of the Blue Nuns on the Coelian Hill, is well known to English visitors to Rome.

The Society of the Sacred Heart is a congregation founded at the beginning of the nineteenth century by St. Madeleine Sophie Barat, and is already to-day one of the great teaching orders of the Church. The Society came to England in 1848 and the English Vicariate has already produced two Mother Generals of the Order, Mother Digby and Mother Janet Stuart. The latter in particular had a profound influence during her life (she died in 1914) and her cause has been proposed for canonisation. She was of Scottish race, the youngest daughter of a Church of England clergyman. Her mother died when she was a young child and, in girlhood, she appears to have lost all faith till she found through the chance picking-up of a book of Ullathorne's a line on the Church which she followed through all the usual difficulties. She even survived an interview with Mr. Gladstone, was received into the Church, and then in 1882 became a novice at Roehampton. Within 12 years she was superior of the English Vicariate with 500 nuns under her rule, and in 1911 she became the Superior General of 6,500 religious.

Mother Stuart had a wonderful freedom of spirit, a serene joyousness and a strong antipathy to Jansenism and all its works. There was about her an atmosphere of the open-air (she had been a keen horse-woman and never lost her interest in such things) which might have degenerated into heartiness in someone who was not through all things lost in God. She had the faculty of drawing people on to undreamt of heights, to the fulfilling of all their powers, but always along the way demanded by the powers of that individual; in fact with her you always come back to that same freedom of spirit which is perhaps so refreshing to find in her because it sometimes seems to be a rarer quality among women than among men. But the greatest thing of all about Mother Stuart was the way in which she remained a contemplative absorbed in the life of prayer amidst her ceaseless activity. Her reliance on prayer may be illustrated by the way in which after she had become Superior of the English Province she decided, despite her great work, to increase her half-hour of afternoon private prayer to an hour in order to " have more and better to give."

Since her death the Society has continued to prosper in this country. In 1929 a convent was opened in Oxford to enable the nuns to study at the University. The most important recent developments have been in the establishment of Training Colleges. The Vicariate and the well-known boarding school that used to be at Roehampton have in the last few years been moved to Woldingham, a large property in Surrey.

We have seen that the modern development of the Dominicans in England dates from the acquisition of Woodchester in 1851. Father Bertrand Wilberforce, a grandson of the philanthropist, was one of the outstanding friars of the succeeding generation and, with his constant work for souls, his unending study, and his compassion for sinners, a worthy fruit of the fervour at Woodchester. In 1884 a school, now at Laxton, was founded. It has been said to represent " perhaps the most deliberate attempt yet made to give educational content as well as outward form to the idea of a Catholic education in modern dress, from the intellectual as well as from the spiritual standpoint; and its teaching is animated by the penetrating Dominican critique of the modern world and the modern mind '''[7].

The modern generation of Dominicans has included some very distinguished friars. Among these Fr. Bede Jarrett must be placed first because it was under his leadership that the English Province gained the important place which it holds to-day. Born in 1881, he was educated at Stonyhurst, clothed in 1898 and sent to Oxford in 1904—" the first swallow of the Dominican Summer," as Fr. Bernard Vaughan so rightly prophesied. He won a First at Oxford, became Prior of St. Dominic's at 33 and Provincial at 35 years of age. It was an office to which he was to be elected four times successively, a record in the history of the 700-year-old English Province. As regards his external work, the founding and building of the Priory of Blackfriars at Oxford will ever be his memorial. But it was Fr. Bede himself and not his work that held such a fascination for those thousands who looked to him for guidance and leadership on the road to God. Amid all his work, his writing, his preaching, and his administrative duties, he was always the same calm, joyous, simple person. " It is rare for a man to grow up into a glorious maturity and still retain all the charm and grace of youth: that is what Fr. Bede somehow managed to achieve." That tribute from a fellow friar is borne out by the picture given of Fr. Bede by those who knew him. He was never ill till his last, short, final illness; wonderfully normal, he had no oddities or fads; he was possessed of a great sense of fun and always full of life and zeal. He was always popular but never spoilt by it. Even as superior he fitted unobtrusively into his community, being most regular at community duties. His writings, most of which were historical, are of value, but as is only proper to one of his order he was greater as a preacher. He had an immense capacity for friendship and it is this, which he exercised so freely for the love of God, that seems his most characteristic gift.

A very different character was Fr. Vincent McNabb, and yet a no less perfect Dominican. An Irishman, educated in Ireland, he was given a maximum of six months by his Headmaster when he heard he had joined the Dominican Novi-

---

[7] H. O. Evennett, *The Catholic Schools of England and Wales*, pp. 74-5.

tiate. And yet for 50 years he followed with all his might the ideal of the Friar Preacher to seek God's glory through prayer, study and teaching. There was something granite-like about him, much as though a mediaeval friar had come alive in our midst. He had a chair in his room on which he never sat, a bed on which he never rested. His apostolate, which carried him many miles, was always done, if at all possible, on foot. Thus every Sunday he walked from his Priory at Hampstead to Marble Arch, lectured from the Catholic Evidence Guild platform, and walked back to Hampstead. It was perhaps on this platform that he could give freest expression to the truths that possessed him. He was a trenchant critic of modern industrial life and of all the social evils, such as birth control, that it generates. He wanted an extension of private ownership and of craftsmanship, in fact of everything that liberates and develops the human person. He loved the poor and defended them against the tyranny of wealth. Biddy in the Basement, a type of the poor struggling mother, was one of his favourite characters. As many of his 30 published works show, he was a theologian of much more than superficial competence, for he remained a student all his life. But he probably would not mind its being said that *The Science of Prayer* was his finest work. For he was above all a man of prayer. He asked that the words, " Lord, Thou knowest all things; Thou knowest that I love Thee " be inscribed on his coffin. They reveal the ideal by which he lived. Belloc has paid him this tribute: " The greatness of his character, of his learning, his experience and above all his judgment, was something altogether separate from the world about him. Those who knew him marvelled increasingly at every aspect of that personality. But the most remarkable aspect of all was the character of holiness. . . . I have known, felt and seen holiness in person."

The third friar who may be taken as illustrating another aspect of Dominican work and influence in modern England is Fr. Hugh Pope. He had a strong, rugged character with a love of that frankness in others that he sometimes so devastatingly manifested himself. He was learned in his chosen field, the Holy Scriptures. His success was based upon relentlessly hard work. From 1914 till his death in 1946 Fr. Hugh held, except for short periods, a succession of offices within his

Order, but neither this administrative work, nor his sermons and conferences (notes for some 4,000 of these were found among his papers) were allowed to crowd out his more scholarly work. This bore fruit not only in the five volumes of *The Catholic Student's Aids to the Bible,* but in a series of books and articles. The caution that marks his treatment of points of exegesis may be more an indication of the dates, 1908 and 1911, when he obtained his Licentiate and Doctorate at Rome than of his natural character. Like Fr. Vincent, he was a great supporter of the Catholic Evidence Guild, which it has been said, " might almost be called his own child."

The Cistercians are another order which has developed rapidly in recent years in England. The Abbey of Mount St. Bernard's met with great difficulties during the second half of the nineteenth century, but with the appointment of Dom Louis Carew in 1910 its fortunes took a turn for the better. This has been more than maintained by his successors Abbot Celsus O'Connell (1929-33) and the present Abbot Dom Malachy Brasil. To-day there is a community of 73 monks with fine conventual buildings and a fine abbey church. Work on the church was recommenced in 1935 to commemorate the centenary of the coming of the monks to Charnwood Forest, and there is now a most impressive building with a retro-choir (the stalls being designed by Eric Gill) and with the High Altar in the transepts. It was consecrated in 1945. Much of the quarrying of the stone and the work of building was done by the monks themselves. There is also a small Cistercian foundation at Caldey, and a recent one at Haddington, made from Roscrea in Ireland.

A memorable event in 1949 was the return of the Carmelites to Aylesford Priory, which had been the first house of the order in mediaeval England. Both branches of the order, the Calced (who have returned to Aylesford) and the Discalced, were active in penal times in England, but both had died out before 1850. The Discalced Carmelites opened a chapel in 1862 in Kensington, the site of their now well known friary, and both branches now have several houses in England.

The Jesuits have in recent times fully maintained the distinction of the English Province. Campion Hall, a hall of residence at Oxford, was opened in 1896, its academic standard has always been remarkably high, and it would be hard to parallel anywhere its successes during the first twenty-five years. It has been said, for instance, that Fr. Martindale's career as a prizewinner (he won eight University prizes) has been beaten only by Gilbert Murray. It was Fr. Martin D'Arcy who, when he was master, engaged Lutyens to build the new Hall, one of the most satisfying of all the modern buildings in Oxford. There are many who can bear witness to the distinction lent to Catholic life at Oxford by Fr. D'Arcy and of the influence of his thought on Catholics and non-Catholics alike.

In education the Jesuits have recognised the great need in England for large secondary schools, and this may now be considered the most important part of their educational work. They have now seven such schools, with an average of about 450 boys in each school.

In several fields the Jesuits have shown themselves innovators. Charles Dominic Plater (1875-1921) wrote in a letter, as a young Jesuit, while on a visit to Belgium, " I am quite mad on the subject of the Belgian retreats for working men. It is really unspeakable—the cure for all our troubles I am sure; the results really miraculous." He returned to England to found a retreat house for working men, the first of four such houses now run by the English Province. He was also the founder of the Catholic Social Guild and therefore of the Catholic Workers' College.

A great friend of his, Fr. Edmund Lester, was to found at Campion House, Osterley, what was probably the first house of studies for late vocations in the world. As a priest at Accrington he came to realise how many vocations were lost to the Church by there being no means for men to remedy a defective early education. The house was started during the First World War and as a result of the wonderful efforts of himself and his successor, Fr. Tigar, nearly 700 late vocations, about half to the Regulars and half to the Seculars, have been given to the Church.

It is only necessary to mention the names of Fr. Steuart, Fr. D'Arcy, Fr. Thurston, Fr. Brodrick, Fr. Martindale and Fr. Frances Woodlock, to indicate that the standard at Farm Street has been fully maintained. Fr. Herbert Thurston lived at Farm Street for nearly 50 years and during that time a spate of some 700 learned books and articles poured from his pen. Whether he was, as a controversialist, engaged against such a foe as Dr. Coulton or, as a hagiographist, revising Butler's *Lives of the Saints,* his work was characterised by a hatred of sham and a love of truth. It would be an impertinence to remind present-day Catholics of the influence for good wielded by Fr. Martindale. Among the other eminent Jesuits it is only possible to mention Archbishops Goodier and Roberts, Fr. Eric Burrows, the Egyptologist, Fr. Lattey and Fr. Sutcliffe, the editors of the Westminster Version of the Scriptures, Fr. Copleston the philosopher, and Fr. Henry Davis, the Professor of Moral Theology. Taken as a whole, it has been a great century in the history of the English Province. Not only has a high standard of excellence been maintained, but there has been a steady expansion. In 1850 there were about 200 members of the Province; to-day there are close on 1,000. Perhaps the most important and permanent work carried out by the members of the Society is that which is directly concerned with the well-being of souls—the absorbing, unspectacular round of retreats and conference to priests, religious communities and layfolk alike.

Recent years have seen an equally remarkable expansion among the Benedictines. This is due in the first place to the creation, alongside the English Congregation, of an English Province of the Cassinese Congregation of Primitive Observance. The earliest founded of those houses now belonging to the English Province is Ramsgate Abbey. Coming from Italy in 1856, the monks were given the seven parishes on the Isle of Thanet to evangelise. The development of the Abbey is due principally to Abbot Thomas Bergh, a liturgiologist of international repute, and Abbot Egan. There is a Preparatory School. Abbot Romanus Rios maintains the tradition for learning.

In 1882 the monks of La Pierre-qui-vire brought the Benedictine Rule to Buckfast, an old Saxon Benedictine foundation which became part of the Savigny reform in the twelfth century. The old monastery had been suppressed in 1536. The first Abbot of the new line, Dom Boniface Natter, was chosen in 1902 at the early age of 36, and was tragically drowned off the coast of Spain four years later. He was succeeded by Dom Anscar Vonier, who in his 32 years as Abbot was to direct and inspire the building of Buckfast as we know it to-day. He made it a centre for showing forth a Benedictine Monastery to the English and telling them something of the Benedictine way of life. The fact that the building of the monastery on the old foundations was largely being done by the monks themselves captured the popular imagination. Abbot Vonier had been a builder in more senses than one. He left a large, fervent community and played his part, through a series of Theological works, in the Thomistic revival in this country.

St. Michael's Abbey, Farnborough, was built between the years 1883 and 1888 by the Empress Eugènie to be a Mausoleum for her husband, the Emperor Napoleon III, and her son, the Prince Imperial. It was taken over by the monks of the French Congregation, and for some 50 years a series of monks such as Dom Fernand Cabrol, Dom André Wilmart, Dom Henri Leclerq, Dom Louis Gougaud and Dom Marius Férotin did scholarly work there recalling the greatest days of the Maurists. But the ethos of the Abbey remained too French to attract English vocations, and the numbers dwindled till in 1947 the French Congregation handed the Abbey over to Prinknash, who were able to send a swarm of monks from their thriving community.

Prinknash Abbey owes its origin to an Anglican community founded by Dom Aelred Carlyle. They had started some sort of community life as early as 1893, and by 1911 were a thriving community on Caldey Island. But they were coming more and more to see the illogicality of their position till finally the liturgical demands of their Visitor, the Bishop of Oxford, precipitated a crisis. Most of the community were received into the Church on March 5th, 1913. After many early difficulties they began to prosper; and in 1937 the Priory was raised to the rank of an Abbey and Dom Wilfrid Upson was blessed as their Abbot. Since then the Abbey has developed very rapidly; not only has Farnborough been taken over, but a foundation has been made in Scotland.

Within the English Benedictine Congregation there has also been much development. With the growth of the monasteries has gone a growth and development in the schools. While this is true of all the houses, it applies particularly to Downside and Ampleforth. Dom Leander Ramsay (later to become Abbot of Downside) initiated the changes at Downside that were to bring the numbers in the school up to 200 by 1914. His aim was to create a Catholic school that had grafted into it those elements which he believed to be valuable in the public school tradition. His work was continued by Dom Sigebert Trafford (also later to become Abbot) till to-day the school at Downside, while remaining Benedictine, can claim to rival the non-Catholic schools on their ground. There has been a parallel development at Ampleforth particularly during the long period of office of the present Headmaster, Dom Paul Nevill, who will rank as one of the great headmasters of the period in England.

Downside has founded two priories, one in 1933 at Worth where there is now the Preparatory School to Downside, and the other in 1896 at Ealing. The latter was made independent in 1947, and shows with a rapidly growing community every sign of vigorous Benedictine life. Among the scholars in the Conventus should be mentioned Dom Hugh Connolly, Dom Cuthbert Butler and Dom John Chapman.

The recent growth of missionary effort within the Church has been reflected in this country. The oldest and most important society taking part in this work is that of St. Joseph for Foreign Missions. Founded by Fr. Herbert Vaughan (later Cardinal) in 1866 as a Congregation of secular priests and lay brothers devoting their lives to the foreign mission, it now has more than 500 members. They work in India, the Upper Nile and in North Borneo, and apart from their large training college in Mill Hill they have two other colleges in this country.

The White Fathers, another missionary order, came to England in 1912. They had been founded in 1869 by Cardinal Lavigerie for the conversion first of the Moslems and later of all pagans in Africa, and the society has spread wonderfully, having now some 1,500 members. In the English Province, erected in 1943, there are about 110 priests and, in this country, eight houses. A most remarkable member of the Province was Archbishop Arthur Hughes, who was till his death in 1949 the first Internuncio Apostolic of Egypt. Very highly regarded by all sections in Egypt and the Middle East, he it was, in effect, who made the appointment of the first representative of the Holy See to a Mohammedan sovereign a practical issue.

The Holy Ghost Fathers are a third missionary order in England; their slow development till very recently (in contrast to their amazing growth in Ireland for example) perhaps emphasizes how comparatively slowly the Church in England is responding to the call for missionary vocations.

The nursing brotherhoods, the Alexian Brothers, Brothers of Charity and the Hospitallers of St. John of God, who between them run in England about ten hospitals and homes, do an invaluable work complementary to that done by the nursing sisters.

The great need for increased Catholic secondary education has already been noted. The Vincentian Fathers, with their large Training College at Strawberry Hill, are helping to meet one need, and a number of congregations such as the Marist Fathers run secondary schools, but it seems likely that in the future the greatest help towards the solution of the problem will come from the teaching brotherhoods. Their contribution is already great. As Mr. Evennett has written, " Their vocation to a hard-working and humble life, with little or no publicity, is one of the highest order, and the quality and extent of their contribution to Catholic education in England deserve to be more generally known and appreciated "[8]. There are seven teaching brotherhoods to-day in England who run, apart from approved, primary and central schools, some 24 secondary schools and three boarding schools. Of these the Christian Brothers de la Salle, who have recently set up an English Province, hold pride of place, but the Christian Brothers of Ireland and the Xaverian Brothers each have a number of efficient schools. The de la Salle Brothers have recently opened a house of studies in Cambridge.

The problem of the secondary education of girls is not nearly so acute as that of boys, for there are about five times as many Catholic schools for girls as for boys in England, i.e., about 460, and the standard of training of the teaching nuns is steadily improving. Indeed, the standard in the better teaching orders is very high indeed, containing as they do

[8] *Op. cit.*, p. 48.

women of intelligence who devote themselves with unsurpassed intensity to the art of teaching.

The religious orders of women have continued to expand rapidly, although recently it has become doubtful whether some of the orders will be able to maintain all their commitments. For there would appear to have been a definite falling off in the religious vocations of women in recent years. Some orders, even in the past, have had to rely perhaps too much on the wonderful abundance of vocations from Ireland. This is no doubt partly due to the lack of zeal and generosity among English girls and to the inadequacy of the way in which the grandeur of the religious vocation is sometimes presented. But it has also been suggested[9] that there is a certain unreal atmosphere in some convents of teaching nuns that does not appeal to the idealism of the modern girl, an emphasis perhaps on a multiplicity of rather sentimental devotions at the expense of a simpler and more virile liturgical spirit, and a prudery which is found doubly repellent when viewed against a background of the excessively free and easy modern world.

It is, curiously enough, some of the strictest and most severely enclosed orders which have developed most rapidly in recent years. For instance, the Poor Clares now have 19 houses in England, many of which have been founded in the last 20 years. But it is among the Carmelites that the growth in contemplative vocations has been most striking. This is due, under God, to a very remarkable woman, Madeleine Dupont.

A foundation had been made at St. Charles' Square, near Notting Hill Gate, from the Carmel of the Rue d'Enfer in Paris in 1878. The early years were very difficult, and it was not an easy task that fell to the lot of Mother Mary of Jesus (as Madeleine Dupont was called in religion) when in 1883 she became Prioress at the age of 32. But God's preparation in this soul had already been profound. Naturally attractive, this slight, small woman was gifted with a keen penetrating mind, an utter fearlessness and a dry sense of humour, and was recognised by her Carmelite superiors as far advanced in sanctity. It was in her twentieth year that Our Lord had made known to her that she would enter Carmel and that her work would be in

---

[9] " The Religious Vocations for Women," by G. W. Shelton, in the *Clergy Review*, XXXIII, 2.

England, a land she already loved so dearly as to be known as
"*la petite Anglaise.*" She had gone to England when the
foundation was first made.

The first years were spent in consolidating the house at
Notting Hill, but the Prioress knew that the period of the
foundations was to come. The first was made in 1907 in
Liverpool, and then for the next 31 years this one house in
Notting Hill was to make no less than 33 foundations, more
than had been made by the great St. Teresa herself. Mother
Mary of Jesus was already 56 at the time when Liverpool was
founded, frail and in constant suffering, yet with indomitable
energy hidden in the slight, straight form. And there were
many signs that all depended on God and was the direct result
of His inspiration and the following of His grace. She could
be so firm in her opinions and so shrewd and even uncompromising in her expression of them that her profound sanctity
and her dependence on God were sometimes lost sight of by
those who built up what has been described by *The Times* as
" the raciest of the Roman Catholic *legenda* of the twentieth
century." There is, however, plenty of material in the every-
day happenings of her life to show how God and Our Lady
worked through Mother Mary of Jesus. The following is typical.
She had been one day praying in the garden when she called
a sister and asked, " Little child, is there a place called
Oban?"

" Yes, Mother," said the sister. " It is in Scotland,
on the coast of Argyllshire."

" Ah!" said Mother Prioress, " Our Lady wants a
Carmel there."

Nothing more was said and some days elapsed before
the Bishop of Argyll and the Isles unexpectedly visited the
Carmel. He said he would like a Carmel for his out-of-the-way
diocese, and suggested Fort William or Rothesay as suitable.
He himself, he said, lived in Oban, but other towns were more
populous and would afford more possibility of support. The
Mother listened in silence but at the end shook her head, and
shyly and deprecatingly, but firmly, said, " I am sorry, my
Lord, but it will have to be Oban."

Later, when a street map of Oban was produced, the
Mother Prioress, without a second's hesitation, indicated a

certain house and said, " That is the house Our Lady wants."

The Bishop, rather aghast, said, " But, Mother, I'm afraid that it is impossible! That house belongs to Major X who I know has no intention of selling."

The house became the site of a new Carmel. And so it was with all the foundations which went on year after year, although there was often a poverty of means which appeared to make the thing impossible. God always responded to the Prioress's limitless trust. Her life has yet to be told. There were her years of terrible conflict with the power of Evil; and there was the appearance of Our Lady to her in a time of particular trial in 1916. And although the judgment of her, and the events in her life, are entirely submitted to the Church, it would seem that in Mother Mary of Jesus the Church in England has been given a most glorious expression of what a religious vocation can be when it is lived to the full in Christ. She died on March 15th, 1942, in the 91st year of her age.

XVI

THE CATHOLIC PRESS, 1850-1950

By J. J. DWYER

THE foundation of *The Dublin Review* is generally attributed to Wiseman and Daniel O'Connell, but the " real makers " were three; according to Wiseman's own account, the idea was first conceived by Michael J. Quin, a journalist from Tipperary. From the very outset, sustained and powerful aid was given by Dr. Charles Russell, of Maynooth; three of the quartet were wholly Irish; hence the title, the green cover and the motto in Celtic characters *Eire go bráth*. It was to be a rival to the Whig *Edinburgh* and the Tory *Quarterly*, and for a long time much of the matter in it was produced in Ireland.

The first number appeared in May 1836; the first two numbers were edited by Quin, the third by the Rev. M. A. Tierney, the fourth and fifth by James Smith of Edinburgh. A permanent editor was then found in the person of H. R. Bagshawe, who acted from October 1837 till the coming of W. G. Ward in 1863, but the presiding genius was Wiseman. The review was his " pet child." His aims were to arouse the torpid Catholic body, to stimulate the Oxford Movement, already promising a rich harvest of conversions, to ensure the co-operation of " old Catholics " and new converts, and in a word, to put Catholicism in England on the map. From the first he stipulated that there were to be " no extremes in politics "—this was necessary on account of the formidable co-operation of O'Connell—and he naturally regarded himself as " representing the theological and religious element in the journal." As the Rector of the English College in Rome, who knew Montalembert and Lamennais, Görres and Döllinger, Gioberti and Rosmini, he represented a European outlook possessed by nobody else in England. His early articles bear witness to his versatility: " The Oxford Controversy," " The Roman Forum," " Italian Guides and Tourists," " Church Architecture of the Middle Ages," " Boniface VIII," " St. Elizabeth of Hungary," " Religion in Italy," " Minor Rites and Offices of the Church." Before very long he had written (August 1839) the article which had a decisive influence on Newman, viz. that on the " Catholic and Anglican Churches " in which he dealt with the Schism of the Donatists. A friend drew Newman's attention to the famous words: *Securus judicat orbis terrarum* which thereafter rang in his ears until his theory of the *Via Media* was " absolutely pulverized." Other notable articles of the period were those of Dr. John Lingard, for instance, on Dodd's *Church History of England,* and " Did the Anglican Church Reform Herself?" and one by Newman, in June 1846, on Keble's *Lyra Innocentium*. The converts soon made their appearance: Christie; Allies; Morris; W. G. Ward; Formby; Capes; Anderdon; Manning. Then, too, began the haunting evil of " the want of adequate means "; it was becoming harder and harder to pay contribu-tors. Meanwhile, the *Dublin* had made a great reputation. The old volumes contained, as Fr. C. Russell wrote later, " treasuries of orthodox erudition " and a complete picture of Catholic life and thought during a quarter of a century.

In 1863 began the Second Series, under " the second creator," the lay professor of Theology, W. G. Ward. Tennyson called him " most generous of Ultramontanes." In personal relations he was, but in print he was the most truculent. About the *Via Media,* as about Tractarianism generally, his mind had been very firmly made up, not unaided by the treatment he had received from his Alma Mater. " The gates of hell," he said " *have* prevailed against the Church of England." He was equally clear about the hidebound, if emancipated, faithful who so disliked the ardour of the Oxford converts: " arguing with English Catholics is like talking with savages." He made little distinction between their cool attitude and the dangerous latitude of liberalising Catholics on the Continent. He could not stand the Munich School and he saw no good in Montalembert, Lacordaire and their followers; nor was he concerned about questions of social justice. " These men would liberalise Catholicism: they would never catholicize

Liberalism." The essence of his complaint was that they were undismayed by what Gladstone[1], some years later, called " the destructive speculations so widely current and the notable hardihood of the anti-Christian writing of the day." Manning knew exactly what he was doing when in 1862 he took over the *Dublin* from Wiseman and put in W. G. Ward as editor. Nevertheless, the review was placed under a triple censorship of the strictest kind—theological, philosophical, and in respect of " ecclesiastical prudence "—and Manning exercised the fullest control. He meant to have nothing resembling *The Rambler,* the more so as one of his special aims at the time was the defence of The Temporal Power.

For all this Ward was the perfect instrument. " You will find me," he wrote to Cashel Hoey, his assistant, " narrow and strong—*very* narrow and *very* strong." He was soon in deep controversy with John Stuart Mill; but while his strongest interests were Theology and Philosophy he was obliged to deal incessantly with topics like The Temporal Power; Catholic Colleges and the National Universities (i.e., Should Catholics be allowed to go to Oxford?); Liberalism in Religion; the " Syllabus " of 1864, and above all the Infallibility. His appetite for doctrinal definition was insatiable and his avowed and ardent desire was to see the scope of Infallibility widened to cover not only encyclicals but briefs and bulls and every injunction and censure that proceeded from the Roman Congregations. Anybody who objected was denounced as " disloyal "; there was certainly no exaggeration in the words used in his epitaph, *Fidei propugnator acerrimus.*

The principal contributors in those years were Ward himself, Manning, Bishop Hedley, Roger Bede Vaughan, O.S.B., the Jesuits Anderdon and Coleridge, Oakeley, W. H. Wilberforce, Allies, Marshall and other converts; Science was represented mainly by St. George Mivart. Newman, who could have done so much, was increasingly alienated and did not conceal it. He denied that Ward was " in any sense a spokesman for English Catholics "; " controversy is his meat and drink and he is never happy except when he is destroying the cohesive unity of Catholic brotherhood "; and in his letter to

[1] *The Vatican Decrees in their bearing on Civil Allegiance,* etc. (1874).

the Duke of Norfolk, Newman alluded to " tyrannous ipse-dixits." Nor can there be any doubt as to who were meant in the famous letter to Ullathorne in 1869 about the " aggressive and insolent faction." The events of the time made the *Dublin* a platform, but Ward's temperament and mentality made it a gun platform, and his influence on the projects and fortunes of Newman cannot be doubted—or be overlooked. Yet he softened in later life and in the 'seventies, when Newman's works were being republished, he made some amends. Nor can there be much doubt that he deepened the general antagonism to the Church, almost certainly that of Gladstone, which became acute during the Vatican Council.

In 1878 the *Dublin* was taken over by that collector of papers, Dr. Herbert Vaughan, Bishop of Salford, and in the January following the new series began with Bishop Hedley, O.S.B., as editor. Book reviews and other features were expanded, the signing of articles was now adopted, and among the contributors we find many notable names: Bishop Clifford; Dr. J. L. Patterson; Bishop of Emmaus; Dr. L. C. Casartelli; Abbot Gasquet, O.S.B.; Father T. E. Bridgett, C.SS.R.; C. S. Devas; W. S. Lilly; while the learned editor took his share with some fifteen articles. At the end of 1884 Dr. Hedley resigned and the Bishop of Salford combined the functions of proprietor and editor till 1892 when he became Archbishop of Westminster in succession to Cardinal Manning[2]. The editorship then devolved upon Canon J. Moyes, theologian to the archdiocese, and was held by him till 1906. Under Canon Moyes a very definitely ecclesiastical character soon prevailed. During his term contributions came from the famous liturgical scholar, Edmund Bishop, such as " The Earliest Roman Mass Book," " The Origin of the Cope as a Church Vestment "; then, too, appeared articles by Mgr. A. S. Barnes, Dom Cuthbert Butler, O.S.B., Fr. W. H. Kent, O.S.C., and J. B. Milburn of *The Tablet*.

With Wilfrid Ward (1906-1915) began the most distinguished period of the *Dublin*, just twenty-eight years after his father's resignation of the same post. The times were very different and though the Irish Question had entered a new

---

[2] He bequeathed the review to the See of Westminster; it is, however, managed by Messrs. Burns, Oates and Washbourne.

phase, as a result of Wyndman's Land Act and the accession of a Liberal government, there was no longer a division into parties among English Catholics; old Catholics and converts were now one body.

But the circulation had gone down again and the *Dublin* was regarded merely as a denominational review. From this position it was soon extricated as much by Ward's policy as by his ability and knowledge. He believed in wide speculative activity but in him this was coupled, as it had not been before, with sound and indeed cautious judgment; before his eyes and his mind he had the double example of his father's *Dublin* and of *The Rambler*. " My desire," he said, " is not to advocate in the *Dublin* one special school of thought but to keep up a certain intellectual level." The disciple and interpreter of Newman—soon to be his biographer—was resolved to combine the orthodoxy of W. G. Ward's *Dublin* with the international outlook and wide-ranging knowledge of *The Home and Foreign Review*. A glance at the first numbers brought out by Wilfrid Ward will indicate both his aim and his achievement. We find articles on " Cardinal Newman and Creative Theology " by the Editor, on " Irish University Education " by the Bishop of Limerick (Dr. O'Dwyer), on " Experience and Transcendence " by Baron Frederick von Hügel, on " Pope Honorius " by Dom John Chapman, O.S.B., on " The Papal Deposing Power " by Canon William Barry. Culture, too, was speedily given its rights: for instance, " Ronsard " by Professor F. Y. Eccles, " Eugène Fromentin " by Professor J. S. Phillimore. Politics soon followed and here both sides were heard; there were articles by Conservatives and Liberals on the Reform of the House of Lords and on the Parliament Act, on the Irish Question by Home Rulers and by Unionists. In this period also appear the first contributions from Bishop Brown, Father Hugh Pope, O.P., Mgr. Ronald Knox, Father Philip Hughes, Fr. Cuthbert, O.S.F.C., Sir Bertram Windle, F.R.S., Hilaire Belloc, Maurice Baring, F. F. Urquhart, Bernard Holland. In July 1908 appeared Francis Thompson's marvellous essay on Shelley, which had been rejected by an earlier editor. Non-Catholics were attracted by this treatment of Literature and by the handling of Politics both home and foreign. To effect all this it needed something more than the wide philosophical spirit of the presiding genius and this was secured by the exceptional range and variety of his friendships.

The Metaphysical Society of the 'sixties and 'seventies was imitated and repeated by the equally distinguished and equally heterogeneous Synthetic Society of which Ward was one of the honorary secretaries. The friend of Huxley and of Father Maturin, of Arthur James Balfour and of Robert Hugh Benson, of George Wyndham and of Bishop Gore, of Sir Alfred Lyall and of Lord Halifax was in a unique position not only to secure contributions but to promote understanding. He thus realised in his conduct of the *Dublin* some of the possibilities of a University and such indeed was his aim. It had already been discerned by Mark Pattison, who had described Newman as " the only philosophical exponent in our language of the Catholic university system." Readers could now judge for themselves how much substance there was in Gladstone's charge that " Rome had equally repudiated modern thought and ancient history."

The Modernist Movement reached its crisis in 1906 and the encyclical *Pascendi* explained and defined the issue. Unluckily the disciple of Newman came under some measure of suspicion, the more so because the French exponents of Modernism had taken trouble, and used much ingenuity, to shelter themselves under that great name. Wilfrid Ward was, moreover, known to be a personal friend of George Tyrrell and of the Baron von Hügel, to be anxious to keep them from dangerous extremes, and, if it might be, to mitigate the shock of collisions. The balance and prudence of his attitude was not understood and reciprocated and for a moment there appeared to be some danger that his editorship would be over-clouded as soon as it began. Thus, the early numbers, on which he was so warmly congratulated by the best judges among English Catholics, were actually impugned in some quarters[3], but before long his success was established and acknowledged. Some idea of the position created for the *Dublin* in those years can be formed by recalling the names of

[3] By Archbishop Bagshawe, then in retirement after his remarkable episcopate at Nottingham, and by Mgr. Croke Robinson. They wrote their complaints to Ward but they did not delate him to Rome.

(National Portrait Gallery)

AUGUSTUS WELBY PUGIN

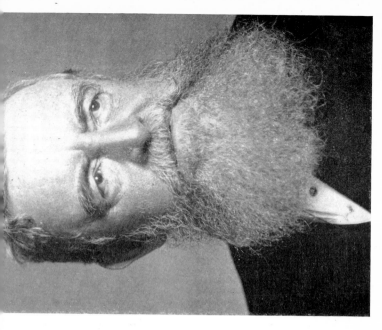

JOHN EMERICH EDWARD DALBERG
FIRST BARON ACTON

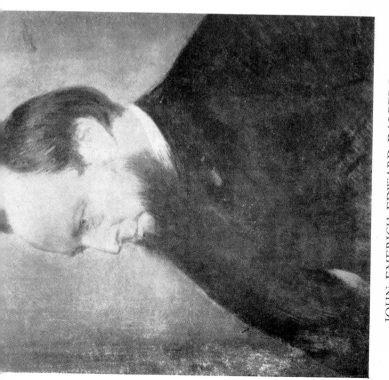

(Picture Post)

GEORGE FREDERICK SAMUEL ROBINSON
FIRST MARQUESS OF RIPON

JOHN HENRY, CARDINAL NEWMAN

FRANCIS AIDAN, CARDINAL GASQUET

FREDERICK WILLIAM FABER
from a pastel portrait

THOMAS EDWARD BRIDGETT, C.SS.R.

COVENTRY PATMORE   (National Portrait Ga
from a portrait by Sargent

[72]

ALICE MEYNELL
from a drawing by Sargent

WILFRID WARD

Mgr. ROBERT HUGH BENSON

PETER GALLWEY, s.j.

Mgr. JAMES NUGENT

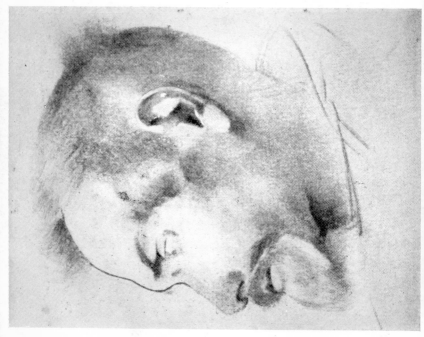

BEDE JARRETT, o.p.

CHARLES DOMINIC PLATER, s.j.

MOTHER JANET ERSKINE STUART,
of the Society of the Sacred Heart

MOTHER MARGARET HALLAHAN
Dominican

MOTHER CORNELIA CONNELLY,
of the Society of the
Holy Child Jesus

MOTHER MAGDALEN TAYLOR
of the Poor Servants of the
Mother of God

[80]

the leading foreign contributors: Cardinal Faulhaber, Abbé Dimnet, Georges Fonsegrive, the Comte de Mun, Charles Du Bos, the Marquis de Chambrun, Eugène Tavernier (*L'Univers*), Don Luigi Sturzo, Professor R. Lanciani. There were others also, for Ward believed in the unsigned article, which, he said, made it possible for " people of importance " to express views which they could not, or would not, put forward over their own signatures. The number and quality of his non-Catholic contributors is surprising: the list is headed by Lord Halifax, Lord Robert Cecil, Lord Hugh Cecil, G. K. Chesterton (not then a Catholic), W. H. Mallock, D. C. Lathbury, Oscar Browning. The *Dublin* had thus become not only a focus for the whole of informed Catholic opinion but also reflected a variety of considered and influential views from outside, the more so because it was known to be free from official inspiration. During Ward's period of editorship he was ably assisted by Reginald Balfour, Bertrand Devas and Stephen Harding, successively, and at the end of the period by Mgr. Barnes who in the last year was his coadjutor. When he retired in 1915 owing to increasing ill health, regret was universal.

Ward has been followed by Shane Leslie, Algar Thorold, Denis Gwynn, Christopher Dawson, T. S. Gregory and T. F. Burns, all of whom have in varying ways continued the tradition and augmented the prestige of the *Dublin*. But no record, however rapid, could conclude without mention of the astonishing amount of work done for the *Dublin* (and for Burns and Oates generally) by the Grand Old Man of the Catholic journalism of the period—Wilfrid Meynell. Though never titular editor, he was for many years almost everything else; and he lived to the age of ninety-four. Under Shane Leslie, History[4] and Biography were, on the whole, the favoured subjects. Under Algar Thorold (1926-1934) some two hundred contributors covered between them the whole field of Catholic interest with the exception of Art and Music and the balance was well maintained though the main interest of the editor was Philosophy and Mysticism. In April 1936

[4] In October, 1922, appeared the first, by Egerton Beck and J. J. Dwyer respectively, of many papers read to the Lingard Society. The last of these to be sent to the *Dublin* was by Abbot Cabrol in April, 1934.

Professor Denis Gwynn, who has done so much to make the story of the last hundred years better known to Catholics, brought out a remarkable Centenary Number containing articles of great value to the future historian of the Catholic Press.

The last part of the chronicle which brings us so near to our own day must be foreshortened. His successor who had to cope with a severe shortage of paper and a notable dearth of books for review, yet managed to produce an admirable Newman Number in October, 1945. In 1947 there were but two numbers, Spring and Autumn. Under Mr. T. S. Gregory's successor, Mr. T. F. Burns, the high level, so long striven for, so sedulously maintained, now appears to be firmly established.

II

Next in seniority comes *The Tablet*.

When Frederick Lucas founded *The Tablet* in 1840 the moment was more opportune than it seemed for such a venture. Emancipation was more than ten years old, the Oxford Movement was developing, and it was soon to be found that not four but eight Vicars Apostolic were needed. O'Connell was still thundering about Repeal. In England it was only eight years since the Reform Act; there was fierce discussion of the Poor Law and the Corn Laws; the Chartists were still active, the " Hungry Forties " had begun.

Lucas, the son of a London Corn Merchant, was educated at University College and was a barrister of Middle Temple. His parents were Quakers, and he was the brother-in-law of John Bright; a solidly built, powerful man, the perfect model for John Bull. In 1839, at the age of twenty-seven, he was received into the Church and, some twelve months afterwards the first number of *The Tablet* came out on Saturday, May 16, 1840. It was headed with a motto from Edmund Burke: " My errors, if any, are my own. I have no man's proxy."

Lucas began with a brief confession of political faith: loyalty to the Crown, adherence to the government of the day (Melbourne's), and the inevitable reference to Ireland: " On the subject of Irish politics it is hard to speak with moderation "—he was to find it hard on most subjects. He went on to explain that, although " No Repealer," he regarded the demand for Repeal as most natural for the inhabitants of a country governed so unwisely and so unjustly. Soon he was to come into contact with O'Connell and to undergo a second, sudden conversion. Meanwhile he could startle English Catholics, many of them Tories, with such observations as: " a large portion of Sir Robert Peel's followers are not sane."

That first year was marked by the usual financial difficulties and a quarrel with his non-Catholic partner, who was also the printer of the paper, with rights over its title, compelled him to call his paper for a short time *The True Tablet*. But O'Connell came to the rescue with influence and with cash, and soon Lucas was in control of the one and only *Tablet*. He enlarged the paper in January 1843 and, as a challenge to the timid, put on its forefront an image of Our Lady and the Divine Infant with the motto: *Sub tuum præsidium confugimus, sancta Dei genetrix*. His comments soon spread wonder and dismay among Catholics who, unused to a newspaper of their own, thought discretion the only policy. Like Carlyle, he was fond of denouncing humbug and cant and his opportunities for so doing were abundant. " Good society," he wrote, " owes us no gratitude and we owe it no allegiance," and he went on to declare that it was " a mass of cowardice, selfishness and religious indifference." When in 1844 the Queen's Colleges scheme (known ever since as the " Godless Colleges ") came out, *The Tablet* asked: " Are the Bishops awake?" When *The Times* and Lord John Russell created the " Papal Aggression " outcry against the re-establishment of the Hierarchy, Lucas's comment was: " The devil is apt to howl when he is hurt." The appearance of *The Tablet* was quaint in those days, tiny print and the general aspect of an ordinary newspaper. Turning over the pages of the first volume, one meets with items such as " Trial of Louis Napoleon "; " Horrible Murder in Barnsley."

The Famine had completed Lucas's conversion on the Irish Question and a visit to Ireland in 1849, when he saw with his own eyes its consequences, had brought a complete change of heart. It was in his nature to become more Irish than the Irish themselves and thus the facts of history and the events of the day combined inexorably to plant discord between English and Irish Catholics. He transferred *The Tablet* to Dublin and before long it was denounced by the Lord Lieutenant as " one of the most offensive and virulent newspapers in Europe "[5]. Later on he became M.P. for Meath, with the active support of the local clergy, and this brought him into sharp collision with the Irish Bishops headed by Archbishop Cullen who prohibited the priests from taking any part in elections. Lucas appealed to Rome and went there in 1854 to explain matters to the Pope. He died not long afterwards, leaving the memory of a fearless[6] and eloquent champion of the Catholic cause.

His successor, John Edward Wallis, who was editor from 1856 to 1868, announced that nothing would be changed; but he soon changed everything. He brought *The Tablet* back to London, a very natural and proper thing, and revoked the policy of Lucas. He was a strong Tory and outraged the feelings of the Irish M.P.s by actually opposing the Disestablishment of the Irish Church. He held with Disraeli that Catholics and Tories are " natural allies " and it was he who began the long association of *The Tablet* with Conservative principles. In this he was not alone for such Catholic sympathy with the Whigs as had been given in return for Emancipation had been dissipated by Palmerston and Lord John Russell by their active support of Victor Emmanuel and Garibaldi.

It was said of Wallis that he detested converts, Irishmen and Dr. Manning. Of the Irish Archbishop he spoke with open contempt: " Paul Cullen, Arch-Whig as well as Archbishop," and Archbishop Cullen for his part declared *The Tablet* to be " the chief difficulty of uniting the English and Irish Bishops." Wallis likewise made constant attacks on *The Dublin Review*, then avowedly Manning's organ. When it was pointed out to him that all this was very bad for busi-

---

[5] Lucas had published very violent attacks on the Irish landlords whom he explicitly accused of having created the Famine by their inordinate selfishness, greed, obstinate stupidity and hardheartedness. They had, he said, " doomed to death by slow murder the whole tenant class."

[6] He had never been a respecter of persons. Here is one of his references to Manning: " The Revd. H. E. Manning, recently ordained, is now proceeding to Rome to commence his ecclesiastical studies."

ness, his reply was that if so, he was very sorry for the business. In 1868 he sold *The Tablet* for a small sum to Father Herbert Vaughan (afterwards Bishop of Salford) who described the transaction as the luckiest investment of his life. The object of the acquisition was to put an end to an embarrassment and to ensure that in the forthcoming debates on Infallibility the paper should not be in the hands of Cisalpines, " Gallicans," or Inopportunists.

The Second Period of *The Tablet* now began. Herbert Vaughan announced himself as the " sole and absolute proprietor." He was, to all intents and purposes, the editor too; eccentric independence had had its day and was seen and heard no more. Fr. Vaughan took as his motto: *Pro Deo, pro Rege et patria,* and explained that the words, in *that order,* proclaimed the principles of the paper. He announced his uncompromising support for Gladstone's policy of Irish Disestablishment and with his habitual bluntness spoke of Disraeli's " crookedness of conduct which is habitual to him but unparalleled in any public man."

During the sessions of the Vatican Council, *The Tablet* brought out special supplements: *The Vatican: A Weekly Record of the Council,* with a mass of documents and reports, while no letters on the side of the Inopportunists were allowed to appear. After the entry of the Sardinian troops (September 20, 1870) into Rome, *The Tablet* got up a special Peter's Pence collection and obtained from readers the not inconsiderable sum of £2,000.

During those exciting times Herbert Vaughan's pronouncements were as absolute as those of his two predecessors. Accusations of " Gallicanism," " disloyalty " and so forth were freely launched and many supporters were alienated by " the confident and rather overbearing tone " of the paper. To the objection that free discussion was not tolerated in *The Tablet* his answer was: " In pure politics, literature and fine arts and every other subject proper to a newspaper, I accept no dependence on any person." Ecclesiastical matters, it should be noted, are carefully excluded from this statement; there, his attitude went without saying. When he became Bishop of Salford in 1872, George Elliot Ranken, his assistant, was appointed editor. Ranken continued quietly on the same lines, particularly in the matter of education and social reforms, until he retired in 1884.

The long editorship of J. G. Snead-Cox, 1884-1920, consolidated the position of *The Tablet* and raised it to the rank of a first-class periodical. The absolute and arbitrary tone now disappeared altogether and the contents of the paper were characterised by lucidity, courtesy and dignity. A just estimate of the temperament and the abilities of the fifth editor can be formed by anyone who reads carefully the *Life of Cardinal Vaughan,* a very admirable specimen of ecclesiastical biography. Snead-Cox, by origin an English country gentleman, was naturally and by conviction a Conservative. His long tenure of the editorial chair covered the period of the two Home Rule Bills and the climax of Parnell's career, and the controversies of the period necessarily found many Catholics, especially those of Irish origin, or Irish affiliations, in sharp opposition to his views. Thus it came to pass that the legend, inveterate in Ireland, that *The Tablet* is " anti-Irish," was confirmed and strengthened. Snead-Cox's answer was that he was not " against Ireland," but against applying political remedies to economic and social evils, and that an English Catholic had the same right to uphold the interests of England as Irishmen had to uphold what they considered the interests of Ireland.

Inevitably Catholics were divided, and very deeply, on those burning questions and in a certain degree it was a fortunate thing when at length the Liberal attacks on Catholic Schools brought the Duke of Norfolk and John Redmond on to the same platform together, on either side of Cardinal Bourne. Later on, others, mostly ladies, complained of Snead-Cox's stiff opposition to the Women's Suffrage Movement. These things, however, did little or nothing to offset the solid merits of the paper. The intellectual and literary side of *The Tablet* had been greatly strengthened, a group of scholars had contributed many articles of lasting value on a variety of subjects proper to a Catholic review, and beyond a few ponderous gibes from the Baron Frederick von Hügel, there was very little criticism from those who actually purchased and read the paper.

J. B. Milburn, who had been Assistant Editor for

twenty-five years, had only a short tenure of the chief post; he died after a long illness, in April 1923. His editorial policy was virtually identical with that of his predecessor, with the same literary merits, and with a special emphasis on Education questions in which Milburn was expert.

The third phase of *The Tablet* began in June 1923 with the advent of Ernest Oldmeadow. He was expressly chosen by Cardinal Bourne from a number of candidates and for thirteen years he was to edit the paper in the closest conformity with the views and wishes of the Cardinal. The curious thing about this partnership was that whereas there had been a certain natural consonance of mind between Cardinal Vaughan and his young kinsman Snead-Cox, there was hardly any discernible similarity of outlook between Cardinal Bourne and Ernest Oldmeadow. The latter was a genial, humorous man of the world with wide interests, a *bon vivant*, too, who could be very witty[7] on congenial subjects. A novelist and a musical critic, with some experience of journalism; more important was the fact that he was a convert from Nonconformity; as a young man he had been a minister at Halifax, Yorkshire. Though very consciously and very emphatically at home as a Catholic, he still retained unconsciously a good deal of Nonconformist characteristics, notably a zest for theological controversy and a decidedly Puritanical attitude in anything that he regarded as a question of morals. He was constantly engaged in polemics with the then editor of *The Church Times*, for whose tactics and views he had an equally strong distaste, and he devoted a disproportionate amount of his attention to the Malines Conversations—but this was apparently under instructions. But, as time went on, no opponent was too insignificant or too inept, the contents of the paper became more and more controversial, and every line of this matter—which did not interest the majority of the subscribers—was written *con amore* by the editor himself in preference to those other topics which the readers naturally looked for in a Catholic review. Under Snead-Cox and Milburn there had always been special articles by Dr. Bernard Ward, Canon Edwin Burton, Dr.

---

[7] For instance his " Francis Downman " wine lists, or such frequent *obiter dicta* as " the *Lauda Sion Salvatorem*, sung to a rollicking tune."

Adrian Fortescue and many other writers of distinction; but when, in the natural course of things, these were no longer available, they were never replaced. Almost the only scholar still writing in *The Tablet* in the early 'thirties was Fr. W. H. Kent, O.S.C., whose " Literary Causerie " had long been one of its best features. This contraction of the scholarly and literary side of the paper was accentuated by the fact that, under the dispositions made by Cardinal Vaughan, the profits were taken for the support of the Archdiocese of Westminster and of the Missionary College at Mill Hill, with the result that, when the circulation began to fall, there was no longer any money for outside contributors. A reviewer likewise got no fee, he merely kept the book as his recompense. For the editor himself the work was a semi-voluntary job—he had his own business to attend to, as well—and so it came to pass that nobody was adequately or even reasonably remunerated. This species of vicious circle brought about a further decline in the circulation. Oldmeadow, however, was of a robust and buoyant disposition and he kept the paper going, writing a large part of every number under various aliases. Throughout he was helped to the very utmost by the unstinted service of G. E. Anstruther. He also took his share of the reviewing; here he relied upon his own versatile mind and fluent pen, but without always realising the difference between general acquaintance with a subject and definite knowledge. Thus, he would cheerfully write a notice of a work on Byzantine Mosaics or Sienese Primitives; he reviewed *The Oxford Book of Medieval Latin Verse*, quite unaware of the identity of its editor. However, he enjoyed to the end the full confidence of Cardinal Bourne, whose mouthpiece he was and he would not have repudiated —he would rather have rejoiced in—the description of himself as " *un écrivain de combat.*" He was created a K.C.S.G. in 1934. His editorship ended rather suddenly in the Spring of 1936 when Cardinal Bourne's successor, Cardinal Hinsley, sold the paper to a group of laymen, Mr. A. H. Pollen, Mr. Douglas Woodruff and Mr. T. F. Burns. It was then sixty-eight years since *The Tablet* had been in lay control.

Under entirely new management *The Tablet* now entered its fourth phase and was immediately recognised as a very different thing. It became a review in the full sense of the

erm.   The new editor, Mr. Douglas Woodruff, came from
Oxford via *The Times*, as an acute student of History and
Politics, possessed of ample experience and with the advantage
of most useful contacts. He lost no time in gathering round
him a band of competent writers who were glad to have a
hand in so promising a venture. The all-important asset of
swift access to real information speedily put the new *Tablet*
into a totally different category from its predecessor, and it now
has a great deal of news that can be seen nowhere else. Another
consequent change was the far wider and more specialized
panel of reviewers, and the appearance, as often as practicable,
of literary articles by writers of distinction.

The war soon brought its difficulties and in particular a
prolonged paper shortage, only recently alleviated. Nevertheless a remarkable Centenary Number was produced on May
8, 1940, with a number of special articles such as: " The
Founder of the Tablet," " The Tablet in Early Victorian
England," " The Tablet through a Hundred Years " and so
on. These contained many interesting views and illuminating
details for which space cannot be found in a single rapid
summary. Thus the obstacles have been ably surmounted and
the increase in circulation has been continuous and is to-day
the largest in its long history.

The Tablet has a valuable documentary feature called
" News, Notes and Texts " covering the activities of the
Church all over the world, but the great strength of the review
is unquestionably its authoritative information and informed
discussion of foreign affairs, both in themselves and as they
affect the Church. A striking tribute was paid to the paper in
1947 by the late Lord Tyrrell of Avon, so well known as Permanent Secretary of the Foreign Office and Ambassador to
France.

III

It is now time to consider briefly a remarkable undertaking which, had it succeeded and become firmly established,
would have had very important results.

The most distinguished and perhaps the most unfortunate review ever published in this country was the Catholic
Magazine called *The Rambler*. It would be easy to collect a

cloud of witnesses to the learning and the intellectual brilliance of its editors and principal contributors, but the testimony of one neutral and disinterested critic, Matthew Arnold, may stand for them all; he said that in no organ of criticism in this country was there so much knowledge and so much play of mind. Yet, like Johnson's *Rambler* it was destined to a short life, with more celebrity than influence.

The Rambler was started as a weekly journal in 1848 by John Moore Capes, a Balliol convert, who was its proprietor for about ten years. It soon became a monthly. Its direction was in the hands of eminent converts, W. G. Ward, Frederick Oakeley and Richard Simpson. It gave general satisfaction and its motto was: *In necessariis unitas, in dubiis libertas, in omnibus caritas*, and Newman agreed to keep an eye on it as unofficial theological adviser. In 1854, however, Simpson became assistant editor and soon there was a change of tone. Richard Simpson, a linguist and a brilliant scholar, had when an Anglican incumbent generally been at variance with his bishop; and he apparently intended to be equally independent of the new Catholic Hierarchy; he was combative and his favourite and familiar element was hot water. In all this he was strongly representative of a band of zealous and injudicious converts who were preoccupied with theological questions and determined to deal with them. The second clause of the motto was stressed. They proclaimed that Religion was the first of human concerns and they were ready to discuss every aspect of it. At the same time, they saw in the political and intellectual upheaval of that time not difficulty or danger but opportunity. The ideals of the moment appealed to them much more strongly than anything traditional and before long, Simpson was making pronouncements so bold that they had the appearance of being inconsistent with the very principles of Christianity. " Modern society," said *The Rambler*, " has developed no security for freedom, no instrument of progress, no means of arriving at truth, which we look upon with indifference or suspicion." Possibly the accent was on the word " we." Another declaration began with the stark formula " while disavowing any interest in the ascetic life and the more intimate relations of religion . . . ." These writers were caught up in the great wave of " Liberalism " which characterised

ie eighteen-fifties and 'sixties, and they called for absolute
reedom in science, and in historical and critical investigation
ithout any regard to the effect upon weaker brethren. By
856 Wiseman had come to think that the tone of *The Rambler*
as a great obstacle to its influence and that by creating dissen-
on it would defeat its own objects; he actually began to fear
iat it would split Catholics into two parties, the " old " and
ie " new."   *The Rambler's* retort was that the hereditary
atholics were a narrow and bigoted clique, not educated
iough to understand modern methods of criticism. This was
ot only dangerous but unfair, because, as they well knew,
ie English Catholics had long been debarred from both
niversities and the Public Schools, while the French Revolu-
on and the Napoleonic wars had made matters worse by
epriving them of access to colleges and seminaries in France.
Viseman's strongest wish was that harmony should be pre-
erved and that there should be no dissensions in face of the
ie. These misgivings were duly expressed by the Cardinal in
s own organ, *The Dublin Review,* and Simpson met them
ith persiflage about views that were *couleur de rose.*

In the meantime Simpson had found a kindred spirit
id a very powerful colleague in the young Sir John Acton.
oth had come very early to that maturity of mind which is
ore important than specific knowledge: by 1858, when Acton
as only twenty-four, they were already in active correspond-
ice, discussing the business of the review and much else on
1 entirely equal footing, though Simpson was fourteen years
der and had had lively experience of editorship. From this
me on, Acton took a larger and larger part in *The Rambler*.
is knowledge was already immense—he was destined to be-
me perhaps the most learned historical scholar that the world
is yet known—but what was, in view of his years, even more
markable was his philosophical grasp, his firm hold of prin-
ple, his ability to assess the value of whatever he had read.
is mind, saturated with Montesquieu, Burke and Tocqueville,
emed to move with ease and certainty in the highest realms
political philosophy, and his judgments, expressed with
enchant clarity, had almost always the tone of long-meditated
inclusions. In all this he reminds us of Pitt when he became
rime Minister at twenty-four.

A great deal of work that is of lasting value and import
ance thus lies buried in the pages of *The Rambler* and of it
successor, *The Home and Foreign Review*, without ever havin,
received due appreciation. It was not understood by th
Catholics of the day and it has remained largely unknown an
unread ever since.

In 1859 the tension increased. *The Rambler* was criti
cised by *The Tablet* and attacked by *The Dublin*. Althoug]
it had the sympathy of the Bollandists, of Montalembert and o
Lacordaire and, naturally, of the majority of German scholars
it was regarded here with increasing distrust. Newman, favour
able at first, was now much disquieted by the theological ex
cursions and suggested " more levity and profaneness." Th
bishops were still more uneasy, but that did not deter Simpson
and his colleagues. They knew that their lordships were no
troubled by speculative difficulties, did not think very much
about the Monophysites, or the Donatists, nor were greatl
moved by chorus-endings from Euripides. Therefore the
could be disregarded. Articles came out on the Relations o
Faith and Reason, on Tridentine Seminaries and their def
ciencies, on Toleration, on Original Sin, and on Eternal Punish
ment; and presently there was a paper inspired, if not writte
by, Döllinger, in which it was stated that St. Augustine wa
the father of Jansenism. This filled up the cup and Simpson
was induced to resign in order to avoid an episcopal censure
Ullathorne then suggested Newman as editor, which seemed t
be such a good solution that Wiseman was actually prepare
to acquiesce in the cessation of the *Dublin* (then at a low ebb)
or its amalgamation with *The Rambler*, deeming that con
tributors would naturally prefer to send everything to th
review edited by Newman. All might have been well; bu
Newman had produced only two numbers, May and July 185
—it was then made bi-monthly by him—when he himself wa
delated to Rome by Bishop Brown of Newport on account o
an article: " On Consulting the Laity in Matters of Doctrine,'
with the result that he was quickly and easily persuaded b
Ullathorne to resign the editorship. The suggestion probabl

[8] In 1858 Acton had observed in a letter to Simpson that the firs
means to be adopted for reviving it was regular payments t
contributors.

came from Westminster, but it was strange that so powerful a mind as Ullathorne's should have been unable to distinguish between Newman and Simpson and failed to realise the importance of what Newman could do. Newman, however, resigned without a struggle though he never got over the shock; " it was," he said, " like the pat of a lion's paw." It was indeed a disaster.

Acton then became editor, with T. F. Wetherell as his assistant; but as the former was often abroad and the latter much occupied elsewhere, while Simpson, the " exceptionally privileged contributor," was always on the spot, the editorship was practically in commission. In this way the review was continued till 1862 when it was decided to make it a quarterly under a new name, *The Home and Foreign Review*, with Acton as editor. He adopted a new motto: *Seu vetus est verum diligo, sive novum,* and he put out a sort of prospectus, which, as pointed out by Abbot Gasquet in *Lord Acton and His Circle,* was almost verbally identical with that of Newman for the bi-monthly *Rambler.* The gist of the statement was that the aim of the review would be to abstain as far as possible from theological discussion, to reconcile freedom of inquiry with implicit faith and while " submitting without reserve to infallible authority, to encourage a habit of manly investigation on subjects of scientific interest." These phrases likewise reflect the purport of an article on " The Catholic Press " in *The Rambler* for February 1859; the aim was simultaneously to educate Catholics and to defend the Church against attacks by the only methods deemed intellectually valid. But the heart of the real difference between *The Dublin* and *The Rambler* lay in the fact that, in practice, the one avoided as far as possible everything awkward and, where it could not satisfactorily explain, endeavoured to explain away; while the other, holding that there was nothing to lose and much to gain by candour, derided all attempts at rehabilitation of " Bad Popes," inquisitors and so on, as mere " whitewashing."

Acton's purpose, however, was not understood. He meant to reproduce in England, so far as he could, the Munich circle, in which he himself had become so deeply learned, or at any rate something as like it as possible. He meant to raise the levels of knowledge, particularly historical knowledge, and to provide Catholics with intellectual leadership, and to help them to equip themselves for some part in public life. He was full of hopes and plans and he even speaks in one of his letters of founding a Lingard Society. The Regius Professorship at Cambridge, which came 30 years later, came much too late.

His own contributions to *The Home and Foreign Review* consisted of articles on contemporary foreign politics and of reviews of books. Of the former it is only necessary to say here that he possessed resources immeasurably greater than those of anybody else in England because to his vast reading he added the knowledge of secrets derived from confidential conversations with important personages in each of the great European capitals. His aristocratic connections thus made him a repository of unpublished information. He was not—like the professors—dependent on either printed or MS sources and he did not believe, as they still do, that *la vraie vérité* is to be found in official letters and despatches. More astonishing still was the work he put into reviews. In a few numbers of *The Home and Foreign* he had notices of more than a hundred books, English, French, German and Italian; in one single number, thirty-one out of sixty-three reviews were by him. His standard was excessively, impossibly, high and he judged writers and scholars, as he did politicians, not by what they knew but by what they did not know[9]; and his capacity for moral indignation was unlimited.

During these years Manning had watched the *Home and Foreign Review* with anxiety and growing hostility. He knew that Acton regarded his views on the Temporal Power (which he was fond of calling " the civil princedom of the Pope ") as absurd, and indeed Manning's statements that the Temporal Power would in due course be the subject of a dogmatic definition were too much for Rome itself. But the crisis did not come through that inflammable topic; it came through the proceedings of two Catholic congresses held abroad in 1863. At the Malines Congress, Montalembert gave two addresses which

---

[9] Excellent examples are quoted by Archbishop Mathew in his *Acton: The Formative Years*; here is one of them: " out of fifteen Lives of Pius V only three are named, and they are not the three best."

caused some commotion in Rome. In the first he spoke of " A Free Church in a Free State "—a slogan invented by Lamennais in *L'Avenir* which had been pirated by Cavour for very different objects—and, in the second, on Intolerance, as expounded by Catholic theologians, declaring that Establishment was wrong in itself and that government neutrality was a better thing than the Catholic Unity ideal of the Holy Roman Empire. More serious still was Döllinger's utterance at Munich; the Professor had called for a complete re-orientation of the Church's policy, for the abandonment of Scholastic Philosophy, for the maximum of speculation and discussion and the minimum of authority. The *Home and Foreign,* i.e., Acton, hailed Döllinger's address as " of rare significance " and declared that it would bear fruit for the whole Catholic world. The first fruit it bore was the end of the review, as Pius IX, December 21, 1863, sent a condemnatory Brief to the Archbishop of Munich, and in April 1864 Acton announced the discontinuance of the *Home and Foreign.* The text of the Brief was printed and followed by a calm and dignified recital of all the facts. Acton said that it was clear that the continuance of the review would result, sooner or later, in direct conflict with Rome and therefore, to avoid grave evils, it was best to withdraw.

Thus ended the most brilliant periodical of the nineteenth century. The loss was incalculable. Had Newman's editorship of *The Rambler* been allowed to continue, with Acton in close alliance as a fount of historical scholarship, the results would have been far-reaching. So powerful an influence could not have been ignored. One thing at any rate is certain; English 19th-century historiography, so provincial and anti-Catholic, would have been very different. The *English Historical Review* would have been founded twenty years sooner, Froude would almost certainly have been demolished; Stubbs and J. R. Green would have learned to write differently; and the intellectual life of the English Catholics would have been immeasurably enriched.

IV

A striking instance of what may come out of small beginnings is furnished by the story of *The Month.*

In response to an expressed wish for a Catholic review which would take an intermediate place between the quarterly *Dublin* and *The Tablet*, or the weekly *Register*, *The Month* was founded in July 1864. It was edited, at least ostensibly, by Miss Fanny Margaret Taylor, a convert, who had been a companion of Florence Nightingale during the Crimean War and who afterwards, under the religious name of Mother Magdalen Taylor, established the Society of the Poor Servants of the Mother of God. It was, however, apparent from the outset that the Jesuit Fathers were closely associated with the venture; the principal article in the first number was entitled " A Few Words for Mary Stuart " by Father Henry Coleridge, the brother of Lord Chief Justice Coleridge. Miss Taylor herself told Father Mathew Russell, S.J., long afterwards, that she regarded Father Gallwey as the real founder of the magazine. She had, at a very early date, proposed to give it up, but he had urged her to continue and before long had taken it over and paid all the bills. Father Gallwey had got James Doyle (not " Dicky Doyle " of *Punch*) to design the cover—Saint George and the Dragon in a kind of cartwheel—with the significant words underneath: " St. George for Merrie England," and it was Doyle who had actually suggested the name, *Month*.

It appears from correspondence that took place between J. H. Newman and the Jesuits that the illustrious Oratorian took a deep interest in the project. He considered that, as things then stood, Catholics should not be unrepresented in the new periodical literature that was developing all around them, and that a well-written Catholic magazine, discussing in a frank and natural way the questions of the hour, and showing good-will towards English institutions, would greatly improve the reputation of Catholics. He was therefore ready with both advice and criticism. His attitude was cautious (" Catholics are not a reading set ") and it was natural that, with his own *Rambler* experience in mind, he was not very sanguine or enthusiastic. He had in particular great misgivings as to the introduction of theological subjects and insisted that care should be taken not to arouse Protestant hostility—at least, that is the way he put it. As regards his own personal willingness to assist, he was lukewarm, and all that could be got from him was the chilly promise that if he were to do anything that was likely to suit them, they should have the first refusal of it.

The first number, that of July 1864, did something to bear out the sub-title, *The Month, an Illustrated Magazine of Literature, Science and Art.* Along with Father Coleridge's criticism of J. A. Froude's treatment of Mary, Queen of Scots, there were the first instalments of two serial stories (one of them by Lady Georgiana Fullerton); an account of the French Salon of 1864, and some personal recollections of Geneva and its environs, an obvious peg for a literary causerie; and there were full-page wood-engravings by Walter Crane. The early numbers contained items like " A Legend of Italy," " A Beauty of the First Empire," " A Wedding at St. Denis " and a good deal of verse, Aubrey de Vere and Denis Florence McCarthy being among the contributors; another was Miss Bessie Rayner Parkes, the future Madame Belloc. In fact, it was to be something very like *The Cornhill*. To the third number Cardinal Wiseman sent one of the last things he ever wrote. But the most remarkable of all, " the greatest distinction of which *The Month* can boast " (as Father Gerard wrote in 1902), was *The Dream of Gerontius*. The waste-paper basket story is a myth; but it has some foundation. According to Aubrey de Vere, Newman had put the poem aside and forgotten it, and then found it when looking for something else. It appeared in May and June 1865.

When Father Coleridge became editor in 1865, he made changes. The price however stood at one shilling and St. George and the Dragon remained on the cover till 1882 while the legend below gave place to a short list of contents. The saint reappeared eventually in 1897, and in 1902 a smaller design by Paul Woodroffe was adopted with space for a full table of contents. The green cover was adopted in 1913 by Fr. J. Keating and the present new one in January 1949. Changes in the title have been as follows: from 1865 to 1873, *The Month: A Magazine and Review;* from 1874-1881, *The Month and Catholic Review;* from 1882 to 1897, *The Month, a Catholic Magazine;* and finally, *The Month* tout court.

Despite Newman's advice, theological and philosophical articles soon began to appear, as was indeed natural, but written with prudence and framed in non-technical language. The literary character of the magazine was, however, very carefully preserved and it has never been lost. An enormous amount of work was now steadily put into it, mostly by the Jesuit Fathers themselves. Father Coleridge who was editor till 1882 must himself have contributed something like two hundred articles. Father Richard F. Clarke, who had been a Fellow of St. John's, Oxford, was the second editor, but his contributions actually ranged from 1870 to 1900. Father John Gerard, of Gunpowder Plot fame, took a giant's share of the work; he was editor from 1894 till 1912, whilst his own articles had started in 1867. So, too, did Father Sydney Smith, whose articles began in 1869 and ended only in 1920, while the famous Father John Hungerford Pollen, contributed a stream of learned historical papers from 1887 till 1924. Other notable contributors were Fathers Francis Goldie, William Humphrey, William Loughnan, Herbert Lucas, John Morris and the amazing Fr. Joseph Stevenson, to whom we mainly owe the Rolls Series. It was perhaps Father John Morris, whose incessant labours in the cause of the English Martyrs will never be forgotten, who did most to communicate this strong historical impulse to the band of scholar-priests who for so many years gave *The Month* its distinctive character. Large tracts of the Reformation period were subjected to methodical and searching study, *ex fontibus ipsis*, the State Papers, the Jesuit archives in England and on the Continent, and all the available contemporary records. Father Pollen, in particular, concentrated his researches upon the Elizabethan persecution, the attitude and behaviour of the Marian clergy and cognate questions. An entirely new framework for the history of the reign of Elizabeth was constructed, and though this was embodied in important books, the first fruits of all this research appeared in *The Month*. The fact that the stream of historical papers was the outcome of teamwork made the gain in cohesion much greater than the loss of variety. A fuller biography of martyrs like Campion, Southwell and Walpole and many more was another object of research and a close connection was naturally created with the work of the Catholic Record Society on the one hand and that of the Catholic Truth Society on the other. James Britten, always in effective liaison with *The Month*, was a frequent contributor and there is no possible doubt that the high standard of the historical papers of the C.T.S. was in the first instance set by the group of Jesuit Fathers above-mentioned.

Meanwhile, the aggressive propaganda of agnostic scientists under the influence of Huxley, Tyndall, W. K. Clifford and the rest was steadily counteracted. Then towards the end of the century came a fresh wave of Anglican controversy. The celebrations, at Ebbsfleet in 1897, of the thirteen-hundredth anniversary of the landing of St. Augustine of Canterbury and his companions, and the almost concurrent condemnation of the validity of Anglican Orders by Leo XIII gave rise to intense and sometimes acrimonious discussion. The hitherto unruffled assurance of Anglican controversialists was considerably shaken.

Fr. Gerard's long editorship[10], which came to an end in 1912, covered a period of difficulty created for the Society and its organ in England by the aberrations of the brilliant but erratic Father George Tyrrell. In the early years of the twentieth century Tyrrell's articles had been an attraction and an ornament of *The Month* as of other reviews. But before long he had plunged with delight into the Modernist movement in which he rapidly became a protagonist, in far closer sympathy with Loisy, Houtin, Laberthonnière and Bremond than with his brethren in the Society, or for that matter, with anybody else in this country. Of the melancholy sequel there is no need to speak here. His last article in *The Month,* bearing the title, " *Semper Eadem,*" appeared in January 1904.

Father Gerard was followed by Father Joseph Keating and a very distinguished period in the long history of the review now began. The new editor introduced alterations in accordance with his own literary tastes; poetry was readmitted and, while continuity was carefully maintained, *belles lettres* began to catch up on history, philosophy and controversy. Another new feature soon became an important part of the review. Instead of " Flotsam and Jetsam " or " Miscellanea " or " Topics of the Month," placed between the articles and

[10] It is curious to note the long editorships of *The Month.* In eighty-five years there have been but six editors, and the latest has held the post only since January, 1949; whereas *The Dublin Review* has had sixteen since its inception in 1836.

the book reviews, " Editorial Comments " now came in front.
These appraisements of current events were informed by the
soundest judgment and by wide knowledge. Judgment, the
most essential of an editor's possessions, was perhaps his forte
and his wise counsel was eagerly sought and deeply appreciated in many other quarters; one need only mention the
Westminster Version of the Sacred Scriptures, the Catholic
Truth Society, the Catholic Social Guild, the Catholic Council
for International Relations. His own articles in *The Month*
were very numerous, not a few dealing with the Irish Question
on which he was well qualified to write. He worked up to the
end (March 1939) and the April issue of that year was filled
with tributes from a wide variety of friends headed by Cardinal
Hinsley.

A glance through the volumes for the nineteen-twenties
will reveal the great range and variety of the contents. Among
many notable things a few may be cited: articles by Fr. Lucas
and Fr. Pollen respectively on Shane Leslie's Life of Cardinal
Manning; a number of " historical revisions " by J. G.
Muddiman of the official stories of the martyrs of the Popish
Plot, and of the traditional fiction of the " Bloody Assizes ";
a series of articles by Fr. Leo Hicks on " Mary Ward and her
institute," on " Father Persons, S.J., and the Seminaries in
Spain," and on " Cardinal Allen and the Society "; Egerton
Beck's refutation, based on the Visitation Records in the
English Episcopal Registers, of Dr. G. G. Coulton's incessant
attacks on monastic morality before the Reformation; and a
series of articles on Astronomy by Father A. L. Cortie, then
Director of the Stonyhurst Observatory. Those years bear
witness also to the intense activity and versatile knowledge of
Father Thurston. There are few numbers that do not contain
a contribution from him. The range is enormous. From " The
Blow in the Rite of Confirmation " or the history of the Cardinal's Hat and many other curious items of recondite
information he passes readily to Alexander VI or Alban Butler
or the Recusant affiliations of John Shakespeare. But these
things were not his speciality. He was an incomparable
detective, and his acute investigation of innumerable cases of
stigmatization, reputed miracles, hypnotism, hysteria,
" spiritualistic phenomena," poltergeists and so forth would

alone have sufficed to make him famous. Of more immediate interest to the devout were his criticisms of the Dominican tradition of the Rosary and the Carmelite tradition of the Scapular; the latter elicited a reply from the erudite Fr. Benedict Zimmerman, O.D.C.

In these volumes also are found the beginning of a long series of contributions from Father C. C. Martindale and the first articles of Father Alban Goodier (afterwards Archbishop of Bombay), Father Francis Woodlock and Father Martin D'Arcy. Here, too, is fiction from the fluent pen of " John Ayscough "—Mgr. Bickerstaffe-Drew. Nor was the ever-growing assertiveness of Agnostic scientists disregarded; while for the exponents of what Newman called " the great Protestant Tradition " in all its forms, whether propounded by the defenders of Anglican Orders or by people who imagine that the Albigenses were Bible Christians, *The Month* had always a full and trenchant reply. Nor were women writers ignored. The issue for July 1920 contained articles by four writers, all well-known at the time, Louise Imogen Guiney, Edith Cowell, Cicely Hallack and Enid Dinnis. In January 1928 there was an article by Eric Gill with the always appropriate title: " The Enormities of Modern Religious Art."

On Father John Murray fell the burden of editing *The Month* during the six years of war and the scarcely less difficult period that followed. Inevitably, political subjects claimed more and more attention and, as the war went on and almost the whole world became more or less involved, all other topics seemed to lose interest and even meaning, so that it became a sort of relief to read charming articles by the Editor on Virgil and able treatment of Reformation subjects by those successors of Fr. Gerard and Fr. Pollen, viz. Fr. Leo Hicks and Fr. James Brodrick, while R. A. L. Smith (a young convert Fellow of Trinity College, Cambridge, whose early death was a great loss to historical studies) wrote interesting papers on Monks and Friars. When the paper shortage became acute, *The Month* appeared six times a year in double numbers; this curtailment lasted from January 1941 till January 1946. During these years articles on spiritual topics were still coming from the pen of the veteran Fr. R. H. J. Steuart whose first contribution had appeared in 1900; but it was gradually becoming evident that in a rapidly changing world, where a profound alteration in tastes and outlook was everywhere emerging, the old current of the famous Jesuit review had spent much of its force and that something fresh was necessary and desirable.

In January 1949 appeared the new *Month,* " New Series No. 1," with a new cover, new title lettering, and a campion flower colophon by Mr. Reynolds Stone. It was virtually a new review with a new editor and a new policy. It proclaimed its intention of appealing to persons with a balanced interest in religion and the humanities, and of providing them with discussions on literature and the arts as well as on philosophy and theology, in other words, those interests that go to make a complete culture. The notion of " specialist house-organ " of the Society was thus openly renounced and the new editor, Father Philip Caraman, quoted with great effect the dictum of Mr. T. S. Eliot (*The Idea of a Christian Society*) that intellectuals should not regard theology as a special study like numismatics or heraldry nor theologians observe the same indifference to literature and art as subjects which do not concern them. The first number of the new series opened with a poem by Thomas Merton; this was followed by articles from M. C. D'Arcy and Frederick C. Copleston (no " Reverend " or " S.J."), Martin Turnell and John Rothenstein. The reviews were by Graham Greene, Deryck Hanshell, Evelyn Waugh, J. L. Russell, D. J. B. Hawkins. The new venture received, deservedly, a very warm welcome from the serious and literary papers, non-Catholic as well as Catholic. *The Times Literary Supplement* paid it great attention, carefully detailing the contents of the first number, while *The Manchester Guardian* and *The Yorkshire Post* each gave a welcoming note. In the issue of September 23, 1949, *The Times Literary Supplement* returned to the subject, reciting the main items that had appeared since January and adding a striking tribute. It was now clear, said the T.L.S., that *The Month* had achieved " a striking success "; " it would be hard to point to a livelier monthly review . . . and harder still to indicate one which had carried out more consistently a precise and civilized intention."

V

Some mention should now be made of several publications which were deemed of interest and importance in their day but which were not destined to survive.

From the end of the eighteenth century there were a number of small Catholic periodicals, most of them with a long title and a short life; their story is too kaleidoscopic to be told in any detail, and in any case nearly all of them are below the horizon of this brief survey. A few of them, however, call for notice if only because they heralded or actually gave birth to more important publications, such as *The Orthodox Journal* and *The Catholic Magazine*, the ancestors of *The Weekly Register*. There was for instance *The Catholic Miscellany*, 1822, which in 1828 became *The Catholic Miscellany and Monthly Repository of Information*. In the same year appeared *The Catholic Journal*, a weekly newspaper, published every Saturday, price 7d. Its object was to further the interests of the British Catholic Association, while disclaiming any connection with the committee of that body. In 1831 came the *Catholic Magazine and Review*, a monthly, published in Birmingham, London and Liverpool; it lasted till 1855. Charles Dolman's *Catholic Magazine*, 1838, price 1s., announced itself as " the only Catholic periodical published in Great Britain "; it ceased publication in 1844. *The London and Dublin Orthodox Journal of Useful Knowledge* which seems to deserve mention, if only for its resounding title, began in 1835 and apparently lasted till 1846.

The Lamp: *A Catholic Journal of Literature, the Fine Arts, etc., devoted to the Religious, Moral, Physical and Domestic Improvement of the Industrious Classes*, was established at York in 1850. It was destined to undergo too many changes to be described here. In 1855 it was being published in London by Charles Dolman. Seven years later it was merely *An Illustrated Catholic Journal of General Literature*, with Miss Fanny Margaret Taylor, the foundress of *The Month*, as proprietor and editor. The magazine had Jesuit support, Fathers Gallwey and Goldie being frequent contributors. In 1870 it was called *A Popular Journal of General Literature*. A year later it was bought by Mrs. Lockhart, mother of Fr. William Lockhart, and became known as *The Lamp: an Illustrated Catholic Magazine,* weekly, 1d., with Wilfrid Meynell as sub-editor. Eventually it came into the hands of Charles Diamond and was put out.

More important than any of the foregoing was *The Weekly Register, A Catholic Journal of Literature, Correspondence and Intelligence,* price 3d., occasionally illustrated, published at 9, Rupert Street, Leicester Square, in 1849. It had vitality and should have been helped by the exciting times in which it had its being, but nevertheless came to a full stop in 1850; then it was re-issued in 1855 as the *Weekly Register and Standard,* price 6d., as the result of one of the amalgamations so frequent at that time, for Henry Wilberforce had acquired *The Catholic Standard* (1849-1855) when Lucas transferred *The Tablet* to Dublin. Henry Wilberforce, to whom Newman dedicated *Callista,* was the son of the Emancipator of the Slaves and the brother of " Soapy Sam," sometime Bishop of Oxford and then of Winchester. He ran *The Weekly Register and Catholic Standard* till 1863, in a sort of covert rivalry to *The Tablet,* whose ultra-Irish tendency and " confident and overbearing tone " he and his friends disliked. The paper took its own line on other questions, too, and at one time was filled with letters from constant readers openly questioning the doctrine of Infallibility or deploring the consequences to be apprehended from a Definition. All that it is now remembered for is the malignant attack of its Roman correspondent on Newman in 1867. This man, by name Martin, was moved to write that the Holy Father had " thought it right to inhibit the proposed mission of Dr. Newman to Oxford " because that distinguished man no longer held a high place in Roman opinion, confidence in him having been shaken by various utterances of his and by his connection with Döllinger. Thus *The Weekly Register* helped to make history. At an earlier period it had taken an active part in the controversies that centred round *The Rambler* and it is mentioned with distaste by Lord Acton in the acrid letter to Newman of June 29, 1860, in which he laments his own position amid " a hostile and illiterate episcopate, an ignorant clergy, and a prejudiced and divided laity." Eventually, when the paper was, according to E. S. Purcell, " in a state of collapse," it was acquired by Cardinal Manning in 1881, " to save it from extinction." Manning, though he held that a bishop must not be " a diner-out nor a waster of time nor a reader of newspapers," was always keenly alive to the influence of the Press—he had acquired *The Dublin* in 1862 and *The Tablet* was similarly acquired by his intimate friend and disciple, Herbert Vaughan in 1868.

Manning gave *The Weekly Register* to Wilfrid Meynell, who, with the help of his brilliant wife and his many friends, ran the paper for the next eighteen years. Under Meynell it sought to reflect Cardinal Manning, whose disciple and fervent admirer he was, with the result that it differed somewhat from *The Tablet*. The latter had become definitely the paper for the old English Catholics under Herbert Vaughan who belonged to them himself. Meynell, who was more versatile and more imaginative, combined some unlikely enthusiasms—for instance, a strange admiration for Disraeli—with his discipleship of the great prelate of Westminster and he also managed to effect the bizarre union of a " Young England " policy with warm support for Home Rule. On the whole, however, *The Weekly Register* never became as effective as, or even a serious rival to, *The Tablet* which throughout the 'eighties and 'nineties under Herbert Vaughan and Snead-Cox had no equal or rival in its own field. Of the two ventures, Meynell's *Merry England* was the more successful.

In 1883, with Lord Ripon and Charles Russell as sleeping partners, Wilfrid Meynell founded and edited the monthly *Merry England* which he carried on with great gusto for twelve years. In this he was wont to express fully and freely his religious, literary and social convictions and he wrote so much that he had to use pseudonyms, such as " John Oldcastle " or " Francis Phillimore " as well as his own name and anonymity. And he had very distinguished contributors: Cardinal Manning, Wilfrid Blunt, W. H. Hudson, Coventry Patmore, George Saintsbury, Lionel Johnson, Katharine Tynan and Alice Meynell. Later, too, came, in *Merry England* in 1888, the first appearances in print of Mr. Hilaire Belloc. But the fame of *Merry England* was above all due to Francis Thompson, for it was Meynell who had discovered him and printed his early poems in that magazine. Few

greater services to literature have been rendered by anybody
in modern times.

VI

We come now to the popular weekly newspapers on
which a very large proportion of the Catholic population have
always had to rely for their information and edification.

The Universe owes its inception to Cardinal Wiseman.
In 1860 there was, despite the repeal of the newspaper tax,
no penny Catholic paper in London and there was very great
need of one. There had been great events in Italy, the battle
of Solferino, the Peace of Villafranca, the expansion of Victor
Emmanuel's Kingdom at the expense of the Papal States,
Garibaldi's descent on Sicily and his subsequent triumphant
advance on Rome. The English Press was full of attacks on
the Pope and on the bishops and clergy of Italy; calumny
and ridicule were unsparing; contradictions and corrections
were useless, as nobody would print them. The majority of
Catholics in this country saw no paper that answered these
attacks, for the sixpenny *Tablet* was beyond their means. So
the Cardinal one day asked the President of the Society of St.
Vincent de Paul if his Society could not do something like what
Louis Veuillot was doing in *L'Univers*. A number of Brothers,
headed by G. J. Wigley, London correspondent of *L'Univers,*
acting in their personal capacity, agreed to try, and eventually
they started the paper on December 8, 1860. It was printed
by Denis Lane, a London Irishman, and edited by Archibald
Dunn. Although editor and staff received no remuneration,
the paper for a long time did not pay. Successive editors were
J. A. O'Shea, James O'Connor, M.P. for West Wicklow, Prior
O'Gorman, Father Alexius Mills. There was a column for
" the Saint of the Week," but no book reviews, for Denis
Lane did not see the use of them, and he was in control.

Later on, the *Universe* scribes, who all possessed the
gift of invective, were wont to revel in ferocious controversy
with *The Rock* and other organs of the Protestant underworld[11]. After the death of Denis Lane the paper was edited

---

[11] Round about 1900 *The Rock* was sued for libel by Father Bernard
Vaughan, S.J., and a very lively trial ended in a verdict for £300
damages against the paper for using opprobrious terms about the
Jesuits. It was also the end of *The Rock* for it had not got the
money and went under. The C.T.S. printed a full report of the
trial.

from 1906 to 1909 by George Elliot Anstruther, K.S.G.[12] The war brought difficulties and by 1917 the circulation had sunk to a very low figure.

Sir Martin Melvin, G.C.S.G., then came to the rescue. The modern technique of production was introduced, news from every part of Great Britain was regularly obtained, " star " contributors, such as Mgr. R. Knox, G. K. Chesterton, Hilaire Belloc, Sir Philip Gibbs, were induced to write articles, and soon there was an enormous increase in the circulation. There was, too, a new editor, Herbert S. Dean, an Oxford convert, who possessed many qualifications for the task. Long before he was received, in 1903, he had been one of the pioneers in England of the Solesmes reform of the liturgical chant. He had likewise a devotion to the Liturgy, and with these classic marks of the cultured convert he proceeded to improve notably the editorial side of the paper. Significantly, he adopted the old *Rambler* motto: *In necessariis unitas; in dubiis libertas; in omnibus caritas*[13]. Recent years however have seen the adoption of ultra-modern methods, the appointment of an American-trained News Editor, the definite precedence of news over views, " snappy " headlines, striking illustrations. Still, nothing succeeds like success, and *The Universe* now has a very prominent place of its own as a comprehensive purveyor of general and local Catholic news with the enormous circulation of 230,000, probably the largest of any religious newspaper in the world.

In 1867 *Catholic Opinion*, A Review of the Catholic Press at Home and Abroad, Saturday, weekly, price 1d., was purchased by Mrs. Lockhart and edited by her son, Fr. William Lockhart, until 1873, when it was bought by Dr. Herbert Vaughan, Bishop of Salford. He used it as an educational supplement to *The Tablet* until 1876, when it was transferred to Father James (afterwards Mgr.) Nugent, of Liverpool, the celebrated Temperance apostle. Father Nugent having acquired an unsuccessful paper, *The Northern Press*

---

[12] Afterwards Organizing Secretary of the C.T.S. (1907-1920) and Assistant Editor of *The Tablet* (1920-1936).

[13] Dean remained editor till 1938. In August 1939 he wrote his own obituary notice, as Sir Edward Clarke had done for *The Times*, and this duly appeared on the appropriate date, August 21, 1942.

& Catholic Weekly Times amalgamated it with *Catholic Opinion* and brought out: *The Catholic Times and Catholic Opinion*: The Organ of the Catholic Body. The first editor was John Denvir, author of *The Irish in Britain*. From the outset is was widely read in Liverpool and the North of England and very soon in London, too. It inevitably became a Home Rule organ, but maintained at all times a tone of moderation and dignity. Mgr. Nugent was succeeded by Fr. Barry, but the bulk of the work was done by P. L. Beazley, who edited the paper for some 27 years. After the First World War its circulation declined; it was acquired in 1926 by Fr. Herbert Vaughan, D.D., nephew of Cardinal Vaughan, and thus became the organ of the Catholic Missionary Society. From 1933 to 1937 it was edited by Dr. Bernard Grimley, and was the only Catholic weekly which had a priest as its editor. It has been modernized without departing from its standards, and maintained a traditional and dignified pace, less rapid perhaps than that of contemporaries, and if the scope is narrower there is a corresponding gain in the coherence of the picture presented to the reader. Under the editorship of Dr. James Walsh, K.C.S.G, it is now meeting with deserved success.

The origin of the first *Catholic Herald* goes back to the days of Cardinal Manning whose ardent desire for the material improvement of the working classes almost equalled his preoccupation with their religious and moral welfare. Under the inspiration of his work for social reform Charles Diamond had in 1884 founded his newspaper avowedly as the organ of " Catholic Industrial Democracy." An eager and restless politician, he soon gained a large following and he was encouraged to create local editions of his newspaper in all the industrial centres where there was a large Catholic population. But his talent for invective got him into trouble and into prison; he lost his influence and his papers lost their circulation. When Diamond died in 1934 *The Catholic Herald* and its numerous satellites were acquired from his estate by a group of laymen who had very different views and intended to appeal to a different public, but they wisely preferred an existing paper with a well-known name to a completely new venture. Their project was to start a fresh kind of Catholic weekly which was not to be a compendium of exclusively, or even specifically, Catholic news, but was to deal with every-day world news of all kinds from the Catholic standpoint. This meant that they would have to write about almost everything. It also meant that they would have to uphold certain standards in conditions where news is generally treated as a weapon. It was felt that there was a real need for such a paper on account of the strong current running in opposition not only to the mission and the claim of the Church but even to the Christian life itself. As long as their religious belief is not openly challenged, Catholics are somewhat inclined to shut their eyes to these tendencies. Many of them, moreover, are accustomed to separate, so to speak, their lives into two compartments, the one closed and almost sectarian, the other indistinguishable from the public, business, or social life of other people. Then, too, there is the opportunity of influencing non-Catholics who are curious about what we believe and do—or don't do—either because they are potential converts or because of a general interest in Religion: these people were thought far more likely to read a " journal of opinion " than a vehicle for specifically Catholic news. Catholics, again, ought to be encouraged to qualify for a more active part in public affairs—which involves sustained discussion. To this end *The Catholic Herald* has always allotted much space for readers' letters, and, as this is an infallible method of creating and retaining their attention, the paper has had its reward—the more so as it does not even enforce brevity on its correspondents. Letters consequently range from the insoluble problem of the right service for Sunday Evening to the most complex questions of world politics.

These strenuous efforts have met with success. *The Catholic Herald*, ably edited by Count Michael de la Bédoyère, has something like 100,000 readers every week and is an established Catholic force. The obvious difficulty of realising its exacting ideal is the heavy demand which it makes upon the staff and in particular the difficulty of holding the balance between the ventilation of opinion on the one hand and, on the other, accuracy and proportion in the collection and reporting of world news.

VII

The Catholic Gazette: A Monthly Review, price 6d., is the organ of the Catholic Missionary Society and it claims attention because it is addressed to the whole of the Catholic body in this country and in a large measure to non-Catholics as well.

The C.M.S. was founded by Cardinal Vaughan in 1902 to work for the conversion of England. As a society of secular priests engaged in the work of giving missions they naturally have their own specific organ, a review of Catholic doctrine and apologetics written in untechnical language. Originally the paper was called *The Missionary Gazette* (10 pages) and the first issue, edited by Fr. Herbert Vaughan, D.D., contained an article on " The Catholic Church and the Working Man " by Fr. Bernard Vaughan, S.J. A new series began in January 1914 (20 pages) with much more space devoted to articles of a doctrinal and apologetic character. In January 1918 the name was changed to *The Catholic Gazette,* with Father Richard Downey, D.D. (now Archbishop of Liverpool) as joint editor, and the *Gazette* now began to cater for more educated readers. Subsequent editors have been Fr. Bernard Grimley, D.D., Canon Joseph Morgan, D.D., Fr. W. Randall, Fr. J. Garvin, D.D., and Fr. G. P. Dwyer, D.D.

After forty years the purport of the controversy has very greatly changed and the *Catholic Gazette* reflects as well as any other organ the transformation of the question: " Catholic or Protestant " into " Christian or Non-Christian."

The price is sixpence. A pleasing feature of the production is excellent print on very good paper.

In this brief survey it is not possible to describe or enumerate the large number of periodicals which may be said to have a limited appeal, or a special or professional clientèle, such as *The Clergy Review,* or the *Catholic Medical Guardian* or the magazines of guilds and societies, and it may be noted that the Catholic body is particularly prolific in monthlies of small format, such as *Stella Maris*. There are, too, over a hundred school and college and seminary magazines, some of which are of venerable age, e.g., *The Ushaw Magazine, The*

Oscotian founded in 1828, or *The Edmundian,* founded in
1841. Exception, however, must be made if only for brief
mention, of *The Downside Review,* founded by Abbot Aidan
Gasquet, O.S.B., in 1882, which is a learned review in the fullest
sense of the term dealing very thoroughly with questions of
theology, philosophy and monastic history; of the interesting
Beda Review, started in 1929 by Mgr. C. L. Duchemin,
Rector of that College; of *Blackfriars,* the organ of the
Dominicans at Oxford, founded in 1920 by Father Bede
Jarrett, O.P., in its distinctive black and white cover designed
by Eric Gill, devoted not only to extending the empire of St.
Thomas Aquinas but to a wide variety of cultural topics; of
Pax, conducted by the Benedictine Fathers of Prinknash; and
of the extremely well edited and excellently illustrated *West-
minster Cathedral Chronicle.*

VIII

Finally, and occupying a special place of its own in
the Apostolate of the Printed Word, without producing a
newspaper, comes the Catholic Truth Society.

The Catholic Truth Society is too well known to need
formal description in these pages, but in any survey of the
Catholic Press it falls to be considered by reason of its intellectual contribution to the common stock of Catholic culture. For
though its primary objects are missionary, propagandist and
apologetic, the character of a large part of its publications in
recent years is such as to bring the Society into line with the
more important of those periodicals which are noticed here.
There has been evolution as well as expansion since the day
when James Britten bought in Paternoster Row a half-crown's
worth of Protestant tracts and pamphlets and resolved upon
the spot to do something like it, for Catholics. The name of
Catholic Truth Society had first been taken by a diocesan
organization in Salford under Bishop Herbert Vaughan (afterwards Archbishop of Westminster and Cardinal) but this effort
did not prosper. James Britten, however, having got together
twelve friends who each subscribed one pound, was able to
convene a meeting in the house of Lady Herbert of Lea, with
Bishop Vaughan in the chair. This was in 1884, and the carefully chosen date was November 5.

The early pamphlets and leaflets were devotional, expository and controversial. The last-named were mostly of the Do-Catholics-Adore-the-Blessed-Virgin? variety, and refutations of Pastor Chiniquy and Maria Monk. But as the field widened the quality improved and before long the infant society had the powerful aid of the Jesuit Fathers at Farm Street.

An immense increase in the diffusion of the C.T.S. publications was secured in 1887 by the adoption of a happy idea of Fr. Rothwell of Manchester. This was the famous C.T.S. Box, whereby the booklets and pamphlets would sell themselves in every church or church porch without the trouble and expense of supervision, reliance being placed on the honesty of those who frequented the church. The courageous experiment was successful and the C.T.S. cases spread rapidly till they covered the country. Now there are 2,500 registered members of the Boxtenders' Association and their work is invaluable.

Nevertheless the growth of the Society involved a tremendous amount of uphill and unpaid work, the bulk of which was done by James Britten. This extraordinary man had a full-time occupation in the Botanical Section of the British Museum and the whole of his immense labour in the cause of spreading Catholic Truth was done in his own time. A convert himself, he had many qualifications for the work. He wrote many of the pamphlets, he was incessantly editing, proof-correcting, travelling, interviewing, speaking in public. He attended, likewise, to the business side and the finances. It was all done with abounding energy and exuberant humour. He was never at rest for a moment. To him the C.T.S. was a crusade. If his tact had equalled his zeal, he would have been superhuman. But, with the defects of his great qualities, it came to pass after many years that other plans and other minds were needed. He was loath to change his methods and deemed that there could be no sure progress except under his control. Eventually the Forward Movement, launched by Cardinal Bourne in 1920, had to be worked without him. But he had done more than any living writer to diminish the stream of anti-Catholic misrepresentation. Nor should the work of Mgr

Cologan and Mr. W. Reed-Lewis, who added the famous Bexhill Library to the resources of the C.T.S., be forgotten.

By this time there had been issued an immense number of pamphlets, well-written, accurate, clear and persuasive, covering many subjects of doctrine, devotion, history, biography, controversy and the like. They were then sold at one penny, and it was not till 1921 that they were, with great reluctance, put up to twopence. Now threepence does not usually cover the cost. Many of them were the work of distinguished writers and scholars and they were wonderful value for the money. To their efficacy in initiating or effecting conversions there is a vast mass of testimony and indeed it is common knowledge.

Along with the Forward Movement came reorganization. The Cardinal appointed Bishop Bidwell as President and Chairman. He was succeeded in 1930 by Bishop Myers and in 1948 by Mgr. C. Collingwood. There were new committees, Executive and General, with a whole-time and salaried General Secretary. Mr. Britten became a Vice-President. Two years later Mr. Reed-Lewis retired and not very long afterwards began the long and fruitful Secretaryship of Mr. J. P. Boland. Advertising and appeals brought up the subscribing membership gradually from a couple of thousand to something like 15,000 in the nineteen-twenties, but it is not, and never has been, enough. The C.T.S. has always been severely handicapped—despite the priceless value of its work—by lack of the support which it ought to have had from clergy and laity alike. If the C.T.S. has not yet got a series of pamphlets covering every point of doctrine, every important historical and controversial issue, the biography of every well-known saint or eminent Catholic, and a great deal more information about the Liturgy, the fault lies with the apathy of the Catholic body, certainly not with the officers and friends of the Society. In view of rising costs and ever-increasing demands the present subscribing membership of 20,000 is totally inadequate.

Yet a very great deal has been done, as a glance through the Annual Reports, the Catalogue and the Classified List of Publications will show. A remarkable feature of recent years is the series of Studies in Comparative Religion, some forty in number, ranging from Ancient Egypt, Babylon and

Assyria down through Greece and Rome, Judaism, Islam, an
Medieval Christianity to Theosophy, Spiritualism, Christia
Science and Communism. Another is Fr. Martindale's admir
able series of liturgical explanations of Holy Week from th
Mass of Palm Sunday to the Easter Vespers on Holy Saturda
evening. The Papal Encyclicals have a special place of thei
own, and current Social Questions have received earnest, care
ful and continuous attention and these two categories ar
likely, in view of the times we live in, to become more an
more important.

History and Biography have been well served all along
For instance, it is quite easy to construct, by selecting an
binding them together, a Catholic History of England—en
tirely in pamphlets. It should begin with Abbot Gasquet'
Short History of the Catholic Church in England, Parts I an
II, and continue with St. Augustine of Canterbury, St
Aidan, St. Cuthbert and so on down to the Reformation
then the Persecution, the Penal Laws, Challoner and the er
of the Vicars Apostolic, Emancipation; and the second volum
may conclude with Wiseman, Newman, and that immorta
sermon, " The Second Spring."

XVII

CATHOLIC ENGLISH LITERATURE
1850-1950

By EDWARD HUTTON

IT was Disraeli who said, in the Preface to *Lothair* (1870),
that " the secession of Dr. Newman dealt a blow to the
Church of England under which it still reels." That
" extraordinary event " if it has " never been explained,"
as that astute and detached observer asserted, has been variously accounted for, not only by Newman himself in his
masterpiece, the *Apologia* (1864), but as an episode, though
an important one, in the Catholic revival all over Europe.
This revival it is maintained was a result of the Romantic
Movement, which in England had produced among other
things the Gothic romances and the novels of Sir Walter Scott.
And it may well be that the Waverley Novels counted for
something in the Catholic revival and not least in England.
Borrow thought so and accused Scott of having debauched the
country. Though Scott's real feeling for Catholicism was
hostile, his excursions into the Middle Ages brought him in
contact with the Catholic Church and, almost inevitably, he
made the Catholicism of long ago and even that of the '45
seem romantic and attractive. His novels brought the idea of
a supernatural society and system back into the very lonely
and insular English mind of the time and he may well have
prepared, not the ground perhaps, but the air. There was,
however, apart from an historical nostalgia, very little sentiment in Newman's conversion, which was accomplished after
that famous journey " amid the encircling gloom . . . o'er
moor and fen, o'er crag and torrent," in 1845. The sentiment
was all the other way. His conversion, which is the major
fact of the Catholic revival in this country, reposed, in any
merely human view of it, on an appeal to the reason through
history. Yet he tells us himself that " the heart is commonly

reached not through the reason but through the imagination
. . . voices melt us, books subdue us." May we not then
detect in the fact that those Latin words—*Securus judicat orbis
terrarum*—haunted him as he describes, something romantic?

It is strange that the Oxford Movement, of which
Newman's conversion was the culmination, should have owed
so little to the great movement in France which began with
Chateaubriand (*Génie du Christianisme*, 1802), Joseph de
Maistre (*Du Pape*, 1821), Bonald, Madame de Krüdener and
their successors. This was probably due to the intellectual insularity to which Protestantism had reduced England, which
had become a Protestant island outside Europe.

But whatever may come to be thought of the relation of
the English movement with its forerunners on the Continent,
it would be difficult to deny that, like them, it was rooted in
Romanticism.

Rome, or at any rate the Emissary from Rome, seems
to have thought so. What could have been more Romantic
than that " Pastoral Letter from out the Flaminian Gate "?
The Flaminian Gate! a term unknown since the fifteenth
century. What could have been more Romantic than the
Letter itself, unless it was the reception of it? Through the
rhetoric of *The Times'* leading article one can almost hear
Drake playing bowls on Plymouth Hoe and the rumour of
the London streets as the " Duke of Smithfield," the " editor
of the *Tablet*," is harried to Tyburn. That tirade, eloquent of
English opinion, the newly-appointed Cardinal Archbishop
of Westminster read " as I was driving through the town
(Vienna) leaning back in my carriage full of satisfaction at the
events of the past month."

The fantastic passion roused by so-called " Papal
Aggression " by which the government, the people and the
press of Great Britain were overtaken produced a reply, a reply
so Christian, so wise and eloquent, that it may well stand at
the head of an examination of the Catholic achievement in
Literature during the last hundred years, between 1850 when
it was written and to-day.

" The Chapter of Westminster has been the first to
protest against the new Archiepiscopal title, as though some

practical attempt at jurisdiction within the *Abbey* was intended. Then let me give them assurance on this point, and let us come to a fair division and a good understanding.

" The diocese, indeed, of Westminster embraces a large district; but Westminster proper consists of two very different parts. To the venerable old church I may repair as I have been wont to do. But perhaps the Dean and Chapter are not aware that were I disposed to claim more than the right to tread the Catholic pavement of that noble building and breathe its air of ancient consecration, another might step in with a prior claim. For successive generations there has existed ever, in the Benedictine order, an Abbot of Westminster, the representative in religious dignity of those who erected and beautified and governed that church and cloister. Have they ever been disturbed by this " titular "? Have they ever heard of any claim or protest on his part, touching their temporalities? Then let them fear no greater aggression now. Like him I may visit, as I have said, the old Abbey and say my prayer at the shrine of good St. Edward and meditate on the olden times, when the church filled without a coronation and multitudes hourly worshipped without a service. . . .

" Yet this spendid monument, its treasures of art and its fitting endowments, form not the part of Westminster which will concern me. For there is another part which stands in frightful contrast, though in immediate contact with this magnificence. In ancient times the existence of an abbey on any spot, with a large staff of clergy and ample revenues, would have sufficed to create around it a little paradise of comfort, cheerfulness and ease. This, however, is not now the case. Close under the Abbey of Westminster there lie concealed labyrinths of lanes and courts and alleys and slums, nests of ignorance, vice, depravity and crime, as well as of squalor, wretchedness and disease; in which swarms a huge and countless population, in great measure, nominally at least, Catholic. This is the part of Westminster which alone I covet and which I shall be glad to claim and to visit as a blessed pasture in which sheep of Holy Church are to be tended, in which a bishop's godly work has to be done by consoling, converting and preserving. And if, as I humbly trust in God, it shall be seen that this special culture, arising from the establishment of our Hierarchy, bears fruit of order, peacefulness, decency, religion and virtue, it may be that the Holy See shall not be thought to have acted unwisely when it bound up the very soul and salvation of a chief pastor with those of a City whereof the name indeed is glorious but the purlieus infamous—in which the very grandeur of its public edifices is a shadow to screen from the public eye sin and misery the most appalling. . . ."

" Voices melt us." The violent agitation died down.

Nicholas Wiseman, the son of an Irish Catholic, settled in Seville, and Xaviera, daughter of Peter Strange of Aylwardston Castle, Co. Kilkenny, was thus Irish on both sides of his family. His great intellectual ability, his urbanity and " the general justice of his mind," together with his fine culture, were to be of immense service to Catholicism in England. Already in 1839 his article in the *Dublin Review* had fundamentally influenced Newman in his approach to the Catholic Church and it is his pen and Newman's that in the first generation of the Catholic revival in this country are the chief instruments in producing a Catholic literature, in distinction from the polemics and the theology of the Reviews, in those difficult and meagre years.

Wiseman published in 1853 three volumes of *Essays on Various Subjects* (from the *Dublin Review*). In 1854 appeared *Fabiola, or the Church of the Catacombs,* a story of the third century which had a considerable circulation, " the first good book," said the Archbishop of Milan, " which has had the success of a bad one." Seven translations, one of them by the author, appeared in Italy and it was translated into most European and many Asiatic languages. Half forgotten as it is, it is still a classic of Catholic English literature. Again in 1858 Wiseman found time to write and publish his still valuable *Recollections of the Last Four Popes* (Pius VII, Leo XII, Pius VIII and Gregory XVI). And about the same time he produced a play in two acts, *The Hidden Gem,* written for the jubilee of his old college of St. Cuthbert's, which was acted in a Liverpool theatre during the year. A volume of sermons, lectures and speeches followed in 1859. In 1863 he lectured at the Royal Institution in London on " Points of Contact between Science and Art " (London, 1863) and again in the same place on " Shakespeare," part of which lecture was posthumously published by Manning, his successor in the Archbishopric, in 1865. Wiseman's reputation as ecclesiastic, scholar and linguist was world wide. He was called the English Mezzofanti. The attempt of Browning to burlesque him in *Bishop Blougram's Apology* (1855) is an admitted libel, which, however, the victim is said to have not unfavourably reviewed in *The Rambler* as a masterly intellectual achievement although an assault on the groundworks of religion.

Meantime with Newman English Catholicism had gained a voice of classic dignity. In 1850 he had published his lectures on *The Present Position of Catholics in England,* an unexpectedly amusing, witty and lively book which astonished George Eliot. The beautiful volume on *The Idea of a University* with his other " University " papers, the best exposition of Catholic educational theory in any language, followed in 1852 and in 1853 anonymously his *Verses on Religious Subjects* (Dublin), to be followed by a volume of hymns. Then in 1856 appeared his second and last novel[1], *Callista: a Tale of the Third Century,* which was far less successful than Cardinal Wiseman's *Fabiola* and is now, I suppose, forgotten, but it recalls in many passages, which only he could have written, his journey in Italy, Sicily and the Mediterranean.

In 1857 Newman published a volume of *Sermons on Various Occasions* in which appeared " The Second Spring " but it is in another and earlier discourse that this famous and beautiful passage on the Catholic Church may be found. : —

" Coming to you from the very time of the Apostles, spreading out into all lands, triumphing over a thousand revolutions, exhibiting so awful a unity, glorifying in so mysterious a vitality; so majestic, so imperturbable, so bold, so saintly, so sublime, so beautiful, O ye sons of men can ye doubt that she is the Divine Messenger for whom you seek?

[1] *Loss and Gain: the Story of a Convert* had appeared in 1848.

" Oh, long sought after, tardily found, desire of the
eyes, joy of the heart, the truth after many shadows, the
fullness after many foretastes, the home after many storms,
come to her poor wanderers, for she it is and she alone, who
can unfold the meaning of your being and the secret of your
destiny. She alone can open to you the gate of heaven and
put you on your way . . ."

Newman had been invited by Wiseman to prepare a
revision of the English Catholic translation of the Bible. This
came, alas, to nothing, but we still have his essay on the
Rheims and Douay version of Holy Scripture, originally published in *The Rambler* (1859) of which periodical at Wiseman's
request he consented to become editor, a position that only
lasted two months (May-July, 1859).

Newman had met difficulty after difficulty in his Catholic career, obstacle after obstacle, when in 1864 an outspoken
attack from Charles Kingsley, a characteristically English
anti-Catholic, gave him the opportunity not only to vindicate
his whole life, but to produce one of the two great autobio-
graphies in the language, the *Apologia pro Vita Sua*, a work
that a distinguished French critic has compared with Pascal's
Lettres Provinciales. The *Apologia* not only annihilated Newman's opponent, it re-established Newman in the respect and
affection of his countrymen and placed him among the im-
mortals of English literature.

In 1865 he published *The Dream of Gerontius* in *The
Month*. It was to be almost his last contribution to pure
literature; thereafter his life was given for the most part to
theology, and unhappily passed under suspicion of ecclesiastical authority here and in Rome, till in 1879 at the urgent
representation of the Duke of Norfolk and other English
Catholic peers, Pope Leo XIII bestowed on him a Cardinal's
Hat, as Cardinal Deacon of the title of San Giorgio in Velabro
and " the cloud was lifted from him for ever." This was, it
seems, the first time a simple priest outside the Roman Curia
had been raised to the Sacred College. *Ex umbris et
imaginibus in veritatem*; it is his epitaph.

In 1878 he had returned to Oxford as Honorary Fellow

of Trinity College and it is there rather than elsewhere his great shade seems to linger.

" Trinity which was so dear to me, which held on its foundation so many who have been kind to me both when I was a boy and all through my Oxford life. Trinity had never been unkind to me. There used to be much snap-dragon growing on the walls opposite my freshman's rooms there and I had for years taken it as the emblem of my own perpetual residence even unto death in my University."

What else in the way of Catholic literature beside these books of Wiseman's and Newman's is there to show during these first decades of the restoration of the Hierarchy? Little save the Reviews, which were filled with matter polemical, theological and historical, but scarcely any pure literature. The fact is that the country did not yet possess a sufficiently numerous and cultured Catholic society capable of producing what might claim to be a literature. The miracle is that in one generation of thirty years or so this tremendous feat was accomplished.

What then do we mean by a Catholic literature? We mean what Newman meant when he thus defined it in the volume we know as *The Idea of a University*. " A Catholic literature," he says, " includes all subjects of literature whatever, treated as a Catholic would treat them and as only he can treat them." That is to say a Catholic literature, like those of Italy, France and Spain, will include History, Biography, Poetry, Prose, Drama, Romance and Fiction, Essays, Belles Lettres, Criticism and so forth, the product of a Catholic culture. That is what had to be accomplished. Let us see how it has been achieved.

I. HISTORY

The small, despised, but far from despicable Catholic remnant in England in the eighteenth and earlier nineteenth centuries had been rather surprisingly strong in the matter of History. To name no others, John Lingard, a Catholic priest, had produced a narrative *History of England* (1819-30), which superseded Hume and in fact remained the most popular general History of England till Green's work appeared, which largely depended upon it. In 1854 it went into a sixth edition, in 1904 it was abridged and continued, and in 1915 it was re-issued in eleven volumes with an additional volume by Hilaire Belloc and an introduction by Cardinal Gibbons. The book was so well founded as to its sources, so moderate and fair, even generous, in its conclusions, that it was denounced by Bishop Milner, but generally accepted by scholars and the public as a standard work.

Lingard had first gained reputation as an historian with his *Antiquities of the Anglo-Saxon Church* (1806-1845) which, while it glorified the Catholic ages, was not found objectionable by the Protestant reader, though eagerly attacked by Bishop Milner. " My occasional ignorance of motives and causes," Lingard wrote, " my inexperience in what is called the philosophy of history, but which often appeared to me the philosophy of romance " excused him from bitter judgments. " Where the authorities are silent I prefer to leave the reader to exercise his own judgment." This cautious and unprejudiced approach succeeded in producing a work of national character and importance. He died in 1851, fondly believing that Leo XII had created him a Cardinal *in petto*, and is buried in the College at Ushaw, which he had done so much to establish.

A far greater scholar than Lingard, among the most learned men in Europe, the greatest ornament of historical learning that modern Catholic England can boast, is John Emerich Edward Dalberg, first Baron Acton of Aldenham (1834-1902). Of Anglo-Italian-German origin and largely bred abroad, educated in Paris, at Oscott, at Edinburgh and Munich, where he studied under Döllinger for six years, he knew Europe and especially Italy well, and when he returned to England (1858-59) it was to begin the collection of his great library of 59,000 volumes at Aldenham. In 1858 he acquired an interest in *The Rambler*, the liberal Catholic monthly periodical which had been started by John Capes and of which Newman was to become editor in the following year for a few months, till under episcopal pressure he resigned, and Acton took his place to write there and in its successor, the *Home and*

Foreign Review, some of the strongest articles that ever appeared in those harried liberal Catholic organs. His output was prodigious. Some of these articles have been republished in the two volumes, *Lectures and Essays in Modern History* (1906), and *The History of Freedom* (1907).

Unfortunately Acton, who was a Whig and a Liberal by conviction, and a close friend of his elder contemporary, Gladstone, with whom he had great political influence and who recommended him for a peerage in 1869, was so deeply involved in ecclesiastical polemic and in the accumulation of documents for his almost chimerical magnum opus, " The History of Liberty," which never was and perhaps never could have been written, that little time and energy were left to produce a book. The two lectures on *The History of Freedom in Antiquity* and *The History of Freedom in Christianity* and the Essay on *Democracy in Europe* (1877) are nearly all that he himself put together, but they are of a very high excellence. In 1886 the foundation of the *English Historical Review* occupied him, and his article on *German Schools of History* is an impressive production which appeared in the first number.

In 1895 he was appointed Regius Professor of Modern History in Cambridge. This splendid appointment produced his inaugural lecture, *The Study of History.* Thereafter he immersed himself in the planning of the great *Cambridge Modern History* which is, in fact, his monument, but which he died too soon to see.

This European rather than English figure towers in silence over his Catholic contemporaries. " I never had any contemporaries," he asserted, and in a sense that was true. " All power tends to corrupt: absolute power tends to corrupt absolutely," he wrote, perhaps not without a glance at Manning and the Hierarchy or even at loftier authority. Yet the Catholic faith was, he declared, when for a moment he feared excommunication, " dearer than life itself." And he maintained that it was in the Middle Ages " were laid the foundations of all the happiness that has since been enjoyed and all the greatness that has been achieved by men." The Reformation he regarded as the " great modern apostasy " and expected a reaction from it. For he saw the Church as the irreconcilable enemy of the despotism of the State and the guardian of the individual's liberty and conscience. Rationalist democracy he regarded as the modern danger. Yet in spite of these most sound opinions—indeed Catholicism had had no such advocate in England since St. Thomas More—the ecclesiastical authorities were suspicious and hostile, perhaps in the main because Acton was the friend, as he had been the pupil, of Döllinger, who was excommunicated after the Vatican Decrees of 1870. But one thinks his famous letters in *The Times* in November and December, 1874, on this very matter of the Infallibility should have reassured them.

Bryce records how—

" Late at night in his library at Cannes, Acton expounded to me his views of how a history of liberty might be written and how it might be made the central thread of all history. He spoke for six or seven minutes only, but he spoke like a man inspired, as if from some mountain summit high in air he saw beneath him the far-winding path of human progress, from dim Cimmerian shores of pre-historic shadow into the fuller yet broken and fitful light of modern time. . . . It was as though the whole landscape of history had been suddenly lit up by a burst of sunlight. I have never heard from any other lips any discourse like this, nor from him did I ever listen to the like again."

" To be with Acton," said another, " was like being with the cultivated mind of Europe. In the deep tones of his voice there seemed to sound the accents of History."

No other historian having the range of Lingard or the profound and wide scholarship of Acton has since appeared among Catholic scholars or indeed elsewhere in England. The times prescribed a more special and concentrated study of particular subjects or periods and in these fields Catholic scholars were not lacking.

And here perhaps may be mentioned in passing, him of whom Newman had said in the *Apologia* that if he wished to point to a straightforward Englishman he should instance the Bishop of Birmingham. William Bernard Ullathorne (1806-89), monk of Downside and a Tory of the old school, was Bishop of Birmingham for thirty-eight years. He was the friend and champion of Newman in the English Hierarchy, and according to Archbishop Mathew regarded Manning " with the suspicion of a mastiff." On one occasion, it is commonly reported, he reminded the Cardinal Archbishop, " I was a Bishop when you was an 'eretic." In 1871 he published in small octavo a *History of the Restoration of the English Hierarchy,* which is still of interest. He was direct and blunt, had no sympathy, as Faber had, with " foreign devotions," of old Catholic Yorkshire stock, a vigorous and forceful preacher—in his sermon " The Drunkard " remarkably so. He was a great son of Downside. England to-day can scarcely hope to see his like again.

Downside, which founded the *Downside Review* in 1882, was to produce indeed a number of distinguished historians, and if the great scholar we now have to meet was not a monk of Downside, it was merely that his poor health would not allow him to take the cowl.

Edmund Bishop (1846-1917) was the greatest English liturgist of our time. Born at Totnes, schooled at Exeter and in Belgium, he employed himself as a young man in the Privy Council Office (Education Department) and spent his free hours in the British Museum examining multitudes of manuscripts. He was received into the Church in 1867. In 1885 he retired and spent the next four years at Downside and from 1892 to 1901 lived with the future Cardinal Gasquet, also of Downside, in London. A bibliography of his publications which were very numerous and scattered, consisting largely of papers contributed to learned reviews, was given (up to 1906) in the *Downside Review* (1906). Among the chief of these may be mentioned the *Collectio Britannica* of some 300 papal letters of the fifth to the eleventh centuries, which he discovered, copied, annotated and published in the *Monumenta Germaniae Historica,* since he could find no means of publication in England. This established his reputation abroad and brought him a tribute from Mommsen. His outstanding publication in this country is the *Liturgica Historica: Liturgy and Religious Life of the Western Church* (Oxford, 1918), containing his identification of the Roman Mass book of Gregory the Great, his studies in the Roman liturgy, and various other essays. In 1909 he published the *Appendix* to the

Liturgical Homilies of Narsai ("Texts and Studies"). In 1890 he had published with his friend Cardinal Gasquet *Edward VI and the Book of Common Prayer,* and in 1908 they collaborated in the publication of *The Bosworth Psalter*. But these and other works that appear in his bibliography by no means exhaust his achievement. His work is the source of much work of the sort by others of his time. He too may be considered as a son of Downside for he not only spent many years in the monastery, but was constantly a guest there and it was only ill health which deprived him of the habit of St. Benedict. He bequeathed his library to Downside, " a unique collection illustrating liturgy," Abbot Butler tells us, " made with exquisite knowledge and endless care, a life-long work of joy."

Bishop's influence was at the root of much of the liturgical and historical learning of his time and his influence was not least to be seen in the work of his friend, Francis Aidan Gasquet (1846-1929). They were born in the same year, the one to die a humble scholar, the other a Prince of the Church.

Dom Aidan Gasquet was a product of Downside, he went to school there, in 1862 he was there professed, in 1878 he was elected prior, and finally, in 1900, second Abbot[2]. In 1903 his name was sent to the Pope by the Westminster Chapter as one of the three it submitted for the vacant Archbishopric. In 1914 Pius X created him Cardinal.

Gasquet's first book and perhaps his best was *Henry VIII and the English Monasteries* (2 vols., 1888-89). It was successful, and perhaps for the first time, in refuting the charges against the English monasteries and convents of the sixteenth century. These charges James Gairdner declared in his review of the book " are now dispelled for ever." This was to be followed by a large number of books on the later Middle Ages and Tudor period. In 1890, as we have seen, in collaboration with Edmund Bishop he published *Edward VI and the Book of Common Prayer*; in 1893 came *The Great Pestilence,* on the Black Death of 1348; in 1895 his eloquent study, the *Last Abbot of Glastonbury*. Many other works were to follow, some technical, like the *Collectanea Anglo-Premonstratensia* (1904-1906), some more generally historical,

---

[2] The first Abbot of Downside was Edmund Ford, perhaps the greatest of the sons of Downside: but he wrote little or nothing.

like *Henry III and the Church* (1905) or *Lord Acton and his Circle* or the *History of the Venerable English College in Rome* (1920). Gasquet's later work was sometimes hurried and superficial. Even in the history of the English College he does not inform us how the College came by its title. Other business had absorbed him. In 1907 Pius X had given the Benedictine Order the work of preparing a revision of the text of the Vulgate and had appointed Gasquet head of the commission. This entailed residence at S. Anselmo in Rome and occupied most of his time. In 1913 to raise money for this expensive enterprise he made a lecture tour in the United States. Immediately after his elevation to the Sacred College the war of 1914 broke out and much of his energy was spent in political work at the Vatican, where the newly-appointed English Ministry to the Vatican needed and received his advice and support. In 1917 he was appointed prefect of the Archives of the Holy See and in 1919 Librarian of the Holy Roman Church and both Archives and Library owe much to his effective organisation.

Gasquet was a man both severe and urbane and of much kindness of heart. He had a sense of humour and a ready wit. To a lady who came to see him during his last illness he is said to have replied, when she asked whether it was true that the next Pope might be an American, " Dear me, how strange it would be to have someone guessing infallibly."

But Cardinal Gasquet was by no means the last of the sons of Downside to distinguish himself in English Letters as an historian.

In 1919 Abbot Cuthbert Butler published his fine study *Benedictine Monachism: Benedictine Life and Rule.* Between 1898 and 1904 he had edited and published in Armitage Robinson's " Texts and Studies " the *Lausiac History of Palladius* with the Greek text and critical notes and a discussion of early Egyptian monachism; and in 1922 his *Benedictine Monachism* was followed by his history of *Western Mysticism* (second edition, 1927) which has become a standard work. His history of the Vatican Council (2 vols., 1930) is the story told from inside, in Bishop Ullathorne's letters, and is an indispensable book.

Then in 1928 another Abbot of Downside published

Studies in the Early Papacy and in the following year his magnum opus, *St. Benedict and the Sixth Century*. This was Dom John Chapman (1865-1933), who had, twenty years before, published *Notes on the Early History of the Vulgate Gospels* (1908), and in 1911 *John the Presbyter and the Fourth Gospel*. He was a scholar of great subtlety and attainment, a man of high courtesy and deep learning, a convert in 1890, the son of a Canon of Ely.

Finally, Downside has given us an historian of the English Monasteries and Religious Houses whose work in its own way may be put beside that of Dugdale. Dom David Knowles, born in 1896, educated at Downside and a monk of that great monastery, now Professor of Medieval History in the University of Cambridge, published in 1929 a book on *The Benedictines*, but his magnum opus appeared in 1940: *The Monastic Order in England*, a history of its development from the time of Dunstan to the Fourth Lateran Council. This fine work was followed in 1948 by a history of the *Religious Orders in England*. Happily, Dom David is still active and we may hope for other fine works from his hand.

Nor must Dom Bede Camm, of Downside (1864-1942), be omitted here. His book *Forgotten Shrines* (1910) is a standard work.

Other historians, not of Downside, were not lacking. And here it ought to be noted that the " Catholic Record Society " was founded in 1904 to print post-Reformation historical material. The forty-three volumes which the Society has sponsored are models of exact and patient editing, and are a mine of information on Recusant and post-Reformation Catholic life.

The Rev. Horace K. Mann (1859-1928), educated at Ushaw, between 1900 and 1910 published the *Lives of the Popes in the Early Middle Ages* (590-1254) in fourteen volumes, and in 1914 a life of *Nicholas Breakspear (Hadrian IV), the only English Pope*. A useful paper from his hand on the *Portraits of the Popes* appeared in the *Papers of the British School at Rome* in 1920 (Vol. IX).

There was, too, the Rev. Adrian Fortescue (1874-1923), who wrote a number of admirable works on the *Orthodox*

Eastern Church (1907), the *Lesser Eastern Churches* (1913), the *Uniate Eastern Churches* (1923). His excellent handbook, *The Mass: a Study of the Roman Liturgy*, was published in 1912, and the *Ceremonies of the Roman Rite Described* in 1919. In the following year appeared *The Early Papacy, to the Synod of Chalcedon in* 451, and in 1923 his last work, the *Uniate Eastern Churches*, on the Byzantine rite in Italy, Sicily, Syria and Egypt. His early death has deprived Catholicism in England of a remarkable scholar.

Even in so brief an essay as this we cannot pass over unnoticed Fr. John Hungerford Pollen, S.J., whose work on the history of the English martyrs was fundamental: *Acts of the English Martyrs* (1896); *Documents Relative to the English Martyrs* (1908). His edition of Kirke's *Lives of English Catholics* (1909), and his *English Catholics in the Time of Elizabeth* (1920), have their importance.

In 1936 David Mathew (born 1902, now Archbishop Mathew) published *Catholicism in England, 1535-1935*, the portrait of a minority, its culture and tradition, a useful and often brilliant book. Archbishop Mathew has also published *Acton—the Formative Years* (1946), the most important study that has appeared of the historian and to be followed by further volumes. Here, too, should be mentioned Maisie Ward's admirable volume on *The Wilfrid Wards and the Transition* (1934), and its complement *Insurrection versus Resurrection*. Fr. Philip Hughes, whose study *The Catholic Question* (1929) gave evidence of his Louvain training, has since written vigorously of the Counter-Reformation in England and is in process of writing a remarkable *History of the Church*, of which three volumes have appeared (1934-48).

An historian and philosopher must bring to an end this brief survey of the work of English Catholicism in History during the last hundred years. I mean Christopher Dawson (born 1889), who was received into the Church in 1914. His volumes from *The Age of The Gods* (1928), a study of the origins of culture, to *The Making of Europe* (1932) and *Religion and the Rise of Western Culture* (1948) are an honour to English Catholic scholarship of our time and may worthily close this record.

II. BIOGRAPHY

In biography the major works produced by Catholics since 1850 have been the series of biographies of the Cardinal Archbishops of Westminster: *The Life and Times of Cardinal Wiseman*, by Wilfrid Ward (1897); *The Life of Cardinal Manning*, by E. S. Purcell (1895); *Henry Edward Manning, his Life and Labours*, by Shane Leslie (1921), an antidote to Purcell; *The Life of Cardinal Vaughan*, by J. G. Snead-Cox (1910); and *The Life of Cardinal Bourne*, by Ernest Old-meadow (1940). If we add *The Life and Times of Bishop Ullathorne*, 1806-1889, by Dom Cuthbert Butler (1926), Ullathorne's *Autobiography* (1891-92), and *The Life of Cardinal Newman*, by Wilfrid Ward (1912), we have what amounts to much more than a history of the Archdiocese of Westminster: it is almost a history of Catholicism in England from 1850 to the death of Cardinal Bourne in 1935. If we add Dr. Burton's *Life and Times of Bishop Challoner*, 1691-1781 (1909), we get a view of that history during the last two hundred and fifty years.

Wilfrid Ward, the author of the lives of Cardinals Wiseman (1897) and Newman (1912), has also written the biography of his father, " Ideal Ward "—*William George Ward and the Oxford Movement* (1889) and *William George Ward and the Catholic Revival* (1893).

It was in 1885 there began to appear a *Literary and Biographical History or Bibliographical Dictionary of the English Catholics from the Breach with Rome in 1534 to the Present Time*, by Joseph Gillow. Three volumes had appeared in 1887 (up to Kemble, John): the rest of the work, all that it seems Gillow left unfinished, was put into two volumes and issued, with the result that the work was always incomplete and in the two last volumes certainly very inaccurate. The work was a magnificent enterprise, issued in the same year as the first volume of the *Dictionary of National Biography*. It should be taken in hand, revised, added to and republished in honour of Joseph Gillow, whose father, too, had always vigorously striven for Catholic recognition.

It was also in 1887 that Wilfrid Meynell published his book on *The Catholic Life and Letters of Cardinal Newman*, a standard work.

A few Lives of the Saints ought to be mentioned beside the famous work *The Lives of the Saints* by Butler which was re-edited, partly rewritten and severely annotated by the late Fr. Thurston, S.J., assisted by Donald Attwater (1926-38).

In 1850 Fr. F. W. Faber (1814-1863), of the Oratory, published a *Life of St. Philip Neri* and in 1855 Lady Georgiana Fullerton (1812-85) published a *Life of S. Frances of Rome*. Far more accomplished and critical than these simple narratives is Edmund Gardner's (1869-1935) *Life of St. Catherine of Siena* (1907), perhaps the best example of the modern scholarly life of a saint in the English language, comparable for scholarship if not in literary charm with Sabatier's *Life of St. Francis*, on which much-loved saint G. K. Chesterton (1874-1936) wrote a brilliant but inaccurate essay in 1923. Quite on the same high plane as Gardner's *St. Catherine* is Fr. Cuthbert's (1866-1939) *Life of St. Francis of Assisi* (1912), a work that was an honour to Franciscan scholarship. Mention, too, should be made of Fr. James Brodrick's studies of *St. Peter Canisius* (1935) and *Blessed Robert Bellarmine* (1928) to say nothing of his two volumes of the history of the Jesuits (1940-46).

I do not know whether I should place as a biography of a saint Evelyn Waugh's beautiful short *Life of Edmund Campion* (1934), the martyr—a fine biographical study and a fine piece of literature.

In 1936 there appeared a remarkable volume, *The Book of Margery Kempe*, 1436. This was a modern version by W. Butler-Bowdon of a manuscript autobiography of the time of Chaucer. Margery Kempe was born in King's Lynn in 1373. Her autobiography, the earliest in the language, lost for many centuries, was discovered by Mr. Butler-Bowdon and published in 1936. Margery was a most fervent Catholic and made pilgrimages to Jerusalem, Assisi, Rome and Compostella. In her book we have a picture of the whole society of her time: a highly important and unique work.

I must not omit to record here other biographical studies of Maisie Ward, her life of Chesterton, *Gilbert Keith*

Chesterton (1944), her biography of her father, William Ward (1934), and her *Young Mr. Newman* (1948).

Of a number of books of Memoirs I will mention: Kegan Paul's (1828-1902) *Memories*(1899), an account of his schooldays at Eton, of his life as an Anglican and of his conversion—a very interesting book; Dr. William Barry's (1849-1930) *Memories and Opinions* (1926)—Mgr. Barry was Protonotary Apostolic and Canon of St. Chad's, Birmingham, as well as the novelist of *The New Antigone* (1887) and *Arden Massiter* (1900), and a prolific author; Lord Braye's *Fewness of My Days* (1927); Mrs. Hugh Fraser's *Memoirs of a Diplomatist's Life* (1899-1911)—in 1914 and 1915 she published her two delightful volumes *Italian Yesterdays* and *More Italian Yesterdays* in which some of her best writing (she was a voluminous novelist) is to be found; and Mrs. Belloc-Lowndes' delightful volumes, *Where Love and Friendship Dwelt* (1943) and *A Passing World* (1948).

Finally, here are some works which have nothing to do with Catholicism: I mean Wilfrid Meynell's *Disraeli* (1893), Algar Thorold's *Life of Henry Labouchere* (1913), Shane Leslie's *Life of Mark Sykes* (1922), Dame Una Pope-Hennessy's *Charles Dickens* (1945) and *Canon Charles Kingsley* (1948) and James Pope-Hennessy's delightful *Monckton-Milnes* (1950).

III. POETRY

It might be claimed that Catholicism can pretend, if not to the foremost, at least to a very important, place in English poetry during the last hundred years.

Aubrey De Vere (1788-1846), not a very important poet, is outside our period and allows us to begin, as is meet and right, once more with John Henry Newman (1801-1890). The earlier verse of Newman is the better, it is full of force and troubled feeling and though often not very poetical is at least not bare and didactic as his later lyrics so often are. It may well be thought that he never surpassed his " Lead Kindly Light,"written in 1833, on his Mediterranean journey, in the strait of Bonifacio. His still earlier verses, " Consola-

tions in Bereavement '' (1828) are beautiful, as is the Tragic
Chorus '' The Elements '' (1833) with its Sophoclean echo:—

> Man is permitted much
>> To scan and learn
>> In Nature's frame:
> Till he well-nigh can tame
> Brute mischiefs and can touch
> Invisible things and turn
> All warring ills to purposes of good.
>> Thus as a god below
>> He can control
> And harmonize, what seems amiss to flow,
>> As sever'd from the whole
>> And dimly understand.

The '' Dream of Gerontius,'' written in 1865 after the
Apologia, is rather a strange than a good poem and certainly
not a great one. It is perhaps best as set to music by Elgar.

F. W. Faber (1812-1863) is a poor poet but a tolerable
writer of hymns which are known all over the English-speaking
world.

But in 1853 we come to Coventry Patmore (1823-1896)
who in that year published *Tamerton Church Tower* in which
appear verses that afterwards formed part of *The Angel in
the House* (1854-1856), the first part of which, *The Betrothed,*
was published in 1854 to be followed in 1856 by *The
Espousals*; in 1860 came *Faithful for Ever,* in 1862 *The
Victories of Love.* The four poems contain a body of fine
poetry, concerned with '' married love '' and contain delightful pictures of English scenery and domestic life. They had
a considerable success and were written before Patmore was
received into the Church in 1864. After he became a Catholic
he published in 1877 *The Unknown Eros and other Odes*
(forty odes in all). His best poetry is generally thought to be
contained in *The Angel in the House* with its glorification of
virtuous and happy marriage; this in spite of an occasional
comic flatness, which provoked Swinburne to parody, is a
considerable and often beautiful achievement. Patmore
ignored Swinburne's raillery: let him sing of pagan love, I
will sing of love blest by Church and Law, he seemed to say;

but for all that *The Angel in the House* is impassioned, emotional, and often very sensuous.

In the Odes, Patmore draws near to the seventeenth-century poets, sometimes at their best but sometimes at their worst: In an abstruse way he confounds spiritual and earthly passion, his religion becomes love, and, as in so much mystical verse, one is often confused with the other. His sincerity, however, is plain. He is at his best, I think, when he leaves this dangerous obsession altogether, as in " The Toys."

> *My little son, who look'd from thoughtless eyes*
> *And moved and spoke in quiet grown-up wise*
> *Having my law the seventh time disobeyed*
> *I struck him and dismiss'd*
> *With hard words and unkiss'd*
> *—His Mother, who was patient, being dead.*
> *Then fearing lest his grief should hinder sleep*
> *I visited his bed*
> *But found him slumbering deep*
> *With darken'd eyelids and their lashes yet*
> *From his late sobbing wet.*
> *And I with moan*
> *Kissing away his tears left others of my own . . .*

There he is human and classical, a master of his difficult rhythm.

The only Jesuit poet of our company, Gerard Manley Hopkins (1844-1889), like Francis Thompson later, was of the school of Patmore and of Donne and the seventeenth century. On occasion he will repeat or imitate Donne's phrases, and in *Justus quidem tu es, Domine,* he seems to prophesy " The Hound of Heaven." For all his queerness and his Meredithian awkwardness, his quite deliberate difficulty, as though he had determined to make English a language only to be deciphered by the learned initiate, he is a fine if not a great poet. If now and then we find an easy musical poem in his work such as " Heaven Haven "—

> *I have desired to go*
> *Where springs not fail,*
> *To fields where flies no sharp and sided hail,*

And a few lilies blow.
And I have asked to be
   Where no storms come,
   Where the green swell is in the haven dumb,
   And out of the swing of the sea.

—we are more likely to come upon one like " Duns Scotus's Oxford " : —

Towering city and branchy between towers
Cuckoo-echoing, bell-swarmed, lark-charmed, rock-racked, river-rounded
The dapple-eared lily below thee; that country and town did
Once encounter in, here coped and poisèd powers . . .

And then we find all clear again in " The Starlight Night."
Look at the stars! Look, look up at the stars!
a beautiful lyric which perhaps no Catholic poet of our time has surpassed. The third edition of his *Poems* was published in 1937 and volumes of his *Letters* are still in course of publication.

Patmore no more than Michelangelo can be held responsible for his followers or successors. The last thing Michelangelo intended was to create a school of mannerists.

Here I must record Adelaide Ann Procter (1825-1864), received into the Church in 1851, who if not a greatly inspired poetess published a large number of verses which were in every drawing room and were indeed in greater demand than the poems of any other writer of the mid-nineteenth century, except Tennyson. Her best work is in her narrative poems, e.g., *The Story of a Faithful Soul* (*Legends and Lyrics*, 2 vols., 1858-1861; complete works, 1905).

Wilfrid Scawen Blunt (1840-1922), who became a Catholic as a child when his mother followed Manning into the Church, was a traveller, politician, breeder of Arab horses and a poet. As a politician he was an eccentric and rhetorical agitator, and as a man of the world a brilliant talker and man of fashion, but as a poet he was an artist and a lover of beautiful things; among them Arab horses. In 1875 he published *Sonnets and Songs of Proteus* and in 1880 added to them. In

1892 *Esther* appeared and in 1893 *Griselda*. A collected edition
of his poems was published in 1914. The Sonnets are Byronic
in emphasis and passion. It is in *Esther*, I think, we get more
closely into touch with his mind. In *Griselda* he is very unequal and this novel in verse is perhaps the least satisfactory
of his poetical works. The fine sonnet on Gibraltar and the
very Shakespearian sonnet in *Esther*—

> *When I hear laughter from a tavern door*

—are in all the anthologies. His *My Diaries* which he published
in 1919-1920 are a mixture of gossip, fact and prejudice, but
make amusing reading.

I doubt whether it would be quite fair to include here
as a Catholic poet Robert Stephen Hawker (1804-1873) of
Morwenstow who, like Wilde, became a Catholic in his last
hours. Everyone knows his " And shall Trelawney die," but
he wrote several notable poems.

Books of verse published under the pseudonym
"Michael Field " were the work of two ladies, Miss Bradley
(1881-1913) and Miss Edith Cooper (1881-1915). Among
these were *Callirrhoe and Fair Rosamund* (1884), *Brutus Ultor*
(1886) and, best known perhaps, *Attila, my Attila* (1895).

We now come to the too notorious " nineties," a far less
Godless and far more civilised moment than that of to-day.
And first I will name the child of Patmore's seventeenth-
century period, Francis Thompson (1859-1907), whose *Poems*
were duly published at the Bodley Head in 1893, to be followed in 1895 (the year of *A Shropshire Lad*) by *Sister Songs*
and in 1907 posthumously by *New Poems*. Thompson was
sometimes a ghost of Crashaw, as in his exquisitely-mannered
poem on " The Dead Cardinal of Westminster," sometimes,
however, he writhed the heart as in his well-known " Hound
of Heaven." His first two books were published in small
quarto because of the length of his lines. Thompson thought
he resembled Cowley and if, like Cowley, he is not a poet of
the highest rank, he has undoubted genius. No one else of
his time could have written " The Hound of Heaven " or for
that matter the opening of the " Victorian Ode " or the
" Ode after Easter."

> *Cast wide the folding doorways of the East*
> *For now is light increased. . .*

Francis Thompson only did not die in misery and dumb because two good Samaritans sought him in the gutter, redeemed him from want and worse, encouraged his genius and collected and published his poems. One of them, Alice Meynell (1847-1922) was a distinguished poet and essayist, the author of a sonnet John Ruskin acclaimed for excellence, of " Renouncement," " The Shepherdess," and other verses to be found in the anthologies. Though not typical of " the nineties " she has their delight in form and the right word. *Preludes* (1875), *Poems* (1893), *Later Poems* (1901), *Last Poems* (1923) are her published volumes of verse.

Several of the poets typical of " the nineties " were Catholics. There was John Gray, born in 1866, who became a priest and Canon of the Edinburgh Chapter. He published a volume of poems, *Silverpoints,* at the Bodley Head in 1893 in a unique and charming format with a cover design by Charles Ricketts, one of the prettiest books of the period, and in 1896 the Vale Press issued his *Spiritual Poems,* chiefly done out of several languages.

Between 1892 and 1894 Elkin Matthews published the two volumes of *The Book of the Rhymers' Club* containing poems by Ernest Dowson and Lionel Johnson. Matthews published *Poems* by Lionel Johnson (1867-1902) in 1895, among them being the well-known lines " By the Statue of King Charles at Charing Cross." Johnson had become a Catholic when he left Winchester. Smithers published *Verses* by Ernest Dowson (1867-1900) in 1896, containing the well-known poem, Dowson's best, with its Horatian title " Non sum qualis eram." His second and last book of verse, *Decorations* was published in 1899, also by Smithers.

I doubt whether Oscar Wilde (1856-1900) can fairly be reckoned among Catholic poets, but he died in the arms of the Church, and wrote those enchanting lines " To Theocritus ":

> *O singer of Persephone*
> *In the dim meadows desolate*
> *Dost thou remember Sicily . . .*

which one remembers, as one does the lovely little ode of Horace, *O Venus regina Cnidi Paphique,* when one is bored

by the melodrama of *Reading Gaol* or tired of the " Regulus "
Ode—except the last two lines.

In 1899 another poet of " the nineties," Lord Alfred
Douglas (1870-1947), published his first book of verse, *The
City of the Soul*; in 1909 appeared *Sonnets* and in 1919 his
Collected Poems. Douglas has an extraordinary mastery of
the sonnet form and is in fact a better poet than his friend
Wilde ever succeeded in being. His ballad " Perkin
Warbeck," too, haunts the memory, where

> . . . *the White Rose of fair England*
> *Turned red on Bosworth field*.

There were other Catholic poets who were at work in,
but were not of, the nineties, such as Fr. J. B. Tabb, who
published a volume of *Poems* at the Bodley Head in 1896.
Chief among them is Hilaire Belloc, born in 1870, whose
Verses and Sonnets were published in 1895 with the well-
known and well-loved poem on " The South Country."
Belloc has written every sort of verse and almost every sort
of prose and I shall have to speak of him again and of his
friend G. K. Chesterton when I come to deal with Belles
Lettres. His verse—he has an extraordinary mastery of the
sonnet—includes not only such a fine achievement as " The
South Country " and such a *tour de force* as the " Heroic
Poem in Praise of Wine " but such a little masterpiece as
" The Statue " : —

> *When we are dead some Hunting-boy will pass*
> *And find a stone half-hidden in tall grass*
> *And grey with age: but having seen that stone*
> *Which was your image, ride more slowly on*.

He is also perhaps the greatest living master of comic verse.

His friend G. K. Chesterton (1874-1936) was received
into the Church in 1922. In 1900 he published *The Wild
Knight and Other Poems* and his well-known *Ballad of the
White Horse* appeared in 1911, a stirring ballad of Alfred
and Guthrum and the battle of Ethandune. Who can forget
the Italian there who, while

> . . . *all the Kings of the earth drank ale*
> *But he drank wine*.

His " Lepanto," possibly his best poem in this style, must be mentioned; his verses, too, on " The Donkey " are a small masterpiece, which only he could have conceived. Nor is he less powerful in his satirical and comic verse such as " Antichrist, or the Reunion of Christendom " and " Wine and Water " all little masterpieces of their kind. He was the master, too, of many forms of writing, and I must speak of him again later in this essay.

In 1902 appeared the first of many volumes of verse by Alfred Noyes: *The Loom of Years* (Collected Poems, 1910-1927) and in 1906 *Sonnets and Short Poems* by Maurice Baring (Collected Poems, 1911) whom I shall speak of again when I come to Belles Lettres. In 1907 Compton Mackenzie, famous as a novelist, published, I think, his only volume of *Poems*.

Finally in 1923 Shane Leslie published *An Anthology of Catholic Poets*. And in 1938 a collection of poems, still incomplete, was made by Louise Imogen Guiney, *Recusant Poets*, from St. Thomas More to Ben Jonson, a most useful and interesting anthology of little-known Catholic English verse.

IV. ESSAYS, CRITICISM, BELLES LETTRES

It is with Newman again I find myself obliged to begin a brief survey of this wide branch of English Catholic Literature. In 1854 to 1858 Newman delivered the lectures or wrote the essays collected in his volume *The Idea of a University*, on " Christianity and Letters," on " Literature," on " Catholic Literature in the English Tongue," on " Christianity and Physical Science " and other similar subjects, and in the many volumes of his collected works we continually come upon essays or lectures, which cannot be neglected, for there in fact is the foundation of the Catholic effort in this sort of writing in England. I do not mean his writings on definitely religious or theological matters, but his immense contribution to Catholic English culture. Nothing of the same quality or plenitude has appeared in England since his death.

He has proved to be not only the main cause, in so far as it was English and not Irish, of the Catholic revival here, which allowed the restoration of the Hierarchy, but his mind has nourished and still nourishes what there is of Catholic culture in England. For lofty intelligence, for beauty and distinction of prose, he is alone; nothing to be compared with either has appeared from our ranks since. It was his writings and Acton's and Ward's (the last chiefly theological in the *Home and Foreign Review*) which drew from Matthew Arnold the tribute, " Perhaps in no organ of criticism in this country was there so much knowledge, so much play of mind."

After Newman and Acton there is a long gap. I do not mean there was a lack of admirable writing on the faith and on religious matters generally. An immense Catholic devotional literature appeared and grew more plentiful every year, but the Catholic contribution to the general literature of culture was small, if not lacking altogether, and when it appears again it is on an altogether less distinguished and more popular level.

There are the numerous works of W. S. Lilly, which appeared from 1884 (when he published *Ancient Religion and Modern Thought*) all through the 'eighties and 'nineties: *A Century of Revolution* (1889), *The Claims of Christianity* (1894), *Christianity and Modern Civilisation* (1903), *Studies in Religion and Literature* (1904), *Idola Fori* (1910), and so forth. Almost if not quite forgotten now, they served their day and purpose.

Nor can we pass over unmentioned Jean M. Stone who in the 'nineties published several useful historical essays, the most important of which is perhaps *Faithful Unto Death* (1892), an account of the sufferings of the English Franciscans during the seventeenth and eighteenth centuries drawn from contemporary records, and a short history of the Franciscan Convent at Taunton which was founded in 1808. This still has value, as have her well-founded historical biographies: *The History of Mary I* (1901) as found in the public records, despatches, private letters and other contemporary documents; *Reformation and Renaissance* (1904) and *Studies from Court and Cloister* (1905), a book of essays, historical and literary, dealing with the sixteenth and seventeenth centuries.

But it is when we come to the epoch of Hilaire Belloc, Gilbert Chesterton, Maurice Baring, and later Christopher Hollis, Shane Leslie and Christopher Dawson that the stream of essays, literary, critical and historical, acquires volume and large variety. Of these six writers the only one who is not a convert is Hilaire Belloc and as a writer it is he who is the most fundamentally and completely Catholic, the most forcible, too, and perhaps the most influential. His work in popular historical studies and essays, indeed in all departments of literature, is among the least insular of our time and though he may not have reached directly a really large audience he has probably influenced those who in journalism and books do reach a very large number of readers. It is his pen which might seem thus to have had in this country the widest and surest influence in our day on the side of Catholicism.

It is impossible in a brief essay such as this to do any sort of justice to his writing or even to name all his works on history, politics, religion, literature and travel, " on anything," as well as his amusing excursions into fiction. His first book was his Volume of *Verses* (1895) of which I have already spoken, but he first attracted wide attention with his *Path to Rome* (1902), one of the best personal " travel books " ever written; and from that time hardly a year has gone by without a book of essays, a book of travel, a biography, a novel, or a book of controversy from his hand. Perhaps his best book is *The Eye Witness* (1908), but it is hard to choose. In 1925 he began to publish a *History of England,* four volumes of which have so far appeared. His general thesis is that religion is the determining force of society; that the inhabitants of this island were never greatly changed in stock by any invasion; and that our institutions derive not from German but from the known and recorded Roman civilisation.

Much these same theses underlie the brilliant *Short History of England* written in 1917 by his friend G. K. Chesterton (1874-1936). Indeed, the mind of Chesterton, who became a Catholic in 1922, would appear to have been largely nourished by the wider culture and less insular experience of Belloc, but his manner of thought, his style of writing, founded as it so constantly is on the exploitation of paradox, are all his own. The genius of the man, one can call it no less, shines through the immense quantity of his work, his lovable innocence of heart and his honesty, sincerity and goodwill His fantastic imagination, which enlivens his novels and stories, his sense of humour everywhere apparent, glorify like a sunbeam his verse, his prose essays and his weekly, almost daily journalism. Perhaps he has not always kept the high level that his friend Belloc maintained in an output only less overwhelming, but everything he wrote was worth reading at the time and much of it has no doubt a permanent value.

Like Belloc, he first published verse, *The Wild Knight and Other Poems* (1900) and *Greybeards at Play* (1900) Perhaps his best-known novel is *The Napoleon of Notting Hill* (1904). He followed it with *England a Nation* in the same year, and in 1905 with one of his best critical works, *Charles Dickens*. His " slovenly autobiography " *Orthodoxy* (1908 was an attempt to express his " ultimate attitude towards life." His " Father Brown " stories have delighted innumerable readers. In 1913 he wrote an essay in the " Home University library " series on *The Victorian Age in Literature* a brilliant and successful piece of literary criticism. His *Short History of England* (1917) is inaccurate perhaps, but life giving; and the same might be said of his *St. Francis of Assisi* (1933). His discovery of Christianity which he relates in *Orthodoxy* is continued, in its relation to mankind, in *The Everlasting Man* (1925). These last two volumes were published after his entry into the Church. His poetry I have briefly touched on above.

The third member of what was almost a personal though not a professional triumvirate was Maurice Baring (1874-1945). A greatly gifted man, a remarkable linguist and a fine scholar (though he always denied it), Baring was a humourist in the best sense of the word and an exquisite artist Received into the Church in 1909 some years after he had resigned from the Foreign Office he had already published in Paris with Lemerre *Hildesheim, Quatre Pastiches* (1899) and from 1902 onwards books seemed to pour from his pen. After serving in the War of 1914-18 he too published a volume of *Poems* (1918) and began what proved to be a whole series of novels of considerable distinction. Possibly, however, his masterpiece is an account of his childhood and youth, *The Puppet Show of Memory* (1922), one of the most enchanting volumes of autobiography ever written, with its moving and delightful picture of late Victorian and Edwardian English life. The volume containing *Punch and Judy and Other Essays,* with papers on Lafontaine, Racine, Taine, French Poetry, Jules Lemaître, Sully Prudhomme and on an anthology of French verse demonstrates his fine taste and wide knowledge of French literature, which was again to be found in his essay on *French Literature* (1927). *Unreliable History* (1934), his imaginative discussions on episodes in ancient and modern history, is a little masterpiece of fantastic learning which in literature is astonishingly manifested in his brilliant and lovely book, *Have You Anything to Declare?* (1936).

Apart from his considerable achievements in literature, Maurice Baring was a unique personality, a man wholly lovable, generous to a fault. Lord Trenchard, Marshal of the Royal Air Force, on whose staff he was in the War of 1914-18, wrote of him: " In the words of a great Frenchman there never was a staff officer in any country, in any nation, in any century, like Major Maurice Baring. He was the most unselfish man I ever met or am likely to meet . . . words fail me in describing this man."

Among other Catholic essayists and critics should be named Mgr. Ronald Knox (born 1888), who has several claims to distinction. As a satirical writer and broadcaster he stands almost unrivalled and as a Catholic (he was received into the Church in 1917) he has published more than one notable work. *A Spiritual Aeneid* appeared in 1918; *The Belief of Catholics* in 1927; *The Mystery of the Kingdom* (sermons) in 1928 and another volume of sermons, *Heaven and Charing Cross,* in 1935; his *Barchester Pilgrimage* (1935) was a tribute to Trollope. To be noted not only as a *tour de force* so far as style is concerned, but as an excellent piece of historical writing, is his *Let Dons Delight* (1939). His most important work, however, and that by which he is most widely known is his translation of the Bible into modern English for which his distinguished scholarship and his skill as a master of English should have fitted him.

Another distinguished writer and essayist of our day is

Christopher Hollis (born 1902, received into the Church 1924), best known perhaps as the author of *The Monstrous Regiment* (1929) and *Death of a Gentleman* (1943). His most important book, however, would appear to be his latest, *Can Parliament Survive?* (1949). He is also the author of a fine life of *Dryden* (1933) and *Glastonbury and England* (1927), together with many other works.

Douglas Woodruff (born 1897), Editor of *The Tablet* since 1937, which paper he has brought to a high position as a literary and political Catholic weekly journal, is the author of several books of distinction, among the best of which is the satire *Plato's American Republic* (1926). He has written monographs on *Charlemagne* (1934) and *Mirabeau* (1936) and in 1935 published *European Civilisation: the Grand Tour*. From his amusing *Tablet* column *Talking at Random* he has published three volumes of selections (1941-44-48).

I have now to record a number of critics of pure literature whose scholarship brings honour to the Catholic name. Edmund Gardner (1869-1935), Professor of Italian, first in the University of Manchester and then in London, was unquestionably one of the best Dante scholars in this country and his three books, *Dante's Ten Heavens* (1898); *Dante and Giovanni del Virgilio* (1902)—which included a critical edition of Dante's *Eclogae Latinae* written with Philip Wicksteed—and *Dante and the Mystics* (1914) are still to be consulted. To these he added in 1930 a study of *The Arthurian Legend in Italian Literature*. In 1900 he published *A Dante Primer* which went into many editions. His interest in everything Italian was eager and he wrote historical handbooks on Florence and Siena and at one time interested himself in Ariosto, so that his *Dukes and Poets in Ferrara* (1904) and *The King of Court Poets* (1906) and his *Painters of the School of Ferrara* (1911) are standard works on the sixteenth-century court of that city. His admirable *Life of St. Catherine of Siena* (1907) I have recorded above. Gardner was a man of singular charm, whose place in Anglo-Italian letters it will be difficult to fill.

Gifted with even greater personal charm was Algar Thorold (1866-1936), a son of the Anglican Bishop of Winchester. He was received into the Church in 1884. In 1904 he published a study of Blessed Angela of Foligno (*Catholic Mysticism*), and in 1907 a translation of the *Dialogue of St. Catherine of Siena*. In the same year appeared a volume of essays, *Seven Masters of Disillusion*, which well represents his literary gifts. In 1913 he published a life of his uncle, Henry Labouchere, noted above.

A writer as gifted in his own way as Thorold is D. B. Wyndham Lewis, who was received into the Church in 1921, and has written many satires and burlesques, but is also the author of two admirable literary studies on *François Villon* (1928) and *Ronsard* (1944). Both these high-spirited works are evidence of his scholarship and research, as are his books on *Louis XI of France* (1930) and *Emperor of the West* (1932), a book on Charles V.

Also of account are the essays of Eric Gill (1882-1940), who was received into the Church in 1913 and was more famous as a sculptor than as a writer. His " Stations of the Cross " in Westminster Cathedral and his work in the Palace of the League of Nations at Geneva and Broadcasting House in London have carried his name all over the world. His books, however, several volumes on life, art and morals, have had a considerable influence, and his *Autobiography* (1940) recorded his spiritual and material adventures during his all too short life.

Two books, one on London and the other on America, should be mentioned—*London Fabric* (1939) and *America is an Atmosphere* (1947)—by James Pope-Hennessy, whose biography of Monkton-Milnes I have already noticed.

I will close this section of my survey with some volumes of the Criticism of Art : In 1927, John Rothenstein (born 1901) published a volume on the art of *Eric Gill,* and in 1928 followed this with a volume on *The Artists of the Eighteen-nineties*. In 1932 appeared his book on *Nineteenth Century Painting*: *A Study in Conflict,* to be followed in 1933 by *An Introduction to English Painting;* John Pope-Hennessy's *Giovanni di Paolo* (1937), his *Sassetta* (1939) and his *Drawings of Domenichino at Windsor Castle* (1948); and, much more general in character, E. I. Watkin's *Catholic Art and Culture* (1942).

Lastly, I must record a most important work by Dr. E. W. Tristram (born 1882), *English Mediæval Wall Paint-*

ings (2 vols., 1944, 1950), certainly the most important work on English mediæval painting ever written.

V. FICTION

Here my survey must be even more superficial. There have been dozens of Catholic novelists, and, good, bad and indifferent, hundreds of Catholic novels, but in the century since 1850 it might be difficult to find among them two master-pieces as fine as *A Simple Story* and *Nature and Art* written by Mrs. Inchbald in the last decade of the eighteenth century or a novelist of our persuasion to compare with his Protestant contemporaries Dickens, Thackeray, Meredith, Hardy, or Henry James[3].

To begin with I cannot but name Lady Georgiana Fullerton (1812-1885), the daughter of the first Earl Granville. She became a Catholic in 1846, but her first novel, *Ellen Middleton*, was written in 1844 before her conversion. In *Grantley Manor* (1847), however, she is a Catholic novelist and it shows a considerable advance on her first book. In 1852 appeared *Lady Bird*, and thereafter her novels were numerous. But she was absorbed in her charitable and religious life, engaged in bringing the Sisters of St. Vincent de Paul to England and in founding with Miss Taylor a new community: the Poor Servants of the Mother of God Incarnate.

Julia Kavanagh (1824-1877), too, must be recorded. Her first book, a tale for children, was published in 1847. In

[3] However that may be, it seems we only just missed being able to enter Thackeray's name in our record. (See F. C. Burnand: *Records and Recollections* 1904.) " I personally have not the smallest doubt that at one period of his life Thackeray was very near becoming a Catholic. So at least he himself gave me to understand and so I have since been informed." Catholicism appears in Thackeray's *Esmond* (1852) (perhaps the finest historical novel in the language) and sympathetically too in *The Newcomes* (1853-55) and elsewhere. *Esmond* was probably responsible for much in *John Inglesant* (1881) which influenced not only R. H. Benson towards the Church. In *Marius the Epicurean,* Pater has some beautiful pages on " the Church in Cecilia's House." These three romances are unlike anything else in English and perhaps in European literature and have something in common. The heroines in Meredith's *Richard Feverel* and Blackmore's *Lorna Doone* were both Catholics.

1853 she published *Daisy Burn*, a domestic novel and there-after a novel almost every year till her death.

I have already spoken of Cardinal Wiseman's remark-able novel *Fabiola*, which appeared in 1854 and had so much success here and abroad, and of Newman's *Callista* of 1856. But the next generation of thirty years was to produce little to our purpose except the novels of Lady Georgiana, and the now-forgotten books of T. F. Smith (1803-1890), though, novel or no, we may remark Sir F. C. Burnand's *Happy Thoughts*, published in 1868.

Then in 1882 there appeared the first of a remarkable number of novels by " Lucas Malet " (1852-1931), Mary St. Leger Harrison, the younger daughter (how time brings about its revenges) of Charles Kingsley, the accuser and adversary of Newman. Mrs. Harrison became a Catholic in 1902 and we cannot therefore claim her books previous to her conversion. We must surrender *Colonel Enderby's Wife* (1885), the *Wages of Sin* (1891) and *Sir Richard Calmady* (1901), but we can claim *The Far Horizon* (1906), *The Score* (1909), *The Golden Galleon* (1910), *Adrian Savage* (1911), *Damaris* (1916), *The Tall Villa* (1920) and other works as coming from a Catholic and a rather Meredithian pen.

It was in 1889 that Mrs. Wilfrid Ward published her first novel, *One Poor Scruple*, to be followed by *The Light Behind* (1903), *Out of Due Time* (1906), *Great Possessions* (1909) and a number of other novels, among them *The Shadow of Mussolini* (1927).

But these " three decker " ladies, of whom " Lucas Malet," in her Protestant novels, was the most distinguished, were quite put in the shade by John Oliver Hobbes (Mrs. Pearl Mary Teresa Craigie, 1867-1906). Mrs. Craigie was received into the Church in 1892. In 1891 she had published her epigrammatic first novel, *Some Emotions and a Moral*, the witty and charmingly cynical flavour of which appealed to the readers of " the nineties." In 1892 her second book appeared, *The Sinners' Comedy*, to be followed by a number of excellent stories: *A Study in Temptations* (1893), *A Bundle of Life* (1894), *The Gods, Some Mortals and Lord Wickenham* (1895), all very successful in their day. *The Herb Moon* (1896), however, was a failure. She now turned to the theatre, and when she failed to convince Sir Henry Irving with a comedy which later appeared as a novel (*The School for Saints,* 1897) she wrote *The Ambassador,* which Sir George Alexander produced at the St. James's theatre in 1898. She followed this again at the St. James's with two other plays, both failures, *A Repentance* (1889) and *The Wisdom of the Wise* (1900). Far from discouraged, she wrote *The Bishop's Move* with Murray Carson. This was her last success in the theatre. Her novels, however, continued to win readers and applause. *The Serious Wooing* appeared in 1901, *Love and the Soul Hunters* in 1902, and *Robert Orange* in the same year. In her last two books, *The Vineyard* (1904) and *The Dream* (1906) she wrote of Catholicism in its contrasts and likenesses to the Protestant view of life and man's relation to God.

John Oliver Hobbes was the most brilliant novelist that English Catholicism could so far claim. Living in and by " the nineties " she had all the gaiety, naiveté and insouciance of that sunset of a golden age[4].

A number of Catholic men of letters belong to " the nineties." I have already spoken of the poets Lionel Johnson, Ernest Dowson, Francis Thompson, Alfred Douglas and others. There remain the novelists or Belles Lettrists, Henry Harland and Baron Corvo.

Henry Harland (1861-1905) was born of an American father in St. Petersburg and educated in Rome and at Harvard University. We can ignore his American, mostly Jewish, novels (*As it was Written, A Jewish Musician's Story* and others) as he himself did after 1890 when he came to live in London. His first two books were *Two Women or One* (1890), *a story of double personality,* and *Mea Culpa: A Woman's Last Word* (1891). In 1893 he published the first book he cared to put on record, *Mademoiselle Miss and Other Stories* which is entirely characteristic of his art and his sentimental and somewhat precious manner. In the following year he became Literary Editor of the *Yellow Book* from its

---

[4] If the reader doubts the naïveté he should have heard Marie Lloyd in a Music Hall or seen Mrs. Campbell and Evelyn Millard in an Adelphi melodrama; and if the light-hearted gaiety, he should have seen Letty Lind dancing on the Gaiety stage or in Shaftesbury Avenue, or have spent a delightful evening at the play, *The Importance of Being Earnest* or *The Liars.*

first volume and in 1895 published his charming volume of short stories *Grey Roses,* one of the " Keynotes Series " with cover design by Beardsley. This was followed in 1898 by another volume of short stories, *Comedies and Errors,* and then in 1900 he had his first great popular success with *The Cardinal's Snuff Box,* a long novel, an exquisite trifle in its delicate form, but inanely sentimental and fundamentally absurd. For this reason perhaps it captured a very large number of readers and tempted the author to repeat an unworthy success—unworthy of the author of *Grey Roses*— and to write *The Lady Paramount* (1902) and *My Friend Prospero* (1904).

A much more intriguing figure of " the nineties " is the unhappy, unfortunate, unpleasant and enigmatic Baron Corvo, that is, Frederick William Serafino Austin Lewis Mary Rolfe (1860-1913). Frederick Rolfe, for such was his real name, was born in Cheapside and schooled in Camden Town, and as an unattached student he worked for a time at Oxford, and presently (1886) was received into the Church, which cost him his employment as a schoolmaster. He then desired to become a Catholic priest and believed all his life in his vocation. He was sent to the Scots College in Rome, but soon dismissed, and then obtained employment in the Sforza-Cesarini family of Santa Fiora and Rome. Dismissed again, he came back to London at last and offered the Bodley Head a number of stories which appeared in the *Yellow Book* (1895-6) and afterwards in booklet form as *Stories Toto Told Me,* and later in an enlarged edition as *In His Own Image* (1901). In that year, 1901, he published *Chronicles of the House of Borgia.* In 1904 appeared his fantastic, autobiographical and famous novel *Hadrian the Seventh,* and in the following year he published *Don Tarquinio : a Kataleptic Phantasmatic Romance.* He then disappeared from the literary world of London and reappeared in Venice, where, after trying to make some sort of living as a gondolier, he died, it would seem of want, misery and starvation, in 1913.

Rolfe was an unpleasant person but much of his unpleasantness and most of his misery sprang from frustration. Had he been able to become a priest he might have lived a happy, well, a happier, life. His exquisite, subtle and fantastic talent was exploited by the London publishers, who no doubt found it hard to sell his queer rococo books.

In His Own Image is based on the folklore stories of central Italy set in a modern frame; but it is not only a beautiful, it is a learned work. A year or two ago Montague Summers arraigned this book in *The Literary Supplement* as having been plagiarised from Busk's *Folk Lore of Rome* (1874), but there is little or nothing in Busk that could account for the stories in *In His Own Image,* which owes its tales to more recondite work—more recondite in England—such as De Nino's *Usi e Costumi Abruzzesi* and the collections of Giuseppe Pitrè.

The Chronicles of the House of Borgia, mannered, rhetorical, and unauthenticated though they are, have more than a grain of truth and historical perception in them, and are, like the former book, the work of an artist, a man of learning and out of the way culture and literary gift. As for *Hadrian the Seventh,* it became at one time almost a best-seller after the author's death, and is to some extent founded on his own experience. In recent years the late A. J. A. Symons started a Corvo cult, and by great perseverance and good luck recovered some, if not all, of Rolfe's lost manuscripts, one of which *The Desire and Pursuit of the Whole* is an account of his tragic life in Venice—a remarkable book.

" Self-styled Baron Corvo " his critics sometimes scornfully call him. Self-styled Baron, but not self-styled Corvo. In the priest John Skelton's (1460-1529) poem, *The Book of Philip Sparrow,* the following line appears:—

> *The raven called rolfe. . . .*

This was surely the origin of the pseudonym of that strange and unhappy figure, Baron Corvo.

Before I turn to writers who though they may have been at work in " the nineties " were not of them, I will just record the novels of Mgr. R. H. Benson (1871-1914), for he was a partner and even a friend of Rolfe's and owed a considerable literary debt to him.

Benson, as is well known, was the son of the Archbishop of Canterbury who called the Catholic Church in England " the Italian mission ": though the Irish mission would have been nearer the mark. Benson was received into the

Church in 1903. He wrote a large number of sensational novels, the sometimes excellent ideas of which he probably got from Rolfe and vulgarised in working them out. It will be enough to mention *The Light Invisible* (1903), *By What Authority?* (1904), *Come Rack, Come Rope, The History of Richard Raynel, Solitary* (1906), his favourite, and the *Lord of the World* (1907), a very popular novel, on the coming of Anti-Christ. Benson's influence through his novels and other writings was considerable and this should, I suppose, count as well as intrinsic value.

Montgomery Carmichael (1857-1936) had already published some undistinguished stories when in 1901 *In Tuscany* appeared, a delightful book on Tuscan towns and types and the Tuscan tongue. In the following year he published *The Life of John William Walshe, F.S.A., edited with an introduction by Montgomery Carmichael.* This was a work of fiction in the form of a biography, the story of a boy who ran away from a Manchester warehouse, boarded a ship and landed at Leghorn where he was met, befriended and educated by a Lord Frederick Markham, a wealthy English milord, Catholic and scholar, living in a great villa near Lucca. John Walshe married Lord Frederick's daughter, became a great Franciscan scholar himself, with a wonderful Franciscan library and died in the odour of sanctity in Assisi. It is a book of great charm and learning and so seemingly real and true that it completely took in Cardinal Vaughan, who declared it " the most glorious book that has come out for years " and demanded to know why he had never been informed of this man and his wonderful life. When he was told it was a fiction, a novel like *Robinson Crusoe,* he was very angry and asked, " Do you mean that the whole thing is a *forgery?* "

Carmichael published several other books, among them *The Solitaries of the Sambuca* (1914), but none with the success of *John William Walshe.* In 1909 he had published a work on the representation of the Immaculate Conception in Art (*Francia's Masterpiece*).

There is much charm, though of a sentimental sort, in the novels of E. Temple Thurston (1879-1933). He, too, began with two books of *Poems* (1895) and one of his numerous stories, *The Greatest Art in the World* (1910), is still remembered, as are the novels *John Chilcote, M.P.*, and *The Circle* by Mrs. Katherine Thurston. Another story teller, Sir Philip Gibbs, K.B.E. (b. 1877), is still with us and famous for his novels, many of them historical.

I have spoken of Belloc, Chesterton and Baring in previous sections of this survey. And though perhaps the only real novelist of these men was Baring, it is not possible to pass over a book like Belloc's *Cruise of the Nona* (1925), though this is scarcely a novel, or Chesterton's *Napoleon of Notting Hill* (1904), and the Father Brown Stories (*The Innocence of Father Brown*, 1911; *The Wisdom of Father Brown*, 1914; *The Secret of Father Brown*, 1927). Baring wrote many charming novels which are perhaps his best work, except, maybe, *The Puppet Show of Memory* (1922). Among his novels are: *Cat's Cradle* (1925), *Daphne Adeane* (1926), *Tinker's Leave* (1927), *Comfortless Memory* (1928), *The Coat Without Seam* (1929), *Robert Peckham* (1930), *In the End is my Beginning* (1931), *Friday's Business* (1932), *The Lonely Lady of Dulwich* (1934).

I now turn to a novelist pure and simple, and one of the most brilliant of our time. Compton Mackenzie was born in 1883 and received into the Church in Italy in 1914. Like Belloc and Chesterton he first published a volume of *Poems* (1907), and then in 1911 there began to appear the novels which made him famous: *The Passionate Elopement* (1911), *Carnival* (1912), *Sinister Street* (1913-1914), *Sylvia and Michael* (1919) and many others. In the 1914-18 War he was in the Gallipoli Expedition and later Military Control Officer in Athens and then Director of the Aegean Intelligence Service. In 1929 he published *Gallipoli Memories*, and in 1931 *First Athenian Memories*. A volume of literary criticism followed in 1933 and in 1936 a book on *Catholicism in Scotland* and in that year he began to publish a new series of novels: *The Four Winds of Love*. In addition to these and many other books, Mackenzie has made himself perhaps the best Broadcaster in Britain, as well as a master of Gramophone technique and lore and the President of the Siamese Cats Club; as a connoisseur of islands he is *facile princeps*, the only runner up being Robinson Crusoe.

Here I should like to record C. K. Scott-Moncrieff (1889-1930), the translator of Proust, one of the best translations of this or any other time, in itself a considerable work of art.

Another genuine novelist, Sheila Kaye-Smith, was received into the Church in 1929 and already famous as the author of *Sussex Gorse* (1916) and other delightful stories about Sussex and Sussex folk, in that year published another Sussex novel *The Village Doctor* (1929). In 1930 appeared *Shepherds in Sackcloth,* and in 1934 *Superstition Corner.* Her latest novel published in 1950 still finds her cultivating her Sussex fields, which in her hands seem to become even more Catholic than the Carthusians and the Capuchins have been able to make them.

I must not omit to record the many novels of Isabel Clarke, almost every one, if not all, of which have a definite Catholic atmosphere and a Catholic dénouement. Indeed, what I especially enjoy in her books—I who insist a novel should have a happy ending—is that finally almost everyone seems on the last page to become a Catholic and so all ends paradisaically, as it should.

Finally I come to the authors of a later generation. Bruce Marshall (b. 1899), Evelyn Waugh (b. 1903) (whose book on Edmund Campion I have already recorded) and Graham Greene (b. 1904). These three authors have won a high reputation with modern readers. Among Bruce Marshall's novels are *Father Malachy's Miracle* (1931), *The Uncertain Glory* (1935), *All Glorious Within* (1944), *George Brown's Schooldays* (1946). Evelyn Waugh, who was received into the Church in 1930, is the author of many novels known and read by everybody who reads novels. *Decline and Fall* (1928), *Vile Bodies* (1930), *Black Mischief* (1934), *Handful of Dust* (1934), to name some of the best known, and then in 1945 he published *Brideshead Revisited.* His *Loved One* (1949) is a masterpiece of cold satire. Not nearly so light in the hand, far more factual and grim are the novels of Graham Greene: *The Man Within* (1929), *Brighton Rock* (1938), *The Power and the Glory* (1940) and *The Heart of the Matter* (1948) are among them.

The return of Catholicism as an intellectual force

throughout Europe, especially apparent since the end of th
First World War, inspired by the fundamental groundworl
of the Neo-Thomists, has begun to make itself felt in thi
field of literature. No longer does the Faith figure in work
of imagination merely as eccentric colour for the better dis
play of some single character in a novel. The Catholic in
tellectual position is now presented as the basic, or at an
rate as a basic, standpoint from which to view the whole c
life. Naturally this development has been much more marke
on the Continent than in England, but the *chefs d'oeuvre* c
such writers as François Mauriac, Georges Bernanos and Pau
Claudel, themselves instances of the renaissance of the Catho
lic intellect in France, have in turn had an influence difficul
to exaggerate upon what promises to be a similar renaissanc
in this country.

The recent work of the two novelists Evelyn Waug
and Graham Greene in England shows a most remarkabl
change from that of the previous generation. In the eighteent
century English novelists represented Catholicism as ludicrou
or intolerable at home, but romantic or pathetic abroad. I
the nineteenth century Catholicism in fiction was at best th
religion for romantic heroes and heroines, with mysteriou
foreign antecedents or connections, not to be taken seriousl
as a possible point of view by the contemporary reader. I
was only at the close of the nineteenth and the beginning c
the present century that the Faith began to be proposed b
imaginative writers as a serious point of view, which the reade
could be invited to consider or even adopt. It is indeed onl
at this point that the first Catholic novelists proper begin t
appear in English literature at all. Belloc and Chesterto
still found it necessary to veneer their proposition with a heav
layer of romance, and indeed in Chesterton's case the atmos
phere of the fairy story is deliberately fostered.

When we consider the work of Catholic novelist
to-day, however, the fairy story atmosphere has entirely dis
appeared. What may well prove to be the last vestige of
is to be found in the well-known novel by Bruce Marshal
Father Malachy's Miracle. Perhaps this particular write
may eventually appear to be the link between the two mode
the two generations, Chesterton on the one hand and Waug

and Greene on the other. For in Bruce Marshall's later work the magical atmosphere is completely absent.

To-day Catholicism is presented by Waugh and Greene as something quite unromantic, quite usual in fact, exceptional only according to its own hypothesis which the writers of course happen to approve and accept.

Evelyn Waugh's *Brideshead Revisited,* which created a certain shock of distaste when it appeared, only did so because Catholicism in this country is still permeated with a minority attitude or inferiority complex. In point of fact it was the first novel by a Catholic devoted to Catholics and Catholicism in England sufficiently serious to be considered as a work of art.

Graham Greene's still more recently published *The Heart of the Matter* created even more controversy among us, not only for the same reason as *Brideshead Revisited,* but in addition because Graham Greene posed a problem in his story which lay within the scope of Catholic theology and answered it, or rather made one of the characters answer it, according to that character's own point of view without any particular gesture of deference to Catholic authority. It would of course have been absurd to have made such a gesture as the book was a novel; Graham Greene was telling a story, he was not writing a theological treatise. For Greene is an artist, not a theologian. His earlier, very powerful novel, *The Power and the Glory,* did not create the same shock merely because the Catholic characters involved were foreigners in a far country.

Perhaps, however, the most striking thing about the Catholic writers of to-day is not their effect upon their co-religionists but their impact upon readers outside the Church. In the solid Victorian and the fairly solid Edwardian and Georgian world, it was necessary to coat Catholicism with a thick veneer of romance to make it attractive; in the frighteningly insecure world of to-day, however, Marshall, Waugh and Greene can profit by showing Catholicism as it really is— the only certain thing in a world whose material being seems to depend tenuously upon some rather obscure hieroglyphics on the back of an envelope in the pocket of an atomic physicist.

VI. RELIGION

In turning at last to the books which have been written on Religion, during the last hundred years, I can only confess my incompetence to deal with them even in the very superficial manner of this survey, though were I competent in this matter it would be impossible so much as to name a tenth of the devotional works which have poured from the Catholic Press[5]. I shall therefore content myself with setting down here what appears to me—a layman, an outsider in this matter, a mere man of letters—to be among the most striking landmarks in this very specialist sort of literature.

In such an objective and extraneous point of view the theological and religious works of Newman seem to tower over the whole century: *The Development of Christian Doctrine* (1845), the *Apologia* (1864), the *Grammar of Assent* (1870) seem to be the most important, and of course his Sermons where *Cor ad cor loquitur*. Not long ago a foreigner and a Jesuit published *A Newman Synthesis* (1930) in which he tried to reconstitute Newman's thought systematically in its completeness, and if not to draw from it a *Summa Theologica* at least to find something like an equivalent.

Then it seems to me the works of the Baron Friedrich von Hügel (1852-1925) hold an outstanding position in the religious literature of the century: *The Mystical Element of Religion as studied in St. Catherine of Genoa and her friends* (1908); *Eternal Life, a study of its Implications and Applications* (1912); *Essays and Addresses on the Philosophy of Religion* (1921) and *The Reality of God* (1931), a posthumous work edited by his friend E. G. Gardner. These works have had a larger influence perhaps on readers outside the Catholic Church, than on those within it.

Among many other notable writers on religion in the period under review are John Dobree Dalgairns the Oratorian (1818-1876), whose *The Devotion to the Sacred Heart of*

---

[5] Though not a devotional work, I take this opportunity to note here that the first translation of the *Fioretti* of St. Francis in English was published by Burns and Lambert in 1864: *The Little Flowers of St. Francis*: translated from the Italian and edited by Rt. Rev. H. E. Manning.

Jesus (1853) and *The Holy Communion, its Philosophy, Theology and Practice* (1856) have passed through many editions. Then there is William George Ward (1812-1882), the only layman who has been a Professor of Theology at St. Edmund's College, Ware, and indeed possibly in any Catholic Seminary. His generosity of temper and largeness of mind had no influence upon his theological rigour. His fragment *On Nature and Grace* (1860) is characteristic of his keen but genial disposition and the same appears in his *Essays on the Philosophy of Theism* (2 vols., 1884). His son, Wilfrid Philip Ward (1856-1916), the biographer of Wiseman and Newman and of his father, also published some essays on religion, *The Wish to Believe* (1882), *The Clothes of Religion* (1886) and *Witnesses to the Unseen* (1893). Nor should Abbot Smith, O.S.B., of Ampleforth (1854-1924) be forgotten as the author of a number of books of meditations. Nor Mgr. A. S. Barnes (1861-1936), the author of *St. Peter at Rome and his Tomb* (1900), *The Early Church in the Light of the Monuments* (1913), *The Martyrdom of St. Peter and St. Paul* (1933), and *The Holy Shroud of Turin* (1934).

An old Benedictine, John Cuthbert Hedley, O.S.B. (1837-1915), Bishop of Newport, has also a strong claim on our remembrance for his *Spiritual Retreat* and *Lex Levitarum*. I ought here again to record Abbot Chapman, O.S.B., of Downside, of whom I have already spoken. His *Spiritual Letters* (1935) is a great book, one of the best works of spiritual reading written in modern times. Nor should the sons of the Society of Jesus go unrecorded: John Rickaby, S.J. (1847-1932), who was writing on Scholasticism before the age of Maritain; Henry Coleridge, S.J. (1822-1893), whose two biographies, *Life and Letters of St. Francis Xavier* (1892) and *Life and Letters of St. Teresa* (1893) are still to be consulted; Archbishop Goodier, S.J. (1869-1939), among whose numerous works *The Public Life of Our Lord Jesus Christ* (2 vols., 1930) is outstanding; Herbert Thurston, S.J. (1856-1939), most learned and most severe of critics whose *Life of St. Hugh of Lincoln* (1898) is a mine of teaching and religion, to say nothing here perforce of his multitudinous contributions to Catholic history, biography and scholarship; and Cyril Charles Martindale, S.J

(b. 1879), happily still with us, whose Sermons are not only a unique religious experience but a delight to simple and scholar alike.

Perhaps I may close this very brief and imperfect section of my survey with the name of Fr. T. E. Bridgett, C.SS.R. (1829-1899), who wrote more than one book of popular devotion and history: *The History of the Eucharist in Great Britain* (1881, new edition with notes by Fr. Thurston, S.J., 1908), and *Our Lady's Dowry; How England gained that Title* (3rd edition, 1891).

Such then, in imperfect outline, is the Catholic achievement in English literature during the last hundred years. And it might seem that what strikes one most, apart from its general magnitude, is the importance and the influence of Newman, the outstanding place occupied by the great Benedictine Abbey of Downside, and the leading position taken by converts in all this transaction.

As for the achievement itself it would seem to be little short of wonderful when we consider that English Catholics in 1850 were not more than 500,000, and that men and women of culture capable of writing an English book were a tiny fraction of that number. That, of course, explains why the work of the converts is so outstanding. As Challoner foretold " a new people " has appeared in our country.

XVIII

THE CARE OF THE POOR

By John Bennett

THE wave of hysteria which swept over the whole country at the restoration of the Hierarchy was not allowed to slow up the work of preparation for the Great Exhibition of 1851, the high water-mark of Victorian pre-eminence in industry. Visitors were not expected to go further than the Crystal Palace and its wonders or to inquire at what a price this victory of free enterprise had been won; this would have led them into places better hidden, the appalling slums of Drury Lane, Clare Market, and Seven Dials, and they might have returned home at least suspicious of the moral excellence of an industrial system which could tolerate such a gulf between wealth and poverty.

The inheritance upon which the restored Hierarchy entered was largely one of wretchedness and poverty, not only in London but throughout the country, and if Cardinal Wiseman sounded a note of triumph from out the Flaminian Gate his Appeal to the English People showed him aware of the problems awaiting him. " Close under the Abbey of Westminster there lie concealed labyrinths of lanes and courts, and alleys and slums, nests of ignorance, vice, depravity, and crime, as well as of squalor, wretchedness, and disease; whose atmosphere is typhus, whose ventilation is cholera, in which swarms a huge and almost countless population, in great measure, nominally at least, Catholic; haunts of filth which no sewage committee can reach—dark corners, which no lighting board can brighten. This is the part of Westminster which alone I covet, and which I shall be glad to claim and to visit, as a blessed pasture in which sheep of holy Church are to be tended."

Already the Chartist movement had shaken the country, but had petered out, and the year of revolutions, 1848, had passed off without major incident. In Parliament Lord Shaftesbury's name had become associated with championship of the oppressed, and factory legislation for the protection of women and children was being forced on to the statute book, though every advance, according to the economic experts, threatened a national collapse.

A major catastrophe had been the Irish potato famine which had flooded the country with hundreds of thousands of refugees fleeing from famine and fever. In 1847 three hundred thousand passed through the gateway of Liverpool alone, of whom one hundred thousand were struck down with fever and dysentery with a death roll of over eight thousand. Most of the survivors fanned out over the country carrying disease with them into the already overcrowded slums. Of twenty-four priests in Liverpool and district eighteen contracted fever; ten, known as the " Martyr Priests," died, as well as ten doctors. To be both Catholic and Irish was a fearful handicap in a country which hated both, and destitution brought many to the workhouse and the gaol. Their faith was a welcome accession to the Church, but their wretchedness added to the many other anxieties of the restored Hierarchy.

Catholic Emancipation had brought considerable relief to Catholics, but they were still denied any religious rights if they were unfortunate enough to enter the workhouse or the gaol. Even in the Army or Navy there was no provision for them. Canon St. John recalls how " Thousands of half-starved Irish poor were dying in the workhouses without the Sacraments, as no priest was allowed to minister to them unless he had been definitely asked for by the patient in each case. The thousands of Catholic children were *all*, without exception, being brought up as Protestants, and no priest was allowed to visit them under any circumstances. Prisoners were compelled to attend Protestant services."

The Crimean War (1854-56) brought Catholic chaplains to the Army through the insistence of Dr. Grant, first Bishop of Southwark, the son of a soldier, who also gained authority to send a few Sisters of Mercy from Bermondsey, and Sisters of the Faithful Virgin from Norwood, under Florence Nightingale to nurse our stricken troops in conditions of incredible hardship. This concession was no doubt due to the fact that our allies, the French, had already sent out Sisters of Charity as a matter of course.

In 1863 the Borough Prisons Act made possible the appointment and payment of chaplains for the spiritual care of prisoners other than those of the Church of England. The first Catholic chaplain to be appointed at a salary of £300 a year was Father Nugent, the Apostle of Liverpool, whose twenty-two years at Walton Gaol inspired his work for children and criminals, for the fallen and for the unmarried mother, and led him to set up the League of the Cross against drink. He used to say: " It was perhaps the best thing that ever happened to me when I was sent to prison. It was there that as chaplain I learned to understand the real nature of the criminal poor, and to study mankind in all its phases. It was that experience which prompted me to deal with crime in its infancy." A grateful city later honoured him by setting up his statue in St. John's Gardens.

The decks had been cleared for action for prison children when, following on a successful Quaker experiment, the Reformatory Schools Act of 1854 enabled voluntary bodies to open schools for children who had formerly been committed to prison. Three years later came the Industrial Schools Act whereby magistrates had authority to commit to schools willing to receive them children who would otherwise drift into a criminal life. They continued to appear in the adult courts until the passing of the Children Act, 1908, which saw the beginning of Juvenile Courts.

The dawn of better days for the workhouse children began in 1859 when the Poor Law Board issued an instruction that by statute law Catholic children under the age of twelve should not be instructed in a different religion, and that a creed register be kept in all workhouses. Certain priests, called religious instructors, were thereby permitted to visit to give instruction to Catholic children, but this had little value in the all-embracing Protestant atmosphere, combined with the passive resistance of the Guardians.

By an Act of 1862 the Guardians were further empowered to board out pauper children in schools certified to receive them at a fee not in excess of what they would cost in the workhouse; this was a permissive Act and promptly became a dead letter. To force the Guardian into action a Poor Law Amendment Act was passed in 1866 enacting that " any parent, step-parent, nearest adult relative, or next of kin of a child not belonging to the Established Church relieved in a Workhouse or District School . . . . (or failing these) then the God-parent of such child, may make application to the said Board (Poor Law Board) in such behalf, and the Board may, if they think fit, order that such child shall be sent to some school established for the reception, maintenance, and education of children of the religion to which such child shall be proved to belong." It further laid down that the Guardians pay such charges as the Board order. This was a distinct advance but it meant detailed investigation of every case submitted before a decision could be reached, and it embittered Guardians still more. Two years later more precise directions were issued for the better keeping of the creed register which in many workhouses had been completely ignored.

The legal position was thus favourable to the Catholic child, whether under the Reformatory and Industrial Schools Acts or under the Poor Law Acts, provided Catholics were willing and able to open and staff schools under the appropriate certificate.

The position was critical; beyond a few small orphanages scattered over the country in the days of the Vicars Apostolic no accommodation was available, nor was it possible to consider lay staffs who would require salaries. Add to this the capital needed to purchase properties and equip schools, and the whole problem became a nightmare to daunt the stoutest heart. Practically the only Sisters to hand were the Sisters of Mercy newly come from Ireland, and of Brothers there were none. Further there was the hatred of the religious habit which Father Dominic experienced in full measure. When Mother Mary of St. Joseph and a companion from the Good Shepherd Convent in Angers arrived in London in 1840 to found the first Good Shepherd Convent at Hammersmith, " they had put off their religious habit, and donned a secular garb consisting of a plain black dress, white net cap, drawn black silk bonnet, with a crepe veil and black cloak. The absence of hair naturally made them appear different from other people, and even the expression of their countenance was different.''

When Dr. Wiseman was transferred from the Midland to the London District as Vicar Apostolic in 1847 he invited the Sisters of the Faithful Virgin from Bayeux to open an orphanage for girls at Norwood, and shortly afterwards he established a corresponding orphanage for boys at North Hyde under the Sisters of Mercy who were already engaged in looking after sick and poor in their own homes in Bermondsey.

To meet the demands of charity he was forced to look abroad for religious communities who were usually only too ready to come and work for the conversion of a Protestant country which was headline news in the Catholic world of those days. Most came from France, many in the spirit of martyrs, all to suffer the severe handicaps of poverty, of a strange language, and the hostility of a Protestant people. Once they arrived a strange thing happened; the floodgates of vocations were opened both here and in Ireland, in God's design, to enable them to meet the ever-increasing calls for their services. Requests to enter came from all classes of society, from well-known Catholic families right through the social scale. Here was an opportunity to help one's neighbour frowned upon as '' methodistical and unladylike '' except in the habit of a religious, and a period of amazing expansion set in as the flower of Catholic womanhood flocked to the convents.

Within one year of the Reformatory Act becoming law in 1854 the Cardinal led the way by opening a reformatory school for boys at Hammersmith. He was closely followed by the Cistercians at Mount St. Bernard's Abbey, Leicestershire. The Fathers of Charity started St. William's, Market Weighton, York, in 1863, and before long took over St. Bernard's from the Cistercians. The Brothers of the Christian Schools who had arrived in England in 1855 had been offered St. Bernard's, and six Brothers had been nominated for the work when the Government stepped in with the objection that an English reformatory school should not be staffed by French teachers.

The Liverpool Catholic Reformatory Association which was early in the field did not at first establish a school, but handed over to the Cistercians £2,000 with the right to board 200 Liverpool reformatory boys at St. Bernard's, the money to remain in trust so long as this number was accepted. The scheme soon broke down, and it was not until 1878 that the Liverpool committee recovered £500.

In 1863 they decided that Liverpool boys needed a ship reformatory, and through the good offices of Father Nugent the Admiralty made over to the committee the *Clarence,* an 84 line-of-battle ship, which the boys conspired to set ablaze and sink in 1884. A second ship of the same name met the same fate in 1899 while the Bishop of Shrewsbury was on board for Confirmations. During these years two other reformatory ships were similarly accounted for in the Thames. After 1899 the *Clarence* was replaced by a nautical reformatory school on land, St. Aidan's, Farnworth, Widnes. Meantime in 1872 Birkdale Farm School had been started by the Liverpool committee for boys not suitable for sea-training.

The Sisters of Charity who had been invited to come to England in 1859 at the request of Lady Georgiana Fullerton, Lady Fitzgerald, Lady Lothian, and other charitable ladies, with the approval of Cardinal Wiseman, and had established themselves at Carlisle Place, Westminster, were approached to open a reformatory for girls in the north of England. In 1860 the scheme was broached at a meeting of Catholic gentlemen held in York with the Hon. Charles Langdale as chairman. The outcome was the reformatory at Howard Hill, Sheffield, where the capital outlay was met by diocesan collections from the northern dioceses. Twenty years later its status was changed to that of an industrial school. It was finally closed in 1931 when the Sisters were transferred to Blackbrook House, St. Helens, to continue similar work.

The first reformatory school for girls in the south of England was opened by the Good Shepherd Nuns at Arnos Vale, Bristol; they had survived the earlier troubles of their first foundation at Hammersmith which had soon been transferred to Windlesham. To-day they have 13 convents, 11 for the rehabilitation of penitents with special emphasis on the training of girls under eighteen, and two approved schools. Owing to war damage Arnos Vale was closed, and a new foundation made at Ashwick Hall, Colerne, Wiltshire. The second approved school, a comparatively recent foundation, is at Troy, Monmouth.

Such were the beginnings of the Catholic reformatories due in large measure to the inspiration of Cardinal Wiseman who was also very early in the field in finding accommodation for children committed to industrial schools. In his first pastoral Archbishop Manning refers to two industrial schools started by his predecessor, St. Nicholas's at Walthamstow for boys, and St. Margaret's in Queen's Square for girls.

The procedure in many parts of the country was to secure an industrial school certificate for existing Homes, the managers retaining the right to admit a proportion of voluntary cases. As the rate of payment at first was only one shilling per head per week from local authorities, with a grant of about the same amount from the Home Office for both reformatory and industrial school cases, they constituted a considerable drain on Catholic charity in any case, even though they developed trades both for the training of the children as well as to try to make both ends meet. Father Nugent's description of the Boys' Refuge is typical: " Here we have a large shoe factory, a printing office where every form of job work is done, and where a newspaper (*The Catholic Times*) is printed each week, a tailor's shop, a joiner's shop, and a paper bag factory. Each boy is taught to work for his own bread as soon as he is fit for labour, and has eight hours work and four hours school each day. There is an instrumental band of 30 performers, and everybody who has a taste for music is taught to read music just as his alphabet." One should add that the chief money spinner was the joiner's shop which included wood chopping, or the sale of firewood, an occupation of little training value.

The government attitude to religious in charge of institutions is well illustrated by happenings at St. George's Industrial School, Liverpool, in 1866. The school had got into low water, and its certificate had been suspended. The managers in order to retrieve the situation had invited the Brothers of the Christian Schools who had come to England in 1855 to take charge. Father Nugent was the spokesman for the managers, and he reported to Bishop Goss: " Sir George Grey (Home Secretary), through the Rev. Sydney Turner

(Inspector) has taken a very decided stand against religious having the management of Reformatory and Industrial Schools. This has added to our difficulties at St. George's, for the Rev. Sydney Turner promised to give us a trial for three months. Owing to difficulties of the same character arising elsewhere with nuns, he now refuses to give back the certificate until he has a definite and satisfactory plan set before him for the future working of the establishment. Last week in company with the Archbishop (Manning) I had an interview with him. At first he was firm and decided that religious from the nature of their vows and pursuits were un-qualified for this special work. . . . He said that he would not for the future recommend the Government to certify any Reformatory or Industrial School which was managed by religious, except there was a responsible committee of manage-ment, and that the only nuns he considered qualified for the work were the Sisters of Charity."

The Brothers were finally tolerated but withdrew after three years through trouble with the managers who had foolishly appointed a lay-secretary, and so set up a divided authority. For some years they conducted the Boys' Refuge for Father Nugent, until in 1886 they transferred to Manchester to take over and purchase Father Quick's Home for boys, known as St. Joseph's, Withy Grove, which had become an industrial school. To-day there are 17 Catholic approved schools for boys of which all but four are under the care of religious, mostly Brothers of the Christian Schools and the Presentation Brothers; the seven girls' schools are all under religious.

The term " Approved School " was preferred under the Children and Young Persons Act, 1933, to " Reforma-tory " and " Industrial School "; they are now schools " approved " by the Secretary of State.

In his first Pastoral Archbishop Manning declared him-self the champion of the Catholic pauper children, and his words carried such weight as to call for a leading article in *The Times,* June 12th, 1866, which was sympathetic if some-what critical. " Nobody here wishes to make public charity the means of religious ' seduction,' or to induce the hungry to sell the soul's birthright. It is out of the question here. But it is the great rule of this country that people must help themselves and take care of themselves, both individually and in classes and sects. . . . If the Roman Catholics really find this to be the awful matter they describe—and on their religion they must—they ought to make out a case, to ascertain the facts thoroughly, putting them beyond disproof, and then ask Parliament whether it does insist on, as they say, a thousand Roman Catholic children being now under compulsion to abjure their religion by the threat of death or hunger. . . . Let them organise a system of protection for the poor, to see either that they are kept out of the workhouses, or that once in they are not compelled to change their faith. The British public has not overmuch confidence in those dismal institutions, and if the Roman Hierarchy will insist on letting the daylight into them, they will be well backed."

It is already clear that the law favoured the Catholic workhouse child, but that the Guardians did not; at least this was the position under the Act of 1862. Two days after *The Times* article the Archbishop held his first St. James's Hall meeting at which he established the Westminster Diocesan Education Fund for the promotion of Westminster diocesan schools, religious inspection of schools, and " the protection of the faith of Roman Catholic children who are chargeable to the Poor Rates or come under the operation of the Reformatory and Industrial Schools Act or the Board of Education Act or any similar Acts of Parliament. (Lastly) the relief or assistance of Roman Catholic poor children in any other manner as the Archbishop shall from time to time direct."

He was speaking on the problem of the education of poor Catholic children in London, but he concentrated on the plight of the workhouse children, acknowledging and commenting on *The Times* article. By arrangement with Bishop Grant of Southwark he spoke for the whole London area. " In the workhouses of London there are one thousand Catholic children educated exclusively and explicitly as Protestants. They attend schools which are Protestant in their teachers, and Protestant in doctrine, and Protestant in their attendance at worship. I will admit that that is not the letter of the statute law; but it is a practical maladministration of the law." He complains that Guardians had resisted the order to keep a creed register as *ultra vires* though it had been issued by the Poor Law Board. One Protestant chaplain had admitted: " I never know of any Catholic children in the house until they come to me and say, ' please, Sir, I do not want to be a Catholic any longer.' I never try to proselytize." The figure of one thousand Catholic children was therefore highly hypothetical, and proved to be a gross under-estimate.

In May, 1867, he announced the purchase at Walthamstow of a school for a hundred girls, and adds: " It is right to report that we have made a strong and constant effort, by application to 15 Boards of Guardians, to obtain the release of our poor children. In two instances only have they consented. In one or two cases the answers were courteous and becoming in manner. Of the rest the least said the better. Thank God the end of this oppression is at hand, and will not much longer be delayed."

To a Liverpool enquirer in 1877, one of the Cardinal's secretaries, Father Seddon, the expert on Poor Law procedure, wrote: " I have pleasure to inform you that the rights of these children as contemplated by the Legislature, are now universally recognised by the several Boards, and there is, I am happy to say, a spirit of fairness gradually year by year supplanting the old prejudices which have in past times acted so injuriously on the faith of our poor children." Twenty-nine Unions and Parishes were now sending Catholic children to Catholic institutions in the London area.

By 1887 there were in Westminster 13 Poor Law schools for 2,000 children, sent by 33 Boards of the Metropolitan District. Thanks to the efforts of other bishops all but four dioceses had provided some accommodation for these children, the exceptions being Middlesbrough, Nottingham, Portsmouth and Liverpool. Bishop Butt was busy redeeming a pledge to house the Southwark Poor Law children with the help of Father St. John. Before the Homes at Orpington were started he was sent up to Hexham and Newcastle diocese to see those already functioning through the initiative of Monsignor Canon Rooney, V.G., particularly St. Peter's, Gainford, which was regarded as a model.

In Birmingham Bishop Ullathorne opened St. Paul's,

Coleshill, in 1884, the forerunner of the splendid group of Homes completed later by Father Hudson.

It was not until 1887 that Bishop O'Reilly began his campaign for Poor Law children with the aim of founding St. Vincent's, Preston, for boys, and Holy Family schools, West Derby, Liverpool, for girls. It remained for his successor, Bishop Whiteside, to complete the scheme with a total of six schools.

The story so far has been concerned with the rescue of children from the prison or the workhouse. Many children managed to steer clear of both, but their plight could be more pitiable, for there were thousands running the streets homeless a hundred years ago. In London the number was estimated to be 30,000, in Liverpool 23,000. Father Nugent described them as huddling together for warmth under railway arches, in empty boxes, over bakers' ovens, behind theatre bill boards. When Lord Shaftesbury challenged Dr. Barnardo to prove his claim that there were thousands homeless in London he was taken to Billingsgate at midnight. They disturbed a heap of barrels covered with tarpaulins from which emerged 73 boys as from an ants' nest. Some 16,000 of these children found their way to prison every year, and thousands more to the workhouse, but this still left many thousands to the charity of the general public, and among them was a considerable percentage of Catholics.

There were many willing hands outstretched to help but on terms which no Catholic could accept even in the last extremity. This was an age of philanthropy by people of strong religious views who regarded the snatching of a Catholic child from the burning as an act pleasing to God. Speaking in support of Bishop O'Reilly's scheme for Poor Law schools at Preston, in May, 1889, Bishop Vaughan of Salford, put the matter very plainly: " The State told them to provide schools if they were not satisfied with the workhouse schools, and the Guardians would have the power to send Catholic children to them, and to support them. Contrast this with the conduct of the philanthropic institutions of the country. They were nearly all Protestant, all absolutely non-Catholic, many of them merely proselytizing institutions, mingled with a great amount of human benevolence. He gave them every credit for making great sacrifices for what they believed to be the best, but they looked upon Catholics as men tainted with disease, and if they could rid their children of the disease in infancy, they believed they were doing a service to the children and to the State. Those philanthropic institutions were not under the general eye of the public or the magistracy of the country—they were not governed by the laws of Parliament. . . . They (the children) were snatched up in courts and alleys. Those private societies had agents who were busy all over large towns and all over the country. . . . They (Catholics) must march with the times, that as the people of England had established by private effort an enormous number of philanthropic institutions for rescuing and educating the waifs and strays of the lower class of society, and were gathering their children, it behoved them as Catholics belonging to the English community not to be behind the times, but to found their own associations for educating their waifs and strays.'' Horrified at the appalling leakage among Catholic children he had set up the first diocesan rescue society three years earlier.

It was not a new problem; it had long worried the Vicars Apostolic, and was part of the inheritance of the restored Hierarchy. One may wonder at their haste to snatch prison and pauper children from the State, yet leave the waifs and strays to the mercy of proselytizing philanthropists. To suggest that nothing had been done would not be true, but against the grave evil too much had depended on individuals and local committees, wholly unco-ordinated, and woefully inadequate.

Bishop Challoner had founded the '' Charitable Society '' for the relief of the poor and to provide Catholic schools, and about the same period the '' Society for Educating Poor Catholic Children '' held its first annual meeting, October 7th, 1764, at the sign of the '' Blue Posts,'' Cockpit Alley. A few working men met in 1796 at the sign of '' The Mariners,'' and from their efforts sprang '' The Laudable Association for the Maintenance and Education of Poor Catholic Children.'' Twelve years earlier the '' Beneficent Society for Apprenticing the Children of Poor Catholic Parents '' had been started. In 1812 the three charities last named were amalgamated into the " Associated Catholic Charities " by Charles Butler, K.C., nephew of Alban Butler, author of the *Lives of the Saints*. Outside London were to be found a few similar societies, but almost the first recorded orphanage was the Catholic Female Orphanage in Liverpool to provide for the respectable orphans of men who died in the wars of Napoleon.

After the restoration of the Hierarchy we read of the heroism of two seamstresses, Elizabeth Twiddy and Fanny Wilson, who in 1857 housed and supported out of their meagre earnings a few orphan girls, and so made possible St. Mary's Orphanage, Hammersmith. Fanny Wilson was a religious of the Daughters of Mary, founded during the French Revolution, bound by rule not to wear a religious habit. This has enabled them to do work in police courts, prisons and for the fallen, normally closed to religious.

In 1859 a worthless Catholic murdered his wife in London, responsibility for the boys of the family falling to the Brothers of St. Vincent de Paul, and for the girls to Lady Georgiana Fullerton, an outstanding convert who died full of good works. The Brothers debated the need for a Home of their own. The president, George Blunt, was annoyed when the proposal was narrowly defeated, so he referred the question to the General Council of the Society in Paris to be assured that the scheme was not within the rules. Still convinced of the urgency of some provision his fellow members and himself undertook to support a small orphanage out of their own pockets as a private venture. A committee was formed with George Blunt, chairman; Renfric Arundell, vice-chairman; John Trivick, treasurer; Archibald Dunn, secretary; the other members being Henry Arundell, J. Sidney Lescher, S. J. Nicholl, John Stuart Knill, George J. Wigley and St. George Mivart. St. Vincent's Home for 20 boys was opened in December, 1859, at Brook Green. Later when accommodation became inadequate the house was handed over to Fanny Wilson for her girls, and St. Vincent's moved to larger premises in Hammersmith, close by the Good Shepherd Convent.

In 1875 after 700 boys had passed through the Home the Brothers made it over to Lord Archibald Douglas (Father Douglas). He moved it to the Harrow Road where he lived on the premises, using his own private means, and for the rest trusting to Providence. Ten years later he returned to Scotland, so Cardinal Manning appointed Father Douglas Hope, an Oblate of St. Charles, to carry on the work. He struggled on like his predecessor until he was forced to give up through ill health.

Meantime the Cardinal had commissioned Father William Barry to start a similar Home in the East End, to which was added responsibility for St. Vincent's in 1889. In addition to his boys' home in Stepney Father Barry soon opened two others, one for little boys, and one for girls, and when shortly he bought a property at Enfield he was better able to classify the children, and signs are evident of some central organisation. But he too was a sick man, and died October 29th, 1894.

Father Berry in Liverpool was engaged on a parallel work at the same time, providing for working boys in a Home begun by the Brothers of St. Vincent de Paul, as well as for boys and girls of school age.

Father Barry was succeeded by his assistant, Father Emmanuel Bans, under the direction of Cardinal Vaughan. His was a period of great expansion, and also in its early stages of grave anxiety owing to the crisis with Dr. Barnardo's Homes. The agreement finally reached by the Cardinal in 1899 had the effect of nearly wrecking the rescue work of the diocese through the added responsibilities it entailed.

Stated simply the quarrel with Dr. Barnardo was due to his motto: " No destitute child ever refused "; in 1887 he admitted that one-fifth of the children he rescued were baptised Catholics, but that he took no account of a child's religion in accepting it. The one question was its destitution. He was an extreme Protestant with a missionary zeal who had come to London from Dublin to prepare himself in the London Hospital for work in China as a medical missionary. During his studies he engaged in missionary work in the East End, and the horrors of child life he met with decided his career. He was an autocrat brooking no interference, who regarded it as his bounden duty to bring up all children in the religion which he followed. It has been estimated that the number of Catholic children who were turned into Protestants in his Homes cannot have been less than 10,000. The fact must be faced that Catholics had not themselves done anything to help these children until they were stung into activity by the revelation of wholesale leakage, too often when the damage was done.

An attempt to reach an agreement with Dr. Barnardo was made in 1887 by Father Seddon on the instructions of Cardinal Manning which at first looked promising. Dr. Barnardo expressed his willingness to refer to the Cardinal, and only to him as head of the Catholic Church in England, any Catholic cases after he had investigated them, and to allow 14 days for action, such action not to include handing a child to the Poor Law. He reserved to himself full independence if nothing were done, and insisted that the annoyance he suffered from priests and lawyers seeking to reclaim children from his Homes should cease.

An impasse was reached on the question of the Catholic children already in Dr. Barnardo's Homes. The Cardinal could not in conscience abate his claim to them while Dr. Barnardo refused flatly to hand them over except under an order of the court. So the struggle went on in the courts with varying success until Cardinal Vaughan accepted Dr. Barnardo's terms in 1899. Canon St. John of Southwark had been prominent in the final negotiations; the agreement has been scrupulously kept by Dr. Barnardo's Homes ever since.

When any problem appeared Cardinal Vaughan ordered a diocesan survey to learn its full extent. He had already done this in Salford over the question of leakage and the danger to faith in which many children were proved to live. The upshot had been two Poor Law schools, one for girls at Tottington, Bury, in 1888, and one for boys at Rochdale about the same time, the former under the Sisters of Charity, from Ghent, and the latter under the Brothers of Charity, of the same congregation. In 1886 he had founded the Salford Catholic Protection and Rescue Society, the first of its kind, with branches in every parish. The Society's first Home for waifs and strays was in Ardwick Green under the community of Sisters he had founded for the Foreign Missions. In 1889 he transferred St. Joseph's Home to Patricroft where he introduced a startling departure from convention by arranging for boys and girls to be brought up in the same Home to prevent the break-up of families. His following the natural law in this particular has been well justified by results. In 1925 a similar Home was opened at Didsbury.

On his translation to Westminster he organised a second survey, and, guided by the results, he established the Crusade of Rescue in 1899 to which he attached the Homes for Catholic Destitute Children already under Father Bans. The West-minster Diocesan Education Fund continued a parallel course, and still does, though Cardinal Hinsley brought the two societies under a unified direction, Canon Craven, now Bishop of Sebastopolis, being the first administrator of both.

In Southwark for many years the pioneer and guiding spirit was Canon St. John who had been driven as a young priest by the importunities of boys begging at the Cathedral presbytery to start a working boys' Home in a disused car-penter's shop. Bishop Butt set up the Southwark Catholic Rescue Society in 1887, one year after Salford. Under Canon Crea the Society assumed the management of all the diocesan institutions for children, and became one of the most complete organisations in the country.

In Liverpool for many years under Archbishop White-side the work centred round Monsignor Pinnington who was the secretary of the Catholic Children's Aid Committee founded in 1899 to serve as an advice bureau on all questions affecting children. Very soon it was driven to provide accom-modation also, but not until 1924 was there any centralisation when the Catholic Children's Aid Committee, and Father Berry's Homes were amalgamated under the Liverpool Catholic Children's Protection Society. Complete centralisa-tion of all children's work was not achieved until 1947.

Under Archbishop Williams the Birmingham Diocesan Rescue Society, founded in 1902, came in Monsignor Hudson's hands to control the various diocesan works for children. The Monsignor's own contribution was St. Edward's for boys in 1906, an orthopædic hospital for children, and St. Joan's semi-cottage Home for girls. Coleshill was also the headquarters for child emigration to Canada.

One of the serious problems confronting all engaged in rescue work has been to safeguard the welfare of those children who would find their way back to the gutter if allowed to return to their worthless families and friends. The most satisfactory solution was to send them overseas to one of the dominions. Canada offered most advantages in the last century because of its strong Catholic population where the children's faith would be best assured.

Father Nugent escorted the first party of Catholic children to Canada on August 18th, 1870. The first Protestant party went out from Mrs. Birt's Homes about the same time; this agency was regarded by Liverpool Catholics as a hot-bed of proselytism. Father Nugent spent nine months in Canada and the United States pleading the cause of both children and families as suitable migrants. " It is estimated that there are at the present time in England and Wales 350,000 children under the age of 16 who are more or less a burden on the parochial rates. I am sure that you will agree with me that poverty is not a crime but a misfortune. These are poor children, and in most large towns there are parish industrial schools for this class. We have one in Liverpool in which there are from 1,200 to 1,500 children. I brought out 24 of these children with me a few weeks ago, all orphans, 12 boys and 12 girls; they were all well instructed in their religion and in book learning. The girls were all in excellent situations within two days at Montreal, four of the youngest being adopted into most respectable families where they will be treated as their own children. The youngest boy was 11, the oldest 15. They had all been accustomed to labour, nine of them had a trade; they all knew how to read and write well, and they had all made their Communion."

Some organisation was obviously needed to protect the children on arrival and disposal; for some years this was quite inadequate. Father Nugent relied on gentlemen of good repute to keep in touch with the children and report to him. Father Seddon who later followed with yearly parties from Westminster depended on local clergy. In 1880 Bishop O'Reilly set up the Liverpool Catholic Children's Protection Society which opened a hostel in Liverpool as a gathering point, and a Canadian hostel in Montreal, with an agent to look after the children.

Father St. John came into the field in the early nineties, and based his work on the plan of Dr. Barnardo's Homes which had started emigration of children in 1882 under their own auspices. Formerly they had used Mrs. Birt's agency. When in Ottawa Father St. John consulted the Archbishop. His Grace pointed out that his clergy could not be responsible for aftercare, and that a Canadian headquarters was required. So came into being the Ottawa hostel called New Orpington Lodge, denoting its Southwark origin.

By 1901 the Liverpool Catholic Children's Protection Society was in low water so Arthur Chilton Thomas, manager of Father Berry's Homes and a barrister, suggested an amalgamation of emigration agencies for more economical and efficient working. The next year Father Bans and himself made a very complete survey of child emigration in Canada, and published a report which set new standards, and recommended a central organisation. Two years later the Catholic Emigration Association took over, with Father Hudson as secretary, and Coleshill as headquarters. The Montreal Hostel was closed, and the Ottawa hostel was renamed St. George's Home. The work was under the control of the rescue societies of Westminster, Southwark, Birmingham and Liverpool; the property was vested in the names of six English bishops; Sisters of Charity of St. Paul from Selly Park were placed in charge. The Home was finally closed in 1934 when emigration ceased after the slump of 1929, but in the intervening years thousands of children had been afforded a new life in a new world.

A fresh chapter opened in 1937 when an agreement was reached under Cardinal Hinsley with the Irish Christian Brothers in Western Australia whose Tardun scheme for boys was in the first class. The Sisters of Nazareth co-operated to look after girls. World War II interrupted this work, and changed conditions, especially the increase in adoptions, have reduced the need for emigration of children.

Monsignor Hudson, our leading authority on child care, founded the Catholic Child Welfare Council in 1929 as a consultative body for the diocesan rescue societies of the country with an annual conference. In its early years not many dioceses were represented; to-day it covers the whole of England and Wales, and is recognised both by the Children's Department, Home Office, and by the major voluntary societies as one of the leading organisations in the country. This is due mainly to the interest of the present Archbishop of Westminster, Cardinal Griffin, who was for several years in charge of the Birmingham Rescue Society and of Father Hudson's Homes until his elevation to the See of Westminster. While all his predecessors were concerned for the welfare of poor children, he is the first to have had actual experience of rescue work.

The latest development has been the formation of the National Council of Associated Children's Homes comprising the Catholic Child Welfare Council, Dr. Barnardo's Homes, the Church of England Children's Society, the National Home (Nonconformist), the Jewish Homes, and the Shaftesbury Homes, for consultation and common action. This is indicative of the change of attitude in the last hundred years, and provides a common front of great strength in approaches to the government in view of the Children Act, 1948. It is significant that the Catholic Child Welfare Council has in its care far more children than any other single body, actually about 15,000.

In its report on children deprived of a normal home life the Curtis Committee, which inspired the Children Act, 1948, paid a tribute to the work of religious having the care of children, mixed with criticism of the isolation of children in convent Homes, the lack of contact of both staff and children with the outside world, and the disadvantage to the children afterwards. It also stressed the need for training of staff of children's Homes, so it is interesting to record that the first full course approved by the Child Care Training Committee, Home Office, was for religious at the Holy Child Convent, Cavendish Square, London, W.1. About 20 religious are following this course each year, apparently a small number but due to the difficulty of sparing Sisters from depleted staffs.

The sad plight of both adults and children afflicted with physical or mental defect, as well as incurables, has ever been the object of Catholic charity which regards them as peculiarly " God's creatures." Provision for them was not always easy, nor was the general community quick to realise their need for classification and education. True the Catholic Blind Asylum for both children and adults was started in

U

Liverpool so long ago as 1841, but this was for long the only effort to provide for any class of defectives. Normally accommodation had to be found for the afflicted in ordinary institutions.

Sometimes a crisis arose, as when the Little Sisters of the Poor, not long established in London, accepted a child born with a head resembling a fish whom no one would care for because of its dreadful appearance. They were reprimanded by their superiors in France as their work was exclusively for old people, and the matter was ultimately referred to the Holy See. The decision was that they must keep their rule, but that any Sisters who were willing to do so might found a new order for such works of mercy. Cardinal Wiseman thereupon called to his help a Breton lady, Victoire Larmenier, who under his direction founded the Congregation of the Sisters of Nazareth to care for cripples and incurables as well as for poor children and old people. This first English foundation after the restoration of the Hierarchy has been of untold help; not only has it flourished exceedingly and set up Nazareth Houses in many large towns and cities of the British Isles, but has spread to the Dominions and to America. The appearance of the Sisters in their daily quest for alms is welcomed by both Catholics and others, and they have relieved the bishops of very heavy financial burdens.

The present Institution of St. John, Boston Spa, for the Deaf and Dumb owes its origin to Monsignor De Haerne, a member of the Belgian House of Representatives, who had done great service to the Deaf and Dumb in Belgium, India and Portugal, and who pioneered the work in England in 1869 in a cottage at Handsworth, Woodhouse, near Sheffield. He financed it for a time until Bishop Cornthwaite of Beverley accepted responsibility. In 1874 the Hierarchy recognised it as the Catholic Institution for Deaf and Dumb for the whole of England; it was transferred to Boston Spa, and the Sisters of Charity who had taken up work for the blind in Liverpool in 1872, now assumed the care of the deaf and dumb as well.

Children who were mentally or physically retarded received little attention from the Board of Education until the closing years of the last century. The Sisters of the Sacred Hearts of Jesus and Mary made this type of work largely their own. Founded by an Alsatian priest, Father Victor Braun, in 1866, they arrived in England in 1870 during the Franco-Prussian War. Their headquarters from 1873 to 1896 were at Homerton until they transferred their Mother House to Chigwell. In 1903 they were constituted an independent Congregation. Already in 1886 they had opened a Home for mentally defective girls at Sudbury; to-day they conduct schools under the Ministry of Education for mentally handicapped boys and girls, as well as open air schools, and schools for heart cases.

The Sisters of Charity were invited by Mr. Potter, St. Hugh's House, Clapham, in 1907, to help in his Cripples' Home; this was moved to Pinner in 1912 when it was certified by the Board of Education, and commenced hospital treatment. It is now a training school for orthopædic nurses. Monsignor Hudson started his orthopædic hospital at Coleshill soon afterwards, made it a training school, and took over the orthopædic clinics for the County of Warwickshire. The Daughters of the Cross opened a school for epileptics and a Home for adults at Much Hadham, Herts., still the only Catholic establishment of its kind.

For low grade mental defectives, men and boys, the Brothers Hospitallers of St. John, who are celebrating their fourth centenary this year, opened a colony at Barvin Park, Hatfield, and the Brothers of Charity of Ghent one at Lisieux Hall, Chorley. The girls and women are catered for at Durran Hill House, Carlisle, by the Sisters of the Sacred Hearts of Jesus and Mary, by the Sisters of Charity at Howard Hill, Sheffield, and by the Daughters of Wisdom at Chorley.

Girls needing protection are under the care of several Communities, but are the special care of the Order of the Good Shepherd. Another Congregation doing similar work is the Poor Servants of the Mother of God, an English foundation by Mother Magdalen Taylor, who was a companion of Florence Nightingale in the Crimea where she became a Catholic. Under the direction of Cardinal Manning and Lady Georgiana Fullerton she developed her work for girls in need, for children, and for nursing.

Many hospitals have been opened over the years by various Communities, and have received wide recognition for their devotion and efficiency, and it is of interest that they have been exempted from the 1948 National Health Service Act when nearly all others have been nationalised. Even the dying find provision under the Irish Sisters of Charity at Hackney, and the Sisters of Charity at St. Vincent's Hospice, Liverpool. For men and boys who are incurable there is the Hospital of St. John of God at Scorton, Yorks.

One social problem to which there has been a complete reversal of attitude in the last hundred years is that of the unmarried mother. Unless she could hide her downfall from the world she became an untouchable with no hand outstretched to help her or her child. No wonder the suicide rate was high, and the chances of survival of the baby correspondingly slight. She was faced with the workhouse or the baby farmer, and in too many cases the bodies of newly born babies were found in ashpits, in trunks, in left-luggage offices, in rivers; all too often verdicts of murder were returned against some person unknown. Some mothers left their babies on door-steps or in vestibules, praying that some kind soul would find and befriend them before it was too late.

The baby farmer flourished on a lump sum or a weekly payment, and soon drew the insurance money on the unfortunate child. Even sentences of hanging for murder did not stop the traffic, nor Acts of Parliament. The first Infant Life Protection Act was passed in 1872, but there were not enough officers to implement it. In 1897 another Act was intended to remedy admitted defects, but was still ineffective, and provisions in the Children Act, 1948, are a reminder that the need for vigilance is still urgent. Machinery on the voluntary side did not exist, and societies risked loss of support if they showed any pity on the ground that they were only encouraging the evil.

So far as Catholics were concerned the first effort to help in a constructive way by providing for both mother and baby, trying to keep them together and teach the mother to care for her baby, was made by the Sisters of the Sacred Hearts of Jesus and Mary when they opened St. Pelagia's Home, Highgate, in 1887. Ten years later Monsignor Nugent invited them to Liverpool to open a similar House of Providence. When he was 81 years of age he at last realised his ambition of setting up a Maternity Home for unmarried mothers which he named the House of Good Counsel. It proved to be too heavy a financial burden, and was closed at his death two years later. Still he had blazed a new trail, and to-day moral welfare work for the unmarried mother is an accepted task of all rescue societies, and religious such as the " Chigwell " nuns have specialised in this admittedly difficult work. One praiseworthy lay effort by the Catholic Women's League is St. Margaret's Home, Leeds.

The hard lot of the illegitimate child has been much lightened by a series of Adoption Acts since 1926 which have given legal security to adopters and to the child, making it a full member of the adopting family under the latest Act which has just come into force. For the deserted or illegitimate child, which may never belong to a family, adoption is surely God's plan, especially when we remember that the Church has recognised adoption from Roman times, and has regulated it in Canon Law. Most diocesan rescue societies have availed themselves of the facilities for adoption by registering as Adoption Societies, and they can point to many hundreds of homes made happy, and children given love and security through adoption.

Another curse of Victorian days was drink, which fell heaviest on the poor, as the gin palace offered an escape for a time from poverty and its attendant evils. In 1843 Father Mathew had campaigned over England for total abstinence with remarkable results here as elsewhere, but with the years the effects wore thin. All the bishops inveighed against the evil, but it was Cardinal Manning who established the League of the Cross in Westminster in 1872 about the same time as Father Nugent in Liverpool. So important did the Cardinal regard his campaign that he tried to attract Father Nugent to London to second his efforts. The Hierarchy were never at one on the question of total abstinence or temperance; Bishop Vaughan who followed the Cardinal on most subjects favoured temperance. Legislation restricting opening hours of public houses, and changing habits, reduced the evil to manageable proportions in the early years of this century.

The Cardinal with his strongly developed social sense considered it a duty of his office to engage in any schemes to ease the hard lot of the poor. He caused something of a sensation when he appeared on the platform at the Exeter Hall in 1872 in sympathy with the agricultural labourers, and he stood in isolation with Cardinal Gibbons of Baltimore when they pleaded the cause of the American Knights of Labour in 1887. Three years earlier he had been invited to serve on a Royal Commission on the housing of the working classes, and in 1889 he was instrumental in settling the long drawn-out London Dock Strike; he well earned the title of " The People's Cardinal." The encyclical *Rerum Novarum* on the Condition of the Working Classes issued by Pope Leo XIII in 1891, the year before the Cardinal's death, must have come to him as an approval of his attitude to the Social Question, of the lonely furrow he had ploughed; his advice had been sought before its publication.

Looking back over a hundred years one cannot fail to realise the change of pattern from the days of Economic Liberalism to the dawn of the Welfare State. Unrestricted competition has yielded place to a planned economy. Freedom to starve, or economic insecurity, has been swept away in favour of social security, at too great a price if it involves the loss of all economic freedom, and the suppression of voluntary action. The plight of our Catholic poor in those early days in a hostile Protestant society demanded the apostolic zeal of the bishops backed by the whole Catholic body if their spiritual welfare was to be safeguarded, and this they achieved mainly by a nation-wide network of institutions. Material destitution was then the root of the problem; to-day the danger lies in a growing moral destitution in a world which is no longer Christian. So the pattern of Catholic action has changed to meet the new conditions.

Catholic institutions are still needed though they also are in process of adaptation to more enlightened standards so far as these are on sound lines. Unfortunately there is a crisis in man-power because the flood of vocations of a century ago has now become a mere trickle, so the problem is to maintain present works while urgent demands have to be refused by the heads of religious congregations for new foundations, especially for the mentally and physically handicapped.

On the other hand more and more Catholic women are

qualifying for social work as a profession, and are holding posts of responsibility in the statutory social services. They too are working for the poor in a framework sadly in need of the influence of Christian principles where religious are not acceptable; so if to their profession they join a sense of vocation, as many do, what is lost in one way is gained in another. The more Catholics help to run the Welfare State the better for the whole community.

The expansion of lay effort in the Catholic body reached a high peak in the years of Cardinal Bourne at Westminster, though the St. Vincent de Paul Society now nation-wide had opened its first conference in London in 1844, 11 years after its foundation in Paris by Frederick Ozanam. To-day it numbers 1,140 Conferences with 8,770 Brothers, and until 25 years ago had no rivals in the field of Catholic lay charity. Its unobtrusive apostolate, seeking no publicity, has its roots deep in Catholic life, a refreshing oasis in a desert of forms and files.

Ireland sent us the Legion of Mary which stemmed from the St. Vincent de Paul Society, and was founded in 1921 by Frank Duff to do battle with the forces of moral destitution under the banner of Mary Immaculate, Mediatrix of all Graces. In its short life its works are legion, and its membership world-wide.

From Belgium came the Young Christian Workers' Movement started by Canon Cardijn in 1925 to attack and overcome the misery and the moral and spiritual wretchedness of working class youth. It is essentially a movement of action to Christianize the environment of work, and to conquer for God the whole life of the worker.

The Catholic Women's League was of native growth before World War I when the members organised clubs for Catholic mothers, as a preliminary to the start of the Union to Catholic Mothers as an independent body. They also saw to the welfare of women and girls emigrating to Canada, and during the two wars became well known through their success in managing canteens for the troops.

These and many other Catholic lay activities were approved by Pope Pius XI when he set up the Catholic Action movement, stressing the duty of the " participation of the laity in the Hierarchic Apostolate of the Church." The layman could no longer hide behind the habit of the religious, and claim that delegated charity was enough.

In his book *Voluntary Action* Lord Beveridge writes: " Diminished influence of the Churches must be taken as one of the changes in the environment of voluntary action." However true this may be of other denominations it is not true of the Catholic Church which has grown in stature and power and influence over the hundred years, so that in social legislation the State reacts on the whole favourably to the Catholic point of view, and may be said to encourage the voluntary co-opera-tion of Catholics where this is possible in statutory schemes. Maybe this is in no small measure due to the keenness of the present Archbishop of Westminster, Cardinal Griffin, who ensures that Catholic interests are adequately represented both personally and through the Catholic Union.

Perhaps that is the measure of difference between 1850 and 1950; from being a hated minority, poor in numbers and in fact, yet throwing all its reserves into the battle for the souls of its children and winning it, to-day the Catholic Church and its Hierarchy of the same metal are known and respected as the only sure guardians of the moral law in a world of Mammon.

XIX

TO-DAY AND TO-MORROW

By GEORGE ANDREW BECK, A.A.

IF an attempt is to be made to assess Catholic progress in this country over the last hundred years, a serious estimate of the present numerical strength of Catholicism ought to be undertaken.

How many Catholics are there in England and Wales to-day? The question, so expressed, must provoke further questioning. What are we to understand by a " Catholic "? Do we include all those baptised according to the Catholic rite, whatever their present religious practice? Or only those who regularly attend Mass and receive the sacraments? According to our choice between such extremes of definition there will clearly be vast difference in our estimates.

The figures published in *The Catholic Directory* year by year have been shown in a previous chapter to be reliable only in a very general way. They are assessments made by parish priests, checked to some extent by the Diocesan authorities, of the number of " practising " Catholics in each parish. Once again the description leaves room for wide divergence of assessment. A practising Catholic may be considered merely as one who has made his Easter Communion and who assists at Mass from time to time, or he may be taken to be a Catholic who is more or less regular in frequenting the sacraments, and perhaps absent from Mass on no more than a few Sundays during the year. It is thus no simple matter to assess, even from the statistics of Mass attendance or Easter duty, the number of Catholics in a parish. As to these, the figure for Easter duties seems, on the whole, to be slightly higher than that for average Mass attendance. Some examples may be of interest. The returns published for the Diocese of Southwark for the last five years are as follows: —

Year	Mass Attendance	Easter Duties
1945	92,702	101,129
1946	117,549	115,350
1947	113,044	121,825
1948	133,003	131,762
1949	144,731	144,190

It is interesting to note that similar figures for 1922 were 74,495 and 79,894. During a period of 27 years the Mass attendance in the Diocese of Southwark has almost doubled. It may be noted also that the estimated Catholic population in the Diocese in 1949 is given as 220,000; which means (using the ratios accepted in the Census of 1851) that 94 per cent. of the able-to-go population does, in fact, attend Mass.

Another example of increase in Catholic practice may be quoted from the Archdiocese of Cardiff. The figures for Mass attendance in 1931 were given as 33,255; in 1949 the figure was 43,956. On the other hand, similar figures for the Archdiocese of Liverpool are 205,476 and 190,724[1], and for the diocese of Salford the figures are 194,821 and 176,502. The Middlesbrough figures show a rise from 35,183 to 41,244. In the City of Birmingham[2] the figures for Easter duties be-

---

[1] The movement of population from Liverpool to parts of Cheshire and Lancashire is attested from other sources. In the Diocese of Hexham and Newcastle, the estimated Catholic population of Northumberland and Durham increased between the years 1921 and 1949 from 206,056 to 246,243. During the same period the Easter Communions increased by 37,322 and the average Sunday Mass attendance by 34,763.

[2] The following is a list of new Churches and Mass Centres opened in the Archdiocese of Birmingham since 1925:—

1928: Holy Family, Small Heath. 1929: Corpus Christi, Stechford (temporary); SS. Peter and Paul, Pype Hayes (temporary); St. Nicholas, Boldmere. 1930: St. Vincent de Paul, Ashted and Vauxhall. 1933: Our Lady of the Rosary and St. Teresa, Saltley; SS. Joseph and Helen, Kings Norton; St. Rose of Lima, Wooley Castle (temporary). 1934: St. Hubert, Warley; Our Lady and St. Gregory, Bearwood; Christ the King, King-

tween 1931 and 1948 have risen from 28,219 to 37,967. Perhaps the most remarkable increase is to be seen in the Diocese of Menevia where, between 1931 and 1949, the Mass attendance figures have risen from 7,415 to 12,250[3].

These figures have, of course, great interest for Catholics, but they do not tell the whole story nor do they relate the Catholic population to that of the whole country. A comparison of this nature can be made at 10-year intervals of the estimated Catholic population, as recorded in *The Catholic Directory*, with the general population as given by the Registrar General. The figures to the nearest 1,000 are given in the following table[4]: —

Year	General Population	Estimated Catholic Population
1911	36,224,000	1,793,000
1921	38,035,000	1,966,000
1931	40,507,000	2,414,000
1949	43,595,000	2,649,000

According to these figures it will be seen that since 1911 the Catholic population may be reckoned to have increased

standing (temporary); Holy Trinity, Sutton Coldfield. 1935: Our Lady of Lourdes, Yardley Wood (temporary). 1936: St. Brigid, Northfield; St. Thomas More, Sheldon (temporary). 1937: Our Lady of the Wayside, Shirley, Birmingham; SS. Mary and John, Gravelly Hill; St. Margaret Mary, Perry Common. 1938: The Holy Name of Jesus, Great Barr. 1939: St. Augustine's Handsworth. 1940: Sacred Heart and Holy Souls, Acocks Green. 1947: St. Teresa, Perry Bar; Mass said in Bradford Arms, Castle Bromwich.

[3] This development in Menevia is further illustrated by the big increase in the number of convents, which has more than doubled since 1913.

[4] The general population figures for 1949 are taken from the Registrar General's *Estimate of the Population of England and Wales* at June 30th, 1949. We may remember that in 1851 the general population was 17,928,000 and the Catholic population has been estimated to have been 700,000.

from under 5 per cent. to over 6 per cent. of the general population.

Most students of this question are persuaded that the figures of the " Estimated Catholic Population " given in *The Catholic Directory* for each diocese are, in fact, very much lower than they ought to be. Returns of the religious denominations of men serving in the armed forces during the war gave a Catholic proportion of almost 11 per cent. To offset premature conclusions from that figure, however, it has been pointed out that, as the Catholic population is admittedly growing steadily, the percentage of Catholics in the younger age groups which were called to national service would be higher than the average for the country, and that, secondly, it must be remembered that both Irish and Scottish recruits served in the armed forces—the former as volunteers in considerable numbers and the latter having a higher percentage of Catholics in their number than is general in England.

A different basis of calculation would be the comparison between the number of Catholic baptisms per year compared with the number of live births in the same year. It may be assumed that Catholic children are in the vast majority of cases baptised within a few weeks of birth and that, in consequence, over a period of several years the baptismal statistics may be taken to represent fairly accurately the Catholic birthrate. The following table gives the elements of this calculation:—

Year	Total Live Births to nearest 1,000	Catholic Infant Baptisms	Catholic Percentage of Total Births
1941	579,000	67,119	11.6
1942	652,000	69,005	10.6
1943	684,000	70,015	10.2
1944	751,000	71,664	9.6
1945	680,000	73,410	10.8
1946	821,000	85,024	10.3
1947	886,000	95,910	10.8

It would seem, from these figures, that it is not unfair to reckon the Catholic population of England and Wales at approximately 10 per cent. of the total population—this, of course, on the assumption that every baptised child continues to be considered a Catholic. The estimate, however, does not take into account immigration, which has undoubtedly increased the number of Catholics in the country since 1939. There are, for example, in the country at the present time, 92 Polish priests who are looking after the welfare of Polish and Central European emigrants whose numbers run to about two hundred thousand. Similarly, no account is taken in these statistics of the immigration from Ireland which in recent years must have been in the neighbourhood of several thousands per year[5].

Finally, in this estimate no account has been taken of the annual number of conversions to Catholicism. Before the war these had grown steadily from over 9,000 in 1917 to 12,065 in 1927, 12,372 in 1928 and 12,075 in 1929. A steady rate of over 12,000 a year was maintained until 1935 when the number declined to 11,648. The figure for 1936 was 10,617 and for 1937 10,651[6].

During the war years, the number of conversions fell off considerably, and the lowest number was reached in 1943 with a total of 8,319. Since the war there has been a steady increase from 10,363 in 1946 and 10,594 in 1947 to 11,520 in 1948. Figures for 1949 are not yet available.

It would seem from the above general survey that the Catholic population of the country—counting as Catholics, the good, the bad and the indifferent—may be estimated to be at least 4,300,000 and quite possibly very near the round figure of 5,000,000.

This general conclusion can be supported from a number of isolated pieces of information. Thus a social survey

[5] According to the census figures, in 1911 there were in this country 375,300 people who were born in Ireland. In 1921 the figure was 364,700, and in 1931 381,100. Everybody is aware that the figure has greatly increased in recent years.

[6] It has been suggested that the Italian Campaign in Abyssinia and the Spanish Civil War had an effect on the general attitude towards Catholicism in this country, and that this may have had some influence on the number of conversions. It is possible that the present change of attitude towards Russia, and the recognition of the part which is being played by European Catholics in resisting Communism, may lead to a more sympathetic attitude towards the Church and a possible increase in the number of conversions. This change of attitude is manifest in the article " Catholicism To-day " published in *The Times* for October 31st, 1949,and discussed on a later page.

of the Tyneside made in 1925 and published in 1928 shows from several points of view that in the Diocese of Hexham and Newcastle Catholics are approximately 9.7 per cent. of the population. In 1924 Catholic marriages were 98 per 1,000 in Northumberland and 101 per 1,000 in Durham. The survey remarks that if the number of Catholic infant baptisms in the whole Diocese, given as 7,434, is correct, and if the general proportion between infants and adults holds good, there must be a Catholic population on Tyneside of 104,500, which is over 12 per cent. of the whole population[7].

A comparison of the number of Catholic and non-Catholic children in Liverpool over a number of years provides another indication of the relative size of the Catholic population. *The Social Survey of Merseyside*, edited by D. C. James and published in 1934, discusses at some length the decline of the Catholic birthrate in relation to the general birthrate of the borough[8].

For the purpose of our present calculations the decline in the birthrate is not important, but a comparison of the numbers in columns (3) and (4) in the table on the opposite page are of interest. They suggest that the Catholics in the city are between 36 per cent. and 40 per cent. of the total population.

---

[7] *See Industrial Tyneside*, by H. E. Mess (Ernest Benn, 1928), p. 135. The survey continues: " If the figures are correct, about 18 per cent. of infants born on Tyneside are baptised by Roman Catholic priests. . . . In Newcastle in 1926 nearly 16 per cent. of all children in public elementary schools were in Roman Catholic schools; in Jarrow in the same year the percentage was over 30.

" There are no figures published or available showing the number of adults on Tyneside who are either nominally or in any real sense Roman Catholics.

" The general effect of the figures is to suggest that the Roman Catholic population is about one-eighth of the total population on Tyneside; in some areas, especially Jarrow, Hebburn and Blaydon, the proportion would be a good deal higher. It can scarcely be doubted that the Roman Catholics are the strongest denomination on Tyneside. They have increased in numbers very considerably in the past ten or fifteen years, and they are active in building churches and schools. Influxes of Irish labourers at various periods in the past have done much to build up their strength. Their birthrate is high; it can be deduced from several sets of figures that it is nearly 40 per cent. in excess of that of the rest of the population; this is explainable in part by their strength in the poorer areas, and in part also by the well-known Roman Catholic opposition to limitation of families."

[8] See Vol. III, Note 1, pp. 547-552.

The following table is given on page 547 of *The Social Survey of Merseyside*: —

ANALYSIS BY AGE OF CHILDREN IN ELEMENTARY AND SECONDARY SCHOOLS
(Liverpool, March 31st, 1931)

Born Year Ended March 31st (1)	Age Last Birthday (2)	Number of Children in		Numbers in Index Form		Index of Liverpool Birthrate for Years shown in Col. (1) (7)
		R.C. Schools (3)	Non-R.C. Schools (4)	R.C. Schools (5)	Non-R.C. Schools (6)	
1918	13	3,522	8,579	68	70	75
1919	12	3,829	8,503	74	69.5	73
1920	11	5,333	12,217	102	100	84
1921	10	5,199	12,242	100	100	100
1922	9	5,472	12,092	105	99	89
1923	8	4,994	11,216	96	92	86.5
1924	7	4,900	11,171	94	91	84
1925	6	4,512	10,898	87	89	82
1926	5	3,431	8,549	66	70	79

Finally, from one of the new housing estates near London the following situation has emerged. It was calculated by the Essex Education Committee that the number of children of primary school age who would require accommodation on the L.C.C. Debden estate would be 1,950.   The Catholic authorities, arguing that 10 per cent. of these children would be Catholics, asked for the provision of a Catholic primary school for 195 children.   According to a recent census, in spite of the fact that only 1,988 houses have been completed out of an ultimate total of 3,850, the number of Catholic children of primary school age on the estate is already 210.   The figures suggest that Catholics on this housing estate will be between 16 per cent. and 20 per cent. of the total population.

The most satisfactory figures would be, as Monsignor Knox has pointed out, the statistics of the number of Catholic funerals year by year.   This would take account of the number of Catholics who lapse, but who end their lives at peace with God and fortified by the sacraments.   It is unfortunate, as Monsignor Knox points out, that " nobody seems to make this lugubrious computation."

Until we have such figures, we may leave the question of the exact number of Catholics in England and Wales as, in practice, insoluble, and content ourselves with saying that the presumption is strong that Catholics born in England and Wales number about 4,300,000 and that the total Catholic population, counting immigrants from Europe and Ireland, must be approximately 5,000,000[9].

[9] A Gallup poll taken in 1947 gave the number of Catholics in England and Wales as 8.7 per cent. of the total population. Fr. C. Maguire in the *Catholic Gazette* for March and April, 1949, estimates the total number at about 3¾ millions.

It has been suggested that had all Catholics remained faithful to their religion and, in particular, had they brought up their children in the Catholic faith, the number of Catholics in this country at the present time would be nearer ten than five million. This is true more particularly of the Irish immigrants of whom a number, separated from their native land, often isolated from the Church and from contact with their own priests, gradually, and almost inevitably, drifted away from the practice of their religion. It is a common experience for priests to find, and particularly in country districts, families with Irish names who, at some moment in the past, turned to one or other of the Nonconformist bodies because there were no facilities for the practice of their own religion. The following

There are signs, however, that, although the percentage of Catholics in the population may remain about the same, a decline in the total number of Catholics may be in sight. Everybody is aware, particularly since the publication of the *Report of the Royal Commission on Population*, that the number of births in this country is about 6 per cent. below replacement level. It is difficult to determine the average size of Catholic families, but a comparison of the ratio of Catholic baptisms to marriages with the ratio of births to marriages for the whole country provides food for reflection. It is possible to obtain the ratio of births to marriages by dividing the number of births for each year by the number of marriages for the same year. This does not give exactly the size of the average family, but it shows the trend which the size of the family is following.

The birth/marriage ratio for the whole country has declined steadily since the beginning of the century. It was 2.6 in 1922, 2.0 in 1932 and 1.25 in 1940. It recovered to 2.48 in 1944 and has been about 2.0 since the war. The Catholic ratio has decreased from 3.49 in 1922 to 2.0 in 1945. It has recovered since then to 2.39 in 1946, 2.75 in 1947 and 2.58 in 1948. It is estimated that a birth/marriage ratio of at least 2.6 is required to enable the population of this country to

quotation from a letter recently addressed to the author from Ireland seems to sum up the position:—

" Old Canon — of — told me of a street of Nonconformist shops every one of which bore a Catholic Irish name. In my own experience, I have met so many old people whose parents came from Ireland but who had never seen a priest or heard Mass in their lives. How can they be expected to call themselves Catholics? Can they be blamed? Only lately in Kent I asked a farmer's wife why she did not attend the Anglican Church which was ten yards from their prosperous farm. She confessed she was Irish; had come over as a land girl in the first world war; married her employer and never gone home or to Mass. I met an old lady in a London hotel which she owned. She had been a barefooted girl on this estate and had six Cockney sons all Protestants. I offered to drive her to Mass if she came home and so on, and so on. . . . The army proportion was good because there were Chaplains, but only roving pastoral Chaplains could collect the strayed sheep to-day."

It is recognised, both here and in Ireland, that this problem is due, in great measure, to shortage of priests, and that a solution lies in more close contact and organisation between the clergy in this country and in the parishes from which the immigrants set out.

replace itself and it seems clear that the Catholic reproduction rate has fallen below this in the past decade and is, at the present moment, just on the border line. *The Report of the Royal Commission on Population* sums up the position, as follows: " There is some evidence—though the statistical information on the subject is scanty—that the trend of family size has differed between people of different religious affiliation. The decline has been slower among Roman Catholics than among Protestants. But the extent of the difference can easily be overstated; there is little doubt that average family size has declined greatly even among the Roman Catholics. Moreover, Roman Catholics of different occupational groups seem to differ in average family size in very much the same way as do non-Catholics."[10]

One question which arises from the consideration of the size of the Catholic population is the provision which needs to be made for the education of Catholic children. Earlier

[10] Para. 72, p. 27.

The reasons for this decline are outside the scope of the present chapter, but it may be worth while to remark that Dr. Lewis-Faning's survey seems to indicate a growing prevalence of birth prevention practices among Catholics. See *Family Limitation and its influence on human fertility during the past fifty years* (Papers of the Royal Commission on Population, Volume I, H.M.S.O., 1949, Table 60, p. 81). See also the remarks made by Dr. H. P. Newsholme in a paper entitled " Family Limitation " published in the *Christian Democrat*, May, 1950.

" The second point in possible palliation is that, of 394 Catholic women questioned, only 269 were married to Catholics, while 122 were married to Protestants and three to men of no religion. It may be that these 125 mixed marriages were predominantly responsible for the 140 cases (as calculated from a table supplied in the Report) in which . . . methods of birth control had been employed. Whatever the extent to which this may reduce the gravity of the charge against so large a proportion of the more recently married Catholics in relation to their manner of family limitation, obviously there is here matter for most serious consideration by Catholics at large.

" There has, in fact, been exposed to our troubled gaze, an ulcer in the body Catholic, an ulcer poisonous to Catholic life in many directions. What is needed is the cautery, whether of human discipline, or of the divine discipline of the Holy Spirit, cleansing, renewing health of outlook, and giving insight and strength of purpose whereby these Catholic couples can recognize and follow the way of married life which God intends for them."

chapters in this book have dealt at considerable length with the history of the Schools' Question, particularly since 1870. The struggle of the Catholic body to make provision for the education of its children has been long and arduous, with recurrent periods of acute crisis, such as those which occurred in 1870, 1902, 1906-8 and of which the " Schools' Crisis " to-day is but another example. The history of the Catholic effort has been one of financial scraping and scratching, of piecemeal and inadequate building, and of heroic sacrifice on the part of the priests, teachers and people. Before 1902 the prospect facing the Catholic lay-teacher was one of hard work under difficult conditions with the constant possibility of being asked to forgo part of the already inadequate salary which the managers of the school had promised to raise.

The ultimate reasons for this insistence by Catholics on a Catholic education for their children is perhaps still not sufficiently understood by non-Catholics. It is true that Catholics are concerned in a general way with demanding freedom of conscience and the natural rights of parents to determine the kind of education which they wish their children to receive. It is true, equally, that the Catholic clergy recognise that in the schools they have the most powerful means of ensuring that the rising generation of young Catholics shall grow up in the knowledge and practice of their religion.

Fundamentally, however, the Catholic attitude to education is, in this country at least, unique. It is not concerned with sectarian advantages or ecclesiastical privilege. It is concerned with something much deeper, the very pith and marrow of education; for the Catholic has an answer, and a complete answer, to the question which even the educationists to-day seem less and less willing to face—what is the purpose of this process, what is it all for? The Catholic concept of the purpose of education has been brilliantly summed up by Mr. H. O. Evennett in his little book entitled *The Catholic Schools of England and Wales*: —

" The hierarchy of values taught by Catholicism is one which runs directly counter to much modern social and moral ideology. It runs counter not only to those idealisms which are constructed upon a frankly secular or hedonistic basis but also to others which would turn, in the chaos of

modern standards, either towards some misty nationalistic
ethic or towards a Christianity interpreted on humanitarian
lines. Death and original sin are the constants in the light of
which the Catholic Church surveys humanity. Life is a
preparatory stage and its values are secondary; fallen man
is a being with a warped nature, doomed during this
planetary stage of his existence to an endless struggle
between an unquenchable propensity towards evil and an
equally unquenchable, nostalgic, striving towards the good,
a struggle in which he is powerfully assisted by the Christian
revelation and its dispensation of Divine Grace. If education
is what remains after we have forgotten all we learnt at
school, the quintessential left by a Catholic education is a
lasting consciousness of the fact and the meaning of death.
Catholic children are brought up to regard death not as some
unhappy, inexplicable fatality which blots the fair cosmic
landscape, and the mention of which embarrasses their
elders, but as the appointed gateway to the next life, through
which all must pass at some moment not of their own choosing. When their school friends die, or their parents, they
find the phenomenon naturally provided for, both ritually
and conversationally. Like the subject of religion itself,
death is spoken of freely and without awkwardness in the
Catholic school. It is the constant theme of Retreats and
Sodality talks. To pass through the gateway of death in the
best possible dispositions towards God and with the best
possible record of behaviour is the very object of life itself,
the purpose for which character is formed and the moral
virtues and even the intellectual faculties fostered. After
death, self-realisation in and through the Beatific Vision in
an eternal happiness, of which we can here form no sensuous
or intellectual concept, is the final end of Man."[11]

---

[11] *op. cit.*, pp. 124-5. The same idea, lacking the clear-cut Catholic
expression, is put forward in the introduction to the Norwood
Report:—

    " We believe that education cannot stop short of recognising
    the ideal of truth and beauty and goodness as final and binding
    for all times and in all places, as ultimate values; we do not
    believe that these ideals are of temporary convenience only, as
    devices for holding together society till they can be dispensed with
    as knowledge grows and organisation becomes more scientific.
    Further, we hold that the recognition of such values implies, for

It is the Catholic claim that there can be no complete conception of education which does not take into consideration the final end of man; and if this is admitted, the necessity for Christian education at once becomes apparent. Pope Pius XI in his encyclical letter on Christian Education has summed up the whole argument in a paragraph: —

" It is therefore as important to make no mistake in education as it is to make no mistake in the pursuit of the last end, with which the whole work of education is intimately and necessarily connected. In fact, since education consists essentially in preparing man for what he must be and for what he must do here below in order to attain the sublime end for which he was created, it is clear that there can be no true education which is not wholly directed to man's last end, and that in the present order of Providence, since God has revealed Himself to us in the Person of His Only Begotten Son, who alone is ' the way, the truth and the life,' there can be no ideally perfect education which is not Christian education."

It is because these eternal and absolute values are involved that Catholic parents and the Catholic clergy adopt such a rigid and apparently " exclusive " attitude on the question of education and insist that the only satisfactory formula is that which makes the school an extension of the home so far as its philosophy of life is concerned, and that the ideal to be sought in season and out of season is that every

most people at least, a religious interpretation of life which for us must mean the Christian interpretation of life. We have no sympathy, therefore, with a theory of education which presupposes that its aim can be dictated by the provisional findings of special Sciences, whether biological, psychological or sociological, that the function of education is to fit pupils to determine their outlook and conduct according to the changing needs and the changing standards of the day. We agree wholeheartedly that scientific method and scientific planning can do much to help in the realisation of the ' good life,' and education which does not avail itself of such aid denies itself one means to the realisation of its ends. But our belief is that education from its own nature must be ultimately concerned with values which are independent of time or particular environment, though realisable under changing forms in both, and therefore that no programmes of education which concern themselves only with relative ends and the immediate adaptation of the individual to existing surroundings can be acceptable."
Curriculum and Examinations in Secondary Schools, H.M.S.O., 1943, p. viii.

Catholic child shall be given a Catholic education by Catholic teachers in an appropriate Catholic school[12].

To some extent, the test of a genuine Catholic outlook on life may be seen in the determination of Catholic parents to send their children to a Catholic school and so carry out the duty which binds their conscience to equip these children as well as possible for the attainment of their last end, which is the very purpose of life. It must, therefore, be cause for some anxiety in the Catholic body that, of the total number of

---

[12] The Communist menace has brought home to many people more vividly than any Catholic propaganda the immense importance of the personal influence exercised on his pupils by the teacher. This was recognised some years ago by the Norwood Committee who, in their Report, included the following passage :—

" In the same way the phrases ' the balance of the curriculum ' and ' breadth of curriculum ' and ' all-round curriculum ' seem to be misleading and indeed to have misled. The phrase ' the balance of curriculum ' throws the emphasis in the wrong place; subjects are not in themselves complementary or antithetic or even antidotic to one another, as they sometimes seem to be regarded; a broad curriculum is not necessarily one in which a large number of subjects is carried continuously through successive forms; nor, we suspect, is the all-round pupil as common as is often assumed when curricula are under construction. To say that a pupil who gives much time to Natural Science should also give some time to English does not mean that of itself Natural Science needs an antidote in the shape of English; but that on the whole, and only on the whole, the scientific interests of pupils, if wrongly guided, attract their attention away from general reading and from standards of clear and easy expression. The curriculum cannot be balanced by opposing, say, Art or Music to the study of Languages or Mathematics. A broad education might be based upon very few subjects handled by a teacher with breadth of outlook. We labour this point because we feel that we are here dealing not merely with a kind of shorthand employed for brevity's sake by those who are engaged in teaching, but with something which has gone deeper, namely, a tendency to regard subjects as having claims in their own right both absolutely and in relation to others without real regard for the supreme consideration, which is the special aptitudes and abilities of the pupils themselves. In the same way we think it difficult to find any principle of what is called integrating the curriculum if it is to take place round a subject or a group of subjects, still less round a single idea, as, for example, leisure or self-expression or activity or citizenship. If anything is to be integrated, it is not the curriculum that must be integrated, but the personality of the child; and this can be brought about, not by adjustment of subjects as such, but by the realisation of his purpose as a human being, which, in turn, can be brought about only by contact with minds conscious of a purpose for him. Only the teacher can make a unity of a child's education by promoting the unity of his personality in terms of purpose."

children who are baptised Catholics, some 30 per cent. fail to find their way into a Catholic school[13].

This figure may well represent the proportion of baptised Catholics who are no longer active in the practice of their religion and who should be deducted from the estimated total of 5,000,000, if the number of " practising " Catholics is to be assessed.

The fact that the 1944 Education Act has made it necessary to survey and plan on a national scale for the provision of Catholic primary and secondary education will probably mean a greater effort than ever to secure that Catholic children do get into Catholic schools. On the other hand, as has been pointed out in an earlier chapter, the mere figures for attendance in Catholic schools may be misleading. Thus, in a survey which was made for the Hierarchy in 1948, it was found that, in the Catholic boarding and day schools catering for boys and girls, out of a total 68,234 pupils 22,521 were non-Catholics; that in girls' boarding schools 47 per cent. of the pupils were non-Catholics and that the figure in the day schools was 42 per cent.

Finally, it may be worth noting that while, in 1947, 27,000 Catholic girls over the age of eleven were in Catholic boarding and grammar schools, the corresponding number for Catholic boys was only 19,000[14].

These figures provoke, of course, a number of reflections. Convent-school education must hold powerful attractions, apart from religion, for non-Catholic parents. In some cases it may be the comparative cheapness of the Convent-school fees which has been a decisive factor; in other cases ease of travel or proximity to the home. But these are not by any means the only reasons. " The influence of these schools is great," wrote Sir Michael Sadler as long ago as 1906, " and the visitor who is allowed to become acquainted with them cannot fail to feel the charm of their refinement." This refinement and its charm have readily attracted non-Catholic parents, and persuaded them to entrust their daughters to the care and influence of the sisters and nuns of

[13] On this question, see *The Tablet*, February 1, 1947.
[14] For details see *Report of the Fifty-first Annual Conference of Catholic Colleges*, pp. 23-28.

the various Catholic teaching orders. (It may be noted that they seem less ready to entrust their sons to the teaching orders of priests or brothers.)

One result of these contacts in childhood will be a steady decrease in anti-Catholic prejudice, and a growing toleration of, and even admiration for, Catholic educational methods. What effect such early influences will have on the souls of these non-Catholic girls and on their ultimate destiny is another question. While there are many who maintain that the seeds of conversion to Catholicism have been sown in childhood, and schools which can point to an impressive number of " Old Girl " converts, there are not wanting those who wonder whether the early contact with Catholic things may not, in fact, produce a form of spiritual inoculation which greatly lessens the impact of Catholicism in later life—an impact which has often been the prelude to conversion.

From the Catholic side, too, there must be grave disquiet at the situation which must exist in those schools where a substantial majority of the girls are not Catholics. Such a situation is a denial in practice of the constantly repeated Catholic claim that we look upon education as a homogeneous and integrated process demanding that Catholic atmosphere which can be supplied only by Catholic teachers and Catholic companions.

One of the underlying principles of the 1944 Education Act, almost unnoticed at first but gradually making itself evident, is the principle that public money shall not be used to assist in the provision of new voluntary school places. In view of the fact that about 30 per cent. of baptised Catholic children are not at present in Catholic schools, it will be recognised that the application of this principle will cause additional financial injustice to the Catholic body in this country.

The great problem for the future will be to find the means whereby the rights of parents, in the matter of education, will be fully recognised, and the present grave financial handicaps which Catholic parents, and others too, now suffer for conscience's sake be thus finally brought to an end. The Catholic community will, it is to be hoped, continue to increase, both absolutely, and in relation to the rest of the population; there is a clear need of administrative machinery which would take account of this growth and relate the facts to the whole question of school provision.

Whatever the size of the Catholic population in this country, Catholic activities seem, at least on paper, to abound. *The Catholic Almanac and Year Book for* 1950 gives a list of 88 Catholic Societies in England and Wales. These Societies cover every aspect of Catholic life from such important and long-standing organisations as *The Apostleship of the Sea,* the *Catholic Education Council,* the *Catholic Evidence Guild,* the *Catholic Truth Society,* and the *Society of St. Vincent de Paul,* to more recent organisations such as *The Catholic Marriage Advisory Council,* the *League of Christ the King,* and the *Sword of the Spirit.* There are also those which have a more restricted appeal, such as the *Apostolate of St. Margaret Mary, St. Cecilia's Guild of Catholic Braillists,* or the *Society of the Magnificat.*

Even a glance at such a list makes clear at once how very serious is the problem of organising Catholic activity, of avoiding unnecessary multiplication of effort, and of preventing overlapping of interest; and how far we still are from the solution. To some extent the existing state of things hinders the work of Catholic lay action. The various societies are concerned either with a particular aspect of Catholic life or the interests and activities of a particular Catholic group. They are not, in the papal sense, Societies for Catholic Action, and they do not seem adapted to the purpose of the Catholic lay apostolate on which Pope Pius XI, and the present Holy Father, have laid such emphasis. The real meaning of Catholic Action has yet to be fully understood, while the implications and organisation of the Catholic lay apostolate have not yet been worked out fully in this country. A great deal has been done in one particular sphere, by means of an adaptation of the Belgian and French technique of the *Jeunesse Ouvrière Chrétienne,* and with the guidance of specially selected priests, to develop the working-class apostolate through the Young Christian Workers. The movement is as yet small in numbers, but it is already exercising a considerable, if restricted, Catholic influence among younger people in the working classes. The question of " Catholic Action " and of the lay apostolate as such, however, has yet to be fully thought out for this country[15].

Reference was made in the first chapter of this book to the establishment in Salford diocese under Bishop Casartelli of the Salford Diocesan Federation. An attempt was made by Cardinal Bourne at a later date to establish a similar federation in the Archdiocese of Westminster. A national body on such lines might be the means of co-ordinating Catholic action[16].

The National Catholic Congresses of pre-war years, held in one after another of the leading cities of the country, although intended mainly to establish means of contact between Catholics, and to encourage Catholics from time to time to take stock of their position, had nevertheless an important influence on local non-Catholic opinion through the numbers which attended them. It may be hoped that these demonstrations of Catholic strength—of particular importance in a mass age—will be revived in the near future.

It seems to be generally admitted that the influence of the Catholic community in England on public life is by no means commensurate with its size, and there seems to be a good case for arguing that, at least until very recent years, this influence has been throughout the greater part of this

---

[15] The Headquarters of the Movement, 43, Offley Road, London, S.W.9, produces important periodical and leaflet literature. Perhaps its spirit and work are best indicated in *Marriage Training Courses* or in the well-produced *New Life*, the monthly review of the workers' apostolate.

[16] At the National Catholic Congress held at Manchester in 1926, the following resolution, proposed by Canon Sharrock, was passed at the Catholic Confederation Meeting:—

" That this Conference appeals to the Catholic body to recognise that Catholic interests demand the formation of one organisation which will gather together the Catholic forces for the promotion and defence of those interests whenever they are attacked by anti-Catholic or non-Catholic forces; an organisation which will unite individuals, parishes and associations without destroying the individuality of either; an organisation which will feed all associations and be fed by them; an organisation which will demand no more from its members than the word ' Catholic ' demands; an organisation which knows no distinction of race, language, sex, class or party; and an organisation which organises Clergy and Laity, and fosters corporate initiative and corporate expression under the guidance of ecclesiastical authority; and, for these reasons, asks the Catholic body to support the Catholic Confederation of England and Wales."

century steadily declining. It has been said that the height of Catholic influence was reached about the period when the Liberal Government of 1906 took office. The Irish influence in the House of Commons was then at its strongest and was later to die away almost entirely. Nothing in Catholic public life has replaced it. A small number of the Catholic gentry and aristocracy still exercised some influence—an afterglow perhaps of the Victorian era under Manning—in a society very different indeed from the society of to-day in which privilege and traditional position are, if anything, a handicap so far as influence on public opinion is concerned. But economic pressure alone, apart from other considerations, is inevitably restricting the opportunity for the exercise of that influence. In this respect, the structure of the Catholic community has changed and is changing rapidly. If there has been a dispersal, particularly since 1939, of the close-knit Catholic centres, and if the migration of industry southward has meant the thinning of Catholic ranks in the northern industrial areas, there has been, at the same time, a deeper Catholic penetration and influence in the middle-classes. In the suburbs round the big cities the typical Catholic is no longer the labourer or the small shopkeeper. Black-coated workers, civil servants, men with responsible positions in Government Departments, in banks and insurance houses, are representative Catholics to-day, together with the owners of small businesses and managers of the big firms. There has been an Irish immigration of a different kind in the medical and the nursing professions, while English-born Catholics and a growing number of educated converts have produced a more balanced and homogeneous community than at any time since the Reformation[17].

Politically, since the withdrawal of the Irish Members, the Catholic influence has, on the whole, been negligible, although the organisation of a " Schools' Campaign " prior to the General Election of February, 1950, was not without success. In general, however, it would seem that Catholics are not actively interested in politics and, apart from the

[17] The steadily improving academic achievements of our Catholic schools is a most encouraging sign. During the year 1949-50 more than 61 Catholic boys gained University open scholarships or exhibitions. The success of Ampleforth, with 17 such awards, was outstanding.

question whether such a policy would be wise, the possibilities of success for the occasionally mooted Catholic Party are not worth consideration.

On the other hand, there are great potentialities in the Catholic body for exercising an influence on specific points of social policy. Such organisations as the Knights of St. Columba have the means of directing large numbers of men to the study of a specific question and, in a more active way, to the holding of large meetings and demonstrations. The best example of lay organisation in recent years has been the formation of Catholic Parents' Associations throughout the country. These associations came into existence at the time when the Education Bill was being discussed in 1943 and their purpose is specifically the protection of parental rights in all social questions, but particularly in education. The organisation is not uniform and there are, for example, associations of both Catholic parents and Catholic parents and electors. Some of the parochial units are particularly strong and active and diocesan organisations with marked initiative and ability are in existence in Salford, Southwark, Leeds and Nottingham. Diocesan organisation is being developed in other parts of the country.

Indeed, it seems clear that, as the distinction between Catholicism and materialism grows sharper, there may be fewer and fewer opportunities of close working together even in the merely political or economic field. As religion is essential to the Catholic, colouring the whole of his outlook even on matters not themselves immediately religious, and as religion becomes more and more irrelevant to the problem of living so far as the materialist is concerned, so will it become more difficult for the Catholic to make those compromises or concessions through which co-operation has been possible. The " other-worldliness " in a Catholic must always be his dominant, if not immediately evident, characteristic. Only in function of this eternal outlook can the " this-worldly " activity of Catholicism be rightly appreciated and understood.

Immediately there arises the question of the place of the layman in the Church and of that proper sharing of the apostolic work of the Hierarchy by the layman which is the core of Catholic action. It has been well said that the Church of Christ is not a society in which there is a governing class. Every member of the Church is a subject of the Church, dependent on the Church's teaching, profiting by the Church's sacraments, subject to the Church's discipline. It is true that there is an *ecclesia docens* and an *ecclesia discens*, but the distinction is not between activity and passivity in the Church. The reception of a sacrament is not merely a passive acceptance, it is *doing* something in the Church and is, in fact, an act of priesthood; the sacramental character impressed on the soul by baptism and confirmation is not just the image of Christ in a general way but is specifically the image of Christ as Priest. Pope Pius XII, in his Encyclical Letter " Mediator Dei " on Christian worship, reminds us that the prayers which the priest says at the Offertory of the Mass are for the most part in the plural and that they indicate that the people have a part in the sacrifice as being offerers of it. " And there is no wonder that the faithful are accorded this privilege: by reason of their baptism Christians are in the Mystical Body and become by a common title members of Christ the Priest; by the ' character ' that is graven upon their souls they are appointed to the worship of God, and therefore, according to their condition, they share in the priesthood of Christ Himself."[18]

It has always been the teaching of the Church, and is specifically so stated by St. Thomas, that the sacramental character is *ad recipiendum vel tradendum aliis ea quae pertinent ad cultum Dei,* and St. Thomas says roundly that these sacramental characters are nothing else than *quaedam participationes sacerdotii Christi*[19].

---

[18] C.T.S. translation, *Christian Worship*, para. 92, p. 43.

[19] On this point, and on the position of the layman in the Church, see the remarkable paper by Father Philip Hughes entitled " The Constitution of the Church " published in the collection of papers read to The Thomas More Society entitled *Under God and the Law*, edited by Richard O'Sullivan (Basil Blackwell, Oxford). After outlining the effect of the sacramental character in the three sacraments of Baptism, Confirmation and Holy Order, Father Hughes adds the following comment:—

" It is in this doctrine that we shall find the key to all the problems of cleric versus layman, and the rule for the conduct of each *vis-à-vis* the other; we shall also find, in the neglect of the cleric to understand this doctrine, to preach it and to apply it, the solution of many dark mysteries in the past history of the Church."

It is perhaps in the realm of literature and philosophical thought—using the term in a very wide sense—that the Catholic influence is more marked at the present time than since the beginning of the century. Novels such as *The Power and the Glory*, *Brideshead Revisited* and *The Heart of the Matter*, have presented the problem of Catholic living in a pagan world in its starkness while, from another point of view, *Late Have I Loved Thee* and *All Glorious Within* show the appeal which Catholicism can make in the midst of modern incertitude. It is this approach to religion, and particularly to Catholicism, which is most easily made to-day, and is a subject of discussion and conversation, wider perhaps than at any time since the height of the Tractarian Movement.   Such adventures into a philosophy of life as T. S. Eliot's *The Cocktail Party* or Charles Morgan's *The Voyage* reveal the hunger for certitude and security, and the readiness to look for that " harder way," which the Catholic knows so well to exist in the Church, which gives him so serene a sense of certitude and security, and which he finds it so difficult to realise that others do not see.

If there is at the present time a greater readiness to discuss Catholicism and to give it a hearing, there is also that amazing lack of knowledge and seeming inability to see for which, as the Catholic recognises, he must, even personally, accept a certain responsibility. Hilaire Belloc underlined this point very clearly when he wrote in *The Cruise of the "Nona"* : " How astonishingly in the modern world we live side by side and know nothing of one another." And he continued in a passage which is as true to-day as it was twenty-five years ago: " But the greatest anomaly of all, the one that has puzzled me most of a hundred such, is the complete ignorance of what the Catholic Church is and means—the ignorance even of what its doctrines may be. One would think it should be a mere matter of encyclopedias and text-books—easy for any one to look up. In nations of Catholic culture, of course, the Church is thoroughly well-known, even by its worst enemies; but in nations not of Catholic culture the absence of all contact with, and of even elementary information upon, this essential thing, is stupefying.

" Here is the corporate tradition which made Europe:

the Thing which is the core and soul of all our history for fifteen hundred years, and on into the present time; the continuator of all our Pagan origins, transformed, baptised, illumined; the matrix of such culture as we still retain. For any European not to know the elements of that affair is to be in a blind ignorance of all his making, and, therefore, of his self. Yet it is perfectly true that the Englishman or Scotsman, cultivated to excess, saturated with the knowledge of all he thinks there is to know, fatigued and cynical after too much sounding of the world, says things with regard to that great affair which show him to be as little acquainted with its essentials as he might be with another planet. He has many Catholic acquaintances; he probably has some reading of his own country before the death of Elizabeth; he is certain to have read Shakespeare—a writer who wrote for and in a Catholic England, and a writer whose whole atmosphere is Catholic. He may justly pride himself upon his knowledge of the architecture, or even the institutions of the Occident before the great sundering of three hundred years ago. Yet, when he is dealing with this mighty business, he says things more grotesque than anything said by any Colonial about that very governing class to which he himself belongs. He produces an effect, when he touches upon the Faith, which—I say it honestly—is as startling and as comic as the effect produced by those ingenuous millionaires from the backwoods who come barging in among the London subtleties of ancient wealth."[20]

Latent interest in Catholicism and in the problem of reunion were made manifest in the remarkable correspondence

---

[20] The same theme, differently expressed, is to be found in Arnold Lunn's two books, *Now I See* and *Within That City*. And long ago, Florence Nightingale wrote in a letter to Manning: " The historic made Schlegel, as you say, a Catholic. But the English have never been historians. Instead of saints they have had great civil engineers; instead of Sisters of Charity they have had great political economists. The Church of England could not have stood in any country but England because she is such a poor historian. I have always thought that the great theological fight has yet to be fought out in England between Catholicism and Protestantism. In Germany it was fought out 300 years ago. They know why they are Protestants. I never knew an Englishman who did and if he enquires he becomes a Catholic." See Leslie, *Henry Edward Manning*, p. 111.

which followed the publication of an article entitled " Roman Catholics and Other Christians," by a Special Correspondent in *The Times* for October 31, 1949. The letters made it clear how general, in face of the growing menace of atheistic Communism, was the anxiety bred by the fact of Christian division. The desire was no less evident for some discussion of at least the possibilities of *rapprochement*. On the whole, the Catholic side appeared intransigent; but as Abbot Butler later put it, in a happy phrase, in the *Dublin Review,* it was rather " intransigence of principle " than " temper of intransigence." And *The Times* leading article of November 29, summing up the discussion, made clear that this very important point has been recognised.

> " Roman Catholics," the leader-writer noted, " are not, in fact, committed, as is widely believed, to the doctrine that all non-Roman Catholics are damned, or to the view that the only channel of divine assistance is the Roman Catholic Church, but they do believe that their Church is the only communion commanded and empowered by God to discharge certain specific, sacramental teaching, and disciplinary functions on earth. In the light of this conviction they cannot, without betraying their conscience, recognise the validity of the claims of other Churches, even by implication. In the sphere of morality, co-operation between Roman Catholics and non-Roman Catholics is, according to Roman Catholic correspondents, far from easy. On many matters of urgent as well as permanent importance, such as the nature of Christian marriage, the differences between them and the other denominations are deep and could not be removed without the abandonment or modification of beliefs which Roman Catholics hold on the strength of what they regard as infallible authority. The obstacles to co-operation, so Roman Catholics maintain, are in practice matters on which compromise could be achieved only at the cost of integrity."

And Abbot Butler in the *Dublin Review* commented acutely though graciously on the non-Catholic attitude of mind:

> " And so I would go further and suggest that the opposition aroused by this intransigence, in so far as it is

SOUTHWARK CATHEDRAL
Pugin's design, never completed

BIRMINGHAM CATHEDRAL

SALFORD CATHEDRAL

LAYING THE FOUNDATION STONE OF
WESTMINSTER CATHEDRAL, in 1895

LIVERPOOL CATHEDRAL   Sir Edwin Lutyens' model

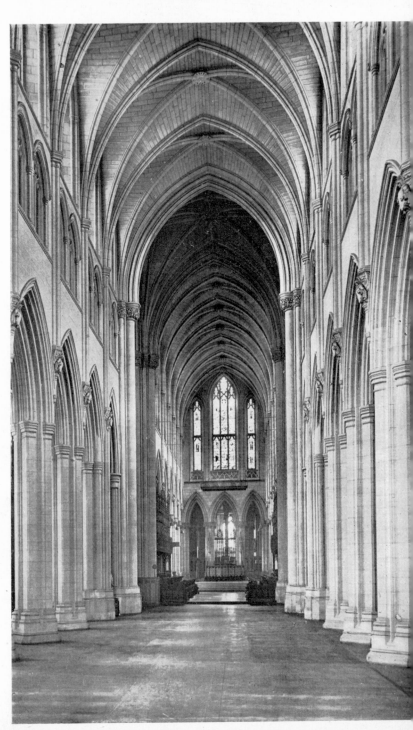

THE NAVE OF DOWNSIDE ABBEY CHURCH

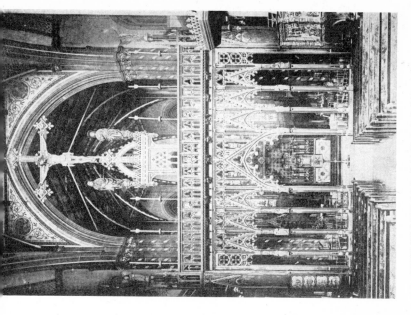

BIRMINGHAM CATHEDRAL, interior

OUR LADY, STAR OF THE SEA, GREENWICH

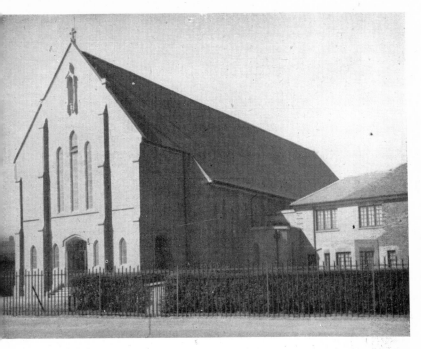

HOLY TRINITY CHURCH, GARSTON, LIVERPOOL

The foundation stone was blessed and laid in October, 1939, and the completed church was solemnly opened in July, 1940. It cost £9,000 and although within a few hundred yards of the Liverpool airport it suffered only superficial damage during the war.

ST. AIDANS, HUYTON, LIVERPOOL

The most recently opened church in the Archdiocese of Liverpool. The nucleus consists of Robin Hangar purchased from the R.A.F., covered with a patented aluminium and having brick porch and baptistery at one end and a sanctuary with sacristies added at the other. It cost approximately £8,000 to complete and was solemnly opened in July, 1949.

SOUTHWARK CATHEDRAL   (Topic
Archbishop Amigo surveys the ruins after the blitz, April, 1941

THE FRIARY, AYLESFORD, KENT
after the Carmelites' return in October, 1949

EUCHARISTIC CONGRESS in 1908
Benediction from Westminster Cathedral balcony

FIRST NATIONAL PILGRIMAGE TO WALSINGHAM
in 1934, Father Vernon Johnson preaching

CORPUS CHRISTI PROCESSION at Middlesbrough

LLANGOLLEN
The Procession entering the Cistercian Abbey of Valle Crucis for Pontifical High Mass sung by Bishop Petit of Menevia, June, 1947

CARDINAL WISEMAN'S TOMB in the crypt of Westminster Cathedral

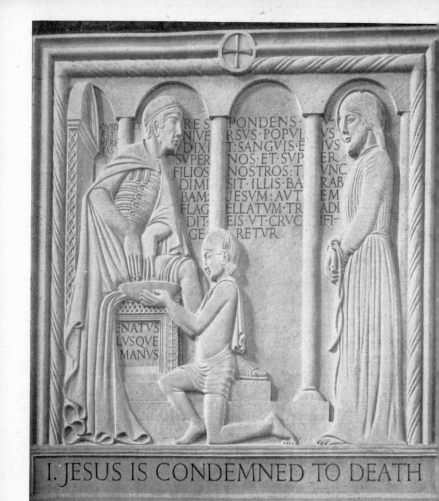

THE FIRST STATION AT WESTMINSTER CATHEDRAL
Stone relief by Eric Gill

an opposition to intransigence *as such*, does not rest upon
a Christian foundation at all, and is not an expression of
charity. Christianity has always maintained that truth is
one and that it is inconsistent with the manifold forms of
error. It has always, too, when faithful to its Gospel source,
maintained that it possesses this truth, that it can formulate
it, and that it can in consequence condemn error. The
hostility to this contention springs not from Christian
charity but—deep down, and often no doubt all unbeknown
to those who share it—from historical and philosophical
relativism and agnosticism. It springs in the last analysis
from the human spirit's horror of encountering the Absolute
within the temporal process. To-day it rejects the Church's
infallible voice as a mediæval anachronism. Yesterday it
inspired Pilate's words to Christ: ' What is truth?' The
day before yesterday it was making terms with the Baals of
Canaan and persecuting the prophets of the unique God
self-revealed on Sinai.

" Now I find that after deprecating the intransigent
temper I have equated our non-Catholic fellow-Christians
with Jezebel! I am sorry. I only mean to suggest that the
claims of absolute truth, whenever published in the world's
market-places and academies, must arouse the bitterest
hostility or amused laughter until they are accepted, or are
by way of being accepted. I can understand and
sympathise with the non-Catholic Christian who honestly
sees in ' Rome ' the scarlet woman of the Apocalypse. For
her claims are indeed such that they must be either tre-
mendously true or abominably false. I am not sure that
it is not harder to sympathise with the man who has ' a
great respect ' for the Catholic Church but will not accept
the ' obedience of faith '."

With some such thoughts in mind, we may turn to consider the possibilities in the second century of organised diocesan
life which opens out before the Church in England. Since
1850 immense changes have taken place, mainly in relation
to the material conditions of living, but reflected inevitably
in the general opinion and outlook of the age. The process of
de-Christianisation which Newman foresaw so clearly has

continued with gathering momentum. Doctrine is at a discount and with its disappearance the inevitable disintegration in morals has taken place.

Signs are not wanting, however, that the drift to materialism is at an end. The fair promises of the conquest of nature held out by the humanitarians of earlier generations are growing more and more suspect to a world which sees itself threatened with atomic destruction, and realises vividly, even if somewhat incoherently, that far more important than the control of nature is man's control over his own appetites and ambitions. Walter Lippman put his finger on the vital spot when he criticised the modern educational process which has not only separated man from his spiritual inheritance but has denied to reason its rightful place as the faculty of government.

" It is this specialised and fundamentally disordered development which has turned so much of man's science into the means of his own destruction. For as reason is regarded as no more than the instrument of men's desires, applied science inflates enormously the power of men's desires. Since the reason is not the ruler of these desires, the power which science places in men's hands is ungoverned.

" Quickly it becomes ungovernable. Science is the product of intelligence. But if the function of the intelligence is to be the instrument of the acquisitive, the possessive, and the domineering impulses, then these impulses, so strong by nature, must become infinitely stronger when they are equipped with all the resources of man's intelligence.

" That is why men to-day are appalled by the discovery that when modern man fights he is the most destructive animal ever known on this planet; that when he is acquisitive he is the most cunning and efficient; that when he dominates the weak he has engines of oppression and of calculated cruelty and deception that no antique devil could have imagined."

Everywhere, at the present time, disquiet and anxiety at what the result of this education may mean are more and more apparent. The human spirit seeks something more permanent and more absolute than mere material security and, even in the midst of his intellectual disruption, man knows that he does not live by bread alone—nor even by bread and circuses. The human mind is made for truth and finds contentment only in certitude. Instinctively man looks for teaching and is ready to seize on dogma, even on the dark dogmas of determinism, if it will bring him certitude and a faith to which his loyalty can adhere.

The day of doctrine is returning, and for that reason alone the situation provides an opportunity and a challenge to the Church in this country. The intellectual security born of certitude, the fruit of " the faith of Christ and the sacraments of the faith " will be perhaps the most powerful argument for Catholicism in the years which lie immediately ahead of us[21].

" The faith of Christ and the sacraments of the faith " —thus is summed up the whole of the Catholic life. Nothing of merely material or statistical significance can replace this spiritual reality and, in consequence, it might well be said that most of what has been printed in the foregoing pages is of only secondary importance in the history of the Church in this country. The ultimate test is the strength of divine charity in the soul of each Catholic, founded on the truth of the *fides Christi,* nourished and sustained by the *sacramenta fidei.* What that test discloses is, of course, the secret of God Himself. It may be hinted at in the figures which have been given of the attendances at Mass at different times and in different places. It could perhaps be more closely determined by the number of weekly and daily Communions in our parish churches and in the chapels of our schools, colleges and convents; for the Blessed Eucharist is the Sacrament *par excellence* of charity, and from that charity is begotten the unity of the Mystical Body. It may be noted, too, in the patient, prayerful queues—a Catholic characteristic long before the queue habit became part of our national life— waiting in the quiet shadows outside the confessional on a Saturday evening. If the history of the Church and, indeed,

[21] In this respect great importance attaches to the revival of the Catholic Missionary Society under Dr. J. C. Heenan. The Oxfordshire mission in 1948 and the General Mission in 1949 are, it is certain, forerunners of a more systematic and persistent effort to make the Catholic Faith more fully known and loved in England.

the history of mankind, seen in its true light *sub specie aeternitatis* is, as St. Paul puts it so tersely to the Ephesians, " the perfecting of saints, the work of the ministry, the building up of the body of Christ," these are the things which finally matter.

The nostalgic yearning for Church unity so apparent at the present time is a recognition that there ought to be this corporate vitality of the Body of Christ, this activity of mutual love—without seeing how to attain it. Part of the work which Catholics in the second century of the restored Hierarchy will need to achieve will be the continued and intensified manifestation of this life of love. " The perfecting of saints " is the purpose for which the Church and the Sacraments exist; the pursuit of holiness remains the primary duty of every Catholic, clerical or lay, and holiness is first all love—love of God and of others in God. St. John Fisher and St. Thomas More were the last canonised English Catholics; and a long period of Catholic history lies between them and the present day. How much the " perfecting of saints " implies a more mature and deep-rooted doctrinal education for layfolk, and a more than perfunctory interest among the clergy in the spiritual life as the " implementing " of the mysteries of the faith, and what measures are best suited to bring this about—these are matters in discussion everywhere nowadays. What is outside all discussion is that any other achievement than " the perfecting of saints " on the part of Catholics, whether individually, or corporately, will be of only minor importance. Here is the purpose for which Catholic schools are founded and conducted; for which the Catholic Press is organised and Catholic societies of all kinds have their activity and function. In this ideal is the right criterion of values, the basis of true judgment on human affairs. Above all and before all, the Church must go about her work which is nothing else than to teach the faith of Christ and to administer the sacraments. For this purpose will she raise up and train her clergy; will she pray for vocations for the priesthood; will she organise and develop her parochial and diocesan life. For this purpose, too, will she have her part in all the movements which make for social justice and better living. Newman's well-known words situate the true standard of Catholic values forcefully and exactly:—

"This, then, is the point I insist upon, in answer to the objection which you have to-day urged against me. The Church aims, not at making a show, but at doing a work. She regards this world, and all that is in it, as a mere shadow, as dust and ashes, compared with the value of one single soul. She holds that, unless she can, in her own way, do good to souls, it is no use her doing anything; she holds that it were better for sun and moon to drop from heaven, for the earth to fail, and for all the many millions who are upon it to die of starvation in extremest agony, so far as temporal affliction goes, than that one soul, I will not say, should be lost, but should commit one single venial sin, should tell one wilful untruth, though it harmed no one, or steal one poor farthing without excuse. She considers the action of this world and the action of the soul simple incommensurate, viewed in their respective spheres; she would rather save the soul of one single wild bandit of Calabria, or whining beggar of Palermo, than draw a hundred lines of railroad through the length and breadth of Italy, or carry out a sanitary reform, in its fullest details, in every city of Sicily, except so far as these great national works tended to some spiritual good beyond them.

"Such is the Church, O ye men of the world, and now you know her. Such she is, such she will be; and, though she aims at your good, it is in her own way—and if you oppose her, she defies you. She has her mission, and do it she will, whether she be in rags, or in fine linen; whether by means of uncultivated intellects, or with the grace of accomplishments. Not that, in fact, she is not the source of numberless temporal and moral blessings to you also; the history of ages testifies it; but she makes no promises; she is sent to seek the lost; that is her first object, and she will fulfil it, whatever comes of it."[22]

It follows from this that administrative and organising ability, no matter how much appreciated in merely human affairs, are of secondary importance in comparison with that pastoral-mindedness of bishop or parish priest which gives him a true concern with the health of soul and the spiritual well-being of his flock. A volume which commemorates the

[22] *Difficulties of Anglicans*, I, 239-41 (The Social state of Catholic countries no prejudice to the Sanctity of the Church, § 4).

centenary of the re-establishment of the Hierarchy may well conclude with a quotation which situates the Church, its ministers and their work, in this just perspective:—

" In the churchman the contest has been frequent, between administration-mindedness and pastoral-mindedness. Where the first is victorious, the ' brainy ' begin to be trained with a view to produce administration-mindedness, and all the ' brainy ' tend to become, by training and by employment, administration-minded; and only the less ' brainy ' are directed to the pastoral cares which are the real business of the priest. In no country more than our own is the witness of history more startling of the ills such a monstrous perversion must bring in its train. And all this is, no doubt, one reason why the administrator *par excellence,* the diocesan bishop, needs to be and—so it is stated—actually is, in the divine view of things, a man already formed and perfected in charity, the *uomo completo,* the saint. Sanctity possessed—a soul utterly surrendered to grace—is the only adequate protection for human nature against the temptations that beset the ruler of his fellows *in spiritualibus*: as essential to the bishop, if he is to do a bishop's work, as a knowledge of music is essential to whoever will conduct a symphony.

" ' Nothing is more helpful than to look on things as they really are,' a modern Pope has reminded us. The Church is both divine and human; and all of us need to consider its constitution in both the senses outlined in this paper[23], and to bear in mind that these are not two points of view, but the two halves that make up a single truth, if we are to understand the past of Catholicism, or its present action, or if, with intelligent loyalty, we are to play our own part as members of the Church, to live consciously as members of Christ, to live by ' the faith of Christ and by the sacraments of the faith.' "[24]

[23] " The ordinary legal sense which this word has . . . those institutions and laws through which authority rules this unity."—Philip Hughes, *op. cit.,* p. 68.

" That which *constitutes* or makes up the Church antecedently to any laws or external activity."—*Ibid,* p. 60.

[24] *Ibid.,* pp. 81-2.

BIBLIOGRAPHY

GENERAL LIST

A

The Annual Register.

The Cambridge Modern History (Vol. X, Ch. 19; Vol. XI, Ch. 1; Vol. XII, Chs. 3, 4, 13 and 25).

The Catholic Directory.

The Catholic Encyclopedia.

The Catholic Who's Who.

The Dictionary of National Biography.

The Dublin Review, No. 369 (April, 1929) and No. 397 (April, 1936).

The Month, No. 901 (July, 1939).

National Catholic Congress, 1926, *Official Report of* (C.T.S.).

Punch.

The Tablet, Centenary Number, May 18, 1940.

The Times.

Whitaker's Almanack.

B

NOTE.—The books in the following list were nearly all published in London, except in the cases where it is otherwise stated.

ANSTRUTHER, G. E., *A Hundred Years of Catholic Progress* (1929).

ATTWATER, DONALD, *The Catholic Church in Modern Wales* (1935).

BATTERSBY, W. J., *St. John Baptist De La Salle* (Vol. I, 1948; Vol. II, 1950).

BEDOYERE, M. DE LA, *Christian Crisis* (1940).

BELL, G. K. A., *Life of Randall Davidson, Archbishop of Canterbury* (1935).

BENSON, A. C., *Life of Edward White Benson, Archbishop of Canterbury* (1905).

BINNS, L. E. ELLIOT, *Religion in the Victorian Era.*

BRADY, W. MAZIERE, *Annals of the Catholic Hierarchy in England and Scotland, 1585-1876* (1877).

BRYCE, J., *Two Centuries of Irish History, 1691-1870* (1888).

BUTLER, ABBOT E. C., *Life and Times of Bishop Ullathorne, 1806-1888* (2 vols., 1926).

—— *The Vatican Council* (1930).

BUTLER, J. R. M., *A History of England, 1815-1918* (1928).

CECIL, ALGERNON, *A Dreamer in Christendom* (1926).

—— *British Foreign Secretaries, 1807-1916* (1927).

CHURCH, R. W., *The Oxford Movement*.

CORNISH, F. WARRE, *History of the English Church in the Nineteenth Century* (2 vols., 1910).

Church and the World, Being Materials for the Historical Study of Christian Sociology. Vol. III: " Church and Society in England from 1800."

DAWSON, C., *The Spirit of the Oxford Movement* (1933).

DENVIR, J., *The Irish in Britain* (1892).

DEVAS, C. S., *The Key to the World's Progress* (1906).

DUNLOP, R., *Life of Daniel O'Connell* (1900).

FABER, GEOFFREY, *Oxford Apostles: A Character Study of the Oxford Movement* (1933).

FAGAN, W., *Life and Times of Daniel O'Connell* (2 vols., Dublin, 1846).

FIFTEEN CLUB, THE (THOMAS MURPHY), *The Position of the Catholic Church in England and Wales during the Last Two Centuries* (1892).

FITZMAURICE, LORD EDMOND, *Life of the Second Earl Granville* (1905).

GASQUET, ABBOT F. A., *History of the Venerable English College in Rome* (1920).

GILLOW, JOSEPH, *Literary and Biographical History, or Biographical Dictionary of the English Catholics from the Breach with Rome (1534) to the Present Time* (5 vols., 1885-87).

GREVILLE, C., *Memoirs, 1818-1860* (8 vols., 1887).

GWYNN, DENIS, *Cardinal Wiseman* (1929).

—— *A Hundred Years of Catholic Emancipation, 1829-1929* (1929).

—— *Life of Daniel O'Connell* (Cork, 1947).

—— *Lord Shrewsbury, Pugin and the Catholic Revival* (1946).

HAILE, M., and BONNEY, E., *Life and Letters of John Lingard, 1771-1851* (N.D.).

HEENAN, J. C., *Cardinal Hinsley* (1944).

HUGHES, PHILIP, *The Catholic Question, 1688-1829* (1929).

—— *Popular History of the Catholic Church* (3rd edn., 1947).

KEBLE, J., and NEWMAN, J. H., *Correspondence, 1839-45* (1917).

HUTTON, EDWARD, *Catholicism and English Literature* (1942; new edn., 1948).

HUTTON, R. H., *Cardinal Newman* (1891).

LEESON, SPENCER, *Christian Education* (1947).

LESLIE, SHANE, *Henry Edward Manning, His Life and Labours* (1921).

—— *The Oxford Movement, 1833-1933*.

—— *Life of Mark Sykes* (1922).

LILLY, W. S., and WALLIS, J. P., *A Manual of the Law specially affecting Catholics* (1893).

LOCKHART, J. G., *Cosmo Gordon Lang* (1949).

MATHEW, ARCHBISHOP D., *Catholicism in England* (1936).

MAY, J. LEWIS, *Cardinal Newman* (1932).

McCARTHY, J. H., *Ireland Since the Union* (1889).

McDONAGH, M., *Life of Daniel O'Connell* (1929).

MESSENGER, E. C., *Rome and Reunion* (1934).

MEYNELL, WILFRID, *The Catholic Life and Letters of Cardinal Newman* (1887).

MIDDLETON, R. D., *Dr. Routh* (1938).

—— *Newman and Bloxam* (1947).

MONYPENNY, W. F., and BUCKLE, G. E., *Life of Disraeli,* Vol. II (1929).

MORLEY, JOHN, *Life of W. E. Gladstone* (3 vols., 1904).

MOZLEY, A., *Letters and Correspondence* (2 vols., 1891).

O'BRIEN, R. BARRY, *Life of Charles Stewart Parnell* (1898).

O'BRIEN, WILLIAM, *Recollections* (1906).

O'CONNELL, J., *Life and Speeches of Daniel O'Connell* (2 vols., 1847-48).

OLDMEADOW, E., *Francis Cardinal Bourne* (2 vols., 1940 and 1944).

PAUL, HERBERT, *History of Modern England, 1846-95* (5 vols., 1904-06).

—— *The Life of Froude* (1905).

PEEL, SIR ROBERT, *Memoirs,* Part I (1856).

PURCELL, E. S., *Life of Cardinal Manning* (2 vols., 1896).

—— *Life and Letters of Ambrose Phillipps de Lisle* (2 vols., 1900).

SMITH, H. L., and NASH V., *The Story of the Dockers' Strike.*

SNEAD-COX, J. G., *Life of Cardinal Vaughan* (1910).

STOCKLEY, W. F. P., *Newman, Education and Ireland* (1933).

THOROLD, ALGAR, *Life of Henry Labouchère* (1913).

ULLATHORNE, BISHOP, *Autobiography* (1891).

VARIOUS WRITERS, *Catholic Emancipation*: Introduction by Cardinal Bourne (1929).

—— *A Tribute to Newman* (Dublin 1945).

—— *Homage to Newman, 1845-1945* (Westminster Cathedral Chron., 1945).

WALSH, P. J., *William J. Walsh, Archbishop of Dublin* (1928).

WARD, MAISIE, *Young Mr. Newman* (1948).

—— *Gilbert Keith Chesterton* (1944).

WARD, WILFRID, *W. G. Ward and the Oxford Movement* (1889).

—— *W. G. Ward and the Catholic Revival* (1893).

—— *Life and Times of Cardinal Wiseman* (1897).

—— *Life of John Henry Cardinal Newman* (2 vols., 1912).

WINDLE, BERTRAM C. A., *Who's Who of the Oxford Movement* (New York, 1926).

WISEMAN, CARDINAL, *Recollections of the Last Four Popes* (1858).

WYNDHAM, G., *Men and Matters* (1914).

—— and MACKAIL, J. W., *Life and Letters of Geo. Wyndham* (2 vols., N.D.).

CHAPTERS I, II AND VI

THE CENTURY 1850-1950—THE ENGLISH CATHOLICS IN 1850
—THE OTHER BISHOPS

Contemporary Writings:

BAYNES, A. D., *History of Eastern England* (1872).

Catholic Directory, The, 1849, 1850, 1851, 1852.

DISRAELI, BENJAMIN, *Endymion* (1881).

Dublin Review, The, 1850, 1851.

ENGELS, FRIEDRICH, *The Condition of the Working Class in England in 1844* (1888).

HOLYOAKE, G. J., *Sixty Years of an Agitator's Life* (1892).

HUSENBETH, F. C., *Life of Dr. Weedall* (1860).

NEWMAN, J. H., *Lecture on Anglican Difficulties*, I (delivered in 1850).

—— *The Idea of a University* (1852).

—— *Sermons on Various Occasions* (1857).

—— *Apologia* (1864).

—— *The Via Media*, II (1877).

—— *Essays, Critical and Historical*, II (1871).

Punch, 1850, 1851.

Reports: The Census of 1851 (4 vols. folio).
    Select Committee on the Law of Mortmain (1851).
    Religious Worship in England and Wales, 1853. (The report of the Registrar-General on the census of this, taken March 30, 1851.)
    Religious Worship in England and Wales, abridged from the Official Report, 1854. (By authority of the Registrar-General.)
    The Catholic Poor School Committee—*Annual Report* for 1851 and 1874.
    Hansard, *Parliamentary Debates*, 1851.

Tablet, The, 1850, 1851.

Times, The, 1850, 1851.

Works by Later Writers:—

ADAMSON, J. W., *English Education, 1789-1902*.

BELL, H., *Lord Palmerston* (2 vols., 1936).

BUTLER, E. C., O.S.B., *Life and Times of Bishop Ullathorne 1806-1889* (2 vols., 1926).

CLAPHAM, J., *An Economic History of Modern Britain* (3 vols.).

ENSOR, C. K., *England, 1870-1914*.

HALEVY, E., *Histoire du peuple Anglais au XIXme siècle* (Vol. IV, 1947).

HAMMOND, J. L., and BARBARA, *Lord Shaftesbury* (1923).

—— *The Age of the Chartists* (1930).

—— *The Bleak Age* (1934, 1947).

—— *Gladstone and the Irish Nation* (1938).

JOUVENEL, B. DE, *Problems of Socialist England* (1949).

MAILLAUD, PIERRE, *The English Way* (1943-44).

MARRIOTT, J. A. R., *A History of Europe, 1815-1923*.

MONYPENNY, F. W., and BUCKLE, G., *Life of Disraeli* (2 vol. edn., 1912).

O'BRIEN, WM., *Recollections* (1906).

ROCHE, J. S., *Prior Park* (1931).

WALPOLE, SPENCER, *Life of Lord John Russell* (2 vols., 1891).

WARD, BERNARD, *The Sequel to Catholic Emancipation, 1830-50* (2 vols., 1915).

WILSON, DOM ANSELM, *Life of Bishop Hedley* (1930).

CHAPTER III

THE RESTORATION OF THE HIERARCHY

BRADY, WM., *Annals of the Catholic Hierarchy* (1877).

LESLIE, SHANE, *From Cabin Boy to Archbishop* (1941).

MILBURN, J. B., *The Restored Hierarchy, 1850-1910* (1911).

Punch, 1850-51 *passim*.

Roman Catholic Question, The—Documents on the re-establishment of the Catholic Hierarchy in England, 1850-51 (contemporary).

Times, The, October and November, 1850.

ULLATHORNE, W. B., *Autobiography* (1891).

See also General List.

CHAPTER IV

DIOCESAN ORGANISATION AND ADMINISTRATION.

Documentary Sources:

Leeds Diocesan Archives. (These are only partly sorted and listed. In this chapter the collection of Roman Documents, Letters and Papers on Finance, and a certain number of episcopal letters have been used. The archives are richest in early nineteenth-century letters and papers, largely those of Bishop Briggs.)

Yorkshire Brethren Manuscripts.

Ushaw College Archives.

Printed Sources:

BENEDICT XIV, *De Synodo Diocesana*.

BINGHAM, *The Sheffield School Board.*

Catholic Directory, The, 1850 ff.

Catholic Encyclopedia, The.

CHARLTON, BARBARA, *Recollections of a Northumbrian Lady* (1949).

Decreta Quatuor Conciliorum Provincialium Westmonasteriensium (1852-1873).

Leeds Synods (and various other Diocesan Synods).

PHILLIPS, *Du Droit Ecclésiastique* (French translation of *Kirchenrecht*).

See also General List.

CHAPTER V

THE ARCHDIOCESE OF WESTMINSTER

ANDREWS, H., *Westminster Retrospect: A Memoir of Sir Richard Terry* (1947).

Dublin Review, The, passim.

HEENAN, J. C., *Cardinal Hinsley* (1944).

HICKS, DOM BRUNO, *Hugh Edmond Ford, First Abbot of Downside* (1948).

L'HOPITAL, WINEFRIDE DE, *Westminster Cathedral and its Architect* (1911).

MATHEW, DAVID, *Catholicism in England* (1936).

SYKES, CHRISTOPHER, *A New Judgement on Cardinal Manning* (MS.).

WARD, BERNARD, *The Sequel to Catholic Emancipation, 1830-1850* (1915).

Westminster Cathedral Chronicle, The, from Jan. 1917.

CHAPTER VIII

CARDINAL NEWMAN

ABBOT, E. A., *Philomythus* (1891).

GLADSTONE, W. E., *The Vatican Decrees, a Political Expostulation* (1874).

—— *Vaticanism* (1875).

MANNING, H. E., *The Vatican Decrees and their bearing on Civil Allegiance* (1875). [A Reply to Gladstone's *Expostulation.*]

NEWMAN, J. H., *Apologia pro Vita Sua* (1864).

—— *Development of Christian Doctrine, Essay on* (1845).

—— *Difficulties felt by Anglicans* (4th edn., 1872).

—— *Grammar of Assent, Essay in aid of* (1870).

—— *Idea of a University,* Part I: " Discourses on the Nature and Scope of a University education " (1852); Part II: " Lectures and Essays on University subjects " (1859).

—— *On the Inspiration of Scripture*: *XIX Century Review* (Feb., 1884).

—— *Letter to the Duke of Norfolk* (1875).

—— *Miracles, Two Essays on* (1870).

—— *My Campaign in Ireland* (privately printed, 1872).

—— *The Pope and the Revolution* (1866).

—— *Present Position of Catholics in England* (1851).

—— *The Second Spring* (1852).

—— *Stray Essays on Controversial Points* (privately printed, 1890).

STOCKLEY, W. F. P., *Newman, Education and Ireland* (1933).

TRISTRAM, H. T., and BACCHUS, F. J., Article, " Newman," *Dictionnaire de la Théologie Catholique*.

WARD, WILFRID, *Life of John Henry Cardinal Newman* (2 vols., 1912).

CHAPTER IX

THE IRISH IMMIGRATION

ATTWATER, D., *The Catholic Church in Modern Wales* (1935).

BURKE, T., *Catholic History of Liverpool* (1910).

Census Reports, The

CHARLTON, BARBARA, *Recollections of a Northumbrian Lady* (1949).

DENVIR, J., *The Irish in Britain* (1892).

YOUNG, REV. URBAN, *Life and Letters of Ven. Dominic Barberi, C.P.* (1926).

—— *Life of Fr. Ignatius Spencer, C.P.* (1933).

—— *The Ven. Dominic Barberi in England* (1935).

See also General List.

CHAPTER X

CATHOLICS AND THE UNIVERSITIES

In addition to the papers mentioned in the first footnote, the following are the principal sources that have been used:

Ampleforth Journal. Various articles, especially: " Oxford and Cambridge," by Bishop Hedley, July, 1896; An account of the first Conference of Catholic Colleges, by Abbot Burge, *ibid.*; " St. Benet's Hall, Oxford," by Dom Justin McCann, Spring Number, 1926; Obituary Notice of Abbot Burge, Autumn Number, 1929; Notes by an Old Amplefordian on Oxford in 1894-95, Summer Number, 1931; " Ampleforth at Oxford, 1893-1938," by Dom Justin McCann, Autumn Number, 1938; Obituary of Abbot Matthews, Spring Number, 1939.

Baeda. (Magazine of St. Bede's College, Manchester.) New Form No. 3, June 1941. Extract from an address to Catholic teachers given by Bishop Casartelli (undated).

BAILEY, CYRIL, *Francis Fortescue Urquhart*: *A Memoir* (1936).

BRAYE, LORD, *The Present State of the Catholic Church in England* (1884).

Clergy Review, October, 1947. Article by the Rev. C. A. Bolton.

Downside Review. Various articles and notices, 1881 onwards.

Dublin Review. Various articles, especially: " The Work and Wants of the Catholic Church in England " (Manning), July, 1863; " University Education for English Catholics," October, 1864; " London University and Catholic Education," by Fr. Henry Tristram, Cong. Orat., October, 1936; " A Chronic Problem in Catholic Education," by the Rev. Philip Hughes, July, 1939; " The Cambridge Prelude to 1895," by H. O. Evennett, April, 1946.

FIGGIS, J. N., and LAURENCE, R. V., *Lord Acton's Correspondence* (1917).

GUY, DOM EPHREM, *The Synods of Westminster*.

Instruction to the Parents, Superiors and Directors of Catholic Laymen who desire to study in the Universities of Oxford and Cambridge. By the Cardinal Archbishop and Bishops of the Province of Westminster (1896).

Lumen Vitæ, 1949-1950. Articles by Father Sebastian Redmond, A.A.

Memorandum on the Universities Question as affecting Catholics (1894). Also: A List of the Signatories to the Petition on the Universities Question addressed to the English Bishops (1895).

Month. Various articles, especially: " The Catholic Colleges and the London University " (1868); and " Newman House " by Sidney Parry (March, 1933).

MURPHY, T., *The Position of the Catholic Church in England and Wales during the last two centuries* (1892).

NEWMAN, J. H., *The Idea of a University*: *My Campaign in Ireland* (privately printed).

NEWMAN ASSOCIATION. Various pamphlets. Notes and information in *Unitas*.

PETRE, MGR. LORD, Various Tracts and Pamphlets on Education.

Report of the Archbishop and Bishops to His Eminence the Cardinal Prefect of the Sacred Congregation of Propaganda on the subject of Higher Catholic Education in England (no date) [1872].

ROCHE, J. S., *A History of Prior Park* (1931).

Special Reports of the members of the Sub-commission appointed at the Conference held in London on November 28th and 29th, 1871, on the evidence received by them (privately printed).

ULLATHORNE, BISHOP WILLIAM BERNARD, *Facts and Documents relating to the Mission and contemplated Oratory at Oxford* (privately printed, 1867).

UNIVERSITIES CATHOLIC EDUCATION BOARD (now the Oxford and Cambridge Catholic Education Board). Reports and Papers.

VON HUGEL, BARON ANATOLE. Papers preserved at Fisher House, Cambridge.

WILSON, DOM ANSELM, *The Life of Bishop Hedley* (1930).

See also General List.

CHAPTER XI

SECONDARY EDUCATION FOR BOYS

ALMOND, CUTHBERT, O.S.B., *The History of Ampleforth Abbey* (London, 1903).

ANON., *Records and Recollections of St. Cuthbert's, Ushaw*, by an Old Alumnus (London, 1889).

AMHERST, W. J., S.J., " History of St. Mary's College, Oscott," in *The Oscotian*, Nos. II-VI.

BARNES, A. S., *The Catholic Schools in England* (London, 1926).

BATTERSBY, W. J., " The Education of the Middle Classes in the 1850's," in *The Month*, September, 1948.

BIRT, H. N., *History of Downside School* (London, 1902).

BRADDOCK, W. J., " The Contribution of Catholics to English Education." M.A. Thesis, London University, 1917.

BUSCOT, CANON, *A History of Cotton College* (London, 1940).

EVENNETT, H. O., *The Catholic Schools of England and Wales* (Cambridge, 1944).

GERARD, JOHN, S.J., *Stonyhurst College* (Belfast, 1894).

GRUGGEN, G., and KEATING, J., *Stonyhurst College* (London, 1901).

GRUNNE, DOMINIQUE DE, O.S.B., " Public-Schools Anglais," in *Revue Générale Belge* (December, 1947).

HUSENBETH, F. C., *A History of Sedgley Park School* (London, 1856).

—— *The Life of the Rt. Rev. Mgr. Weedall, D.D., President of St. Mary's College, Oscott* (London, 1860).

PETRE, REV. HON. W., *The Position and Prospects of Catholic Liberal Education* (London, 1878).

ROCHE, J. S., *A History of Prior Park College and its Founder, Bishop Baines* (London, 1931).

WARD, BERNARD, *History of St. Edmund's College, Old Hall* (London, 1893).

WARD, W. G., " Catholic Colleges and Protestant Schools," in *The Dublin Review* (1878).

—— " Special Report upon the Evidence Supplied to the Sub-Commission on Higher Catholic Education; appointed at the Conference held in London, November 28th and 29th, 1871," by Rev. E. J. Purbrick.

—— " A Review of the Studies of the Past Five Years," in *Downside Review, Vol.* III.

CHAPTER XII

EDUCATIONAL WORK OF THE RELIGIOUS ORDERS OF WOMEN

ANON., *Leaves from the Annals of the Sisters of Mercy*, by a Member of the Order of Mercy, Vol. II (New York, 1883).

—— *The Life of Cornelia Connelly, 1809-1879, Foundress of the Society of the Holy Child Jesus,* by a Member of the Society (London, 1922).

—— *The Congregation of Jesus and Mary: Cameos from its History* (London, 1917).

—— *Sister Mary of St. Philip, 1825-1904,* by a Sister of Notre Dame (London, 1920).

CHAMBERS, M. C. E., *The Life of Mary Ward* (2 vols., London, 1882).

—— *St. Mary's Convent, Micklegate Bar, York* (London, 1887).

DEVAS, F. C., S.J., *Mother Magdalen Taylor: Foundress of the Poor Servants of the Mother of God* (London, 1927).

DRANE, A. T., *Life of Mother Margaret Hallahan* (London, 1869).

GOBILLOT, RENE, *Les Sœurs de St. Paul de Chartres* (Paris, 1938).

LAVEILLE, MGR., *L'Abbé Jean Baptiste Debrabant, Founder of the Congregation of La Sainte Union des Sacrés Cœurs, 1801-1880* (Exeter, 1934).

MARTIN, M. DE S.J., *Ursuline Method of Education* (1946).

MARTINDALE, C. C., S.J., *The Foundress of the Sisters of the Assumption, Mother Marie-Eugénie Milleret de Brou* (London, 1936).

MONAHAN, MAUD, *Life and Letters of Janet Erskine Stuart* (London, 1922).

O'LEARY, M., *Education with a Tradition* (London, 1936).

O'REILLY, BERNARD, *St. Angela Merici and the Ursulines* (London, 1880).

SIMEON, CHANOINE, *La Congrégation des Dames de l'Instruction Chrétienne, Notice Historique* (Liège, 1927).

STANISLAUS, FR., F.M.C., *Life of the Viscountess de Bonnault d'Houet, Foundress of the Society of the Faithful Companions of Jesus, 1781-1858* (London, 1916).

ERSKINE, JANET STUART, *The Education of Catholic Girls* (London, 1911).

WHELAN, DOM BASIL, *Historic English Convents of Today* (London, 1936).

Reference Works:

ANSON, PETER F., *The Religious Orders and Congregations of Great Britain and Ireland* (Worcester, 1949).

STEELE, F. M., *The Convents of Great Britain* (1925).

CHAPTER XIII

THE STRUGGLE FOR THE SCHOOLS

Official Documents:

Annual Reports of the Catholic Poor School Committee, 1847-1905.

Annual Reports of the Catholic Education Council, since 1905.

Minutes of the Committee of Council on Education, 1848-99.

Annual Reports of the Board/Ministry of Education, 1899 to date.
Studies and Articles:

ALLIES, MARY H, *T. W. Allies* (1907).

BATTERSBY, W. J., " Middle Class Education " (*Month*, September, 1948).

BEALES, A. C. F., " Beginnings of Catholic Elementary Education in the Second Spring " (*Dublin Review*, October, 1939).

—— " Religious Education in England, Past, Present and Future " (*Sword of the Spirit*, 1944).

—— " Some Delusions of Catholic Education " (Bradford C.P.E.A., 1944).

—— " Catholic Education in England " (*Lumen Vitæ*, Louvain, Vol. I, No. 3, 1946).

—— " The Free Churches and the Catholic Schools " (*Month*, November-December, 1943).

——" The Catholic Schools Crisis of 1950 " (Catholic Social Guild, 1950).

BECK, GEO. ANDREW, A.A., Articles in *The Tablet*: " More Catholic Children than Schools," 2nd February, 1947; " Future of the Catholic Grammar Schools," 10th May, 1947; " Our Falling Population," 29th May, 1948; " The Drift in Education, " 10th July, 1948; " The Schools after Five Years," 9th July, 1949; " Bishops, Schools and General Elections, 1885 and 1950," 14th and 21st January, 1950.

EVENNETT, H. O., *The Catholic Schools of England* (Cambridge U.P., 1944).

GILBERT, SIR J., " Education " (in *Catholic Emancipation, 1829-1929*, B.O. & W., 1929).

HOWARD, C. D. H., " The Parnell Manifesto of 1885 and the Schools' Question " (*Engl. Hist. Review*, January, 1947).

O'LEARY, M., *The Catholic Church and Education* (B.O. & W., 1944).

PIUS XI, POPE, *Divini Illius Magistri*: *the Christian Education of Youth*, 1929 (Catholic Truth Society).

QUIRK, T., *The Education Question*, 1943 (privately printed).

—— *The Education Act of 1944 and the Voluntary Schools*, 1946 (privately printed).

SMITH, R. A. L., *The Catholic Church and Social Order* (Longmans, 1943).

SOMERVILLE, C., S.J., " The Catholic Secondary Schools " (*Month*, May-June, 1943).

Sword of the Spirit. "Education" (Report of Education Committee), 1944.

Tablet, The, Text of Statements of the Hierarchy and of the Ministry of Education during the 1949-50 Crisis (16th July, 5th November, 3rd December).

See also General List.

CHAPTER XIV

GROWTH OF THE CATHOLIC COMMUNITY

ATTWATER, DONALD, *The Catholic Church in Modern Wales* (1935).

BARNES, MGR. A. S., *The Catholic Schools of England* (1926).

FITZGERALD, P., *Fifty Years of Catholic Life and Progress* (2 vols., 1901).

FLETCHER, REV. P., *Recollections of a Ransomer* (1928).

GWYNN, DENIS, *Lord Shrewsbury, Pugin and the Catholic Revival* (1946).

MATHEW, DAVID, *Catholicism in England* (1936).

—— *Acton, the Formative Years* (1946).

See also General List.

CHAPTER XV

DEVELOPMENT OF THE RELIGIOUS ORDERS

A

The Catholic Directory, 1850, and the following years.

The Downside Review, especially Centenary Number, November, 1914.

The Ampleforth Journal.

The Month.

" Letters and Notices," a private Magazine (Jesuit).

Pax.

Blackfriars.

Historical Guide to Buckfast Abbey, by Dom John Stephan.

The Story of the London Oratory, by H. M. Gillett (1946).

The London Oratory (various writers): Souvenir, 1949.

Religious Houses of the United Kingdom—compiled under authority (1887).

Farm Street, by Bernard Basset, S.J. (1948).

B

ANSON, PETER F., *The Religious Orders and Congregations of Great Britain and Ireland* (1949).

—— *Benedictines of Caldey* (1940).

BARNES, MGR. A. S., *The Catholic Schools of England* (1926).

BATTERSBY, W. J., *St. John Baptist De La Salle* (1948).

BUTLER, DOM CUTHBERT, *Life of William Bernard Ullathorne, O.S.B.* (1926).

CAPES, H. M., *Life and Letters of Fr. Bertrand Wilberforce, O.P.* (1912).

CHANTAL, F. DE., *Julie Billiart and Her Institute* (1938).

DEVAS, F. C., S.J., *Mother Magdalen Taylor* (1927).

DRANE, A. T., *Life of Mother Margaret Hallahan* (1869).

EVENNETT, H. O., *The Catholic Schools of England and Wales* (1944).

FLETCHER, J. R., *The Story of the English Bridgettines of Syon Abbey* (1933).

HICKS, DOM BRUNO, *Hugh Edmund Ford, First Abbot of Downside* (1948).

MARTINDALE, C. C., S.J., *Life of Bernard Vaughan, S.J.* (1923).

—— *Life of C. D. Plater, S.J.* (1922).

MONAHAN, MAUD, *Life and Letters of Janet Erskine Stuart* (1922).

MURPHY, J. N., *Terra Incognita, or The Convents of the United Kingdom* (1876).

STEELE, FRANCESCA M., *The Convents of Great Britain* (1902; revised edn., 1925).

—— *Monasteries and Religious Houses of Great Britain* (1903).

TIGAR, CLEMENT, S.J., *Edmund Lester, A Memoir* (1937).

TRISTRAM, HENRY, *Newman and His Friends* (1933).

WHELAN, DOM BASIL, *Historic English Convents of Today* (1936).

WEYAND, NORMAN (edited by), *Immortal Diamond: Studies in Gerard Manley Hopkins, S.J.* (1946).

CHAPTER XVI

THE CATHOLIC PRESS.

ACTON, LORD, *Letters to Mary Gladstone* (1904; 2nd edn., 1906), with long memoir by Herbert Paul.

BARRY, CANON W., *The Papacy and Modern Times* (1911).

BERKELEY, G. H., *Italy in the Making* (2 vols., 1932, 1936).

BODLEY, J. E. C., *Cardinal Manning and Other Essays* (1912).

GASQUET, ABBOT, *Lord Acton and His Circle* (1906).

GLADSTONE, W. E., *The Vatican Decrees* (1874).

HORGAN, J. J., *Frederick Lucas, Founder of " The Tablet "* (C. T. S. Ireland, N.D.).

HULL, ELEANOR, *A History of Ireland*, Vol. II (1931).

" JANUS " (DOLLINGER), *The Pope and the Council* (1869).

KNOX, R. A., *Let Dons Delight* (1939).

LUCAS, EDWARD, *The Life of Frederick Lucas, M.P.* (2 vols., 1886).

MATHEW, DAVID, *Acton, The Formative Years* (1946).

ORSI, PIETRO, *Italia Moderna* (5th edn., 1923).

PETRE, M. D., *Modernism* (1918).

RIETH MULLER, C. J., *Frederick Lucas, a Biography* (1862).

RUSSELL, LORD JOHN, *Later Correspondence of*, 1840-78 ed. by G. P. Gooch (2 vols., 1925).

THUREAU-DANGIN, P., *La Renaissance Catholique en Angleterre* (2 vols, 1899).

WARD, MAISIE, *The Wilfrid Wards and The Transition* (1934).

—— *Insurrection versus Resurrection* (1937).

WOODWARD, E. L., *Three Studies in European Conservatism*: *Metternich, Guizot, the Catholic Church* (1930).

—— *The Age of Reform* (1938).

YOUNG, G. M., *The Victorian Era*: *Portrait of an Age* (1936).

See also General List.

INDEX

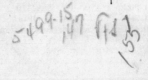